TELE ⬛ COMMUNI- CATIONS POLICY for the 1990s and beyond

Walter G. Bolter•James W. McConnaughey•Fred J. Kelsey

M. E. Sharpe, Inc.
Armonk, New York
London, England

Library of Congress Cataloging-in-Publication Data

Bolter, Walter G.
    Telecommunications policy for the 1990s and beyond/ by Walter G. Bolter,
  James W. McConnaughey, Fred J. Kelsey.
        p. cm.
    Includes bibliographical references.
    ISBN 0-87332-586-9
        1. Telecommunications policy—United States. I. McConnaughey, James W.
II. Kelsey, Fred J. III. Title.
HE7781.B65   1990
384′.068—dc20   89-10803
                                                                          CIP

Cover design by Ted Palmer

The tables that do not include specific information regarding the source are
compiled from estimates of the Bethesda Research Institute.

Printed in the United States of America

ED   10 9 8 7 6 5 4 3 2 1

CONTENTS

LIST OF ABBREVIATIONS

ABI   American Businessphones, Inc.
ACD   automatic call distributor
ADAPSO   Association of Data Processing Service Organizations
ADR   Applied Data Research
AL   access line
AmSat   American Satellite Company
ANI   automatic number identification
AR   average revenue
ARCO   Atlantic Richfield Company
AT&T   American Telephone and Telegraph
ATTIS   AT&T Information Systems
AUTOVON   Automatic Voice Network
AWA   Australian CPE manufacturer

B.C.Tel   British Columbia Telephone
B.W.   Business Week
BABT   British Approvals Board for Telecommunications
BAPCO   BellSouth Advertising and Publishing Company
BAT   Bay Area Teleport
BC   typo; should be "BT"
BOC   Bell Operating Company
BRC   Bell regional holding company
BRI   Basic Rate Interface
BRI   Bethesda Research Institute, Ltd.
BSA   Basic Serving Arrangements
BSE   basic service element
BSI   BellSouth International
BT   British Telecom
BUTN   Broadband Universal Telecommunications Network

CA   connecting arrangement
CALC   customer access line charge
CATV   cable television
CBI   Cincinnati Bell
CBIS   Cincinnati Bell Information Systems
CCIS   Common Channel Interoffice Signaling
CCLC   carrier common line charge
CCRA   Consumer Communications Reform Act
CCSA   common control switching arrangements
CEI   Comparably Efficient Interconnection
CI1   Computer Inquiry I
CI2   Computer Inquiry II
CNCP   Canadian National/Canadian Pacific

CNI	calling number identification
CNIS	Call Number Information Service
CNS	complementary network services
CO	central office
CO-LAN	central office based local area network
COCOT	customer owned coin operated telephone
CPD	consumer productivity dividend
CPE	customer premises equipment
CPI	Consumer Price Index
CRTC	Canadian Radio-television and Telecommunication Commission
CSP	Customer Specific Pricing
CSX	a U.S. corporation
DBP	Deutsche Bundespost
DBS	direct broadcast satellite
DBT	typo; should be DBP
DDS	Digital Dataphone Services
DEMS	digital electronic message services
DGT	prior acronym for the currently constituted France Telecom
DGT	Spanish regulatory body
DID	direct inward dialing
DOJ	Department of Justice
domsat	domestic satellite
DOV	data over voice
DP	data processing
DPS	dividend per share
DR	division of revenues
DRA	Division of Ratepayer Advocate
DSO	digital signal level 0
DTS	digital termination service
EAS	extended area service
EC	European Community
EDI	Electronic Document Interchange
ENFIA	exchange network facilities for interstate access
EPS	earnings per share
ESP	enhanced service providers
FCC	Federal Communications Commission
FCI	Forward Call Information
FD	followship demand
FDC	fully distributed costing/costs
FM-SCA	frequency modulation—subsidiary carrier authorization
FTC	Federal Trade Commission
FTS	Federal Telecommunications Service
FX	foreign exchange

HBO	home box office
HDTV	high definition television
IC	interexchange carrier
ICA	International Communications Association
ICC	Illinois Commerce Commission
ICC	Interstate Commerce Commission
IDA	Integrated Digital Access (UK)
IDC	International Digital Company
IDCMA	Independent Data Communications Manufacturers Association
IDS	Information Delivery Service
INS	Information Network System
Intelsat	International Telecommunications Satellite Organization
IO	industrial organization
IRC	international record carrier
ISDN	Integrated Services Digital Network
IXC	interexchange carrier
JSP	jurisdictional separations process
KDD	Kokusai Denshin Denwa Co., Ltd.; Japanese international carrier
KTAS	largest of Denmark's independent telephone companies
LAC	long run average cost
LAN	local area network
LATA	local access transport area
LEC	local exchange company
LMC	long run marginal cost
LMS	local measured service
LPSN	local public switched network
LPTV	low power television
LRAC	long run average cost
LRIC	long run incremental cost
LT&T	Lincoln (Nebraska) Telephone and Telegraph
MAN	metropolitan area network
MC	marginal cost
MCC	miscellaneous common carrier
MDS	multipoint distribution services/system
MFJ	Modification of Final Judgment
MIS	management information systems
MITI	Ministry of International Trade and Industry (Japan)
MOU	minutes of use
MPL	Multischedule Private Line
MPT	Ministry of Posts and Telecommunications (Japan)
MR	marginal revenue

MS	migration strategy
MSA	Market Service Area
MSO	multiple system operator
MTS	Message Telephone Service/telecommunications (basic long distance) service
MTSO	Mobile Telecommunications Switching Office
NARUC	National Association of Regulatory Commissioners
NEC	Japanese electronics firm
NET	New England Telephone
NFD	nonfollowship demand
NIC	Nippon Information and Communications Company
NPRM	Notice of Proposed Rulemaking
NRRI	National Regulatory Research Institute
NTIA	National Telecommunications and Information Administration
NTS	nontraffic sensitive
NTT	Nippon Telephone and Telegraph
NURE	Network Utilization Rate Element
OCC	other common carrier
OECD	Organization for Economic Cooperation and Development
OFS	operational fixed microwave radio service
OFTEL	Office of Telecommunications (UK)
OID	outgoing individual dialing
ONA	Open Network Architecture
OSP	outside plant
PABX	private automatic branch exchange
PBX	private branch exchange
PLVN	Private Line Voice Network
POP	points of presence
POTS	plain old telephone service
PRI	Primary Rate Interface
PSA	Public Service Announcement
PSB	Public Service Board
PSN	public switched network
PSTN	Public Switched Telephone Network
PTC	primary toll carrier
PTI	Pacific Telesis International
PTO	Public Telecommunication Operator (UK)
PTT	Post Telephone & Telegraph (administrations)
PUC	Public Utility Commission
RBOC	Regional Bell Operating Company
RCC	radio common carrier
RHC	Regional Holding Company
RPI	Retail Price Index

RSA	rural service area
RSC	regional service company
RTT	major supplier of telecommunications services in Belgium
SBS	Satellite Business Systems
SCC	specialized common carrier
SDN	software defined network
SFC	Australian CPE manufacturer
SIC	standard industrial classification
SLC	subscriber line charge
SMATV	satellite master antenna television
SMC	short run marginal cost
SMDI	Simplified Message Desk Interface
SNA	system network architecture
SNET	Southern New England Telephone
SPCC	Southern Pacific Communications Company
STS	shared tenant services/systems
SWB	Southwestern Bell
SWBT	Southwestern Bell Telephone
TBL	Telecommunications Business Law (Japan)
TRAC	Telecommunications Research and Action Center
TS	traffic sensitive
TVA	Tennessee Valley Authority
TWX	teletypewriter exchange
USOA	Uniform System of Accounts
USSI	a satellite carrier
USTA	United States Telephone Association
USTS	U.S. Transmission Systems
UTS	universal telephone service
VAN	value added network
VGS	voice grade service
VOS	value of service
VSAT	very small aperture terminal
VSR	Voice Storage and Retrieval
VTNS	virtual telecommunications network service
WAN	wide area network
WATS	Wide Area Telephone Service
WUI	Western Union International

PREFACE

This book presents a description and analysis of the volatile environment of the telecommunications industry after the breakup of the former Bell System on January 1, 1984. An analytical economic framework is established that is carried through to the events now occurring within the industry both on a nationwide scale and with a global flavor. The groundwork thus laid leads into an exploration of the future of telecommunications. The development of these scenarios considers various aspects of technology and regulatory innovations in addition to market structure and public policy considerations.

TELE ⊜ COMMUNI-CATIONS POLICY for the 1990s and beyond

CHAPTER I

TELECOMMUNICATIONS: THE NEW BEGINNING

We believe competition, or more precisely regulated competition, or government allocation of the market, is adverse to
the interest of the public.
> – John D. de Butts, AT&T
> Chairman of the Board, 1976[1]

Competition is the answer for telecommunications.
Technology dictates it. Regulators, legislators, and the
industry must work vigorously to ensure that competition can
flourish.
> – Jack A. MacAllister, U S WEST
> Chairman of the Board, 1985[2]

A. Industry Evolution and the Forms of Change

Few sectors of the U.S. economy have experienced greater changes since
their inception than telecommunications. The industry has undergone a
remarkable transformation in terms of its major catalyst, technology, as well
as the more reactive factors of market structure, and the public policies that
have adapted to its evolution. In its earliest form, telecommunications found
itself rooted in the technology of Morse's telegraph of the 1840s. After a
brief period of public ownership, it has been characterized by a reliance on
private provision of electronic communications service. But there has been
little other evidence of stability during its existence.

For instance, industry technology has evolved from telegraphy to
telephony and then to multi–medium telecommunications suited to the nascent
"Information Age." As new stages of technology have unfolded, industry
structure has changed. At times, a multiple vendor environment has
predominated. During other periods, however, monopoly has prevailed, with
market dominance by a few entities. Typically, market power has accrued to
the technological innovator, as evidenced initially by dominance of the
telegraph giant, Western Union, and, subsequently, by the telephone based
empire of the Bell System and its successors.

At some points, public policy has been accommodating and facilitated
industry trends already underway. At other times, it has tended to delay
changeover. Consistency has not been a watchword. Notably, public policy
has changed from an early espousal of laissez–faire to a program of vigorous
regulatory oversight. More recently, the regulatory regime has been
succeeded by institution of procompetition policies and their deregulation.
With current trends toward industry rationalization in evidence, many predict
that in the future reregulation may be in the offing.

1

B. The Postwar Period

The forces of telecommunications' underlying technologies have not been kind to new entrants. Indeed, during more than two–thirds of this century, near monopoly has prevailed in the domestic segment of the industry. As recently as the mid 1960s, AT&T's familial Bell System and Independent telephone companies were still the sole authorized providers of both local and long distance telephone service. Users could turn only to Western Union as an alternative and this was restricted to their public telegraph needs since a series of mergers and government fiat had produced sole source supply even in this area. Residences had no choice but to rent telephones, which were usually black in color, from the local exchange carrier, while businesses could look no further than the local telephone company for their office switchboards.

Until the late 1970s, provision of international communications was also characterized by the fewness of suppliers and product homogeneity. AT&T furnished all voice grade traffic that was transmitted from the U.S. by under–sea cable. Comsat, a quasi–government entity created by Congress, accounted for satellite–bound traffic as part of the International Telecommunications Satellite Organization, or "Intelsat," consortium of country representatives. Finally, data transmissions such as telex or teletypewriter exchange (TWX) were the province of the international record carriers, or IRCs, particularly RCA Globcom, ITT Worldcom, and Western Union International (WUI).[3]

This relatively tranquil setting gave way subsequently to turbulence and diversity. Rapid technological change caused the supplanting of analog electromechanical switching systems with state–of–the art digital electronics. Similarly, wideband fiber optics transmission made the facilities of microwave and satellite based carriers obsolete for some purposes and soon became the transmission mode of choice for long distance and, increasingly, local telecommunications. Simultaneously, a new round of competitive entry intruded upon the halcyon existence of regulated telephone companies in both service and customer equipment arenas.

C. The Bases of Evolution for the 1990s and Beyond

In the 1980s, these forces for change would affect and, in turn, were impacted by new public policy directions. Often supported and sometimes prodded by the courts, the Federal Communications Commission (FCC) has initiated procompetitive and deregulatory policies during this decade that significantly altered rules of entry and pricing in telecommunications markets. Reluctant to change at first, state public service commissions subsequently caught up with or even overshadowed the FCC in some cases (e.g., Nebraska and Vermont) in implementing new deregulatory policies.

The most far reaching of all changes, however, was the market restructuring triggered by the 1982 consent decree, which settled an antitrust suit brought against AT&T and its affiliates eight years earlier by the Justice

Department. This Modification of Final Judgment or "MFJ" broke up the Bell System on January 1, 1984, creating in its wake seven Region Bell Operating Companies and a smaller AT&T. The RBOCs, as they were called, would be permitted by the MFJ to conduct business only in certain markets, and many of their operations would be subject to state or federal regulation. Despite these constraints, the Bell entities remained sanguine about diversification. For example, the Chief Executive Officer of one of the RBOCs remarked soon after divestiture:

> What percentage of [our] net income will come from our unregulated subsidiaries? Eventually, I hope all of it will. We intend to move more and more of our operations out from under regulation, as every aspect of our business is increasingly subject to competition.[4]

In turn, a streamlined AT&T, which was freed from the restrictions consigned by a 1956 consent decree, could enter virtually any market. But, AT&T's top priority was apparently to maintain and even boost its market share in its "core businesses." These were long distance communications, network equipment, and customer premises equipment.[5] The company's strategy to strengthen these operations was deemed by AT&T's leadership to be "critical to . . . success in data networking and the international arena," which represented additional target areas.[6]

Thus, by the end of 1980s, technology, market structure, and public policy were again synchronized, albeit all had shifted from their positions of barely a decade earlier. Technological innovation had permitted entry, entry altered service provisioning, and policy adjusted -- with unprecedented severity. Still, few observers stood ready to predict that no further changes lay ahead.

The purpose of this book is to describe and analyze the volatile environment of post divestiture telecommunications as this country adjusts to industry changes and enters the "brave new world" of the 1990s and beyond. To provide a basis of investigation, in Chapter II we adopt an analytical economic framework. As supported by the tenets of industrial organization, which is a branch of theoretical and applied economics, we utilize the structure–conduct–performance paradigm as a methodology for analysis. This reliance on economic principles as a preferred means of reviewing public policy making has been on the rise during the 1980s. For example, agencies such as the FCC have recently demonstrated a heightening acceptance of the approach as shown in the following language excerpted from a Commission decision that was initiated to determine the proper limits of regulation:

> We reasoned, based upon the well–established teachings of modern welfare economics, that a firm without market power does not have the ability or incentive to price its services unreasonably, to discriminate among customers unjustly, to terminate or reduce service unreasonably or to overbuild its facilities.[7]

After establishing a theoretical framework, the chapter examines the underlying bases of the goals and objectives of government intervention. Various rationales for regulation of public utilities are reviewed, ranging from the well publicized case of "natural monopoly" to lesser known arbitration theories. The discourse then turns to antitrust policy, another major form of intervention, whose discussion is couched in terms of the aforementioned structure, conduct, and performance paradigm.

Chapter III then attempts to focus the generalized analysis and make it specific to this country's telecommunications sector.   Utilizing our methodological tools, the first section traces the origins of the industry and the emergence of the regulated monopoly franchise.   Next, the primary technological, structural, and policy catalysts for change that gripped the industry from the formative era of the 1950s through the early 1980s are probed. This sets the stage for an examination of the "new beginning" for telecommunications as the Bell System is split up and public policy makers grapple with this radical restructuring of an institution.

In Chapter IV traditional rate of return/rate base regulation is reviewed, followed by an assessment of the relative advantages and shortcomings of other   major   approaches.   Specifically,   the   chapter   investigates   such nontraditional policy alternatives as social contracts and price cap plans, incentive regulation, rate stabilization, deregulation, and separate subsidiaries, including their major applications in state and federal settings.

Chapter V examines the dramatic impact of the introduction of new technology in the 1980s. Particular emphasis is placed on the application of new transmission and switching facilities, which revitalized local and long distance telecommunications networks.   The surge in construction of innovative fiber optics and digital plant are described, along with the emergence of new network services made possible by the capabilities of these facilities.

The important phenomenon known as "bypass," which pertains to the circumvention of the local public switched network, is analyzed in Chapter VI. Its evolution and causes, as well as its current incidence and prospects, are carefully addressed in the context of a fast changing industry structure that alternatively has been viewed as both a result and cause of the appearance of bypass.

Chapter VII provides a perspective of the new global environment of telecommunications.   This analysis includes a structural profile of long distance and local network service providers, resellers and information offering suppliers, equipment vendors, and the many industry "players" of various national origins that are having an impact in the U.S. setting. A demand or services view of telecommunications is set forth next, with a review of the history and recent changes in service offerings of the burgeon—ing array of new companies now operating in this country. Chapter VIII then furnishes a complementary supply based analysis with international overtones. Regional Bell Company ventures into overseas telecommunications and current conditions in major foreign markets are discussed, as well as the status of key developments such as ISDN in Canada, Western Europe, and Japan.

Finally, Chapters IX and X explore the future of telecommunications in the United States generally and with specific reference to the last monopoly "frontier" of local exchange. In particular, Chapter IX evaluates the validity of the Huberian[8] view of the evolving telecommunications industry and examines the implications for public policy in such areas as interconnection, deregulation, removal of MFJ restrictions, and a new round of divestiture. In turn, Chapter X presents prognostications of industry performance of the major local exchange telephone companies from a financial perspective based on the policy expectations expressed.

Notes

1. "Public Regulation of the Telephone Company Was Long Evolution," *AT&T News*, March 10, 1976, p. 2.

2. "Commentary: Competition is the Only Way," *Financier*, June 1985, p. 51.

3. Other, much smaller IRCs at that time included TRT (owned by United Fruit), U.S. Liberia–Radio (once controlled by Firestone Tire and Rubber Co.), and French Cable.

4. See "How some key players see the new era," *Telephony*, January 16, 1984 (remarks attributed to Jack MacAllister, CEO, U S WEST).

5. AT&T, *1986 Annual Report*, pp. 1, 2; *1987 Annual Report*, pp. 2, 3.

6. AT&T, *1987 Annual Report*, p. 2.

7. FCC, *First Report and Order*, 85 FCC 2d 20, 21 (CC Docket No. 79–252), released November 28, 1982.

8. Peter Huber, consultant to the Justice Department, set forth his expectations regarding the technological transformation of the local public switched network as part of the MFJ Court's triennial review of the need for line of business restrictions on the Regional Bell Companies.

CHAPTER II

AN ANALYTICAL FRAMEWORK FOR PUBLIC POLICY ASSESSMENT

A. Introduction

This chapter outlines an analytical framework for examining public policy alternatives generally and with specific application to the telecommunications market setting. It explores the rationale for government intervention in terms of microeconomic theory and industrial organization, giving special weight to alternative industry structures and measures of market power. Finally, it delves into policy vehicles for intervention, such as regulation and antitrust, seeking to acquaint the reader with the rationale for departing from free market or laissez–faire principles.

In the discussion below, considerable attention is directed toward the major economic models of competition, namely perfect competition, pure monopoly, monopolistic competition and oligopoly.[1] The distinguishing characteristics of these basic market models are shown schematically in Figure II–1 using various criteria. Of course, perfect competition is primarily a theoretical construct, in that it requires full knowledge of all input and output options, transferability of resources, product homogeneity, and absence of any pricing power. This market structure cannot be attained. Even instances of "pure competition," under which the perfect knowledge and resource transferability assumptions are relaxed, have been rare in the U.S. economy and not of significant market magnitude or economic consequence.

Conceptually situated further along the continuum in Figure II–1 are other theories of the firm, which are often differentiated from competitive models in terms of the number of suppliers. Other distinguishing factors are entry barriers, product differentiation, price–cost margins, advertising, innova- tion, allocative efficiency, and market power. These are reviewed in descend- ing order of market competitiveness, starting with the multifirm pure competition and monopolistic competition, and concluding with oligopoly and monopoly. The teachings of industrial organization, which is the specific branch within the field of applied economics that deals with market structure and organization, are then proffered as a framework for analyzing the basic market forms, their conduct, and economic performance. Subsequently, the concept of market power is probed, including an examination of several significant definitions and measures.

The basic objective in describing these models is to lay the groundwork of fundamental understanding, insights, and economic tools that will be drawn upon later in the analysis. Specifically, these will be used to examine the workings of telecommunications markets and the tenets of current public policy making. Accordingly, the essential theoretical distinctions that economists believe lead to the need for differing approaches to industry developments, such as regulation or antitrust, are presented for review and

6

Figure II–1

BASIC MARKET MODELS AND THEIR DISTINGUISHING CHARACTERISTICS:
A SIMPLIFIED SCHEMATIC

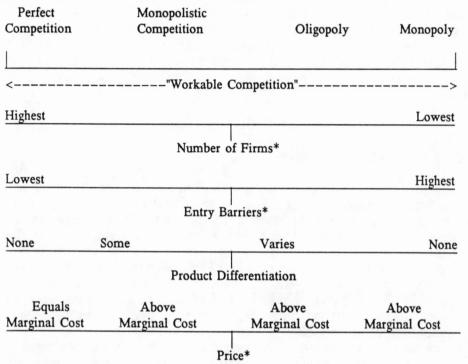

Perfect Competition	Monopolistic Competition	Oligopoly	Monopoly

<———————————————"Workable Competition"———————————————>

Highest			Lowest

Number of Firms*

Lowest			Highest

Entry Barriers*

None	Some	Varies	None

Product Differentiation

Equals Marginal Cost	Above Marginal Cost	Above Marginal Cost	Above Marginal Cost

Price*

* Long run equilibrium.

evaluation.   Of course, application of these constructs will ultimately be subject to the unrelenting critique of marketplace forces themselves.

The first section below provides the theoretical underpinnings for later examination of the telecommunications industry and affords needed benchmarks for evaluating the performance of this sector.   The constructs furnished are also beneficial in a prospective sense since they permit "educated guesses" concerning the future workings of telecommunications markets, especially in reaction to application of new policy initiatives.   And, resultant findings can be utilized to test the validity of the many hypotheses currently proffered for this industry's behavior and for other applications.[2] Although this section will concentrate on neoclassical economic theory, it will also touch on alternative models of firm behavior.

The second section analyzes the principal rationales that have been advanced in support of regulation of public utilities.   Essentially, these rely on the premise that regulation can effectively override the pursuit of self interest by the major players in the industry, and produce results not unlike those that would obtain with a laissez–faire or market directed approach.

The various *raisons d'etre* for regulation and underlying theoretical bases are also discussed.

The other fundamental method involving governmental intervention traditionally employed in this country, *viz.*, antitrust policy, is analyzed in the third section of this chapter.[3] This discussion focuses on the nature and function of the institution, and its application particularly *vis-à-vis* the regulatory approach. In addition, it analyzes the application of the structure–conduct–performance paradigm in various instances of antitrust enforcement. The section concludes by considering the broader implications of the ongoing evolution of the antitrust form of public policy in the United States.

B. Market Theory and Pricing

1. Behavior of Competitive Markets

As noted, perfect competition provides a fundamental conceptual design for characterizing market behavior. As a theoretical construct, it is distinguished from other models of market structure by the impersonality of supplier and consumer conduct and by the absence of rivalry among the individual firms.

The model of perfect competition is based on the following assumptions:

(1) Large numbers of buyers and sellers. The quantity of the good bought by any buyer or sold by any seller is so small relative to the total quantity traded that the changes in these quantities leave market price unaffected.

(2) Homogeneous products. The technical characteristics of the product as well as the services associated with its sale and delivery are identical. There is no way in which a buyer could differentiate among the products of different firms. Because there are large numbers of sellers and because products are homogeneous, the individual firm in pure competition is a price taker. As a result, the demand curve it faces is infinitely elastic, indicating that the firm can sell any amount of output at the prevailing market price.

(3) Free entry and exit of firms. It is presumed that there are no barriers to entry or exit from the industry. This is because if barriers did exist the number of firms in the industry would be reduced, and thus that each one of them could acquire power to affect the price in the market.

(4) Profit maximization. The sole goal of all firms in pure or perfect competition is profit maximization. In addition, consumers will maximize their total utility to the exclusion of other objectives.

(5) Absence of government regulation. There is no need for government intervention in the market such that tariffs, excise or sales taxes, subsidies, rationing, etc. are never initiated.

The above assumptions, taken alone, characterize a market structure which economists call "pure competition." Although pure and perfect competition are often used interchangeably, they are technically different. For "perfect competition" to exist the following additional assumptions must also be satisfied:

(6) Perfect knowledge or information.   There is perfect information in the sense that all buyers and all sellers have complete information on the prices being asked and offered in all other parts of the market. Information is free and costless, and complete certainty exists about future developments in the market.

(7) Perfect mobility of factors of production.   Distribution of raw materials is not restricted or monopolized, and labor is not unionized so that workers may move freely between jobs.

If these various assumptions are satisfied, then any individual firm will perceive that demand for its products is insatiable at the prevailing price. In other words, at the existing market price a firm would be able to increase its production without having to reduce price to encourage additional sales. Graphically, the demand curve facing each firm in a (perfectly) competitive market will appear to be horizontal, with both the additional (marginal) revenue and average revenue per unit equal to price.

However, while firms may alter output with impunity, they may not increase price. Should they do so, it is assumed that other suppliers exist who will capture the entire market share of the offending entity. Thus, under these market conditions, firms must act as "price takers." While they can sell as much as they are capable of producing at the prevailing market price, they have no market power with which to influence or alter that price. As a result, a short run profit maximizing level of output will come to exist where additional volume unit (marginal) cost equals market price, and, simultaneously, marginal revenue, with marginal cost increasing at this point.

In the short run, pursuit of profit maximization may result in supranormal profits, normal profits, or even losses. This is because average cost per unit of production may be below, equal to, or above the market set price, which is also the average revenue for a given firm. In the long run, however, free entry and exit would ensure that each surviving firm will earn normal profits. This is because price will be driven to a level where it equals the minimum long run average cost of production. Eventually, all firms will be forced to utilize the same least cost plant, and thus, under long run equilibrium conditions, short run marginal cost (SMC), long run marginal cost (LMC), and long run average cost (LAC) will be equal, and these will, in turn, equate with price (P), average revenue (AR), and marginal revenue (MR). Expressed as an equation, $SMC = LMC = LAC = P = AR = MR$.

Of course, the above discussion provides essentially a static analysis of perfect competition. Particularly in telecommunications, attention should also be directed to the impact of dynamic changes on the model. For example, a shift in market demand will have varying impacts depending on whether the industry exhibits constant, increasing, or decreasing cost characteristics. At any given point, changes in industry conditions may "swamp" the predicted effects on variables based on analysis of individual firm behavior.

Important exogenous dynamic changes could result from increases in some firm's fixed or variable costs. For instance, in the fixed cost case, the equilibrium position of a firm would not be affected in the short run. However, in the long run, the firm will not be able to cover its higher than average total unit costs and will be faced with bankruptcy. As a result, under new equilibrium conditions, for a time industry output will be lower, prices higher, and there will be fewer suppliers. Concerning the variable cost situation, there will be short run effects including an increase in price and a decrease in output. But when a new long run market equilibrium is reached, the quantity produced will be lower and the price higher when compared to initial equilibrium levels.

2. Competition and Social Welfare

The model of perfect competition yields significant results when viewed from the perspective of efficiency and welfare economics. In particular, after all adjustments, conditions of "Pareto optimality" will be achieved under which the economy's resources and output will have been allocated in such a way that no reallocation can make anyone better off without reducing the welfare of at least one other person.

Three sets of marginal conditions must be met before maximum welfare (*i.e.*, the attainment of a Pareto optimal equilibrium) can be reached. First, the marginal rate of substitution between any pair of consumer goods must be the same for all individuals who consume both goods. Second, the marginal rate of technical substitution between any pair of inputs must be the same for all producers who use both inputs. Third, the marginal rate of transformation in production must equal the marginal rate of substitution in consumption for every pair of commodities and for every individual consumer of both. The perfect competition model satisfies these requirements because of its assumption that producers maximize profits. As a result, this form of market organization theoretically results in optimal consumptive, technical, and allocative efficiency.

Unfortunately, perfect competition still falls short of being an all purpose or ideal benchmark for comparison with other market forms. For instance, serious questions arise concerning the attainability or even the desirability of many conditions and assumptions inherent in the model. Notably, the model necessitates that the sole goal of the firm is profit maximization, which may be unrealistic in practical terms. Indeed, writers such as Herbert Simon and others suggest that the firm in reality "satisfices" rather than maximizes profit.[4] In other words, business firms aim at only a satisfactory rate of profit, consistent with other objectives, rather than the maximum figure. Firms may abandon the attempt to maximize short run profits for several reasons, *e.g.*, the calculations required may be too complex, volatile, or insensitive to ongoing conditions, or the needed data may not be normally recorded or available on a timely basis. Indeed, some attribute the success of the Japanese in foreign markets (including telecommunications) to their ability to weight short term earnings at a lower level in favor of a more long run strategy.

Others suggest additional options as an alternative to focusing on profits. For example, Baumol suggests that maximization of total sales is more important in many cases than maximization of profits.[5] Another view is that of Berle and Means, who insist that given the modern corporation's separation between ownership and control, managers may often ignore the desires of stockholders for profit maximization.[6] Furthermore, the organizational complexity of the modern day corporation may effectively preclude installation of a single unified (and consistent) goal of profit maximization.[7]

Growth maximization has also been advanced as a primary corporate objective.[8] For instance, MCI in recent years has undertaken ambitious, but profit draining, construction programs as a means of enhancing its market position. Accordingly, it has acquired interests in some markets for short term position and presence, which were subsequently abandoned. Galbraith even suggests that simple preservation of the infrastructure of the corporation may be the overriding goal of many firms.[9] The deeply ingrained corporate culture which apparently existed within the old Bell System may be illustrative of this point.

Besides profit maximization, perfect competition's assumption that consumer sovereignty will be completely embraced in any market is probably unrealistic. This ignores the wishes of producers to minimize costs and market constraints. Going back to Henry Ford, even the color of a product may be "standardized." Franchise power of utilities also enters the equation, as in telephony where for many years American consumers could only lease a limited variety of telephones.

Notably, the achievement of maximum economic efficiency (the Pareto optimum) under perfect competition may well result in underemphasizing other important goals, such as equity and product diversity, that may be considered equally valid by many people. For instance, a social goal such as maintenance of universal telephone service, i.e., availability of basic local service at affordable rates, is currently a key objective for many public policy makers.

These various concerns about departures from realistic conditions are especially significant given the insights provided by Lipsey and Lancaster's "theory of the second best." In essence, this theorem states that if one of the conditions for Pareto optimality cannot be fulfilled, then the best obtainable situation can, in general, only be achieved by departing from all the other Paretian conditions. Thus, partial or incomplete progress toward the attainment of all aspects of perfect competition may, in fact, not constitute progress at all toward optimal conditions.

There are additional theoretical reasons why perfect competition has not been embraced as the sole standard for performance. Indeed, even if all markets conformed with the constructs of perfect competition, it may still not be possible to achieve the desired Pareto optimum. This is because of the likely existence of market failures. Examples include the presence of economies of scale.[10] external benefits, or public goods which could result in an underallocation of resources to a sector, as marginal social benefits exceed marginal social costs. Similarly, from a Pareto optimality viewpoint, the existence of external costs (*e.g.,* pollution) could result in an overallocation of resources to that sector, since marginal social benefits are less than marginal social costs.

Finally, the perfect competition model may yield unsatisfactory results from a macroeconomic perspective. For example, the rapid adjustments of price inherent in that scheme may well lead to extreme instability in employment in the economy, confidence threatening movements of capital across international borders, or even stock market and accompanying dislocations tantamount to "black monday."

3. Workable Competition

Given the infirmities of the perfect competition model as a standard for evaluation, economists have long sought alternatives that might be more pragmatically suited to this mission. In this regard, many scholars, including J.M. Clark, Corwin Edwards, Walter Adams, and others, have attempted to develop the concept of "workable competition."[11] Under this approach, the key operational task involves the defining of minimum criteria which can be used to judge real world conditions. A number of such criteria have been set forth over the years in the economics literature.[12] For example, many support the view that the number of sellers should be targeted at a level at least as large as scale economies permit. Also, firms should be encouraged to strive to achieve whatever their goals may be in an independent manner and without collusion. Inefficient suppliers and customers should not generally be shielded as a matter of policy and in no event on a permanent basis. Further, profits should be realizable only at levels just sufficient to reward investment, efficiency, and innovation.

Unfortunately, the workable competition standard demonstrably possesses shortcomings of its own. As might be expected when there is a departure from the most facilitating or "frictionless" conditions, the construct suffers from lack of precision or rigor, and in some formulations is beset with value judgments. As a result, investigators must weigh the practical advantages of this method against use of a less precise methodology relative to the perfect competition model.

4. Noncompetitive Conditions

As noted, there are instances, such as the commodities market and stock exchange, where behavior may more closely approximate that envisioned under perfect competition, but the vast majority of markets fail to satisfy at least some and often many of the conditions necessary for perfect competition. The array of such exceptions are termed *market imperfections*. These should be distinguished from *market failure*, which represents the inability of a private market, whether perfect or imperfect, to provide certain goods in the proper quantities to reach optimal conditions.[13]

Economists have traditionally attempted to capture various types of market imperfections in three basic models: pure monopoly, monopolistic competition, and oligopoly. The major characteristics of each of these models is examined below. In addition, a summary review of proper costing and pricing is provided as a means of setting the proper background for this discussion.

Of course, use of the marginal approach to analyze the pricing of goods and services and factors of production in a market context, has a long and rich history, with significant contributions having been made in this area by such notable economists as Marshall, Pareto, Walras, and Wicksell. Indeed, a key segment of this analysis, termed marginal cost pricing, has been generally embraced as the socially advantageous form of pricing in most markets.

Marginal cost pricing is the natural result of market pressures in a perfectly competitive setting since average and marginal revenue are identical. The model's requirements for profit maximization, namely that marginal revenue be equated to marginal cost, necessarily implies that price also equals marginal cost. Under conditions of imperfect competition, however, profits will not be maximized when price equals marginal cost, because average revenue exceeds marginal revenue. Hence, marginal cost pricing under imperfect competition will only occur through intervention, *e.g.*, regulation or taxation.

In the case of a regulated monopolist that participates in both unregulated and regulated markets, *e.g.*, a telephone company, the basic notion of marginal cost pricing (theoretical and applied) has come under fire by some economists.[14] Of course, in a natural monopoly setting, the equating of price and marginal cost would not allow the firm to meet its "revenue requirements" as set by the appropriate regulatory agency (see *supra*). This is because under regulation the firm has a legal right to recover profit, while perfect competition "permits" a firm to lose money. Indeed, the marginal cost approach suffers from a number of serious shortcomings when it is applied to regulated firms. For instance, this analysis is typically very difficult to implement because of the paucity of available data. In addition, marginal cost pricing tends to focus on the single goal of economic efficiency to the exclusion of other goals or objectives, which often have equal or even greater standing because of applicable utility statutes. Finally, marginal cost pricing may not be conducive to achieving the social optimum, because of certain institutional factors which govern behavior of the regulated monopolist, *e.g.*, the need to set price in the context of meeting a total revenue requirement.

Because of these practical constraints, other theories have been developed which seek to establish prices that are "optimal departures" from marginal cost pricing. Most prominent has been "Ramsey pricing," formulated by Ramsey in the 1920s and refined by such economists as Baumol, Bradford, and others.[15] These authors maintain that optimizing requires that such pricing departures be set equal to the reciprocal or inverse of the elasticity of demand for a given offering. Under this concept, prices in relatively inelastic (monopoly) markets would normally be higher than those in relatively elastic (competitive) sectors. The resultant price or rate structure would be designed to serve as a benchmark pricing system for the multiple services provided by a regulated firm. This approach, however, also has deficiencies. For example, incentives are provided for strategic cost shifting between markets. This may be masked by the focus on estimating demand elasticities. Moreover, the inverse elasticity principle only merits consideration as a second best solution because of the revenue requirement constraint imposed on pricing in a regulated industry, and the social unacceptability of unfettered prices set by monopoly.[16]

An alternative pricing philosophy which may be used in a regulated sector is fully distributed costing (FDC). Essentially, this concept immediately recognizes the need to allow the regulated firm to recover all of its costs, including a fair rate of return, and incorporate other social goals besides economic efficiency (*e.g.*, equity, accountability) in its price setting processes. Under FDC, embedded historical costs are allocated among the various services offered by the firm under usage, original cost causation or other schemes which are public interest as defined by regulatory authorities.

Criticisms have also been directed at this approach. For instance, Kahn argues:

> Quite simply, the basic defect of fully distributed costs as a basis for rate making is that they do not necessarily measure marginal cost responsibility in a causal sense. They do not measure by what amount costs would be increased if additional quantities of any particular service were taken, or by what amount costs would be reduced if the service were correspondingly curtailed. They are average costs: the allocations among the various services are often made in part on the basis of the relative number of physical units of consumption or utilization by each, and the total allocated dollars are then divided by those physical units to get the unit costs. Also, being apportionments of historical costs, even when they do accurately reflect historical responsibility for the incurrence of these costs among the respective users, they do not provide a reliable measure of what will happen to costs in the future if particular portions of the business are expanded or dropped. Therefore, they do not tell whether a particular service is really profitable or unprofitable, in the sense that its continued provision at existing rates makes a net contribution to company revenues over and above the costs for which it is responsible, or whether, instead, it is a burden on the other subscribers.
>
> This is a defect, of course, only to the extent that marginal costs diverge from average.[17]

Basic premises for pure FDC based pricing may be eroded when historically monopolistic markets become less insulated from competition and are regulated to lesser degrees. As this phenomenon becomes more widespread, new methodologies have evolved, such as the stand alone or own−service cost approach.[18] This methodology basically attempts to segregate and separately develop rates for those services of a regulated firm that are subject to monopoly supply. In telecommunications, for example, such separation currently appears logical for local exchange service costs *vis–à–vis* those of toll offerings. This option represents a generic category under which the more industry specific "VGS" (voice grade service) approach would fall.[19] Requirements for tying the revenue generation, capital expenditures, and capital recovery processes together are often associated with VGS methods.

On balance, there is no theoretically or practically flawless set of pricing principles applicable to a regulated industry. Alternatives are numerous, however, especially when the industrial sector in question exhibits a high proportion of common costs,[20] or is experiencing substantial competition and selective deregulation. These conditions would apply in the case of telecommunications. For some, an acceptable approach for those services which remain under the aegis of a regulatory commission would be simply to set a pricing range whose boundaries are based on methodologies grounded in marginal cost and stand alone approaches. Alternative regulatory approaches relating to pricing, rate of return, or other areas are discussed in the next chapter.

5. Monopoly

Under the concept of pure monopoly there is only one seller, no close substitutes for the monopolist's product exist, and there are effective barriers to entry. In practice, a monopoly may occur for any of a myriad of reasons, such as sole control of a key productive input by a single firm, existence of scale economies in some segment of the supply process, grants of patent rights, or an award of an exclusive government franchise. In telecommunications, supply of basic service by a local telephone company provides a classic example of the latter possibility. Historically, local companies have been assigned legal monopolies in return for accepting rate–of–return/rate base regulation administered by public service commissions. Even with the development of privately supplied local service alternatives in recent years, past grants of these franchises remain a difficult obstacle for new entrants to overcome in many jurisdictions.

Because the monopolist is the only firm producing a particular product, the demand curve for the firm's output is necessarily the same as the market demand curve for the product itself. Thus, the monopolist's demand curve is negatively sloped and price must be reduced to increase sales, unlike the case of perfect competition where it is horizontal and a firm can sell all it wishes at the going price. As a result, for the monopolist average revenue (or price) and marginal revenue are not the same. Product cost characteristics, however, are not dissimilar. Like the perfectly competitive firm, the average variable cost, marginal cost, and average cost curves facing the monopolist are also U–shaped.[21]

Under monopoly or competition, the firm will achieve its goal of short run profit maximization by equating marginal cost with its marginal revenue. The competitive firm's output level or supply curve can be found by altering price, which is always equal to marginal revenue, and finding the corresponding intersection on the marginal cost curve. However, for the monopolist, there is no unique supply curve that can be derived from marginal cost. Given demand, the monopolist simply picks a unique, profit maximizing point of operation. But, if the shape or level of the demand curve changes, a particular price can result in a wide variety of output levels or, conversely, the same quantity may be offered at different prices.

Long run equilibrium for a monopolist can be characterized by economic profits or even losses. These conditions would be avoided in competitive markets by the occurrence of entry or exit. From a social perspective, this is unreasonable and, indeed the output of a monopolist tends to be lower and priced higher than under perfect competition. Notably, if the monopoly firm expands its long run economic equilibrium output, it could utilize a plant with lower average cost and be more efficient. In short, the lack of competition theoretically leads to technical (or X) inefficiency and production costs at each output level which are higher than they would otherwise be under perfect competition. As a result, in theory, there will be loss of consumer welfare attributable to the operation of monopoly.

There are several special features of monopoly that merit close examination. For example, price discrimination occurs when buyers are charged different prices for the same good. While instances of at least some preferential treatment for long standing or "valued" customers is not unusual, prospects of socially excessive price discrimination have been cited as one of the traditional reasons for instituting public utility regulation (see *infra*). In the absence of regulation or market pressures, where the price elasticity of demand is not the same in all markets in which the monopolist operates, the firm may be able to boost its profits dramatically by charging discriminatory rather than uniform prices.

Another unusual case includes bilateral monopoly, which occurs when a single seller faces a single buyer in the same market. Under these circumstances, the "winner" of this marketpower struggle and, hence, the equilibrium price and output parameters are theoretically indeterminant. Another specific circumstance is that of the multi–plant monopolist, who produces a homogeneous product. Maximization of profits in this setting requires the distribution of total production between each plant so that the level of output at each facility occurs where the marginal costs are equal to each other and to (the common) marginal revenue. Of course, in all of these cases, price, output and resource allocations will differ from the ideal set under the perfectly competitive model.

As noted, the existence of monopoly conditions in the telecommunications sector has been a common occurrence since the industry's beginnings. For example, Western Union possessed an unregulated telegraph monopoly in numerous geographic markets during the latter half of the 1800s. The emergence of telephony in the late 1870s did inject an element of competition. But ultimately, this only traded one monopoly for another. After a period of competition in telephony, during the early 1900s AT&T embarked on an aggressive acquisition program, which created monopoly telephone operations in a number of locales.[22] Many of these persist today.

6. Monopolistic Competition

Perfect competition and pure monopoly represent theoretical extremes of market organization. Accordingly, there clearly exists a need for additional models, which may be used to analyze and predict the outcome of intermediate market structures. In response, especially since the 1930s, economists have looked to the basic economic models of monopolistic competition and oligopoly to provide insights into this middle ground. Instances of such intermediate conditions are not uncommon in most industries, including telecommunications. For example, the current market for customer premises equipment approximates the model of monopolistic competition, which will be discussed below.

On the continuum of economic models, monopolistic competition is nearest to perfect competition. A monopolistically competitive industry is characterized by a large number of firms which produce similar but not identical products. This capacity for product differentiation means that these firms are able to influence price, *i.e.*, they face a negatively sloped demand curve. In the long run, under monopolistic competition no excess profits are sustainable because firms can freely move into the industry and produce a different brand of the same product utilizing the best technology, *i.e.*, under identical cost conditions. Notably, this model embraces the fundamental assumptions of the perfect competition construct, except for the introduction of the factors of product heterogeneity and nonperfectly elastic demand curves.

The long run equilibrium position under monopolistic competition differs from perfect competition results in that price does not equal long run marginal cost, and production does take place at minimum cost levels. That is, equilibrium occurs on the downward sloping segment of the long run average cost curve, rather than at its lowest or minimum cost point. In capsule, long run equilibrium under perfect competition requires that MC = MR = AC = P, while monopolistic competition in the long run dictates that MC = MR and AC = P but that P is greater than MC. As a result, the latter will yield a lower output and a higher price than would result under perfect competition. However, normal profits will be obtained in both cases in the long run. Compared to the pure monopolist, monopolistic competition is superior, occasioning higher output, lower prices, and lower profits.

Economists disagree as to the overall impact of monopolistic competition on social welfare. This is because the theoretical advantages attending product differentiation and diversity must be weighed against the socially disadvantageous "excess capacity" and the apparent existence of too many undersized firms. Several strong criticisms have been leveled at the model of monopolistic competition, especially as this construct was envisioned by Chamberlin. For example, some argue that if the assumption is made that all firms have the same demand and cost curves, then it is not persuasive that a downward sloping demand curve should apply to the situation. Others have questioned the magnitude and even the existence of excess capacity in Chamberlin's model. Finally, as was true respecting criticisms of both the perfectly competitive and monopolistic models, there appear to be too few real world markets which are accurately portrayed by the monopolistic competition construct for it to be used as a pragmatic standard. The net result, as observed by Mansfield, Ferguson, Gould and others, is that the model has not occupied a central role in the analysis of markets behavior.[23]

7. Oligopoly

Oligopoly is another fundamental type of intermediate model of market behavior falling between monopoly and perfect competition. Subsumed in the broad category of oligopoly are a number of specific theories. Although the possible variations among these different theories are manifold, the essential feature of each of them is the high degree of mutual interdependence between suppliers. The extremely limited number of firms operating in the market—place and impeded entry conditions are other hallmarks of most of the theories of oligopoly.[24] The majority of specific oligopoly formulations may be broken down into two categories: noncollusive and collusive arrangements.

As the name implies, under noncollusive oligopoly arrangements it is assumed that suppliers have made no tacit agreements or "understandings" among themselves to operate independently. An early example of this formulation was Cournot's construct of duopolistic behavior. That is, under Cournot's model, each seller assumed that the other's output was unaffected by his own; each then adjusted their prices and output until after a series of iterations the position of equilibrium was reached. The specific output and price levels that result under this formulation again lie somewhere between the outcomes fostered under pure monopoly and perfect competition but much closer to monopoly. Forty—five years after Cournot's work, Bertrand developed another model of duopoly. His work differed from Cournot's in that Bertrand assumed that each firm would expect its rival to keep its price constant, irrespective of the other firm's decisions about pricing. The main criticism of both models relates to their requirements that firms do not learn from experience.

Subsequent models departed from this notion, in the sense that they assume that few firms are conscious of their interdependence. But the Chamberlin model explicitly recognized such interdependence and showed how firms may noncollusively decide to set identical prices and to maximize their joint profits. The chief criticisms of the Chamberlin model are that it ignores entry and fails to recognize that joint profit maximization is impossible without some collusion (i.e., unless all firms have identical costs and demands).

The kinked demand model developed by Sweezy has been oft sited as a notable attempt to explain the persistence of rigid or "sticky" prices in oligopolistic markets. Essentially, Sweezy postulated that under certain conditions a discontinuity arises in the marginal revenue curve so that only wide variations in cost conditions will cause price to change. The underlying kink in demand causing the discontinuity may be a result of behavior where a firm believes all competitors will match any price decrease, but not a price increase. Sweezy's formulation is now generally viewed as an incomplete theory of oligopolistic pricing in that it does not explain the price and output decisions of the firms or level of price at which the kink will occur, and does not define the level at which price will be set in order to maximize profits.

The duopoly construct of Stackelberg also represented a refinement of Cournot's model[25] based on its use of more sophisticated assumptions. Stackelberg presumed that one of the two duopolists will take into account the predictable actions of the naive duopolist in its profit maximizing calculations. Under these tenets, a stable equilibrium will occur since the naive firm will act as a follower. However, if both firms are sophisticated, then both will want to act as leaders and disequilibrium will exist, resulting either in a price war or a perceived need for collusion. The Stackelberg model, however, was otherwise largely restricted to the assumptions made by Cournot.

Theories based on the assumption of collusion among oligopolists abound. A "cartel" exists when a formal agreement has been reached between firms in an oligopolistic market to cooperate with regard to certain variables, *e.g.*, price and output, in order to reduce uncertainty and risk. In practice, of course, tacit arrangements may be preferred. Overall, there are two main theories of cartels. One model assumes joint profit maximization through collusion by members in the industry. Although the model explains that the monopoly solution is easy to obtain in theory, pragmatically there are many reasons why joint profit maximization in a cartel arrangement does not actually occur. These include such explanations as difficulty in determining market demand and marginal cost, fear of government interference or entry, desire to retain a good public image, and inherent rigidities of cartel negotiations and results.

Theories which rely on the premise that market shares are allocated through nonprice competition or quotas have also been postulated. These cartel models presume that such sales sharing mechanisms would result in proper output allocations if the marginal cost facing all firms is equal. In actuality, an efficient distribution of production is unlikely to occur because shares will reflect many noneconomic factors typically introduced during a negotiation process.

Price leadership represents a more common form of collusion because, unlike a formal cartel, this arrangement permits members nearly complete freedom regarding production and selling activities.[26] The literature identifies several types of price leadership.[27] For example, low cost price leadership may occur where two firms vying in the same market have unequal costs. The supplier with the more efficient plant cost will set a comparatively low price, which will have to be matched by the high cost firm even though at this price the second firm does not maximize profits. The second firm chooses to follow because it prefers to sacrifice some of its profits rather than lose market share or ultimately risk erosion of all of its profits in a possible price war.

The instance of dominant firm price leadership may arise in an industry where one firm possesses a substantial share of the total market and all the remaining firms are minuscule both in terms of size and market share. The dominant firm maximizes profits by equating its marginal cost to marginal revenue; while the smaller firms simply act as price takers. These firms may or may not maximize profits, depending on their individual cost structures. Long distance telephone service may represent an example of the functioning of this model, since MCI and other small carriers have frequently patterned their rate structures after the industry's dominant firm, AT&T (see *infra*). Barometric price leadership represents a variation of dominant firm price leadership. Under this construct, the identity of the leader can change over time and its power may not always be pervasive. For example, a given price initiative may be followed depending on how closely the change reflects market conditions that are faced by all.

Conditions amenable to the emergence of collusive price leadership may exist in an industry where each of the firms has similar demand, cost, and market shares. Under such operating conditions, price leadership may be exhibited with little disparate behavior and no overt collusion.   Price initiatives by any of the firms would presumably be quickly recognized as attractive by all the remaining suppliers in the industry and be whole-heartedly adopted. In the airline industry, for example, nonrefundable fares were rapidly utilized by all the major carriers, which are quite similar in operation, after their introduction as a means of enhancing aircraft loading and profits.   The major criticisms of the price leadership models include: (1) the lack of precision in determining market variables that is inherent in these models, *e.g.,* which price should be used as the signal; and (2) the practical reality of "price shading" or concoction of special discounts or other arrangements for preferred customers, especially by the smallest firms, when demand declines.

Of course, some theories of oligopolistic behavior do not fall neatly into any of the above categories. For instance, game theory, as originated by von Neumann and Morgenstern, has an unusual niche. Under this approach, in various situations of conflict and cooperation, the investigation centers on whether self-seeking behavior by the participants involved will lead to a determinate equilibrium.[28] Game theory attempts to catalog the complete specification of what a participant will do under each contingency of the context or game. Although promising, this construct has not yet provided results which could lead to a comprehensive theory of oligopoly. But the model is conducive to use of high speed computer conducted experiments of oligopolistic behavior, and may yield results sufficient for important decision making in many circumstances.

Another important approach is the average cost or cost-plus pricing construct. Under this model, the firm is assumed to price equal to its total average cost, which includes a certain net profit margin. There are various average cost pricing formulations which differ respecting the manner of arriving at the estimate of the average cost which will be charged as price. Actual use of average cost pricing practices by industry has been widely supported by empirical studies.

There is considerable controversy, however, over the extent to which this pricing method is compatible with profit maximization. But some economists strongly aver that the average cost theory is essentially no different from marginal analysis techniques.[29]

The limit pricing approach pioneered by Bain also has found support.[30] This theory centers on the manner in which established firms within an industry would set price if prevention of new entry were a key objective. Where some barriers to entry exist such as high capital costs, an entry forestalling price might be set just below the minimum long run average cost of the most advantageously positioned potential entrant. Subsequent refinements of the original Bain model have been made by Sylos, Modigliani, Bhagwati, and Pashigian, but these have largely resulted in complicating representation of the process.[31] While appealing from a technical perspective, the refined models' results still hinge on the necessity of agreement (at least within certain bounds) between existing firms in the industry concerning the advisability of utilizing a limit price and the level at which it should be set.

Utilization of limit pricing and predatory prices (see next section) encompass strategies which an incumbent firm may use in a natural monopoly setting. In each case the broad intent is to deter entry by other firms, but while limit pricing is probably legal, predation clearly is not. Predatory pricing may represent a *per se* antitrust violation, but is difficult to prove in practice. On the other hand, limit pricing is generally not unlawful but may have effects that are quite difficult to distinguish from those of predatory pricing.[32]

Among the constructs which depart from traditional reliance on profit maximization are Williamson's model of managerial discretion and the behavior model of Cyert and March.[33] Williamson's work focuses on the premise that managers have sufficient discretion to pursue policies which are intended to maximize their own utility. Pursuit of this objective may often not be consistent with profit maximization. A major drawback of this approach is that it fails to deal with the core attributes of most oligopolies, namely, interdependence and strong rivalry. On the other hand, Cyert and March's theory centers its attention on the internal organization of the firm, and in particular, its internal efficiency. As a result, the more traditional question of allocative efficiency receives inadequate expositions. The approach also fails to fully address industry equilibrium or the effect of actual or potential entry.

In summary, economists' attempts to describe and model the behavior of oligopolistic firms, which demonstrably represent the most prevalent structural condition in the U.S. economy, have engendered a variety of explanatory theories. Most have at least some degree of applicability. However, none of the constructs has emerged as a standard, owing to the widely differing situations that these models attempt to describe. Few conditions can be deemed to be of universal applicability, although oligopoly does seem to consistently feature a small number of firms that recognize their interdependence.

In addition, oligopoly does appear to normally promote collusion as a means of increasing profits, decreasing uncertainty, and controlling the entry of new firms. Yet, collusion is not simple to achieve or sustain and, thus, appearances of oligopolistic behavior may be inherently short lived or unstable. They would obviously be difficult to fully document or catalog because the more direct and blatant forms of collusion are patently illegal. And, typically firms can privately gain by cheating on any agreement, which would lead to their abrogation. For these reasons, collusion or oligopolistic arrangements may not have the profiteering or distortive effects that one might expect.

Generally, oligopolistic prices and profits will be higher than those under both perfect competition and monopolistic competition, but lower than those that would exist under conditions of pure monopoly. However, the net social welfare effects of nonprice competition under oligopoly, *e.g.*, advertising and product differentiation, are unclear. In such cases, the advantages of diversity must be weighed against the potential for erecting barriers to entry. The outcome of this particular calculus for the various telecommunications markets is critical, given the proliferation of new products and services and the associated flurry of promotional activities.

C. Applicability of the Economics of Industrial Organization

1. The Basic Approach

Industrial organization (IO) economists, led by Mason, Bain, Clark, Scherer, and Stigler, have developed a special taxonomy and analytical framework for examining markets.[34] This approach, quite apart from other contributions of traditional or neo-classical analyses, focused on market structure, conduct, and performance. As with most economic exposition, basic conditions may be segmented initially into supply and demand categories. On the supply side, these conditions include such factors as the state of technology, the extent of unionization, and the location and ownership of raw materials. Also important are product characteristics, the timing of production, the historical origins of the product or firm, and business attitudes and public policies. Concerning demand, relevant conditions include price and cross elasticities of demand for the product, and the rate of growth and variability of demand. Additionally, the purchasing methods used by consumers, "lumpiness," *i.e.*, the timing of orders, and the nature of the products that are marketed must be examined.

The emphasis of IO concerning *market structure* typically pertains to analyses of the number and size distribution of sellers, number of buyers, degree of product differentiation, existence of barriers to entry and vertical integration, cost methodologies, and conglomerateness. Examination of *conduct*, on the other hand, usually concerns strategic policies and behavior of firms in a given market. It includes review of such factors as pricing policy, product strategy and advertising, production policies, research and innovation, coercion, legal tactics, and plant investment. Finally, investigation of *performance* involves summary or "bottom line" assessments outcomes, *e.g.,* of such elements as extant allocative and technical efficiency, levels of employment and inflation, progressiveness, equity and quality of product.

The industrial organization framework affords an opportunity for the systematic examination of the aforementioned four basic economic models of the firm and market organization. A variety of options are presented for analysis as price and cross elasticities of demand range from quite elastic for perfectly competitive industries to quite inelastic for the pure monopoly sectors. Other characteristics are discernible including concentration, industry rigidity, and product stability. Notably, perfect competition includes a significant number of firms, no entry barriers, and homogeneous products. Monopolistic competition is characterized by a large number of firms, free entry and exit, and heterogeneous products. In turn, oligopoly exhibits few firms, potentially sizeable barriers to entry and either homogeneous or heterogeneous products. A pure monopoly by definition has one supplier, impenetrable barriers, and a unique product.

Less easily and definitively classified, the elements of conduct and performance nonetheless fit this scheme. While the perfectly competitive firm has the ability to set output levels but not price, the monopolistic competitor has some discretion as to both price and production levels; the monopolist, as usual, is virtually the master of his own destiny. Because firms in the industry generally recognize an interdependence, the oligopolist may or may not have more flexibility in terms of setting price and output levels compared to other market types; this will depend on the nature of arrangements entered into by oligopolistic firms. Along with the monopolist, the latter will enjoy considerably more latitude compared to firms in other types of markets. Economists differ as to the intensity of research and development efforts conducted under the various market scenarios.[35] There also exists some haziness among theoreticians and empiricists concerning legal tactics among different market structures as well.

In general, pursuit of profit maximization seems to lead to normal profits for firms in pure competition and monopolistic competition arenas in the long run, and supranormal profits for the other two market types over the same period. In terms of allocative efficiency, perfect competition theoretically yields the ideal results while pure monopoly leads to welfare losses. Because of product differentiation, however, the performance of the other two market types in this regard is uncertain. Also subject to dispute is the performance of monopolistic competition, oligopoly, and monopoly in the area of technical efficiency. The perfect competitor achieves optimal levels of performance here. The expected results of each model regarding full employment, progressiveness and equity still remain subject to vigorous debate.

The causal relationship between the different elements of the structure–conduct–performance nexus is an area of considerable controversy, both theoretically and empirically. Bain believes that the pivotal link is between structure and performance, *i.e.*, conduct is relatively unimportant.[36] Hence, concentration and barriers to entry -- not collusion -- are seen to dictate performance results. In particular, high concentration levels and high barriers to entry are claimed to lead to excessive profit levels and other undesirable social results. In contrast, advocates of the Chicago school survivorship approach, *e.g.*, Stigler, believe that concentration is relatively unimportant but that collusion should be the focal point of any such analysis.[37]

There is considerable support in the economic community that structure, but also conduct, are important determinants of performance. Baldwin, Greer, Scherer, and others seem to ascribe significance to both the structure and the conduct elements in terms of ultimately determining a given market's performance.[38] Viewed this way, the intermediate relationships of structure–conduct and conduct–performance may shed new analytical light on the process and thereby permit better predictions and statistical studies.

Some economists believe the proper investigatory approach resides elsewhere. The behavioral school downplays the importance of the structural concatenation, instead emphasizing the importance of the firm's internal organization.[39] Certain economists, such as Alfred Kahn, exhort researchers to reevaluate current thinking in industrial organizations and develop new theoretical etiologies:

> I guess what I am really urging is a continuation of the trend of closer integration of industrial organization with microeconomics and microeconomic policy generally; breaking out of the structure–behavior–performance box in the many situations where that framework seems not very useful; a recognition that the range of available micro policy instruments and the need for imaginative new institutional arrangements extends far beyond the various categories of competition and monopoly, and the range of policy instruments far beyond the antitrust laws.[40]

2. Market Power Analysis

Market or *monopoly power* is the ability of one or more firms to influence or control the price of a product or service or to exclude competition. Only a truly competitive market insures that absolutely no market power exists. Otherwise, any analysis of markets must necessarily take into consideration the issue of market power.

The issue of market power is significant in a public policy sense. Most economists and public policy makers would recommend application of either existing antitrust statutes or other forms of government intervention when they perceive a firm's market power to be excessive. If an industry exhibits characteristics of a "natural monopoly," then public utility regulation is deemed by many to be appropriate for the surviving firm.[41]

Market power may arise for any of a number of reasons. First, patent rights to an essential process or technique will insulate, at least in part, a firm from market competition as others are precluded from legally adopting the practice during the pendency of the patent(s). For example, the nascent Bell System solidified its market presence during the latter 1800s through use of its basic telephone patents. Second, absolute cost advantages, *e.g.*, control over nonreproducible resources or an ability to secure a lower cost of capital, will deter entry in many cases. Some believe that the size of the predivestiture AT&T, the world's largest corporation in terms of assets, conferred upon it a unique ability to attract capital financing.

Third, scale economies may exist such that the minimum efficient scale of plant is so large in relation to market size that only one firm can operate efficiently. The Bell System traditionally argued that its network exhibited such economies at least at the transmission level.[42] Fourth, product differentiation achieved through, *e.g.*, extensive advertising may create strong brand loyalty among consumers and thereby discourage entry as found by Comanor and Wilson.[43] As discussed below, Western Electric, AT&T, and the Regional Bell Operating Companies have enjoyed "premium price" or other advantages of incumbency. Moreover, an increase in market share generally denotes a concomitant increase in market power. And finally, other forms of structure, *e.g.*, vertical integration and conglomerateness, may well enhance one's market power.

Less settled than the question of whether market power exists is the issue of the extent or degree of power for a given firm. Numerous approaches have been developed in the attempt to measure its incidence. Some have theoretical bases, while others are primarily statistical measures of structural power. Several of the most significant methods are examined below.

Among the statistical measures that should be discussed is the straightforward calculation of the number of firms in a given market. The main advantages of this approach are its ease of computation and its sensitivity to changes over time. Its basic disadvantage is that it totally ignores market shares and thus is a very unbalanced approach.

A second type of computation centers on market share, *i.e.*, the proportion of an industry's sales or output controlled by one firm. Using the Justice Department's June 14, 1984 "Merger Guidelines" in conjunction with the Herfindahl–Hirschman Index (see below), firm market shares greater than 42.5 percent apparently indicate the existence of market power. Studies have been undertaken whose results show that in general, firm shares and rates of return are directly related.[44] A possible drawback of the measure is that it may be misleading: if a more efficient firm increases its market share by producing at a lower cost, then its profits would rise because of greater efficiency, not market power. However, available evidence does not support an embrace of the efficiency argument in lieu of the market dominance thesis.[45]

A third technique is the Lorenz curve, which is a construct used in the calculation of firm inequality and concentration in an industry. The extent to which the measured Lorenz curve deviates from the hypothetical line of absolute equality indicates the degree of inequality within the sample. The Gini coefficient numerically characterizes the Lorenz curve by measuring the departure between the curve actually observed and the curve that would appear if all firms had equal market shares. As the Lorenz curve approaches the "equality line," the area of concentration declines and the Gini coefficient approaches zero, indicating less inequality. Conversely, as the two curves diverge, the coefficient approaches one and there is deemed to be more inequality among firms.

The Lorenz curve and associated Gini coefficient incorporate firm size into the measure of structural power.[46]   In this sense, they therefore represent an improvement over a simple number–of–firms approach.   In another sense, however, they are deficient in that they assign too much weight to inequivalences of firm size, thereby underemphasizing the effects of firm number. Nonetheless, the shape of the Lorenz curve and the value of the Gini coefficient are sensitive to errors in determining industry size. The more firms one includes, the higher the indicated degree of inequality tends to be.   In addition, one distribution of firms might be more equal than another over one range, less equal over a different range, and yet register the same coefficient.   Finally, the data requirements would be enormous: market shares of every firm in the industry would need to be secured to compute these measures.

One of the most popular statistical measures is the concentration ratio, which shows the percentage of total industry sales, capacity, employment or output that is contributed by the largest few firms in a given market.   Such ratios are most commonly computed for four, eight, twenty or fifty firms in an industry.   The attractiveness of this method stems from the fact that it addresses both the number of firms and inequality for firm market shares. However, it inherently has several disadvantages.

First, it is less detailed than the Lorenz curve in that it describes a size distribution of only some of the firms in the industry.   Second, the ratio is very sensitive to how one defines the market.   A concentration ratio will be overstated if inappropriate products are included or if the relevant market is smaller in scope than nationwide.   In turn, the concentration ratio will be understated if reasonably good substitutes are excluded and import competition in that market is significant.   Third, there are certain data problems in using this technique.   For example, industry and product class definitions for Census Bureau standard industrial classification (SIC) codes often do not provide the type of data that economists need.   In addition, it may be difficult to separate sales of given firms and relevant markets from those in other markets.

The Herfindahl–Hirschman index is a summary measure which is calculated by summing the squares of the sizes of firms in a given market.   Units of measurement may be sales, assets or employment.   It is similar to the Gini coefficient, but overcomes the latter's main drawbacks.   In general, the value of the index increases as the number of firms decreases or the inequality among the number of firms in the industry increases. The maximum value obtainable is 10,000, for a pure monopolist.

The measure is supported because of its treatment of firm size, both absolute and relative, within a given market. Further, the index simultaneously considers all firms in the market. Its primary deficiency is the basic difficulty in obtaining necessary market share data. This need is particularly acute for the largest firms because squaring of market shares in the formula more heavily weights the values for these firms.

Two indices have strong theoretical economic underpinnings. The Rothschild index is a measure of market power that utilizes a comparison of two types of negatively sloped demand curves that a firm may face.[47] If the firm believes that its rivals will match any price changes which it initiates, then the relevant demand curve is the "followship" or "constant share" curve. On the other hand, if the firm assumes that its rivals do not change their prices in response to its price moves, then the applicable curve is the "nonfollowship" or changing market share" demand curve. In this situation, the firm can gain customers if it lowers its price below that of its rivals or, conversely, lose some of its business by instituting a boost in price level above that of its competitors. It is possible that the firm may find either one or the other curve apropos, depending on the specific segment of the market.

The Rothschild index may be calculated by dividing the slope of the nonfollowship (NFD) demand curve by that of the followship (FD) curve. A computed value of zero would indicate perfect competition and a flat NFD curve, while a value of one would reflect a pure monopoly market and, therefore, identical NFD and FD curves. Market power would, of course, be greater the closer the index value came to equaling one.

While intellectually appealing, the index suffers from two serious drawbacks: 1) it is virtually impossible to secure the requisite data to calculate any values; and 2) it is devoid of any supply or cost elements.

Another theoretical measure of market power is the Lerner index.[48] The index is calculated by dividing the difference between price and marginal cost for a given product by its price. Under conditions of perfect competition, price equals marginal cost and therefore the index equals zero, as was the case with the Rothschild construct. Similarly, a pure monopoly would yield a value of one, and intermediate market structures would result in positive values less than one.

In short, under this approach, the degree of market power is gauged based on the ability of the firm to deviate from true marginal cost. Underlying assumptions include: 1) the firm must pursue profit maximization and charge only one price; 2) marginal cost can be measured and is indepen-dent of market structure; and 3) the dominant firm and its rivals are presumed to be well-informed about market conditions.

The Lerner index is the most commonly used measure of market perfor-mance that estimates departures from an ideal competitive structure. It has a number of advantages. The method theoretically permits direct calculation of the allocatively inefficient deviation of actual price from marginal cost associated with monopoly. Unlike the Rothschild index, it utilizes both demand and cost variables. The Lerner index varies with the elasticities of demand and supply facing the firm as well as market shares. It does not overemphasize a single variable, *e.g.*, number of firms or market share, which is a drawback inherent in certain other market power estimators. The approach is a measure of actual misconduct (but is not a gauge of potential monopoly behavior).

The index also possesses a few disadvantages. It is static rather than dynamic; this, however, is also characteristic of other market power measures. Second, obtaining data on marginal costs or ratios of price to marginal costs is quite difficult in practice. A reasonable surrogate in practice is the substitution of either average total cost or average variable cost. A variation on this theme is to use a ratio of actual profits to unit cost. Since economic theory teaches us that in the long run monopoly profits will generally be supranormal and competitive profits can be expected to be normal, such profit indices are also potentially useful measures of market power.

These measures have proven to be of more than academic interest. For example, the Majority Staff of the House Subcommittee on Telecommunications relied on the Lerner index as an important gauge of AT&T's monopoly power in the long distance and terminal equipment markets.[49] Calculations of Herfindahl–Hirschman Indices have been developed relating to intrastate interexchange markets.[50] Moreover, the link between high concentration and high profits has been demonstrated in many U.S. markets.[51]

D. Market Theory in Perspective

Several conclusions follow from this discussion of theoretical models of the firm and market organization and their applicability to the telecommunications industry. First, perfect competition and pure monopoly are useful analytical tools for economists. However, there are many real world markets (*e.g.*, telecommunications) that do not resemble the structure–conduct–performance paradigm of these two models, a fact that has led theoreticians to search for new explanatory constructs. A number of "intermediate" models have been introduced which fall broadly into the categories of oligopoly, monopolistic competition, or the behavioral school.

Second, while attractive as a standard for comparison of performance for real world firms and markets, the perfect competition model has proven to be theoretically less than perfect because of market failures, "second best" problems, and questionable assumptions and competing objectives. The quest for a replacement has resulted in a workable competition standard whose practicality probably makes it a superior standard, but which suffers from indecision and the need for subjective judgments. More recently, "market contestability" has been proffered by some as a more realistic conceptual benchmark (see *infra*).

Third, the preceding points underscore the need for more research into the theory of the firm and market organization. Nonetheless, the "state of the art" in industrial organization has provided us with some useful insights for our examination of the telecommunications industry. For example, the current dominance of AT&T in many telecommunications markets and submarkets, plus the increasingly important role played by other large corporations, moves this analysis towards consideration of oligopoly and other similar models of imperfect competition. Among existing theories which we have reviewed, price leadership (especially the dominant firm construct) and limit pricing models would particularly seem to merit a closer look.[52]   In addition, the increasingly important role apparently played by strategic behavior coupled with structural characteristics (e.g., the dynamics of rapid entry and eventual market rationalization) should also be scrutinized.

Next, the swirling debate concerning the extent of market power in a number of telecommunications arenas should exhort us to find a meaningful measure of that phenomenon. Our review of available techniques leads us to embrace the Lerner or Herfindahl–Hirschman indices, or both, whenever feasible as a means of lending rigor to any such analysis. Indeed, as noted above, tests of the Lerner gauge have already been conducted by researchers with respect to predivestiture AT&T. Further, given the significant structural changes now occurring in the industry and the excellent prospects of continuing change for at least the near term, there appears to be a particular need for "fresh" empirical research. In short, much work needs to be done in the realm of case studies and cross–section analyses in the telecommunications sector.

Finally, the continuation of robust new entry coupled with the existence of significant market imperfections in the telecommunications industry during the early post divestiture period may signal the need for new and innovative public policies, at least in the short run. We will examine in the next section the conceptual justification for government intervention in the U.S. economy, followed by an exposition of the theory and role of regulation as it pertains to our analysis.

E. Goals and Objectives of Governmental Intervention

In any form of economic system (e.g., capitalism, socialism), formulation of societal goals or objectives must necessarily be undertaken. How is the "correct" mix of goals chosen in this country, and by whom? Of course, public policy makers, both those who are elected and those who receive appointments, determine the mix, guided ultimately by the voters (either acting individually or as part of a special interest "bloc"). A much more difficult question concerns the "best" means to achieve these objectives. The optimal blend of market forces and government intervention is something, as they say, about which "reasonable men will differ."

The neoclassical roots of American capitalism dictate that market based solutions be found wherever possible. Competition in the marketplace can potentially lead to welfare maximization to an extent not obtainable through actions by the state, *ceteris paribus*.

In practice, the market mechanism alone may be insufficient to achieve optimal economic prosperity. First, the conditions required to reach this nirvana, *viz.*, "perfect competition," are rarely met in the real world. Second, market "imperfections," *e.g.*, the possession of excessive market power by one or more firms in an industry, may necessitate government activism. The imperfections of the market do not, of course, imply that governmental action will be an improvement, only that it should be considered on its merits.

Market "failures" may also arise, such that an unfettered market mechanism may yield unacceptable results. For example, an unscrupulous polluter may continue to pass the costs of his dubious deeds (*i.e.*, contaminated air, soil or water) onto society unless dissuaded by a nonmarket solution, such as a tax. Of greater interest for our purposes is the case of a "natural monopoly," where the existence of scale economies and a decreasing long run average cost (LRAC) curve in the relevant portion of the demand curve prevents marginal cost pricing and profitability.[53]

Moreover, public decision makers may not share mainstream economics' emphasis on efficiency. If this is so, then even competition under the requisite set of conditions for efficiency may not unequivocally be the policy prescription desired by society. Greater economic security or equity considerations such as a more fair distribution of wealth may be accorded significant weight by the public. Adoption of these goals may well require less emphasis on efficiency.

Basically, competition allowed to flourish in an open marketplace may be the best way to achieve economic efficiency in many instances; this presumes that such distortions as the aforementioned imperfections and failures, as well as "second best" problems, do not intercede, and that the state can do no better despite higher transaction costs.[54] Under some circumstances, solely a government solution may be required for assuring social wellbeing. A good that can be supplied at no extra cost to consumers beyond the first one, and whose availability is not reduced after the initial unit is "consumed," cannot be successfully provided and distributed by the market. If attempted, the experiment would be beset by a "free rider" problem, thereby dashing hopes of an efficient allocation of resources through the price mechanism. Thus, such "public goods" as police and fire protection and national defense should be handled by a state authority.

What, then, is the proper role of government in an avowedly market based economic system? There is no easy answer to this question. Milton Friedman, a leading spokesman for libertarian economists, believes the state should be limited to three specific functions: 1) to legislate and enforce laws, and adjudicate disputes; 2) to intervene in order to counter technical monopolies and overcome "neighborhood" (*i.e.*, externality) effects, such as pollution; and 3) to supplement private charities and families in protecting the "irresponsible" (*e.g.*, the mentally ill, children).[55] On the particular subject of technical monopolies, he argues that only under certain circumstances, *viz.*, where the good or service is a necessity and the provider's market power is sizeable, could government regulation or ownership conceivably be a "lesser evil" than private monopoly.[56] Overall, Friedman regards the achievement and maintenance of economic (and noneconomic) freedom as a social goal of paramount importance, the basis for his belief in democracy and its prerequisite, a free market.

Other economists would expand the scope of legitimate government authority. Paul Samuelson, a major architect of the Keynesian "new economics," avers that government should strive to establish an economic and legal framework as well as promote efficiency, equity and stability. State intervention should occur wherever 1) the market performs imperfectly or fails altogether; 2) externalities or "spillover effects" are needed to reflect an inequality of social and private costs or benefits; 3) income redistribution is sought; and 4) discretionary fiscal (*i.e.*, government spending or taxation) and monetary policy are deemed necessary to combat inflation or unemployment. Regulation is considered appropriate in cases of "natural monopoly," but periodic government failures are a reality which must be recognized.[57]

Phillip Klein, an institutionalist, specifically disputes Friedman's views, extending the latter's umpire analogy:

> The public sector is . . . more than the umpire Friedman permits it to be. It is also part manager and part coach, as well as a sometime player. Even if it never carried the ball, however, the public sector would still play a role greater than mere keeper of the rules, because like all umpires it has a view of the whole that is distinctive and is a crucial complement to the view of the other players. No doubt in football umpires are consulted before critical rules are changed because they have a perspective on the way the game goes that no one else has. They cannot and should not change the rules by fiat or alone, but their view is a valuable input.[58]

Those with a philosophical bent toward economic planning would assign a greater role to government. For example, Gerald Sirkin points to the four general bases for government intervention: 1) provision of "non–market products" (*i.e.*, public goods), such as parks, roads, and national defense; 2) attempted improvement of the functioning of markets; 3) efforts to correct "inherent defects in the market mechanism"; and 4) optimization of the savings rate.[59] The market improvement function (number two) would include facilitation of information flows for decision makers, promotion of effective competition, increased resource mobility, and economic stabilization through appropriate fiscal and monetary measures. Amelioration of market failures (number three) would become a necessity in the case of "external" economies or diseconomies (whereby one firm's actions impose nonmarket benefits or costs upon another, *e.g.*, unpatented basic research available to everyone); consumer irrationality; "unavoidable monopoly" (which must be regulated); uncertainty and risk (requiring better dissemination of information); and emergency resource reallocations. Government intervention would also be prudent where "monopoly" (*i.e.*, a single supplier) exists in a given market, or income redistribution or supplementation is needed. Sirkin cautions us, however, that government decision makers, like the market, are imperfect, and urges a market based solution in "close call" instances because the market better promotes economic freedom.

W. Arthur Lewis, a social democrat and a 1979 Nobel Prize recipient for economics, would add that other "defects" mandating state intervention include 1) the inability of the market mechanism to "humanize the wage relation" because workers do not own the tools and machinery with which they work; 2) the need to regulate foreign trade; and 3) the wastefulness of the market economy attributable to heavy advertising.[60] Lewis posits that only the state can assure competition and the effective working of the market economy; this is ideally achieved through "inducement" whereby the state "manipulates the market to secure its objectives."[61]

What can be surmised from this diversity of learned opinion with respect to government's rightful duties in a capitalist economy? Several broad themes seem to emerge. First, when in doubt as to the proper policy route, public decision makers should opt for a market based solution. Second, a legitimate role for prudent government intervention clearly exists. At minimum, the state is needed to function as rule maker, and policeman and judge. It should create incentives for efficiency by choosing (at the behest of its electorate) the market mechanism. When the mechanism malfunctions, discretionary policies which utilize the market (e.g., taxes), and surrogate market prescriptions (e.g., rate base/rate of return regulation) should be specifically applied. Some measure of distributional equity and macroeconomic stabilization should also be implemented. A general "rule" on the role of government in the economic system may be enunciated: government intervention should be considered where the "invisible hand" is inherently deficient. Public participation can sometimes correct the occasional failures of the marketplace. Thus, government action of some sort is plainly required where "natural monopoly" conditions prevent the coexistence of profit maximization and allocative efficiency. Market power not stemming from significant economies presents a more vexing problem. Delineations of egregious monopoly control must be carefully developed before the state's role can be defined.

Thus, both economic regulation and antitrust policy in a broad sense seem to have a solid theoretical foundation, in terms of mainstream economic theory and desirable objectives for the economy. Subsequent sections in this chapter address these traditional forms of U.S. public policy.

F.   Rationales for Regulating Public Utilities

1.   Overview

Conceptually and in practice, public utility regulation is an instrument of economic control most sharply characterized by its complex, seemingly Delphic nature. The subject is one about which pundits vociferously "agree to disagree." A lack of consensus begins with the definition of "public utility" itself: many would concur with the assessment that this entity is "easy to recognize but difficult to describe."[62]

Many interpretations exist. For example, Farris and Sampson observe:

> We have seen that there are no valid universal criteria by which we can define a public utility in economic terms. Legally speaking, the situation is almost vague. The courts have been somewhat erratic and inconsistent in applying the concept of "business affected with a public interest," and they now seem to have abandoned this function to legislative bodies. For practical purposes, then, it would not be far wrong to assume that a public utility is any business which an appropriate legislative body declares to be a public utility! Nevertheless, we commonly think of public utility operations as being confined to certain privately owned or publicly owned organizations in the areas of communications, energy, transportation, and water supply, and sometimes sewage and garbage disposal.[63]

Kahn acknowledges the fuzziness of the public utility concept but asserts:

> And yet there is such a thing as a public utility. The line between these and other types of industries is a shadowy area; and it shifts over time. But there remains a core of industries, privately owned and operated in this country, in which, at least in principle, the primary guarantor of acceptable performance is conceived to be (whatever it is in truth) not competition or self–restraint but direct government controls––over entry (and in many instances exit), and price, and conditions of service––exercised by administrative commissions constituted for this specific purpose. In this respect, the public utilities remain a fairly distinct group, comprising the same industries that 60 to 80 years ago would have been given essentially the same designation and regulatory treatment––the generation, transmission, and distribution of electric power; the manufacture and distribution of gas; telephone, telegraph, and cable communi– cations; common carrier transportation, urban and interurban, passenger and freight; local water and sewerage supply (to the extent at least that these continue to be provided by privately–owned companies); and, in a sense at the periphery, banking.[64]

Shepherd and Wilcox succinctly define "public utility" as a "vernacular phrase for a common carrier [which] may be privately or publicly owned."[65] In turn, a "common carrier" is a "franchised utility required to serve all customers at the regulated prices."[66]

Notions of the proper characterization of the concept may be extracted from the writings of Bonbright as well as Garfield and Lovejoy. Classifying the term "public utilities" as "one of popular usage rather than of precise definition," Bonbright delimits the idea as:

> . . . any enterprise subject to regulation, including price regulation, of a type designed primarily to protect consumers . . . [applies] only to those enterprises subject to regulation as a matter of long–run policy rather than as a temporary expedient in wartime or in some other emergency.[67]

Garfield and Lovejoy attempt to differentiate between "public interest" and "public utility":

> The latter concept is narrower than the former and is included in it. Regulation in the public interest apparently can encompass virtually any type of business activity if there is adequate reason. In cases of other than utility industries, a prime consideration is the adequacy or inadequacy of competition in a broad sense. Too much or too little competition may generate the need for some controls. In contrast, a utility has some rather definite characteristics that make extensive regulation a necessity.[68]

Most economists agree, however, that among these "rather definite characteristics" necessitating regulation are those which collectively may be called a "natural monopoly."[69] These and other justifications for public utility regulation are discussed below.

2. Natural Monopoly and the Control of Monopoly Power

Simply stated, a "natural monopoly" occurs when: (1) long run average costs (LRAC) are declining over the entire range of a given market as determined by the relevant portion of the demand curve); and (2) the market in question is local, *i.e.*, confined to a particular geographic area.[70] Figure II–2 illustrates this basic concept graphically. Curve LRAC represents both economies and diseconomies of scale. Point X marks the minimum on the curve: to the left of X are points on LRAC that indicate unit costs that decline as output increases (*e.g.*, Point Y); to the right, unit costs rise as the quantity supplied is boosted (*e.g.*, Point Z).

In economic terms, Point Y hypothetically corresponds to two oligopolists, or "duopolists," that equally divide the market established by industry demand curve D_1. That is, each duopolist supplies $Q_{d1,2}$ which equals one half of the total market. As is shown, the resulting unit cost for each is $LRAC_{d1,2}$, which is significantly greater than the unit cost enjoyed by a monopolist ($LRAC_{RM1}$). In such a case, public policy makers should consider a regulated monopoly industry structure to maximize industry efficiency or other goals.

A second nonoptimal situation is portrayed by Point Z. Original demand curve D_1 increases, *i.e.*, shifts to the right, yielding D_2. If the LRAC curve remains the same, then a monopolist would produce at a point on the curve where diseconomies occur, *viz.*, $LRAC_{RM2}$. Under these conditions, a firm's efficiency is not maximized since lower firm output levels would yield lower unit costs.

Figure II–2

NATURAL MONOPOLY AND ECONOMIES OF SCALE:
TWO NON–OPTIMAL CASES

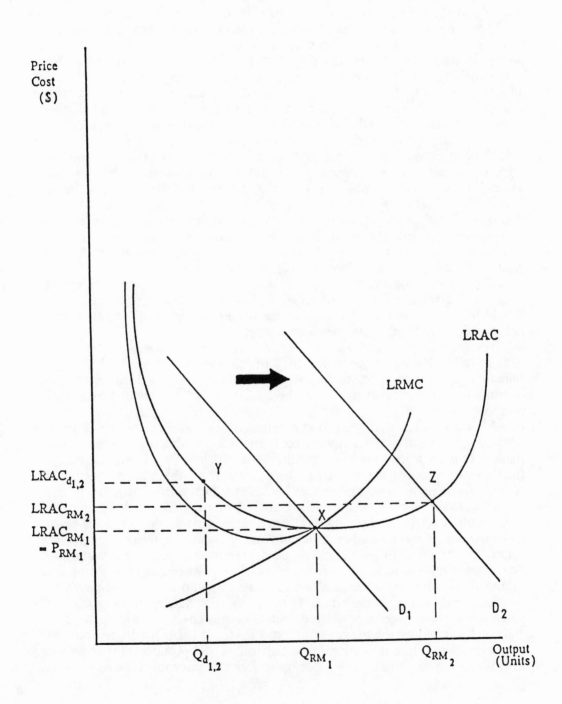

Elaboration on our use of "efficiency" seems appropriate at this point. More precisely, *economic efficiency* has primarily two components, allocative and technical. *Allocative efficiency* relates to the way in which society's scarce resources are allocated among the goods and services produced by the economy. Resources are said to be allocated efficiently when it is not possible to change the distribution of resources, increasing quantities of some goods and reducing quantities of others, without making some one worse off than before. That is, if it is possible to reallocate resources and make some people better (in the sense that they prefer the second situation to the first) while making no one else worse off, then the existing pattern of resource allocation is not efficient. This is called the Pareto criterion, after the economist V.F.D. Pareto.[71] If a particular allocation of resources is efficient in this sense, then it is called "Pareto optimal" (see discussion *supra*).

In a competitive market, allocative efficiency (*i.e.*, Pareto optimality) would be achieved if a firm set its price at marginal cost (P=MC) and there were no externalities (*e.g.*, social costs are not internalized by the firm, such as the societal cost of pollution). In a natural monopoly setting, setting P=MC would yield a price less than average costs (because the MC curve declines "faster" than the long run average cost curve), and the firm's revenue requirement would not be achieved. This, of course, complicates the picture and has resulted in a raging debate concerning optimal pricing for a regulated monopoly (see *supra* and Chapter IV).

The other basic type of efficiency is *technical* or *X efficiency*. This refers to the relationship of output to inputs; a technically efficient outcome would be one where output is maximized for a given level of (input) cost, or cost is minimized for a given level of output.

There actually is a third, albeit much less used, concept of efficiency. This is called *Y efficiency*. Inefficiency of this sort would arise where a firm fails to supply potential customers who are willing to pay a price which yields a profit to the firm, and may arise because of a lack of competitive market pressures.

All three efficiencies may occur concurrently. A firm which is pricing optimally, producing at its lowest cost, and taking advantage of all existing market opportunities which are profitable is efficient in all three senses. A firm can be efficient in one, two, three or none of these areas. Generally, X and Y are likely to occur together because of their similar origins.

In essence, the discussion has centered on a static analysis and cost minimization, given an existing long run average cost curve. Optimal pricing and promotion of allocative efficiency in the current telecommunications setting is addressed in greater detail elsewhere in this book; for purposes of this exposition on scale economies, it is shown graphically as Point X in Figure II–2. Improved technical (X) efficiency could be depicted graphically by a lowering (*i.e.*, downward shift) of the existing LRAC curve, such that a given output level would now have decreased unit costs. In Figure II–3, this shift is illustrated by the movement from $LRAC_1$ to $LRAC_2$. In practice, this might be caused by a technological breakthrough in a production process (*e.g.*, manufacturing of single mode fiber optics) or a significant innovation (*e.g.*,

Figure II–3

NATURAL MONOPOLY AND ECONOMIES OF SCALE:
EFFECTS OF TECHNICAL EFFICIENCY CHANGES

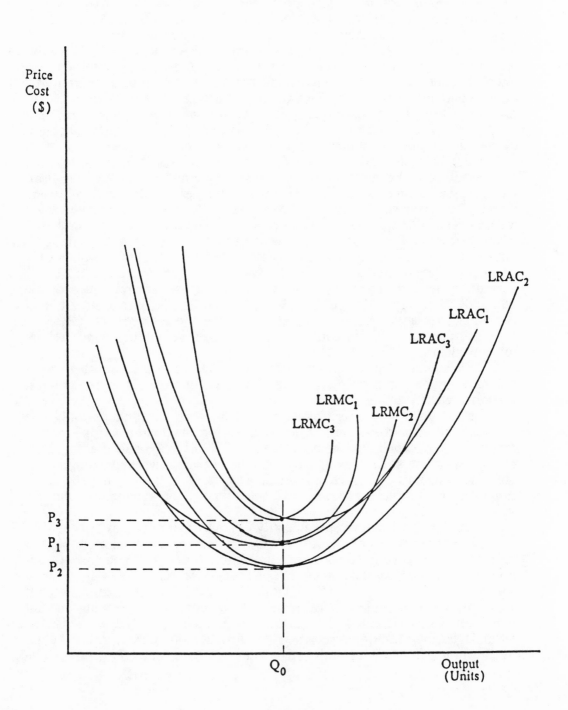

paired cable replacing open wire for local transmission of telephone calls). A decrease in technical efficiency ($LRAC_1$ shifting upward to $LRAC_3$) could occur as use of a scarce resource becomes more costly with existing or even new technology (*e.g.*, congestion or "crowding" in the radio spectrum band allocated to satellite transmission). In this example, the same output Q_0 is attained regardless of the LRAC curve shift so that the unit cost effect ($P_i = LRAC_{i\ MIN}$) for a given quantity supplied can be readily seen.

Economies of scale can occur for any of several reasons. Broadly, economies may arise with respect to the manufacture of a single product or multiple products,[72] and may involve a single plant or multiplant operations. Scale economies may be "real" (*e.g.*, in production, advertising, marketing, research and development, or transportation) or pecuniary (such as borrowing or raising capital through equity issues). Diseconomies may surface because of managerial problems inherent in a large corporation.

Figure II–4 illustrates why regulation of a natural monopoly may be theoretically superior in terms of society's welfare and viability of the firm. As discussed above, a profit maximizing supplier would produce where marginal revenue equals marginal cost (*i.e.*, MR=MC). The unregulated monopolist's price P_{UM} would be higher and his output Q_{UM} lower than that resulting from perfect competition.[73] Under conditions where scale economies obtain relative to market demand, this strategy would additionally yield a situation where marginal cost is always lower than average total costs, preventing the monopolist from recovering his investment regardless of the output level chosen. If regulation were introduced, the firm's output level could be increased to Q_{RM} by setting the price equal to average costs (P_{RM}), thereby more closely approximating the "competitive solution" and welfare maximization.

The discussion thus far has presented a straightforward linkage between a natural monopoly and scale economies. In fact, the issue is more complex, both theoretically and in practice.

For example, it has been assumed that the industry produces only one product and that economies of scale exist for the market's total output required by the applicable demand curve. This is only one limiting case; multiproduct industries are not only possible but are much more common in the U.S. economy. In such instances, economies of scope may be more important than scale economies and determinative of a natural monopoly state.[74]

Moreover, the extent or sustainability of scale economies may vary widely in a given industry. For instance, an industry may be a natural monopoly in only certain facets or operations, *e.g.*, provision of local telephone service but not customer premises equipment. Scale economies might only apply over a specific range of outputs (*i.e.*, "locally") rather than the entire output ("globally"). And technological change may unravel an existing natural monopoly by overcoming the latter's inherent cost advantage. Different technologies may feature varying degrees of scale economies such that failure by the monopolist to "keep up–to–date" may not make competition infeasible.

Figure II–4

NATURAL MONOPOLY AND ECONOMIES OF SCALE:
REGULATION VS. FREE MARKET

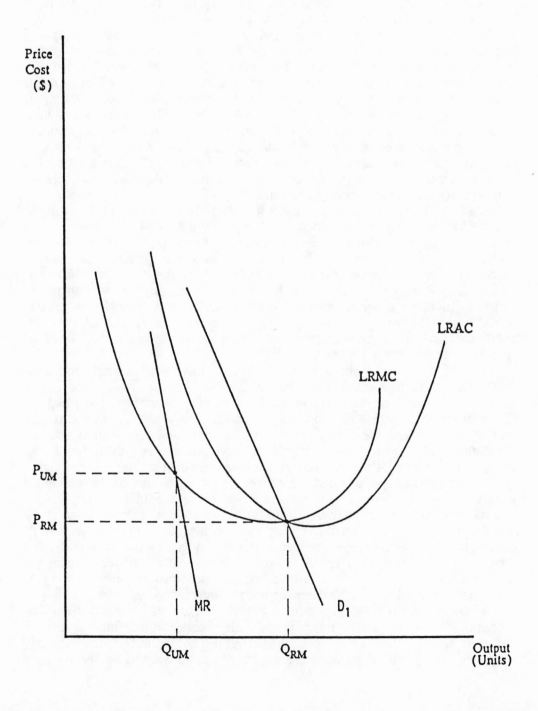

Thus, both the relative costs of alternative technologies and the level of market demand (along with scale or scope economies) appear to be critical determinants of a natural monopoly.

In the recent industrial organization literature several major new concepts have emerged with respect to the natural monopoly debate. Economists affiliated with the now dismantled Bell System have been principal contributors to these new theories, which first surfaced during the late 1970s. Baumol, Bailey, Panzar and Willig developed the theory of "sustainability" as a means to explain the seemingly counterintuitive notion that a natural monopoly may be vulnerable to successful entry by "uninnovative" competitors even if it is producing and pricing efficiently and earning no economic profits.[75] Under such circumstances, regulators may seek to bar entry which would threaten the viability of a socially advantageous monopoly. Criticisms of the theory center on its assumptions, e.g., the unrealistic premise of an "idealized regulatory process"[76] or the use of an alternative assumption of output maintenance (vis-à-vis a lack of a price response) by the monopolist once confronted by entry, thereby ameliorating most sustainability problems.[77]

A second model of entry into natural monopoly sectors was introduced in the 1970s. Called "game theory," the construct was pioneered in a telecommunications setting by Faulhaber and refined by Sharkey.[78] In one such model, firms pursuing unconstrained strategic pricing and output strategies can achieve a stable equilibrium if potential competition is significant. A demand side model has also been formulated, where buyers form coalitions in order to extract more favorable terms from firms. As in the case of the sustainability theories, the game theory models possess shortcomings, such as indeterminate equilibria (noncooperative) or "costless" formation of coalitions (cooperative).[79]

More recently and perhaps more importantly in view of current conditions in the U.S. telecommunications industry, Baumol, Panzar, Willig, and Bailey conceived a theory of "contestable markets" as an explanation and predictor of behavior in a regulated monopoly market with unconstrained exit and entry.[80] In essence, the theory postulates that potential competition acts to constrain market power by a regulated monopolist. For example, if the monopolist's pricing does not reflect the marginal cost of providing a given service or product, then rapid entry by firms with similar technological capabilities would occur. This market disciplining would even apply to a natural monopoly which may be forced by "hit-and-run" entry to price at the social optimum.[81] In a perfectly contestable market there are no "sunk costs" of entry, i.e., irreversible investments borne for a specific use that have virtually no economic alternative use. It is also assumed that the monopolist's prices are fixed for a certain amount of time, and that consumers respond to price differences with a shorter lag.

A noncontestable market is one in which barriers to entry permit a monopolist to behave anticompetitively. Entry barriers are defined to include any cost borne solely or at least primarily by an entrant in an industry. Fixed costs and scale economies are generally not considered by the theory's supporters to function as such barriers. Apparently only sunk costs serve to bar entry by increasing the risk faced by potential entrants. Some have alleged that AT&T's attempts to use the regulatory process during the 1970s to deny interconnection to specialized common carriers were evidence of a strategy to erect sunk cost barriers.[82]

Economists differ as to the degree of usefulness of the model. Contestable market theory proponents suggest it should supplant the traditional perfect competition construct as the benchmark for evaluating public policy initiatives in an industrial organization context. These advocates emphasize the importance of incorporating into any such model the ability of firms to initiate changes in market prices, an element not currently found in the perfect competition theory. Moreover, contrary to accepted teachings, the new theory posits that market power may be absent despite a paucity of firms in a given industry such as may exist in telecommunications and airlines. For this to occur, a number of conditions requisite for market contestability must be met, i.e., a lagged response by the incumbents to entrant's price reductions, durable capital goods and industry personnel that are economically transferable between alternative uses, and easy access to the market.[83]

Others are less convinced by this theoretical approach. Criticisms include: (1) an overemphasis with respect to cost and other supply conditions vis-à-vis demand factors;[84] (2) the inappropriate deemphasis on dominant firm behavior;[85] and (3) a preoccupation with "ultra-free entry" as a new conceptual standard for industrial organization when, in fact, the analysis only examines a "specialized, extreme set of conditions" which rarely exist in practice.[86] In addition, some assert that the existence of time lags allows incumbents to earn supranormal profits and forestall entry, and that technology may create sunk costs that constrain a market's contestability. Moreover, a recession may lead to depressed capital markets and thereby raise the cost of exit, while an economic expansion could afford entry without threatening the incumbent's monopolistic prices.[87]

These three models all attempt, *inter alia,* to explain the dynamics of a regulated natural monopoly subject to competitive entry. A fourth theory, espoused by the "Chicago School" of economics, posits that the incidence of natural monopolies is neither significant[88] nor in need of public regulation.[89] Friedman argues that:

> . . . the areas in which technical considerations make
> monopoly a likely or a probable outcome are fairly limited.
> They would offer no serious threat to the preservation of a
> free economy if it were not for the tendency of regulation,
> introduced on this ground, to spread to situations in which it
> is not so justified.[90]

Posner similarly emphasizes his view about the doubtful efficacy of regulation, especially as it would adversely affect a dynamic industry such as telecommunications:

> The benefits of [public utility] regulation are dubious,
> not only because the evils of natural monopoly are

exaggerated but also because the effectiveness of regulation in controlling them is highly questionable. At the same time, regulation costs a great deal and would probably cost much more if serious effort were made to prevent the undesirable side effects on efficiency that profit regulation fosters.

. . . Communications is a contemporary example of an industry undergoing rapid technological changes that are apparently opening up a host of new competitive opportunities. In general, the tempo of change in the economy seems to be increasing. The most pernicious feature of regulation would appear to be precisely its impact on change--its tendency to retard the growth of competition that would erode the power of regulated monopolists. To embrace regulation because an industry is today a natural monopoly and seems likely to remain so is to gamble dangerously with the future. To impose regulation on the basis of a prophecy that the industry will remain monopolistic forever may be to make the prophecy self-fulfilling.[91]

The "public interest" theory presents a poignant contrast to this line of reasoning. Essentially, the theory states that the function of public utility regulation is to protect the consumer against potential or actual abuses of monopoly power. Primary objectives of the regulator are perceived to be the promotion of efficiency and the minimization of maldistribution of income by the monopolist.[92] This regulation is basically intended to function as a "substitute for competition."[93] Criticisms of the theory's premise center on its "negative role" and questionable efficacy relative to competition in providing incentives for good performance.[94]

A more recently developed model in the public utility literature is the "dominant firm/strategic behavior" theory.[95] Using a market rules paradigm approach, the construct is premised on the need for a transitional mechanism for regulating the dominant firm in an industry destined to become structurally contestable, *i.e.*, characterized by a lack of major entry barriers and multiple substitute services. It is assumed that different markets will "evolve" at different rates, *e.g.*, interexchange markets more rapidly than local exchange markets. Under this theory, market rules would include, *inter alia*, a rate structure which reflects the use of generic facilities rather than the current services, no tariff restrictions on resale or shared use, and a ban on price boosts by the dominant firm after a competitor exits a given market.

Before turning to other major rationales for public utility regulation, the discussion on natural monopoly must be suitably completed. Many economists would join Baumol, Eckstein and Kahn in defining this market condition:

An industry is said to be a natural monopoly when it is characterized by economies of scale over the entire range of output that the market will take.[96]

Some other economists would supplement the "economies" feature with certain additional characteristics:[97] (1) Demand elasticities that vary by markets, with at least one market highly inelastic (*e.g.,* local phone service or residential electricity); (2) sharp and regular fluctuations in output (*e.g.,* peak vs. off peak calling traffic); and (3) direct physical connections (*e.g.,* gas hook ups or telephone drop wire and local loops).

3. Other Rationales for Regulation

Besides "natural monopoly" conditions and the concomitant need for control of market power, other major explanations or theories concerning the existence of public utility regulation include: (1) Self–interest theories (*i.e.,* "capture" of regulators by the regulated; "interest group"; "coalition building"); (2) Theory of the status quo; (3) Equity–stability theory; (4) Avoidance of destructive competition theory; and (5) Arbitration theories. Each is discussed below.

a. Self–Interest Theories
One type of "self–interest" rationale is the "capture" theory, re–cast in economic terms by Stigler.[98] This "theory of economic regulation" attempts to explain who will benefit and who will be harmed by regulation, the nature of that regulation, and its effect on allocative efficiency. The basic premise of the Stigler model is that "regulation is acquired by the industry, and is designed and operated primarily for its benefit."[99] Essentially, the demand for regulation is not determined by consumers who are seeking protection from monopoly power (as per the "public interest" theory); rather, this function is shaped by firms seeking to use regulation to their own best advantage. This may include such activities as collusion, barring entry, thwarting competitive responses from existing rivals, or securing favorable treatment from the government (*e.g.,* subsidies). In turn, regulation is supplied by political jurisdictions willing to participate on a *quid pro quo* basis, *i.e.,* an exchange of favors. On balance, political support of industry is perceived as potentially of great benefit to regulators while the adverse effects of regulation on consumers are regarded as small, hidden, and not likely to cause political problems. The history of transportation regulation is considered by advocates to be support for the theory's validity.

Deficiencies have been found to exist, however. A number of "real world" exceptions have been identified in telecommunications (*e.g.,* the FCC's procompetition policies, despite enormous pressure from AT&T during the 1960s and 1970s)[100] and other regulated sectors (such as railroads, natural gas transmission, nuclear energy). Thus, there is considerable evidence which contradicts the predictions of this theory.[101]

Closely related to the economic theory of regulation is the "interest group" model, which is a political science construct that envisions regulation as a good that may be exchanged for votes.[102] Criticisms include the lack of rigorous theory for predicting the role of the various interest groups, and the exclusion of all nonpolitical factors.

According to the "coalition–building" theory, regulators attempt to create a "coalition of support" to ensure their wellbeing.[103] This goal allegedly explains observed agency policies of rate averaging, cross subsidization, and income redistribution. Critics point to the theory's simplistic thesis which ignores public "sunshine" and debate.

b. Theory of the "Status Quo"

Developed by Owen and Braeutigam, this model is based on the notion that regulatory lag and other administrative characteristics of public service commissions are a smoke screen for the agencies' true objective, *viz.*, to preserve the *status quo* from market–induced shocks.[104] Such perturbations would include higher risk and uncertainty, the threat of substantial financial losses, and "noise" in the planning process. Benefits accrue to those who accept the existing regime, whose costs are borne by those who favor change, *i.e.*, an opportunity for the market to operate. As in the case of the "capture" models, this rationale fails to explain many occurrences, such as regulators who are embracing change.[105]

c. "Equity – Stability" Theory

This theory stresses that regulation attempts to introduce nonefficiency goals through administrative–judicial systems rather than promote efficient markets.[106] Goals such as fairness and stability take precedence over efficiency considerations. Congress is perceived to be the driving force behind this philosophical thrust. Drawbacks of the construct center on its one dimensional focus (*viz.*, equity) which belies the current public policy emphasis on competition and efficiency. Examples are the new reliance on the market place and deregulation in such traditionally regulated sectors as the airline industry, trucking, railroads, pipelines, and telecommunications.

d. Avoidance of Destructive Competition

Brandeis and others have argued that competition under certain conditions could be destructive and, therefore, socially undesirable.[107] Markets which are capital intensive, where fixed costs represent a relatively high percentage of total costs, and excess capacity is commonplace may be susceptible to financially disastrous episodes brought on by "ruinous" competition. Substantial underutilization of capacity could precipitate vigorous price "wars" which, given the industry cost structure, could cause prices to plummet significantly before settling out at average variable cost (below which the economic justification for continuing to operate generally disappears). In an industry characterized by scale economies in the relevant demand range and entry, the problem could be exacerbated.

This defense of regulation has been subject to considerable criticism. For example, firms could obtain capital to keep their facilities operating rather than resort to injurious pricing strategies. If borrowing could be arranged based on expected future upswings, then perhaps operations should be ceased. In the latter situation, the market could well be signaling that an inefficient overinvestment had occurred.

Secondly, industries that fit the large fixed investment prerequisite include, *e.g.*, metals such as copper or steel--not transportation or airlines (as is usually argued) where high fixed costs are not an intractable problem.[108]

e. Arbitration Theories

Two basic models are classified as arbitration theories.[109] First, Baldwin advances a "political" theory of regulation which identifies a mediation function as an agency's *raison d'etre*.[110] In order to prevent a possible political backlash from losing parties whose dispute has been arbitrated by the government, an independent regulatory commission is established which is removed from political control and the potential ire of the losers. A second variation is Goldberg's "contract" model where a regulatory commission functions as an agent for consumers in their "bargaining" with producers.[111] Contracts are consummated by the two groups and subject to periodic re-negotiations and interpretations.

As with the other theories, this type is not broad enough to explain all "real world" rationales for regulation. Both are simplistic: the political theory ignores the impact of higher authorities, *e.g.*, courts that hear appeals of commission decisions, while the contract model tends to reduce regulatory operations to two-party bargaining.

The next section examines antitrust policy, the other major form of government oversight affecting the structure, conduct, and performance of public utilities and other types of telecommunications firms.

G.   Antitrust Policy

1.   Overview

"Antitrust policy" refers to programs designed to control the growth of market power exercised by firms. The term encompasses antimonopoly policy, as well as attempts to curb restrictive practices. Originally intended to deal with groups of amalgamated companies called trusts, the policy in later years has come to include individual firms and groups of cooperating firms called cartels.

As in the case of economic regulatory policy, antitrust policy is a mechanism for public control of business enterprise. Both trace their roots to the late 1800s, and both are essentially legal vehicles that lean heavily on theoretical and empirical economics. General goals of U.S. public policy toward business include achievement of socially optimum levels of resource use (output, prices, costs), progressiveness, full employment and stability of aggregate employment.

In addition, certain microeconomic objectives are ideally pursued by governmental programs. These objectives include technical and allocative efficiency, robust rates of innovation, and a desirable level of product differentiation and selling cost. Of course, our particular concern in this section is the performance of the telecommunications industry in these areas.

Why is there need for an antitrust policy? A number of different reasons have been proffered. Most students of antitrust concur with Dewey's conclusion that all antitrust court decisions at least reflect "a commitment to smallness and decentralization as ways of discouraging the concentration of discretionary authority."[112] Neale adds that the role of special interests, especially those concerned with small business, cannot be overlooked.[113] Some more cynical observers insist that the full employment act for attorneys and economists would dictate such a policy. Apparently few experts in the field would do away with antitrust enforcement altogether; however, vigorous debate continues as to the shape and extent of such public policy.

As discussed above, debate seems to center on the "true" relationship of structure to conduct and each of these factors' effects on performance. Bain and his followers stress the importance of the structure–performance nexus, downplaying the significance of conduct.[114] In contrast, Scherer and others emphasize the importance of examining both structure and conduct, pointing to the greater explanatory power afforded by this approach.[115]

Some economists (e.g., Stigler) have posited that the direction of causation flows from conduct to structure to performance.[116] Under this scenario, public policy should discourage collusive activities but refrain from attempts at deconcentrating markets which are of that nature because of significant economies of scale.

In fact, Williamson asserts that the policy pendulum has incontrovertibly swung toward the primacy of conduct as a determinant of performance:

> The 1960s, 1970s, and 1980s can each, I think, be usefully characterized as an antitrust era. Specifically, concentration and entry–barrier analysis flourished in the 1960s. Efficiency analysis gained ascendancy in the 1970s, and I expect the 1980s to be the period when the analysis of strategic behavior comes of age.[117]

The brouhaha has not been limited to academic economists. Attorneys, although having significant differences in this area, seem united in their condemnation of the state of the art in the economics of industrial organization. Of course, those who wear both legal and economic hats have a special set of conflicts all their own! And public policy makers anxiously await the outcome so they can "get on with it."

The policy task of choosing between antitrust and (economic) regulation can be particularly frustrating. Reasonable men may differ as they are wont to do. The existence of scale economies suggests a demarcation in theory but in practice such characteristics are frequently subject to much empirical debate. Intertemporal considerations may also be important as sagacious determinations may change over time. For example, airlines, trucks, railroads, natural gas, broadcasting, and telecommunications have all been heavily regulated historically. This was true until recently, that is, when each has been deregulated to varying degrees. Some unquantifiable portion of the explanation may be assigned to changed conditions (e.g., a blistering rate of technological change in telecommunications) but another unknown part may be attributed to changing social priorities (e.g., efficiency increasing in importance relative to equity concerns, such as the current emphasis on cost based rates in telecommunications).

Thus, it is difficult to pinpoint the reasons for the relative public policy mix at any one point in time. In fact, a U.S. Appellate Court Judge argues that, technically, antitrust policy should not be thought of as a direct substitute for regulation, except in the case of predatory pricing where it may remove the "excessive competition" rationale for regulatory intervention:

> Rather, it is the unregulated market which is often the alternative to regulation. The function of antitrust is to make that unregulated market a competitive one.[118]

Nonetheless, the practical answer to the apparent dilemma is that ultimately the courts decide.[119] Perhaps the most significant test case in recent history was the landmark Department of Justice – AT&T antitrust action filed on November 20, 1974, where issues such as the "exclusive" versus the "primary jurisdiction" of the FCC with respect to AT&T were debated for some 30 months.[120] The outcome was predictably complex; both regulators and antitrust agencies could legally claim jurisdiction over certain aspects of the Bell System's structure, conduct, and performance.[121]

2. The Foundations of Antitrust

Although a discussion of U.S. antitrust laws and policy must delve into case law, no attempt will be made here to analyze these areas in an exhaustive fashion, especially given the myriad of legal actions that have been taken and the complex legal theories that are at issue. Instead, this part will generally set forth the major statutes, findings and themes that have evolved. This, in turn, will provide the bases for a more detailed examination of the telecommunications sector.[122]

Among the fundamental statutes underlying U.S. Federal antitrust policy that provide a basis for the analysis herein are: (1) the Sherman Act of 1890, (2) the Clayton Act of 1914, and (3) the Federal Trade Commission Act of 1914. The framework of analysis for this part, as in the case of earlier sections, will concern economic theories of the firm and markets. Thus, these major laws, and related court interpretations, will be examined in terms of structure, conduct, and performance.

3. Structural Concerns

a. Description

Three fundamental sections of the antitrust laws focus on structural aspects of industries. For instance, Section 2 of the Sherman Act addresses monopolization practices:

> every person who shall monopolize, or attempt to monopolize, or combine or conspire with another person or persons, to monopolize any part of the trade or commerce among the several States, or with foreign nations, shall be deemed guilty of a misdemeanor, and, on conviction thereof, shall be

punished by fine exceeding $50,000, or by imprisonment not exceeding one year, or by both said punishments, in the discretion of the court.[123]

Early attempts at enforcement of this statute were generally unsuccessful. For example, pivotal initial cases against the whiskey, sugar refining, and cash register trusts were dismissed, either by the government or the courts. However, by the beginning of the second decade of the 1900s, the Supreme Court shifted its position, and issued two new landmark decisions. In 1911, the Court held that the Standard Oil Company of New Jersey and the American Tobacco Company had illegally monopolized the petroleum refining and cigarette industries, respectively. Predatory pricing and a host of other offenses were found. At that time, the Supreme Court set forth its "rule of reason," which held that trade restraints are not necessarily illegal *per se*.

In 1920, Court interpretations made a radical turnabout when it ruled that U.S. Steel had not monopolized the steel industry, and that even if it did possess monopoly power, it had certainly not exercised that power. Hence, this case determined that only "bad monopolists" (*i.e.*, those engaging in monopolistic tactics such as predatory pricing or exclusionary practices) should be found guilty of unlawful conduct, and that a "good monopoly" such as U.S. Steel should not be prosecuted. Similar Court decisions involving American Can, United Shoe Machinery, International Harvester and Eastman Kodak strengthened this pronouncement.

Another major judicial action occurred twenty–five years later in the *Alcoa* case when a circuit court ruled that Alcoa had illegally monopolized the aluminum ingot market despite the absence of any unreasonable practices. In short, the Court concluded that a firm's monopoly power, if found to be sufficiently great, would be illegal when consciously maintained. This decision, coupled with the findings in the *American Tobacco* case of 1946, significantly modified the lessons established in prior antitrust cases. In addition, Judge Hand in the *Alcoa* case established the precedent that 90 percent "is enough to constitute a monopoly; it is doubtful whether 60 or 64 percent would be enough; and certainly 33 percent is not."[124] In consequence, definitions of market and market share henceforth became pivotal considerations in deciding antitrust violations.

The heyday of Section 2 enforcement occurred during the late 1940s with major decisions concerning A&P and motion picture exhibition chains. Joined by the findings in the *United Shoe Machinery Corporation* decision, the courts demonstrably proved that they would find a firm guilty of monopolization despite the absence of unlawful heinous practices. It seemed that structure by itself might be sufficient grounds for finding violative conduct under Section 2 of the Sherman Act. But a 1956 decision, which found DuPont innocent of monopolizing production of cellophane, dampened this conclusion.

Few, if any, decisions by the Supreme Court in the period up to the 1970s are of landmark importance. Perhaps the closest instance of a precedential case was *U.S.* v. *Grinnell Corporation,* et al., decided by the Supreme Court in 1966. In that case, the Court underscored the critical importance of determining both market share and the relevant market in gauging monopoly power. Further, the Court refined monopolization criteria under Section 2 to include the possession of monopoly power in the relevant market, and willful acquisition or maintenance of that power.

Among three recent lower court decisions, two relate to alleged practices of IBM. In 1978, IBM was exonerated by a district court for monopolizing or attempting to monopolize four computer markets as alleged by Memorex Corporation. That same year, an appellate court found in favor of Greyhound Corporation that IBM had apparently attempted to monopolize the computer leasing market. Although Eastman Kodak was absolved of certain alleged wrongdoing as claimed by Berkey Photo Incorporated, an appellate court decided that Kodak's agreement with Sylvania and General Electric to time the introduction of their new camera systems could well be the basis for a jury finding that Kodak, as a monopolist, unreasonably restrained trade.

In telecommunications, a major suit was brought under Section 2 of the Sherman Act against AT&T in 1974. This was resolved by a consent decree filed on January 8, 1982, culminating in a significant reorganization of the firm and the industry. This pivotal case will be discussed in greater detail below.

A second structure–related statute is Section 7 of the Clayton Act. This section prohibits mergers when the effect may be to substantially lessen competition or to create a monopoly. To correct deficiencies in the Sherman Act (which could be used to prosecute merged companies only after they combine), this section became part of the Clayton Act which was passed in 1914. In 1950, the Celler–Kefauver Act was passed to amend Section 7. Originally useful only for banning anticompetitive mergers that resulted from the purchase of stock, Section 7 was amended to include the purchase of assets. Prior to this modification, only five mergers were dissolved under Section 7 of the Clayton Act.

Two seminal merger cases have been successfully prosecuted under Section 7. In 1962, the Supreme Court ruled in *Brown Shoe Company* that a proposed merger between Brown Shoe Company and Kinney Company was to be disallowed. The thrust of the Court's finding was that both the horizontal and vertical aspects of the merger were perceived to probably lessen competition in the future. In short, the Court concluded that those mergers which may lead to a significant reduction in competition should be prohibited.

Subsequently, the Supreme Court overruled a lower court decision in *Von's Grocery Company* concerning a proposed merger between Von's Grocery Company and Shopping Bag Food Stores in the Los Angeles area. This action established the precedent that mergers which resulted in increased concentration would be banned. This post–1950 tendency of the courts towards a hard look at mergers has been softened considerably during the last few years as a result of more lenient standards utilized by the Department of Justice.[125]

A third and final statute that centers on structural reform is Section 8 of the Clayton Act. This statute bans interlocking directorates for corporations whose assets are larger than one million dollars.

Court interpretations of alleged illegal behavior under structure oriented statutes of the antitrust laws are generally guided by a doctrine called the "rule of reason." Rather than a mechanical application of a given statute, this doctrine requires an in depth examination of the history, motivations, and competitive significance of the given alleged violation. As Neale has observed, the rule of reason is essentially a rule of construction.[126]

b. Significance

In essence, U.S. antitrust policy with respect to structure relies heavily on the use of "relevant market" definitions, measures of market power and concentration such as market shares and Herfindahl Indices and evidence of barriers to entry. This general acceptance of these economic tools of analysis by the courts and the government bestows credibility on the use of these methods for examining the workings of specific industries for both positive and normative purposes. Armed with this imprimatur, our examination of the telecommunications sector will draw significantly upon these criteria.

4. Firm and Market Conduct

a. Price Fixing

Antitrust statutes designed to cope with violations related to the behavior of firms include the Sherman, Clayton and Federal Trade Commission Acts. Under the provision of Section 1 of the Sherman Act:

> every contract, combination in the form of trust or otherwise, or conspiracy, in restraint of trade or commerce among the several States, or with foreign nations, is hereby declared to be illegal.

In contrast to Section 2 of the Sherman Act, this section requires a showing of only *per se* violations in order for illegality to be established. The *per se* doctrine may be regarded as a rule of evidence, *i.e.*, the mere demonstration that an alleged misconduct has in fact occurred is sufficient to make a showing of unlawfulness.[127] Despite the generally less activist stance of the Chicago School and the Reagan administration, antitrust enforcement during the 1980s has apparently remained vigorous with respect to price fixing and bid rigging.

Historically, Section 1 has been used to prosecute explicit collusive pricing activities, *e.g.*, price fixing and market divisions. In the first major price fixing case (in 1897), the Supreme Court overturned two lower court rulings and established that Congress intended that any such restraint of trade would be unlawful *per se*. Two years later, Circuit Court Judge William Howard Taft found in *Addyston Pipe* that six manufacturers of cast iron pipe were guilty of fixing prices through use of a bidding cartel, rejecting the defendant's argument that this had permitted them to avoid a ruinous price war.

Perhaps the most significant judicial precedent in this area was the *Trenton Potteries* case of 1927. Ruling that 23 manufacturers of vitreous pottery fixtures were guilty of conspiring to fix prices and to limit production, the Supreme Court concluded that such agreements in principle may be unreasonable or unlawful restraints, even "without the necessity of minute inquiry as to whether a particular price is reasonable or unreasonable as fixed."

Notwithstanding the Court's "anomalous" 1933 *Appalachian Coals* decision which sanctioned a joint selling company in a depressed bituminous coal industry, the 1927 stance was affirmed in the Supreme Court decision in the 1940 *Socony-Vacuum Oil Company* case. In an attempt to avoid "ruinously low prices," twelve major petroleum refining companies had bought excess oil that had flooded the market. Rejecting their argument, the Court stated that "any combination which tampers with price structures is engaged in an unlawful activity."

Application of the *per se* prohibitions against explicit price fixing has been consistently applied since that time. However, a number of borderline situations for which there has been no clear-cut solution by the courts also exist. Trade associations are a good example. While the blatant practice of firms in an industry gathering to agree on prices, output and market shares is clearly unlawful, the practice of information exchange through these associations is more difficult to resolve. In general, courts have apparently followed a modified *per se* approach that borders on a rule of reason philosophy. Such factors as the nature of the information exchanged and the characteristics of the industry's structure are typically considered in a court review of any information exchange allegation. In short, courts are cognizant that certain types of information exchange may be beneficial in allowing a market to function more efficiently.

However, price fixing is only one means of controlling prices. Another more indirect way is for firms to reach agreements setting forth how they will compete with one another through the use of market allocations. There are several types of market division agreements; *e.g.,* markets may be allocated on the basis of geographic area, classes of customer, or types of product.

Courts now generally invoke a *per se* rule in dealing with market division arrangements. Judicial interpretations in this area date back to the aforementioned *Addyston Pipe* case of 1899, where the major producers of cast iron pipe were castigated for market allocation arrangements as well as for price fixing. Ensuing cases did not always seem to embrace a particular doctrine, however, and it remained until the *Topco Associates* case of 1972 to firmly establish the use of the *per se* rule in such cases. Here the Supreme Court ruled that a cooperative scheme involving small and medium sized supermarket chains to allocate sales of the Topco brand of products that they sold was a means to restrain competition and hence was *per se* illegal. In short, the courts have determined that market division arrangements are unlawful *per se* whether or not price fixing agreements are also involved.

b.   Cartelization

Cartelization is an explicit means of collusion whereby both price fixing and output allocation occur. Not surprisingly, the courts have adopted a *per se* doctrine in this area as well. Unlike in many foreign companies where such market organizations are encouraged, however, formal cartels have been virtually eliminated from American industry as a result of the antitrust laws in this country.

A significant attempt at cartelization involved the electrical equipment manufacturers in the 1950s. General Electric, Westinghouse, Allis Chalmers, and twenty-six other firms in the industry were indicted in 1960 for criminal conspiracies and outright collusion in product pricing in twenty separate lines. Proceedings uncovered such tactics as the use of code names, clandestine meetings, and a "phases of the moon" pricing system for sealed bid switch gear. Instances of such blatant conduct, however, have been extremely rare in recent antitrust history. Typically, more subtle activities appear to appeal to those who would circumvent the intent of the antitrust laws.

Gray areas under the aegis of Section 1 of the Sherman act include boycotts and vertical territorial restrictions. Boycotts arise when a group of firms in concert refuses to deal with another firm for the express purpose of coercing or even destroying that firm. In practice, the courts have found that boycotts directly aimed at limiting or excluding competitors are *per se* illegal, *e.g.,* the 1914 *Eastern States Retail Lumber Dealers Association* case and the 1966 *General Motors Corporation* decision. Other concerted refusals to deal, however, are usually but not always tested under a rule of reason approach; *e.g.,* the 1971 *Fashion Originator's Guild of America* case. The Supreme Court has shown a lack of consistency in its rulings concerning vertical distribution arrangements. Hence, it has shifted from a *per se* doctrine as expressed in the 1967 *Schwinn* case to a rule of reason thrust articulated in its 1977 *GTE Sylvania* case.

c.   Price Discrimination

Section 2 of the Clayton Act is designed to combat anticompetitive behavior. The essence of this section is to prohibit price discrimination:

> that it shall be unlawful for any person engaged in commerce, in the course of such commerce, either directly or indirectly, to discriminate in price between purchasers of commodities of like grade and quality, where either or any of the purchases involved in such discrimination are in commerce, . . . where the effect of such discrimination may be substantially to lessen competition or tend to create a monopoly in any line of commerce, or to injure, destroy, or prevent competition with any person who either grants or knowingly receives the benefit of such discrimination, or with customers of either of them: Provided, that nothing herein contained shall prevent differentials which make only due allowance for differences in cost of manufacture, sale, or

delivery resulting in the differing methods or quantities at which such commodities are to such purchasers sold or delivered. . .

This language was amended in 1938 by the Robinson–Patman Act, which was designed to meet the complaints of small business that larger competitors were eliciting lower discriminatory prices from their suppliers. Specifically, the Robinson–Patman Act states:

> that it shall be unlawful for any person engaged in commerce, in the course of such commerce, knowingly to induce or receive a discrimination in price which is prohibited by this section.

The crux of the Robinson–Patman Act is that for a violation to occur, different prices must be charged on an interstate basis to different purchasers of the same like product such that the effect of the pricing must be to lessen competition substantially. The landmark case in this area is the 1966 *Borden* Supreme Court decision in which the Court ruled that the Borden Company was guilty of selling essentially the same quality of milk at two different prices in two different markets.

Although vigorously enforced throughout most of its history, Robinson–Patman cases have been relatively few and insignificant in recent years largely because many, including members of Congress, the FTC, and scholars believe that the essence of the Act is anticompetitive.[128] Overall, then, the usefulness and incidence of Robinson–Patman Act cases has diminished substantially in recent years, succumbing to widespread criticism of its consequences of discouraging price competition and promoting price uniformity.

d. Tying Arrangements

Section 3 of the Clayton Act is designed to deter and to punish those who would use tie–in arrangements, requirements contracts and exclusive dealing agreements for anticompetitive purposes. More specifically, this section of the antitrust statutes states:

> that it shall be unlawful for any person engaged in commerce, in the course of such commerce, to lease or make a sale or contract for sale of goods, wares, merchandise, machinery, supplies or other commodities, whether patented or unpatented, for use, consumption or resale within the United States . . . or discount from or rebate upon, such price, on the condition, agreement, or understanding that the lessee or purchaser thereof shall not use or deal in the goods, wares, merchandise, machinery, supplies or other commodities of a competitor or competitors of the lessor or seller, where the effect of such lease, sale, or contract for sale or such condition, agreement, or understanding may be to substantially lessen competition or tend to create a monopoly in any line of commerce.

Tying contracts are those whereby a customer who wants to buy a certain product from a given seller is also required to buy some other product or products exclusively from that same seller. Under Section 3 of the Clayton Act, the *sine qua non* is the substantial lessening of competition or the tendency to create a monopoly. Section 1 of the Sherman Act may also be invoked where such practices are perceived to be restraints of trade.

The history of judicial cases pertaining to these sections of the antitrust laws has been anything but straightforward and unambiguous. The landmark Supreme Court decision in this area is the *IBM* case of 1936. In the 1930s, IBM had required users of its machines to also buy all of its punch cards made by others and thereby prevent the loss of goodwill to IBM. It also insisted that since it already possessed a patent on its machines, it would not be attempting to extend its monopoly position by requiring this tie–in arrangement.

Rejecting these arguments, the Supreme Court found that the effect of such actions had been a substantial decrease in competition in the punch card industry and that the company's goodwill could have been maintained by simply requiring certain specifications to be met concerning these cards. This ruling seemed to emphasize the judicial preference for following a rule of reason approach in determining the outcome of tie–in cases under Section 3.

This tone seemed to change markedly thirteen years later in the *Standard Oil Company of California* case in which the Supreme Court ruled that "tie–in agreements serve hardly any purpose beyond the suppression of competition." In another landmark case, decided in 1947, the Supreme Court found International Salt guilty of violations of both Section 3 of the Clayton Act and Section 1 of the Sherman Act. In that case, the Court determined that it is "unreasonable *per se* to foreclose competitors from any substantial market" through the use of tying contracts.

Subsequent decisions in this area similarly seemed to send multiple signals when viewed collectively. See, *e.g., Supreme Court* case *Fortner Enterprises, Inc.* vs. *United States Steel Corporation,* where the Court in 1969 seemed to cite U.S. Steel's tie–in arrangement with homebuilders as a *per se* violation, only to invoke a rule of reason in 1977 in deciding that U.S. Steel had no demonstrable market power in the credit market. Given this history regarding tie–in arrangements, it appears that no "final" precedents have yet to emerge in this area.

e. Requirements and Exclusive Dealing Contracts

Requirements contracts involve situations where a buyer agrees to purchase all of its needs for a given commodity or commodities from a particular seller. The pivotal case in this area of antitrust law is the aforementioned *Standard Oil of California* case, also called the *Standard Stations Decision* of 1949.

In the 1940s, Standard Oil of California consummated agreements with a number of independent gasoline retailers such that the latter could only purchase their gasoline and, in some cases, certain gasoline related products from Standard. Upon review of the facts, the Supreme Court determined that

Standard Oil had foreclosed a substantial share of commerce and that its agreements with independent retailers were illegal.

This decision impacted requirements contracts and other exclusive dealing arrangements in several important ways. First, it underscored the importance of the factor of foreclosing a substantial share of a concentrated and impeded retail market as a sufficient basis for which a court could conclude that competition has been substantially diminished. Second, the Court developed a different standard for exclusive dealing contracts *vis-à-vis* tying arrangements under Section 3 of the Clayton Act. An approach closer to but still not tantamount to a rule of reason approach was established for cases involving exclusive dealing contracts. This contrasted with the apparent tendency for the Court to prefer in many instances a *per se* approach concerning tying arrangements. In *Standard Stations*, the Court not only looked at the volume of sales standard created under the *International Salt* case, but also considered, albeit not in great detail, the economic effects of the foreclosure, *e.g.*, market shares. Third, its use of a 6.7 percent market share standard for the threshold evaluation of exclusive dealing arrangements signaled a "hard line" approach by the courts toward exclusive dealing arrangements.

f.   Federal Trade Commission

A major milestone related to antitrust statutes dealing with firm and market conduct was passage of the Federal Trade Commission Act in 1914. This Act, *inter alia,* established the Federal Trade Commission (FTC) as an administrative and adjudicatory agency charged with enforcing the nation's antitrust laws. The FTC was given the specific power to enforce Section 5 of the Act, which now states in its amended form that "unfair methods of competition in or affecting commerce, and unfair or deceptive acts or practices in or affecting commerce are hereby declared unlawful."

The Wheeler–Lea Act (1938) imposed a ban on unfair or deceptive acts or practices; and the Magnuson–Moss Warranty–Federal Trade Commission Improvement Act of 1974 included the words "in or affecting commerce" in order to broaden the jurisdiction of Section 5. Unlike the Sherman Act where felonies are punishable by either fines or imprisonment or both, the FTC Act as amended, like the Clayton Act, carries no criminal penalties. The FTC and the Department of Justice together are responsible for enforcement of the Clayton Act; but only the Trade Commission may enforce the FTC Act.

In practice, the FTC with the Justice Department also has jurisdiction over the Sherman Act because of the Court's interpretation of the broad mandate given to the FTC under Section 5 of the FTC Act. The FTC's enforcement powers include ability to issue cease and desist orders; to file complaints and pursue prosecution, terminating in either a court decision or decisions or else a consent decree; and to issue industry guides and trade regulation rules as a more general means of enforcing Section 5 of the FTC Act. While such guides are an informal means of presenting FTC views on various subjects, the trade regulation rules issued by the Trade Commission have the same standing in law as actual legislation.

The breadth of the FTC's prosecutorial powers is substantial under Section 5 of the FTC Act. Besides the enabling provisions of the aforementioned amendments to Section 5 of the Act, a series of Supreme Court decisions has widened the FTC's powers to prohibit practices that offend public policy or cause substantial injury to consumers. See, *e.g., FTC v. Sperry and Hutchison, Co.,* 405 U.S. 233, 244–45 (1972).

In addition to a myriad of cases involving such issues as advertising and deception, the Commission has been involved in numerous Robinson–Patman case activities. The FTC has also sought in the past to achieve structural reorganization in such industries as ready–made breakfast cereals and petroleum refining. Under the broad umbrella of Section 5, the Trade Commission is not required to prove the individual elements of either a Clayton or Sherman Act violation. Rather, the FTC has been empowered to arrest trade restraints and other anticompetitive conduct in their incipiency without the need to demonstrate outright violation of the Clayton or Sherman Act.

Further, the FTC has historically overseen such activities as resale price maintenance, *i.e.,* the establishment of floor prices by manufacturers below which retailers may not sell their products. Hence, the Miller–Tydings Resale Price Maintenance Act of 1937 represented enabling legislation for an endorsement of such practices under Section 1 of the Sherman Act.

g. *Significance*

The U.S. antitrust laws in the realm of firm or market behavior also provide insights which are useful for our scrutiny of telecommunications activity in this country. While this book makes no conscious attempt to perform an antitrust analysis, the precepts and methods employed in those undertakings may provide insights for our purposes. For example, evidence regarding market allocations or price fixing would certainly suggest anticompetitive conduct in a given market. However, tying arrangements and especially exclusive dealing contracts may not always be indicative of dubious market behavior. Clearly the use of market share, definitions, and foreclosure would seem to be endorsed as acceptable methodologies for economic inquiry.

5. Structure and Conduct: The Case of Oligopoly

Antitrust laws are reasonably clear about the anticompetitive nature of such flagrant abuses as price fixing, market and allocation schemes, and even to a certain extent, the attempts at monopolization by single firm monopoly markets. These statutes become relatively uncharted waters, however, when the focus becomes oligopolistic market structures, *i.e.,* where explicit collusive activities are superseded by tacit and even parallel conduct and single firm dominance gives way to market power by several firms. This subject is of particular interest, of course, as it pertains to telecommunications and its emerging oligopolistic structure in a number of markets.

The desirability of the oligopolist in terms of economic theory has already been discussed: such factors as performance in the realm of research–and–development and product differentiation must be weighed against the effects of such a structure on output and prices. Experts disagree as to the wisdom of discouraging oligopolies through antitrust laws, but most concur that to date these laws have generally been ineffective in reaching such market forms.[129]

The late 1940s were apparently the high water mark for those who would pursue oligopolies under the antitrust statutes. In the 1946 *American Tobacco* case discussed above, the Supreme Court declined to review the determination by two lower courts that the big three of the cigarette industry, *viz.,* American Tobacco, Reynolds, and Liggett and Myers, were guilty of price fixing based on circumstantial evidence. In declining to review the case, the Supreme Court stressed that "no formal agreement is necessary to constitute an unlawful conspiracy."

Two subsequent cases filed under Section 5 of the FTC Act seem to confirm the thrust of the *American Tobacco* case concerning the legal dubiety of the conscious parallelism approaches. Both cases involved the use of basing point pricing formulas, *i.e.,* the use of pricing schemes where delivered prices are computed using freight charges from major designated geographic areas. See *FTC* v. *Cement Institute, et al.,* 333 U.S. 683, 712–21 (1948); and *Triangle Conduit and Cable Company, et al.* v. *FTC,* 168 F. 2d 175 (1948).

The precedential value of *American Tobacco* and subsequent cases in the late 1940s was soon tarnished by new judicial decisions. Parallel business behavior in the dairy and film distribution markets and several drug industries was deemed by the courts to be lawful under existing antitrust statutes. See the 1954 *Theatre Enterprises, Inc.,* 1950 *Peveley Dairy Company,* the 1959 *Eli Lilley and Company, et al.,* and the 1970 *Charles Pfizer and Company, Inc., et al.* cases.

In short, as observed by Scherer, "parallelism plus" would need to be established before illegality could be demonstrated.[130] See *Naumkeag Theatres Company* v. *New England Theatres, Inc. et al.,* 345 F. 2d 910, 912 (1965). Proof of advanced knowledge of impending rival actions by firms in an industry plus such factors as "price protection plans" that discourage price cutting and the publication of "how–to books" for calculating bidding prices appear representative of the behavior that would be required to accompany mere parallel firm conduct. Price leadership behavior in general is apparently acceptable under existing antitrust laws except where there is evidence that the leading firm attempts to coerce other firms into following its lead, or unless it can be demonstrated that an agreement among price leadership participants is designed to facilitate price fixing arrangements. See, *U.S.* v. *International Harvester Company,* 274 U.S. 693, 708–9 (1927) and *U.S.* v. *United States Steel Corporation, et al.,* 251 U.S. 417, 447 (1920).

The lack of success of pursuing oligopolies under the antitrust statutes has been perhaps even more pronounced under Section 5 of the FTC Act than it has been in the cases of Section 1 and Section 2 of the Sherman Act, discussed above. In 1972 under the doctrine of "shared monopoly," the FTC alleged that Kelloggs, General Mills, General Foods, and (initially) Quaker Company collectively possessed monopoly power that earned excessive profits and that effectively deterred new entry into the cereals market. The FTC originally sought divestiture of Kelloggs into several firms and the requirement that any firm could produce virtually any of Kelloggs' products as a punitive measure. This bold initiative never got out of the judicial starting blocks, however, as the Justice Department dropped it in January 1982.

A somewhat similar case brought by the Commission against the eight leading petroleum refiners was dismissed shortly prior to that time. Overall, the political misfortunes of the FTC in the latter 1970s and the "hands off" policy of the Reaganites during the 1980s resulted in no significant "shared monopoly cases" filed in court. In view of the current and recent historical status of the oligopoly as the major market structure in the United States, it would seem likely that the issue of the applicability of antitrust laws to the oligopolistic form of market organization will continue to be a subject of vigorous debate. Certainly the prevalence of such market structures in a number of telecommunications markets renders this subject of great interest for the analysis undertaken in this book.

6. Performance Factors

U.S. antitrust statutes have historically focused on structure and conduct. This policy direction was undoubtedly developed in deference to the widespread belief that structure or conduct, or both, are decisive determinants of the performance of an industry or market. Given the premium that Americans place on the value of democracy and entrepreneurial abilities, there has also been a certain reluctance historically for Congress to pass performance–oriented legislation. Broadly defined examples of performance laws include the Emergency Price Control Act of 1942, the Economic Stabilization Act of 1970s, and the Full Employment and Balanced Growth Act of 1978. In the telecommunications sector, the 1934 Communications Act requires, *inter alia*, universally affordable telephone service in this country, and recent legislation has targeted communications and other equipment markets for improved trade access to foreign countries such as Japan and Europe.

7. Antitrust Exemptions

Finally, several significant exemptions to the antitrust laws should be mentioned. One such area is agricultural marketing, *e.g.*, growing cooperatives and joint fishing co–ops. A broad exemption has been granted for labor. Section 6 of the Clayton Act, which asserts "that the labor of a human being is not a commodity or an article of commerce," coupled with later legislation, *e.g.*, the Norris–LaGuardia Act of 1932, have resulted in a general insulation from the antitrust laws of the activities of trade unions directed to promoting the interests of their members. Resale price maintenance agreements, *i.e.*, "fair trade laws," the Webb–Pomerene Act of

1918 which effectively protects American exporters from antitrust prosecution, and insurance and banking services are all at least partially immune from these laws. More recently, public policy makers have sought to enhance the competitiveness of U.S. companies in foreign markets by easing existing restrictions on some forms of cooperative activity (see below).

8.   Antitrust Policy in Perspective

According to Neale in his classic book, *The Antitrust Laws of the U.S.A.*, two concepts form the underpinnings of U.S. antitrust law: (1) American distrust of economic power and authority; and (2) a reliance on judicial process to disperse such power among private entities.[131]   This view contrasts markedly with the traditional British perspective where power is supposed to be facilitated rather than hampered, with appropriate safeguards instituted to protect minorities. In fact, our antitrust focus is essentially unique compared to the prevailing attitudes in the rest of the world.

In this country, legal and political considerations have traditionally formed the backbone of our antitrust policy. Economics has also assumed an important role in this area but has historically been relegated to a lesser status for three reasons. First, the pursuit of firm and market efficiency may not be consistent with other social goals such as equity or "political realities." Second, the state of economic theory is such that many of its precepts are the subjects of considerable debate, *e.g.*, the causal relationship between structure, conduct and performance. Third, those who are legislators and judges in this country are typically lawyers or other "non–economists" by trade and frequently have little or no training in economics.

The appointment of William F. Baxter, however, in 1981 as Assistant Attorney General in charge of antitrust policy at the Department of Justice represented a significant departure from customary practice: his reliance on economic theory and his espousal of economic efficiency and a crackdown on price fixing as the paramount objectives of his regime signaled a new emphasis on the "dismal science" for grappling with antitrust matters.[132]   His successors under the Reagan administration generally continued this policy direction.[133]

The broad goal of U.S. antitrust policy today is to maintain competition. Inadequacies of common and statutory laws prior to the late 1800s in combating the flagrant abuses of the giant "robber baron" trusts led to the establishment of the three basic antitrust laws. The Sherman Act was designed to thwart monopolization and to prevent "restraints of trade." The Clayton Act was passed to halt market behavior that would "substantially lessen competition" or "tend to create a monopoly." And the Federal Trade Commission Act was primarily created to frustrate "unfair methods of competition."

A major element of maintenance of competition is control of market power; this has also been one of the principal rationales of regulation (see *supra*). Market or monopoly power may be acquired through (or manifested in) mergers, predatory or fixed or discriminatory pricing, nonprice exclusionary practices or other means.   Significant entry barriers would appear to be necessary to sustain such dominance in the long run.

In practice, the market power issue is extremely complex.   Its identification and measurement is not easy or straightforward; indeed, the myriad of measurement techniques and the reams of case law attest to the difficulties involved.   A prerequisite for these determinations is the proper definition of a given market.   Correct identification of the "relevant market" through such measures as cross elasticities of demand is crucial to the outcome of a structure–related antitrust case, and is frequently important for resolution of more conduct oriented proceedings.

For antitrust cases, courts have evolved two fundamental doctrines of judicial interpretations, the *per se* and the "rule of reason" approaches.   The courts have tended to designate business activities which have no perceived redeeming value as *per se* violations, *i.e.*, automatically violative of the antitrust statute once their existence has been demonstrated.   This approach possesses the following advantages: (1) it creates a "bright line" of demarcation between lawful and unlawful practices, which reduces uncertainty and may deter would–be violators; and (2) it permits savings for those parties who would otherwise be engaged in lengthy and costly litigation. Disadvantages of this philosophy (*i.e.*, advantages of the "rule of reason" doctrine) include: (1) some activities that are not clearly detrimental may be penalized, *e.g.*, fixing prices to reach scale economies; and (2) the accused may be unfairly deprived of the "right" to defend their behavior.

9.   Performance of the Antitrust Laws

With regard to restrictive agreements such as price fixing, exclusive dealing and boycotts, Neale believes that of the late 1970s "there is little doubt that detection and enforcement [were] reasonably effective in this field."[134] Concerning the effectiveness of antitrust in the realm of actual or attempted monopolization, Neale notes the existence of various economic and legal criticisms, but concludes that the "genuine impact of Section 2 [of the Sherman Act] on business conduct probably counts as a success in most American eyes."[135]   He argues that this is so because "it seems probable that what has been done by the courts under Section 2 . . . has reflected public opinion in the United States pretty accurately."[136]   Further, he opines that "if monopoly power as such cannot be avoided, at least its exercise is beset with legal checks, and this is a large part of what is expected of antitrust as a 'constitution' for the economy."[137]

Antitrust laws have become less broad and enforcement more selective during the 1980s.   Thus, while price fixing and bid rigging apparently continue to be vigorously pursued, other areas such as predatory pricing and horizontal and vertical mergers have been challenged much less readily.   As the Chicago School influence has increased, efficiency considerations have usually overcome any equity or other social concerns.   Moreover, potential competition has been frequently invoked as a factor diminishing the importance of an existing high level of concentration or market power.

Consequently, a number of observers have criticized the prevailing antitrust system of the 1980s. For example, Robert Pitofsky, the dean of Georgetown Law Center and a leading antitrust authority, asserts that "the antitrust laws as enforced by the government today are the most lenient in 50 years."[138]

The impact of antitrust on oligopolistic markets, however, has apparently been slight. Notwithstanding the 1946 *American Tobacco* case and the initiation of shared monopoly suits, government attempts at structural reorganization of various oligopolies have been largely unsuccessful. Except for episodes of *per se* violations of exclusionary conduct, *e.g.*, price fixing and cartelization, oligopolies have usually proven to be beyond the effective reach of antitrust laws. For example, courts have not generally viewed the practice of price leadership as unlawful unless coercion or price fixing is involved. "Conscious parallelism" in general has not been successfully challenged unless other factors such as evidence of relatively explicit collusion, *e.g.*, advance notice of a rival's actions, have been convincingly demonstrated.

An issue in this area that is even more fundamental than lack of U.S. success in prosecuting oligopolies is whether these markets should properly be the focus of antitrust scrutiny. As discussed previously, economic theory suggests that such market structures result in mutual interdependence which likely leads to misallocation of resources through lower output, higher prices, and greater profits relative to a perfectly competitive industry.

Many economists would agree that empirically, high seller concentration seems to be correlated with, and is a necessary condition for, higher profits, especially when accompanied by entry barriers.[139] Concerning the relationship between concentration and invention/innovation, Scherer concludes after surveying the various studies on the subjects:

> What is needed for rapid technical progress is a subtle blend
> of competition and monopoly, with more emphasis in general
> on the former than the latter, and with the role of
> monopolistic elements diminishing when rich technological
> opportunities exist.[140]

In short, there may exist rather compelling economic reasons which could warrant a reassessment of current U.S. antitrust policy towards oligopolies in general. On the other hand, the emergence of global markets and the concern over U.S. competitiveness have caused some public movement towards relaxation of existing restraints on, *e.g.*, cooperative or joint research projects among American companies.[141] Some legislation has been passed, such as the 1984 National Cooperative Research Act, which permits companies to jointly conduct basic research, and more bills will apparently be initiated by the Bush administration.[142] Major research consortia have been established in recent years in such diverse areas as glass bottles, computers and semiconductors, and boiler pumps for power plants. In December 1988 a Presidential commission urged the creation of several consortia comprised of industry, government, and university laboratories for research in superconductivity, a pioneering technology with potential applications in power transmission, computers, and public transit.[143]

This form of market structure has become a "burning issue" in antitrust circles during the 1980s and the debate promises to continue during the next decade. Oligopolistic settings featuring dominant firms, implementation of the MFJ, and other areas apropos to telecommunications are discussed in the sections below.

APPENDIX II–A
SOME BASIC CONCEPTS

The underlying basis for economics is scarcity. At any point in time, resources are available only in limited quantities and must be allocated among competing uses. In turn, the resulting products and services must be distributed among consumers, either currently or in the future. Economics, then, is the study of the production, distribution, and consumption of these scarce resources, *viz.*, land, labor, capital, and entrepreneurial ability.[144]

The discipline is essentially a science in its methodological approach and an art in its application. However, the increasing use of sophisticated methods of quantification such as mathematical economics and econometrics as well as the refinement of theoretical economics have moved economics closer to being a science in recent times.[145] This social science may be broadly categorized as both basic and applied. Basic economics emphasizes principles and theories, while applied economics is the employment of these concepts for policy purposes.

The study of economics is generally divided into macroeconomic and microeconomic branches. As the name suggests, macroeconomics examines the workings of the economy as a whole. Macroeconomists analyze the behavior of such aggregates as total output, employment, national income, and the general price level. Their efforts are concentrated on such social problems as inflation and unemployment. The economy may also be viewed in disaggregated fashion, a perspective known as microeconomics. More specifically, this branch studies individual industries and firms, their products, costs, and prices. Practitioners concentrate, *inter alia,* on the effects of various market characteristics on each market's economic performance. Both macro– and micro– types of inquiry use supply and demand analysis, and also embody theoretical and empirical methods.

The basic concepts of economics may also be dichotomized by the "what is" as opposed to "what ought to be" approach. Dating back to the times of John Stuart Mill some 150 years ago, the distinction is succinctly captured today in the terms "positive" and "normative" economics. Positive economics concerns the development and testing of verifiable hypotheses through analysis of data. This approach proffers no assessment of the desirability of any economic event or occurrence. In contrast, normative economics yields evaluations of economic phenomena, *e.g.*, "good," "bad," "unpredictable." This "welfare theory" perspective embraces ethical goals which are not typically derived from economic analyses. Simply stated, the difference may be considered to be "facts" vs. "value judgments."[146]

Given this framework, other fundamental terms or concepts may be briefly discussed.[147] Market mechanism as used in this text is a system in which individuals or other entities may freely buy or sell inputs or outputs, guided by their own goals and tastes and by relative prices which, in turn, are free to change in response to the market decisions of the various players. Where the system does not or can not function in this manner, market failures or imperfections may be at work. Market failures (*e.g.*, where "externalities" prevent the equating of private and social costs or benefits) arise even though a market may be "perfectly competitive." Also, market imperfections distort the operation of a free market because of deviations from one or more of the conditions requisite for "perfect competition." The manifestation of this imperfection is called market power when a firm or group of firms in an industry possesses an ability to significantly affect the price of a good or service (e.g., supply of local telephone service).

Opportunity cost and economic efficiency are two of the most fundamental concepts in economics. Developed as a principle by nineteenth century neoclassicists,[148] opportunity cost is essentially the value of a foregone or sacrificed alternative which represents the "next best use" of an economic good. For example, the opportunity cost of manufacturing wartime products would be foregone consumer goods –– the classic "guns and butter" policy debate. Construction of a telephone network or oil pipeline means that the resources employed there may not be concurrently utilized in alternative gainful uses. If scarcity of resources were not a factor in all economic decisions, the value of foregoing the best alternative use of resources would be zero. However, given the limited availability of resources in the "real world," the opportunity cost of an economic decision is always positive.

Accountants and economists subscribe to different concepts of cost. The former interprets cost to be those that appear on a profit–and–loss statement, i.e., recorded money flows. In contrast, the economist would examine the foregone benefits of a particular action. For example, the lost profits accruing to an alternative investment (e.g., opting not to put money in a U.S. Treasury bill but, instead, to provide capital for a new commuter airlines) must be included in any computation of opportunity costs. Such calculations may be performed with respect to either the private or public social benefits involved.

For an economist, efficiency has several dimensions. First, allocative efficiency occurs where a change in a resource allocation that makes someone better off cannot be achieved without making someone worse off.[149] An optimal output is deemed to be that output combination which would result from individual consumers choosing commodities priced at true costs of production in perfectly competitive markets. Second, technical or "X" efficiency occurs where an output is produced at the least (opportunity) cost or, alternatively, output is maximized for a mix of inputs. More succinctly, economic efficiency may be thought of as an absence of waste.

Notes

1. Appendix II–A provides a brief review of basic economic concepts and terminology as a rudimentary introduction to the analytical "tools" described in this chapter.

2. To be useful, these models need not have completely realistic assumptions or always pertain to precisely quantifiable factors or elements. Rather, as Milton Friedman has shown, the value of these models lies in their ability to predict performance. See "The Methodology of Positive Economics," *Essays in Positive Economics* (Chicago: University of Chicago Press, 1953), pp. 1–43.

3. Another policy option is public enterprise, *i.e.*, entities owned and operated by the government sector. Although an important institution in Europe and Asia, public entrepreneurship has had only limited application in this country *e.g.*, electric power generation by the Tennessee Valley Authority (TVA) since the 1930s and provision of telephone service during World War II. Some countries in recent years have shown a tendency to retreat from public ownership in certain areas of their economies (for example, the British and Japanese in domestic telecommunications).

4. See, *e.g.*, H. Simon, *Models of Man* (New York: John Wiley and Sons, 1957); and R. Cyert and J. March, *A Behavioral Theory of the Firm* (Englewood Cliffs, N.J.: Prentice–Hall, 1963).

5. Appendix II–A provides a brief review of basic economic concepts and terminology as a rudimentary introduction to the analytical "tools" described in this chapter.

6. See A. Berle and G. Means, *The Modern Corporation and Private Property* (New York: Macmillan, 1952).

7. See O. Williamson, *Economics of Discretionary Behavior* (Englewood Cliffs, N.J.: Prentice–Hall, 1964).

8. See, *e.g.*, D. Mueller, "A Life Cycle Theory of the Firm," *Journal of Industrial Economics*, Vol. 20, July 1972, pp. 199–219.

9. J. Galbraith, *The New Industrial State* (Boston: Houghton Mifflin Company, 1967).

10. This subject is examined in greater detail below in the discussion on natural monopolies.

11. See S. Sosnick, "A Critique of Concepts of Workable Competition," *Quarterly Journal of Economics* (August 1958), pp. 380–423, and H. Liebhafsky, *American Government and Business* (New York: John Wiley and Sons, Inc., 1971) for a review of the literature on the subject.

12. See F. Scherer, *Industrial Market Structure and Economic Performance* (Chicago: Rand McNally, 1980).

13. The classic treatment of this subject is contained in F.M. Bator, "The Anatomy of Market Failure," *The Quarterly Journal of Economics*, Vol. 92, August 1958.

14. See, *e.g.*, W.H. Melody, "Interservice Subsidy: Regulatory Standards and Applied Economics," in H.M. Trebing, ed., *Essays on Public Utility Pricing and Regulation* (East Lansing: Institute for Public Utilities, Michigan State University, 1971); and W. Bolter, "The FCC's Selection of a `Proper' Costing Standard after Fifteen Years – What Can We Learn from Docket 18128?," in Trebing, ed., *Assessing New Pricing Concepts in Public Utilities*, (East Lansing: Division of Research, Michigan State University, 1978).

15. See F. Ramsey, "A Contribution to the Theory of Taxation," *Economic Journal*, Vol. 37, March 1927, pp.47–61; W. Baumol and D. Bradford, "Optimal Departures from Marginal Cost Pricing," *American Economic Review*, Vol. 60, June 1970, pp. 265–83; and E. Zajac, *Fairness or Efficiency: An Introduction to Public Utility Pricing* (Cambridge, Mass.: Ballinger Publishing Co., 1978).

16. For an elaboration on this subject, see W. Bolter, J. Duvall, F. Kelsey, and J. McConnaughey, *Telecommunications Policy for the 1980s: The Transition to Competition* (Englewood Cliffs, New Jersey: Prentice–Hall, Inc., 1984), pp. 83–88.

17. A. Kahn, *The Economics of Regulation*, Vol. I (New York: John Wiley & Sons, Inc., 1970), pp. 151–52.

18. See, *e.g.*, W. Bolter, Testimony, Formal Case No. 814, Public Service Commission of the District of Columbia, December 1984; and R. Gabel, W. Melody, R. Warnek and W. Mihuc, *The Allocation of Local Exchange Plant Investment to the Common Exchange and Toll Services on the Basis of Equalized Relative Cost Benefits* (Research paper supported by the Kansas Corporation Commission), May 23, 1983.

19. See W. Bolter, "Restructuring in Telecommunications and Regulatory Adjustment," *Public Utilities Fortnightly*, July 5, 1984, pp. 15–22.

20. Common costs are often the overhead costs of the firm or those associated with multipurpose facilities. It may be difficult to find any rational allocative basis for ascribing such costs to specific services in some instances.

21. See *e.g.*, Harry M. Trebing, *New Dimensions in Public Utility Pricing* (East Lansing, Michigan: Institute of Public Utilities, Michigan State University, 1976).

22. As discussed below, the 1913 "Kingsbury Commitment" bound AT&T to refrain from further takeovers of other telephone companies.

23. See *e.g.*, E. Mansfield, *Microeconomics, Theory and Applications* (New York: W.W. Norton and Company, Inc., 1970) and C. Ferguson and J. Gould, *Microeconomic Theory* (Homewood, Illinois: Richard D. Irwin, Inc., 1975) for a review of these criticisms.

24. The market for large switching systems used in telephone company central offices and provision of long distance telephone service probably both fit the oligopolistic model.

25. At the time of the 1985 MCI/IBM agreement to become financially intertwined, some predicted that a duopoly (with AT&T) would eventually emerge in interstate long distance markets. Because of their keen awareness of each other's corporate aims and the long history of interfirm supply of computers and communications to one another, IBM and AT&T were expected to compete more in line with a duopoly arrangement model than more vigorous competitive designs. At the end of the 1980s, IBM's presence in these markets has actually diminished as AT&T, followed by an increasingly independent MCI and US Sprint, have been the principal "players."

26. As an example, throughout much of their early history MCI and other larger long distance entrants have generally patterned their prices after AT&T's service rates and rate structure, only making changes necessary to preserve rate differentials or gradually increase their market shares.

27. For a seminal work on the subject, see J. Markham, "The Nature and Significance of Price Leadership," *American Economic Review 41* (December 1951).

28. J. von Neumann and O. Morgenstern, *Theory of Games and Economic Behavior* (Princeton, New Jersey: Princeton University Press, 1944).

29. See, *e.g.*, C. Cole, *Microeconomics* (New York: Harcourt Brace Jovanovich, 1973).

30. J. Bain, *Barriers to New Competition* (Cambridge, Mass.: Harvard University Press, 1956).

31. For a discussion of these refinements see A. Koutsoyiannis, *Modern Microeconomics* (New York: John Wiley and Sons, 1975).

32. See W. Sharkey, *The Theory of Natural Monopoly*, (Cambridge: Cambridge University Press, 1982), pp. 146, 159–164.

33. See O. Williamson, *The Economics of Discretionary Behavior* (Englewood Cliffs, New Jersey: Prentice–Hall, 1964) and R. Cyert and J. March, *op. cit.*

34. For the pioneering work in this field, see E. Mason, "Price and Production Policies of Large–Scale Enterprise," *American Economic Review*, Supplement 29 (March 1, 1939), pp. 61–74; and "Monopoly in Law and Economics," *Yale Law Journal*, Vol. 47 (November 1939).

35. See, *e.g.*, J. Schumpeter, *Capitalism, Socialism, and Democracy*, (New York: Harper and Row, Publishers, 1942) and E. Mansfield, *The Economics of Technological Change* (New York: W.W. Norton, 1968).

36. See, *e.g.*, J. Bain, *Industrial Organization* (New York: John Wiley and Sons, 1968).

37. See, *e.g.*, G. Stigler, "A Theory of Oligopoly," *Journal of Political Economy* 72 (February 1964).

38. See W. Baldwin, *Market Power, Competition, and Antitrust Policy* (Homewood, Illinois: Richard D. Irwin, 1986), pp. 107–119; D. Greer, *Industrial Organization and Public Policy* (New York: Macmillan Publishing Co., Inc., 1984), pp. 206, 400–401; and F. Scherer, *op. cit.*, pp. 7, 294–295.

39. See, *e.g.*, H. Simon, *op. cit.*, and R. Cyert and J. March, *op. cit.*

40. A. Kahn, "The Relevance of Industrial Organization," in J.V. Craven, ed., *Industrial Organization, Antitrust, and Public Policy* (Boston: Kluwer–Nijhoff Publishing, 1983), p. 16.

41. The rationale for public utility regulation and antitrust enforcement is discussed *infra*.

42. See, *e.g.*, Bell Laboratories, *Engineering and Operations in the Bell System (1980)*, p. 98.

43. W. Comanor and T. Wilson, *Advertising and Market Power* (Cambridge, Mass.: Harvard University Press, 1974).

44. See, *e.g.*, W. G. Shepherd, "The Elements of Market Structure," *Review of Economics and Statistics*, 54 (February 1972), pp. 25–37; J. Dalton and S. Levin, "Market Power: Concentration and Market Share," *Industrial Organization Review*, 5 No. 1 (1977), pp. 27–35; and D. F. Lean, J. D. Ogur, and R. P. Rogers, "Competition and Collusion in Electrical Equipment Markets: An Economic Assessment" (Washington, D.C.: FTC Staff Report, 1982).

45. See D. Greer, *op. cit.*, pp. 413–414.

46. See *Telecommunications in Transition: The Status of Competition in the Telecommunications Industry*, House of Representatives, 97th Congress, 1st Session, Committee Print 97–V, November 3, 1981, Appendix C.

47. See K. Rothschild, "The Degree of Monopoly," *Economics* (February 1942), pp. 24–40.

48. See A. Lerner, "The Concept of Monopoly and the Measurement of Monopoly Power," *Review of Economic Studies* (June 1934), pp. 157–75.

49. See *Telecommunications in Transition: The Status of Competition in the Telecommunications Industry*, U.S. House of Representatives, *op. cit.*, p. 407.

50. See, *e.g.*, Testimony of Walter G. Bolter and James W. McConnaughey, Docket 05–TI–104, Public Service Commission of Wisconsin, December 1987.

51. Statistical studies have demonstrated this relationship for a myriad of industries and sectors. For example, see the pioneering article by Joe Bain, "Relation of Profit Rate to Industry Concentration, American Manufacturing, 1936–40," *Quarterly Journal of Economics*, 65 (August 1951), pp. 293–324. More recent significant works include, *inter alia*, M. Mann, "Seller Concentration, Barriers to Entry, and Rates of Return in 30 Industries, 1950–60," *Review of Economics and Statistics*, 48 (August 1966), p. 296–307; L. W. Weiss, "Quantitative Studies of Industrial Organization" in M. Intrilligator, *Frontiers of Quantitative Economics* (Amsterdam: North–Holland Publishing Company, 1971), pp. 363–403; W. G. Shepherd, "The Elements of Market Structure," *op. cit.*; P. D. Qualls, "Concentration, Barriers to Entry, and Long Run Economic Profit Margins," *Journal of Industrial Economics* (April 1972), pp. 146–158; and S. A. Rhoades and J. M. Cleaver, "The Nature of the Concentration – Price/Cost Margin Relationship for 352 Manufacturing Industries: 1967," *Southern Economic Journal* (July 1973), pp. 90–102. For surveys of these and numerous other studies supporting the basic high concentration – high profits linkage, see L. W. Weiss "The Concentration – Profits Relationship," in *Industrial Concentration: The New Learning*, edited by H. Goldschmid, M. Mann and F. Weston (Boston: Little Brown, 1974), pp. 196–201: and S. A. Rhoades, "Structure–Performance Studies in Banking: A Summary and Evaluation," Staff Economic Studies, No. 92 (Board of Governors of the Federal Reserve System, 1977), "Updated," Staff Economic Studies, No. 119 (Board of Governors of the Federal Reserve System, 1982).

52. Mutual interdependence and conscious parallelism seem to have characterized at least part of the telecommunications sector historically. For example, a Western Electric Analysis of a rival's crossbar community dial office (a small switching system) in the early 1970s concluded that "if Western's price is 10% more than Nippon's, we'll get the whole market, if it is 20% more we won't get anything." See p. 673, *Proposed Findings of Facts and Conclusions of the Common Carrier Bureau's Trial Staff*, Vol. II, FCC Docket No. 19129, Phase II, Charges for Interstate Telephone Service, Transmittal Nos. 10989, 11027, 1165, and 12303. The international record carriers, provider of such services as telex and TWX, have historically employed pricing strategies appropriate for a tight oligopoly. The recent acceleration of pro–competition and deregulatory policies by public decision makers have caused significant changes in both domestic and international telecommunications markets, impelling theoreticians and policy makers to re–evaluate these traditionally insulated arenas. And other common carriers such as MCI and SPC (now US Sprint) have established a market niche in intercity telecommunications by maintaining a fairly stable relative discount rate compared to the market leader, AT&T.

53. The situation of natural monopoly and other proffered rationales for government regulation are explored *infra*.

54. "Second best" problems, in an economic sense relate to the notion that unless all markets are efficient (*i.e.*, "pareto optimal"), then it is not certain that any other number of efficient markets will yield maximum social welfare.

55. See M. Friedman, *Capitalism and Freedom, op. cit.*, pp. 22–36.

56. *Id.*, p. 29. The views of Friedman and other "Chicago school" economists with respect to rationales for regulation are discussed in more detail in the next section.

57. P.A. Samuelson and W.D. Nordhaus, *Economics, op. cit.*, pp. 47,721–22.

58. P.A. Klein, "Institutional Reflections on the Role of the Public Sector," in M.R. Tool, ed., *An Institutionalist Guide to Economics and Public Policy, op. cit.*, p. 64. Klein and Friedman may be more in synch on the propriety of economists making (normative) policy recommendations. The former asserts:
   As students of the game economists can't be above it. The agent who analyzes the distribu-
   tion of guns and bullets cannot get away with saying he doesn't care who wins the war.
   Even if he advocates distribution by random draw, by lottery, or by any other arbitrary
   system, the fact that he devotes himself to the special problems of how munitions are
   deployed means *eo ipso* that he is involved in where and what they lead to. (*Id.*)
Friedman has been a policy advisor to Presidents Nixon, Ford and Reagan.

59. G. Sirkin, *The Visible Hand: The Fundamentals of Economic Planning*, (New York: McGraw–Hill Book Company, 1968), pp. 8–42.

60. W.A. Lewis, *The Principles of Economic Planning* (New York: Harper & Row, Publishers, 1969), pp. 12–14.

61. *Id.*, pp. 20–22, 28–29.

62. See M. Farris and R. Sampson, *Public Utilities: Regulation, Management, and Ownership* (Boston: Houghton Mifflin Company, 1973), p. 18.

63. *Id.*, p. 29.

64. A. Kahn, *The Economics of Regulation*, Vol. I, *op. cit.*, p. 10.

65. W.G. Shepherd and C. Wilcox, *Public Policies Toward Business* (Homewood, Illinois: Richard D. Irwin, Inc., 1979), p. 292.

66. *Id.*

67. J.C. Bonbright, *Principles of Public Utility Rates*, (New York: Columbia University Press, 1961), pp. 5–6.

68. P.J. Garfield and W.F. Lovejoy, *Public Utility Economics*, (Englewood Cliffs, New Jersey: Prentice–Hall, Inc., 1964).

69. See, *e.g.*, Bonbright, *op. cit.*, pp. 10–17; Garfield and Lovejoy, *op. cit.*, pp. 15–19; Kahn, *op. cit.*, p. 11; C.F. Phillips, Jr., *The Economics of Regulation: Theory and Practice in the Transportation and Public Utility Industries* (Homewood, Illinois: Richard D. Irwin, 1969), pp. XX; and *The Regulation of Public Utilities: Theory and Practice* (Arlington, Virginia: Public Utilities Reports, Inc., 1984), pp. XX.

70. This oversimplification, adopted here for conceptual ease, will be addressed below.

71. For the original discussion see esp. V. Pareto, *Manual of Political Economy*, 1909. Also see J.A. Schumpeter, "Vilfredo Pareto," *Ten Great Economists from Marx to Keynes*, (Oxford: Oxford University Press, 1951).

72. This may also involve economies of scope, where joint production of two goods may incur lower costs than separate production of each (see discussion *infra*).

73. For the seminal article on measuring welfare loss attributable to monopoly, see A.C. Harberger, "Monopoly and Resource Allocation," *American Economic Review*, May 1954.

74. "Subadditivity of costs," *i.e.*, the situation where (1) one firm can produce a given output at a lower cost than two firms regardless of the allocation of output between the two, or (2) one firm can produce two goods jointly at a lower cost than individually for any mix of a given output level, is a necessary and sufficient condition for natural monopoly. Thus, such a market may evolve if either product–specific scale economies or multiproduct (scope) economies exist to a significant degree relative to market demand.

75. See especially J. Panzar and R. Willig, "Free Entry and the Sustainability of Natural Monopoly," *Bell Journal of Economics*, Spring 1977, pp. 1–22; and W. Baumol, E. Bailey, and R. Willig, "Weak Invisible Hand Theorems on the Sustainability of Natural Monopoly," *American Economic Review*, June 1977, pp. 360–65.

76. W. Bolter, J. Duvall, F. Kelsey, and J. McConnaughey, *Telecommunications Policy for the 1980s: The Transition to Competition* (Englewood Cliffs, New Jersey: Prentice–Hall, Inc. 1984), p. 76.

77. W. A. Brock and J. A. Scheinkman, "Free Entry and the Sustainability of Natural Monopoly: Bertrand Revisited by Cournot," D. S. Evans, ed., *Breaking Up Bell: Essays on Industrial Organization and Regulation* (New York: North–Holland, 1983), pp. 231–252.

78. See G. Faulhaber, "Cross Subsidization: Pricing in Public Enterprises," *American Economic Review*, Volume 65, pp. 966–977; and W. Sharkey, *The Theory of Natural Monopoly* (Cambridge: Cambridge University Press, 1982), esp. Chapters 5, 6, and 8.

79. W. Sharkey, *op. cit.*

80. The landmark writing on the subject was published in 1982 by W. Baumol, J. Panzar, and R. Willig. See *Contestable Markets and the Theory of Industry Structure* (San Diego: Harcourt, Brace, Jovanovich, 1982). For important contributions see also E. Bailey and J. Panzar, "The Contestability of Airline Markets During the Transition to Deregulation," Law and Contemporary Problems, Vol. 44, 1981, pp. 125–46; E. Bailey, "Contestability and the Decision of Regulatory and Antitrust Policy," American Economic Review, Vol. 71, 1981, pp. 178–83; and W. Baumol and R. Willig, "Fixed Cost, Sunk Cost, Entry Barriers and Sustainability of Monopoly," *Quarterly Journal of Economics* Vol. 96, 1981, pp. 405–32. For a concise discussion of the topic, see Bolter, Duvall *et al. op. cit.*, pp. 63–66.

81. W. Baumol, E. Bailey, and R. Willig, "Weak Invisible Hand Theorems on the Sustainability of Natural Monopoly," *op. cit.*, pp. 350–65.

82. See G. Brock, *The Telecommunications Industry: The Dynamics of Market Structure* (Cambridge, Massachusetts: Harvard University Press, 1982), p. 356; and D. Evans, ed., *Breaking Up Bell*, *op. cit.*, p. 47.

83. See, *e.g.*, E. Bailey and A. Friedlaender, "Market Structure and Multiproduct Industries," *Journal of Economic Literature*, Vol. 20, September 1982, pp. 1024–48.

84. M. Spence, "Contestable Markets and the Theory of Industry Structure: A Review Article," *Journal of Economics*, Vol. 21, September 1983, pp. 981–90.

85. Bolter, Duvall *et al.*, p. 66.

86. W.G. Shepherd, "'Contestability' vs. Competition," *American Economic Review*, September 1984, pp. 572–85.

87. A. Helwege and A. Hendricks, "Three Problems in Applying Contestability to Regulated Markets," *Review of Industrial Organization*, Vol. 2, Number 2 (1985), pp. 132–143.

88. The issue of whether or not the telecommunications industry itself exhibits economies of scale or other characteristics of a natural monopoly remains a source of much debate. The recent consolidation of suppliers faced with an apparent glut of capacity in long distance telephony suggests that such economies may at least exist in intercity transmission networks.

89. For a good review and critique of this group's positions, see H.M. Trebing "The Chicago School versus Public Utility Regulation," *Journal of Economic Issues*, Vol. X, March 1976.

90. M. Friedman, *Capitalism and Freedom* (Chicago: The University of Chicago Press, 1962), p. 129.

91. R.A. Posner, "Natural Monopoly and Its Regulation," *Stanford Law Review*, Vol. 21, February 1969, pp. 635–37.

92. For a detailed discussion of basic theories of public utility regulation, see H. Trebing, "Equity, Efficiency, and the Viability of Public Utility Regulation," in W. Sichel and T. Gies, eds., *Applications of Economic Principles in Public Utility Industries* (Ann Arbor: University of Michigan, 1981), pp. 17–30.

93. See J. Bonbright, *op. cit.*, p. 10.

94. Kahn, *Economics of Regulation*, *op. cit.*, pp. 22–25.

95. For a detailed exposition of the theory as it applies to telecommunications, see Bolter, Duvall *et al.*, *op. cit.*, pp. 66–121. For a pioneering article on strategic firms conduct, see R. Caves and M. Porter, "From Entry Barriers to Mobility Barriers," *Quarterly Journal of Economics*, Vol. 91, May 1977, pp. 241–62.

96. W. Baumol, O. Eckstein, and A. Kahn, "Competition and Monopoly in Telecommunications Services," p. 5, Bell System Exhibit No. 46, FCC Docket No. 19129, Phase II.

97. See, *e.g.*, C. Wilcox and W. Shepherd, *op. cit.*, pp. 271–72.

98. G. Stigler, "The Theory of Economic Regulation," *The Bell Journal of Economics and Management Science*, Vol. 2, Spring 1971, pp. 3–21. See also "Free Riders and Collective Action: An Appendix to Theories of Economic Regulation," *Bell Journal of Economics and Management Science*, Vol. 5, Autumn 1974, pp. 359–65.

99. *Id.*, p. 1.

100. For a good case study of one such episode, see J. P. Fuhr, "Antitrust and Regulation: Forestalling Competition in the Telecommunications Terminal Equipment Market," *Review of Industrial Organization*, Spring 1988, pp. 101–126.

101. See H. Trebing, "Public Utility Regulation: A Case Study in the Debate over Effectiveness of Economic Regulation," in M. Tool, ed., *An Institutionalist Guide to Economics and Public Policy* (Armonk: M.E. Sharpe, 1984), pp. 199–226.

102. For articulation of this viewpoint, see A.F. Bentley, *The Process of Government* (Chicago: University of Chicago Press, 1908) and D.B. Truman, *The Government Process: Political Interests and Public Opinion* (New York: Alfred Knopf, 1951).

103. See H. Trebing, "Public Utility Regulation," *op. cit.*, p. 214.

104. B. Owen and R. Braeutigam, *The Regulation Game: Strategic Use of the Administrative Process* (Cambridge, Mass.: Ballinger, 1978).

105. For example, see "Illinois Bell is First to Allow Competition for Local Services," *Communications Week*, July 8, 1985, p. 1; and "Vermont Official: Deregulate New England Tel," *Communications Week*, July 15, 1985, p. 8.

106. See H. Trebing, "Public Utility Regulation," *op. cit.*, pp. 214–15.

107. See, *e.g.*, Brandeis' dissenting opinion in *New State Ice Co. v. Liebmann*, 285 U.S. 262, 280–311 (1932); and A. Kahn, *The Economics of Regulation*, *op. cit.*, pp. 7,9.

108. See discussion in Breyer, *op. cit.*, pp. 30–32.

109. See G. Brock, *The Telecommunications Industry*, *op. cit.*, pp. 10, 11 for a description of the two theories discussed in this part.

110. J.R. Baldwin, *The Regulatory Agency and the Public Corporation: The Canadian Air Transport Industry* (Cambridge, Mass.: Ballinger, 1975).

111. V.P. Goldberg, "Regulation and Administered Contracts," *The Bell Journal of Economics*, Vol. 7, Autumn 1976, pp. 426–48.

112. D. Dewey, "The New Learning: One Man's View" in *Industrial Concentration: The New Learning*, H. Goldschmid *et al.*, eds. (New York: Praeger Publishers, 1971), esp. p. 13.

113. A. Neale, *The Antitrust Laws of the U.S.A.* (London: Cambridge University Press, 1977), pp. 431–32.

114. See, *e.g.*, J. Bain, *op. cit.*

115. See, *e.g.*, F. Scherer, *op. cit.*

116. See, *e.g.*, G. Stigler, "A Theory of Oligopoly," *Journal of Political Economy*, Vol. 72 (February 1964).

117. O. Williamson, "Antitrust Enforcement: Where Has It Been, Where Is It Going?", in J. Craven, Ed., *Industrial Organization, Antitrust, and Public Policy*, *op. cit.*, p. 42.

118. See S. Breyer, *Regulation and Its Reform* (Cambridge, Mass.: Harvard University Press, 1982), p. 161.

119. Under the U.S. system of "checks and balances," the U.S. Congress or the President may theoretically steer this policy course. But since the early 1900s, with passage of the landmark Clayton and Federal Trade Commission (FTC) Acts, little new antitrust legislation has been enacted. The President, primarily through the Department of Justice and the FTC, implements existing antitrust policy and may change the nature of the enforcement appreciably. See, *e.g.*, "'Efficiency' Becomes Yardstick for Mergers," *Washington Post*, March 24, 1985, p. H1. However, any such course of action typically must withstand one or more court tests, *e.g.*, the Justice Department's prosecution of AT&T in 1974–81.

120. See *United States v. AT&T*, 552 F. Supp. 131 (1982), *aff'd sum nom Maryland v. United States*, 103 s. Ct. 1240 (1983).

121. See Slip Opinion, p. 9, filed August 11, 1982, by Judge Harold H. Greene, U.S. District Court for the District of Columbia, *United States v. AT&T*, *op. cit.*

122. For an excellent review of U.S. antitrust laws, policy, and decisions, see Neale, *op. cit.*; Scherer, *op. cit.*; P. Areeda, *Antitrust Analysis: Problems, Test, Cases* (Boston: Little, Brown and Company, 1974 and 1978 *Supplement*); and D. Greer, *Industrial Organization and Public Policy* (New York: Macmillan Publishing Co., Inc., 1980).

123. This section was amended in 1974 and 1976 to increase penalties up to one million dollars and felony status and to broaden enforcement.

124. It is interesting to compare this to the 1984 Justice Department "Merger Guidelines," which identifies 42.5 percent as the potential threshold for firm market power. See discussion *supra*.

125. See, *e.g.*, "U.S. Attorney General Signals Shift in Policing Big Corporate Mergers," June 25, 1981 *Washington Star News.*

126. Neale, *op. cit.*, p. 27.

127. *Id.*

128. See, *e.g.*, E. Gellhorn, *Antitrust Law and Economics in a Nutshell* (St. Paul: West Publishing Co., 1981). pp. 369–82 and Greer, *op. cit.*, p. 363.

129. See, *e.g.*, Areeda, *op. cit.*, p. 240 and Greer, op. cit., p. 203.

130. Scherer, *op. cit.*, pp. 519–25.

131. Neale, op. cit., pp. 430–31, 478–79.

132. This new emphasis on economics is not necessarily tantamount to pursuit of a "hard line" in antitrust enforcement.   In fact, some observers believe that the opposite result has occurred.   See, *e.g.*, "Attorney General: Competition Doesn't Require Many Firms," *Washington Post*, June 25, 1981; "Antitrust Chief Speaks Kindly of Big Mergers," *New York Times*, March 9, 1984, p. D3; "Antitrust Officials Unlikely to Challenge Pending Mergers During Reagan's Term," *Wall Street Journal*, June 28, 1985, p. 2; "Antitrust Law Changes Planned," *Washington Post*, November 28, 1985, p. F1; and "Justice Shifts Antitrust Responsibilities–Switching Initial Review to Economists Said to Further Weaken Merger Movement," *Washington Post*, December 11, 1986, p. D9.

133. See, *e.g.*, "Price–Fixing is Targeted by New Antitrust Chief," *Washington Post*, January 10, 1984, p. D7, and "'Efficiency' Becomes Yardstick for Mergers," *op. cit.*   See generally "Scales Tip Against Antitrust Statutes," *Insight*, June 15, 1987, pp. 8–17.

134. Neale, *op. cit.*, p. 432.

135. *Id.*, p. 448.

136. *Id.*, p. 441.

137. *Id.*, p. 448.

138. "Scales Tip Against Antitrust Statutes," *Insight*, June 15, 1987, p. 11.

139. See, *e.g.*, Greer, *op. cit.*, pp. 295, 405–415 and Scherer, *op. cit.*, pp. 267–95. For an opposing view, see, *e.g.*, H. Demsetz, *The Market Concentration Doctrine* (Washington, D.C.: American Enterprise Institute, 1973).

140. Scherer, *op. cit.*, pp. 438, 407–37.

141. See, *e.g.*, "Baxter Spells Out Plan to Let Industry Set Up Joint Research Efforts," *Washington Post*, May 11, 1983, p. D7; and "Senate Approves R&D Cooperation Bill" *Washington Post*, August 1, 1984, p. F1.

142. "A New Spirit of Cooperation," *New York Times*, January 14, 1986, p. D1; and "Commerce Secretary Nominee Backs Relaxed Antitrust Laws," *Washington Post*, January 25, 1989, p. F2.

143. "Consortia Urged for Superconductor Research," *Washington Post*, January 4, 1989, pp. A1, A6.

144. For the classic exposition defining economics, see L. Robbins, *An Essay on the Nature and Significance of Economic Science* (London: Macmillan, 1935).

145. Mathematical economics concerns the use of quantitative techniques to explain economic phenomena.   Econometrics is a branch of statistics whereby economic hypotheses are tested and economic parameters are estimated.   In theory, econometrics involves numerical measurement while mathematical economics is purely abstract.   In practice, the distinctions are frequently blurred.

146. For a good discussion of the complexities of the subject, see M. Blaug, *op. cit.*, pp. 129–56.

147. Many of these notions are examined in greater detail in Chapter II above.   Other independent sources which may be profitably read are P.A. Samuelson and W.D. Nordhaus, *op. cit.*; C.R. McConnell, *Economics Principles, Problems, and Policies* (New York: McGraw–Hill Book Company, 1969); and W.J. Baumol and A.S. Blinder, *Economics Principles and Policy* (New York: Harcourt Brace Jovanovich, 1982).

148. Jean–Baptiste Say and Nassau William Senior were among the principal contributors.

149. This is called a "Pareto optimum" after the Italian economist–engineer Vilfredo Pareto.   For a more detailed discussion of economic efficiency, see Chapter II *supra*.

CHAPTER III

TELECOMMUNICATIONS DEVELOPMENT AND PARAMETERS

A. Origins of U.S. Telecommunications: The Road to Monopoly

1. Background

a. *Early Development of Telegraphy*

It is instructive to trace the development of electronic communications in this country and the evolution of a regulatory governmental approach. The American experience has special characteristics, which contrast with reliance on governmental direction and even public ownership in some countries, and, often, much more vigorous interventionist tactics and interference with market processes. However, this country's philosophy has evolved considerably over time, as can be surmised from a brief examination of the early days of telegraphy and telephony.

Of course, the U.S. telecommunications industry traces its roots to the invention of the telegraph in the 1830s by Samuel F. B. Morse.[1] Diffusion of this technology languished, however, until 1843, when Congress passed the Telegraph Act. This led to the construction and development of a federally owned facility operating between Washington, D.C. and Baltimore in 1844. However, Congress refused to purchase the patent rights to the technology in 1846, thus permitting private commercial development and ownership of telegraphy. Significantly, at that time, it established the American practice of private sector provision of electronic communications services, subject to the guidance of public policy.

For the remainder of the decade, as many as fifty small telegraph companies began operations in various regions of the country. In 1851 Mississippi Valley Printing Telegraph and New York Telegraph merged, and later combined with United States and American Telegraph to form the Western Union Telegraph Company. By the end of the Civil War, Western Union had emerged as this nation's first great industrial monopoly and its biggest corporation.[2]

From this period until the early 1900s, a number of public policy makers recommended that Congress declare a government monopoly over all electronic communications in this country. Reasons given by some Congressmen and most U.S. Postmasters General centered on the "postal nature" of telegraphy, advantages of "institutional efficiency," and the "monopolistic tendency of the business."[3] Among others advocating public ownership of Western Union were President Ulysses S. Grant, labor leader Samuel Gompers, Supreme Court Justice H. B. Brown, Senators Henry Clay and Charles Sumner, and Prof. Morse himself. Despite this "agitation," no such nationalization occurred, and Congress did not embrace regulation as a policy prescription until 1910. That year, the Interstate Commerce Commission (ICC) was chartered to regulate Western Union's interstate activities.

b.   Emergence of Telephony and the New Industry Structure

Although some competition arose in the late 1800s (*e.g.*, the Postal Telegraph Company), a much more formidable threat to Western Union would prove to be the invention of the telephone.[4]   In March 1876, Alexander Graham Bell was granted his first telephone patent, narrowly securing these rights before a rival inventor, Elisha Gray, could finalize his claim. Lack of early commercial success, however, led Bell's backers to offer the telephone patent to Western Union for $100,000, a sum which would not have even covered development expenses that had been incurred. Although initially declining to participate in the fledgling telephone business, by 1878 Western Union perceived the significance of the technology and decided to enter the market.   Toward this end, the Company acquired the patents of Gray, Thomas Edison, and Amos Dolbear.

The ensuing legal confrontation between Western Union and the entity formed by Bell's group was resolved in 1879. In a negotiated settlement, Bell agreed not to enter the telegraph business during the pendency of the disputed patents and compensated Western Union for lost patent royalties. In return, Western Union agreed to drop its patent suits against Bell and to withdraw from telephony for seventeen years.

In actuality, this agreement established the basic monopoly service and product structure for domestic U.S. communications, as divided between Western Union and Bell, for roughly the next 100 years. With the exception of the aforementioned Postal Telegraph entity, Western Union would not experience significant entry into its telegraph business until its public message telegraph (or "telegram") service would be opened to competition by the FCC in 1979.[5]   And, AT&T's Bell System would not relinquish its predominant monopoly position in the telephone market until the familial ties were severed on January 1, 1984 as part of the "Modification of Final Judgment" (MFJ) settlement of a pending antitrust suit.[6] Technically, the Bell patent monopoly endured until 1893. But, by this time, Bell had already well established telephone operations in the major markets of the day, and evolved quickly into a financially powerful, soon to be dominant corporation.

Yet, with the expiration of the Bell patents, a number of new telephone companies, or "Independents," did begin operations.   While often serving outlying areas, these were sometimes in competition with the "Bell System." Bell's initial response was to rapidly boost its own operations. For instance, Bell's number of telephones served grew by over 1,000 percent between 1893 and 1907.[7]

Subsequently American Telephone and Telegraph Company (which became the parent holding company of the Bell corporate family in 1901), under the guidance of President Theodore Vail, inaugurated an acquisition policy when confronting formidable rivals or seeking to expand its base of operation. Indeed, between 1907 and 1910 the Bell System acquired control of 495,000 Independent company telephones.[8] This marked the beginning of a merger movement which reduced the number of Independent operating companies from more than 9,000 in 1922 to 4,114 in 1957, and then to approximately 1,400 on the eve of the AT&T divestiture on December 31, 1983.[9]

Notably, one of AT&T's prime acquisition targets was Western Union. In 1909, AT&T bought a controlling (30 percent) interest in the telegraph giant, and Vail assumed the presidency of the new combined entity. The newfound synergy was noteworthy: now telegrams could be sent and delivered by telephone, conferring an enormous advantage for the affiliated Western Union over its chief rival, Postal Telegraph.[10] At this point in time, AT&T effectively dominated both the telephone and telegraph businesses, which were the two major forms of electronic communications.

c.   Evolving Governmental Policy Toward Telecommunications

Alarmed at these developments, public policy makers at the state and national levels intervened. In 1907 Wisconsin and New York established the first state regulatory commissions. Their actions were followed by 28 other states during the next six years.[11] Also, during the period 1904 to 1919, some 34 states passed laws which rendered unlawful the Bell System policy of refusing to interconnect its facilities with those of the Independents.[12] In 1910 Congress authorized the Interstate Commerce Commission to oversee interstate common carrier wire and radio communications.

AT&T's competitors petitioned the Justice Department for relief from conditions of market concentration. Indeed, the 1912 Presidential campaign of Woodrow Wilson revealed a growing public sentiment favoring restraints on monopoly practices. During the same period, Postmaster General Burleson and others were lobbying Congress to nationalize electronic communications in this country.

In response to these pressures, and to avoid antitrust actions, N. C. Kingsbury, an AT&T Vice President, sent a letter to the U.S. Attorney General in 1913 committing his company to certain ameliorative conditions. AT&T agreed to curtail further acquisitions of competing Independent telephone companies and to connect its system to the facilities of Independents for purposes of toll service provision. In addition, the company averred that it would sell all of its holdings of Western Union stock. At the time, this represented an investment estimated to be $30 million in value.

This "Kingsbury Commitment" signified a major redirection in the structure and conduct of the U.S. communications industry. Once more, two private entities emerged as dominant players viz., AT&T and Western Union. But, the former product division that separated the companies did not reappear. Although purging itself of Western Union stock, AT&T acquired a leading position in the private line telegraph market which it apparently did not relinquish upon divestiture.[13] In addition, U.S. telephony was assured of the ongoing presence of non-AT&T supply. But the continued existence of Independent companies as a group did not represent traditional competition, since these firms' and Bell's customers were split territorially. The Bell System's presence was in "most of the profitable service areas," while the Independents typically operated in rural or smaller districts.[14] During World War I, the communications industry was placed under the control of the federal government. However, daily management remained the responsibility of the companies. Moreover, despite some sentiment at the time, nationalization of the sector did not come to pass after the war ended.

d. The Changing Fortunes of Telegraphy and Telephony

Over the first half of the 1920s, Western Union enjoyed revenue growth spawned by the general economic prosperity of the period in this country. Nevertheless, its share of the communications market was decreased by customer defections to both long distance telephone service and to the newly introduced "Air Mail" services. Although buoyed by resurging demand by the country during World War II, telegraphy has experienced a secular trend of a declining market presence since the mid 1920s.

As shown in Table III–1, toll telephone (the principal telephonic competitor to telegraphy) experienced a steadily increasing share of the long distance communications revenue "pie," growing from 59.5 percent in 1926 to an estimated 79.1 percent in 1949. Domestic air mail revenues also rose in relative (and absolute) terms, boosting that sector's share from 0.2 percent in 1926 to 5.3 percent some 23 years later. In contrast, telegraph revenues of telephone companies and especially nontelegraph carriers (i.e., Western Union and Postal Telegraph) declined substantially, plummeting a combined 24.7 points over the same period. Indeed, the President's Communications Policy Board warned in its March 1951 Report to the White House that this shift in the character of the demand for telegraph service has seriously threatened the continued existence of the Western Union system as a private enterprise.[15]

During the 1970s and early 1980s domestic toll telephony has continued to dominate among modes of U.S. communications, commanding 69 percent of the market by 1983 (see Table III–2). Air mail has added to its share during this period, exceeding 29 percent by the year before the Bell System breakup. Telegraphy continued its slide, however, registering only 1.3 percent of the total by 1983.

2. Monopoly Nature of the Industry

An important factor in analyzing telecommunications trends and strategic opportunities involves recognition of the industry's underlying driving forces and economic aspects. These inexorably survive changes in governmental policies, alliances, and shifts in market position and ownership. In this regard, a crucial variable is supply characteristics and tendencies toward concentration. This special aspect of telecommunications is discussed below from the standpoint of technology, economics, demand, and policy views.

a. Technological Perspective

Historically, after an early period of competition from the 1890s to World War I, the telephone industry evolved into a regulated monopoly, consisting of Bell companies and the Independents operating out of monopoly franchised territories. Use of this restricted, government imposed entry barrier reflected the consensus that the telecommunications market was a "natural monopoly,"

Table III–1

DISTRIBUTION OF COMMUNICATIONS REVENUES
Trends: 1926 to 1949

Year	Air Mail*	Telephone Companies Tphn. Toll#	Tgph.	Western Union/ Postal Telegraph	Total+
1926	0.2%	59.5%	3.9%	36.4%	100%
1929	0.9	64.3	4.5	30.4	100
1934	1.5	65.1	5.0	28.4	100
1939	3.8	68.2	4.5	23.5	100
1944	7.9	71.3	3.6	17.2	100
1949	5.3**	79.1**	2.9	12.7	100

Source: *A Report by the President's Communications Board*, March 1951, pp. 83, 84.

* Includes domestic air mail, letter, card, and parcel post revenues.
# Includes message, private line, and miscellaneous toll revenues.
+ May not sum due to rounding.
** Preliminary data.

Table III–2

DISTRIBUTION OF COMMUNICATIONS REVENUES
Trends: 1975 to 1983

Year	First Class and Air Mail*	Domestic Toll Service+	Domestic Telegraphy	Total#
1975	27.0%	70.6%	2.4%	100%
1980	25.5	72.7	1.8	100
1983	29.8	69.0	1.3	100

Source: U.S. Department of Commerce, *Statistical Abstract of the United States, 1987*, Table 901; FCC *Statistics of Communications Common Carriers*, Tables 16 and 23.

* Items mailed at first class rates and weighing 12 oz. or less. Beginning in 1977, category includes air mail which was discontinued as a separate class.
+ Includes toll revenues for all Bell System and Independent telephone companies and for AT&T's Long Lines.
# May not sum due to rounding.

characterized by economies of scale over the entire range of output that would be demanded by users. Generally, economies of scale are said to exist where a given percentage increase in inputs (*e.g.*, labor and capital) to the productive process results in a greater percentage increase in output. In economic terms, the phenomenon occurs where long run average costs (LRAC) are declining over the entire range of output in a given market as determined by the relevant portion of the demand curve.

Scale economies can occur for any of several reasons and for different production conditions. For example, economies may arise with respect to the production of a single product or multiple products. And, economies of scale may be "real" (*e.g.*, arising in production, advertising, marketing, research and development) or "pecuniary" (*e.g.*, related to the raising of capital through equity issues). In the case of telephony, most industry observers have singled out cost savings in the large volume "production" of services in the network as the source of economies, especially in the transmission of calls.

Besides scale economies, the telephone natural monopoly has been thought to exhibit demand elasticities that vary by markets, with at least one market being highly inelastic (namely, basic local service). Moreover, sharp and regular fluctuations in output are known to occur (*e.g.*, peak versus off–peak calling traffic). Finally, private controlled connection points, which are effective opportunities to prevent entry, are readily evident in telephony, including the direct physical connections needed to access the network (such as a customer's "local loop" or "drop wire"). All of these alleged long term characteristics support the technological view of telephony as a natural monopoly, and, in the absence of other factors or policy criteria, would dictate the long term accommodation of users and policy makers to this underlying aspect of the industry.

b. Economic Perspective

Given its interrelated technical characteristics, the telephone sector developed under a regime of joint network planning, with franchised monopoly carriers providing local exchange service under either the mantle of the Bell System or as one of the Independent companies. AT&T's Long Lines Department supplied long distance toll service in conjunction with the Bell local companies and the Independents. Private line services were also furnished jointly over the same facilities used for long distance service. Vertical integration of service, manufacturing, and R&D operations were commonplace. For example, AT&T and the Bell Operating Companies' (BOCs) equipment and research needs were supplied internally by Western Electric and Bell Laboratories, while those of the General telephone companies were satisfied by wholly controlled Automatic Electric, Sylvania, and GTE Laboratories.

This structure gave rise to several important economic characteristics of the industry. For instance, the constituent Bell operating companies became highly capital intensive and large in financial resources, employment and other aspects. In turn, this enormous size enabled the telephone carriers to meet huge growth in customer demand in the precompetitive environment and also to reap economies of operation. Finally, the structure led to the development of overwhelming "market power," whereby the telephone companies could introduce services or equipment, as well as retire plant facilities in their respective territories, on a timetable often virtually undisturbed by the threat of alternative sources of supply.

Other economic implications resulted from this arrangement. Even if legal restraints (such as franchises and patents) could be overcome, potential entrants were confronted with overwhelmingly high costs of entry to compete nationwide or across all services. Confronted with barriers, including the aforementioned economies and the need for substantial capital expenditures for facilities, the telephone companies appeared to have little to fear from new entry.

The concomitant monopoly power of their positions afforded the telephone companies with the ability to discriminate among customers, sometimes with regulatory approval and support (e.g., in the case of charging higher rates for business customers than their residential counterparts for a given service). But, the potential for predacious discrimination and cross subsidy was tremendous even without regulatory approval, since no cost of service studies were required by regulatory commissions for many years. As history shows, once such analyses were performed, there were compelling indications that less than full equanimity in pricing or service treatment had been practiced. For example, the FCC's "seven way" cost study results that were developed for the Bell System in 1964 indicated that unreasonable cross subsidization among services may have been taking place for some time (see discussion below).

c. Customer Perspective

Under the franchised monopoly regime extant in telephony historically, users came to expect "one stop shopping" and "end-to-end service." There were several major advantages of this arrangement from the customer's vantage point. For instance, these included choices uncomplicated by multiple vendors, a concomitant minimum of confusion, and relatively clear-cut lines of carrier accountability and responsibility, especially respecting service quality and reliability.

Disadvantages, however, were also significant. For example, the obverse of uncomplicated choices was the limited array of available carrier products and services from which to choose. Users did know easily enough who to contact for their telecommunications needs. But there were few or no alternative sources of supply in most cases, especially where the subscriber's local exchange carrier or long distance provider was incapable of meeting a user's special requirements or problems. Since market entry was strictly regulated by the local public service commission or the FCC, resources and timing for meeting out-of-the-ordinary user needs were essentially controlled by the established carriers.

In this environment, new network offerings were introduced on a restrained basis and were largely predictable. Also, terms and conditions of supply were not always reflective of technical limitations. For instance, customer premises equipment (CPE) was strictly leased, and not bought or sold by users. In addition, domestic long distance service was limited to voice grade services, such as ordinary long distance Message Telephone Service (MTS) and Wide Area Telephone Service (WATS), which was used for flat rate calling within a given geographic zone or "band." Both these toll and local offerings were provided on an analog network comprised of primarily electromechanical (e.g., step–by–step or crossbar) switches, and transmission modes such as microwave radio, coaxial cable, and paired copper wires. "Point–to–point" private lines were available for those with usually high traffic or specific needs for voice or data services. Telegraphy could also be utilized for data needs. Finally, overseas communications from the United States represented another restricted market. The limited options encompassed the offerings of AT&T (for voice grade transmissions via undersea cable), the international record carriers or IRCs (for record or data needs), and, eventually, Comsat, which was established as a quasi–governmental entity (for mainly voice services and television needs offered via satellite).

Communications typically represented an important but relatively small part of the budgets of residences, vis–à–vis other utility needs, and those of businesses. In the latter case, small and most large firms historically did not designate a specific telecommunications operation within their organizations. Instead, most assigned these functions to a data processing or administrative department. Typically, communications management was concerned more with avoiding the imposition of problems upon line or day–to–day operations rather than planning or strategic objectives.

d. Policy Perspective

As recently as the mid 1960s, public policy makers still promoted a monopoly supply structure for the domestic communications industry. Three basic types of offerings existed at that time much as they had earlier in the century. These were: a) switched local and long distance telephone services; b) telegraph and teletypewriter exchange offerings (telex or TWX); and c) various private line services. The Bell System and the Independent telephone companies were the sole authorized suppliers of public telephone services, both local and long distance (MTS and WATS). Western Union retained its monopoly in the provision of public telegraph messages, and was soon to gain (in part, through acquisition from AT&T) a monopoly position in the market for teletypewriter exchange services. Only in the realm of private line services was any "competition" permitted, and even here the AT&T–Western Union duopoly offered dominant competing interstate lines for the lucrative business of high volume communications users, mainly in the area of telegraph grade and voice grade services.

The nature of the industry's structure, i.e., the paucity of competition, was not surprising in view of the easily defined, limited, and homogeneous markets involved. From this vantage point, the telephone and telegraph sectors fit the classic view of natural monopolies, which, accordingly, would require only one supplier in each of these instances. Concerning the private line market, services were needed in such substantial volumes by customers that the dominance of the huge AT&T and Western Union carriers was not surprising to industry observers.   Indeed, only the existence of private networks and a few inconsequential entrants (such as MCI) upset this traditional well–ordered market structure.

And, through most of the 20th century, government decision makers had viewed telephone companies as not unlike their energy counterparts.   Thus, these "public utilities" were regulated in "the public interest."   This fit well with concepts constituting the cornerstones of what would become standard telecommunications public policy in the U.S., namely, the attainment and maintenance of universally available and affordable telephone service.

Interestingly, the primary architect of this "universal service" goal was the Bell System's own founding father, Theodore Vail.   Through the years, it would become the public interest standard against which telephone companies would be evaluated.   Long time AT&T executive Alvin von Auw noted that "As [Alexander Graham] Bell invented the telephone, so Vail invented the Bell System."[16]   And, under the guidance of Vail (and his successors), the Bell System "family" of telephone operating companies, manufacturing arm (Western Electric), and research laboratories (Bell Labs) emerged as the world's largest company during most of this century.[17]   Over time, largely through Vail's synergistic efforts, these and other U.S. telephone companies came to be considered by public officials as the structural "natural monopolies," which was Vail's view, and thus, had to be publicly regulated (albeit privately owned).

Within this natural monopoly framework, the goal of universal service was in its primacy through roughly the first one hundred years of telephony (1876–1976).

Consistent with Vail's own strategy of fostering Bell's expansion, the industry invested tremendously toward meeting this objective.   By the end of this period, it had been essentially achieved, although socially costly both in terms of the resources devoted to the industry (about 10 percent of all U.S. investment by the 1970s), and in the sense that it was apparently attained without adequate public oversight.   To illustrate this phenomenon, consider that through the early 1930s, federal regulation of telephone rates, practices, and charges was deemed to be practically nonexistent.   This deficiency was attributable to the lack of a Congressional mandate and to insufficient funding and attention of the Interstate Commerce Commission (ICC).[18] Similarly, state regulation of operating companies by the 1930s was frequently ineffective because of funding problems, far ranging duties over multiple utilities, and the increasing complexities of the business, particularly AT&T's emerging long distance network and its complex vertical operational arrangement.[19]

To remedy some of the authority and organizational problems of regulation at the federal level, Congress passed what was believed to be remedial legislation in the 1930s, namely the Communications Act of 1934 ("the Act").   Superseding the Mann–Elkins Act of 1910, which had expanded the ICC's authority of telephone and telegraph carriers, the Act created the Federal Communications Commission (FCC).   But, the latter's mandate from

Congress simply formalized the Vail inspired public policy universal service objective in Section 201:

> . . . to make available, so far as possible, to all the people of the United States a rapid, efficient, Nation–wide, and world–wide wire and radio–communication service with adequate facilities at reasonable charges . . .[20]

The governmental view of regulation, excepting universal service, has not been based on precise standards during most of this century. For example, pricing concepts embraced by regulators have generally not been founded on achieving cost based rates. Instead, "value of service" (VOS) principles have been the driving force behind rate determinations. When coupled with universal service objectives, at the state level the VOS approach has led to a number of rate structure perturbations; these include categorically higher telephone rates for business vis–à–vis residential customers. Similarly, city dwellers have faced higher rates as a group than rural subscribers, despite frequently higher service costs in outlying areas. Not until the mid 1960s did message unit (i.e., per call) pricing begin to gain acceptance, initially among businesses in large cities and later in smaller urban areas and residences.

The FCC has engaged, perhaps to a lesser degree, in such price discrimination, setting long distance MTS rates for weekday evenings and nights, and weekends at uniformly lower levels than peak period usage during the business day. Unlike at the local level, toll rates have been metered for both distance and duration of call, but these charges also did not precisely reflect underlying costs. Other long distance services, such as WATS and TELPAK (both volume business–oriented offerings), also appeared to have utilized noncost based rates (see the discussion below).

A special policy focus during the post–World War II period has been defense considerations. Concerns about developing and maintaining a secure, reliable system of communications, especially during wartime, have occupied the interests of Congress, the Pentagon, and the FCC. As a result, a high priority has been accorded national security issues. Stress has been placed upon a single, coordinated telephone network, construction of the more secure cable technology for use in transmission facilities domestically and for over–seas calling, and system redundancy.

Overall, these sundry policy objectives appear to have been largely met during the monopoly era of telecommunications, albeit in varying degrees among the respective jurisdictions. However, apparently a "price" has been paid for these successes, in the form of economic discrimination, and possibly inefficiency and lagged rates of innovation and technological change. Many observers believe that constraints on entry of potential competitors and acceptance of noncost based rates has produced distorted investment and pricing signals, which have resulted in nonoptimal industry performance. This scenario was seemingly compounded by rather ineffective regulation, especially in many state jurisdictions. There, commissions were typically beset by inadequate resources, and, in some two–thirds of all states, the existence of multistate Bell Operating Companies which tended to complicate jurisdictional authority and oversight. Consequently, users suffered in terms of less diversity and choice, higher prices, and frequently unmet communications needs.

B.   Bases for Policy Redirection and Competitive Entry

Several key occurrences led to the AT&T divestiture fundamental remaking of the traditional structure and policies of the U.S. telecommunications industry. These include: (1) the constraints placed on AT&T and the Bell System by a 1956 antitrust consent decree; (2) the technological revolution that began during the 1950s and 1960s; (3) FCC policy changes (sanctioned by the courts), that promoted competition and deregulation; (4) the Commission's landmark "Computer II" proceeding; and (5) perceived Bell System abuses. Each of these is discussed below.

1.   Antitrust Restrictions on AT&T: The 1956 Decree

In 1949 the Department of Justice brought an antitrust suit against the Bell System, charging restraint of trade and other monopolistic abuses pursuant to the Sherman Act.[21] After seven years of litigation, the parties settled the case through consummation of a consent decree. In return for preservation of the Bell System structure, AT&T agreed, in effect, to operate only in traditional, regulated telephone markets. The 1956 decree had two important implications for regulatory policy in this country. First, the existing regulatory framework and the public utility concept were essentially bolstered by the agreement. Second, the constraints placed upon permissible activities of AT&T and other Bell System members would need to be re-evaluated as events dictated. As described below, a series of significant changes would soon commence which would eventually necessitate a modification of the constraints of the 1956 decree, as well as other traditional public policy programs.

2.   Convergence of Computers and Communications

A revolution in computer and electronic technology, born in the 1950s and accelerating during the 1960s, greatly expanded the United States' communications capabilities. Moreover, the occurrence concomitantly inspired and initiated a groundswell of new demands in the area of terminal, or customer premises, equipment and the aforementioned private line sector. Such breakthroughs as the transistor, remote batch and time sharing techniques, integrated circuits, and the minicomputer manifestly possessed tremendous potential for applications in the communications arena. These innovations beckoned technical expertise which existed outside (as well as inside) the traditional telephone and telegraph industry. As a result, technological achievements rapidly began to render obsolete certain aspects of the aforementioned industry structure prior to, and during, the mid–1960s. Moreover, new technology caused the traditional regulatory boundaries between regulated communications and other unregulated activities (such as computers) to erode, necessitating a reassessment of conventional regulation and the 1956 consent decree.

3. FCC Policy Changes

Clearly, the most important institutional catalyst for new public policy directions in telecommunications since 1934 has been the directives of the FCC. For example, decisions by the Commission precipitated eventual court sanctioning of competitive provision of customer premises equipment in interstate and intrastate markets, as well as opening transmission services markets to competition.

Notably, the agency's *Carterfone* case was a key proceeding leading to such results. Traditionally, telephone company tariffs had expressly prohibited the connection of any customer owned communications equipment to telephone company lines or facilities. However, in 1968, the Commission issued a landmark decision stemming from an antitrust suit brought against AT&T by Thomas Carter on behalf of his manufacturing firm.[22] In essence, the FCC ruled that AT&T's prohibitions on terminal equipment interconnection were unlawful. The FCC generally embraced an earlier (1956) ruling of the U.S. Court of Appeals for the District of Columbia Circuit, which found that a telephone subscriber had an intrinsic right to use the public telephone network for private gain as long as the public's welfare is not compromised.[23] Eventually, AT&T responded by filing new tariffs which permitted ratepayers to acquire and interconnect their own terminal devices, provided that telephone company used connecting arrangements (CAs), which were designed to protect the telecommunications network from the potential harm of utilizing nontelephone company equipment.

In implementing its new policies, the FCC conducted numerous studies of the carrier initiated CA program, as well as reviewing the report and conclusions of a federal/state Joint Board, which was convened during 1972–75. The Commission ultimately ascertained that institution of a federal certification/registration policy for certain customer provided equipment was the preferred approach.[24]

Under this plan, any terminal equipment which passed the FCC's technical standards could be attached to the telephone network without use of a telephone company connecting arrangement. In advocating this program, the FCC argued that the carrier CA policy was unlawful and unjustifiably discriminatory. The Commission believed that telephone company provided equipment ostensibly did not need such a protective device while identical customer supplied terminals would (and did) require costly connecting arrangements from the carriers. The validity of the decision, which was vehemently opposed by some, was eventually upheld by the courts.[25]

Over the years, the FCC's registration program, established under Docket 19528, has included numerous types of telephone handsets, key systems, private branch exchanges (PBXs), and inside wiring. Moreover, as discussed below, other Commission actions have brought about the detariffing and eventual deregulation of CPE under Title II of the Communications Act. In addition, in the context of FCC Docket 80–286, CPE has been removed from the jurisdictional separations process of apportioning costs between the inter–state and intrastate arenas.

Besides equipment markets, the Commission has laid the policy ground–work for competitive entry and reduced regulation in many service related areas. For example, the private line arena has been a major source of regulatory, legal, and technological changes. Until the latter part of the 1950s, provision of such services required an enormous investment in facilities and a securing of requisite rights–of–way. AT&T and Western Union proved to be the only substantial and lasting participants during much of that decade. With the widespread use of microwave radio as a means of transmitting messages, however, the potential for competition increased significantly as capital requirements markedly diminished and rights–of–way problems also lessened. Subsequently, large corporations, with high volumes of internal communications traffic, petitioned the FCC to allow them to construct lines for their own personal use. The Commission affirmed the right of these firms to do this in its 1959 *Above 890* decision, and agreed to apportion needed radio frequencies for such endeavors.[26]

Not unexpectedly, numerous requests for the furnishing of private line services on a common carrier basis followed. In 1969, the FCC finally authorized MCI to build and operate a private line microwave system between Chicago and St. Louis.[27]   By 1970 a variety of new carriers were categorically allowed to compete with the interstate offerings of telephone companies. The culmination of this FCC inquiry into the desirability from a public interest standpoint of promoting competition in this market was the *Specialized Common Carrier* ruling of 1971.[28]   That decision is noteworthy because of its stress on the need to meet user requirements for specialized private line communications (especially for data transmission), as well as the advantages of multiple suppliers.

The following year, the Commission promulgated its "Open Skies" policy, announcing that competition would be allowed in the new domestic communi–cations satellite sector for reasons similar to those enunciated in its earlier competitive findings.[29]   The FCC further ordered that AT&T and the Independent telephone companies could not legally deny interconnection of specialized carrier lines to the telephone companies' networks; this position was subsequently upheld in 1975 by a United States Appellate Court in Philadelphia.[30]   A variety of entrants were subsequently authorized by the Commission to operate in such areas as "value added" packet switching networks (1973 and 1974),[31] resale and shared use (1976),[32] and domestic public message services (1979).[33]

The arrival of the 1980s brought a myriad of changes to the telecommu–nications sector, many of them again inaugurated by the FCC. For instance, an examination of the competitiveness of various markets was undertaken, leading to streamlined regulatory treatment of such "nondominant" providers as new domestic satellite service providers or "domsats," miscellaneous common carriers, newer interexchange service market entrants, such as MCI, and telex/TWX service providers other than Western Union.[34] Entities such as AT&T, the Bell Operating Companies (BOCs), Independent telephone companies, and Western Union (in the 1970s and early 1980s) were classified as "dominant." These firms remained subject to "full regulation."

Application of regulation was also limited on a service basis, due to the continued blurring of the distinction between statutorily unregulated computers and data processing (DP) services and regulated communications offerings. These problems initially led the FCC to adopt a mixed definitional scheme. This was established in Computer Inquiry I (CI1) in the early 1970s.[35] In summary, under CI1, only "pure" communications and hybrid communications services were made subject to regulation; DP and hybrid DP offerings were unregulated. Eventually, this scheme was abandoned in favor of new demarcations set forth in Computer Inquiry II (CI2) as discussed below.

4. The FCC's Computer Inquiry II Solution

As noted, the Commission's initial attempt to distinguish between computers and data processing (DP) services, the mixed area of data communications, and pure communications offerings culminated in its decision rendered in the First Computer Inquiry. In that proceeding, the FCC established a special regulated hybrid communications category under the definitional scheme where DP was determined to be "incidental" to message switching. Separately, an unregulated hybrid data processing category was defined where message switching was considered "incidental" to the service (see Figure III–1). The agency then imposed structural separation upon all communications carriers providing one million dollars or more of DP services annually. The notable exception to this scheme was AT&T, which apparently could only offer tariffed common carrier services pursuant to the 1956 consent decree.

The CI1 approach sufficed for several years, but by 1976 the Commission inaugurated a new proceeding in response to the emerging need for a revised definitional system. In 1977 the agency proposed to now redefine the CI1 scheme of services as "voice," "basic nonvoice," and "enhanced nonvoice." The first two could be provided directly by carriers but enhanced nonvoice could only be offered under a resale structure (see Figure III–2). Customer premises equipment's (CPE) regulatory status hinged upon whether or not more than a "basic media conversion" was performed. In this Second Computer Inquiry, the FCC attempted to determine the most appropriate regulatory framework for the provision of CPE and enhanced services by telephone companies and other entities. But, by the end of the 1970s, the agency had not settled upon a specific new scheme.

In 1980 the Commission issued its landmark *Final Report* in Computer Inquiry II which, ironically, would prove to be anything but the final ruling on the subject.[36] The FCC deemed that both the CPE and "enhanced services" markets were sufficiently competitive to warrant their deregulation in both interstate and intrastate jurisdictions. "Basic services" would continue

Figure III–1

THE FCC'S COMPUTER INQUIRIES:
"Computer I" (Docket No. 16979)

- DP INDUSTRY ENVIRONMENT: central host computer + remote batch processing

- FCC established hybrid communication and hybrid DP boundary for common carrier regulation

  STANDARD:
  single integrated service DP incidental to message
  switching = "hybrid communication"
  M/S incidental to DP = "hybrid DP"

- MAXIMUM SEPARATION POLICY: structural separation imposed for all carriers providing DP services ($1 million cutoff)
  Separate from Regulated Carriers
  - computer facilities
  - employees
  - advertising & marketing
  - officers

- NOT APPLICABLE TO AT&T
  Assumption: AT&T could only offer tariffed common carrier services under the 1956 consent decree interpretation

to be regulated (Figure III–3).   These markets were deregulated on a "bifurcated" basis, such that new CPE and enhanced services were removed from Title II regulation sooner than existing offerings.   For CPE, the transition established for state tariffed Bell equipment was January 1, 1986 and for Independents, between December 31, 1987 and December 31, 1990. Concerning any existing enhanced services, the deadline for detariffing was January 1, 1983.

For AT&T and the Bell Operating Companies (and initially GTE), the Commission ruled in 1980 that CPE and enhanced services could only be provided through fully separate subsidiaries.   The "maximum separation" principle established in the agency's CI1 proceeding relating to the provision of data processing services by certain carriers was generally embraced in CI2 as well.   Reasons set forth by the FCC for initiating a separate subsidiary condition for Bell entities centered on their potential use of extant market power in basic network services.   This could be employed either to improperly shift costs   from unregulated to regulated   activities or to discriminate against their competitors' products and services.   Soon after the January 1, 1984 divestiture, the structural requirement was extended to the new Regional

Figure III-2

THE FCC'S COMPUTER INQUIRIES:
"Computer II" (Docket No. 20828)

- EVOLUTION

- *Notice* (1976): *Supplemental Notice* (1977): Definition Proposed: Functions

- *Tentative Decision and Further Notice of Inquiry and Rulemaking* (1977):

  New Definitional Structure Proposed
  - Services: pipeline as basic building block introduced
  - "Voice" and "basic non-voice" services could be directly provided: but "enhanced non-voice" offerings offered only under resale structure
  - CPE: regulatory scheme based on whether CPE performed more than a basic media conversion function

- FURTHER NPRM OPTIONS
  - Exclude all enhanced non-voice service from Title II
  - Deregulate all carrier provided CPE
  - Limit structural separation to certain carriers

Bell Operating Companies (RBOCs)[37] (CC Docket No. 83–115). But, the Commission would soon retreat from even this refined mode of regulation.

To understand the further evolution of the computer inquiries, it is well to explore briefly the ongoing difficulty of allocating common communications plant costs. Indeed, the FCC has attempted to ascertain cost by service for over two decades. In early 1964, in response to allegations by Western Union that the Bell System had historically utilized its monopoly voice services to cross subsidize its other offerings, the Commission directed AT&T to develop the costs and earnings of each of its seven major interstate service classifications for the 1964 test year.[38]

As shown by Table III-3, the results of the seminal "seven way" cost study seemingly supported those that claimed Bell's monopoly services earnings cross-subsidized other offerings in an unreasonable manner. Thus, although the company's overall rate of return was 7.5 percent, the competitive services (Telpak and private line telegraph) earned substantially less than the monopoly service, *viz.*, 0.3 percent and 1.4 percent vs. approximately 10.0 percent. These findings led to the Commission's general telephone investigation in Docket No. 16258, initiated in 1965, and, ultimately, to the FCC investigation into proper costing methodologies in Docket No. 18128.[39]

Broadly, the Commission attempted in Docket No. 18128 to weigh the relative merits of fully distributed costs (FDC) and long run incremental costs

Figure III–3

THE FCC'S COMPUTER INQUIRIES:
Computer II and Network Services

- SERVICE DIVIDED INTO TWO TYPES: basic or enhanced

    1. Basic Services: common carrier offering of transmission capacity
        (pipeline)
            – Does not include voice and data storage retrieval
        Basic Services are regulated under Title II
            – For example; ordinary telephone service
            – Private lines for voice, video, data, etc.
            – Resale of basic service

    2. Enhanced Services: services offered over common carrier transmission
        facilities used in interstate communications, which employ computer
        processing applications that act on the format, content, code,
        protocol or similar aspects of the subscriber's transmitted informa–
        tion; provide the subscriber additional, different or restructured
        information; or involve subscriber interaction with stored information.
        These include:
            – Business management systems (inventory)
            – Text editing services
            – Information retrieval services (mail box and data base services)
            – Data processing services

(LRIC). It chose the former as preferable. More specifically, the agency
developed a forecasted FDC methodology, called revised Method 7, as its
accepted cost allocation approach. Generally, two drawbacks became evident
with these procedures: (1) the inherent difficulties in allocating plant on the
basis of forecasts and (2) the problems of reconciliation of forecasted and
actual costs on a *ex post* basis. Indeed, in Docket No. 20814, the *Multi–
Schedule Private Line* (MPL) case, an FCC administrative law judge concluded
that a new cost manual and system of audit control were needed, since AT&T
had failed to implement the cost standards set forth in Docket 18128 (1979).
   Subsequently, the Commission supplanted Method 7 with an FDC method
based on relative use or "historical cost causation." The so–called Method 1
overcame the aforementioned forecasting and reconciliation problems.
Method 1 was employed in the new interim cost manual and included use of a
reduced number of service categories: MTS, WATS, private line and ENFIA
(exchange network facilities for interstate access). Yet, the Commission's
approach to cost allocation continued to evolve (or vacillate as described by
less kind observers) beyond this stage.
   In particular, the FCC increasingly sanctioned competitive entry and had
undertaken deregulatory initiatives during the pendency of Docket No. 18128

Table III–3

FCC "SEVEN WAY" COST STUDY
Bell System Interstate Rate of Return on Net Investment
12 Months Ended August 31, 1964

Service Classification	Rate of Return
Message Toll Telephone (MTS)	10.0%
Wide Area Telephone Service (WATS)	10.1
Teletypewriter Exchange Service (TWX)	2.9
Private Line–Telephone	4.7
Private Line–Telegraph	1.4
Telpak	0.3
All Other*	1.1
Total All Interstate Services	7.5%

Source: AT&T Exhibit 81, Attachment A, p. 4, FCC Docket 14650.

* Principally video transmission.

and follow–on proceedings. This changed the status of many telecommunications markets and carriers at the same time that the FCC was attempting to establish administrative cost allocation standards. In effect, these standards were being defined for problems whose boundaries were continually changing. Moreover, in the early 1980s, the rapid rate of technological change and advent of competitive pressures increased further. This led the Commission to accelerate and expand its procompetition policies and in the process, exacerbated the difficulties of cost allocation.

In addition, a major new effort to deregulate, or at least relax, regulatory constraints was launched, as the rigors of competition in a number of markets were perceived by the agency to warrant additional retrenchment from traditional regulation. The "Competitive Carrier" and "Computer II" proceedings inaugurated during the 1970s represented attempts to identify these markets and streamline regulation where appropriate. Ultimately, these caused enhanced services, CPE, and inside wire (Docket 79–105) to be detariffed. Simultaneously, many carriers were deregulated.

But, traditional service subsidies became less feasible in the new deregulated, multisupplier environment, prompting the Commission to pursue the establishment of cost based rates and unbundling. One of the legacies of *Specialized Common Carrier Services* and *Execunet II* was implementation of a system of "access charges" for interconnection to exchange facilities used for provision of interstate (and intrastate) services (Docket 78–72). And, there were numerous revisions to the jurisdictional separations process (Docket 80–286), which allocates telephone company plant and related expenses between the interstate and intrastate jurisdictions.

Similarly, changes to the Uniform System of Accounts, or USOA (Docket 78–196) were proposed during this period, and an interim cost allocation manual (ICAM) was developed using the aforementioned Method 1 historical approach (Docket 79–245). Depreciation rates were also accelerated to reflect the plummeting lives of many types of plant used to provide services in a multiple firm setting. At the same time the Commission sought to accommodate the new offerings afforded by technological innovation, such as cellular radio based telephony (Docket 79–318 and 83–1096), digital electronic message services, or DEMS (Docket 79–188), and direct broadcast satellite, or DBS (Docket 80–603). Administratively, the use of lotteries was initiated to replace comparative hearings in order to expedite Commission grants of radio licenses in such areas as cellular (markets 90 and below), low power television or LPTV, and certain private radio services (Docket 81–768).

In essence, the intercity operations of AT&T, along with the rest of the Bell System, beginning in the 1960s experienced a period of substantial and turbulent change. This involved an unprecedented upheaval in their operating environment which was fueled by technological imperatives and sanctioned by unsympathetic governmental (especially FCC) and judicial determinations. The pre–*Carterfone* days of omnipresent monopoly markets in the communications industry were succeeded by the advent of competition in the terminal equipment and specialized common carrier arenas initiated during the 1960s and early 1970s. These forces accelerated during the 1970s and early 1980s, but nonetheless paled relative to the continuing market power of the Bell System.

5. Bell System Abuses: Potential, Alleged, and Actual

The Bell System's immense size and market breadth in U.S. communications historically conferred it with enormous monopoly power. A brief review of Bell's strategic behavior during its history confirms the directed use of that power in many instances to the detriment of its competitors and to thwart the normal play of market forces. For instance, beginning as far back as 1879, when AT&T (voice) and Western Union (nonvoice) divided up the nation's electronic communications markets, AT&T undertook aggressive expansion and, later, market "protection" programs. AT&T acquired its manufacturing arm, Western Electric, in 1881 and generally refused thereafter to sell Western's equipment to nonBell companies. A strong market presence was solidified through the 1890s via Bell patent infringement suits against others. Simultaneously, the vigorous Bell growth policy entailed absorption of rivals (including Western Union) and denial of long distance interconnection to Independent telephone companies. Eventually, this strategy became too abusive, and the aforementioned "Kingsbury Commitment" was exacted by the government in 1913 to mitigate such practices.

This action apparently halted neither Bell's aggressiveness nor its priorities for long. For instance, by 1925, AT&T had already completed its integration strategy by creating an in house research arm, Bell Telephone Laboratories. And, by the beginning of World War II, the Bell System was servicing over 85 percent of American's telephones. At this point, Bell was essentially in control of communications in this country. As a result, Bell has been a special target of antitrust actions over the years. For instance, the Justice Department initiated two major antitrust suits against the Bell System prior to the 1980s in addition to gaining its Kingsbury Commitment. In 1949, an action was sought to have the court require the divestiture of Western Electric (see below). Despite a strong case against the Bell entities the parties, instead, opted to settle the case. The consummated 1956 consent decree limited the permissible scope of Bell activity to tariffed communications offerings in return for leaving the Bell System structure intact.

A new suit was filed 18 years later, seeking redress of alleged antitrust activities and a drastic structural remedy. This would include divestiture of Western Electric and potentially Long Lines, some if not all of the BOCs, or Bell Labs. By 1977 the presiding court determined that the FCC did not have exclusive jurisdiction over the defendants, thereby permitting the suit to proceed. A period of extensive discovery and stipulated agreements of facts among the parties ensued. The trial itself finally began on January 15, 1981, but was interrupted by negotiations among AT&T and the Justice Department concerning settlement of the case as occurred with the prior suit.

On January 8, 1982, the parties filed a proposed "Modification of Final Judgment" (MFJ) which would vacate the 1956 Decree and substitute various structural and injunctive provisions. On August 24, 1982 the proposed settlement was approved with modifications by Judge Harold Greene. The court specifically pointed to Bell's anticompetitive conduct in service and CPE markets and the entity's inherent ability to wield economic power. In essence, the court concluded that the divestiture from AT&T of its local operations as represented by the Bell Operating Companies was in the public interest. Despite vociferous complaints by some parties to the proceeding, Judge Greene's actions were subsequently affirmed by an appellate court.[40]

Notably, many private actions have also plagued Bell over the years. Indeed, by 1982 AT&T, Western Electric or other members of the Bell System were confronted with 29 private antitrust suits, as well as the Justice Department's action.[41] These suits, while smaller in scope than that filed by the Justice Department, often had large initial judgments associated with them. For instance, MCI at one point was awarded a preliminary judgment of $1.8 billion in 1980 albeit the amount was subsequently reduced to $113.4 million.[42]

The FCC concurrently faced problems stemming from the Bell System's vast size and substantial market power. Critics both within and outside the agency contended that the Commission could not regulate Bell despite findings of likely abuse of its market power such as the above mentioned 1964 "seven way" cost study. Notably, in the 1970s prior to divestiture, the FCC determined that the rates for such AT&T interstate services as "Hi-Lo," Multi-Schedule Private Line (MPL) and Digital Dataphone Services (DDS) were unlawful and in some regards anticompetitive.[43] No legal WATS tariff existed during this decade, prompting an exasperated FCC Commissioner to remark that the agency had ". . . essentially lost control over the rates Bell charges customers."[44] And, a Common Carrier Bureau Task Force report issued in 1974, after documenting numerous anticompetitive abuses by the Bell System, even recommended divestiture of Western Electric.[45]

Moreover, Judge Harold Greene of the AT&T divestiture Court excoriated the Commission in the course of reviewing the merits of the proposed settlement. As he observed in 1982, the FCC's inability to effectively regulate "a gigantic corporation with almost unlimited resources in funds and gifted personnel" was hardly surprising in view of this agency's "problems of supervision" and the FCC's status as a "relatively poorly–financed, poorly–staffed government agency."[46]

In summary, public policy, confronted by rapid technological change, burgeoning competition, unsatisfied customer needs, and the sizable market power of the Bell System, simply could not control the situation. As a result, a most drastic step was taken that even Bell could not ignore, namely, the largest corporate restructuring in the history of this nation.

C. Structural Change and Public Policy: The New Beginning

1. Overview

The decade of the 1980s has witnessed changes in the structure of the U.S. telecommunications industry to an extent unparalleled in this century. Some of the impetus has been exogenous in the sense that it preceded and even contravened existing public policy. For example, one can persuasively argue that the aforementioned computer revolution of the 1950s and 1960s effectively prodded policy makers to permit entry into traditionally closed communications markets. A case might also be made that anticompetitive conduct by monopoly service and equipment providers intended to stifle new entrants compelled public decision makers to accommodate incipient competition. Others may aver that the process is both interactive and iterative such that public and private forces impact each other in a dynamic setting.

Whatever the direction of causation, the preeminence of structural reform as a policy initiative in telecommunications has been evident during this decade. Government promotion of entry and competition through deregulation, structural separation, and divestiture has been achieved in varying degrees at various levels.

Clearly, the objectives of public policy makers with respect to telecommunications now draw heavily on economic theory and analytical techniques. Broad goals currently center on the proper "mix" of regulation and deregulation, on the balance of natural monopoly and competition. Reliance on the market mechanism, a strong emphasis on creating incentives for efficiency, and promotion of innovation and technological change have all been accorded priority status by government decision makers.

While most public policy objectives have been microeconomic in nature, their achievement has frequently had macroeconomic consequences. Thus, the recent policy initiatives of competition and deregulation have led to such results as significant lay offs of employees. For example, between 1984 and mid 1988 AT&T, the communications giant which has been undergoing significant organizational changes during this decade, reduced its work force from 373,000 to 313,000 employees (*i.e.*, by over 16 percent) in a cost cutting program designed to enhance its competitiveness in consumer phones, business information systems, and long distance calling.[47] Actions of this nature and magnitude ultimately could affect such macroeconomic goals as "full employment" and minimal price inflation.

In the following sections, we briefly trace the role of structural objectives and, more broadly, economics in recent telecommunications policy development. Our examination begins with the FCC, followed by other major "players" in the industry; the States, Congress, the Courts, NTIA, Justice Department, Industry, and Consumers. Next, the complexities of setting public policy goals are explored. Finally, the initial impact of the AT&T divestiture on the former members of the Bell System are set forth.

2. Recent Public Actions

During the past two decades, the foundations of public utility regulation in telephony and other telecommunications markets have begun to erode as the sector has undergone fundamental structural changes. This change has occurred neither evenly nor with the same public policy resolve over the period. Basic catalysts have included technological change, competition, and deregulation.

Traditional goals of equity and efficiency continue to be important in setting such public policy, with efficiency being afforded more emphasis than in the past. A concise recounting of this policy changeover follows.

a. Federal Communications Commission

Although the Congress is the entity with primary responsibility for setting national telecommunications policy, the Commission in recent years has largely assumed this role. As the central agency in telecommunications matters, the FCC will be examined in more detail than other industry players.

Indicators of the rising influence of economic thought at the agency are the public positions taken by high ranking Commission members. Prior to the 1970s, the FCC did not strongly support competition as a way of life in telecommunications, nor did it set forth pricing and costing standards which would reflect all carriers' relative service costs and facilitate competitive entry. Rather, the Commission reluctantly ventured into the new *modus operandi* in response to pressure from the courts or determined entrepreneurs.[48]

During the 1970s, the FCC began to assume a more active procompetitive stance. Entry was championed for some markets (*e.g.*, terminal equipment) but not for others (*e.g.*, Message Telephone Service, or MTS; Wide Area Telephone Service, or WATS) in the middle part of the decade. Thus, the FCC Chairman in January 1976 stated that liberal terminal interconnection policies should be viewed as a "blessing and not a curse."[49] However, he cautioned that "I do not believe that any encroachment by specialized carriers upon traditional MTS or WATS services should be tolerated."[50]

This commitment to procompetitive policies and a reduced reliance on regulatory measures continued in the last years of the decade. For example, the Chief of the Common Carrier Bureau posited in September 1977:

> In summary, it appears to me that there are demonstrable and significant deficiencies, both theoretical and actual, in the concept of a regulated telecommunications monopoly. These deficiencies lead me, and have led the FCC, to prefer a measure of competition in specialized telecommunications equipment and service markets, as a better means of stimulating technological and service innovation and efficiency operations, and of controlling the charges, terms and conditions of such service offerings in the public interest.[51]

Concerning the impact of these policies on the achievement of universal service, he observed that competition may well be the best way to satisfy this objective in the future.[52]

However, the FCC's reluctance to extend cost based competition to most services continued, even after an appeals court ruled that the Commission had to show why competition should not be permitted in the MTS and WATS markets.[53]

Subsequent Commission policy makers have also embraced the dual goals of competition and deregulation. In October 1978, the FCC's Chairman asserted that "[w]hatever else the future holds for us, you will find me supporting a telecommunications system that reinforces open competition and reduces the need for government regulation."[54] As the decade ended, some officials within the agency called for "regulation only where competition is not possible."[55]

The importance of economics in general and structural remedies in particular as tools for policy analysis at the Commission became evident by the beginning of the 1980s. For example, the Chief of the Common Carrier Bureau emphasized in January 1980 that "[n]eoclassical economies . . . guides much of the policy that the FCC and other regulatory agencies are pursuing today."[56] Moreover, he stated:

> [D]o we believe that the principal purpose of Title II of the Communications Act, and indeed of all public utility regulation, is to procure economically efficient outcomes for consumers or to permit the achievement of broader social policies? The answer, of course, is both.

> But just as it is fashionable for regulators today to lean toward structural approaches in the structure/conduct debate, it is only honest to disclose that one of these views enjoys more favor today -- at least in the Common Carrier Bureau -- than the other.

It is probably fair to say that as between social engineering and social Darwinism, those responsible for the management of the Common Carrier Bureau tilt toward the "economic efficiency" end of the spectrum. In economic regulation, long run economic efficiency should take primacy precisely because this best serves the interests of consumers.[57]

The successor regime at the Commission accelerated deregulatory programs (called "unregulation" by the Chairman)[58] and assigned even greater relative significance to the efficiency objective. These so-called "Reaganites" viewed free markets as the most efficient way to bring telecommunications goods and services to the public -- and the "cornerstone" of U.S. deregulation philosophy.[59] Competition has been regarded as the means to eliminate the "skewing force" of government intervention.[60] And, the "success of our mission" in the short run was perceived to depend "crucially on the speed with which we can continue to dismantle fifty years of accumulated restrictions in the marketplace that earlier Commissions erected."[61]

Perhaps the most succinct policy statement of this FCC's agenda was enunciated by the Chairman on February 17, 1982 before a House subcommittee:

> I welcome structural and other approaches, whether legislative or antitrust-initiated, that further the development of full and fair telecommunications competition.
>
> The Federal Communications Commission is committed to deregulation of competitive telecommunications markets. We believe that the interplay of competitive market forces can best determine the services that should be available to the public. For this reason, the FCC is strongly promoting new entry and the development of new services. And, when deregulation is not yet possible, in markets where competition is still developing or where competition is imperfect for reasons beyond the FCC's control, the FCC is committed to regulatory improvement and development of transitional measures that promote the development of competition.[62]

Some four years later in a widely discussed law journal article, the Chairman, the Common Carrier Bureau Chief, and a Special Counsel in the Bureau articulated their vision for all U.S. telecommunications markets, urging, *inter alia,* competition solutions and trial deregulation of all telecommunications markets in the various states.[63]

The Reagan Commission also stressed that competition and universal service are both achievable.[64] However, as pointed out by the Common Carrier Bureau Chief in November 1982:

> Increasing competition in interexchange services and the growing prospects of bypass of local exchange facilities strains the ability of the present system to sustain both fair competition and universal service . . .[65]

Other objectives have been adopted by the FCC. In its access charge proceeding, the agency established four goals which would be achieved in a "reasonable balance" in setting the rates that interexchange (long distance) companies must pay to use the facilities of local exchange companies.[66] These include preservation of universal service, prevention of uneconomic bypass, development of an efficient pricing system, and elimination of unlawful discrimination.[67]

Although conduct oriented deregulation often seemed to overshadow structural remedies under this FCC regime, market structure remained a concern to some at the agency. For example, an FCC Commissioner in March 1985 stated:

> After twenty–five years of procompetitive policymaking, what role remains for the FCC in the immediate post divestiture period? Is it time for the FCC to step aside?

> The critical question here is timing. In my view, the Commission should neither confuse nor equate the success of its open entry policies with the arrival of workable competition in interexchange services. For this reason, I do not believe that the Commission should move precipitously to deregulate AT&T's basic interexchange service in a pre–equal access environment by presuming that the interexchange market is now workably competitive. Rather, the Commission must recognize that [it] is a time of demonopolization, not deregulation. To those who are thinking "natural monopoly," I say that that may be a self fulfilling prophecy if the Commission moves too fast . . .[68]

Moreover, the need for continued public intervention for the short term was acknowledged. Thus, the Senior Legal Advisor in the Chairman's Office emphasized in July 1986 that "during the transition away from a monopoly to the Shangri–la of telecommunications competition, government is still playing a very active role."[69]

The Commission has also been seeking statutory language that the "public interest favors competition, rather than regulated monopoly."[70] The goals have been applied (with predictably less but growing success) to international telecommunications markets where governments share the FCC's traditional universal service objective but not necessarily its preference for competition.[71]

These new or modified objectives have wrought operational changes at the Commission. Hearingless proceedings and informal measures, such as letters, have replaced formal hearings on rate base, expenses, and rate of return. Structural and especially accounting safeguards in many cases have supplanted more direct, interventionist modes of regulation. Rates have been unbundled, tariff filing periods have been shortened, detailed cost and demand studies in support of tariffs have been reduced, and pricing flexibility has been permitted to combat uneconomic "bypass" of telephone facilities by nontelephone companies. Resale of carrier offerings by others is also allowed.

Not all at the FCC have been completely enamored with recent Commission proclivities. One Commissioner registered the following criticism concerning choices made between conflicting objectives:

> . . . [There is a need] to resolve the tension between the notions of full and fair competition and universal service. In balancing these issues, it is what is best on the whole for the American consumer which should be controlling. Sometimes this will mean the acceptance of trade offs in favor of competition and somewhat to the disadvantage of universal service. With increasing frequency, it may also mean making trade offs in favor of universal service. In the past few years, the FCC has been reluctant, in the name of the sanctity of the Chicago School of Economics, to make this type of trade off.[72]

The current emphasis on economic efficiency apparently will continue for some time. The Commission's "Computer II" deregulatory initiatives are being supplanted by new policies featuring fewer governmental constraints on traditionally regulated carriers, viz., AT&T and the Bell regional companies. In particular, structural safeguards are being removed in favor of greater opportunities for efficiency. New approaches "would turn on economic analysis and policy considerations."[73] Interestingly, the Commission has assigned increasing importance to deregulation and conduct related policies as structural change has been left to the dynamics of the marketplace.

b. States

Traditionally, regulation by the states has emphasized equity. Universal telephone service, i.e., basic, reliable service which is affordable and available on a virtually ubiquitous basis, has generally been regarded as paramount. Economic goals (e.g., efficiency) have been considered important but have been accorded lower priority in cases of conflict with the universal service objective.[74]

With the onset of rapid technological change, procompetitive and deregulatory actions by the courts and the FCC, and the AT&T divestiture, the states have been under enormous pressure to reevaluate their priorities. Unlike in the past, when their regulatory approaches in the broadest sense were relatively monolithic, the states have now responded in diverse fashion. For example, some states are not allowing unfettered competition in local exchange markets (e.g., North Carolina, West Virginia) while others are much more liberal in permitting such activity (e.g., Nebraska). Soon after divestiture the Iowa State Commerce Commission recently became the first state to deregulate Centrex, a leased telephone company offering which competes with customer–owned PBX systems.[75] Significant deregulatory bills have been passed in a number of states. Several major alternatives to traditional rate base regulation have been initiated, as is discussed in some detail below. Conversely, some states have appealed the FCC's recent preemption of their ability to impose structural safeguards on the BOCs or Independent telephone companies.

Through all of the turmoil, however, the states appear to be unwilling to abandon the traditional universal service goal. As of July 1, 1989, 44 states, the District of Columbia, and Puerto Rico have been certified by the FCC to participate in one or more of its federal lifeline assistance plans.   Under these programs, low income ratepayers may either have their fixed local service charges waived, their connection charges paid by federal and state governments ("Link Up America"), or both.[76]

c.   Congress and the Courts

The U.S. Congress makes telecommunications policy and the courts have a major impact on its implementation through their interpretation of statutes. Most Congressional and court actions revolve around the Communications Act of 1934 ("the Act") and the nation's antitrust laws.

New legislation designed to revise or supplant the Act was introduced in Congress on several occasions in the late 1970s and early 1980s. Although no bill has successfully navigated the legislative process to date, the attempts coupled with regular oversight (and other) hearings concerning the FCC have undoubtedly left the Congress's imprimatur on U.S. telecommunications policy.

The legislation proffered during this period has generally reflected developments in the industry. For example, the ill–fated 1976 "Consumer Communications Reform Act" (CCRA) sought to overturn the burgeoning competition in many telecommunications markets and basically return the industry to the precompetitive era. Dubbed the "Bell Bill" by its detractors because it was vociferously supported by the Bell System, the CCRA represented an unsuccessful structural based attempt to prohibit the "wasteful or unnecessary duplication of communications lines" introduced by competitive entry.[77]

Two bills, S. 898 (Telecommunications Competition and Deregulation Acts of 1981) and H.R. 5158 (the Telecommunications Act of 1981), represented a Congressional attempt to legislatively identify their preference for the workings of the market place as the means to assure universal service, efficiency, and innovation. The specific objectives embodied in each differed somewhat: the House version emphasized maintenance of universal service and the need for a transition period before deregulation could occur, while the Senate bill stressed rapid deregulation of markets to afford the immediate benefits of competition. Both achieved early success but ultimately did not pass muster of the full Congress.

The courts were also busy rendering decisions interpreting the Act and ruling on antitrust suits during that time. They have ratified the FCC's procompetitive policies in a number of markets, e.g., private lines, enhanced services, and terminal equipment, and reversed it in some others, e.g., MTS and WATS services.[78] In addition, the Commission's authority to preempt state jurisdiction in a myriad of areas has been affirmed, e.g., terminal equipment, enhanced services, resale of intrastate WATS, digital termination service (DTS), multipoint distribution systems (MDS), and jurisdictional separations of expenses, plant, and revenues. The Supreme Court recently dealt the FCC's preemption authority a substantial setback, however, in the realm of depreciation and potentially other areas.[79]

Moreover, the courts have been a hotbed of antitrust litigation in recent years, with telephone companies or their manufacturers the focus of most suits. By 1983, some 30 suits were pending against AT&T alone. Unquestionably the most significant of these was the proceeding that culminated in the 1982 consent decree between AT&T and the Department of Justice. This "Modification of Final Judgment" (MFJ) has had a far reaching effect on numerous aspects of telecommunications policy. For instance, the action achieved the most significant corporate divestiture in over seventy years (*i.e.,* since Standard Oil's breakup in 1911) and radically restructured the telecommunications industry. In essence, the decree as modified was approved by Judge Harold H. Greene because of its structural ramifications, *viz.,* that it:

> effectively opens the relevant markets to competition and prevents the recurrence of anticompetitive activity . . . with-out imposing undue and unnecessary burdens upon other aspects of the public interest.[80]

The Judge stressed that diffusion of economic power "in order to promote the proper functioning of both our economic and our political systems" was both a goal of the antitrust laws and necessary in this particular case.[81]

That universal service is a critical concern to the court has also been made clear. Judge Greene concluded that the divestiture of the Bell operating companies from AT&T was in the public interest because, *inter alia,* neither local telephone rates nor service quality need be adversely affected.[82] Subsequent to divestiture, the court has unequivocally criticized the Bell regional companies for pursuing diversification into unrelated markets more aggressively than their pursuit of the satisfaction of the "public desire [for] good local telephone service at reasonable rates."[83]

d. Executive Agencies

There are two primary organizations within the executive branch which significantly impact U.S. telecommunications policy: the National Telecommunications and Information Administration (NTIA) and the Department of Justice. With respect to telecommunications markets, both seek to promote competition and its perceived concomitant, economic efficiency. NTIA has supported the Justice–AT&T concept of enhancing competition through the divestiture of the Bell System, rather than through exclusive reliance on public utility regulation. The agency also has recommended an easing of restrictions on the BOC entry into unregulated businesses and Computer II structural safeguards for the BOCs and AT&T. In addition, it has cautioned against protecting competitors *vis–à–vis* the competition.[84] Conversely, the Department of Defense, a major telecommunications user, sought to have the Justice Department suit against AT&T dropped, on the theory that only a fully integrated Bell System network could provide responsive and secure nationwide military communications. The Carter Administration promoted a new emphasis on competition and improved management of a streamlined regulatory process. With "Reaganomics" came new commitment to a deregulatory and "free market" policy thrust.[85] Judge Greene and others have questioned the resolve of the Justice Department in enforcing the decree during the mid and late 1980s.

e.   Industry and Consumers

The views of the industry's carriers have undergone changes over time. Like the states, telephone companies during the 1970s did not openly embrace the notion of competition promulgated by the courts and the FCC.   In September 1973 the AT&T Chairman called for a structural remedy antithetical to entry, i.e., "a moratorium on further experiments in economics" and declared that:

> . . . we believe that there is something right about the
> common carrier principle. There is something right about
> regulation. And––given the nature of our industry –– there is
> something right about monopoly –– regulated monopoly.[86]

He equated the public interest with the Bell System goal of assuring the "widest availability of high quality communications service at the lowest cost to the entire public."[87] These viewpoints were actively promoted at both the FCC and Congress during most of the 1970s.[88]

By the end of the decade, AT&T's opposition to competition and deregulation had lessened. The new Chairman indicated in February 1979 that he was ready to "contemplate –– even to encourage –– deregulation" of terminal equipment.[89] In return, he urged a softening of the 1956 consent decree which confined AT&T to regulated markets.[90]

During the post divestiture period, AT&T and the new Bell entities have accepted competition and actively sought deregulation.[91] For example, AT&T now believes that "free competition is exactly the objective that should be set for interexchange telecommunications markets."[92]

U S WEST, one of the seven new Bell regional holding companies (BRCs), in no uncertain terms decries regulation and welcomes full competition:

> Bring on the competition . . . We have learned from our past
> that regulation cannot shelter us from competition. So,
> today, wherever we find competition, we advocate
> deregulation . . . Start thinking of us as a growth company.
> If you haven't already, you will soon. We are not a utility.
> And we are not acting like one.[93]

Virtually all Bell operating companies (BOCs) point to the significant threat to their continued viability and the ratepayers' wellbeing posed by "bypass," i.e., circumvention of the local exchange companies' plant or services, in a world where only the BOCs are regulated.[94]

Other industry groups also generally support competition and deregulation today. For many, the most important issue is timing. In particular, inter-exchange carriers (IXCs) are concerned that the dominant firm in the industry (AT&T) should not be deregulated before the market is sufficiently mature. Without an adequate transition, these carriers believe their financial future as effective competitors to AT&T is anything but sanguine.[95]   During this transition period, some have sought increased government participation to mitigate the potential for market place abuses or otherwise to assist the workings of the market mechanism.   Initiatives have included requests for a "moratorium" on AT&T pricing plans and acceleration of BOC conversion of their central offices to an "equal access" capability.   One IXC sought and, in a court challenge, won the right to continue to have its services tariffed and on file at the FCC.[96]

Historically, consumers have had little input in establishing public policy.[97]   Universal service, a principal concern of residential users, is a goal expressed, at least in theory, in the statutory language of the Communications Act itself.   Large users (*e.g.*, manufacturers, banks) have traditionally relied on trade associations and/or "in-house" regulatory and Congressional liaisons to convey their objectives to government decision makers.   Today residential users are also represented in the process by consumer organizations such as TRAC (Telecommunications Research and Action Center) and Consumer Federation of America.

Figure III-4 illustrates in capsulized form some of these general trends in public policy with respect to telecommunications.   The next section describes difficulties inherent in achieving many of these goals concurrently.

3.   Setting Goals in Telecommunications: Tradeoffs, Primacy, and Other Complications

a.   *The Impossibility Theorems*

Achievement of all public policy goals is difficult in any industry, and telecommunications is no exception.   Tradeoffs are inevitable, and it is the task of the American electorate through its government to choose the "correct" mix of goals.   Most basic for our purposes is the determination of the appropriate balance between government intervention and the marketplace, *i.e.*, social control (especially regulation) and competition.   In the chapters that follow, we show how basic economic principles are affecting the traditional telecommunications industry.   It is hoped that once equipped with these "tools," those who establish or impact upon social policy may be better able to both evaluate options and develop optimal policies in the future.

Economists differ as to the "attainability" of the joint goals of competition and regulation.   Almarin Phillips (and former AT&T Chairman John deButts, among others) believes that the existence of substantial economies of scale and scope require regulation of telephone companies as "natural monopolies."[98]

Others express views diametrically opposed to the "natural monopoly" argument.   Robert Crandall states that competitive entry and new technology render traditional regulation "extremely difficult and perhaps impossible."[99]   Misallocation of resources, cartelization of the market, and the "long-run strangulation" of AT&T through imposition of selected regulatory constraints present a "very strong case for pushing ahead with deregulation."[100]

Figure III–4

THE TELECOMMUNICATIONS INDUSTRY:
GENERAL TRENDS IN PUBLIC POLICY

- FULL REGULATION ------------------> DEREGULATION OF
  (Pre Late 1960s)   MANY CARRIER OFFERINGS
                                            (Today)

- EMPHASIS ON UNIVERSAL ------------> EMPHASIS ON MAXIMIZING
  SERVICE AND PREVENTION   EFFICIENCY
  OF ANTICOMPETITIVE   (Today)
  BEHAVIOR
  (Predivestiture)

- SIGNIFICANT CONSTRAINTS ON --------> ERODING CONSTRAINTS ON
  CARRIER INTERACTION WITH   SUCH INTERACTION
  UNREGULATED AFFILIATES   (Today)
  (Predivestiture)

Economists Cornell, Kelley, and Greenhalgh assert that not only is:
> . . . increased competition in the common carrier
> communications industry . . . compatible with the
> achievement of social goals, but also that many of the goals
> may be unattainable without competitive forces . . . We
> believe that unless those competitive deregulatory principles
> are applied, the dominant telephone utilities will share the
> fate of the railroads.[101]

Alfred Kahn is no less adamant. Calling the current blend of regulation
and competition an inefficient "halfway house,"[102] he asserts that:
> The sooner we find ways of terminating the uneasy marriage
> between regulation and competition, wherever remotely
> feasible, the better. The grounds? Fundamental incom–
> patibility.[103]

Many economists and commissioners have probably adopted a less extreme
position, accepting that tradeoffs are both possible and desirable. Harry
Trebing, for example, concludes that:
> In essence, regulatory reform, improved performance, and
> greater competition should not be perceived as contradictory
> objectives, but rather as complementary ways to promote the
> public welfare.[104]

Trebing believes that by adding four objectives to the traditional regulatory
goals of controlling monopoly profits, preventing price discrimination, and
assuring adequate service the regulatory process can be improved. These
objectives include: 1) the promotion of the form of industry structure most
conducive to superior performance; 2) the formal recognition that equity and

income distribution are collectively a major objective of regulation; 3) the establishment of a priority system for allocating available "supplies" of communication during shortages; and 4) the control of social costs is a valid objective of regulation.[105]

The Chief of the FCC's Office of Plans and Policy in the mid 1980s also indicated his concurrence regarding the feasibility of coexistence of certain goals, *e.g.*, between cost based rates and universal service. Thus, higher local rates caused by the need to realign costs and prices in a competitive environ-ment is not seen as incompatible with the traditional "affordability" objective of the Communications Act and regulation.[106]

b.   *Jurisdictional Conflicts and Other Complexities*

In practice, the establishment of social goals and other public policy making tasks are complicated by the frequently blurred demarcations between governmental jurisdictions. For example, jurisdictional friction between the FCC and the states has been manifested in numerous ways over the years, resulting in various court tests, assertions of federal preemption, and pleas for reconciliation[107]

Differences have also arisen between the FCC and the court presiding over the implementation of the MFJ. The Commission's General Counsel has asserted that:

> The case law is fairly clear that it is the antitrust laws, not the regulatory statute, which must give way in cases of irreconcilable conflict . . . FCC laws stand as law unless reversed by a circuit court of appeals . . . The District Court lacks jurisdiction to review or abrogate any decision of the FCC.[108]

In contrast, Judge Greene states that:

> regulation under the Communications Act is neither sufficiently explicit nor sufficiently pervasive to allow it to stand in the way of the enforcement of the antitrust laws.[109]

Besides such complications, public policy making in telecommunications today seems more complex in another sense: the number of points of view. In the pre-divestiture era and especially before the onset of competition, lobbying groups were readily identifiable and their positions often predictable. Currently, many of the traditional allies (*e.g*, the Bell entities) have divergent interests. As observed by the Common Carrier Bureau Chief in August 1985:

> There are more lobbyists [today], less focused and more confusing . . . The question of who is competing with whom is getting very confused.[110]

c.   *Some Practical Problems*

Other considerations also affect the decisions of government. For example, many experts believe that any policy promoting competition instituted by public officials must take into account the issue of predatory pricing. Identification and detection of such practices have proven to be quite difficult, *e.g.*, distinguishing between price discounts established as a legitimate response to competition and unlawful below–cost pricing by a dominant firm. AT&T has alternately been accused and exonerated of engaging in predatory pricing by industry observers.[111]

Proper measurements can also be elusive. A definition must be agreed upon to determine, *e.g.*, whether or not competition has adversely impacted either the viability of a telephone company or the maintenance of universal service. In fact, no such consensus has emerged, leaving the field to a variety of measures such as customers or revenues "lost," facilities or systems "stranded," or actual or potential losses attributable to bypass.[112] Measurement of the "relevant market" is another matter critical to an assess–ment of the sector's competitiveness, especially in antitrust analyses. Clearly, a given level of firm interaction may or may not qualify as "competition" depending on one's definition of the market in question.

Despite these complexities, our analysis proceeds with the most significant structural change of the 1980s, *viz.*, the dissolution of the Bell System.

4.   The Bell Transformation

On the eve of divestiture, the Bell System was a corporate "giant among giants" (see Figure III–5). AT&T was the world's largest nongovernmental employer, and was also overwhelmingly the largest company in terms of assets. Compared with the 500 largest corporations in the United States in 1982, AT&T ranked first in major categories such as assets and net income, and finished second in sales. By 1982 AT&T's profits totaled almost $7.3 billion. Bell entities services 146.2 million telephones in 6,784 exchanges located predominantly in major metropolitan areas in the 48 contiguous states, accounting for well over 80 percent of the U.S. total. AT&T's Long Lines commanded over 90 percent of the long distance market. Western Electric loomed as the world's largest manufacturer of telecommunications equipment ranging from "no frills" telephone handsets to sophisticated electronic switch–ing machines. And Bell Labs' basic research budget surpassed the total for the rest of U.S. industry.

Essentially, the Modification of Final Judgment (MFJ) as revised by Judge Greene on August 24, 1982 separated the 22 Bell Operating Companies[113] from AT&T and combined them into seven Regional Bell Operating Companies (see Figure III–6). The latter, in turn, were in each case comprised of a parent Regional Holding Company (RHC), several BOCs, and various unregulated subsidiaries. Under the agreement, AT&T relinquished its local exchange (and certain long distance toll) operations in return for removal of the constraints of the 1956 decree. In turn, the newly created Regional Bell Operating Companies received the BOC franchised local monopolies, but had to be granted waivers by the court in order to operate in most other telecom–munications markets.

Despite the throes of divestiture, AT&T remained the most expansive telecommunications firm in the world on January 1, 1984. AT&T retained $35.6 billion in assets notwithstanding the actual loss of almost $114 billion in

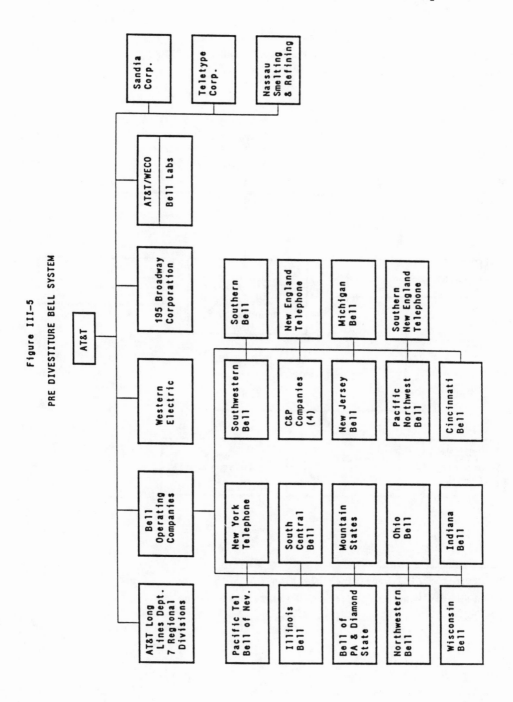

Figure III-5
PRE DIVESTITURE BELL SYSTEM

Figure III-6
EARLY POST DIVESTITURE: THE NEW AT&T

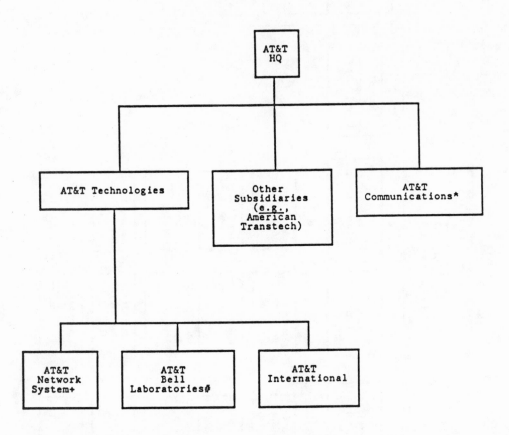

---

*   Formerly AT&T Long Lines Division.

+   Formerly Western Electric Co. and Teletype Corp.

∮   Formerly Bell Telephone Laboratories.

assets to the BOCs and a year end "write down" of $4.2 billion.[114]   Only Exxon and General Motors had higher totals among the largest U.S. corporations on that date.[115] The divestiture agreement assigned AT&T approximately 385,000 employees, a future that was surpassed only by General Motors' total of 748,000.[116] The company's 1984 revenues of $33.2 billion would rank it above all other firms which primarily have a telecommunications focus.[117]

Western Electric, the Bell System's manufacturing operations, has been primarily absorbed by a new organization called AT&T Network Systems (see Figure III–6). The successor to Bell Telephone Laboratories is AT&T Bell Laboratories and AT&T Information Systems (ATTIS) succeeded American Bell as the company's enhanced service and customer premises equipment subsidiary. AT&T International was created to focus on foreign customers through wholly and partly owned operations. AT&T Technologies was created as an umbrella organization for these entities in the emerging corporate structure. AT&T Communications replaced the now defunct Long Lines Division as the long distance service operations. Other specialized affiliates also were created, such as Ameritech Transtech for shareholder relations.

The seven Regional Bell Operating Companies that arose from the 22 reconstituted BOCs represent the Northeast (NYNEX), Mid–Atlantic (Bell Atlantic Corporation), Southeast (BellSouth Corporation), Midwest (American Information Technologies Corporation –– "Ameritech"), Southwest (Southwestern Bell Corporation), the Mountains and Great Plains (U S WEST), and the Far West (Pacific Telesis Group) (see Figure III–7).

Under the terms of the MFJ, the operating companies each provide exchange, exchange access, and information access. In addition, the Regional Companies may operate various subsidiaries as of January 1, 1984, these typically include cellular radio telephone service, CPE, directory, and other services. Each RHC also owns a regional service company (RSC) and an equal share of Bell Communications Research (Bellcore). These entities supply certain technical and administrative functions for principally their owners (albeit other customers exist such as Cincinnati Bell and Southern New England Telephone Company).

A snapshot of the new Bell entities during the early post divestiture period affords a useful benchmark for later comparisons. Clearly, AT&T emerged on January 1, 1984 as the dominant member of the group in terms of assets ($36 billion) and employees (385,000) as shown in Table III–4.

AT&T's share of the total assets was 22.6 percent; the next closest entity was BellSouth (13.5 percent). In turn, the proportion of Bell employees accounted for by AT&T (39.5 percent) greatly exceeded that of the second largest member, again BellSouth (10.2 percent).

A similar scenario obtains with respect to comparisons of total operating revenues, net operating revenues, and net income (Table III–5). Using pro forma data computed for the twelve month period ending June 30, 1983 reflecting divestiture requirements, the statistics for AT&T swamp those for the RBOCs viewed individually. Thus, AT&T's imputed operating revenues ($67.6 billion, or 52.4 percent of the Bell total) dwarfed those of BellSouth's ($10.5 billion, or 8.1 percent). In a similar fashion, net operating revenues

Figure III-7

POST DIVESTITURE: THE SEVEN REGIONAL BELL OPERATING COMPANIES

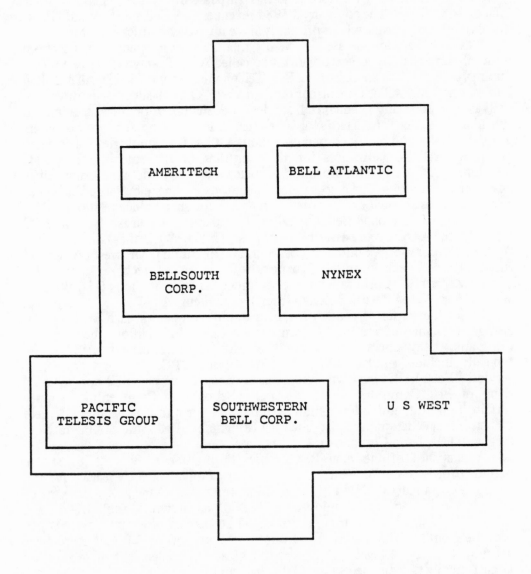

Table III–4

ASSETS, ACCESS LINES, AND EMPLOYEES
AT&T and the RBOCs
January 1, 1984

Company	Total Assets*		Network Access Lines+		Employees+	
	$ Bil.	Rank	Mil.	Rank	Thous.	Rank
AT&T	36.0	1	NA	NA	385.0	1
Ameritech	16.9	6	14.0	2	79.0	6
Bell Atlantic	17.3	4	14.2	1	80.0	5
BellSouth	21.5	2	13.6	3	99.1	2
NYNEX	18.5	3	12.8	4	98.2	3
Pacific Telesis	17.2	5	10.9	5	82.0	4
Southwestern Bell	16.5	7	10.3	7	74.7	8
U S WEST	15.6	8	10.6	6	75.0	7
Total	159.5		86.4		973.0	

* Quarterly Reports.

+ *AT&T Information Statement and Prospectus*, November 8, 1983, pp. 6–13.

($20.4 billion, or 50.4 percent) and net income ($7,188.0, or 49.7 percent) for AT&T overshadowed those of the RBOC leader, BellSouth ($3.7 billion, or 9.1 percent; and $1.4 billion, or 9.6 percent, respectively).

Among themselves, the RBOCs at the beginning of divestiture manifested various rankings depending on the measure used (see Tables III–4 and III–5). As discussed, BellSouth was the leader in various revenue, asset, and employee categories. In terms of number of network access lines, however, its figure (13.6 million) was surpassed by both Bell Atlantic and Ameritech, which are service providers in two of the most mature and densely populated regions. These two companies and NYNEX generally placed in the second tier of rankings below BellSouth. Exceptions were Pacific Telesis' fifth place rating with respect to total assets ($17.2 billion) and access lines (10.9 million). Typically, though, PacTel ranked at the top of a third tier, followed by either Southwestern Bell or US West.

From this starting point, AT&T and the RBOCs (nee Bell System) have embarked on strategic programs that often vary widely. This penchant for individuality may perhaps be seen most poignantly in the corporate logos chosen by the entities (see Figure III–8).

Probably no other entity has had to endure the financial and operating "shocks" recently experienced by AT&T. Divestiture, coupled with rapid technological change, increased competition, and regulatory reform have caused the company to undergo a wrenching downsizing of assets and staff. In addition, a major effort has been expended to revamp the traditional corporate culture which was rooted in the predivestiture monopoly era. Also

Table III–5

REVENUES, NET REVENUES, AND NET INCOME
AT&T and the RBOCs
12 Months June 30, 1984
(Proforma)

Company	Total Operating Revenues		Net Operating Revenues		Net Income	
	$ Bil.	Rank	$ Bil.	Rank	$ Mil.	Rank
AT&T	67.6	1	20.4	1	7.2	1
Ameritech	8.9	4	3.1	4	1.0	4
Bell Atlantic	8.7	5	2.8	5	1.1	3
BellSouth	10.5	2	3.7	2	1.4	2
NYNEX	10.0	3	3.4	3	1.0	5
Pacific Telesis	7.9	6	2.1	8	1.0	6
Southwestern Bell	7.9	7	2.6	6	0.9	8
U S WEST	7.6	8	2.5	7	0.9	7
Total	129.1		40.6		14.5	

Source: *AT&T Information Statement and Prospectus*, November 8, 1983, pp. 6–13.

a series of reorganizations have taken place, complementing holdover organizations such as AT&T Network Systems with new ones, including Data Systems, Business Markets, General Business Systems, and Federal Systems Groups.

Despite these difficulties AT&T has devised and moved forward on a three pronged–strategy unencumbered by the constraints of the 1956 decree.[118] First, AT&T intends to retain and strengthen its current leadership in core businesses such as long distance service, communications equipment for businesses and residences, and telecommunications network equipment.

Second, AT&T seeks to provide integrated data networking for corporate and government users, stressing connectivity between disparate systems. A key to this strategy is deemed to be a vanguard position for the company with respect to Integrated Services Digital Network (ISDN). Broadly speaking, ISDN is an engineering concept featuring a public end–to–end digital network in which time division switches and digital transmission paths accommodate multiple services originating at subscriber locations.[119]

Third, the company, is vigorously pursuing international telecommunications business. This pursuit is seen as consonant with the globalization of markets, especially in the new "Information Age." Consequently, AT&T is participating in joint ventures in such countries as Italy, the Netherlands, Korea, and Taiwan.[120]

In turn, the RBOCs have developed their own particularized strategies since divestiture. The heart of their operation, of course, continues to be the provision of local telecommunications services. While all have diversified

Figure III–8

POST DIVESTITURE: THE NEW BELL ENTITIES

AT&T

 Bell Atlantic

*BELL*SOUTH

NYNEX

PACIFIC TELESIS
Group

USWEST

 Southwestern Bell
Corporation

 Bell
Communications
Research

into new telecommunications and certain nontelecommunications markets, each has sought endeavors tailored to their corporate goals, customers' needs, and constraints imposed by government. For example, Southwestern Bell has placed considerable emphasis on its cellular telephone and yellow pages businesses. Bell Atlantic regards Centrex, CO–LAN, and other central office based services as flagship offerings and is actively promoting new data services. US West has pursued wide ranging activities, such as financial services, real estate, and fleet (trucking) businesses.

In addition, BellSouth has recently bolstered its cellular operations with the acquisition of MCCA, and has been a pioneer in fiber–to–the–home trials. NYNEX's special interests lie with "integrated solutions" for large business customers, and the company has also been vigorously arranging joint agreements with European countries which would utilize the region's gateway position to Western Europe. And Pacific Telesis has relied on its booming cellular and paging businesses (as well as its local network) for growth.

A glance at Table III–6 reveals the relative robustness of the new Bell entities during the post divestiture era. On the basis of computed "market values," AT&T achieved number one ranking among the top U.S. telecommunications firms during the period 1986 through 1988.[121] The RBOCs accounted for eight of the next nine slots, with only GTE (ranked sixth, fifth, and seventh in 1986, 1987, and 1988, respectively) preventing a clean sweep by the recombined former Bell System members.

That these entities continue to wield substantial monopoly power today is asserted by such public policy makers as the Judge whose court retains jurisdiction over the implementation of the 1982 consent decree. Thus, in December 1988, Judge Greene observed that his refusal to rescind existing "line of business" restrictions on the RBOCs with respect to manufacturing, provision of long distance service, or origination of information service content was rooted in such concerns:

> The Regional Companies are perhaps unique in modern
> America in the breadth of their economic and political
> power.[122]

The MFJ, then, has created large, financially robust companies whose core businesses survived the breakup and apparently continue to confer market power on these entities.[123] Given this scenario, we next turn to considerations of various public policy alternatives with respect to these dominant carriers in the next chapter.

Table III–6

THE TOP 25 TELECOMMUNICATIONS FIRMS
Ranked by Market Value

Ranking				
March 1989	March 1988	March 1987	March 1986	Entity
1	1	1	1	AT&T
2	2	2	2	BellSouth
3	7	5	6	GTE
4	3	3	3	Bell Atlantic
5	6	8	7	Pacific Telesis Group
6	5	6	5	Ameritech
7	4	4	4	NYNEX
8	8	7	9	Southwestern Bell
9	9	9	8	U S WEST
10	10	12	10	MCI
11	11	10	11	United Telecom
12	13	NR	NR	McCaw Cellular Communications
13	12	11	12	Contel
14	14	13	13	Centel
15	15	14	14	Southern New England
16	NR	NR	NR	Contel Cellular*
17	16	NR	NR	Citizens Utilities
18	17	15	15	Alltel
19	NR	NR	NR	U S WEST NewVector+
20	18	21	NR	Metro Mobile CTS
21	19	16	17	Cincinnati Bell
22	24	NR	NR	Cellular Communications
23	26	NR	NR	Telephone & Data Systems
24	NR	NR	NR	U.S. Cellular+
25	20	19	NR	Mobile Communications

* Ten percent public offering in 1988.
+ Spun off from Telephone & Data Systems in 1988.
NR = Not Ranked.

Source: "The Top 1000 Ranked By Industry," *Business Week*, "1989 Special Issue," pp. 268–69; April 15, 1988, p. 284, April 17, 1987, pp. 154–56; April 18, 1986, p. 180.

Notes

1. For accounts of the nascent U.S. communications industry, see R.L. Thompson, *Wiring a Continent* (Princeton, New Jersey: Princeton University Press, 1947); Federal Communications Commission, "Report on the Investigation of the Telephone Industry in the United States," H.R. Doc. No. 340, 76th Congress, 1st Session (1939); and John G. Glover and R.L. Lagal, eds., *The Development of American Industries* (New York: Simmons – Boardman Publishing Corp., 1959), Chapter XXXII.

2. R.L. Thompson, *op. cit.*, pp. 442, 446.

3. See "Government Ownership of Electrical Means of Communication: Report to the Postmaster General by a Committee of the Post Office," including Appendix A. – "Historical Resume of the Agitation for Government Ownership of the Telegraph and Telephone in the United States," U.S. Senate, 63rd Congress, 2nd Session, Document No. 399, pp. 1–43 and 144–145, Washington, D.C. 1914.

4. For a good discussion of the early days of telephony, see "Report by the Federal Communications Commission on Domestic Telecommunications Policy," released September 27, 1976, esp. Attachment B, pp. 3–13 (hereafter referenced as FCC Report on Domestic Telecommunications Policy).

5. Domestic Public Message Services (PMS), 71 FCC 2d 471 (1979), *aff'd. sub nom. Western Union Telegraph Company v. FCC,* No. 79–1352, slip opinion (D.C. Cir. Sept. 3, 1981). See Discussion *infra.*

6. *United States v. Western Electric Co., Inc. et al.,* 1982–2 Trade Cases, Par. 64,900 (D.D.C. 1982), *summary affirmance sub nom. Maryland et al.,* 51 U.S.L.W. 3632 (1983).

7. Based on data supplied in FCC Report on Domestic Telecommunications Policy, *op. cit.*, p. 6.

8. See United States Telephone Association (USTA), "The Ring of Success: The Independent Telephone Movement in America," p. 8.

9. *Id.*, p. 1; "The Rapid Growth of Independent Telephone Holding Companies," *TE&M,* October 1, 1973, p. 130; Francis X. Welch, *Sixty Years of the Independent Telephone Movement* (Washington, D.C.: USITA, 1957), p. 22.

10. See, *e.g.*, John Brooks, *Telephone: The First Hundred Years* (New York: Harper & Row, Publishers, 1976), p. 134.

11. Harry M. Trebing, "Public Utility Regulation: A Case Study in the Debate Over Effectiveness of Economic Regulation," p. 201 in M.R. Tool, ed., *An Institutionalist Guide to Economics and Public Policy* (Armonk, New York: M.E. Sharpe, Inc., 1984).

12. FCC, *op. cit.*, p. 6.

13. President's Task Force on Communications Policy, Staff Paper Five, "The Domestic Telecommunications Carrier Industry," (Washington, D.C., 1968), p. 37.

14. USTA, *op. cit.*, p. 9; FCC Report on Domestic Telecommunications Policy, *op. cit.*, p. 9.

15. *Telecommunications: A Program for Progress. A Report by the President's Communications Policy Board,* (Washington, D.C.: March 1951), pp. 98, 99.

16. A. von Auw, *Heritage and Destiny* (New York: Praeger Publishers, 1983), p. 5. Von Auw was *inter alia,* Vice President – Assistant to the Chairman of AT&T from 1969 to 1981.

17. In 1937, AT&T's Bell System possessed total assets in excess of $5 billion, "constituting the largest single aggregation of wealth ever concentrated in private hands." See C.I. Wheat, "The Regulation of Interstate Telephone Rates," *Harvard Law Review,* Vol. 51, pp. 849–50. Some 45 years later its gross assets exceeded $148 billion as Bell remained the largest private entity in the world. See FCC *Statistics of Communication Common Carriers,* 1982, p. 28. The Bell System and other facets of telephone common carriers are probed in greater detail below.

18. "The Preliminary Report on Communications Companies" (H.R. Report No. 1273, 73d Cong. 2d Session (1934), submitted April 18, 1934 ("The Splawn Report"). For a detailed history of early federal telephone regulation, see C.I. Wheat, *op. cit.* Other good accounts of nascent telephony include, *e.g.*, J. Brooks, *Telephone: The First Hundred Years* (New York: Harper and Row, 1975); and R. Gabel, "The Early Competitive Era in Telephone Communications, 1893–1920," *Law and Contemporary Problems*, Vol. 34, Spring 1969.

19. C.I. Wheat *op. cit.*, p. 847.

20. See Communications Act of 1934, as amended, 47 U.S.C. Section 201.

21. *United States v. Western Electric Co., Inc. and American Teleph. & Teleg. Co., Inc.*, Civil Action No. 17–49 (D. NJ, filed January 14, 1949).

22. *Carterfone*, 13 FCC 2d 420 (1968), *aff'd. on recon.*, 14 FCC 2d 571 (1968).

23. *Hush-a-Phone v. FCC*, 238F. 2d 266 (1956).

24. FCC Docket No. 19528 equipment registration program.

25. See *North Carolina Utilities Commission v. F.C.C.*, 537 F2d 787 (1976); 552 F. 2d 1036 (1977).

26. *Allocation of Microwave Frequencies Above 890 Megacycles*, 27 FCC 359 (1959).

27. *Microwave Communications, Inc.*, 18 FCC 953 (1969).

28. *Specialized Common Carrier Services*, First Report and Order, 29 FCC 2d 870, *aff'd on recon.*, 3 FCC 2d 1106 (1971), *aff'd sub nom. Washington Util. and Transp. Comm'n v. FCC*, 513 F2d 1142 (9th Cir.), *cert. denied*, 423 U.S. 836 (1975).

29. *Second Report and Order*, 35 FCC 2d 844 (1972).

30. *Bell Telephone Company of Pennsylvania v. FCC*, 503 F. 2d 1250 (1974) *cert. denied*, 423, U.S. 886 (1975).

31. *Packet Communications, Inc.*, 43 FCC 2d 922 (1973); *Graphnet Systems, Inc.*, 44 FCC 2d 800 (1974); *Telenet Communications Corp.*, 46 FCC 2d 680 (1974).

32. *Resale and Shared Use of Common Carrier Services*, 60 FCC 2d 261 (1976), *recon.*, 62 FCC 2d 588 (1977), *aff'd sub nom. Amer Tel & Tel Co. v. FCC*, 572 F.2d 17 (2d Cir.), *cert. denied*, 439 U.S. 875 (1978).

33. CC Docket No. 78–96, *Graphnet Systems, Inc.*, 67 FCC 2d 1059 (1978); *Domestic Public Message Services (PMS)*, 71 FCC 2d 471 (1979) *reconsideration*, 73 FCC 2d 151 (1979).

34. Policy and Rules Concerning Rates for Competitive Common Carrier Services and Facilities Authorizations Therefor, CC Docket No. 79–252 *Competitive Carrier Rulemaking*, Notice of Inquiry and Proposed Rulemaking, 77 FCC 2d 308 (1979); First Report and Order, 85 FCC 2d 1 (1980) (*First Report*); Further Notice of Proposed Rulemaking, 84 FCC 2d 445 (1981); Second Report and Order, 91 FCC 2d 59 91982) (*Second Report*), *recon.*, 93 FCC 2d 54 (1983); Second Further Notice of Proposed Rulemaking, FCC No. 82–187, 47 Fed. Reg. 46,791 (Oct. 14, 1983); Third Further Notice of Proposed Rulemaking, 48 Fed. Reg. 28,292 (June 21, 1983); Third Report and Order, 48 Fed. Reg. 46,791 (Oct. 15, 1983); Fourth Further Notice of Proposed Rulemaking, 96 FCC 2d 922 (1984); Fifth Report and order, 98 FCC 2d 1191 (1984) (*Fifth Report*); Sixth Report and Order, 99 FCC 2d 1020 (1985) (*Sixth Report*), Sixth Report *vacated sub nom. MCI Telecommunications Corp v.. FCC*, No. 85–1030 (D.C. Cir. July 9, 1985).

35. *Computer Inquiry* (Tentative Decision), 28 FCC 2d 291 (1970), *Final Decision*, 28 FCC 2d 267 (1971), *aff'd in part sub nom. GTE Service Corp. v. FCC*, 474 F2d 724 (2 Cir. 1973).

36. Second Computer Inquiry, *Final Decision*, 77 FCC 2d 384, *modified on reconsideration*, 84 FCC 2d 50 (1980), *further modified on reconsideration*, 88 FCC 2d 512 (1981), *aff'd sub nom. Computer and Communications Indus. Ass'n v. FCC*, 693 F.2d 198 (D.C. Cir. 1982), *cert. denied*, 461 U.S. 938 (1983),

aff'd on second further reconsideration, FCC No. 84–190 (released May 1984).

37. See Policy and Rules Concerning the Furnishing of Customer Premises Equipment, *Enhanced Services and Cellular Communications Equipment by the Bell Operating Companies,* 95 FCC 2d 1117 (1984), *aff'd sub nom. Illinois Bell Telephone Co. v. FCC,* 740 F2d 465 (7th Cir. 1984), *aff'd on reconsideration,* FCC No. 84–242, 49 Fed. Reg. 26056 (1984), *aff'd sub nom. North American Telecommunications Assoc. v. FCC,* 772 F2d 1282 (7th Cir. 1985).

38. Report of the Telephone and Telegraph Committees in the Domestic Telegraph Investigation, Docket No. 14650, p. 200.

39. 7 FCC 2d 30,31 (1965); 6 FCC 2d 177,180 (1966) (Docket 16258); FCC 68–388 (1968); 13 FCC 2d 853; FCC 68–756 (1986); FCC 69M–197 (1969); 18 FCC 2d 76 (1969); 20 FCC 2d 383 (1969); 21 FCC 2d 495 (1970); 27 FCC 2d 151 (1971); 30 FCC 2d 503 (1971); 33 FCC 2d 522 (1972); 34 FCC 2d 839 (1972); FCC 72M–1528; *AT&T Private Line Rate Cases,* 61 FCC 2d 587 (1976); *Memorandum Opinion and Order,* released June 13, 1977, FCC 77–385 (Docket 18128).

40. *United States v. Am. Tel. & Tel. Co.,* 552 F. Supp. 131 (D.D.C. 1982), *aff'd sub nom. Maryland v. United States,* 46 U.S. 1001 (1983).

41. See Western Electric *Annual Report Form 10K* for the year ended December 31, 1982, p. 11.

42. See, *e.g.,* "Court Limits Damages Award to MCI," *Washington Post* May 29, 1985, p. F1.

43. *Final Decision,* Docket 19919; *Final Decision and Order,* September 20, 1979, Docket 20288; any *Final Decision and Order,* January 5, 1977, Docket 20814.

44. May 27, 1976, "Concurring Statement of Commissioner Washburn Re: Docket 19989, WATS," p. 1 appended to *Final Decision and Order,* 59 FCC 2d 715 (1976), released June 2, 1976, in that proceeding.

45. See *Statement and Recommendations of the Common Carrier Bureau's Trial Staff,* FCC Docket No. 9129, Phase II, issued February 2, 1976 to Administrative Law Judge David Kraushaar.

46. Slip Opinion, *United States of America v. American Telephone and Telegraph Company et. al.,* filed August 11, 1982, p. 64.

47. See, *e.g.,* "AT&T Will Lay Off 1,000 More Workers at Louisiana Factory," *Wall Street Journal,* August 12, 1985, p. 10; "24,000 AT&T Jobs to be Eliminated at Major Division," *New York Times,* August 22, 1985, p. A1; "AT&T Says It Will Take $6.7 Billion Writedown," *Washington Post,* December 2, 1988, p. G1.

48. For a description and analysis of FCC policies toward competition see Chapter IV *infra.* See also W.G. Bolter, "The Continuing Role of Federal Regulation in the Transition to Competition in Communications," *Issues in Public Utilities Regulation,* 411 (H. Trebing, ed. 1979).

49. "Trends in Telecommunications," *Telecommunications,* January 1976, p. 231 (Quote attributed to FCC Chairman Richard E. Wiley).

50. *Id.,* p. 24.

51. Remarks by Walter R. Hinchman before the Securities Industry Association, New York, New York, September 14, 1977, pp. 17–18.

52. *Id.,* pp. 28–29.

53. Remarks by Walter R. Hinchman before the ICA, Las Vegas, Nevada, May 15, 1978, esp. pp. 11–12. See ("Execunet I") *MCI Telecommunications Corp. v. FCC,* 561 FCC 2d 365 (D.C. Cir. 1977), and ("Execunet II") *MCI Telecommunications v. FCC* (D.C. Cir. No. 76–1635, decided April 14, 1978).

54. Remarks of Charles D. Ferris before the 81st Annual Convention of the United States Independent Telephone Association, Atlanta, Georgia, October 11, 1978, pp. 3–4.

55. "Telecommunications Regulation and Competition in a Post–Industrial Society," by Nina W. Cornell before the Armed Forces Communications and Electronics Association, January 11, 1979, p. 1.

56. "Remarks by Philip L. Verveer before the Federal Communications Bar Association, January 25, 1980, p. 4.

57. *Id.*, pp. 4–5.

58. Testimony of Mark S. Fowler before two subcommittees of the Energy and Commerce Committee of the U.S. House of Representatives, September 21, 1981, p. 4.

59. "U.S. Global Telecommunications: The Popcorn Principle," Address by Mark S. Fowler, FCC Chairman, before the Georgetown University Center for Strategic and International Studies, Washington, D.C., February 26, 1985, p. 2.

60. Address of Mark S. Fowler, FCC Chairman, before Infotel '82 Conference, Washington, D.C. March 30, 1982, p. 9.

61. See, *e.g.*, Statement of Mark S. Fowler, FCC Chairman, before the Subcommittee on Telecommunications, Consumer Protection, and Finance of the House Committee on Energy and Commerce, April 19, 1983, p. 3.

62. Statement of Mark S. Fowler before the House Subcommittee on Telecommunications, Consumer Protection, and Finance, February 17, 1982, p. 1.

63. Mark S. Fowler, Albert Halprin, James D. Schlichting, "Back to the Future: A Model for Telecommunications," *Federal Communications Law Journal*, Vol. 38, No. 2, August 1986, p. 147.

64. Mark S. Fowler, "U.S. Global Telecommunications: The Popcorn Principle," *op. cit.*, p. 7.

65. Remarks of Gary M. Epstein before the National Association of Regulatory Utility Commissioners, 94th Annual Convention and Regulatory Symposium, Boston, Massachusetts, November 11, 1982, pp. 1, 11.

66. *MTS and WATS Market Structure*, CC Docket No. 78–72, Phase I, 93 FCC 2d 241 (1983) at para. 89.

67. *Id.* at paras. 74–88.

68. Remarks of Mimi Weyforth Dawson before the USTA 10th Annual Seminar for Institutional Investment Analysis, New York, New York, March 25, 1985, pp. 9–10. See also Anne P. Jones, FCC Commission "The 1982 AT&T Consent Decree and the Future of Telecommunications Competition," Presented at the Fifth Annual Public Utilities Conference on Regulation and the Rate Making Process, October 22, 1982, p. 25; and "State and Federal Telecommunications Regulation: Background and Blueprint," Address by Mark S. Fowler, FCC Chairman, before the National Association of Regulatory Utility Commissioners, Los Angeles, California, November 29, 1984, p. 12.

69. "The Shorter Shadow of Government Over American Telecommunications," Remarks by Janice Obuchowski at Telecom Pacific '86, Hong Kong, July 3, 1986, p. 9.

70. Statement of Mark S. Fowler before the House Subcommittee on Telecommunications, Consumer Protection and Finance, *op. cit.*, p. 10.

71. At least some officials at the Commission are optimistic about foreign countries embracing competitive solutions in their markets. See, *e.g.*, Commissioner Mimi Weyforth Dawson, "Communications Deregulation in the United States and its Effect on the International Marketplace," Remarks presented to the 1983 Telephone Summit Conference, June 22, 1983, esp. p. 6.

72. Remarks by Commissioner Joseph R. Fogarty before the Yale Workshop in Public and Private Management Class, New Haven, Connecticut, April 5, 1983, pp. 5, 12, 13.

73. "Making Perceptions Match Reality," Remarks of Commissioner (later Chairman) Dennis R. Patrick before the 1985 USTA Public Relations Seminar, Washington, D.C., September 4, 1985, p. 12. For a good discussion of these changing FCC programs, see Kathleen B. Levitz, "Separate Subsidiaries, the Interim Cost Manual, and AT&T Divestiture" in P. Mann and H. Trebing, eds., *The Impact of Deregulation and Market Forces on Public Utilities: The Future Role of Regulation* (East Lansing, Michigan: MSU Public Utilities Papers, 1985), pp. 209–228.

74. See, *e.g.*, Katherine E. Sasseville, Commissioner, Minnesota Public Utilities Commission "Competition in Communications," before the 1977 NARUC Annual Studies Program, August 9, 1977; and Testimony of John E. Bryson, Chairman, California Public Utilities Commission, before the House Subcommittee on Telecommunications, Consumer Protection, and Finance, February 2, 1982.

75. See, *e.g.*, *Communications Week*, June 10, 1984, p. 1.

76. According to Dr. Larry Povich of the FCC's Common Carrier Bureau, one state (California) offers a lifeline program with a state means test and a 50 percent subscriber line charge (Plan 1), and 26 states and the District of Columbia waive the SLC (Plan 2) as of July 1, 1989. In addition, 39 states, the District of Columbia, and Puerto Rico participate in "Link Up America's" connection program.

77. See, *e.g.*, "A Bill for Ma Bell," *Time*, October 4, 1976, pp. 78–79.

78. See Execunet I and II *supra* and Second Computer Inquiry, 77 FCC 2d 384 (1979) (Final Decision) *aff'd on reconsideration* 84 FCC 2d 50 (1980), 88 FCC 2d 512 (1981), *aff'd sub nom.*, *CCIA v. FCC*, 693 F.2d 198 (D.C. Cir. 1982), *cert. denied sub nom. Louisiana P.S.C. v. United States*, 461 U.S. 938 (1983). See also Remarks of FCC Commissioner Tyrone Brown before the Federal Communications Bar Association, October 12, 1978 and FCC News Release No. 8357, "Commissioner Brown Faults Agency for Permitting Court of Appeals to Become a Super FCC, Offers Prescription for FCC to Regain Initiative," issued same day.

79. *Louisiana Public Service Commission v. FCC*, 106 S. Ct. 1890 (1986).

80. See Slip Opinion issued August 11, 1982, *United States v. Am. Tel. and Tel. Co., op. cit.*, p. 35.

81. *Id.* at pp. 57–58.

82. *Id.*, at pp. 65–68.

83. See Slip Opinion, issued July 26, 1984, pp. 63–64; and Hearings on interpretation of the 1982 consent decree as modified, August 9, 1985, Tr. 4.

84. NTIA, *Issues in Domestic Telecommunications: Directions for National Policy*, July 1985; any Testimony of David J. Markey, Administrator, NTIA, before the Senate Communications Subcommittee, September 5, 1985.

85. See, *e.g.*, "Government Regulation: Where Do We Go From Here," Transcript of a Round Table Discussion, sponsored by the American Enterprise Institute, December 19, 1977, p. 4.

86. J.D. deButts, "An Unusual Obligation," before NARUC convention, Seattle, Washington, September 20, 1973, p. 4.

87. See, *e.g.*, *id.*, and Testimony of J.D. deButts, AT&T Chairman, before the Senate Subcommittee on Communications, March 21, 1977.

88. See, *e.g.*, "Cut Back the Competition, AT&T Asks the FCC," *Washington Star*, October 5, 1973 p. E–13; and "A Bill for Ma Bell," *op. cit.*, p. 78.

89. "AT&T Chief May Encourage End of Telephone Regulation," *Washington Star*, February 24, 1979, p. C–6.

90. *Id.*

91. For a detailed account of the Bell breakup, See W.B. Tunstall, *Disconnecting Parties (Managing the Bell System Break-up: An Inside View)* (New York: McGraw–Hill Book Company, 1985).

92. Lawrence Garfinkel, "Interexchange Telecommunications Markets in Transition," *Public Utilities Fortnightly*, July 21, 1983, pp. 30, 32–33.

93. Advertisement, *Fortune*, October 17, 1984.

94. See Chapter VI for a discussion of nonBOC studies.

95. See, *e.g.*, Booz Allen & Hamilton, "Prospects for Major Facilities–Based Other Common Carriers," March 1985, prepared for GTE Corp.

96. See, *e.g.*, "AT&T Competitors Seek Price Freeze," *Washington Post*, June 18, 1985, p. E1 *Telecommunications Reports*, September 2, 1985, pp. 1–3; "FCC, MCI Waging War Over Mandatory Detariffing of Long Distance Rates," *FCC Week*, March 4, 1985; and "Appeals Court Outlaws FCC's Forbearance Stance," July 20, 1985, p. 16.

97. See, *e.g.*, W.B. Tunstall, *op. cit.* pp. 191–92.

98. A. Phillips, "The Impossibility of Competition in Telecommunications," unpublished manuscript, 1982, pp. 6–7. For similar sentiments, see J.D. deButts, *e.g.*, Address to Bell System President's Conference, May 12, 1972.

99. R.W. Crandall, "The Impossibility of Regulating Competition in Interstate Communications Markets," a paper delivered at the Eastern Economic Association meetings, May 12, 1979, p. 2.

100. *Id.*, p. 16.

101. N.W. Cornell, D. Kelley, and P.R. Greenhalgh, "Social Objectives and Competition in Common Carrier Communications: Incompatible or Inseparable?," presented at the Michigan State University Public Utilities Institute's Eleventh Annual Conference in Williamsburg, Virginia, December 10–12, 1979, p. 2.

102. A. Kahn, "The Next Steps in Telecommunications Regulation and Research," *Public Utilities Fortnightly*, July 19, 1984, p. 17.

103. A. Kahn, "The Uneasy Marriage of Regulation and Competition," *Telematics*, Vol. 1, September 1984, p. 16.

104. H.M. Trebing, "Motivations and Barriers to Superior Performance Under Public Utility Regulation," *Productivity Measurement in Regulated Industries* (New York: Academic Press, Inc., 1981), p. 394.

105. Harry M. Trebing, "Broadening the Objectives of Public Utility Regulation," *Land Economics*, February 1977, pp. 1110–11.

106. Testimony of P.K. Pitsch before the Select Committee on Aging, Subcommittee on Housing and Consumer Interests, June 30, 1983, p. 4.

107. In one recent instance, Commissioner Henry M. Rivera noted the existence of this tension and emphasized the need for continued improvement in federal–state relations. Address before the Western Conference of Public Service Commissioners, Salt Lake City, Utah, July 1985.

108. Jack D. Smith, "Reconciling the Antitrust Laws and the Communications Act in the AT&T Divestiture," Address before the Administrative Law Section of the Bar Association of the District of Columbia, Washington, D.C., March 20, 1985, pp. 5, 9. See also remarks of FCC Commissioner Anne P. Jones, *op. cit.*, p. 3.

109. Slip Opinion, *United States v. AT&T, Supra*, p. 42. (Footnotes omitted.)

110. "The Telephone Lobby: No Longer a One–Company Shop," *New York Times*, August 4, 1985, p. F7 (quote attributed to Albert Halprin).

111. See, *e.g.*, W.H. Melody, "Standards for Judging Predatory Pricing in Telecommunications," in H.M. Trebing, ed., *New Challenges for the 1980s* (East Lansing: Michigan State University, 1981); and L. Garfinkel, "Interexchange Telecommunications Markets in Transition," *op. cit.*, p. 31.

112. For a discussion of bypass measurement frailties, see *infra.*

113. At the time of divestiture, AT&T was minority owner of Cincinnati Bell, Inc., and Southern New England Telephone Company, but owned 100 percent of the remaining 21 BOCs.

114. AT&T, *1984 Annual Report,* p. 18.

115. "Fortune 500" rankings, *Fortune,* April 30, 1984, p. 276.

116. "Fortune 500" rankings, *Fortune,* April 29, 1985, p. 267.   If AT&T's access charge payments are not subtracted from its revenues, then the resulting revenue figure of $53.8 billion would have placed it behind only Exxon, General Motors, and Mobil Corp.

117. *Id.,* p. 277.

118. See AT&T *1987 Annual Report to Stockholders,* pp. 2–3.

119. This and other facets of network revitalization are examined in Chapter V.119.

120. More specifically, AT&T possesses a 22 percent ownership interest in Italy's Ing. C. Olivetti & Co., S.P.A., a 60 percent interest in a joint venture with the Dutch firm, N.V. Philips (now called AT&T Network Systems International).   In Asia, AT&T is involved in two joint ventures with Korea's Lucky Gold Star Group in semiconductors (44 percent) and fiber optics (50 percent), and owns 50 percent of AT&T Taiwan Telecommunications, a supplier of large electronic switching systems.

121. "Market value" as computed by *Business Week* researchers equaled the share price on a given March date (*e.g.,* March 18 in 1988) multiplied by the latest available common shares outstanding.

122. These assertions relating to market power are examined in greater detail in subsequent portions of the book.   See especially Chapters VII and VIII.

123. Address by Judge Harold Greene before the Communications Week Symposium, December 8, 1988, p. 10.

CHAPTER IV

APPLICATION OF POLICY ALTERNATIVES IN TELECOMMUNICATIONS

A. Introduction

A brief synopsis of the discussion thus far may be helpful in keeping our perspective. Earlier, we presented an analytical framework for investigating the telecommunications sector that invokes the theories of the industrial organization branch of economics (see Chapter II). Specifically, the methodology used herein draws heavily on the widely accepted structure–conduct–performance paradigm for assessing the workings of a given industry. The goals and objectives of government intervention were described, and the roles of this country's two major forms of intervention, *viz.*, public utility regulation and antitrust, were explored.

Subsequently, this framework was used to examine the structural and related conduct and performance characteristics of a changing telecommunications industry (see Chapter III). The evolution of the sector was analyzed from an organizational and public policy perspective as it passed through stages of unbridled competition and laissez–faire, regulated monopoly, and emerging competition and deregulation. The events leading to the 1984 AT&T divestiture were identified, and then the initial effects of the largest corporate restructuring in history were assessed.

The purpose of this chapter is to examine the merits of alternative public policy approaches for the post divestiture telecommunications environment. In the sections that follow, we describe rate of return/rate base regulation[1] as it has traditionally been applied to communications markets and evaluate its effectiveness in today's conditions. Next we revisit the MFJ to lend perspective to the changed ground rules of post divestiture telecommunications. Finally, policy alternatives designed to cope with the characteristics of modern telecommunications markets are discussed. In particular, we will focus on the relative advantages and deficiencies of each and their current utilization by public policy makers.

B. Rate of Return Regulation

As discussed in Chapter III, public utility regulation in telecommunications began in the early 1900s in response to perceived abuses by suppliers, especially the Bell System. By 1913 almost two–thirds of the states had established regulatory commissions, and the Interstate Commerce Commission had jurisdiction over interstate wire and radio communications provided on a common carriage basis. For the next 50 years, federal regulators at the ICC and, later, the FCC addressed carrier profits and rates informally (*i.e.,* through "continuing surveillance"), if at all. The FCC basically eschewed a formal public review of such matters as profit criteria, prices and cost structure, equipment procurement, and interconnection until the mid 1960s. In contrast, the state commissions have been concerned with these issues for much of this century. With a few exceptions, however, they were perceived prior to divestiture as more passive than federal regulators with respect to rate of return, rate structure, and competition.[2]   This "rate of return/rate base" regulation sought to control the monopoly power of subject telephone companies by constraining their total earnings and revenues in a manner intended to approximate results determined in an effectively competitive market. Generally, state public service commissions have attempted to ensure a "fair" rate of return, a "used and useful" rate base, and "just and reasonable" rates for companies entrusted with bringing telephone service to the public.

A company's "revenue requirement" is the gross amount of revenue allowed to be collected in a given "test year" from its customers, typically pursuant to "tariffs" filed with and approved by the regulatory agency. Thereafter, the company will normally submit evidence to the commission supporting a further revenue requirement claim used to justify proposed rate changes. The commission will then decide the proper magnitude of the company's revenue requirement and make any rate changes in accordance with the agency's policies regarding rates and rate structures. This revenue requirement process involves regulatory oversight with respect to the proper size of the utility's depreciated assets, the allowed rate of return, and the reasonableness of claimed operating expenses and taxes.

Historically, this form of regulation has been employed during an era when telephone service in this country has been widely acclaimed as the best in the world. Although complex in many facets, the process has apparently served telephone ratepayers well in terms of providing good service at afford-able rates.

Several criticisms have been directed at this regulatory method in recent years. Alleged deficiencies of this traditional approach include the creation of undesirable incentives to overinvest (i.e., to "pad the rate base") and generate nonoptimal levels of operating expenses. Moreover, the perceived problems inherent in this "cost plus" process have allegedly been compounded by noncost based pricing of services. As a result, distorted economic signals may have been sent to investors, ratepayers, and competitors. Indeed, wasteful outcomes could have been promoted, both in terms of resource misallocations and technical (higher than least cost) inefficiencies.

Further, detractors claim that the historical governmental limits placed on entry by potential competitors have hindered innovation. NTIA asserts that rate base regulation is very costly to implement, involving direct expenditures estimated to be one billion dollars annually. Even larger indirect costs are attributed to the process

> . . . by discouraging efforts to minimize production costs, dampening regulated firm's incentives rapidly to innovate, and, potentially, facilitating possible anticompetitive behavior.[3]

A number of factors have acted to change the relatively predictable environment of franchised monopolies, which rate of return regulation was originally designed to control. None has been more significant for regulators than the Modification of Final Judgment, which will be addressed in the next section.

C. The Bell System Divestiture

One of the policy alternatives available to government decision makers centers on antitrust relief. After being targeted by two major suits by the Department of Justice pursuant to Section 2 of the Sherman Act (see Chapter II) and numerous treble damage private actions, AT&T agreed to dissolve the Bell System's familial ties through the 1982 consent decree. As discussed above, the Modification of Final Judgment broke up the major integrated telecommunications firm in the country on January 1, 1984, creating seven Regional Bell Operating Companies and a new, smaller AT&T. In return for relinquishing over three fourths of its assets and approximately one half of its net operating revenues and net income, AT&T was freed from the 28 year restraints of the 1956 consent decree and a probable adverse ruling[4] in the pending Justice Department antitrust suit initiated on November 20, 1974.

In addition, the RBOCs were allowed to operate subject to "line of business" restrictions on the markets in which they could lawfully operate. On the day of divestiture, the Bell companies were permitted by the MFJ decree to offer only exchange or other basic services (e.g., cellular mobile telephony), exchange or information access, yellow pages directories, and customer premises equipment. Publication of yellow pages and use of the traditional Bell name and logo represented judicial victories for the RBOCs over AT&T.[5]   Concurrently, the FCC authorized the BOCs to provide "enhanced services," creating confusion and uncertainty with respect to the MFJ's prohibition concerning information services. Both enhanced service and CPE supply by the RBOCs would be allowed by the FCC on a deregulated basis. The Commission required establishment of separate subsidiaries for any Bell CPE or enhanced service provision. Explicit MFJ bans existed, however, relating to Bell offering of interexchange services, manufacture of telecommunications equipment (including CPE), and provision of "any other product or service, except exchange access service, that is not a natural monopoly service actually regulated by tariff." (Section II(D) (3)).

The decree's Section VIII(C) represents the judicial gauntlet through which the RBOCs must pass in their attempts to shuck existing market prohibitions. Specifically, the constraints will be rescinded only:

> . . . upon a showing by the petitioning BOC that there is no
> substantial possibility that it could use its monopoly power to
> impede competition in the market it seeks to enter.

Since January 1, 1984, the RHCs have been permitted to enter a variety of new markets, generally subject to four conditions: (1) the new enterprise must be operated through a separate subsidiary; (2) such subsidiary must obtain debt financing only on its own credit; (3) the estimated net revenues from all conditioned operations of a Regional Company must not exceed ten percent of such company's net revenues; and (4) the monitoring and visitorial provisions of section VI of the decree shall apply to the subsidiary.

In early 1987 the public debate regarding the "first triennial review" of the decree commenced with the filing of a government sponsored analysis with the Court. Justice Department consultant, Dr. Peter Huber, who is a mechanical engineer and lawyer by training, submitted a report to the Department relating to his examination of the telecommunications industry. Basically, *The Geodesic Network: 1987 Report on Competition in the Telephone Industry* concludes that the industry is structurally competitive as vertical consolidation of vendors and dispersed consumption of switching have replaced the traditional hierarchial ("pyramid") telephone network. Using these findings as factual predicates, the Justice Department initially recommended removal of the line-of-business constraints for information services, manufacturing and out-of-region interexchange services. Subsequently, the Department withdrew its proposal concerning interexchange offerings because of the perceived difficulties in locating the boundary between in-region and extra region services. The linchpin to the DOJ recommendations was the assumption that regulators would be able to prevent or mitigate any anticompetitive conduct by the RBOCs.

Most parties commenting on the proposals urged the court to either reject the Justice Department recommendations or at most accept only limited aspects of the proposals. An ad hoc coalition comprised of interexchange carriers, information service providers, manufacturers, publishers and others was particularly vocal in its disagreement with the DOJ position.

On September 10, 1987 Judge Greene issued an Opinion regarding the Court's view of the results of this first formal scrutiny of the MFJ implementation. Based on his examination of the record, the Judge concluded that:

> it is clear that . . . no substantial competition exists at the present time in the local exchange service and that the Regional Companies have retained control of the local bottlenecks.[6]

[footnote removed]

The Court refused to remove existing constraints on provision of interexchange services by the Bell Companies, including long distance inter-LATA and mobile (*e.g.,* cellular) services, because the entities were perceived to retain the ability to impede competition on a significant scale.

Similarly, the Judge averred that removal of the manufacturing restriction was not warranted. Rationale given for retention of the ban included, *inter alia,* the Companies' continuing "bottleneck" control of the local exchanges, the large (70 percent) proportion of total U.S. telecommunications equipment purchases represented by the seven Bell Regionals, and the expectation that BOCs would have the incentive to buy from their in-house suppliers and, thereby, return the telecommunications equipment market to the monopolistic, anticompetitive tendencies of the past.[7] In a subsequent (December 3, 1987) order, Judge Greene clarified that the manufacturing ban pertained to equipment design and development as well as fabrication.[8]

With respect to provision of information services, the Court ruled that the reasons cited in 1982 and 1984 for preserving the ban remained valid. The decision reasoned that "the same incentives and the same abilities" to act anticompetitively continue to exist.[9]   In fact, the Judge surmised that the need for these line of business restrictions is greater now than before the Bell System was segmented because more of the latter's operations were regulated.[10]

Overall, the Judge dismissed arguments made by both the Justice Department and the RBOCs that FCC regulation -- unlike before -- is capable of preventing unlawful abuses by those wielding monopoly power derived from their bottleneck exchanges.   Instead, the Court posited that the FCC is currently less able and likely to regulate vigorously because of, *inter alia,* fewer resources and a lesser resolve.[11]   Concerning unlawful cross subsidization, the Opinion indicated that the problem has never been greater.[12]

In addition, the Court chided the Justice Department for its reliance on the Commission's new "Joint Cost" methodologies for separating costs between regulated and unregulated operations of dominant carriers and the FCC's "Computer III" "Open Network Architecture" (ONA) and "Comparably Efficient Interconnection" (CEI) equal access requirements since these programs are largely untested and still developing.[13]   In particular, ONA was regarded as inadequate as a deterrent because (1) it applies only to one fourth of all access lines (*i.e.,* those served by digital switches); (2) no collocation is currently available for enhanced service providers at the BOCs' central offices; and (3) the concept only applies to current technology.[14]   The Court strongly suggested that the Regional Bell companies' cross subsidization activities since divestiture may have contributed significantly to rising local telephone rates and expressed concern that the problem would escalate as MFJ restrictions were relaxed.[15]

However, the Court decided to permit the RBOCs to participate in transmission of information services.   Citing the salutary experience of the French with respect to low cost Minitel (videotex) services, Judge Greene stated that, on balance, it would be appropriate to allow the RBOCs to provide an information–service infrastructure consisting primarily of various low–level gateway functions that are distinct from information content.   This would include such offerings as data transmission, address translation, some protocol conversions, billing arrangements, and limited introductory information content (*e.g.,* provider listings).   Provision of electronic yellow pages and terminals as part of the infrastructure would remain verboten.[16]

Finally, the Opinion concluded that Section II(D)(3) should be deleted from the decree.   Although the decision expressed concern about the potential for cross subsidization with respect to nontelecommunications ("unrelated") businesses, it determined that this was outweighed by the relative paucity of joint and common costs and the apparent lack of interest by potential competitors in maintaining the restriction.

Today, Regional Bell activities are permitted by MFJ waiver grants in 18 line of business areas (see Figure IV–1).   These include: advertising; cellular monitoring and consulting services; computer sales, service and maintenance;

Figure IV-1

RBOC ACTIVITIES PERMITTED BY MFJ WAIVER GRANTS
(July 15, 1989)

- Advertising
- Cellular Monitoring & Consulting Services
- Computer Sales, Service, & Maintenance
- Financial Services
- Fleet Services
- Foreign Business Ventures
- Insurance
- Multi-LATA Paging
- Non-Tariffed Billing Services
- Office Equipment
- Out of Region Cellular and Paging
- Print Media
- Real Estate
- Software (Operating Company; External)
- Telephone Answering Services and Voice Storage & Retrieval (VSR)
- Training and Education
- Time & Weather
- Equipment Lease Financing

financial services; fleet services; foreign business ventures; insurance; multiLATA paging; nontariffed billing services; office equipment; out of region cellular & paging; print media; real estate; software; telephone answering services and voice storage & retrieval (VSR); training & education; time & weather; and equipment lease financing.

Overall, the Regional Companies are currently allowed to operate in a variety of markets and submarkets by the Court and the FCC (see Figure IV-2). Thus, Regional Companies or their affiliates may provide exchange and other basic services, exchange or information access, *non*-electronic yellow page directories, as well as the aforementioned information ("gateway") transmission services, nontelecommunications offerings, and services authorized by MFJ court waiver grants. The FCC also permits the Regional Bell entities to supply CPE or enhanced services without structural separation once Commission approval of Bell ONA plans or compliance with other nonstructural conditions is received.

Finally, as discussed above and set forth in Figure IV-3, the Bell Companies may not legally engage in certain activities. Proscriptions continue to apply to the provision of interexchange services, information services where control of content is significant, and equipment manufacturing prohibition was removed, as well as the four conditions heretofore applied to this "catch-all" restriction (see above).[17]

Figure IV–2

PERMITTED ACTIVITIES FOR THE RBOCS
(July 15, 1989)

* Exchange and Other Basic Services
* Exchange (Information) Access
* Yellow Pages (Nonelectronic)
* CPE Provision*
* Enhanced Services+
* Information ("Gateway") Transmission
* Nontelecommunications Activities#
* Activities Authorized by MFJ Court Waiver Grants

* Removal of structural separation requirements pending FCC approval of RHC compliance/accounting plans.

\+ Removal of structural separation requirements pending FCC approval of RHC compliance/accounting plans, other nonstructural conditions, and ONA plans.

\# Requirement for court approval rescinded in Judge Harold Greene's September 10, 1987 Opinion.

Figure IV–3

PROHIBITED ACTIVITIES FOR THE RBOCS
(July 15, 1989)

* Interexchange Services
* Information Services (Control of Content)
* BOCs: " . . . Any Product or Service, Except Exchange Telecommunications and Exchange Access Service, that is Not a Natural Monopoly Service Actually Regulated by Tariff" (Section II(D)(3) of the 8/82 Decree)

    – Repealed by MFJ Court (September 10, 1987)

Other rulings have followed, with the most important clarifications being set forth in an order issued on March 7, 1988 and June 13, 1989.[18] Specifically, in the earlier ruling the Court relaxed the information services restriction to permit the Regional Companies to provide such services as protocol conversion, voice storage and retrieval, voice messaging, and electronic mail. Freed of these constraints by the Court, the BOCs have sought permission from the FCC to offer various information services. For

Figure IV–4

STATUS OF RBOC LINE OF BUSINESS REQUESTS*
(July 15, 1989)

- 125 Waiver Requests Submitted by RHCs

  – 20 Pending Before DOJ

  – 9 Approved by DOJ and Pending Before the Court

  – 91 Approved by DOJ and Judge Greene

  – 5 Requests Withdrawn or Rejected

    (a) STS (2) – Withdrawn
    (b) Interexchange Service for NASA – Rejected
    (c) Acquisition of Electronics Firms that Sell Refurbished
        Central Office (CO) Equipment to IXCs – Rejected
    (d) Provision of Electronic Publishing/Directory Services
        – Rejected

*   As a result of the removal of Section II(D)(3) from the MFJ consent
    decree pursuant to Judge Harold Greene's September 10, 1987 Opinion, the
    Justice Department no longer tracks "nontelecommunications" waiver
    requests.

instance, CEI proposals have been submitted relating to voice messaging
services, voice mail, audiotex, protocol conversion, and videotex gateways,
with some success.   However, requests by Bell Atlantic Corp., BellSouth,
Corp., and Southwestern Bell Corp. to provide electronic publishing and
electronic directory services were denied by the MFJ Court in the June 1989
order.   In his rejection, the Judge cited substantial concerns about the
Regional companies' ability to unlawfully subsidize these information content
offerings.

Since divestiture was implemented on January 1, 1984, the RBOCs have
submitted well over 100 "line of business" waiver requests to the Justice
Department and Judge Greene.   Excluding "nontelecommunications" related
requests formerly addressed by the now rescinded Section II(D)(3), the count
as shown in Figure IV–4 is 125 (July 1989 data).   Of this number, 20 are
pending before the Department and nine approved by DOJ are currently
before the Court.   In all, the Regional Companies have received (full)
approval for 91 of their "telecommunications" requests.[19]   Five requests have
been withdrawn or rejected: two concerning shared tenant services (STS),
which is a means of aggregating traffic in a business park setting to afford
services or rates otherwise infeasible for medium and small users; one per–

taining to provision of interexchange service for a government agency (NASA); one involving the proposed acquisition of an electronics firm, and one relating to the offering of electronic publishing and electronic directory services.

D. Nontraditional Policy Alternatives

1. Overview

Such forces as the AT&T divestiture, technological change, and competition have brought about a fundamental revamping of the U.S. telecommunications industry structure during the 1980s. Since the breakup of the Bell System, the states as a group have been actively pursuing varying programs of regulatory reform. This has included generally increasing carrier flexibility to respond to the market place and in some cases instituting regulatory forbearance. After a relatively slow rate of acceptance compared to federal policymakers, deregulation and regulatory flexibility now exist in some form in most state jurisdictions.

Initially, several states resisted the procompetition policies espoused at the federal level, but most jurisdictions have now embraced this philosophy for at least certain toll markets.

For example, virtually all multiLATA states permit both facilities based and resale competition in interLATA toll markets. In addition, more than one–third of all states allow facilities based competition in intraLATA toll areas, and many more have sanctioned multiple entry in the resale market. Moreover, the right of price flexibility has been granted to AT&T (and other IXCs) in a majority of state jurisdictions. Other changes have been made to ostensibly encourage competition while maintaining universal telephone service including, *e.g.*, authorization of local measured service (LMS) and price flexibility for local exchange companies (LECs), and institution of "lifeline programs" for the poor.

A number of major alternatives to rate of return/rate base regulation have been developed in recent years with respect to dominant carriers, and five are explored below in terms of their relative merits and current utilization. These approaches include: (1) social contract/price cap plans; (2) incentive regulation; (3) rate stabilization; (4) deregulation; and (5) separate subsidiaries. Each is discussed below.

2. Social Contract/Price Cap Plan

The basic elements of this approach include stable local exchange rates which may only be changed based on a predetermined index (*e.g.*, Consumer Price Index) or factors (such as government tax increases). These rates are typically set at existing levels initially. Ceilings on overall rate of return established under traditional regulation would be abandoned. Other contractual terms usually include requirements for high service quality, and public access to a complaint mechanism at the regulatory commissions. In return, local exchange carriers often enjoy price flexibility, or even deregulation for designated, nonbasic services.

In January 1989, the PSB approved the "Modified Vermont Telecommunications Agreement." The revised social contract essentially freezes its basic business and residential telephone rates through 1991 in exchange for reduced regulation of new service offerings. Other provisions include the right of NET to offer new services after 15 days public notice; blocking mechanisms for any 976 service it offers; and the promise to spend $284 million for improvements in equipment and facilities.

Advantages of this method are several. Subscribers to a carrier's monopoly services are given some assurances that their rates will be less volatile, if not fixed or stable in nature. Further, regulatory costs are reduced as price adjustments may be made "automatically" in compliance with the agreed upon formula. The plan encourages efficiency by the carrier, since the lower the operating costs incurred, the higher the profits reaped. Return levels are typically not controlled in a social contract arrangement, and thus the operating company keeps all or at least some earnings increments.

Drawbacks exist as well. Existing rates are frequently not cost based, so ceilings may build in and perpetuate distortions. Coupled with the ability to flexibly or freely price nonbasic services, anticompetitive cross subsidization could occur. Incentives exist for maximizing profits but these would not necessarily promote service quality in the absence of either vigorous, economic competition or commission oversight. Choice of an improper price index could result in either excessive or deficient basic service rates, sending the wrong "signals" to potential entrants, investors, and users. Moreover, the finite duration of a given social contract or price cap trial (usually several years long) could cause the subject carrier to bias the outcome by only behaving in an exemplary fashion during that time period. Some view the approach as a precursor to the implementation of a "sunset provision" to state regulation of telecommunications.[20]

The best known proponent of the social contract concept has been the State of Vermont. In January 1987, the state government and the New England Telephone Company (NET) announced a proposed agreement which would require NET to stabilize its basic telephone rates, limit increases for services (such as an intrastate long distance offering, WATS, and Centrex), invest in a statewide network modernization program, and, at the same time, assure the continuation of high standards of service quality. The agreement insures no price increases through 1988 and limits monthly price increases over the five year life of the agreement. For residences, increases are limited from 35¢ to $1.70 annually, and for businesses, the maximum increase is two percent annually. This agreement incorporates former Vermont Public Service Board (PSB) Chairman Louise McCarren's social contract proposal and will place the risk associated with inflation on NET. Although the plan does not guarantee NET a reasonable return on its investment, it also does not limit NET's ability to earn. Before the agreement could be effectuated, legislation had to be enacted to authorize the Public Service Board's

consideration and approval. In June 1987, the Governor signed this enabling
legislation but the final agreement would be subject to approval and oversight
by the PSB after completion of a full public hearing of its terms and
conditions in early 1988.

At the conclusion of this hearing, the PSB stated that it had several
concerns about the new legislation, including the need for a longer period for
frozen basic rates and the return of any surpluses to ratepayers. In
response, NET and the Department of Public Service renegotiated the
"Vermont telecommunications agreement" and submitted it to the PSB for
approval in late August 1988. Among the proposed changes are a six month
increase in the length of the original three year contract. Another suggested
revision is the elimination of a provision heretofore allowing NET to increase
its basic rates if unforeseen events substantially impacted telephone company
earnings. Other changes involve increased consumer access to rate information and the ability to block unwanted services.

The concept of the "social contract" as a replacement for formal rate
regulation faces several definitional and management problems that are rooted
in the history of and ongoing changes in service provisioning by telephone
companies. Experience at the federal level in telecommunications since the
early 1960s demonstrates that defining which services should be subject to the
contract can be a precarious undertaking.

Under a service oriented approach to a social contract, services are often
grouped into three general categories:
1. Basic/monopoly services
    • subject to social contract
2. Basic/competitive services
    • some competition exists, but not effective
    • subject to rate of return/rate base and other conventional
      regulation
3. Enhanced/information services
    • nonbasic or basic services for which effective competition exists
    • not subject to regulation (deregulated)
    • deregulated

To attain a workable plan, the above scheme requires clear definition of
the services which fall in each category and specification of the boundaries
between service categories, customers, and service providers.

Concerning service definition, the way in which services are "packaged"
for marketing has changed over time even though the underlying engineering
characteristics of these offerings have remained largely the same. For
instance, "plain old telephone service" (POTS) as a conduit to basic long
distance service (MTS) was supplemented in 1961 by AT&T's marketing of so-
called wide area telecommunications service (WATS). WATS essentially
provided the user with the same technical characteristics of ordinary MTS,
except that WATS furnished calling volumes to larger users in a bulk,
discounted fashion.

In the late 1970s, the FCC commenced an investigation which ultimately
found that WATS and MTS were "like" offerings. Yet, in the 1980s, the

Commission permitted the repackaging of WATS as a new, high capacity (and further discounted) service known as Megacom. Similarly, simple private line services were repackaged as Telpak discounted private line offerings by AT&T in 1961. Telpak, like WATS, was a marketing (pricing) rather than an engineering change in a basic offering.

In the 1980s, a more refined private line offering called software defined network (SDN) emerged as competition for simple private line network offerings. SDN is a switched service which gives the large user considerable control over services which can substitute for traditional private lines and provides substantial discounts over regular switched telephone service. Finally, dialing plans such as Reach Out America, which provide calling time by the hour rather than by the traditional time and distance formula, constitute still further marketing developments. Service changes have occurred for both the switched and unswitched services, but the corresponding and associated engineering innovation has been minuscule.

With respect to network boundaries, until relatively recently in the telephone industry, the local and long distance telephone companies controlled all parts of the system, including customer premises equipment (CPE), local transmission and switching, and long distance services. The erosion of this unity by regulatory, legal, and technical changes has been underway for some time. Terminal equipment was progressively deregulated by the FCC in the *Carterphone, Dataspeed 40/4,* and *Computer Inquiry II* proceedings.

Seemingly clear distinctions between basic and enhanced services have become increasingly blurred. For example, in recent years the standing of network channel terminating equipment as part of basic offerings has been subject to controversy. In the future, the status of terminal equipment now being introduced to facilitate conversion to an ISDN environment should be similarly contested.

Boundaries between physical parts of the network have also been changed as competition and deregulation have grown. The MFJ created the LATA structure with long distance companies providing service between LATAs and local companies providing service only within LATAs. Within LATAs, the local company must interface with its customers as well as with the interLATA carriers. The definition of the customer boundary, the network interface, is subject to change. Provision of the network channel terminating equipment required for code and protocol conversion between some CPE and the local telephone network might be basic or nonbasic in nature depending on the application. Whether the protocol conversion function should be part of the network services or part of CPE owned by the customer is an ongoing boundary definitional problem.

Changing service definitions and the regulatory boundaries of phone company services and systems can have major impacts on costs and revenues. For example, the lucrative yellow pages and billing services have been removed from the "basic" service category and treated as information services (unregulated). This would eliminate some costs formerly assigned to basic service ratepayers, but even more revenues would be lost, resulting in upward pressures on the rates of remaining services classified as basic.[21]

Technical changes in the network are leading to wholly new services which not only cause reallocation of costs within a general category of services, but can also vitiate a fixed regulatory scheme. For example, as noted, an integrated services digital network (ISDN) subsumes in its flexible service capabilities both private line and POTS/MTS type services.

This task of characterizing services and defining boundaries is nontrivial. The number of services offered by telephone companies now runs into the hundreds. Moreover, in some states the LECs reject regulation by service and promote regulation based on the network elements used in providing services. This alternative approach is related to the concept of Open Network Architecture (ONA) in which each service is provided by assembling individually priced, discrete system resources. This approach does not aid in determining which services should be subject to a social contract, traditionally regulated, or deregulated.

The social contract approach may require an ongoing mechanism to characterize new, repackaged, and updated service offerings as Basic/Monopoly, Basic/Competitive, or Enhanced/Information services. Otherwise, constantly changing service offerings and new technology could mean regulation of services that have become competitive or lack of regulation of services that are without effective competition.

Very closely related to the "social contract" is the "price cap" approach. Under this plan, basic telephone rates would also be generally frozen in return for pricing flexibility for the local company's competitive services. As before, basic rates could be changed on the basis of nonmarket factors or relationships to preset indices. Constraints on earnings would still be eliminated. The major difference between the approaches appears to be procedural. That is, the social contract involves negotiations between the carrier and the state, whereas the price cap approach does not *per se*. However, both methods are characterized by *quid pro quos* and "package deals" which feature the same basic elements of monopoly ratepayer protections in return for greater marketplace freedoms for the local telephone company. In practice, this fine distinction is often overlooked, and the terms are frequently used interchangeably.

Social contract/price cap arrangements have been proposed in numerous states and adopted in a few. Plans have been sponsored by telephone companies and legislators in such states as Idaho, Utah, Arizona, Washington, Ohio, Texas, Florida, Maryland, Virginia, West Virginia, and the District of Columbia. Besides Vermont, the approach has been legislatively adopted in Idaho after three years of promotion by Mountain Bell and its supporters. Initially designed to deregulate all intrastate services in the state, the bill underwent several revisions before eventual passage.

More specifically, a social contract bill, which would freeze basic rates in return for a service—by—service review for deregulatory purposes, was introduced into the Idaho legislature in 1987. Although passed by both houses, the governor vetoed the measure because of concerns about possible adverse effects on universal service. In particular, he criticized the lack of a complaint mechanism at the Public Utility Commission (PUC) and the inability of public policy makers to reimpose regulation if circumstances warrant.

As finally passed, HB 687 preserves PUC jurisdiction over basic rates, service quality, customer deposits, and disconnection of service. The plan requires that the commission develop a cost allocation process for regulated services. Those offerings considered to be "highly competitive," such as Centron, state toll, WATS, and custom calling, were deregulated. The governor signed the bill at the end of March 1988.

In May 1989 the Arizona Corporation Commission and Mountain Bell (d/b/a US WEST) agreed to freeze basic rates through 1991. The deal was concluded after more than a year of negotiation.

Policymakers may apply price caps (*i.e.*, ceilings) or bands (ceilings and floors)[22] to other than local exchange carriers. For example, in August 1987, the FCC proposed to implement price cap regulation for AT&T, the dominant interexchange carrier, and the Regional Bell Operating Companies. In May 1988, the Florida PSC announced that it was considering such a two year experiment with AT&T, which also includes a requirement to serve the entire state and to maintain statewide averaged rates. In March 1989, the FCC adopted price cap regulation for AT&T, the dominant interexchange carrier at the interstate level (see Chapter IX).

3. Incentive Regulation

This form of regulation requires that commissions continue to establish rates of return for regulated carriers, but permits the latter to share earnings that exceed authorized levels with ratepayers.

Among its alleged advantages are the creation of incentives for cost minimization and efficiency. Process or service innovation by the carrier could be translated into productivity increases or other cost reducing measures, thereby boosting the firm's profitability. If the increase exceeds the commission approved rate, then the carrier is allowed to retain a portion of the higher earnings. Stockholders presumably benefit, as well as ratepayers who are recipients of lower rates, refunds, and or heightened innovation. By retaining limits on earnings, the commission can theoretically prevent those with market power from reaping the monopoly profits.

The approach in its purest form has certain disadvantages. Affected carriers would not be able to flexibly price to meet competition. And, maintenance of good service quality is not necessarily a concomitant of the pursuit of profits. Indeed, many would argue that quality may well be sacrificed on the road to higher earnings in a weakly competitive setting.

The concept of sharing excessive earnings with ratepayers was publicized in May 1986 by Pacific Bell as part of a general rate case. Although the outcome of the California proposal has not yet been determined, the approach has been embraced in other jurisdictions. For instance, New York, Wisconsin, and Florida have each adopted variants of this plan. Perhaps the best known of the adopted commission plans is that of New York. After enduring seven general rate cases in eight years (1978–1985), each lasting an average of eleven months, the New York Public Service Commission (PSC) in early 1986 solicited proposals for reducing the number of such proceedings. New York Telephone Company responded with a proposal for a three year period of no general rate case filings (albeit it would still be permitted to pass through FCC imposed costs), and a rate of return on equity no higher than 14 percent. The PSC and New York Telephone each proposed revisions which were eventually adopted.

Thus, in May 1986, the New York Public Service Commission approved a moratorium plan precluding New York Telephone from filing a general rate case before September 1987, with certain rate adjustments effective in August 1986 and 1987. In April 1987, the New York PSC approved a plan which was negotiated by the PSC, New York Tel, politicians, and consumer groups. The plan basically extended the rate case moratorium through January 1, 1991. The agreement not only stipulated that no general rate increase prior to January 1, 1991 would be permitted, but would implement up to $700 million in rate reductions. Notably, beginning in August 1989, actual earnings for the previous July through June period would be reviewed with one-half of the excess over the currently authorized 14 percent return on equity refunded to the ratepayers and the other one-half to be retained by New York Telephone. In effect, New York has opted for a regulatory program that combines a rate cap with an incentive earnings plan.

In an approach similar to New York's, Wisconsin adopted a combination incentive/price cap plan with an effective date of August 1, 1987. In its July 1987 order, the Wisconsin PSC lowered Wisconsin Bell's return on equity from 14.25 percent to 13.5 percent. However, the PSC concluded that the local exchange carrier could keep earnings between 13.5 and 14.0 percent. Any excess between 14.0 and 15.5 percent, in turn, would be shared equally between the company and the state's ratepayers. Where earnings fell below 12.5 percent, Bell would be allowed to request rate increases. In August 1988, Wisconsin Bell petitioned the PSC to change its regulatory focus from "what the company earns to the prices the customers pay," i.e., a changeover to a price cap approach similar to that proposed by the FCC.[23] Six months later, the company proposed a three year rate ceiling plan for virtually all telephone services through 1992. In return, it seeks to be able to flexibly change prices below the ceiling for most services, and to broaden its rate of return range to between 10.75 percent and 14.5 percent on total investment.

In October 1988, the Florida Public Service Commission ordered Southern Bell to share its earnings above 14 percent on equity with customers. For the range 14 to 16 percent, users receive 60 percent of the "excess"; above 16 percent, customers are refunded 160 percent. A three year rate stability plan was also authorized by the FCC.

4. Rate Stabilization

Under the rate stabilization approach, carrier rates are generally reduced if earnings exceed authorized levels and, conversely, rates will rise if earnings are deficient. Advantages of this approach include: a) an automatic mechanism for triggering rate changes, and b) a theoretical means to prevent monopoly profits by dominant firms. One disadvantage is that the trigger can only be effectuated when the excess is discovered by the agency, *i.e.*, regulatory lag may occur. Another is that the program in its purest form does not include a provision for pricing flexibility.

Alabama and New Jersey currently have such plans in effect. In November 1986, the Alabama PSC approved and implemented a Rate Stabilization and Equalization plan similar to those used for the state's electric and gas utilities. This approach limits South Central Bell's rate of return to a PSC prescribed range of 11.65 to 12.30 percent. Any earnings beyond this range will force rate reductions; earnings below this range necessitate rate boosts. The plan establishes priorities regarding which services would be affected by improper earnings levels. An independent audit completed in May 1988 concluded that South Central is in full compliance with the program and that the quality of Alabama regulation has improved. Although somewhat like the incentive regulation method discussed above, there is no provision to share excess earnings among carriers and their ratepayers.

Begun on July 1, 1987, New Jersey's program is a hybrid of several plans. New Jersey Bell's services were initially divided between two categories. For those deemed to be "competitive," rate of return regulation was rescinded. These "Group I" offerings included Centrex, yellow pages, high capacity special access services, public data network, CO–LAN (a central–office based local area network), billing and collection, and coin services. Concerning all other ("Group II") services, rates are to be frozen until June 30, 1990. If exogenous factors do not impact these rates or the CPI remains under 4.5 percent annually, then the freeze would be extended for three more years.

If Bell's earnings are in excess of the authorized level, then Group II rates would be lowered. Quarterly "surveillance" data are collected for both groups. Although similar to Alabama's plan, New Jersey's approach uses rate freezes and apparently does not utilize a wide rate of return range. By way of contrast, Michigan sets a return range and employs rate bands for its interexchange carriers, but does not currently make use of a rate adjustment mechanism for excess or deficient earnings.

5. Deregulation

Service by service deregulatory proposals have been introduced in numerous states, with varying degrees of success. The major benefits of this approach go to the heart of the regulatory/deregulatory debate. That is, where competition is effective, regulation should be reduced or eliminated to facilitate innovation, productivity, and other marketplace benefits. Conversely, drawbacks center on the imprudence of deregulating where carriers exhibit substantial market power and competition is weak.

U S WEST has vigorously promoted deregulation and enjoyed considerable success. As of April 1989, thirteen of the fourteen states in the RBOC's operating territory had approved some form of deregulation. Specifically, one (Nebraska) had completely eliminated rate of return regulation; and several (e.g., Colorado, Idaho, Minnesota, North Dakota, and Oregon) had deregulated particular competitive services. Moreover, seven states, (Washington, Utah, Arizona, Oregon, North Dakota, Iowa, and New Mexico) have initiated flexible pricing policies.

On January 1, 1987, Nebraska became the first state to deregulate all telephone services, including basic local exchange service, pursuant to enacted legislation (L.B. 835).[24] Under the new law, the Commission's jurisdiction is limited to rates for basic local exchange service. And, it may only review increases upon petition by a specified number of affected customers (e.g., two percent for companies with more than 250,000 lines), or if the rate increase is greater than 10 percent. Only a 90 day notice period is required in all other cases. The Commission has no control over the rates for other services offered by telephone companies in the state. New services with nonregulated rates can be implemented with 10 days notice to the Commission.

In return for the deregulation aspects of L.B. 835, the LECs have to maintain the caps on local exchange rates for five years. With respect to the pricing of access services to interexchange carriers (IXCs), the Commission will retain jurisdiction for the purpose of resolving differences that the IXCs and the local exchange carriers cannot resolve through private negotiations. InterLATA toll service is also deregulated, but rate deaveraging is prohibited until September 1991 and intraLATA competition was delayed until January 1989.

The first two years of implementation of L.B. 835 in Nebraska have seen some problems emerge. For instance, there have been cases where customers were given insufficient, if any, notice of impending rate increases and then backbilled.[25] Confusion and uncertainty to both customers and the local exchange carriers occurred. The Commission has recommended several changes and with regard to customer notification, suggested that adequate notification be achieved through PSC actions.[26]

Other areas that the Commission believed to be in need of reevaluation are the instances of skyrocketing rates (e.g., 400 percent increase in AT&T's private line rates) and the necessity of deregulation even in areas where natural monopolies exist. The Commission favors a strategy of regulated monopoly service while deregulating services that operate within the framework of workably competitive markets.

A brief anecdote underscores the early problems experienced under the new deregulatory regime in Nebraska and the critical role of the PSC even today. In October 1987 residents of Ceresco, a suburb of Lincoln, sought to have their community become part of the Lincoln telephone exchange.[27] The request was made because of the strong ties Ceresco citizens believe current- ly exist between the two geographic areas. Two the of town's three schools could only be reached through long distance calling. Ceresco is located less than 15 miles from Lincoln and less than a mile from the current perimeter of Lincoln Telephone and Telegraph's (LT&T) toll free local service.

than $22. Subsequently, LT&T informed Ceresco community leaders that the company was not interested in providing the service at any cost.[28]

Irate Ceresco residents filed a complaint with the Nebraska Commission. Under the new deregulatory law, the PSC has the authority to order a carrier to provide EAS but has jurisdiction solely over quality, *i.e.,* not rates. However, the rates for an EAS must be approved by 65 percent of the community before the service can be supplied.

In a February 1988 letter to its Ceresco customers, LT&T outlined its reasons for opposing the EAS petition.[29]   First, the company would need to install new switching and transmission equipment to provide EAS. Second, there would be lost revenue from elimination of existing long distance calling from Ceresco to Lincoln.   Third, the large increase in basic telephone rates for Ceresco residents –– now estimated to be $28 more than current local rates –– would not benefit many of the community's members who make relatively few toll calls currently and, thus, would be unfair.   Finally, the new local calling capability priced on a flat rate basis would give "false signals" to callers, who could greatly increase their volume of calls at no extra billing cost but could require LT&T to build more facilities to handle the higher demand.

Ceresco customers remained unhappy, pointing toward the company's spiraling EAS rate estimates.   Moreover, they claimed that LT&T's offer to install local telephone lines in the two schools came far too late and only after pressure was applied by citizens.[30]

On May 2, 1988, which was three days before a scheduled PSC hearing on the EAS dispute, LT&T's executive vice president wrote a letter to the Commission delineating a conciliatory proposal.[31]   This showed the impact of Commission intervention and the continued need for a governmental role even under deregulation.   Apparently, the prospects of hearings by the PSC evoked some changes in LT&T's previous positions.   Specifically, LT&T proposed the following:[32]

a) Upon proper proof of a 65 percent "community of interest" showing, allow Ceresco to become part of the Lincoln exchange at a rate of $14.70 per urban residential single–party line per month;

b) This EAS service would be optional to each Ceresco customer, *i.e.,* each resident could choose between the $7.70 existing local rate and the new EAS rate; and

c) If the subscription level to this EAS service should drop below 50 percent of all lines in Ceresco, LT&T would have the right to petition the PSC to discontinue the service.

The letter concluded that:

We will await your decision on whether or not the Ceresco hearing, scheduled for May 5th, would be required.   If it is not, appropriate information regarding this proposal will be disseminated to the Ceresco community.[33]

Legislation permitting PSC deregulation of certain services is being con–sidered in Georgia, but has recently been passed in Mississippi.   In April

1987, Bell of Pennsylvania offered a novel *quid pro quo* to the state. That is, in return for deregulation of all services except local exchange, Bell would freeze basic rates for three years and would contribute $100 million over a five year period to Pennsylvania's economic development fund. Amidst a great furor, Bell and the state's Independents recommended a new plan whereby five services (billing and collection, operator services, yellow and white page directories, and mobile/paging services) would be targeted for deregulation. In return, a six year phaseout of the revenues for these services would be undertaken to ameliorate any adverse impact on ratepayers.

A second major arena where traditional regulation has given way to deregulatory and competitive solutions is the State of Illinois. Illinois is recognized as one of the leaders in taking a vigorous procompetitive stance. While criticized by some as excessive in relation to market conditions, both the legislature and Illinois Commerce Commission (ICC) have nonetheless sought to further the goals of competition in the state. For instance, in June 1986 the ICC approved the Consensus Exchange Plan which restructures rates in MSA 1[34] (including Chicago and other areas in the northeast portion of Illinois) along with revised and generally higher charges for business private line services in the state. The new rate plan was designed to be revenue neutral and reduces widespread pricing inconsistencies that existed for the unmanageable myriad of 93 calling plans for residence and business customers. One purpose of the restructure was an attempt to bring rates closer to actual network usage costs. In addition, rate restructuring was deemed necessary as a matter of fairness and in response to the pressures of improving technologies and advancing competition.

The Illinois Legislature passed legislation (Illinois Public Utilities Act) that allows intraLATA competition and local exchange competition beginning January 1, 1989. IntraLATA toll rate deaveraging is also permitted under the new act. Under the deaveraging plan, primary toll carriers (PTCs) may be established within each MSA in Illinois with the toll market shares of carriers operating within each MSA determining the identity of the PTC in that MSA. For instance, the PTCs are divided up as follows: Illinois Bell-3; GTE-6; Continental-1; and Illinois Consolidated-1. The designated PTC is responsible for setting toll rates and determining its MSA revenue requirements, as well as general oversight of toll service within the MSA.

AT&T's interLATA MTS offering in Illinois was declared to be competitive and is now deregulated, but WATS and private line remain under regulation. AT&T has since reduced its MTS rates and has agreed not to deaverage them.

The Act has provided IXCs and LECs the flexibility to price certified services to meet strategic objectives. Furthermore, rates can be developed on a case-by-case basis as the need arises. The only requirement embodied in the Act is that a marginal cost study must be on file with the ICC, on a proprietary basis, for each competitive service. The Commission also has the authority to establish rules to insure that prices are at or above marginal cost. In order to meet competition for the local loop, Illinois Bell proposed a rate restructuring at the end of 1988 that, if approved, will result in higher residential rates while lowering charges to businesses. The LEC proposed a rate plan similar to New York Telephone Company's incentive regulation scheme.

6. Separate Subsidiaries

A regulatory option of recent years is that of the separate subsidiary. Under this concept, a carrier's operations may be segmented for purposes of public scrutiny through the use of separate books, officers, and facilities. It might also involve the imposition of conduct related restrictions, such as permitted interactions between the separated entity and its parent or affiliates. The "separate sub" approach has been typically applied to "dominant carriers" by the FCC, i.e., telecommunications firms which operate in both regulated and unregulated markets and which possess "market power." As defined by the Commission in its "Competitive Carrier" proceeding, market power refers to the

> . . . control a firm can exercise in setting the price of its
> output. A firm with market power is able to engage in
> conduct that may be anticompetitive or otherwise inconsistent
> with the public interest. This may entail setting price above
> competitive costs in order to earn supranormal profits, or
> setting price below competitive costs to forestall entry by
> new competitors or to eliminate existing competitors.[35]

Similar to the previous policy alternatives discussed in this chapter, the separate subsidiary approach may be used in lieu of traditional regulatory methods. However, unlike the other alternatives viewed in a normal setting, the separation mode may also be used to complement rate base/rate of return regulation. For example, a telephone company's monopoly business could be subject to traditional regulation while the company's competitive operations must conform with separation requirements.

The attractiveness of "maximum separation" short of divestiture centers on its effectiveness in highlighting transactions between the separated affiliate and other members of the corporate family. Inter service cross subsidization and cost shifting between operations become more difficult to achieve when physical separation of financial accounts, management, and plant is implemented. Accounting safeguards alone do not afford this level of protection to ratepayers because commingling of costs may occur. Given the high level of joint and common costs in telephony, this arrangement may facilitate abuses by carriers operating in both regulated and unregulated markets.

More stringent than a wholly owned separate subsidiary would be one in which the dominant carrier is only a minority owner of the affiliate. This construct not only highlights interactions but also changes fundamental corporate incentives. In this mode, the goals and objectives of the subsidiary would theoretically not be controlled by the dominant carrier but, rather, by other considerations such as the market place. In contrast, there would be substantial pressure upon corporate managers and directors of the wholly owned subsidiary to conform to the strategic directives of the parent.

Disadvantages of this structural approach also exist.   By physically separating functions such as joint marketing or common facilities, certain synergies may be lost.   Moreover, less extreme forms of safeguards such as commission prescribed cost allocation methodologies or other nonstructural conditions may provide adequate protection for ratepayers without unfairly hamstringing a dominant carrier.

a.   Federal Communications Commission

At the FCC, advocates and opponents of the separate subsidiary concept have each prevailed at different points in time.   Two distinct trends have emerged during the past two decades, and are discussed in turn.

The U.S. experience with the notion of structural separation and the "separate subsidiary" concept as regulatory tools essentially traces its origins to policies instituted by the FCC during the early 1970s.   This approach was created to be a vehicle for fostering fair, arm's length competition for the participants in a given communications marketplace.   An alternative to more radical prescriptions such as divestiture and denial of mergers, the separate subsidiary is a compromise solution designed to balance the often–competing objectives of preventing anticompetitive activities and preserving corporate incentives and prerogatives.   Hence, structural and accounting safeguards have been instituted over the years in a number of instances, both for internation–al and domestic services, and in a variety of tailored combinations in the attempt to protect the interstate ratepayers' interests.

The Commission has issued a number of decisions in recent years ordering the establishment of separate subsidiaries to insure "maximum separation," *i.e.*, requiring that in certain situations communications common carriers form separate corporate entities for the provision of particular services.   The aforementioned "Computer I" proceeding inaugurated the policy to separate activities subject to regulation from nonregulated operations involving data processing.[36]   In general, the Commission believed that without appropriate safeguards, the provision of data processing by communications common carriers could adversely affect statutory obligations of these carriers to provide adequate communications services under reasonable terms and conditions, and impair effective competition in the sale of data processing services.

To insure maximum separation, the Commission required in this case that any communications common carrier wishing to provide data processing services be permitted to do so only through separate affiliates or subsidiaries utilizing separate books of account, separate officers, separate operating personnel, and separated equipment and facilities devoted exclusively to the rendition of data processing services.

The Commission has issued several other decisions since the *First Computer Inquiry* requiring the establishment of separate corporate entities to provide for maximum separation.[37]   In many of the early cases, an established international carrier petitioned the Commission for authority to provide a new service in the domestic market.   Before such a service could be offered, however, the Commission required that the international carrier form a separate subsidiary to provide the service, and that the subsidiary be subject to several conditions. In the more recent cases cited, a domestic carrier typically petitioned the Commission to allow it to provide additional communications services, either through the acquisition of another domestic firm or via internal expansion. Again, the Commission required the establishment of a separate subsidiary subject to several conditions.

The major reasons for the requirement of separate corporate entities was to insure that the established carriers not create the potential for unfair competitive practices, such as underpricing of new services as a result of cross subsidization from the old ones. For example, the Commission wanted to assure itself that RCA Globcom, an established international carrier, would not provide cross subsidies to RCA's domestic satellite activities, and thus give these activities an unfair competitive advantage *vis-à-vis* other potential domestic satellite entrants. Additionally, the Commission wanted to assure itself that in no way would the proposed domestic service affect the international operations. Again, by way of example, in the Comsat case, the Commission wanted assurance that Comsat's venture into the domestic satellite market, through its separate corporate entity, Comsat General, would in no way impair Comsat's ability to discharge its statutory responsibilities with respect to its Intelsat activities.

In addition to simply requiring the established carriers to form separate subsidiaries for their new operations, the Commission set forth several conditions under which those subsidiaries should operate. These safeguards generally stipulated separate accounting records, marketing functions, management, and physical contact. Moreover, equipment purchases had to be conducted on an arm's length basis, and nondiscriminatory interconnection was mandated. The Commission also established reporting requirements.

The separate subsidiary concept was again utilized by the FCC as a regulatory tool in the *Second Computer Inquiry*.[38] This and related proceedings represented a far reaching attempt by the Commission to re-draw traditional lines of regulation, given the emergence of competition and the existence of rapid technological change.

On April 7, 1980, the Commission adopted the *Final Decision* in the *Second Computer Inquiry,* thereby establishing the policies and procedures that have completely removed enhanced communications services from Title II regulation and would deregulate all customer premises equipment in stages. As modified subsequently by a *Reconsideration Order* and a *Further Reconsideration Order,* Computer II states that only basic services must continue to be regulated by the Commission, while enhanced services have been detariffed and deregulated since January 1, 1983.[39] A "basic service" is a transmission service limited to the common carrier offering of transmission capacity for the movement of information. An "enhanced service" is any service offered over common carrier transmission facilities which provides the customer additional, different or restructured information or permits customer interaction with stored information.

A fundamental result of the Computer II decisions was the predivestiture imposition of structural separation requirements upon AT&T for its provision of enhanced services and CPE.   The original separation conditions as set forth in the *Final Decision* were primarily established to mitigate the potential for cross subsidization or other anticompetitive conduct of AT&T and GTE.   The Commission's action, succinctly embodied in Section 64.702 of the FCC's Rules, essentially instituted restrictions on, *inter alia,* sharing of officers and certain other personnel, switching equipment, and product specific advertising.   Arm's length transactions between the subsidiary and manufacturing or research affiliates were required, and the affiliated carrier could not discriminate in favor of the subsidiary with respect to interconnection and customer proprietary information.

On reconsideration, 1980, the FCC established specific criteria for determining the need for structural safeguards in a given case.   In assessing whether separation requirements should be maintained, consideration was to be given to: 1) a carrier's ability to engage in anticompetitive activity through control over "bottleneck" facilities, *i.e.,* local exchange and toll transmission facilities, on a broad national geographic basis; 2) a carrier's ability to engage in cross subsidization to the detriment of the communications ratepayer; 3) the integrated nature of the carrier and affiliated entities, with special emphasis upon research and development and manufacturing capabilities that are used in conjunction with, or are supported by, communications derived revenues; and 4) the carrier's possession of sufficient resources to enter the competitive market through a separate subsidiary.

Using these guidelines, the Commission concluded that GTE did not possess market power on a national scope sufficient to warrant structural separation.   Moreover, the FCC decided to "wait to see if competitive abuses develop" before applying the separate subsidiary mechanism to additional carriers.[40]   In 1981, it was determined that the four criteria, on balance, dictated imposition of the "separate sub" requirement on the two minority-owned BOCs.

The "Modification of Final Judgment" (MFJ) which led to the divestiture of AT&T significantly impacted Computer II's separation requirements.   The structural safeguards imposed on Cincinnati Bell Inc. and Southern New England Telephone Company in an earlier Commission decision were removed "as a result of the changed circumstances created by the MFJ."[41]   The consent decree also caused the Commission to terminate its investigation of AT&T's now defunct intrasystem agreements (*e.g.,* the license contracts) and to consider the arrangements of GTE, United, and Continental Telecom (Contel) at some later date.[42]   The Commission originally intended, *inter alia,* that the issue of whether Western Electric's manufacturing and R&D activities should be separated would be examined during the license contract review.[43]

Consummation of the MFJ moved the FCC to re-evaluate the need for structural separation for the entities which comprised the Bell System prior to its dismantling.[44]   On November 23, 1983, the Commission decided that a set of modified structural conditions should be applied to the divested Bell operating companies.[45]   Basically the BOCs were allowed lesser restrictions concerning CPE billing, marketing, and maintenance, as well as administrative services and corporate organization (*e.g.,* an unincorporated division would be an acceptable substitute for a separate subsidiary). The Commission believed that this relaxation of the separation requirements was warranted because of significantly changed circumstances brought about by the AT&T divestiture. Thus, the BOCs would not be affiliated with Western Electric, would not participate in the interLATA market, and would reenter the CPE arena without an established market share. Continued use of the basic separate structure approach was affirmed, however, because it was deemed to be the most cost–effective regulatory tool to protect ratepayers from bearing the costs of providing competitive products and services and to promote competition.[46]

On reconsideration, the revised structural conditions were affirmed.[47] The decision concluded, in part, that "not every one of these four factors need to be satisfied to impose structural separation."[48]

The *BOC Separation Order* also asserted that the FCC intended to "review the appropriateness of the separation conditions [as modified] within two years" after the BOCs had complied with the new set of conditions "in light of prevailing circumstances." The agency reemphasized that accounting by itself would provide the public less protection against "improper cost shifting" than would structural separation. Further, it ascertained that accounting separation can be both more difficult to oversee and a much more intrusive method of agency monitoring.

This order represented a watershed ruling regarding structural separation; soon thereafter, the FCC abruptly reversed the policy in the face of the ISDN and fiber optic revolution and, of course, the MFJ.

Accordingly, the Commission has vigorously pursued new deregulatory initiatives and other regulatory changes. Thus, the *Third Computer Inquiry,* or *Computer III* (Docket 85–229) was launched on August 16, 1985 through a Notice of Proposed Rulemaking designed to reassess the new telecommunications environment for enhanced services. Concurrent with the initiation of this proceeding was a significant change in the philosophy underlying *Computer II,* especially with respect to the perceived need to require structural separation for the enhanced service and CPE operations of both AT&T and the Regional Bell Companies.

More specifically, since the mid 1980s the Commission has systematically removed "separate sub" requirements for AT&T and the Bell companies contingent on the implementation of certain nonstructural safeguards.[49] The agency conditionally rescinded structural requirements for AT&T relating to CPE and enhanced services through orders adopted in September 1985 and May 1986, respectively; similarly, the Regionals were released from this constraint respecting CPE and enhanced services in November and May of 1986, respectively. In its June 1986 order in the *Third Computer Inquiry* the FCC asserted that complete structural relief for the entities is predicated upon: (1) FCC approval of "Open Network Architecture" (ONA) plans which were filed on February 1 1988, that satisfy "Comparably Efficient Interconnection" (CEI) requirements and additional unbundling conditions through a set of tariffed "basic service elements" that, in turn, support enhanced services offered by BOCs and their competitors;[50] (2) the filing of detailed accounting plans that comply with the requirements set forth in the FCC's *Joint Cost* proceeding (Docket 86–111); and (3) adherence to requirements concerning network information disclosure and customer proprietary network information.   The agency preempted all state attempts to impose structural conditions on intrastate provision of enhanced services.

In its Computer III reconsideration order, released May 22, 1987, the Commission concluded that competitive considerations dictated that (nonstructural) safeguards be retained for AT&T. CEI and ONA requirements were "generalized" for the BOCs and AT&T, with less stringent rules made applicable to the latter (*e.g.*, "service specific CEI" would be substituted for unbundling). Concerning independent telephone companies, no CEI/ONA or nonstructural conditions would be imposed by the Commission for the foreseeable future. However, states would be permitted to institute nonstructural safeguards which are no more strict than those established for the BOCs by the FCC.

b. The Courts

The Modification of Final Judgment agreed to by AT&T and the Department of Justice specifically circumscribes the activities in which the post divestiture regional companies and their affiliates may participate. More particularly, the original January 8, 1982 consent decree limited BOCs to the provision of exchange, exchange (and information)[51] access services, and the provision of natural monopoly services ". . . actually regulated by tariff" (Section II (D)). Subsequently, the U.S. Court for the District of Columbia modified the agreement to permit the BOCs to provide, but not manufacture, CPE and to continue to publish the Yellow Pages. Court approval must be obtained before the Bell regions may engage in any other line of business.[52]

In *Opinion* issued July 26, 1984,[53] the Court set forth the standards and procedures that it would use in ruling upon any motion for waiver of existing MFJ constraints. Among other things, the Court asserted that it would not consider granting any regional company permission to enter the equipment manufacturing, interexchange service, or information service markets at this time.[54] The Court established four conditions which the petition must meet before its waiver could be authorized:

1. *The regional companies are required to conduct competitive activities through separate subsidiaries.* The Court opined that such structural safeguards are appropriate where there is a "substantial possibility that the Operating Companies could impede competition." It also stated that conducting activities through such subsidiaries would make intracompany transactions more apparent and that cross subsidization or other anticompetitive conduct therefore could be more easily prevented or rectified. The Court refused to define specifically the form that the subsidiaries should take, apparently leaving at least the initial stage of that task to the Department of Justice.
2. *Subsidiaries engaged in competitive enterprises must obtain their own debt financing on their own credit, and no entity affiliated with the regional company may guarantee the debt in any manner that would*

permit a creditor, on default, to have recourse to the assets of an operating company. The Court asserted that use of operating companies' financial resources or credit for new ventures created a potential for cross subsidization and tended to jeopardize the financial soundness of the operating companies.

3. *The total estimated net revenues from activities for which waivers are granted must not exceed ten percent of a regional holding company's total estimated net revenues.* The Court reasoned that such a limitation serves to protect the nation's telecommunications service from injury due to failure of management to devote sufficient attention to regulated activities and ensures that the bulk of the investment of the RBOCs remain in exchange telecommunications–related activities.

4. *Each regional holding company seeking a waiver must agree in its application that the monitoring and visitorial provisions of Section VI of the Decree apply to its proposed competitive activities.*[55]

The Court directed the regional companies to submit any line of business waiver request to the Department of Justice. Each such motion would necessarily be accompanied by a detailed proposal describing the products or services to be offered, the specific means of provision, and the conditions proposed for avoiding the various problems identified in the *Opinion.* The Court ordered the Department of Justice to examine the requests, in conjunction with the petitioning regional company and "all other interested parties."

As discussed above, some 125 waiver requests for telecommunications offerings are either pending before the Justice Dept. or the MFJ Court, have been approved, or have been rejected or withdrawn. On September 10, 1987, Judge Greene eliminated the applicability of the four conditions regarding nontelecommunications endeavors but retained the criteria for telecom–munications related requests.

The same Court presided over the entry of another consent decree terminating an antitrust complaint brought by the Department of Justice regarding the proposed acquisition of Southern Pacific Communications Company (SPCC) by GTE Corporation. The complaint alleged that the acquisition could: (1) serve to substantially lessen competition in the provision of interexchange telecommunications services (particularly where GTE operates local exchanges); and (2) create a substantial probability that GTE will monopolize information services in markets which it serves.[56]

Essentially, the Court approved the proposed merger ". . . only because of the strictness and firmness of the decree's injunctive and separate subsidiary provisions."[57] Cross subsidization concerns have been dealt with primarily by requiring GTE to maintain total separation between the local telephone companies and the newly acquired companies.

Most fundamentally, the GTE operating companies may not provide interexchange services, but may offer information services -- albeit only through separate subsidiaries or divisions and on an equal and nondiscrimina–tory basis. In fact, the companies may engage in virtually any line of business, related or unrelated to telecommunications, subject to the decree's separation requirements.

c.   U.S. Congress

Although no formal legislation establishing structural changes in the telecommunications industry has been promulgated since 1943,[58] clear sentiments favoring structural remedies periodically surface.

For example, in H.R. 5158, a bill to amend the Communications Act of 1934 to revise provisions of the Act relating to telecommunications, a number of separate requirements were proposed as a means to assure fair competition and prevent cross subsidies in the long distance telecommunications market. These requirements were reported to the House Energy and Commerce Committee by the Subcommittee on Telecommunications, Consumer Protection, and Finance on March 25, 1982. Recommended conditions included, among others, separation between the subsidiary and its affiliates, arm's length transaction, and nondiscrimination.

d.   The States

During the 1980s individual states have had little leeway in adopting structural conditions for dominant carriers. Their jurisdiction has been preempted by the FCC with respect to regulation of enhanced services and CPE.[59] Originally forbidden under *Computer II* to exempt the Bell companies from the separation requirement for intrastate regulatory purposes,[60] the states are now forbidden to impose structural conditions on the CPE operations of either the BOCs or the independents. They may, in fact, impose only those nonstructural conditions consistent with the FCC's policies under *Computer III*.[61] Thus, the latitude available to states to deviate from the framework established in *Computer II* is apparently quite narrow.

Despite these constraints, some states have proceeded with structural inquiries. One notable action taken by a state is the recent proceeding before the Alaska Public Utilities Commission whereby a stipulation was reached concerning, *inter alia,* the need for separation requirements for Pacific Telecom, Inc.[62] In August 1987 the California PUC issued a Notice of En Banc Hearings on alternatives to cost of service regulation for local exchange carriers. In the Phase II portion of the proceeding various interested parties filed testimony that set forth potential regulatory schemes for PacBell. Among the issues addressed, the parties proposed structural remedies for the carrier's operation in a competitive marketplace. Characteristically, varying degrees of separation and control were proposed to attain and maintain safeguards against the potential cross–subsidization of competitive services by monopoly ratepayers of basic services. A discussion of three proposed scenarios with respect to regulatory separation follows.

The first approach was set forth by PacBell. In brief, the company does not believe there should be any separation of basic and competitive services. Rather, there are or will be sufficient safeguards in place to protect monopoly ratepayers from unfairly supporting competitive offerings. The company claims that it will provide enough cost information to allow the PUC to ascertain and rule on cross-subsidy issues. PacBell's basic plan is to provide rate stability in the form of unindexed price caps for residential customers in return for relaxed regulation of its competitive services. Earnings achieved above a benchmark level would be equally shared with consumers and the company, and the carrier alleges that it will absorb earnings deficiencies. This so called "concession" may be pure rhetoric because it is doubtful that the company's stockholders would permit management to allow PacBell to suffer economic losses when it was constitutionally entitled to earn a fair and reasonable return.

A second proposal was advanced by the Division of Ratepayer Advocate (DRA). The DRA, which is a part of the PUC, supports an accounting separation approach to regulation.[63] PacBell would be divided into two accounting based entities, monopoly services and new/competitive offerings. This dichotomy was struck as representing the balance between accountability and economic efficiency which is required to meet the requirements of the technology and other changes taking place in telecommunications. Thus, it was emphasized that the competitive entry should not be a fully separated wholly owned subsidiary because inherent economies of scale and scope associated with a single operation would be lost or diminished under such an arrangement. The DRA proposal recommended that the competitive entry be organized along semiautonomous lines with separate profit centers. Also, there would be total flexibility as to the pricing of competitive services. Figure IV-5 depicts the pricing plan set forth by the DRA.

The DRA plan permits sharing of excess profits up to a ceiling and then returns all profits above the ceiling to basic services ratepayers. However, none of the losses associated with competitive services, if they occur, will be shared with basic service customers. The DRA opined that basic ratepayers have already taken considerable risk in developing new Information Age technology and services.[64] For instance, substantial sums were spent on R&D, capital items, and training before new nonbasic services could be brought on line if, indeed, all the new offerings are marketed. These efforts were funded by PacBell's mammoth base of captive basic service ratepayers.

Furthermore, DRA believes that the natural synergy between basic and competitive services has developed over the years and is not directly quantifiable in terms of how much each entity benefits. For instance, extant billing and other customer related functions provide an immeasurable benefit to new services. As noted by the DRA, the greatest synergy may be the vast customer base along with extensive financial and technological resources of PacBell in relation to competitors.

Finally, the proposal set forth by Bay Area Teleport (BAT) is at the extreme end of the regulatory separation continuum, i.e., it has proposed a divestiture of PacBell's competitive and unregulated services into a separate entity. The remaining entity would continue to be regulated as a monopoly on a cost of service basis. In order to assure fair and equitable competition PacBell would be required to permit direct connection to their central offices on terms that are equal in price, quality, and terms as are the comparable services provided to the competitive entity of PacBell. Essentially, BAT has

Figure IV–5

DRA PRICING PLAN

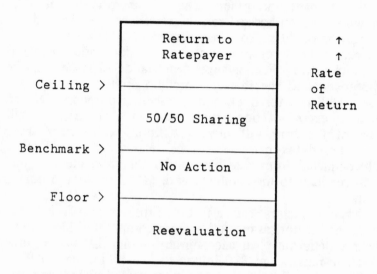

proffered the approach associated with the divestiture of the Bell System in 1984, only at a greater degree of disaggregation. The major impetus to the proposal is the control of bottleneck access facilities by PacBell which results in the potential for anticompetitive behavior with respect to competitors. Thus, BAT maintains, the benefits of competition may not be attainable subject to these obstacles.

7. Policy Constraints

Regardless of the public policy approach employed, certain real world constraints must be recognized and addressed. For example, use of physical plant in providing communications services results in the loss of value of the asset over time due to such factors as physical deterioration and economic obsolescence. This loss in service value, or consumption of the asset, is known generically as depreciation. In an accounting sense, depreciation of an asset is treated as an annual cost of production, and is classified as a capital expense which occurs during the generation of revenues. The process of determining what portion of the capital cost of plant should be charged to expense in each year of the service life of a property is known as depreciation accounting.

Depreciation occupies a unique niche within the cost structure of a telecommunications firm. Rather than being a fixed cost, it is based on estimates of the remaining life, salvage, and cost–of–removal of each class of depreciable property, as well as on the property grouping methods and calcu–

lational procedures employed. Additionally, while part of operating expenses, depreciation does not entail any current expenditure of funds.

Accumulation of these annual charges is known as accrued depreciation. Under traditional regulation, accumulated depreciation is a deduction from the original cost of plant and other assets in determining the rate base of a carrier to which the authorized rate of return can be applied in calculating the return portion of the revenue requirement.

The specific choice of policy alternative does not obviate the need to allow for depreciation. For instance, depreciation expense must be computed for tax purposes, and the rate and method applied are separate and apart from those established for book and ratemaking purposes. Nevertheless, tax depreciation in excess of book may result in a significant addition to the funds flow of the firm. If these tax timing differences are normalized, significant deferred tax balances can be created. Deferred taxes, an asset, are usually deducted from rate base under the rationale that they represent an interest–free loan to the company and, therefore, should not earn a return for investors.

A variety of factors can affect a firm's rate of depreciation. For example, carriers' historical insulation from competition likely led to a depreciation reserve deficiency[65] in telecommunications that was estimated by the FCC in 1987 to range from $10 billion to $26 billion nationally.[66]

With the permissibility of entry in many telephone company markets, regulatory commissions have been forced to allow carriers to accelerate their capital recovery. Technology, too, impacts the depreciation process, shortening the economic life of embedded plant and making it more difficult for regulators and telephone companies to defer recovery of capital.

Countervailing considerations complicate the process: deferral of depreciation translates into lower rates in the short term, yet such a policy over the long run promotes inefficiency and yields inadequate capital recovery. In contrast, faster recovery prevents burdensome and costly deficiencies in the future but puts pressure on prices in the short term. Both regulated and unregulated firms must grapple with these considerations.

A second factor which all policy schemes must take into account is interconnection. As discussed in Chapter III, refusal by telephone companies to interconnect their individual networks caused chaos in the early days of communications. Despite the myriad changes of the 1980s, the need for access continues and, in fact, is critical to the future viability of competition in such markets as interexchange services, information services, and customer premises equipment. The interexchange "equal access" program instituted by the MFJ, the 1987 GTE–Justice Department consent decree, and the FCC, and the latter agency's ONA program for enhanced service provision demonstrate policy makers' cognizance of the importance of the function. Whether full regulation, total deregulation, or some alternative in between is adopted, interconnection is essential to the proper functioning of the U.S. (or any) telecommunications network.

8. General Observations

In virtually all cases where state governments have enacted legislation to change the way telephone companies should be regulated, the local commissions have retained their roles as the overseers of the carriers they regulate. At the same time that they have been directed to generally increase competition and relax regulation, these agencies have been given greater flexibility to deal with changes occurring within the industry. Their primary responsibilities appear to be the maintenance of universal service, protection of service quality from degradation, and ensuring that basic monopoly service ratepayers do not subsidize the competitive or unregulated offerings of carriers. Some public service commissions face "sunset" provisions; for example, the telecommunications portion of the Florida public utility law is currently scheduled to expire on October 1, 1989. In the majority of cases thus far, however, state legislatures appear to recognize the importance of commission oversight of local communications on an ongoing basis albeit with a new mandate.

We now turn our attention to the technological revolution of the 1980s and its implications for the public switched network. The next two chapters address the technological revitalization of the public network and the phenomenon called "bypass."

Notes

1. As a means of short hand reference, we will frequently use either rate base or rate of return regulation in this context.

2. For an evaluation of communications regulation historically, see W.G. Shepherd and C. Wilcox, *Public Policies Toward Business* (Homewood, Illinois: Richard D. Irwin, 1979), pp. 345–373.

3. *NTIA Regulatory Alternatives Report*, No. 87–222, issued July 1987, p. 5.

4. In 1981, Judge Greene's Court concluded that because of ineffective regulation by the FCC, AT&T was able to violate the antitrust laws in a number of ways over a long period of time with respect to interexchange services and equipment procurement. See *AT&T*, 552 F. Supp at 168, 170, and nn. 154, 155; *United States v. Am. Tel. & Tel. Co.*, 524 F. Supp. 1336, 1348–57, 1364–75.

5. A notable exception to Judge Greene's order was the ruling that the word "Bell" could be retained in the name of its world famous laboratories, Bell Labs.

6. *Slip Opinion, U.S. v. Western Electric Company, Inc., et. al.*, Civil Action No. 82–0192, filed September 10, 1987, at pp. 35–36.

7. *Slip Opinion* at p. 79.

8. *Slip Opinion, U.S. v. Western Electric Company, et al.*, Civil Action No. 82–0192, filed December 3, 1987.

9. *Id.*, p. 114.

10. *Id.*, p. 120.

11. *Id.* pp. 123–124.

12. *Id.*, p. 125.

13. ONA and CEI are two elements of the FCC's Third Computer Inquiry, a policy initiative which is currently attempting to replace CI2's separate subsidiary requirements with access, accounting, and other nonstructural conditions. See discussion *infra*.

14. *Id.*, pp. 138–143.

15. *Id.*, pp. 157–161.

16. *Id.*, pp. 173–203. This prohibition was reaffirmed in the MFJ Court's June 13, 1989 Opinion.

17. *Id.*, pp. 207–210.

18. *Slip Opinions, U.S. v. Western Electric Company, Inc., et al.*, Civil Action No. 82–0192, filed March 7, 1988 and June 13, 1989.

19. Including the nontelecommunications–related figures would boost the above tallies considerably. For example, the total number of waiver requests submitted (*i.e.*, telecommunications and "unrelated") as of February 20, 1988 was 182, and the total number of grants equaled 122.

20. See, *e.g.*, Douglas N. Jones, *A Perspective on Social Contract and Telecommunications Regulation*, NRRI–87–5, June 1987, p. 23.

21. In many state jurisdictions, yellow page profits are credited to basic services to offset the problem discussed.

22. Bands are currently used in such states as Washington and Michigan, and have been proposed in Florida.

23. See, *e.g.*, "Wisconsin Bell Asks PSC to Consider Price Regulation as Rate of Return Alternative," *Telecommunications Reports*, August 29, 1988, p. 45.

24. On March 11, 1987 the District Court issued a decision upholding the 1986 telecommunications law.   Opponents believed the deregulation bill is unconstitutional because it abdicates the PSC's constitutional responsibility to regulate utilities. Implementation of the new law was delayed until May 1987.

25. Nebraska Public Service Commission, *1987 Annual Report on Telecommunications to the Nebraska Unilateral Legislature*, January 5, 1988, p. 14.   See also *1988 Annual Report*, January 5, 1989, p. 2.

26. *Id.*, p. 53.

27. "Ceresco businessmen discuss phone changeover with LT&T," *Lincoln Star*, October 25, 1987.

28. "PSC: Ceresco should apply for more telephone service," *Lincoln Star*, February 17, 1988.

29. Letter dated February 19, 1988 from James E. Geist, LT&T President, to "Ceresco Customers."

30. "Ceresco citizens say town singled out," *Lincoln Journal-Star*, February 28, 1988.

31. Letter dated May 2, 1988 from Frank H. Hilsabeck, LT&T Executive Vice President, to Nebraska PSC.

32. *Id.*, p. 1.

33. *Id.*, p. 2.

34. An MSA is a marketing service area similar to a LATA, except that it is generally smaller in its geographical area.

35. *In the Matter of Policy and Rules Concerning Rates for Competitive Common Carrier Services and Facilities Authorizations Therefor*, First Report and Order, 85 FCC 2d 1 (1980), CC Docket 79–252.

36. *Computer Use of Communications Facilities*, 28 FCC 2d 267 (1971).

37. See, for example, *U.S. Transmission Systems, Inc.*, 48 FCC 2d 859 (1974); *ITT Domestic Transmissions, Inc.*, 62 FCC 2d 236 (1976); *Communications Satellite Corporation*, 45 FCC 2d 444 (1974); *CML Satellite Corporation*, 51 FCC 2d 14 (1975); *RCA Global Communications*, 56 FCC 2d 660 (1975); and *Satellite Business Systems, et. al.*, 62 FCC 2d 997 (1977); *GTE-Telenet Merger*, 72 FCC 2d 111 recon., 72 FCC 2d 516, *recon. denied*, 84 FCC 2d 18 (1979); *Comsat Study*, 77 FCC 2d 564 (1980); *Amsat-Fairchild-Continental Joint Venture*, 80 FCC 2d 254 (1980); *Second Computer Inquiry*, Tentative Decision, 72 FCC 2d 358 (1977), *Final Decision*, 77 FCC 2d 384 (1980) (Final Decision), *reconsideration*, 84 FCC 2d 50 (1980), *further reconsideration*, 88 FCC 2d 512 (1981), *aff'd sub. nom.*, *CCIA v. FCC*, 693 F. 2d 198 (D.C. Cir. 1982) *cert. denied*, 461 U.S. 938 (1983) *aff'd on second further reconsideration*, FCC 84–190 (released May 4, 1984).

38. *Notice of Inquiry and Proposed Rulemaking (Notice)*, 61 FCC 2d 103 (1976); *Supplemental Notice of Inquiry and Enlargement of Proposed Rulemaking (Supplemental Notice)*, 64 FCC 2d 771 (1977); and *Tentative Decision and Further Notice of Inquiry and Rulemaking (Tentative Decision)*, 72 FCC 2d 358 (1977).

39. *Amendment of Section 64.702 of the Commission's Rules and Regulations (Second Computer)* 77 FCC 2d 384 (1980) *(Final Decision)*, *reconsideration*, 84 FCC 2d 50 (1980), *further reconsideration*, 88 FCC 2d 512 (1981), *aff'd sub. nom. CCIA v. FCC*, 693 F. 2d 198 (D.C. Cir. 1982) *cert. denied*, 461 U.S. 938 (1983) *aff'd on second further reconsideration*, FCC 84–190 (released May 4, 1984).

40. 84 FCC 2d 72 (1980).

41. *Memorandum Opinion and Order*, FCC 83–74, released February 25, 1983.

42. *Report and Order*, CC Docket No. 80–742, FCC 83–601, released January 16, 1984.

43. *Further Reconsideration Order,* 88 FCC 2d 547 (1981).

44. Initially, the states were empowered by the Commission to determine the need for structural separation requirements for independent carriers consistent with the terms of the Computer II decisions. *Memorandum Opinion and Order,* FCC 84–190 released May 4, 1984. Subsequently, the FCC preempted this ability. *Memorandum Opinion and Order,* adopted November 25, 1986.

45. *Report and Order,* CC Docket No. 83–115, 95 FCC 2d 1117 (1984) (*BOC Separation Order*).

46. *Id.,* 1139.

47. *Memorandum Opinion and Order* (Reconsideration), FCC 84–252, released June 1, 1984.

48. *Id.*

49. This removal pertains to the entities' CPE and enhanced services operations.   Structural separation requirements still apply to the Regional Companies' cellular telephone businesses.

50. Both CEI and ONA are vaguely defined at present.   CEI is an interim concept that seeks to provide a mechanism for equal interconnection for enhanced service providers; it is generally regarded as "service specific" in nature and not unbundled to the extent envisioned for ONA.   Similarly, ONA is a nebulous concept that broadly encompasses the notion that a local exchange carrier offers (on a nondiscriminatory basis) elements of its network *at any level* needed by its customers, especially respecting provision of enhanced services.

51. "Information services" are the offering of a capability for the generation, acquisition, storage, transformation, processing, retrieval, utilization, or making available information which may be conveyed by telecommunications, *e.g.,* videotext, some forms of electronic mail, electronic publishing services, data processing services, telephone–operated burglar alarm systems, and some office management systems.   Such services do not include any use of any such capability for the management, control or operation of a telecommunications system or management of a telecommunications service. Decree, Section IV (J).   See also Opinion, filed December 13, 1984, *U.S. v. GTE* (D.D.C.), n. 46.

52. See *United States v. AT&T,* 552 F. Supp. 131, 187 (D.D.C. 1982), *aff'd. sub nom. Maryland v. U.S.,* 103 S. Ct. 1240 (1983).

53. *United States v. Western Electric and AT&T,* Civil Action No. 82–0192.

54. *Slip Opinion* at 46.

55. *Id.* at 48–58.

56. *Complaint,* filed May 4, 1983, *U.S. v. GTE.*

57. *Slip Opinion, U.S. v. GTE Corporation,* Civil Action No. 83–1298, filed December 13, 1984, p. 16.

58. That year, Congress passed legislation that eventually caused AT&T to sell its TWX operations to Western Union in 1971.

59. 77 FCC 2d at 428–29; 84 FCC 2d at 99.

60. See 88 FCC 2d at n. 34.

61. *Order,* CC Docket No. 86–79, adopted November 25, 1986.

62. *Stipulation,* Dockets U–83–55 and U–83–76, released October 12, 1984.

63. See, "Report on Alternative Regulatory Frameworks for Local Exchange Carriers, Phase II" (*Report*), Docket I. 87–11–033, by Division of Ratepayer Advocates, California Public Utilities Commission, September 19, 1988.

64. See Section 7 of *Report.*

65. This deficiency reflects the difference between what regulators have allowed as a depreciation expense and what should have derived using economic concepts of depreciation.

66. FCC, *Report on Telephone Industry Depreciation, Tax, and Capital/Expense Policy* (Washington, D.C.: FCC, 1987)y

CHAPTER V

NETWORK TECHNOLOGICAL REVITALIZATION

A. Introduction

Although the ubiquitous use of digital technology in telecommunications may be considered to be in its start–up phase, substantial costs have already been expended to prepare and equip telephone company networks to handle perceived "Information Age" demand. For instance, it is virtually a foregone conclusion in the U.S. that by the mid to late 1990s most of the telcos' end offices will contain digital switches. At the end of 1987 almost one–third of the nation's switches were digital offices as can be seen in Table V–1. This was up from 13 percent in 1984 and growth continued through 1988 as the relative number of BOCs' digital switches increased to 34 percent from 22 percent in 1987. Digital switches are even more prominent for independent telephone companies. In 1988, 51 percent of local switches were digital which served 61 percent of the access lines of the ten largest independents.

Future growth may even accelerate as fiber in the loop is deployed and the Integrated Services Digital Network (ISDN) becomes the reality touted by the BOCs and other telephone companies. The cost to develop and market a new digital switch is not trivial, amounting to over one billion dollars. Special features such as equal access, ISDN, and Centrex can substantially inflate this figure by a factor of from 2.5 to 3.5.[1]

The level of investment in transmission facilities and switching equipment over the past five years has no precedent. Indeed, the capacity and capabilities of the carrier network now becoming available with regard to future revenue generation is staggering. These potentialities must be similarly viewed as an imposing competitive advantage by new entrants.

Of the over $70 billion spent by the BOCs in the U.S. since divestiture, more than half was spent on relatively new technologies. These include optical fiber transmission systems and new digital switching facilities. As a result, carriers now have in place easily expandable modular switching systems, and transmission systems whose capacity in many instances is "dependent only on the equipment at each end."[2]

The telecommunications industry has experienced substantial growth along with rapid technological changes over the last several decades. New firms have entered the industry, bringing consumers differentiated and new products and services. At the same time the productive and communications capacity of the industry has expanded greatly. The open entry policies implemented by the Federal Communications Commission (FCC) and, more recently, the divestiture of the Bell Operating Companies (BOCs) from the integrated Bell System in 1984 have created new opportunities for industry growth and expansion.

From what was once a reasonably well defined telecommunications system, a market structure has evolved that is rapidly changing, complex and some–

Table V–1

CENTRAL OFFICE TECHNOLOGY
Share of U.S. Total

Central Offices	1984	1985	1986	1987
Step–by–Step	47.3%	45.8%	40.0%	38.7%
Cross Bar	15.6	13.0	11.1	10.7
Electronic–Analog	24.2	19.5	19.8	18.2
Electronic–Digital	13.0	21.6	29.0	32.4
	100.0%	100.0%	100.0%	100.0%

Source: Bethesda Research Institute, Ltd. (BRI), estimates.

what amorphous. Few among suppliers, major telecommunications users, and new entrants have a solid basis upon which to formulate market plans, let alone design their strategic initiatives.   The forging of alliances with long distance manufacturing, research and even foreign entities hinges on assessments that are technological, demand, and regulatory sensitive.

The local network portion of the industry is at the same time both the most historically stable area of the market and the area of most opportunity. In a sense, local exchange is the "last frontier" and is about to undergo the technological, demand, entity, and market adjustment pressures that have already passed through manufacturing, long distance and terminal equipment areas of the network.

B. The Local Network

Prior to the 1980s and the onslaught of extensive telecommunications competition, the "telephone network" was largely synonymous with the local and long distance telecommunications services and facilities provided by the predivestiture Bell System and its independent telephone company partners. But with the dismantlement of the Bell System in 1984 and entry of both domestic and foreign service providers, traditional notions of an integrated, fully compatible and coordinated network must be reviewed and revised. No longer may users look to do "one stop shopping" with a sole supplier of services and facilities nationwide.   This is particularly evident in the "last mile" area of reaching to and from connected points, namely, local exchange markets.

In a general sense, any distribution system (transportation, communication, water, energy, or even financial credit) may be viewed as a system of interconnected elements. More pointedly, networks may be conceived as a set of nodes or distribution centers, combined with a set of links that interconnect individual pairs of nodes.[3] While economies result even when subsets of nodes are combined, least cost scenarios are likely to occur when discrete facilities can be utilized in common for the array of potential subscribers thereby furnishing access to many widely dispersed locations and possible uses.

A singular concept of product flow or traffic is also essential to defining telecommunications and other networks. Generally, "traffic" may be viewed as the flow of a particular quantity of output through a network.[4] Often times, traffic units can consist of multiple dimensions. For instance, telecommunications traffic may consist of ordinary telephone voice conversations or more complex units such as data, video and audio transmissions. These distinctions may stem from facility capabilities or be more intrinsic.[5]

Combining the general notion of a network with the special case of providing telecommunications transmission permits at least a broad definition of a communications network, namely, a system of interconnected, and possibly disparate, facilities designed to carry voice, data, and other traffic units between a multiplicity of users, locations and services for a variety of ultimate uses. Within this broad perspective, telecommunications networks can be further disaggregated from two additional, related viewpoints. First, telecommunications distribution systems may be examined in terms of their physical components. From this vantage, analyses may proceed toward the concept of a "facilities network." Considering economic factors as predominant, the analytical tool of a facilities network may be viewed as production or supply–side oriented.

Alternatively, telecommunications distribution may be examined in terms of the variety of industry services that are provided. This second view is consistent with the concept of telecommunications distribution as a traffic directed network,[6] and is demand or service oriented. From this vantage, a common ubiquitous system would be simply the interconnected set of traffic networks sharing common facilities. Individual traffic networks, in turn, would subsume the variety of arrangements of communications channels, such as local loops and trunks, certain switching arrangements, and station equipment, that are designed to handle specific types of traffic.

A facilities network consists of three physical components, namely: (1) station equipment; (2) transmission facilities; and (3) switching systems. Of course, station equipment, usually located on the customer's premises, allows the user to initially access network services. Transmission facilities consist of various transmission mediums (e.g., paired cable, coaxial cable, or optical fiber) and electronic equipment located at points along the transmission path that transport information between and among various points or nodes of the network. Much of the electronic equipment of a facilities system is devoted to only maintaining the integrity of the communications signals transported by transmission plant.

Finally, switching systems perform the function of interconnecting transmission facilities at various locations and under different operating conditions within the facilities network and also routing traffic through the distribution stages. Increasingly, program controlled digital facilities are performing the switching task. This is shown by Figure V–1, which is a graphical representation of the telephone system as it is used for message (switched) services.

Figure V–1

PLANT USED FOR MESSAGE SERVICES

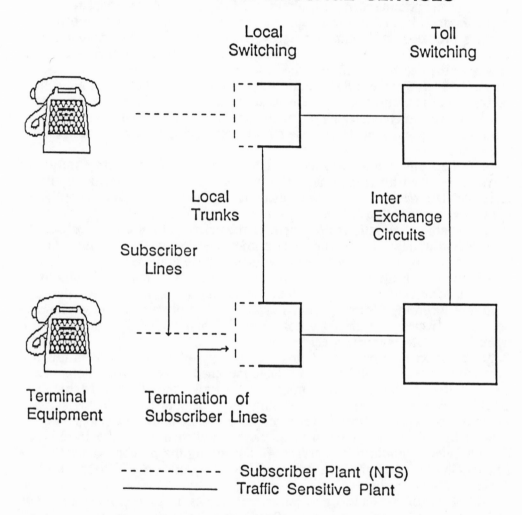

Local
Switching

Toll
Switching

Local
Trunks

Inter
Exchange
Circuits

Subscriber
Lines

Terminal
Equipment

Termination of
Subscriber Lines

— — — — — — Subscriber Plant (NTS)
—————— Traffic Sensitive Plant

Notably, it shows that the local network portion of the system excludes functions that embody toll switching, interexchange circuits, and associated trunks between local and toll switches. While not important from a facilities view, of course, station equipment (customer provided equipment or CPE) is no longer provided as a part of the basic services offered by local exchange companies (LECs) in this country.

Prior to divestiture, one could easily delineate several major traffic networks distributions systems that used facilities on both a shared and dedicated basis. These included: (1) the Public Switched Telephone Network (PSTN); (2) Private Line Voice Networks; (3) Private Line Data Networks; and (4) Program Networks. The PSTN is defined in terms of various switched network services that constitute the bulk of traditional business and residential telephone traffic.   More specifically, these services include: local exchange "plain old telephone service" (POTS); ordinary telephone toll (Message Telecommunications Service or MTS); Wide Area Telecommunications Service (WATS; In WATS or its successor, 800 Service); supplemental services provided by the direct services' dialing capability; Automated Calling Card Service; DIAL–IT network communications service (900 Service); and services provided by circuit switched digital capability.   The various types of traffic carried by the PSTN basically represent potential communications between any two end points in the switched network.   The PSTN furnishes a capability for interconnecting virtually any home or office in the country with any other with the shared use of common facilities being its key essential attribute.

Private Line Voice Networks (PLVN) refer to the telecommunications services provided by circuits and, sometimes, switching arrangements, dedicated for the exclusive use of one customer or a group of allied users.   These networks can be nationwide in scope and typically provide voice communications for large corporations or government agencies.   PLVN services may be switched or nonswitched.   The most numerous, unsophisticated nonswitched private line networks are point–to–point in nature and may serve as few as two stations.   Multipoint networks interconnect a number of stations at different locations and may include signalling arrangements to alert the station of incoming communications.   Nonswitched private line networks may be interconnected at carrier central offices, although they are not switched through associated switching equipment.

In addition to nonswitched private line networks, the predivestiture Bell System provided several thousand private switched voice networks to governments and large business customers.   The trunks and lines used by these dedicated systems are private line circuits that interconnect switching systems either at a customer's location, for example, a private branch exchange (PBX), or at a central office.   Examples of private switched networks include the Federal Telecommunications Service (FTS) serving the civilian agencies of the Federal Government and the Automatic Voice Network (AUTOVON) serving the United States military.

Other traffic based distribution arrangements include private line data networks and program networks.   Data networks provide channels for data transmission at various speeds and bandwidths.   Such systems also encompass telegraph channels.   Program networks are designed for radio and television broadcasters to distribute program material simultaneously to a number of affiliated stations.   Program networks also share transmission facilities with other private networks and the PSTN.

At divestiture, the PSTN constituted the largest traffic based distribution arrangement in terms of both equipment utilization and "through–put" or volume in the predivestiture Bell System.   Given its quantitative significance for Bell at that time, the PSTN was often loosely viewed as synonymous with the nation's telephone facilities prior to 1984.   The PSTN effectively included both the facilities used to provide ordinary local exchange service and the switching and transmission facilities used to provide long distance telephone service.

Referencing Figure V–1, note that in terms of facilities the "local network" encompassed station equipment located on the customer's premises, which was connected by loop plant to a local switching system situated in a central office. The predivestiture local network may also have included one or more tandem switches that served any given exchange area. The Bell System toll network also utilized a toll switching hierarchy that interconnected all independent and Bell System local telephone companies to provide long distance switching and transmission.

The 1984 breakup of the Bell System effectively formalized the separation of the toll traffic distribution from the local network. Divestiture also created an industry structure where exchange area networks supply local exchange discrete access and local concentration and distribution services to multiple interexchange carriers, enhanced service providers, and end users. In particular, the FCC's open entry policies, together with divestiture, have resulted in an industry organization where multiple exchange carriers interconnect (but do not necessarily integrate) with many types of users, including both private and public interexchange carriers.

C. The Economics of Technological Advancements

1. First Costs

At the present time, the outlook appears to be favorable for the input prices that telephone companies must pay when they install new plant and equipment. This is true, in part, because newer technologies, such as digital switching and digital transmission over optical fiber cables, are frequently much less expensive relative to plant capacities than are the older technologies. In most major telephone companies digital technology is supplanting analog applications in both toll and local networks, fundamentally affecting switching, transmission, and terminal equipment as the carriers are actively evolving their public switched networks toward the ISDN.

Broadly speaking, ISDN is an engineering concept that contemplates a public, end–to–end switched digital network in which time division switches and digital transmission paths accommodate multiple services originating at subscriber locations. It will eventually be able to accommodate such broadband applications as video and high speed data, in addition to standard voice, medium speed data, facsimile and telemetry services.

The BOCs have undertaken dozens of ISDN trials, and orders from customers have exceeded 50,000 lines. Several BOCs have been more aggressive and have already tariffed services that utilize the ISDN concept. Essential elements for the widescale evolution of ISDN are digital switching and fiber optics transmission. The rate of investment in such facilities has been extraordinary since divestiture, involving a level of expenditure suited less to demand growth rates than strategic market designs.

As noted above, one crucial result of the telcos' investment strategies is that the proportion of switching systems that are digital has climbed dramatically.   Optical fiber transmission facilities have shown rapid expansion as well.   From 1984 to September 1988 the BOCs experienced an increase from 239,000 fiber miles to about 1,400,000 fiber miles. The total of 1.4 million fiber miles represents a 23 percent increase over year–end 1987 figures.   In fact, as recently as 1982, there was virtually no fiber in service.   This growth is shown graphically by Figure V–2.

Telephone carriers have recognized the economic advantages of this technology from the outset. For example, in its application to the FCC for authority to construct one of the earliest digital systems, which was a route between Washington and Boston, AT&T pointed out that "constructing a lightwave system was about 20 percent less expensive than the alternative of increasing the capacity of existing analog facilities."[7]

One of the major sources of savings cited in that application was the reduced requirement for signal regeneration.   Repeater spacing at the time (1983) was seven kilometers, which is not competitive with today's standards for optical cable, but was a substantial improvement over the existing system, eliminating the need for outside plant electronics on many of the short haul links.

Another important source of savings was fiber's efficient use of very expensive duct space in metropolitan areas.   A single fiber operating at a data transmission rate of 45 megabits per second (Mb/s) could replace 28 copper pairs that operated at the old rate of 1.5 Mb/s.

The introduction of fiber optics into the network has not been completed, of course, especially in the local exchange. The majority of switches are still not capable of being easily integrated into the ISDN applications, and most transmission plant is still not fiber, so more investment will be required in the future. But the costs of new installations are declining rapidly, to the point that even the cost advantages AT&T attributed to digital systems in 1983 now seem insignificant. This is due primarily to the fact that increased use of fiber cable has allowed manufacturers to achieve significant economies.

Economies of production for fiber optics are apparent from the history of manufacturers' prices for fiber cable.[8]   In 1980, the price of single mode fiber was averaging $2.62 per cabled fiber meter. But, it costs less than one–tenth of that today, and most observers expect continued price reductions. Officials responsible for the production process at AT&T, where costs have been reduced by increasing the "draw rate" (the speed at which fiber is drawn through the furnace) to more than 10 meters per second without any degrada–tion in fiber performance, say "the technology is not fully mature and it is likely that even higher rates should be achievable."[9]

A report for NASA prepared by IGI Consulting, Inc., predicts that cable costs will go as low as $.12 per meter by 1995. New England Telephone is predicting that fiber prices in 1994 will be only half as high as they were in 1986.[10] Southwestern Bell is forecasting annual price reductions of 10 to 15

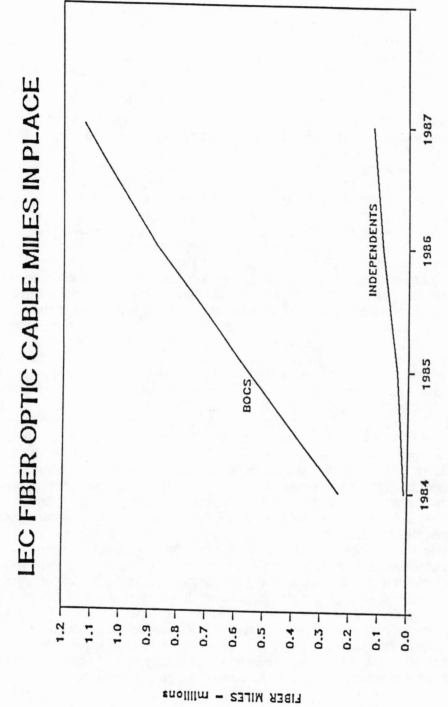

Figure V-2

LEC FIBER OPTIC CABLE MILES IN PLACE

Source: Communications News, August 1987, p. 36.

percent for fiber cable over the next five years, as well as annual reductions of 10 to 15 percent in prices of digital loop carrier systems, 15 to 20 percent in optical device prices, and 37 percent in laser prices.[11]

Randall Park, of Lightguide Systems, also forecasts a decline in prices for terminal equipment for fiber systems, due in part to the fact that manufacturers' input prices have been going down. High quality LEDs, for example, have dropped in price from $200 to $10 in recent years.[12]

Digital switching costs are also declining, having fallen 17 percent in the last three years.[13] While this is not as impressive as the savings in fiber costs, the outlook for switching equipment is good. The market is very fragmented, leading Daniel Kelley, senior economic analyst for MCI, to conclude that "the equipment local carriers buy is going to fall in price."[14]

The cost effectiveness of digital switches is derived from the economies and efficiencies associated with electronic technology, e.g., the availability of solid state technology. The establishment of a digital network has also resulted in network administration efficiencies with development of the Common Channel Interoffice Signaling (CCIS) system, which enables call set-up to be implemented over independent packet circuits. To see this, consider that with the analog network call paths are established sequentially through the voice path from origination to destination. Each step of the network is utilized in order to provide ringing to the called party. The entire network is used even if the call is unanswered for whatever reason.

CCIS, on the other hand, utilizes a unique packet switching path for signaling alone which is independent of the voice path from origination to destination. Calls are momentarily held until signaling is completed at the termination point, and only then is the call put through if the called party is available. If not, the call is terminated without having used the network and, thereby, facilitating its more efficient use. Other advantages accrue to the telcos with the implementation of CCIS. These are: faster call set-up and take-down which reduces post-dialing delay and reduces trunk and switching equipment holding times; increased information carrying capacity that permits new and improved customer services; 2-way signaling; compatibility with international signaling; improved reliability of address information; and improved flexibility.

Table V-2 shows how the initial cost of digital switches compares with other technologies. The substantially lower cost per line and per CCS more than offset the high fixed cost of digital switches. (Table V-3 shows how the per line cost of digital switching comes down as the size of the central office increases.) Another estimate of switching costs is that with analog technology the cost is $220 per line versus $190 for digital.[15] An Ameritech study found that over an eight year period one vendor tripled its digital switches' processing power, reduced power consumption and physical size by 40 percent, yet was able to lower the cost of the switch by 20 percent.[16]

2. Operating Costs

Carriers' operating costs are also experiencing a downward trend. This

Table V–2

COMPARISON OF ANALOG AND DIGITAL SWITCH COSTS
Analog Growth Versus Conversion to Digital
($000)

	5,000 Lines	10,000 Lines	20,000 Lines
Digital			
5ESS: Host	$ 2,395	$ 3,510	$ 5,740
5ESS: Remote	1,400	––	––
DMS – 10	1,265	––	––
DMS – 100: Host	1,841	3,036	5,426
DMS – 100: Remote	1,149	––	––
Analog			
5XBAR	2,875	5,750	––
Step–by–Step	3,190	––	––
Electronic	1,095	2,190	4,380

Source: New England Telephone Company submission in D.P.U. 86–33 and BRI estimates.

may be due, in part, to the newer technologies, especially the lower provisioning and maintenance costs associated with fiber optics and digital switches.[17]

There are operating savings that carriers expect to derive from technological changes which are particularly impressive. The evolution to a digital network means both a reduction in current costs and an increase in capacity, which may lead, in turn, to future economic benefits, through increased revenues and lower costs for expanding and rearranging the system.

The savings in current costs manifest themselves in virtually every area of operation.[18] For example, power costs are reduced due to the low power consumption of fiber systems. Installation costs are also lower because of the lower number of repeater sites, and because cables are small and lightweight, require less security protection, and can be converted from one type of use to another merely by changing electronics.

In addition, the lower number of repeater sites also leads to savings in maintenance costs, which are even further reduced because optical cables are less susceptible to corrosion and electrical or radio interference. Moreover, the greater processing power of the digital switches used with optical cables offers opportunities for automatic remote diagnostics, as well as automatic records keeping and traffic monitoring, all of which contribute to maintenance

Table V–3

DIGITAL CENTRAL OFFICE INVESTMENT
Comparisons of Per Line Costs for Various Office Sizes
($000)

Lines	AT&T No. 5ESS	Northern Telecom DMS–100
1,000	$ 1,503	$ 885
2,000	863	562
3,000	650	454
4,000	543	401
5,000	479	368
6,000	436	347
7,000	406	331
8,000	383	320
9,000	365	311
10,000	351	304
11,000	339	298
12,000	330	293
13,000	321	289
14,000	314	285
15,000	308	282
16,000	303	279
17,000	298	277
18,000	294	275
19,000	290	273
20,000	287	271

Source: New England Telephone Company submission in D.P.U. 86–33 and BRI
estimates.

savings.[19] For instance, the New England Telephone Company, which has extensively studied the relative cost savings, reports that "the fiber system maintenance costs were approximately one–fifth those of the copper cable facilities."[20]

It has been noted by many observers in the industry that investment in new technologies by LECs has resulted in substantial productivity gains and cost reductions. In this regard, the Ameritech study noted above found that since 1950 the number of employees required to support 10,000 access lines steadily decreased from 300 to less than 50 in 1985.[21] During this period, one–sixth as many employees were able to service six times as many calls.

The substitution of capital for labor was the reason cited for the improvements in productivity.

Lower operating and maintenance costs also are cited by the industry as being benefits of digital switches. Reasons for this are: less moving parts; increased processing speed per unit of traffic; reduced number of operators with the advent of automated directory and credit card functions; automated recordkeeping and remote diagnostic routines; improved traffic data tracking capability; and increased reliability. Also, the deployment of digital switches provides greater opportunities for the offering of new services and features although it has not yet been demonstrated that sufficient demand will be realized.

Efficiency and productivity measures can also be seen on Tables V–4 and 5. The first exhibit depicts revenues per telephone employee from 1984 to 1988 for the major LECs and indicates substantial improvements in the measurement. For the RHCs, increases over the time period range from 18 percent (Ameritech) to almost 37 percent (BellSouth) with an average of about 29 percent. Thus, it would appear that LECs have been able to improve their revenue per employee streams during the turmoil that has followed divestiture, including any revenues lost to bypass. Whether this is a reaction to perceived competition is not clear, but the results do point out the LECs' ability to remain viable. It is also interesting to note that the comparable revenue per employee in Japan was only $64,000 in 1984, or about two–thirds of the U.S. figure. This suggests that U.S. LECs may be operating more efficiently than their Japanese counterparts.

Table V–5 shows an overall increase in access lines per telephone employee for the LECs from 1984 to 1988 of about 22 percent. The average in 1984 was about 156 lines per employee which increased to 191 in 1988. Thus, LECs in the U.S. have been able to provide and service more access lines with less employees since 1984.

3. Fixed Cost Facilities

The declining cost of fiber optic cable is not the only aspect of the new technologies from which the entrenched dominant carriers are deriving a cost advantage. In fact, the savings that these firms are experiencing from technical improvements are even more impressive than the reductions in manufacturers' equipment prices.

Even before AT&T's digital system for the northeast corridor was in place, longer wavelength laser systems had been introduced. These reduced the signal loss in fibers, and, as a result, increased the repeater spacing from 7 kilometers to 25 kilometers. In the first year of the route's operation (1984), the carrier added these longer wavelength lasers in the corridor, permitting AT&T to skip three–fourths of the repeaters anticipated by the original plan. At the same time, system capacity was increased threefold by adding wavelength–division multiplexing.[22]

Technical improvements have not slowed since 1984. Continuing "research and development of discrete lightwave sources and detectors has improved the

Table V–4

TELEPHONE COMPANIES
Revenues Per Employee
($000)

	1984	1985	1986	1987	1988
Ameritech	$ 108	$ 119	$ 123	$ 122	$ 127
Bell Atlantic	102	115	126	133	134
BellSouth	101	114	122	126	138
NYNEX	101	112	126	130	131
Pacific Telesis	102	115	123	125	134
Southwestern Bell	100	111	114	119	128
U S West	103	111	120	126	133
GTE	87	96	105	109	117
Cincinnati Bell	91	97	103	113	94
SNET	94	100	106	108	116
Contel	72	75	83	88	95
United	78	84	91	103	82
Centel	95	95	100	104	110

Source: Annual Reports.

Table V–5

TELEPHONE COMPANIES
Lines Per Employee

	1984	1985	1986	1987	1988
Ameritech	193	205	207	210	215
Bell Atlantic	189	207	211	218	224
BellSouth	158	175	187	196	205
NYNEX	148	164	183	182	193
Pacific Telesis	149	167	171	185	198
Southwestern Bell	157	166	179	186	196
U S West	165	172	191	202	205
GTE	116	123	128	135	146
Cincinnati Bell	159	162	169	174	186
SNET	124	131	130	137	147
Contel	94	97	98	109	107
United	137	147	156	172	181
Centel	––	155	168	182	193

Source: Annual Reports.

performance and lowered the cost of current transmission systems."[23] The standard measure of optical capabilities is the product of bit rate and repeater spacing. This measure shows continued improvement. Repeaterless spans of 40 kilometers are now "typical with transmission rates up to about 420 Mb/s,"[24] and "repeaterless span lengths between 55 and 60 km are possible."[25]

The record of bit rates times repeater spacing, as that measure applies to systems in commercial use, is shown by Figure V–3. Notably, the vertical scale for the figure is exponential, reflecting the fact that the improvements have been exponential and it is impractical to capture these on a linear measure. In fact, this parameter has actually improved by a factor of ten approximately every three years, while the cost of optical fiber capacity has been decreasing at a similar rate. The resultant unit cost reductions are illustrated by the same figure.

At the end of 1987, the fastest operating commercial system in the United States was the AT&T link between central offices in Oakbrook and Plano, Illinois, on which four lines operating at 417 Mb/s are multiplexed, to yield a combined transmission rate of 1.7 Gb/s. U.S. Sprint has a 1.13 Gb/s system in operation between Relay, Maryland, and Washington, D.C. It is the first leg in a 568 mile route that will eventually reach from Relay to Fairfax, South Carolina. And MCI has recently installed a similar system in a 969 mile route connecting Chicago to Longview, Texas, via St. Louis and Memphis.[26]

This progress is very likely to continue well into the future. "The trend is for transmission costs to continue to drop rapidly, so high–capacity transport will be available at relatively low costs."[27] As IGI reports to NASA, "optimistically, bit rates may continue to double every year... to ...something on the order of 400 gigabits per second [400,000 Mb/s] by 2000."[28] Such achievements are incredible, from a historical perspective. IGI avers that realizing these figures "seems unlikely," but A. Javed and P. MacLaren of Northern Telecom find that the transmission rate is indeed expected to continue to double every year. They point out that "a single mode fiber can support in the order of 100,000 GHz of bandwidth" and "presently perceived transmission systems of the near–future would exploit less than 0.005 percent (4.8 Gb/s) of this tremendous fiber capability."[29] Experimental developments are still well ahead of present commercial applications and this progress shows no sign of slowing.

IGI acknowledges that, "fiber optic cable potential capacity is very large, and the capacity limit has not yet been defined, much less realized." But the report also delineates what the authors consider to be a more realistic forecast of technical capabilities. Yet, even this forecast projects transmission rates to reach 8.1 Gb/s by the end of the century, with repeater spacing of 250 kilometers.[30] The conclusion reached was that, "the larger cables may not be used to their maximum capacity during their installation lifetime (20 years)."[31]

Switching capacities have also been increasing, though not quite as rapidly as the cable capacities. Patrick White of Bellcore reported that, "The

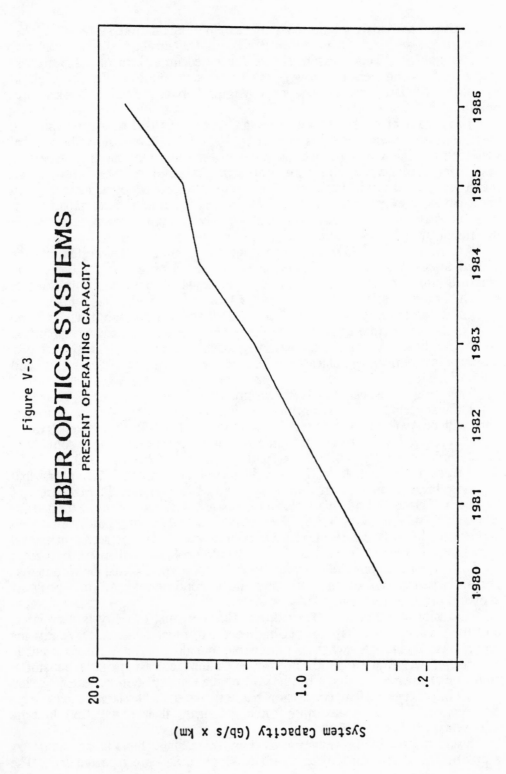

Figure V-3

FIBER OPTICS SYSTEMS
PRESENT OPERATING CAPACITY

1ESS switch, first introduced in the mid 1960s, could process 115,000 calls per hour, while its successor, 1AESS handles 240,000 calls per hour. Current generation digital switches, such as the DMS100 can process 330,000 calls per hour."[32]

Implications of these prognoses for telephone companies, among other things, include a rapidly increasing revenue generating capacity in the network with minimal additional investment. Even the topology of the network can be simplified, reducing the amount of transmission cable required to serve a given configuration of nodes. This stems from the fact that the high bandwidth and low regeneration requirements of fiber have made route costs less sensitive to distance, so circuitous routes can be used, patching large amounts of traffic through intermediate switches.[33]

An example of the economies associated with new technologies can be seen on Figure V–4 which shows how fiber optic costs vary with the cross section size of cable. For comparative purposes the data is presented for circuit lengths of one and five kilometers. The graph clearly demonstrates that economies occur as the cable cross section increases. However, there is a point where the unit cost effectively stabilizes such that there is virtually no difference in costs from one cross section to the next. As expected, the cost for a five kilometer circuit exceeds that of a one kilometer circuit. The difference between the two narrows as the number of circuits increases. For instance, at a cross section of 240 the ratio is 2.0 to one whereas at 2,016 circuits the ratio is 1.2 to one.

D. Technological Advancements: Transmission

1. Fiber Optics

Telecommunications firms are the largest users of fiber optics technology by far in the United States. Most of these are carriers (or carriers' carriers) and for these companies, fiber is utilized as a backbone medium on major routes for the transmission of their customers' voice and data communications traffic. To date, fiber has mainly been deployed for toll markets with a growing emphasis on the use of fiber in the high density interoffice and feeder portions of the local exchange. Fiber applications in the loop that link customers directly to the switched network are likely to remain the area of least application in the near future. However, as the economics of fiber facilities continue to improve, as indicated by declining production costs of the cable technology, associated electronics and other related factors, fiber will increasingly appear as the medium of choice in the distribution portion of local outside plant. This bodes quite well for suppliers of fiber since, in terms of mileage, about 90 percent of potential circuit usage of fiber is in the local loop.

If it is assumed that fiber will be the most preferred transmission medium in the local loop in the future, revenues from new services and applications must be found to assist in the initial financial support of fiber in the distri-

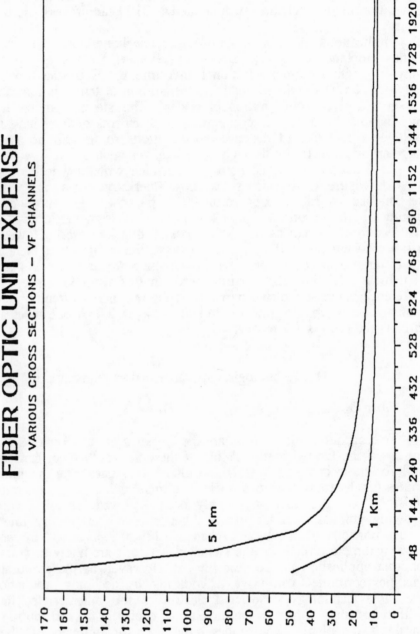

Figure V-4

FIBER OPTIC UNIT EXPENSE

VARIOUS CROSS SECTIONS — VF CHANNELS

bution portion of the loop. That is, carrying costs to fund new construction must be covered until the full benefits and savings associated with improved production, installation, and maintenance are realized at higher traffic loads. Available evidence suggests that the potential for these new revenues may presently exist. Thus, under the right marketing and regulatory conditions, the central office digital switching implementation strategies now being undertaken by most local exchange telephone companies can be realized in certain markets and will assure favorable prospects for fiber loops.

At the present time, telecommunications firms account for some 70 to 85 percent of the United States fiber optics market. Program, voice, and data transmission are among the activities employing fiber optics, in both local and wide area systems. As noted above, telephone entities have made much greater application of fiber optic facilities in the toll area, especially along key north/south and transcontinental traffic corridors. For instance, it is estimated that less than 20 percent of installed fiber is used for local transmission.[34]

Additional evidence of this distribution pattern can be gleaned from a comparison of the growth of installed fiber optic miles of the Regional Bell Operating Companies (RBOCs) *vis-à-vis* those of the major interexchange carriers (ICs) such as AT&T, MCI, and US Sprint. For example, from 1985 to 1986, RBOCs' fiber miles increased by 72 percent, whereas IC fiber miles grew by 99 percent, with both having approximately the same installed base in 1985. Notably, the majority of the RBOCs' installations have been for inter-office trunking, with increasing emphasis on the high density feeder line portion of the local loop.

The most optimistic projections of new investments in optical cable transmission for long distance services by the end of the decade foresee installations of about six billion dollars in additional facilities. This added investment in fiber is expected to boost the nation's toll capacity by a factor of at least five for the public switched long distance network. It is also anticipated that this construction will spur further local carrier investment. For instance, about $1.0 billion was spent by the BOCs to install fiber during the 1987–1988 period alone to take advantage of and work in concert with the interexchange facilities that are in place and those soon to be added.[35] By 1997 it is expected that $1.3 billion will be spent in that year alone.[36]

This part of the section will discuss the economics of fiber in the local loop, inclusive of the "last mile" or distribution portion. However, during the early implementation phase of fiber placement in the loop, economics alone may not be sufficient to justify installation. Thus, additional revenue sources obtained from services that appeal to and meet the needs of users will be required. Stated another way, if fiber in the "last mile" is not economically feasible for local telephone companies initially, then new services must be developed that attract customers and help support new plant additions during the start–up period. Of course, another, and perhaps more likely, outcome is that basic service ratepayers will have to bear the burden of new technology costs without obtaining any significant benefits. Once construction is well under way, economic forces such as production efficiencies, operating economies, and "learning curve" factors will be realized and may provide net overall benefits to the telephone companies for their decisions to deploy this technology on a broad scale.

a. Fiber in the Local Loop

The local loop is the link between customer premises equipment (CPE) and the end office switching location of the telephone company. The facilities used to provide this function, outside plant (OSP), are divided into three components: feeder, distribution, and drop wire.[37] Large capacity feeder routes originate at the end office to remote switching bundling points where they are divided into lower capacity groupings known as distribution cables. The distribution facilities continue on to customer locations where the final connection is made to CPE via drop wires, or, in some cases, interior inter-faces. Generally, the distribution segment of the loop is shorter in length and smaller in capacity (cross section) than feeder cables.[38] The following discussion will analyze the feeder and distribution portions of the local loop, *i.e.*, the OSP from the central office to the drop wire interface.

Presently, fiber optic plant appears to be taking hold in selected single user local area networking applications. This plant is also utilized in wiring for shared tenant and industrial park projects. But, its deployment for conventional applications in the distribution, or "last mile," portion of the loop is clearly still in its infancy.

Some companies are setting a faster pace in applying fiber locally. For instance, Illinois Bell is providing tariffed local services over fiber loops in downtown Chicago. Pacific Bell is another leader, having installed local fiber loop plant in several San Francisco and Los Angeles applications. Bell Atlan-tic and BellSouth are also moving ahead. For example, Chesapeake and Potomac Telephone Company of Maryland, a Bell Atlantic company, activated a new switch connecting local fiber plant in Columbia, Maryland, in the fall of 1986. BellSouth's Southern Bell affiliate will be employing strictly fiber optic–coaxial cable system facilities for a planned community application in Florida. Mountain Bell, Southwestern Bell, and New Jersey Bell are also conducting fiber trials.

The use of fiber for high capacity feeder cables and distribution cables installed for large business customers will continue to grow through the early 1990s. On the other hand, relatively slower growth of optical cable in the distribution portion of loop plant for other customers can be anticipated over the near term. This stems, in part, from fiber's limited availability in the past, its high installation costs, and technical complexity of installation at the distribution level. However, not all of these factors are likely to remain a barrier as new development proceeds as noted above.

For instance, the complexity of new fiber installation is rapidly lessening as new techniques and equipment become available. Similarly, the facility costs of installations are shrinking, as the price of (single mode) fiber per foot has dropped rapidly. And, prices for fiber optic associated electronic components have shown similar recent declines, with projections of additional reductions of as much as 20 percent per year in the near future. Over the next ten years some forecasters have predicted an overall reduction of as much as 50 percent in installed fiber optic system costs. For example, AT&T estimated that the cost of fiber optic cable would decline by a factor of eight by the end of 1988.[39]

One of the reasons for the steady decline in fiber cable prices is that learning curve cost savings related to production have not been exhausted. It is anticipated that yields from raw materials can still be increased and efficiencies improved during the production process. Another factor leading to lower costs is in fiber placement. Improvements in installation methods have reduced associated labor costs by over 50 percent thereby cutting overall costs. Also, splice costs have been reduced by over 70 percent due to fewer required splices and increased knowledge of the function by employees. Figure V–5 shows how fiber optic prices have declined since 1981 and are expected to continue to fall to the year 2000 (using 1987 as the base year).

Once installed, fiber is alleged to have a substantial advantage in operating costs over other transmission options. Accordingly, the economics of selecting a transmission medium for local distribution may begin to shift toward fiber, particularly in applications where capacity needs, space limitations, and operating costs play a central role.

b. Cost of Transmission Media

Generally, the economics of media selection are dependent on installed (or investment) costs[40] of each facility, as well as the operating costs of the given technologies. Of course, if these two types of costs are considered separately, minimization cost analyses may suggest installation of different facility mixes for the same application.

For instance, optical cable's higher installed costs *vis-à-vis* other media have diminished its attractiveness for lower capacity and shorter distance uses. This disadvantage of fiber owes to the fact that the actual production costs of the cable are relatively high at the present time. The higher costs are also a function of the newness of the technology, the extensive electronics required for most applications, and the difficulty in the actual process of installation, particularly in the splicing of cables and "laboratory" environment that needs to be established for this task.

On the other hand, fiber usage is claimed to generally involve lower operating costs than other technologies. Fiber can also be reconfigured and expanded much more easily than other media, and is much less subject to corrosion and the repair and maintenance costs necessitated by corrosion.

Installed cost tradeoffs for transmission media are usually determined by the route cross section (number of channels) and accompanying length of haul. Weather conditions for the application are also a significant cost factor. This is especially true in certain geographic areas where electrical storm activity is common. Notably, investment costs of loop facilities are dependent on the costs of associated electronics, such as multiplexing and transmitting/receiving equipment; the production costs of the media itself,

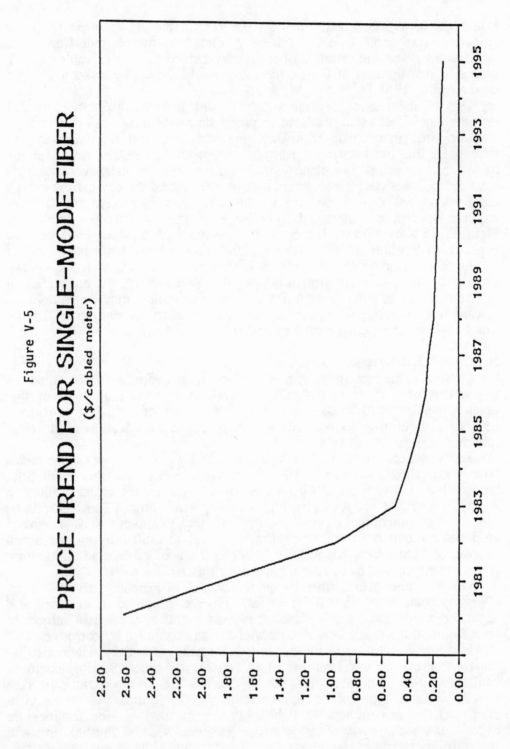

Figure V-5

PRICE TREND FOR SINGLE-MODE FIBER

($/cabled meter)

such as cable and antennas; and land, support structures, and other implementation costs (e.g., for real estate, engineering and construction).

Various technologies have some area of operation in which each exhibits
some cost advantages. For instance, in the case of analog copper wire, no
multiplexing costs are incurred, and the cost of the wire itself and wire
installation are both lower than comparable costs for optical fiber. However,
as the length of haul increases, analog copper wire includes very high charges
for load coils (and other range extending devices), which are required to
prevent signal degradation. And, as the number of channels increases, more
copper wire pairs must be added (at a rate of one pair per channel).
Expectedly, analog wire is competitive with other technologies for some very
short haul systems with small cross sections (low channel counts) but not
under other conditions of use.

In contrast, copper wire that is utilized on T-1 digital carrier systems
suffers less from signal degradation. Consequently, it incurs lower range
extension costs than analog wire. Fewer wire pairs are required, because the
digital signal can be multiplexed. Of course, the process of multiplexing adds
costs (for transmitting and receiving equipment) which tends to somewhat
offset the economies associated with T-1 systems. Overall, though, the
economies of digital wire suggest that it is preferable to analog wire on
longer routes, at least for the smaller systems. But it is generally not
competitive with fiber at higher cross sections (See Figure V-6).

From an investment viewpoint, the high "front end" costs of fiber and
microwave make these technologies impractical for small, short haul systems.
Fiber and microwave systems demonstrate sizable economies, however, as the
length and cross section of the application increase. Indeed, microwave costs
are completely insensitive to distance for the range of most existing loop
lengths, provided a line-of-sight connection can be established between the
two ends of a route.

Fiber system installed costs are partially distance sensitive because of the
costs of cable and cable installation. But, while these costs are much higher
per mile than those of a comparable copper installation, fiber systems do not
incur range extension costs, at least up to about 15 miles for multimode and
50 miles for single mode. And, of course, range extension charges are the
costs that make long haul copper systems relatively uneconomical.

The ability of fiber to expand to accommodate growth along a given route
is considerable, with the capabilities improving constantly with each new
advance in the technology. Present capability is more than ten times the
capacity that was possible prior to the advancement from multimode to single
mode fiber. This expandability of fiber opens many possibilities, e.g., to
increase the number of subscribers along a given cable route merely by adding
electronic transmitting and receiving equipment at each end of the route. In
contrast, copper wire systems in many urban centers are often crowded into
inadequate duct space. In many sections of the country, these systems can
only be expanded by installing entirely new conduit. Such installations may
not even be possible, and, would, at a minimum, incur the consequent costs of
trenching, backfilling, and repaving.

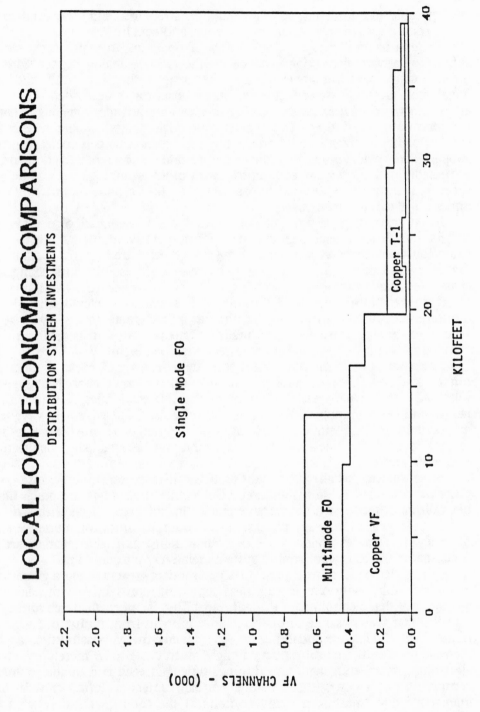

Figure V-6

LOCAL LOOP ECONOMIC COMPARISONS

DISTRIBUTION SYSTEM INVESTMENTS

Fiber has unique cost advantages in those areas of the country where there is frequent, severe thunderstorm activity. Thunderstorms can cause extremely damaging electrical potentials to surge through copper wire systems. These lightning surges can even produce explosive results in an electrical system connected by copper wire, as well as arching, dielectric failures, and fused conductors.[41]

This problem should not be minimized. A day of thunderstorm activity will generally induce at least one surge of 1,000 to 1,300 volts peak on aerial or buried copper cable. This is several hundred volts beyond the dependable voltage limitation of the best surge protectors in use today. Some sections of the country, such as the Gulf Coast and the eastern slopes of the Rocky Mountains, experience more than sixty days of thunderstorm activity each year. Other areas, such as southern Florida, record more than a hundred thunderstorm days. In these locations, high repair costs, coupled with the less quantifiable costs of service down time, should be factored into the comparative costs of copper wire networks.

In recent years, dangers of equipment damage resulting from lightning surges have been compounded by increasing use of solid state electronics in central office and station equipment. The integrated circuits that are at the heart of such equipment are extremely susceptible to surge damage. Even lower voltage static discharges that are induced by remote lightning strikes are capable of damaging some types of solid state equipment. These voltages may be below the levels necessary to trip surge protectors installed on the cables. Under such circumstances it may be prudent to consider alternatives to simply installing expensive electrical protection devices on copper systems. That is, the most cost effective approach may be to remove such systems in favor of optical fiber facilities that do not conduct electrical charges.

It is also important to note significant cost differences between single mode and multimode fiber. For instance, splicing is a much more difficult, time consuming process with single mode fiber although recent improvements in the operation have reduced the differentials. Connecting the smaller strand sizes of the single mode systems is a very labor intensive, lengthy process even for skilled personnel. It requires use of special microscopes and other equipment, which are unnecessary in a multimode installation. To offset these factors, proponents of single mode systems point toward the more flexible, greater capacity and easier expandability attributes of the alternative. In some cases, single mode might eventually save the owner of a system considerable installation cost, especially where expansion is continually necessary.

For any given application, system cost comparisons are substantially influenced by the specific values of individual cost factors and the varying extent to which different technologies are affected by these factors. For instance, the costs of rights-of-way, which directly impact both fiber and copper cable systems, are highly dependent on the specific application's location. Similarly, the engineering and real estate costs for microwave installations are dependent on locational circumstances.

There are also noncost factors to consider respecting selection of a transmission technology. These considerations may be determinative in some cases. Although not always subject to quantification, they cannot be considered any less important than the cost factors. For example, in an urban environment, limited duct space or pole capacity may make the installation of bulky copper cables totally impractical. Accordingly, selection may be limited to fiber cable or microwave radio. Separately, limited availability of interference free radio spectrum could rule out the use of microwave. Under these circumstances, the choice may narrow to fiber or copper.

Fiber's flexibility provides it with at least two advantages over other technologies. First, this medium is capable of serving a diverse mix of transmission modes, *e.g.*, voice, data, and video. Second, as noted, the size of a communications system, in terms of the number of channels, can be easily altered without incurring significant new investment costs or stranding previously deployed investment. Relative to microwave radio, fiber would also be favored in those installations where transmission security is of special concern. Properly installed, optical fiber is extremely difficult to tap into or jam without detection.

As a selection factor, the system reliability criteria would favor fiber. As discussed, in areas that experience considerable electrical storm activity fiber is advantageous since it is unaffected by electrical interference. In contrast, copper systems are susceptible to serious damage from lightning strikes. Fiber is also more reliable than microwave because microwave radio systems must often be utilized at high frequencies, since these are the only levels not yet congested in some urban areas. In such situations, microwave facilities may provide unacceptable service due to severe signal attenuation (*e.g.*, during heavy rainfall).

The most important noncost factor favoring fiber may well have little to do with flexibility, reliability, security or the other noncost criteria discussed above. Instead, fiber installation may be most favored by the prospects of further technological advancement. The other technologies discussed are quite mature in their life cycles, and are now progressing in terms of innovation, cost reduction, and capacity and feature enhancements only at the slower rate characteristic of older technologies. But, optical fiber, especially in the local loop, is still relatively in its formative years. As a result, communications managers choosing to install fiber systems can expect that the economics and efficiencies of their systems will improve substantially as the technology continues to progress. In fact, single mode fiber, which is now the mode of choice in most field applications, was only introduced into commercial use in late 1983, with Continental Telephone's installation of a 37 kilometer line between Norwich and Sidney, in south central New York State.

As a barometer of improvement and change in optical technology, consider the constant increase in the limiting distance for repeaterless transmission of coherent, large bandwidth signals. In the field of optical research there have been various "hero" experiments, in which industry laboratories have been increasing this limit, measured in bit-kilometers per second (distance times transmission speed). Of late, these increases have come almost predictably. For instance, in early 1984 the reported record was a 120 kilometer transmission at one gigabit (one billion bits) per second or 120 billion bit–kilometers. Within a year, Bell Labs had pushed the record to 1.37 trillion bit–kilometers by multiplexing 10 signals of two gigabits each, and transmitting them over a fiber of 68.3 kilometers. At the same time, the bandwidth for a single fiber channel had been increased to four gigabits, and this was transmitted 117 kilometers, for a nonmultiplexed record of 468 billion bit–kilometers. Even a multimode fiber, which normally requires repeaters at much shorter intervals than single mode fibers, has been used for a 1.3 gigabit transmission of 103 kilometers. New records continue to be broken on a regular basis.

These experiments demonstrate the rapid rate of change in fiber technology and suggest that the potential for even lower unit costs than predicted is feasible. Although these continuing technological advances may have more applications for longer distance toll transmissions, the local service market should also benefit from lower costs. Other research objectives, such as in–fiber repeaters and optical switches, are important for applications in multi–drop distribution systems, such a subscriber loop networks. Repeaters and switches are generally required whenever a transmission route branches, which happens frequently in local distribution networks. At present, when repeaters and switches are encountered, it is necessary to translate the lightwave signal into an electrical signal, send it through the equipment, and translate it back to a lightwave signal on the other side. The economics of fiber networking would be much improved if switching and regeneration could be accomplished without going through such a translation process.

But, the in–fiber repeater is still only in the conceptual stage. On the other hand, some working models of optical switches have already been developed, and appear to be close to commercial applications. Both a mechanical model, in which a fiber is physically moved back and forth to make or break a connection, and an electro–optical device, in which a light wave guide changes its transparency in response to changes in the electrical field around it, are operational. An all–optical model, using a second beam of light to change the transparency of a medium through which the signal beam is moving, is still in the developmental stage. Such a model will be implemented as fiber becomes more pervasive and the provisioning cost of optical switches reach economical levels. These changes will greatly enhance the ability to provide lower cost loop facilities.

2. Radio Based Transmission

Initially, radio technology was used for long distance applications by common carriers and private companies. However, technological advances have driven costs down such that radio has found more widespread use. Over the last several years the short haul (10–15 miles) microwave market has grown substantially. The systems are often utilized as short hops between customers, to provide connections to long distance carriers, and to intercon–nect customers with LECs' central offices.

Short haul microwave systems are generally easy to install, operate, and maintain, and do not require regulatory approval for rights of way. These systems are usually small with equipment including a two foot antenna, an outdoor radio unit, and an indoor interface module at each end of the link. The small size of the electronics permits its mounting along with the antenna. Systems are often installed on rooftops or even window sills and operate at up to 45 Mbps which is ideal for T–1 carrier or video transmission. Although technology improvements and a ten percent growth rate in sales of short haul systems have brought costs down, there are environmental problems that still remain. These include a requirement for line of sight between the transmitter and receiver, and sensitivity to terrain, building structures, and weather disturbances. Another drawback to microwave is its high start–up cost. Overall, though, the market continues to flourish. For instance, from 1982 to 1986 capacity grew by a factor of over 12.[42]

Short haul microwave is often cited as a viable alternative to bypassing the local network and statistics appear to support this contention. In 1986, microwave captured almost 30 percent, or $4.1 million of the bypass market whereas by 1991 the comparable figures are expected to be 43 percent and $92 million[43]   Bypass microwave systems are mainly used by businesses in the nation's larger cities.

Digital termination services (DTS) are an authorized use of the frequency spectrum for local distribution of long distance voice/data/video communications using point–to–point microwave. This service provides complete bypass of local telephone company loop facilities and switches for larger communications users or groups of users. DTS is expected to dramatically lower the cost of local loop services, spanning the last several miles from the local node of an interexchange carrier to the customer's premises.

DTS networks, in which local nodes of the DTS company can be interconnected to each other to provide local private line services as well as connected to various interexchange carriers, are also possible with microwave technology. Improved data compression systems and the use of Ku and Ka frequency bands will also lower the costs of DTS systems and increase use. However, interference from microwave congestion could inhibit development of these systems in the long run. Additionally, telephone operating companies may become not only the biggest providers of digital termination systems, but could eventually bypass DTS with low cost, high capacity fiber optic loop transmission systems.

As in the case of cellular radio, the number of FCC applications for DTS permits is quite large. Some of the companies offering DTS are positioning themselves to bypass both long distance and local common carrier networks. Both private and interexchange common carrier companies are positioned to provide end–to–end data communications combining their extant long distance networks with new DTS facilities. Reselling of either DTS or end–to–end capacity is, of course, entirely possible as the number of applicants exceeds available spectrum. However, the market for DTS has not yet taken off as many predicted. This potentially significant bypass technology for high capacity usage has had limited applicability to date.

Another radio–related technology is infrared which operates above the microwave range.   It has several advantages over traditional microwave. These are the lack of stringent regulatory rules, licensing requirements, and frequency coordination concerns. Capacity is virtually limitless and implemen– tation costs are minimal.   The operating range for infrared, however, is significantly smaller than microwave which limits its use.   The compactness and simplicity make infrared an excellent choice for links between buildings, across streets, and for temporary and emergency requirements.   Once the technology is further developed, it is expected to be employed as a means of bypassing the local network.

Cellular radio has expanded greatly during the last six years (see Figure V–7) as costs have come down and the BOCs have entered the market. Subscribership continues to grow, with virtually no subscribers in 1983 to where there were over 1.9 million by year–end 1988. Development is under– way to enhance cellular to a digital mode, but it appears that this offering is several years ahead.   Once this occurs, though, individual channel capacity will increase by a factor of four and quality will improve.   Thus, to a great extent the congestion that is now building up will be alleviated.

3. Additional Options

Cable television (CATV) had already grown to the level of more than 43 million subscribers by the beginning of 1988, which constitutes almost 50 percent of U.S. households having television.   Uninterrupted growth is anticipated especially since regulation has decreased substantially and financial resources are now available from several well–heeled corporate investment sponsors.[44] Forty five percent of the industry is owned and managed by the ten largest multiple system operators (MSOs).   It is not impossible that the BOCs may eventually provide a viable alternative to CATV once fiber optics becomes prevalent in the local loop and if regulatory prohibitions are lifted. These large carriers would view cable as a lucrative extension of their soon–to–be local fiber networks.   But, importantly, the deployment of fiber may obsolete the immense coaxial cable investment incurred by present CATV companies.

Home satellites also offer competition to CATV. Despite the drawbacks of a high initial cost and degree of exactness with respect to installation, growth has especially centered on rural areas and among the more affluent. At the end of 1987, it was reported that there were already 1.7 million satellite dishes for direct access already in use by homeowners.[45]

T–1 digital carrier was the first Bell System short haul digital transmis– sion line and was initially used in a commercial application in 1962.   T–1 systems can save from 10 to 50 percent on telecom expenses for users with the right usage characteristics.   Because of this, growth in T–1 multiplexers is expected to grow by over 25 percent per year into the 1990s from less than $300 million to over one billion dollars. The popularity of T–1, which carries 24 channels on two cable pairs, has been enhanced as prices have come down drastically.

Figure V-7

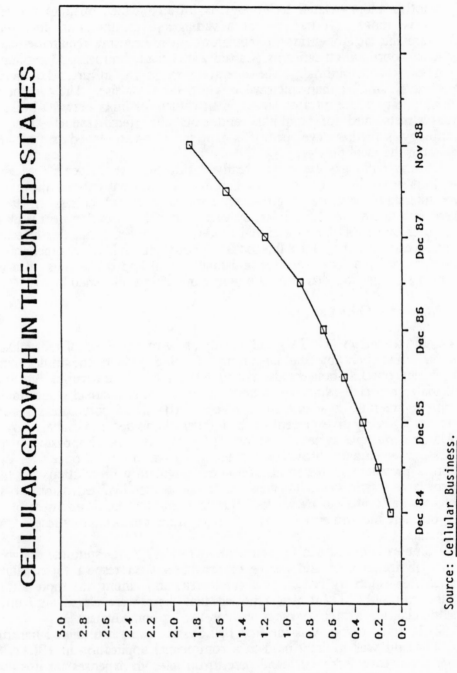

CELLULAR GROWTH IN THE UNITED STATES

Source: Cellular Business.

E. New Technology Deployment

Some of the fiber optic trials undertaken by the LECs in the U.S. have produced results that suggest some significant fiber deployment may be accounted for in the last mile of the local loop by as early as 1989. Indeed, on a wide scale, Southwestern Bell (SWB) believes that the actual economic crossover between copper and fiber will occur no later than 1995.[46] One of the key parameters leading to the view that wholesale fiber deployment is in the offing is the expectation that costs associated with lightwave technology will continue to decline.

For instance, SWB expects a 10 percent drop in fiber cost, 15 percent in electronics, 15–20 percent in optical devices, and 37 percent in laser prices over the next several years. Analyses by the company indicate that it might be beneficial to pay a premium for fiber at a date earlier than 1995 in order to avoid constructing network overlays in the future to use broadband services. SWB determined that the anticipated expansion to broadband service justified a 10 percent premium for fiber over copper in early 1991, and a 25 percent premium in 1989. Besides trends toward lower costs of fiber cable and electronic components, professed needs for the facilities also stem from the increasing use of concentrators and remote switching units which intrins-ically favor fiber construction over copper.

According to Southern Bell, trial results have suggested that fiber can be the economic choice in the loop under certain circumstances by late 1989.[47] While this conclusion relies on the oft–predicted continued decrease in the cost of electronics, it also assumes reduced upkeep in life cycle, remote provisioning, reduction in field visits, and portability of electronics to meet dynamic network requirements.

Yet, these scenarios do not envision the wide ranging replacement of embedded copper cable or plant now in the local loop. Rather, fiber will be most economically deployed in new construction and replacements, or in other applications where special economics or requirements so dictate. Thus, it will likely not be until the 21st century when everyone will have access to the network over a fiber loop.

Decisions to deploy fiber in the local network are most often based on economic studies conducted by the LECs. Typically, the economics of altern-ative provisioning schemes are analyzed and the plan with the most favorable net present value (or other decision–making criteria) is chosen. The usual choice is between copper and fiber. Currently, if the results of the economic analyses were adhered to, copper would almost always be installed. However, in practice this is not the case. In some instances, companies are becoming somewhat liberal by accepting up to 15 percent cost penalties for the case of fiber economics. This allegedly reflects a need of providing for future unknowns. Not the least of these are the advent of hoped–for demand for information services, as well as potential entry of long distance, foreign, and alternative providers in exchange markets.

The fiber optics market is dominated by only a few suppliers as can be seen on Table V–6. In the cable segment, AT&T has the largest share at 35

Table V–6

MARKET SHARES FOR FIBER OPTICS SUPPLIERS

Fiber Optic Cable		Optoelectronics		Carrier Systems	
AT&T	35%	AT&T	25%	AT&T	56%
Siecor	29	NEC	21	Rockwell	10
Ericsson	11	Fujitsu	15	Northern Tel	5
Northern Tel	10	Northern Tel	13	GTE	3
ITT	9	Rockwell	12	Lynch	3
Pirelli	3	Telco Systems	8	R–Tec	3
Sumitomo	2	Ericsson	2	Granger	2
Others	2	Stromb.–Carlson	2	ITT	2
		ITT	1	Ericsson	1
		Others	1	NEC	1
				Siecor	1
				Others (24)	13

Source: *Communications News,* September 1987, p. 61.

percent with Siecor right behind at 29 percent. The top five firms control over 90 percent of the market. AT&T also has a slight advantage in optoelectronics, which includes digital subscriber loop carrier systems. The top five suppliers control 86 percent of this market. AT&T dominates carrier systems supply with a 56 percent share. The next highest company, Rockwell has a 10 percent share, and no other firm has more than five percent of the market.

It is suggested by the industry that various services could be offered more feasibly and efficiently over fiber loops. If priced appropriately, revenues from these services could aid in the initial support of fiber in the distribution portion of the loop until production and other efficiencies are attained to a greater degree and make the economics of the "last mile" more attractive to telephone companies. These services would generally utilize broadband, high volume transmission capacity such as envisioned for CATV and information services. Regulators will most likely wish to establish safe-guards to insure that basic monopoly service ratepayers are not required to support, through higher rates, the initial deployment of fiber in the loop, especially when it may not yet be economical on a stand alone basis. Other discretionary and competitive services should bear these costs since they will be the major benefactors of fiber installation.

The bulk of enhanced services are most effectively provided via digital switches. A review of BOC data indicates that digital is the replacement technology of the future in virtually all cases. Many of the BOCs plan to have all–digital switching by the early to late 1990s. In this regard, U S West planned to increase the percentage of lines served by digital switches from 17 percent in 1987 to 25 percent in 1988. Southern Bell

(BellSouth) has a goal of replacing all analog switches with digital switching in the next decade. Similar strategies apply to other BOCs. For instance, NYNEX more than tripled its digitally served customers from 1985 to 1987. That company projects spending of $3.0 billion to replace 800 electromechanical switches over a six year period. Overall, in 1987 the BOCs digital switch installations increased by 180 percent over the 1985 level. This widespread deployment of digital switches will facilitate the offering of services appropriately provided over fiber loops.

One such service is cable television which passes 80 percent and has penetrated almost 50 percent of television households in the United States. These 43 million subscribers can be expected to grow to over 60 million in the 1990s. From 1982 to 1986 growth was 48 percent, and from 1987 to 1990 growth is expected to be about 19 percent (See Table V–7). Likewise, current annual construction is over $1.4 billion, up from the 1987 figure of $1.2 billion, with no appreciable showdown likely for the foreseeable future.[48]

The continuing growth in CATV and the availability of high capacity fiber loops would appear to offer an opportunity of tremendous synergistic potential. That is, the cable companies have a product desired by customers[49] and the telephone companies have the facilities to provide services more efficiently and with a greater array of options. Although current regulatory constraints will have to be addressed, there is no technological reason that CATV cannot be provided via fiber loops leased from the local telephone company. Such a merger would be advantageous to both entities, with consumers the ultimate beneficiary of more and improved enhanced services.

In this regard, recommendations recently initiated at the federal level indicate that regulatory constraints on telephone company participation may be relaxed. Both the FCC and the National Telecommunications Information Administration (NTIA) called for an easing of prohibitions that prevent telephone companies from providing transport facilities to CATV operators and other video suppliers. There is one fundamental difference between the recommendations of the two federal entities. The FCC concluded in Docket 87–266 that telephone companies should be permitted to provide CATV services, including programming content.[50] Further comments have been solicited by the Commission with the expectation that the FCC will eventually recommend changes in the Cable Act of 1984 to the U.S. Congress. NTIA, on the other hand, did not go as far as the FCC and in a report released in June 1988 recommended that telephone companies be allowed to provide video dial tone, but not programming content.

The FCC and NTIA both view their actions as fostering competition and bringing broadband services to the home. Also, it was anticipated that enactment of the proposals would encourage the development and deployment of fiber optics in the local loop. Of course, Congress will make the final determination in this matter, and it is not expected that such a decision will be forthcoming in the near future.[51]

On average, CATV subscribers pay about $20 for monthly service which includes basic service plus optional premium services such as Home Box Office (HBO) and Showtime.[52] For each $2.00, or ten percent of CATV revenues,

Table V-7

U.S. CABLE INDUSTRY GROWTH THROUGH 1990

Year	Television Households (mil)	Homes Passed (mil)	Basic * Subscribers (mil)	% of TVHH	Pay + Subscribers (mil)	% of TVHH
1975	69.6	19.9	11.1	16	N/A	N/A
1976	71.1	22.0	12.1	17	0.5	1
1977	73.3	24.9	13.2	18	1.5	2
1979	76.3	32.7	16.0	21	5.3	7
1981	80.7	44.0	22.6	28	11.8	15
1982	82.8	49.1	28.2	34	15.9	19
1983	83.5	53.6	30.3	36	17.9	21
1984	84.6	60.0	33.0	39	19.8	23
1985	86.3	64.6	36.1	42	21.7	25
1986	87.8	69.6	41.7	47	24.1	27
1987	89.3	72.5	42.7	48	26.0	29
1988(e)	91.0	75.8	45.5	50	28.7	32
1989(e)	92.8	79.1	48.3	52	30.9	33
1990(e)	93.9	81.8	50.7	54	33.0	35

(e) = estimated.

* Number of subscribers to basic cable service, some of whom will also take "pay" services such as HBO. Basic tier services often include local broadcast channels, all-news stations, etc.

+ Pay subscribers pay a monthly fee to receive premium services on a per channel basis or as a "tier" of services. A small percentage of pay subscribers can also receive programming on a pay-per-view basis.

Source: *Cablevision*, March 14, 1988.

that could be charged to cable companies for rental of fiber loops, about $1.0 billion of revenues would be realized by local telephone companies, based on current CATV subscribership. Revenues of this magnitude, which are expected to grow by at least five percent as CATV subscribership continues to increase, could assist in the initial support of fiber in the distribution portion of the loop.

Videotex services are also predicted to grow in the future. The number of videotex terminals is expected to increase significantly to some 435,000 by 1990 with associated revenues of approximately $1.0 billion. This figure could be substantially higher in 1990 and for future years if the French approach to providing low cost terminals is implemented. Concomitantly, additional usage would be generated on networks that appear to have an abundance of capacity, thereby resulting in more efficient use of telecommunications facilities. Videotex services can be offered over the same facilities as CATV, and for certain market groups, such as hotels and motels, economies can be achieved by combining services on fiber. Thus, the fiber loop with its high capacity would appear to be well suited for many videotex applications with associated revenues flowing to local telephone companies for rental of the lines.

On a more global perspective, there are various estimates of the information services market that utilize local loops. Figures vary up to $47 billion of annual revenues. Apart from the current national debate as to whether the BOCs should be allowed to provide such services, local loops are often required for many of the information services. The use of fiber in the loop could facilitate the offering of these services by providing for sufficient capacity, improved performance, and cost efficiencies. These qualities would generally tend to accelerate the emergence of new information services.

Access to information services is often claimed to be most efficiently provided by LECs over their exchange networks and fiber loops could facilitate more effective connection to providers of information services. On–line data bases can be more efficiently accessed and thereby rates for related services can be minimized. Under this scenario, local telephone companies will be able to generate revenues to maintain and continue fiber growth in the loop so that all customers can ultimately realize the benefits of fiber optic technology. Once the initial implementation is achieved, the technology could become self sustaining (at least) well into the next century.

Despite the apparent benefits of fiber optics in the local loop, the key element to the success of fiber deployment is whether demand for these new services will materialize in sufficient quantities. Unless the LECs can market (either to end users or service providers) new services such as CATV, videophone, security systems, video databanks, High Definition Television (HDTV), home banking, etc., the viability of fiber in the distribution portion of the loop, the "last mile," is questionable. Of course, regulation at the national and local levels will also have an impact on the deployment of fiber in the loop.

As noted above, an important issue that needs to be resolved as the nation and the world move into the Information Age relates to the needs and desires of consumers with respect to services. If there is insufficient demand, the best technology in the world might have little value, with the likely possibility that monopoly customers will have to pay for it.

Notes

1. Thomas McPhail, "A History of Telecommunications," in M.F. Estabrooks and R.H. Lamarche, *Telecommunications: A Strategic Perspective on Regional, Economic and Business Development*, The Canadian Institute for Research on Regional Development (Ottawa: 1986), p. 27.

2. John Bourne, "Technology as Service Enabler: Balancing the Strategy," Proceedings of FibreSat 86, International Conference on Satellite and Fibre Optic Communications, September 1986, p. 378.

3. Examples include two airports (nodes), connected by air service (links), or two communications switches (nodes) connected by transmission facilities (links).

4. For instance, the quantity may be passengers, wattage, gallons of water, telephone calls, etc.

5. As telecommunications networks evolve toward all–digital technologies, traditional traffic distinctions, such as voice and data defined with reference to analogue technology, will lose their meaning.

6. The concepts of facilities and traffic networks are not without controversy. Some have viewed the concept of a traffic network largely as a way to segment markets and implement price discrimination (*i.e.*, establishing different rate levels and rate structures for the use of identical network facilities with identical economic costs by different user groups).

7. R.J. Sanferrare, "Terrestrial Lightwave Systems," *AT&T Technical Journal*, Jan./Feb., 1987, p. 97. The route was completed in 1984.

8. For comments on manufacturer's economies of scale, see Randall E. Park, "Economic Viability of Fiber Optics for Local Area Networks," Proceedings of FibreSat 86, International Conference on Satellite and Fibre Optic Communications, September 1986, p. 390.

9. D.P. Jablonowski, U.C. Paek and L.S. Watkins, "Optical Fiber Manufacturing Techniques," *AT&T Technical Journal*, January/February 1987, pp. 33–44.

10. New England Telephone and Telegraph Company, *Depreciation Rate Study* (1987), Intro., p. 12, filed with the Massachusetts D.P.U. in Case No. 86–33.

11. Myron Keller, area manager for loop technical planning, Southwestern Bell, at the Fifth Annual Bypass Conference sponsored by Phillips Publishing, Inc., April 4, 1988. Mr. Keller's comments were reported in *Lightwave*, April 7, 1988, p. 34.

12. Randall E. Park, *op. cit.*

13. Bethesda Research Institute, Ltd., estimate.

14. Daniel Kelley, Proceedings of the George Washington University Policy Symposium: Federal/State Price–of–Service Regulation, December 1987, p. 83.

15. Testimony of Patrick E. White, Docket D.P.U. 86–33, Commonwealth of Massachusetts, January 5, 1987, p. 20.

16. "A Case for Capital Investment," *Telephony*, February 2, 1987, p. 58.

17. Other factors making a contribution include savings in taxes, depreciation and labor costs.

18. The potential cost savings identified here are set forth in Bethesda Research Institute, Ltd., "Benefits of Full Universal Service as a National Policy Goal," Fall 1987, p. 11. They are described in more detail in James J. Leto, "Reaching New Dimensions in Communications Efficiency;" Randall E. Park, "Economic Viability of Fiber Optics to Local Area Networks;" and G.P. Kurpis and P.C. Merriman, "Applications of High Capacity Fiber Systems in Bell Canada's Network;" in Proceedings of FibreSat 86, International Conference on Satellite and Fibre Optic Communications, September 1986, pp. 373, 388, and 455.

19. Patrick E. White, *Op. Cit.*

20. *Ibid.*, p. 37.

21. "A Case for Capital Investment," *Op. Cit.*

22. R.J. Sanferrare, *op. cit.*

23. R.W. Dixon and N.K. Dutta, "Lightwave Device Technology," *AT&T Technical Journal*, Jan./Feb. 1987, p. 80.

24. C.H. Gartside, A.J. Panuska, P.D. Patel, "Single–Mode Cable for Long–Haul, Trunk, and Loop Networks," *AT&T Technical Journal*, Jan./Feb. 1987, p. 84.

25. *Ibid.*, p. 93.

26. Michael Warr, "Fiber Gets Faster – Again," *Telephony*, November 16, 1987, p. 58.

27. J.L. Cummings, K.R. Hickey, B.D. Kinney, "AT&T Network Architecture Evolution," *AT&T Technical Journal*, Jan./Feb. 1987, p. 10.

28. IGI Consulting, Inc., *U.S. Long Distance Fiber Optic Networks*, October 1986, Vol. II, p. 14.

29. A. Javed and P. MacLaren, "Fiber Loops for Residential Services – the 1990's Revolution," Proceedings of FibreSat 86, International Conference on Satellite and Fibre Optic Communications, September 1986, pp. 434 and 439.

30. IGI Consulting, Inc., *op. cit.*, p. 24. The report provides much greater detail regarding expected future technical developments, especially the transmission speed improvements that can be achieved through a move to lasers operating at longer wave lengths. Also, J.E. Rogalski, "Evolution of Gigabit Lightwave Transmission Systems," *AT&T Technical Journal*, Jan./Feb. 1987, provides considerable insight into future developments at pages 39–40.

31. IGI Consulting, Inc., *op. cit.*, Vol. I, p. 34.

32. Patrick White, *op. cit.*, pp. 20–21.

33. Based on an example from John Bourne, director, corporate development, Bell Northern Research, "Technology as Service Enabler: Balancing the Strategy," Proceedings of FibreSat 86, International Conference on Satellite and Fibre Optic Communications, p. 380.

34. Specific estimates range from 7 to 17 percent. See, *e.g.*, *New York Times*, November 13, 1986, p. D8, and *TE&M*, July 1, 1987, pp. 78–79.

35. *Telephony*, Jan. 12, 1987, p. 42 and Jan. 18, 1988, p. 39.

36. *Communications Week*, May 9, 1988, p. 31.

37. Transmission facilities that run between telephone company offices are also designated as OSP but are referred to as trunks. These trunks can carry local and/or toll traffic.

38. For instance, a 1983 study of Bell System loops showed that average feeder and distribution lengths were 10,448 feet and 1,888 feet, respectively. Ram R. P. Singh, "The LAST Bell System Subscriber Loop Survey," *Telephony*, October 5, 1987, p. 32.

39. "AT&T Plans Fiber Optic Network," *The Washington Post*, November 9, 1984, p. B2.

40. Installed costs include material, installation labor, and other one–time costs incurred to get a facility into a turn–key mode.

41. The dangers of thunderstorm activity and the recommended engineering response to those dangers are noted in various sources. See *e.g.*, Rural Electrification Administration, *Telecommunications Engineering and Construction Manual*, Section 801, October 1982.

42. *The Geodesic Network, 1987 Report on Competition in the Telephone Industry,* (*Huber Report*), Peter W. Huber for the Department of Justice, January 1987, Table L.15.

43. "Bypass Market Study Shows Microwave and Fiber on Rise," *Communications News,* February 1988, p. 4.

44. Some of these are: Coca–Cola, the New York Times, Time Inc., Warner Communications, and RJR Nabisco.

45. Many Roads Home: The New Electronic Pathways, NAB, April 1988, p. 126.

46. "Lightwave in the Loop," *Lightwave,* April 1988, p. 35.

47. *Id.*

48. *Cablevision,* February 15, 1988, p. 58.

49. These CATV subscribers are also customers of the telephone companies for the most part.

50. However, one of the three FCC commissioners, Patricia Diaz Dennis, favored the NTIA proposal with respect to programming content.

51. *Lightwave,* November 1988, p. 6.

52. Premium services vary according to the packages established by suppliers. For instance, one cable company may include ESPN in its basic service grouping whereas another supplier may offer ESPN as a premium service.

CHAPTER VI

THE EVOLUTION OF BYPASS

A. Definition and Description

1. Bypass Defined

Since it was first advanced as a public policy issue in telecommunications, apparently in 1980,[1] the concept of telephone company "bypass" has been defined in a variety of ways. Most definitions include the basic notion that facilities of local exchange carriers (LECs) are circumvented in some manner by alternative means of communications. Beyond this core description, however, many variations have been set forth over the years during the ongoing debate.

For instance, as an element of bypass, some have stressed the circumvention of exchange carrier facilities that are utilized in the provision of long distance service. Others, while still emphasizing the facilities dimension, broaden the focus to include the use of nonnetwork plant to furnish alternative local offerings. Still others believe that the concept encompasses the use of alternative facilities, both toll and local plant.

Alternatively, bypass may be viewed as the use of nonLEC services in lieu of local, toll, or any telephone company offering. This perspective will generally produce a different bypass result relative to a facilities focus wherever a telephone company engages in nontraditional (*e.g.*, foreign business ventures, real estate consulting services) or even traditional services (such as "yellow pages" directory operations). These activities do not utilize (regulated) telephone plant or other resources in the usual sense. In this broad service oriented interpretation, the definition of bypass is essentially considered to be tantamount to that of the general term "competition."

Depending on one's definition, bypass ventures can take many forms. They can involve ownership of private systems (including private microwave, and fiber optic networks), or subscription to nonLEC bypass services (for example, interactive cable television, or digital termination systems). Other manifestations may include direct interconnection to interexchange carrier (IXC) points of presence ("POPs"). This may occur through private lines provided by bypass vendors or LECs, or customers may subscribe to "teleport" multiple technology networks featuring antenna "farms" and fiber optic "rings" around urban centers. The effects of bypass may be felt on a state or interstate basis, or at the intraLATA or interLATA level.[2] These alternative services may carry voice, data or video, and may be transmitted over analog or digital based technologies.

Many LECs argue that a highly expansive definition of bypass is most appropriate. Under this approach, it is presumed that any communications traffic that occurs in a given area should be handled by the local telephone company. For example, Bell Atlantic asserts that "[i]n common usage" the term

. . . refers to the origination and/or completion of telecommunications by end users, interexchange carriers, or other
providers of communications services without the use of the
local exchange carrier's services or facilities.[3]

Bell Communications Research, the central services organization for the
seven Regional Bell Companies, similarly supports a broad definition, but
excludes private lines, as does AT&T's conceptualization.[4] A number of LECs,
especially the RBOCs, would include virtually all those services that
technologically could be provided by these local carriers.[5]

As a further point of departure, certain other industry parties have
defined bypass as traffic circumventing the public switched network (PSN),
rather than avoiding the LEC.[6] The concept that traffic that does not travel
over LEC facilities or, more restrictively, over the public switched network,
can be called bypass is itself disputed by some. For example, some users and
suppliers of alternative services argue that particular communications such as
video and high speed data are not examples of bypass. That is, such traffic
should not be included since it generally cannot be transmitted through the
local exchange even if the alternative services did not exist.[7]

Local telephone service in this country is predominantly[8] supplied by Bell
Operating Companies. Pursuant to the "Modification of Final Judgment" which
dismantled the Bell System on January 1, 1984, the BOCs were severed from
AT&T's long distance operations. This decree specifically limits the operating
companies to provision of intraLATA offerings but does permit the BOCs to
offer interLATA and intraLATA access services. In a small, single LATA
jurisdiction such as the District of Columbia, there is no "intrastate"
(District) or intraLATA toll. Thus, no intraDistrict access to the local
exchange exists.

InterLATA access services consist of two basic types: switched and
special. Switched access for IXCs is charged on the basis of per minute
usage, which contributes to the cost of the local public switched network
(LPSN). In contrast, special access for private line services is typically
assessed on a flat, per monthly arrangement which may make no contribution
to the fixed costs of LPSN facilities. Private systems avoid use of all local
telephone company "plant" and, accordingly, do not defray the costs of the
public switched network.

As a benchmark for analysis, the term "bypass" or more particularly,
"local bypass," is defined herein as the intraLATA circumvention of the public
switched network of the local telephone company, whether by privately owned
or leased alternative services or facilities. This definition encompasses
telephone company (and nonLEC) private lines, as well as private systems.
Such circumvention only includes those services which could have been
provided by the local exchange carrier.[9] As a result, local bypass may be
viewed as a specialized form of competition, relating to local public switched
network facilities and services that historically were considered to be the
domain of the monopoly franchise of the LECs.

This demarcation is adopted to reflect the most significant public policy
aspects of bypass. More specifically, it is rooted in the notions that: (1)

local exchange carriers have traditionally provided basic communications on a nondiscriminatory, affordable, and virtually ubiquitous basis, and, thus, should remain financially viable; and (2) maintenance of such "universal telephone service" (UTS) and attainment of other social objectives in the post divestiture environment require measured public policy initiatives which center on the LPSN.

2. Types of Bypass

Given the above definition of local telephone bypass, specific forms of such activity can be meaningfully classified from a public policy perspective. Figure VI–1 presents our categorization of local bypass.

This system of classification sets forth distinctions based upon whether the bypass is undertaken by the LEC (or its affiliates) or by other entities, whether such activity is motivated by economic or service related factors, and whether the bypass is achieved through carrier or private facilities.

Perhaps the most fundamental categorization is one based on the source of the bypass offering being provided. Many regard the term "bypass" as synonymous with "external bypass." This occurs when customers use nonLEC facilities which effectively circumvent the local public switched network. Such bypass is generally obtained through private systems or IXCs.

The counterpart to this category can be termed "internal bypass," which exists when the facility or service that is used by the customer instead of the LPSN is provided by an LEC (or its affiliate). Examples include the LEC's private lines or cellular radio services provided by affiliated entities.[10] Local telephone companies in major urban centers in this country generally provide private lines or (local) channel services. The seven RBOCs, GTE, Contel, Centel and many other telephone companies market cellular mobile telephone service through affiliates in various U.S. markets. Construction and maintenance of communications networks for universities furnishes another illustration. Notably, Bell Atlanticom has contracted to provide, install and maintain Temple University's new fiber optics based system. These facilities would circumvent the local switched network of another Bell Atlantic entity, Bell of Pennsylvania.[11]

Internal bypass is often not recognized as such because the alternative service or facility that enables the user to replace regular switched service is provided by the telephone company. The use of carrier provided private lines or bypass facilities may detract from the support of local switched service. In several respects, this is not unlike bypass provided by nonLEC sources. If, however, private lines are underpriced and do not recover their associated revenue requirements, a local exchange company ironically could be better off financially by losing such traffic to external bypassers, rather than to internally provide private lines.

One form of external bypass involves capture of one LEC's customers by another. For instance, LECs from other areas ("foreign LECs"), *i.e.*, franchised carriers not affiliated with a given local telephone company, may directly, or through sister companies, construct and/or operate fiber facilities

Figure VI–1

BYPASS CLASSIFICATION SCHEME

	Internal		External	
Economic				
Uneconomic				
Noneconomic				
	Carrier ("Service")	Facility	Carrier	Facility

that divert traffic from that telephone company.   Other vehicles for such activity include private communications systems built and maintained by foreign LECs (*e.g.*, campus or industrial park intrasystem networks), or competing LEC owned facilities which users secure through contractual leases or tariff in lieu of services obtained from their local telephone company.

Cases of foreign LEC bypass are apparently not uncommon. For example, Centel Business Systems, a subsidiary of Centel Corporation (the fourth largest nonBell telephone company), has designed and installed an advanced voice/data telecommunications system that will connect three campuses of the University of Michigan.[12] This contract displaced telephone service provided by Michigan Bell. NYNEX Business Information Systems has agreed to design, install, and service two customized fiber optic intraLATA networks for Digital Equipment Corporation in Massachusetts and New Hampshire, thereby circum- venting its sister company, New England Telephone Company.[13]   In the District of Columbia, one of the two cellular franchises (*Cellular One*) is majority owned by Southwestern Bell Corp., one of the Regional Bell Operat- ing Companies.

These contracts illustrate cases where an unregulated affiliate of an LEC circumvents the services of another LEC. As a result of a recent FCC ruling in its *ARCO* case, users may be permitted to interconnect their private systems to the local exchange of their choice if the action can be demonstra- ted to be "privately beneficial without being publicly detrimental."[14]

For purposes of public policy making, one of the most important distinc- tions between forms of bypass activity concerns the difference between "economic" and "uneconomic" bypass. Although both may serve to reduce local telephone company revenues, their respective impacts on allocative efficiency may differ significantly. Cost based rates or prices form the basis for any economic bypass decision, while noncost based rates create the potential for uneconomic circumvention of LEC facilities. According to economic theory, the failure to set prices on the basis of costs will lead to distortions in (relative) prices, misallocations of resources, and general inefficiency. The resulting "uneconomic" bypass may specifically be attributable to local telephone company costs that are artificially increased or rates that are otherwise inflated, or bypass providers whose costs are underallocated or prices understated.

For state regulators, establishing the distinction between economic and uneconomic bypass activity is critically important, but, in practice, may be quite difficult. Uneconomic bypass is undesirable because it is wasteful and sends false economic signals to the industry. Under certain circumstances it might also threaten universal service and the LEC's financial stability. In contrast, economic bypass, by definition, occurs when LEC and bypass prices are cost based, and, hence, may be technically termed to be "economically efficient" solutions, albeit concerns respecting universal service and carrier viability still remain. However, the determination of whether a particular rate is cost based can be an extremely complex, even illusory, process. This applies, in particular, where common and joint costs of the local network must be allocated to an individual service offering.

Another major distinction concerns bypass activity stemming from service factors, or "noneconomic" bypass. Noneconomic bypass arises when a telephone company fails to meet users' nonprice requirements, causing them to seek alternative sources of supply. These may include such considerations as service quality, reliability, system features, availability, flexibility, and, generally responsiveness to customer needs. For example, unsatisfactory telephone service repairs may drive businesses critically dependent on communications to develop new solutions. This form of bypass may occur whether or not prices of LEC services are cost based.

As indicated by Figure VI–1, internal or external bypass may occur for any of these reasons, viz., economic, uneconomic, or noneconomic. It is not inconceivable, for example, that LPSN circumvention could be attained through customer subscription to a local carrier channel service for uneconomic and noneconomic reasons.

A final distinction of importance to public decision makers concerns differences between facility and carrier bypass. *Facility bypass* relates to private ownership of communications systems or networks that circumvent the LEC's local switched network. *Carrier bypass* involves the use of nonLPSN transmission plant to connect a given user and an interexchange carrier. Basically, telecommunications users may employ LEC private line tariffed services (called service bypass), as well as other leased or privately owned means to directly interconnect to AT&T or other IXCs.

In practice, these differences between facility and carrier forms of bypass are blurring. Carriers, acting through affiliates, are deeply involved in building private bypass systems for businesses and universities. An example is FiberLAN, Inc., a company formed by BellSouth (a Regional Bell Operating Company) and Siecor (a fiber system manufacturer) to design and install fiber optic based local area networks (LANs) for business use.[15] Private bypassers are now allowed by the FCC to resell excess capacity on private microwave systems in competition with the common carriers.   Shared tenant systems (STS) operations may concentrate user needs such that bypass is facilitated. Ameritech Communications currently is an STS provider, and AT&T at one time engaged in such activity.[16]

Moreover, carriers may engage in or promote bypass of their own facilities in the pursuit of customers. For example, an Illinois Bell unit and Alpha Communications have joined together to provide various telecommunications services and products to tenants in Chicago office complexes in a teleport configuration which will bypass Illinois Bell's own local switching center.[17] Ohio Bell publicly announced its intent to purchase a 20 percent stake in a privately held satellite–based Ohio Teleport Company.[18] And Diamond State Telephone Company recently installed "one of the largest private fiber optic networks in the world" for a Delaware corporation.[19]

B.   The Development of Bypass

1.   Historical Perspective

In practice, telephone "bypass" is not new. Telephone company supplied private lines have circumvented the switched network for approximately one hundred years. In the late 1870s, there existed Western Union's public telegraph offerings and also private telegraph lines, which were installed by, *inter alia,* Atlantic Refining Company and Tidewater Pipeline Company. Competitive alternatives to the Bell network also arose with the emergence of new telephone companies when the original Bell patents expired in 1893. This continued unabated until consummation of the "Kingsbury Commitment" in 1913, which essentially established the longstanding U.S. telephone industry market structure comprised of Independents and the Bell System.

During the 1940s, there were additional new communications ventures. For instance, several companies, including Raytheon, Philco, Dumont, IBM, General Electric, and Western Union, initiated efforts to build private micro– wave systems which were designed to meet these companies' internal communications needs and, generally, the requirements of the early television broadcast market. These efforts were generally unsuccessful in large measure because of the entities' failure to obtain the requisite regulatory permission to proceed.   In 1949, Keystone Pipeline Company contracted with Federal Telephone and Radio Corporation, an affiliate of International Telephone and Telegraph Company, to replace its leased wireline facilities in Pennsylvania with the world's first industrial microwave system. AT&T met these threats directly, engaging in a massive development and construction program which resulted in a nationwide microwave system by the end of the 1940s that the FCC accorded utility status.

In the 1950s, many large users put into place a myriad of private micro– wave systems. Many systems grew out of demands for special types of service, or the needs for service to particular (remote) regions not served by telephone companies. Others were built when individual firms or industry groups possessed high levels of internal demand, which made private facilities more economically attractive than common carrier service. Included among the applicants for private microwave frequencies were the railroads, oil and gas pipeline companies, cable television (CATV) systems, state and local governmental entities, and rural broadcasting stations. As in the late 1940s, all were initially limited to one year restricted licenses with attendant risks of nonrenewal.

In 1954, however, two North Dakota television stations, with other broad-casting support, requested rule changes permitting private microwave use for intercity television relay whenever savings could be realized over common carrier services. Since the availability of common carrier services was not to be considered, this proposed rule change clearly threatened the extant video monopoly. In 1958, the FCC determined that broadcasters could obtain facility licenses without regard to availability of AT&T video channels. Such licenses would not be granted, however, if interconnection with common carrier lines was required. While not legitimizing the concept of competitive supply, this case indicated that FCC policies might finally reflect supply options made possible years earlier by microwave radio.

Thus, by the end of the 1950s, private microwave systems appeared to offer significant service, cost and technical advantages relative to convention-al telephone service in several applications. Moreover, having reversed its earlier position, the FCC sanctioned the construction and operation of such systems that achieved certain technical standards in its *Above 890 Mc* deci-sion.[20] This landmark 1959 ruling basically marked the beginning of the "modern era" of telecommunications regulation whereby alternatives to telephone company offerings would not necessarily be viewed by policy makers as inconsistent with the public interest.

2. Impetus for Bypass

As discussed throughout this book, the U.S. telecommunications sector today is the product of major technological forces, increased competitive entry, and a myriad of facilitating public policies instituted by federal and state agencies, the courts, and the U.S. Congress. These fundamental changes to the U.S. telecommunications environment have specifically had a profound effect on local bypass. Several basic variables have been found to exist which tend to influence the nature and extent of local bypass. Concerning demand related factors, the specific needs of the various types of users will help determine the level of bypass activity, as will the demographics of a given state or region. Supply side considerations center on the availability of technologies which are both cost effective and technically feasible, and the existence of alternative communications sources.

a. Demand Factors: User Incentives
The decision of users to bypass the local exchange carrier's LPSN is driven by many factors, among them service, technology, price, and govern-mental policy. It is possible that technology will play a deterministic role in

the evolution of bypass over the longer term, as it has in the United States at several other points in the past. For example, new technology, especially economical microwave systems, permitted facilities based private communications to become a reality for many companies in the 1960s. Of course, the advance of transmission technology through intensive research also reduced costs of long distance service, at a pace much faster than for local loop plant. This, in the view of some observers, permitted the industry to direct a flow of funds financed by long distance offerings to the local service arena. Similarly, changes in the pricing of local exchange and access service were undertaken in several jurisdictions in the post divestiture environment to redirect this flow to suit competitive and other goals.

Local bypass has been in evidence since at least the 1950s. The underlying technology continues to grow in sophistication and to decline in cost, especially in recent years. New services also continue to evolve. But the plethora of new pricing schemes now being undertaken by LECs and sanctioned by federal and state policy makers are likely to leave some local telephone services overpriced or underpriced relative to alternative services or facilities. Additionally, if state regulatory commissions allow additional forms of bypass and the FCC continues to act aggressively in a "procompetitive fashion," bypass will present ongoing policy problems.

One of the most powerful incentives to bypass is, of course, the unavailability of a needed service from the LEC. Long delays in service provisioning can also drive users to alternative carriers and systems. Even at a relatively high price, bypass will take place if a business requires a service or installation schedule that is unavailable from the local telephone company.

Other service or nonprice factors can also motivate bypass of the LPSN. An exchange carrier's lack of responsiveness to maintenance, service change, and accounting needs can motivate a search for alternative service. And, potential bypassers may place high value on service reliability, security, or direct control of the service. Experience or reputation of the supplier may also be accorded top priority by local service customers.

Governmental policy can be a major factor in the bypass decision of an organization. For instance, shared tenant systems (now allowed in some form in over half of the states) make it possible for small users to take advantage of bypass systems and services by pooling demand in an industrial park or office building. Similarly, an FCC decision to allocate additional spectrum to private microwave and digital termination systems would increase bypass opportunities.

Court decisions may also impact the attractiveness of bypass. For example, the MFJ Court's September 1987 and March 1988 Opinions retained existing bans on RBOCs engaging in manufacturing and interexchange activities, but relaxed certain aspects of the information service prohibition. Thus, similar to GTE, Contel, United and other LECs, Bell Operating Companies may now lawfully offer information "gateways" and such services as electronic mail and voice messaging. These enhancements may encourage users otherwise set on leaving the public network for reasons of features or costs to remain on the LPSN. Moreover, court, state commission, and FCC decisions relating to state regulation of information services, carrier and end user access charges, and depreciation could impact the price, availability, and dissemination of bypass.

b. Supply Factors: Available Technologies

Over the longer term, the most important incentive for users to bypass the local exchange carrier could hinge upon technological change. Technology directly affects the feasibility of most forms of local bypass, and ultimately defines the boundaries of bypass service features. Today, if the local exchange company does not provide a technologically and economically feasible service, another carrier or the user will likely fill the void. Technology plays a bypass role similar to that of governmental regulation and market demand in determining whether bypass will take place and what carrier or user will be responsible.

Although there are over a dozen major bypass technologies extant in the U.S. today,[21] the individual technologies may be conveniently grouped into four broad categories. These include (a) radio based systems, (b) cable based systems, (c) intraoffice systems, and (d) multiple technology ("multitech") systems.

Some of these technologies have been employed for a number of years (e.g., point–to–point microwave), while others are relatively new (such as lasers or infrared). Each of these represents a medium that enables customers to communicate without using portions of a telephone company's existing facilities. Customers may obtain needed services by individually or jointly owning or leasing distribution systems which utilize varying combinations of these bypass technologies. Alternatively, these services may be provided by nonLEC suppliers using the same technologies. To date, bypass technologies have gained varying degrees of acceptance among providers and users, offering different "mixes" of features and capabilities. Each of these alternatives is discussed below.

(1) Radio Based Systems

Bypass is afforded by a variety of microwave and other radio based technologies. Since 1959, major corporations have been legally permitted to establish private microwave systems for intrafirm data and voice point–to–point communications in the 2, 6, 18, and 23 GHz spectrum "bands." These user owned networks typically may be deployed relatively quickly once licenses are received from the FCC. Other advantages sometimes cited for these systems are user control, no right–of–way requirements, high capacity, and possible scale economies as additional channels are added. Drawbacks in the use of microwave systems include (a) a sensitivity to adverse weather conditions and line–of–sight obstructions such as buildings and rugged terrain; (b) a need to employ (scarce) spectrum; and (c) reduced reliability, security, and privacy (e.g., compared to cable systems).

The major potential for growth would appear to be in the frequency range above 18 GHz, which is less congested in most major cities. Moreover, these high frequency systems are less costly in terms of equipment, such as radio antenna and towers, and also installation.   The new antennae are smaller: the 23 GHz systems require antennae 1.5 to 3 feet in diameter while 2 and 6 GHz typically use ones 6 to 10 feet.   Short haul 18 and 23 GHz radios are generally used for applications of under 15 miles.

A digital termination system (DTS) is another bypass technology which employs radio signals.   DTS systems can form a wideband local distribution network that transmits high speed digital electronic message services (DEMS) on a two-way basis.   These systems employ small rooftop antennae in a limited (7 to 10 miles) service region, such as a metropolitan area, and use intercity terrestrial microwave and satellite links to form end-to-end digital data communications networks. DTS technology features low power microwave transmitters, with higher speeds and potentially superior quality compared to that afforded by telephone company point-to-point or point-to-multipoint offerings.   A primary attraction is its relatively short installation time. Flexibility will be another advantage as voice applications develop in the future.   As with private microwave systems, major disadvantages of DTS center on its susceptibility to interference and concerns relating to spectrum scarcity.   The technology also exhibits a limited capacity overall and can be expensive relative to leased line alternatives such as T1 when subscribers are widely dispersed. Nonoptimization for voice applications also appears to be a deterrent.

After considerable regulatory delays at the developmental stage, cellular radio is a recently introduced mobile communications medium which will permit each assigned frequency channel to be used many times within a given service area through the establishment and coordination of a system of zones or "cells."   As the subscriber unit (e.g., a car) travels in a defined area that offers cellular service, a radio connection will be "handed off" while the unit passes through a grid of cells.   This uninterrupted calling is accomplished through the functional control afforded by a central computerized switched called a Mobile Telecommunications Switching Office (MTSO).

A major advantage of cellular radio is that it permits more efficient use of the spectrum relative to existing mobile telephone offerings.   Its availability will significantly increase service accessibility for existing and prospective users. Numbering over 1.7 million subscribers by August 1988, the cellular service business is expected to experience strong demand during the next five years.[22]   An early concern by many observers that cellular technology, particularly terminal equipment, would be too expensive for all but the largest business customers during the next several years appears to have been unduly negative as equipment prices and service rates have decreased rapidly.   An anticipated problem is that capacity shortages will cause deterioration in service quality. A current disadvantage is that cellular service continues to be bothered by heavy precipitation, lightning storms, and the close proximity of some microwave towers.

FM-SCAs (frequency modulation -- subsidiary carrier authorizations), or simply FM subcarriers, are another potential radio based vehicle for bypass.

Until April 7, 1983, the FCC restricted FM radio station use of subchannels to services of a broadcast nature, *e.g.,* background music in shopping centers. A subchannel is essentially an inaudible ultrasonic signal that can be added to the regular program signal of a FM radio station, or to the audio signals of television stations. The signal can be picked up through decoders or special receivers, *e.g.,* paging devices which display text data. Applications include translation of voice, music, text, and data; generation of control signals for traffic lights; and operation of teletype machines.

An advantage of FM–SCAs is that heretofore largely unused spectrum may be productively utilized on a 24–hour basis. The medium offers transmission speeds up to 19.2 Kbps at relatively low costs. One drawback concerning such systems is that only specially targeted, one–way signals, such as data and paging, may be transmitted, thereby significantly limiting its attractiveness as a bypass medium. Limited bandwidth is another disadvantage. A third problem pertains to "multipath," where terrain or other obstacles create conflicting signals or other distortions.

Thus far, several types of terrestrial, or land based radio systems have been discussed as means of bypassing the local switched network or, more broadly, LEC facilities. Satellites represent a significant radio based bypass alternative featuring space and earth station subsystems. Satellite transmission and switching achieved through customer owned earth stations can be used to bypass the local switched network, as well as long distance carriers to create private end–to–end systems. Bypass would take place whether the terminals are owned by a private corporation (for its personal communications needs, shared use, or resale) or by a domestic satellite ("domsat") carrier as elements of its network.

The primary advantage inherent in satellite technology is lower costs over long distances (*i.e.,* distance insensitivity) relative to many other technologies. In the course of utilizing satellites for this reason, a customer may also bypass the local exchange for video, voice, or data applications. Another attractive feature of a satellite system is its large capacity. A disadvantage *vis–à–vis* terrestrial microwave, is the medium's characteristic delay and echo during transmission of information. Another centers on its distance insensitivity: therefore a cost effective "breakeven" or "crossover" point occurs for C–band (4 to 6 GHz) satellites at relatively close in mileage relative to distance–dependent terrestrial communications.

In 1980 the first Ku–band satellite was launched into geosynchronous orbit. The deployment of these satellites made customer premises applications feasible because of smaller antennae for earth stations and relatively simple frequency coordination. Very small aperture terminals (VSATs) are used predominantly with Ku band networks, and feature efficient transmission, relatively easy growth up to a certain capacity, and a single vendor solution. A major disadvantage is the severe effect of rain attenuation on Ku–band. The main application of satellite technology has become private data networks for multipoint communications among corporate branches, *i.e.,* for links to specific sites.

(2) Cable Based Systems

Two–way or interactive broadband coaxial cable represents another potential means of bypassing local exchange plant. The technology is best suited for point–to–point communication within a 10 to 15 mile range. Traditional cable television (CATV) systems exist in a number of communities. To date, such systems have mainly provided entertainment programming and have offered only very limited high speed data service applications. One of the few successful companies thus far, Manhattan Cable TV Co., Inc. in New York generated only $1.5 million in local private line revenues in 1986, or less than 2 percent of New York Telephone's total for that service. Voice grade service offerings may be provided in the future over institutional cable networks or two–way interactive cable systems.

Cable television may eventually become one of the more significant bypass technologies because of widespread accessibility for users, and economic incentives for CATV operators to offer two–way services. Cable systems, however, have significant technical problems with two–way applications as they are optimized for the one–way dissemination of television signals. High CATV installation costs are currently an important drawback to offering alternative data transmission services from the perspective of the provider. There are also substantial regulatory, reliability, and capability concerns, and accessing buildings can be a lengthy, complex process. An institutional obstacle may be the possibility that many cable operators are not comfortable with non–entertainment endeavors, which may bring about partnerships with LECs (see below). Security problems can be mitigated through the use of encryption devices but can be costly.

Fiber optics is another cable based system with possible bypass application. Voice or data transmission through thin glass filaments or "fibers" has become economically feasible for operational systems only during the last several years. Current "lightguide" transmission applications include uses in local networks (generally singlemode technology except for certain multimode uses such as in LANs), long distance communications (singlemode), and military systems (*e.g.,* underwater acoustic sensors using singlemode fibers). Future uses may include teleconferencing and high speed matrix switching functions. Optical fiber is particularly attractive for large volume communications between locations at least 5 miles apart.

Advantages of a fiber optics system include its high capacity, relative ease of installation (compared to copper cable), low operating and maintenance costs, minimal susceptibility to interference, and high reliability. Recent production cost reductions, improved fiber attenuation, and greater longevity of light sources add to the attractiveness of fiber optics. Main shortcomings include its relatively rapid design obsolescence and relatively high overall costs for mobile and rural communications or, generally, applications where low capacity may be needed. Right–of–way problems will also serve to detract from its perceived usefulness.

As originally developed in 1962, the T1 digital carrier was a telephone company short haul (metropolitan area) system using paired cable. The technology was used initially for interconnecting local central offices, using

D-type channel banks. In 1977 AT&T added T1 multiplexing capability to its DDS offerings, thereby introducing the technology to customer premises.

In its basic form, the T1 system carries twenty-four voiceband channels on two pairs of wires and has a transmission range of approximately 50 miles. T1 is widely regarded today as any digital communications system functioning at a synchronous data rate of 1.544 Mbps. In recent years T1 and other T carrier systems have employed paired and coaxial cable, digital microwave radio systems, and fiber optics. The latter lightwave systems provide high capacity and high quality transmission which makes them attractive for short haul or long haul applications. Besides terrestrial facilities, digital satellite has been developed for use in a T1 (multiplexing) mode. Their deployment has gained in popularity as satellite orbital lives have recently been extended, yielding satellite T1 link prices that are 35 to 70 percent below those of typical terrestrial services.

T1's attractiveness to users center on its increasing ability to economically multiply (*i.e.*, "multiplex") the number of signals that a given circuit may transmit. Thus, T1's DS-1 digital signal carries 48 voice grade channels at 1.544 Mbps. As T1 costs continue to fall and slower speed private line rates rise, T1 demand has been increasing. The higher DS-3 capacity data and voice communications lines are beginning to gain popularity, with the cost of one DS-3 line equivalent to the cost of eight to ten T1 circuits. Other advantages of T1 systems are easier (user) management of fewer lines, large capacity, and the utilization of "backbone" networks for back up and disaster reasons. Disadvantages pertain to the cost of the approach for smaller users, which may not have the capacity requirements to justify a T1 application. T1 capability may be obtained either through public or private networks.

(3) Intraoffice Systems

The growth of internal business telecommunications and the dispersal of computing capacity throughout major business and university campuses has increased the need to tie together the many sources of information within organizations. Electronic private branch exchanges (PBXs) are being developed as a means of enhancing local intracorporate information flows. PBXs are small, private switchboards which historically have provided businesses with internal telephone switching capabilities. With the advent of the electronics and software resolution, PBXs can also be programmed to furnish advanced telephone functions such as speed dialing, least cost routing, and call forwarding. These switchboards serve as the hub of the modern office, shepherding voice and data transmission and making intrafacility "smart" devices compatible. The newest generation of PBXs using digital techniques permits simultaneous transmission of voice and data and can handle information from communicating word processors, multifunction electronic copiers, and various generic types of computers (*i.e.*, from mainframe to personal computers).

PBXs pose a different type of bypass "problem" for LECs and public policy makers than does the more familiar facility or carrier bypass. Calls switched by a PBX in an office setting are connected to the local exchange network through trunks, which concentrate the traffic and thereby utilize the transmission facilities more efficiently. In contrast, subscribers served by a conventional local loop are each individually connected to the central office by a dedicated access line as in the case of an LEC's Centrex service. Thus, "bypass" occurs in the narrow sense that traffic is aggregated such that (1) fewer LEC access lines are obtained and (2) it becomes more feasible to connect to a private line or private bypass facility. As such, PBXs may facilitate circumvention of LEC facilities or services but does not present a bypass threat in the usual sense.

Local area networks (LANs) are often high speed intrafacility "data pipelines" that permit communication among an office's computers, as well as other intelligent devices. LANs use coaxial cable or, more popular of late, fiber optics to provide data, image or text communications within one building or several contiguous buildings. Significant voice applications may be possible in the future.   LANs may be interconnected to form metropolitan area networks (MANs). Certain applications of LANs and presumably the typical MAN represent means to communicate without using the local public switched network.

A fundamental advantage of a LAN is its ability to increase the value of the various "smart" machines in an office through integration. For example, this technique permits coordination and avoidance of data redundancy logjams. Deficiencies inherent in the arrangement include the fact that currently different types of computers often cannot communicate with each other on the same local area network; the industry's unresolved quest for a standard office technology; office inside wiring complexities; and the limited range of many LANs (often less than a mile).

LAN sales are currently brisk and are expected to grow; however, many in the industry view local area networks as currently delivering only a fraction of the potential benefits promised and, ". . . thus far, have not lived up to their name."[23]

Atmospheric optical systems, such as infrared and lasers, are lesser known, line–of–sight bypass technologies. The boundary between radio and optical communications is beginning to blur as infrared and laser systems begin to come into use. Both are largely unproven. These technologies' primary current use is by the military, which may find their secure, jam–resistant features especially attractive. Infrared's main applications thus far have been in data transmission. In this use, infrared may have costs comparable to those of microwave radio. Lasers can transmit voice and data, and can be used for video conferencing or even videotex. This technology may be particularly attractive for remote locations.

Both of these technologies do not require FCC licenses in order to be used, and both avoid large start up costs. Another advantage is a short installation time; indeed, a portable laser system may be installed in a few days. They appear to be suitable especially for links between buildings and for emergency or temporary applications. Disadvantages include these systems' limited range (less than 1 mile), line of sight limitations, and susceptibility to atmospheric conditions such as electrical storms or dense fog.

(4) Multitech Systems

Rather than employing a single technology, some bypass systems use multiple technologies to effect circumvention of local telephone company plant.   For instance, teleports, which combine real estate development, telecommunications, and information processing, integrate various technologies to create customized services for the tenants of executive offices or industrial parks. Technologies employed in connection with these "smart" or "intelligent buildings" may include, *inter alia,* satellites (*e.g.,* master TV antenna systems [SMATV] and "antennae farms"), fiber optics, coaxial cable, microwave links, and value added networks, and electronic PBXs. Teleports may be especially attractive to small businesses, since by aggregating their buying power, these users may secure services which might not be affordable or otherwise obtainable. In practice, shared tenant services have experienced only limited success thus far.

Other mixed technology uses exist as well. For example, in the past MCI has employed microwave links in combination with interactive cable in experiments in Omaha and Atlanta. And mobile communications providers are combining satellite technology with cellular telephony to address needs of rural and other users.

c. Supply Factors: Alternative Communications Sources

Alternatives to the local public switched network have existed for years. Private microwave has been used since the 1940s by select customers (*e.g.,* utilities and government), and since the late 1950s by businesses. Originally confined to intrasystem applications, private microwave networks may not legitimately have their excess capacity marketed to other users. Private line alternatives to the LPSN have been readily available to subscribers since the last century, both on a toll and local (channel) basis.

Suppliers of the newer technologies are apparently becoming more evident. For example, by the end of 1984, six metropolitan areas had teleport facilities available. Currently more than 20 cities have at least one teleport, including New York, Boston, San Francisco, and Washington, D.C.[24] Manufacturers of fiber optics number among their ranks AT&T, Corning Glass, Fujitsu, ITT, Pirelli, and SIECOR, and LEC and nonLEC providers of private fiber communications networks are numerous.   Cellular service has been licensed by the FCC in more than 270 major medium, and small metropolitan areas, as well as rural service areas (RSAs).[25] Cable television companies, some with interactive capability, currently serve approximately 50 percent of U.S. TV households.[26] Satellite links through VSAT arrangements seem to be widely available, and supply of such "niche" technologies as infrared, lasers, and FM–SCA exists albeit on a much smaller scale than other modes of bypass. The emergence of trade associations for teleport, cellular, STS, and bypassers in general (such as Association of Local Alternative Transmission Services) attests to the growing presence of such suppliers.

Potentially the single most significant source of bypass activity is AT&T. It appears that AT&T's predominance in long distance, ubiquitous network, and technical capabilities is being marshalled to penetrate the local exchange area. AT&T has maintained that the company would not actively attempt to bypass the local facilities of its former Bell Operating Company units despite alleged strong customer interest.[27]   However, AT&T has adopted a more aggressive approach, offering new services such as Software Defined Network (SDN) and Megacom, encouraging direct connections between large users and its points of presence, and introducing new microwave systems designed for private facility bypass.

AT&T's development of new private line tariffs in 1985 signifies an early attempt by the company to adjust to increasing competition in some parts of the private line market. Adopted by the Federal Communications Commission in late 1985, the AT&T tariffs represent a major restructuring and repricing intended to position AT&T to effectively compete for private line business. These new tariffs create new service options and opportunities for the user through the unbundling and repricing of services which were formerly integrated in AT&T's end–to–end offerings.

Prime examples of this ongoing unbundling and repricing of services include the shifting of revenue requirements from relatively competitive data services to less competitive voice grade offerings, and the reduction in relatively competitive long haul rates and concomitant increases in short haul. AT&T also continues to make adjustments in its private line tariffs to further improve its position relative to local operating companies and the other interexchange carriers.

Similarly, AT&T's WATS pricing has seemingly followed a pattern that adheres to the principle of increasing rates for services that it deems to be less competitive and decreasing rates for the services it considers more competitive. For AT&T's WATS service, this has meant a decreasing discount from MTS equivalent service for large users as the length of haul increases. This approach is consistent with the view that WATS service for large users is less subject to competitive inroads and thus may be overpriced relative to the service obtained by medium users of WATS. Some maintain that these changes reflect a judgment by AT&T that its huge market share will enable the company to subsidize its competitive services by increasing the rates of services less subject to competitive inroads. As an example, October 1988 AT&T notified its customers that WATS pricing would be changed from mileage bands to a distance sensitive rate structure.

AT&T is also offering three new high capacity services: Accunet (T1) Switched 56, Megacom, and the Software Defined Network (SDN). Unlike private lines which use dedicated facilities, all three of these new services use the switched network. All also continue the trend observed for private line tariffs toward unbundling of local access channels from the line haul function and instituting separate charges for extra services. These switched services differ from private lines in that they are billed on a monthly access charge basis with additional time and distance based usage charges.

The similarity of AT&T's new services to ordinary switched telephone service appears to be consistent with the company's competitive push toward instituting usage based rates. Existence of such rates would help position AT&T for intense head–to–head competition with other interexchange companies, and, eventually, with the BOCs' local exchange and intraLATA toll services.

Each of AT&T's new services appears to be targeted toward the needs of high volume customers. These users have traditionally employed normal private lines or have required high speed service. AT&T's new services represent a step in the company's evolution toward the Integrated Services Digital Network (ISDN) concept. Under this approach, there is an emphasis on strong user selection capabilities, *e.g.,* on a real time basis for only the needed amounts of specific services and under usage based prices.

Elimination of the local access charge discount offered other common carriers (other than AT&T), as well as the spread of equal local access for all long distance carriers, will tend to reduce AT&T's relative costs to accessing the local telephone networks and could reduce price competition in long distance service. The LECs and other common carriers (OCCs) have complained to the FCC that these changes and AT&T's new services will cause large customers to circumvent the local network and implement private and carrier bypass alternatives, presumably including direct connection to or by AT&T. The lifting of the structural separation requirements imposed on AT&T may also enable the company to provide local bypass facilities integrated with interexchange services.

Of course, concern over these changes may stem primarily from fear that AT&T will use its new found market freedom under the divestiture agreement and its market presence to reintegrate the most profitable parts of the old Bell System. Reaching out to large users, AT&T could bypass local exchange companies entirely. The company clearly has the capability to furnish the technically sophisticated pathways needed by large users for both switched and unswitched voice and data directly to its points of presence.

In effect, AT&T may be able to offer the largest users of communications services very attractive "one–stop shopping" on highly competitive terms. Recent AT&T strategic pricing initiatives at the interstate level may presage such an occurrence. The company has developed several controversial tariff packages which have been approved at least tentatively by the FCC. In early 1985, AT&T proposed a broadening of Tariff No. 12 to include a customized network for the Department of Defense. With Tariff 12 filings, AT&T can offer custom designed networks incorporating a mix of voice and data services for large business users at a fixed price, usually at significant discounts from tariffed rates. In 1986, the company sought permission to provide a Digital Tandem Switched Network for General Electric. Subsequently AT&T requested approval for Tariff 12's Option I and Option II plans for DuPont and Ford Motor Co., respectively. The FCC approved all of these proposals subject to the results of pending investigations. Currently AT&T seeks authorization to offer an expanded customized network (Option III) to American Express.

In September 1986, the Federal Communications Commission granted at least temporary approval to the carrier to offer volume discounts to Holiday Corp. pursuant to new Tariff 15. The tariff allows AT&T to offer a specific customer below–tariff pricing if a competing carrier has made such an offer (as MCI did in this instance). Moreover, AT&T received authorization to offer switched service discounts to business users with multiple locations ("Multi–Location Calling Plan"). In October 1988 the FCC approved AT&T's request to offer the General Services Administration a one year rate stabilization plan in lieu of monthly rates for existing common control switching arrangements (CCSA), an intercity private line service. Despite vehement arguments presented by numerous parties to reject each of these proposed tariffs, the FCC has apparently cleared the way for AT&T to engage in selective pricing. For its part, AT&T has stated that it will decide on a case–by–case basis whether to respond to competitors' price offers to customers, observing that any attempts by the carrier to initiate price cutting might be viewed as anticompetitive behavior.[28]

The IXC may, in fact, be acting more aggressively in promoting its capability as a one stop communications source. For example, AT&T recently "drove the situation, although the application was developed jointly" involving the installation of a direct microwave link between a Carter Hawley Hale Stores' facility in Anaheim, California and AT&T's point of presence in Santa Ana some 8 to 10 miles away.[29] This arrangement bypasses local facilities of Pacific Bell.

3. Strategic Responses to Bypass

Local telephone companies have become vigilant in the protection of their existing and potential revenues from encroachment by other carriers or private forms of local exchange bypass. Regulatory commissions at both the state and federal levels are increasingly concerned with the potential threat to universal service from bypass of the LECs by their largest, and often most profitable customers. A number of alternative strategies have been offered to public policy makers striving to address the alleged bypass problem. Among these are pricing changes, regulatory and judicial relief, and service related improvements.

a. Repricing Strategies

Clearly price is not the only factor controlling user decisions to bypass the local network. However, it is a highly visible one which involves both the LECs and the regulatory commissions. Of course, pricing changes must be made based on knowledge of the types of bypass such changes are meant to control. All other things being equal, attempts to suppress economic bypass, based on a cost advantage enjoyed by the bypassing entity, are likely to be futile if competitors' prices accurately reflect these differences. Such attempts may produce allegations of cross subsidies among telephone company services. Similarly, no reasonable pricing changes can suppress noneconomic bypass which is motivated not by price differentials, but by the user's search for a service not provided by the LEC.

Nevertheless, deaveraged or flexible rates, incremental or marginal cost pricing for services featuring new technology, and various nontraffic sensitive (NTS) cost recovery plans have all been advanced as possible policy prescriptions for addressing uneconomic bypass.

Local exchange companies (with requisite regulatory approvals) could deaverage telephone company prices for services on highly competitive routes or could otherwise be allowed to charge prices to meet market conditions. As described in Chapter IV, a number of such formal proposals have been introduced before regulatory agencies during the 1980s, and include, *inter alia,* social contract/price cap plans, incentive regulation, rate stabilization, and deregulation.

Implementation of these alternative regulatory plans might enable local telephone companies to compete on a more equitable basis with their less regulated rivals. Such policies might also help preserve universal telephone service where it may be threatened by excessive local price increases, including those that could result from bypass.

Another approach centers on pricing services using new technology at incremental or marginal cost instead of system wide average costs. The LECs argue that incremental or marginal cost pricing could help induce these companies to modernize, and become more competitive with bypass providers. Purportedly, it would also aid in the maintenance of universal service. A concern under this approach is the avoidance of cross subsidy and discrimination among communications users.

These repricing schemes are widely proposed, but not widely implemented. The reasons relate mainly to the implementation problems associated with the subjective judgments as to which markets are competitive, what a "reasonable" price range would be, and the determination of incremental or marginal costs. Theoretical questions are also relevant, such as the reliance on economic efficiency to the exclusion of other goals and the perhaps overriding question of how the LEC's total revenue requirement would be met under the current regulatory scheme.

Another repricing approach is to shift the bulk of local loop costs that do not vary with use to the specifically defined "cost causative" customer. The original FCC plan to shift all nontraffic sensitive cost recovery to the end user[30] has not come to fruition: while business subscribers may be assessed as much as $6.00 per line per month, residential ratepayers have paid $3.20 per line per month since December 1, 1988, with the last scheduled access charge boost to $3.50 implemented on April 1, 1989. Consumer and Congressional objections to making local customers pay all these costs have kept the FCC favored reduction in charges for long distance carriers from becoming a reality. The separation of local and long distance service providers means, of course, that NTS costs imposed on interexchange carriers in the form of higher local access rates, make bypass systems look more attractive to large users and carriers than would otherwise be the case.

The Federal Communications Commission concluded that, in light of structural and technological changes in the industry during the 1970s and early 1980s, these perceived "subsidies" were inducing larger users to bypass the local network, and potentially draining off substantial revenues from local companies or reducing support for high cost local loop plant.   These allegations have never been incontrovertibly proven. However, the FCC has proceeded with actions which instituted a dual access charge system. Some of the NTS costs are being imposed on a flat rate basis on local subscribers as the end user or "subscriber line charge" (SLC), while a portion continues to be paid by the interexchange long distance carriers.

Those interstate NTS costs not recovered through end user charges may be recovered from the interexchange carriers through the carrier common line charges (CCLCs).   Because political pressure has forced the FCC to retreat from its original plan of recovering all NTS costs from end users, various alternatives for continuing to recover the majority of NTS costs from interexchange usage sensitive charges have been proposed.   The purported problem, of course, is to recover the NTS costs from the interexchange carriers without aggravating bypass of the local telephone company.

Several general approaches are possible to eliminate the threat of bypass induced by the use of CCLCs.   For instance, competitive entry could be limited by forbidding the interconnection of private lines in carrier switches or forcing customers to use the local public switched network. An alternative is to effectively tax bypass, an approach represented by the FCC's $25 per month charge on private lines that can access the local switched network through a "leaky" PBX.   These and other approaches may tend to discourage technological innovation and perpetuate "inefficient" pricing.

b.   Relaxation of Public Policy Constraints

Regulatory policy pertaining to areas in addition to the setting of prices and cost recovery schemes can also form a part of the response to the threat of bypass.   Streamlined tariff filing procedures designed to reduce cost support and shorten tariff implementation periods would permit LECs to respond to any competition on a more timely basis. However, adoption of these procedures where substantial market power exists could undercut incipient competition.

The use of contractual arrangements in lieu of tariffs is another vehicle which might be profitably employed to persuade large users to remain with the telephone company. By tailoring contractual terms to the specific needs of its customer, the LEC may more flexibly market its offerings to those threatening to bypass the local public switched network.   Again, the advantages of such lessening of regulatory constraints are enhanced viability of the local company and, potentially, protection of universal service.

Drawbacks in allowing LECs to enter into private contracts with customers would also exist.   There would be difficulties *a priori* in determining when contracts might be appropriate. Further the use of such agreements might become vehicles for market place misconduct, particularly if combined with noncost based rates or prices.

As detailed in other chapters, the RBOCs at the federal level have sought to have the MFJ "line of business" restrictions relaxed if not eliminated. Although the Bell Operating Companies or their affiliates cannot currently manufacture telecommunications (or other) equipment and cannot offer interexchange services, many areas of commerce are available to these entities as MFJ and FCC restrictions are eased. Independent companies have no such constraints but interestingly, GTE, the largest nonBell LEC, has voluntarily reduced its participation in the interexchange market and is shedding a significant segment of its manufacturing business, *viz.*, switching equipment.[31]

The Bell Operating Companies have also been vigorously pressing state legislators and regulatory commissions to free them from most intrastate regulations. For the BOCs, complete deregulation of competitive offerings of all LECs and equal regulatory treatment of all competitors represent serious policy options. Potential outcomes of such a policy range from greater efficiency and innovation to the creation of a new monopoly if the LECs are able to leverage the market power of their local networks to gain control of a significant share of toll traffic. Many states have resisted implementation of deregulation proposals, at least as long as the LECs still possess substantial intrastate market power, believing such an action would likely have disastrous consequences for competition and local ratepayers.

Some states have tried to eliminate the problem of LEC bypass through the institution of regulatory constraints. Options include imposition of a ban on some types of bypass service, restrictions on the installation of private bypass facilities (where enforceable), and tariff changes. These are intended to help the LECs compete or even to compel use of the local public switched network as part of a public policy commitment to universal service. Restrictions on local bypass are the most severe policy options. For instance, such requirements might cause some companies to relocate to other states, and may dampen technological innovation, cost reduction efforts, and efficiency.

Deregulation of supposedly competitive intrastate telecommunications services is also an active policy option. Indeed, some states have allowed intrastate competition in a number of competitive areas. Among the RBOCs, U S WEST has promoted deregulation vigorously, and enjoyed considerable success. As of April 1988, twelve of the fourteen states in this RBOC's operating territory have approved some form of deregulation. Specifically, one (Nebraska) completely eliminated rate of return regulation; and several (*e.g.*, Colorado, Idaho, Minnesota, North Dakota, and Oregon) deregulated particular "competitive" services. Moreover, seven states (Washington, Utah, Arizona, Oregon, North Dakota, Iowa, and New Mexico) have initiated flexible pricing policies.

c. Improving Service Capabilities

Telephone companies and their affiliates are also employing the aforementioned bypass technologies to bring new services to customers in an increasingly market driven industry. Local distribution plant now consists largely of copper wire strung to subscribers' premises on poles. This strengthening of the existing local plant is taking place as necessary through new technologies such as packet switching, local area data transport systems, and digital electronic switching. Often, local telephone companies or their affiliates provide these bypass systems themselves.

Ultimately, fiber optic distribution systems are likely to supplement considerable copper wire and microwave facilities, especially if ubiquitous high speed data capabilities are to be available to most users of the local switched network. In the interim, major local telephone companies (e.g., New York Telephone, and Southern Bell) are installing fiber loops through business centers to serve data transport that otherwise might be lost to technologically advanced private bypass systems.

There is, of course, a substantial risk that the telephone subscriber with the most inelastic demand, namely the small business and residential ratepayer, will be forced to subsidize some of the costs of serving other customers and permitting LECs to compete or diversify. There is also risk that an unrestrained upgrading of facilities could raise rate levels in general and actually increase bypass. Yet, if LECs' largest customers are neglected for technological, financial, and service reasons, these customers may be forced to move toward external bypass at the expense of telephone company switched network offerings or private lines.

To suppress bypass, local exchange companies must not only have plant that is capable of providing services at reasonable prices, but also must be responsive to customer needs in ways unrelated to price and capacity. Availability, flexibility, reliability, maintenance, technical quality, and even good billing practices may be pivotal in retaining large customers, clearly those which are the LEC customers most likely to have practical bypass options. Poor nonprice performance by the telephone company can drive users to private lines, competing carriers, or totally private bypass systems.

The importance of quality in determining one's commercial success would seem to be well established. Thus,

> . . . many experts rank poor quality as the No. 1 drag--on
> U.S. productivity and competitiveness--and the chief
> opportunity to trim prices and enhance profits.[32]

Concerning the choice of a long distance carrier, most Americans apparently believe that quality of service and reliability are more important than cost in selecting a carrier.[33] Indeed, only AT&T among all IXCs was ranked in the top 20 of "high quality" companies as determined in an American Society for Quality Control/Gallup poll.[34] Bell Communications Research, the RBOC's centralized technical and service organization, apparently shares this view with respect to LECs as well:

> As providers of telecommunications service, telcos should not
> be surprised that quality service is in demand. . . . It is now
> evident that customers are motivated not only by cost, but
> perhaps more important, by the quality of the service they
> are purchasing. Some customers may even be willing to pay
> more for improved service.   There is evidence that

inadequate service may cause customers to bypass the local exchange.[35]

Of course, the local telephone company has wide latitude in meeting customer nonprice needs. However, telephone company complacency could turn this opportunity into a strong motivation for large users to bypass the local network. Nonprice factors can be of central importance in a bypass decision involving new services or technologies, especially where both telephone company and nontelephone company entities face similar costs.

Local telephone companies have strengthened themselves against the unregulated technologies and services that threaten their long term predominance. For instance, the RBOCs have vigorously pursued regional and cross regional operations as part of a strategy apparently designed to establish new sources of revenue in unregulated markets, and to generally "test the water" of new business opportunities. These moves strengthen the BOCs against bypass threats from other entities, such as AT&T, because they extend the reach of the regional companies nationwide and allow them, where expedient, to bypass their own BOCs. This approach may also leave the BOCs with less net access revenue. For this reason, they may press the need to raise rates, especially for basic telephone service where competition is less threatening. In any event, this strategy at least keeps the revenues within the BOCs' corporate "families."

C. Bypass Evidence and Prospects: An Overview

1. Current Incidence

Myriad studies of the nature and extent of local bypass in various states, regions, and nationally have been undertaken by public and private organizations.[36] Bethesda Research Institute, Ltd. (BRI) has examined many of these studies and conducted extensive bypass analyses and surveys of its own.[37] Appendix VI–A contains a synopsis and critique of major studies sponsored by LECs or nonexchange companies.

These surveys and studies tend to leave one with an inconsistent or otherwise incomplete view of the extent and depth of bypass activity in recent years. Part of the problem is that many of the studies define bypass slightly differently and most ignore some relevant factors. For example, an estimate of revenue loss to bypass must not only be based on a reasonable definition of what bypass is, but must also explain the basis on which the traffic "loss" is calculated. Usually, the losses are not calculated from a base of actual current revenues, but rather on the assumption that all local revenues other than those received by the local telephone company are "bypass losses."

Despite an increasing awareness and incidence of offerings that circumvent the LPSN, it is evident that local exchanges continue to be dominated by local telephone carriers. Although the use of alternative sources has undoubtedly increased, there has been no convincing demonstration in any of these studies that current levels of bypass in the various local markets have thus far seriously impaired either maintenance of universal telephone service or the financial vitality of local carriers.

Prominent public policy makers who have examined the bypass issue apparently believe that the problem is not one of major proportions. Judge Greene of the court overseeing the Modification of Final Judgment has held this view for more than five years. For example, the Judge opined in July 1983 that:

> The Court . . . does not consider bypass to be an immediate large-scale problem . . . There is no reason to believe that bypass on a large scale is imminent.[38]

By September 1987 his review of the record led him to the same basic conclusion:

> The complete lack of merit of arguments that economic, technological, or legal changes have substantially eroded or impaired the Regional Company bottleneck monopoly power is demonstrated by the fact that only one-tenth of one percent of *interLATA traffic volume, generated by one customer out of one million, is carried through nonRegional Company facilities* to reach an interexchange carrier. Huber report at 3.9, Table IX.5. To put it another way, 99.9 percent of all interexchange traffic generated by 99.9999 percent of the nation's telephone customers, is today carried entirely or in some part by the Regional Companies (or their equivalents in the territories served by the independents). *The Department of Justice found only twenty-four customers in the entire United States who managed to deliver their interexchange traffic directly to their interexchange carriers, bypassing the Regional Companies.* Department of Justice report at 80–81. It is clear, therefore, and the Court finds, that no substantial competition exists at the present time in the local exchange service, and that the Regional Companies have retained control of the local bottlenecks.[39]
>
> (footnote omitted; emphasis in original text)

In an August 9, 1988 speech before the American Bar Association, the Judge emphasized that the ". . . monopoly of the local bottleneck is still just as powerful as it was."[40] He basically reaffirmed this assessment in another speech presented to a conference on December 8, 1988, and in an opinion issued June 13, 1989.[41]

Observers on both sides of Congress also have not found bypass to be a substantial occurrence. For example, on December 10, 1984, the House Small Business Committee stated that the:

> . . . current level of bypass is not significant today . . . It is very clear from testimony presented to the [Committee's Special Task Force on Telephones] that the current level of bypass is minimal compared to the annual growth rate of the telephone industry.[42]

Doubts have also been expressed in the Senate about the magnitude of the bypass problem. The need for lower carrier common line access charges (and concurrently higher end user charges) has also been questioned.[43]   The Department of Justice, in a September 1986 letter to the Chairman of the House Energy and Commerce Committee, asserted that:

> while there have been some notable instances in which local exchange facilities have been bypassed, there is no substantial evidence that the ability of users to bypass the local exchange is so widespread as to eliminate the practical ability of the BOCs to disadvantage competition in the provision of [interexchange] and information services.[44]

Apparently, the FCC agrees with these assessments concerning the current extent of bypass. In July 1985, Chairman Mark Fowler asserted that he was "not yet" concerned by the current level of bypass.[45]   In November 1986, the Chairman declared that "uneconomic bypass of the network has become less of a problem."[46]   On February 5, 1987, the Commission in response to interrogatories from House Energy and Commerce Committee Chairman John Dingell stated that bypass has been held to a small level.[47]   The FCC apparently believes that this assessment applies to small telephone companies as well as large ones, positing in December 1986 that it has "again [been] presented with no evidence that all or most small company [access] rates are constrained by bypass, and it is unlikely that bypass prevents excess rates at this time."[48]   In December 1988 the agency reimposed a usage charge for interexchange carrier access to local telephone company exchanges for originating traffic, again citing the relative insignificance of the bypass threat.[49]

The National Telecommunications and Information Administration (NTIA), the executive branch's advisor on telecommunications policy, recently found that:

> . . . while concentration of revenues geographically and/or within customer groups may increase opportunities for competitive entry in theory, other factors may limit the incidence of competitive entry in practice. For instance, even where customers secure transmission capacity from nonRHC [Regional Holding Companies] sources, they seldom abandon the local exchange network totally. While it can be advantageous for firms to use nonRHC facilities for communications in certain locations (e.g., company offices within a city), organizational and individual calling requirements generally necessitate access to a calling universe outside of the firms' private networks and hence connection to an RHC network switch (and probably to an interexchange switch as well).[50]

In addition, the agency ascertained that:

> Further, competitive transmission systems frequently are unable economically to duplicate the redundant connectivity of RHC facilities. Therefore, users continue to connect to

the local exchange network to ensure reliable communications
should their own facilities fail under certain conditions (*e.g.,*
power outages). Connection to an RHC network also allows
users of private communications systems to engineer their
systems to facilities that can be relied upon to accommodate
peak traffic overflow from their private systems.

Moreover, for some services, high levels of revenue
concentration may be misleading. For example, although
larger customers generate a substantial percentage of the
RHCs' business exchange services, those customers may not
be viable targets for competitive providers. The RHCs'
business exchange services give customers access to all other
telephones within the designated exchange area. A competitor would not likely incur the massive facility and
switching investment required to duplicate that calling
capability.[51]

(footnotes omitted)

The study also determined that the "high concentration of switched access
revenues in large cities may not imply a commensurate level of competitive
vulnerability" albeit a "different conclusion appears warranted" in the "busiest
wire centers."[52]

Overall, based on data obtained from the Bell operating companies (BOCs),
their competitors, interexchange carriers, and large user groups, NTIA
concluded that:

Whatever the precise degree of RHC vulnerability attributable
to concentration of revenues, the RHCs have thus far not
experienced significant revenue losses. Business exchange
service revenues, though significantly concentrated among
high volume customers, increased for all RHCs between 1984
and 1985. IntraLATA private line revenues, which are even
more concentrated among high volume users, also increased
between 1984 and 1985, in a majority of cases in excess of
15 percent.[53]

A review of certain indicators seems to confirm these assessments. As
shown in Table VI–1, total operating revenues for LECs grew by $7.5 billion
between 1984 and 1987. The two largest revenue components, subscribers'
station and access revenues, which represent approximately 70 percent of the
total, experienced growth of $3.5 billion and $4.1 billion, respectively. Even
though local private line revenue grew at a faster rate (17.8 percent) than
one of these categories, *viz.,* subscribers' stations (13.6 percent), the growth
of the latter in absolute terms was more than 20 times that of local private
lines. Toll private line revenues actually declined by almost $11 million
during the period. In essence, it would appear that LEC revenue growth
volumes in total and for local switched services since divestiture have
swamped the corresponding growth in service bypass.

The LECs' telephone plant in service also rose during the post divestiture

Table VI–1

LEC GROWTH RATES: OPERATING REVENUES
Post Divestiture (1984–87)
($ Million)

Item	1984	1987	Average Annual Change	Average Annual Growth
Operating Revenues Total	$63,839	$71,351	$2,504	3.8%
Selected Services:				
Subscribers' Station	25,650	29,134	1,161	4.3
% of Total	40.2%	40.8%		
Public Telephone	1,241	1,471	77	5.8
% of Total	1.9%	2.1%		
Local Private Line	887	1,046	53	5.6
% of Total	1.4%	1.5%		
Access Revenues	18,758	22,898	1,380	6.9
% of Total	29.4%	33.0%		
Message Toll	7,289	8,264	325	4.3
% of Total	11.4%	11.6%		
Toll Private Line	1,228	1,217	(4)	(0.3)
% of Total	1.9%	1.7%		
Directory Advertising and Sales	2,834	1,712	(374)	(15.5)
% of Total	4.4%	2.4%		

Source: FCC, *Statistics of Communications Common Carriers*, for the years ended December 31, 1984 through 1987, Table 14.   These statistics are provided by those LECs reporting annually to the FCC, about 90% of industry.

period despite any external bypass incursions. This plant grew $34.5 billion, or 21.6 percent over the three–year interval 1984–87 (Table VI–2).[54]

Similarly, the number of access lines (ALs) in service has been growing (see Table VI–3), suggesting that any external bypass that may exist is impacting LEC growth in this area *vis-à-vis* the existing customer base. Concerning service bypass, the growth in the number of switched access lines (in total and for the major components) exceeded that of special ALs during 1984–87. More specifically, total switched access lines (10.1 million, 10.2

Table VI–2

LEC GROWTH RATES: TELEPHONE IN SERVICE
Post Divestiture (1984–87)
($ Million)

Item	1984	1987	Average Annual Change	Average Annual Growth
Telephone Plant in Service	$159,798	$194,343	$11,515	6.7%

Source: FCC, *Statistics of Communications Common Carriers*, for the years ended December 31, 1984 through 1987, Table 14. These statistics are provided by those LECs reporting annually to the FCC, about 90% of industry.

Table VI–3

LEC GROWTH RATES: ACCESS LINES IN SERVICE
Post Divestiture (1984–87)
(000)

Item	1984	1987	Average Annual Change	Average Annual Growth
Access Lines in Svc. (No. of Lines) Switched ALs:				
Main	87,660	97,045	3,128	3.4%
PBX & Centrex	9,178	10,049	290	3.0
Other	2,015	1,880	(45)	(2.2)
Total	98,853	108,974	3,374	3.3%
Special ALs	1,129	1,996	289	20.7%
Total ALs:				
Business	27,148	32,106	1,653	5.8%
Public	1,619	1,629	3	0.2
Residential	71,216	77,236	2,007	2.7

Source: FCC, *Statistics of Communications Common Carriers*, for the years ended December 31, 1984 through 1987, Table 14. These statistics are provided by those LECs reporting annually to the FCC, about 90% of industry.

percent) and the two principal subcategories, main ALs (9.4 million, 10.7 percent) and PBX/Centrex ALs (871,000 and 9.5 percent) have grown more than special access lines (867,000 and 77 percent), both absolutely and relatively during the span. Thus, similar to the revenue case above, service bypass as gauged by the number of special access lines may be losing ground to the LECs' growth in switched ALs.

Moreover, notwithstanding circumvention of the local public switched network, local calling volumes over the LPSN have risen since the breakup of the Bell System. From 1984 to 1987, the total number of local calls increased by almost 30 billion, or 9.0 percent, nationally (Table VI–4).

Viewed individually or as a group, the RBOCs' claimed bypass revenue losses[55] do not demonstrably offset the companies' reported post divestiture revenue growth (see Table VI–5). Thus, bypass as a percent of revenue growth ranges from 11 percent for BellSouth to 71 percent for Ameritech. Although Bell Atlantic registered the highest regional bypass figure ($859 million), its robust growth in revenue places it third (39 percent in terms of this ratio) behind Ameritech (71 percent) and Southwestern Bell (55 percent). Overall, even by their own calculations, RBOC bypass losses eroded only one–third of their revenue growth.

The post divestiture bypass era has thus far not adversely affected the nation's largest telecommunications firms, at least collectively speaking. Based upon "market value,"[56] the identities of the firms in the top twelve grouping has virtually not changed from March 1986 to March 1989 although some shifting has occurred within that echelon (see Table III–6). Among the twelve, ten are LEC based companies, *i.e.*, the seven RBOCs, GTE, United Telecom, and Contel (the other two are IXCs, AT&T and MCI). Although many factors determine these rankings, it can be reasonably concluded that the level of bypass activity has not been so severe as to harm the viability of these firms as perceived by the financial community.

One of the primary concerns about the bypass phenomenon centers on its impact on universal telephone service (UTS). Using the FCC's telephone penetration calculations as a surrogate for UTS, the trend since divestiture has generally been an increasing level of penetration (see Table VI–6). For example, from November 1983 to July 1988, the penetration increased 1.4 percentage points. Adjusting for any seasonality, much the same pattern emerges: +1.1 percentage points from March 1984 to March 1988; +1.2 from July 1984 to July 1988; and +0.9 from November 1984 to November 1987. Similarly, the annual average increased from 91.6 to 92.4 percent, or .8 percentage point, from 1984 to 1987. Such a trend would likely be inconsistent with a relatively high level of bypass, which in its extreme form would involve a large scale exodus of large users, concomitantly rising local rates, and a decline in the number of residential subscribers able to remain on the network.

Table VI-4

LEC GROWTH RATES: CALLING VOLUMES
Post Divestiture (1984-87)
(Million)

Item	1984	1987	Average Annual Change	Average Annual Growth
Local Calls*	327,483	357,056	9,858	2.9%

* Includes completed and incompleted calls.

Source: FCC, *Statistics of Communications Common Carriers*, for the years ended December 31, 1984 through 1987, Table 14.   These statistics are provided by those LECs reporting annually to the FCC, about 90% of industry.

Table VI-5

COMPARISON OF REVENUES LOST TO BYPASS
WITH REVENUE GROWTH: 1984-1987
($ Million)

	Total Bypass	Revenue Growth	Bypass as a Percent of Revenue Growth
Ameritech	$ 840	$ 1,190	71 %
Bell Atlantic	859	2,208	39
BellSouth	283	2,638	11
NYNEX	418	2,510	17
Pacific Telesis	330	1,306	25
Southwestern Bell	443	812	55
U S WEST	374	1,164	32
	$3,547	$11,828	30 %

Sources: RBOC April 1988 monitoring studies and Annual Reports.

2. Prospective Bypass

Few would disagree with the prognosis that circumvention of the local public switched network will continue to exist in the future. For example, specialized user requirements for management and control of their communications network (*e.g.*, electric utilities) may necessitate utilization of facility bypass for some. Others may select a bypass medium for service or cost reasons. Certain users may seek alternatives because of an LEC's torpid

Table VI–6

TELEPHONE PENETRATION RATES IN THE UNITED STATES
Post Divestiture

Date	Percentage of Households With Telephones %*
November 1983	91.4
March 1984	91.8
July 1984	91.6
November 1984	91.4
March 1985	91.8
July 1985	91.8
November 1985	91.9
March 1986	92.2
July 1986	92.2
November 1986	92.4
March 1987	92.5
July 1987	92.3
November 1987	92.3
March 1988	92.9
July 1988	92.8
Annual Average:	
1984	91.6
1985	91.8
1986	92.3
1987	92.4

* Critical values for determining a statistically significant difference in telephone penetration over time at the 95% confidence level for sampling done in the U.S. are .5 for comparison of the same month in nonconsecutive years and .4 for consecutive years. Concerning annual averages, the critical values are .3 for nonconsecutive years and .2 for consecutive years. Where changes in the indices are less than or equal to these critical values, the changes are likely to be due to sampling error *vis-à-vis* changes in the telephone penetration.

Source: *Telephone Subscribership in the U.S.*, September 1988, Tables 1 and 7, p. 4; Census Bureau Data.

adaption of "state of the art" technology, for example, the BOCs as a group are apparently making the transition to digital switching in their networks at a slower pace than AT&T and major Independent telephone companies.[57] Ironically, the latter could pose a service bypass threat to a given BOC by encouraging users in the BOC's serving area to select a "foreign exchange" (FX) tie in to the digital office of a neighboring Independent. A recent calamity at an LEC's facilities has apparently prodded many users to consider bypass in the future. On May 9, 1988, a fire swept through Illinois Bell's Hinsdale central office, effectively halting communications for hundreds of thousands of individuals and businesses in and around Chicago for weeks. As a result of the crisis and given the technological options that exist, several satellite, microwave and long distance vendors have reportedly been "swamped with inquiries and requests for proposal" regarding primary and backup bypass networks.[58]

Bypass activity may also be increased by facilitating public policy. In recent years, for example, the FCC has permitted licensees of private operational fixed microwave radio service (OFS) systems to lease excess capacity on their networks to "other eligible entities" (1985). The agency also approved AT&T's Software Defined Network tariff which affords users direct interconnection to the IXC (1986).

However, several other factors apparently exist which may act as counterweights to those conditions deemed favorable to bypass.

One such factor relates to user demand. No matter how wondrous the available technologies are, circumvention of the LPSN will not occur unless customer needs are met by the bypass vehicle. For facilities bypass to occur, users must have the necessary resources, expertise, time, and desire to own and operate a private network. Although less burdensome, carrier or service bypass will only take place if users' service and price requirements are best met by the alternative. Other user characteristics which could forestall or otherwise prevent utilization of bypass might be lack of information or acumen, a small communications budget, or an aversion to change.

Indeed, in some instances, the early promise of a major bypass technology has not been realized. For example, despite initial enthusiasm by suppliers with respect to digital termination systems (DTS), users have not flocked to the medium because of its high cost and nonoptimization for voice applications.[59] In fact, as of mid October 1988, fourteen of sixteen BOCs have withdrawn or forfeited their applications for construction permits for digital electronic message services (DEMS) –– the FCC's nomenclature for DTS–type offerings.[60]

Another bypass mode which has experienced sluggish demand is shared tenant services (STS) and intelligent buildings. A recent supplier "shakeout" claimed, among others, the industry–leading Sharetech partnership between AT&T and United Technologies in 1986.[61] A year later, AT&T sold Sharetech's offspring, Intelliserve.[62] On July 11, 1987, the *Washington Post* reported that:

> Despite the strong push from people selling equipment for
> shared telecommunications, integrated building services and
> central in–house computers, developers and leasing agents say
> that the majority of office tenants do not need, or want, a
> smart building.

Many have touted two–way cable television as a significant bypass vehicle, but few systems apparently are operational at present. As of July 1988, only three out of 35 state commissions responding to a NARUC survey indicated that any interactive CATV systems were in service in those states.[63]

After a slow start, technologies such as infrared and FM subcarriers have been attracting some users. However, these are "niche" media which would have only a very limited impact on the local public switched network: infrared requires an unobstructed line–of–sight setting and is functional for distances of less than one mile; and FM–SCA is a one–way data transmitter which would generally supplant an LEC's dedicated services (*i.e.*, private lines) rather than an LPSN offering.

Microwave is a proven technology, with private systems in use beginning in the 1940s. Lately the market has been in transition, with primary applications moving away from long distance and repositioning as a short haul, high frequency alternative. Manufacturers of these systems have been experiencing difficulties. One of the leading suppliers, Wang Communications Inc., has been losing money and is rumored to be exiting the business.[64] A spokesman for another vendor, Loral Terracom, recently observed:

> A lot of people are confused and waiting to see if the [microwave] market will stabilize. There's a lot of uncertainty about what's coming . . .[65]

The recent growth in demand for teleport applications has been rapid. Although some project that total revenues could reach one billion dollars by 1997, only $91 million in revenues was generated in 1987.[66] The VSAT market began strong with receive–only stations but may have slowed of late due to certain technical deficiencies.[67]

Fiber optics, T1 multiplexers, and cellular are currently three of the most attractive "bypass" technologies. In fact, all three have been adopted and widely deployed by LECs or their affiliates, thereby meeting (or beating) these technological challenges.

The telephone industry apparently has concluded that the key to combatting bypass is to deploy fiber in the loop and to develop ISDN capability.[68] During the past few years, installation of fiber in the feeder and distribution portions of the "local loop" has been accelerating. Southern Bell has been a front runner in implementing "fiber to the home," with projects underway in Florida and North Carolina. Southwestern Bell and AT&T are jointly conducting a trial in Kansas, and U S WEST, Ameritech, and other RBOCs are considering similar residential broadband service undertakings in other areas. In essence, "[e]ach BOC has undertaken the development of fiber in core areas where they consider bypass a threat."[69]

LECs are aggressively implementing ISDN architecture, as well. Currently, there are over 50 trials under way, and Illinois Bell has recently inaugurated the first U.S. ISDN tariffed service.[70] As a precursor to ISDN, LECs have been offering T1 and digital Centrex services on the public switched network. For most local telephone companies, T1 circuits are their fastest growing business. Between 1986 and 1987, the BOCs enjoyed a 40 percent increase in demand for public network T1 services.[71]

Prospects for a broadband ISDN public switched network during the 1990s appear to be quite favorable. This may well include a partnership with CATV companies to bring entertainment and information services to the public. In June 1988 the National Telecommunications and Information Administration

(NTIA) recommended letting local telephone companies offer "video dial–tone" through fiber optics supporting high speed data and video.[72] The following month, the FCC tentatively concluded that legal restrictions preventing telephone companies from owning cable television systems should be removed.[73] Under current regulations, the large nonBell LECs are prohibited from offering cable services in their own exchange areas, and BOCs are prohibited from the business altogether. With this obstacle removed, there is considerable sentiment among industry observers that the LEC's ISDN broadband network would be the transmission conduit of the future used by CATV companies to bring their entertainment programming to homes.[74] Moreover, the new public switched network would also convey video, voice and data information services on a ubiquitous basis to residences and businesses.

Through a series of acquisitions, Bell companies are apparently partners in nine of the "A block" (nonwireline) systems in the top twelve U.S. cellular markets.[75] Of the nine, eight involve a Bell controlling interest, *i.e.*, RBOCs are the managing partners of the nonwireline operations in these markets, and each is typically paired with the subsidiary of another Bell company operating the area's wireline slot. As of late 1987, eight of the top ten cellular phone companies nationwide in terms of number of potential customers were LEC affiliates (seven RBOC subsidiaries, GTE Mobilnet).[76]

Local exchange carriers are responding to the bypass challenge in a variety of ways. Bell Atlantic and other LECs have initiated central office based local area networks, or CO–LANs, as a means to provide the functionality of an on–site LAN without the burdens of capital investment, obsolescence, and maintenance. The offering is particularly attractive to Centrex users as a low cost precursor to ISDN capability. Some LECs (*e.g.*, Pacific Bell) have eschewed STS in favor of "vertical marketing," which targets geographically scattered but professionally similar users (such as doctors or lawyers).[77] These offerings tend to bolster the LPSN.

Some LEC tactics, however, serve to further bypass. For example, Pacific Telecom owns a 50 percent stake in San Francisco's Bay Area Teleport, and at least two BOCs are financially involved with teleport ventures.[78] Virtually all RBOCs have CPE subsidiaries that market PBXs and LANs that compete directly or indirectly with their LEC affiliates' offerings. Interestingly, the Bell equipment sales units have been "gaining ground in PBX and key system sales, while [BOCs are] holding steady in centrex services."[79]

Moreover, LECs or their affiliates have constructed private fiber optics networks for customers, and the affiliates frequently operate cellular franchises in the same geographic markets as their sister operating companies. Ironically, AT&T has reportedly been marketing digital microwave bypass systems to the CPE units of RBOCs and certain Independents, who assert that "if they don't [market these systems], someone else will."[80]

LEC based companies today apparently have begun to retreat from the nontelecommunications diversification trend of recent years.[81] Concurrently, there has been increased emphasis on "one stop shopping" solutions for telecommunications customers. For example, Illinois Bell and U.S. Sprint jointly won a contract to build a new backbone voice, data, and video network for the state of Illinois.[82]

In New York, NYNEX companies teamed with IBM and Eastern Microwave to install a T1 backbone network for the state. IBM will provide T1 multiplexers, and Eastern Microwave will supply long distance services. Reportedly, the "lion's share" of the contract will go to NYNEX and its subsidiaries. New York Telephone will furnish all required local T1 lines. NYNEX Information Solutions and its subsidiaries will provide project management, system integration, and network management. In turn, NYNEX Business Information Systems will supply CPE and maintenance. NYNEX Systems Marketing served as NYNEX's sales representatives during the negotiation.[83]

Nonprice factors apparently play a critical role in the bypass decision making process of many large users.[84] Such factors as responsiveness to customer "needs," maintenance, and technical quality of service are all performance areas which the local companies can substantially impact. The significance of this finding is that the success of LECs would appear to be "in their own hands" and not a function of regulatory fiat.

Price may also be an important criterion for potential bypassers. It is also an area of their local exchange operations over which telephone companies have less control, given the current regulatory environment. Recent initiatives by regulators, however, have tended to lessen the threat of uneconomic bypass. Thus, the Federal–State Joint Board and the FCC have acted during the 1980s to (1) implement flat end–user charges for residential, small business, and large users; and (2) provide LECs, with the concurrence of state regulatory officials or the Joint Board, the flexibility to implement optional alternative interstate tariff provisions for the recovery of carrier common line costs. And in October 1988, the FCC ruled that LECs that meet six financial and policy guidelines will be given limited freedom to strategically price private high–capacity data lines.

Notably a trend may be developing which would not only block local bypass but could erode it to some degree, as well. Some large users, such as Westinghouse Communications Corp. and Sears Communications Network, Inc., are testing feature group access arrangements with local carriers (Bell Atlantic and Southwestern Bell operating companies, respectively).[85] Under Feature Group D ("equal access"), customers would be allowed to use the shared public switched network rather than private lines ("special access") to interconnect their private long distance networks. In effect, the corporation's private network would be designated as the interexchange carrier of choice, rather than selecting a long distance company. In this way, service (private line) bypass would be eliminated, and carrier bypass (*i.e.*, direct connection to an IXC) would be prevented.

Appendix VI–A

BRI ANALYSIS OF POST DIVESTITURE BYPASS STUDIES[86]

A. The FCC's Evidence

In April 1987 the FCC submitted four major studies to Congress which purportedly summarize the bypass issue and additional studies that delve into specific aspects of the bypass problem. The major bypass studies cited by the FCC embrace ones issued by the Federal Communications Commission (1984), the General Accounting Office (1986), and The National Regulatory Research Institute (1984). Also included is Dr. Peter Huber's recent (1987) report on competition in the telephone industry prepared for the Department of Justice as part of its triennial review of the Consent Decree by which the local Bell operating companies were divested from AT&T.

The FCC report was intended to provide a comprehensive look at bypass of local telephone switched services. "Bypass of the Public Switched Network"[87] is essentially a summary of more than 30 volumes of bypass studies and testimony submitted to the Commission by various communications firms. In this study the FCC adopted a limited definition of bypass to those alternatives to the local public switched network which avoided the payment of access charges:

> Bypass is the transmission of long distance messages that do
> not use the facilities of local telephone companies available
> to the general public, but that could use such facilities.

The focus is on bypass of the local network by long distance communications because of the possible negative effect on other subscribers.

The FCC study also recognized that the major form of bypass, under its definition of the phenomenon is service bypass. This primarily takes the form of private lines, *i.e.,* leasing unswitched local service from the telephone company. Further, it notes that bypass is not dependent on any particular technology, although microwave systems are currently the most frequently used medium of transmission.[88] In this study, microwave systems growth is reported to be a relatively modest five percent per year between 1979 through 1984. As to the use of technology by the telephone company *vis-à-vis* the bypasser the report states:

> There are no current technologies, or combinations of tech-
> nologies, used in bypass applications which are not also
> available to carriers. Carriers, however, may rule out certain
> technologies based on reliability or maintenance factors. It
> appears that interexchange carriers are concentrating on
> fiber and microwave systems.[89]

Although the Commission concludes from this study that bypass is a growing problem threatening the revenues supporting the local public switched network, large telecommunications customers and user groups commented that the problem of bypass is not as widespread or as serious as concluded by the telephone industry and the FCC. Indeed, these groups argued that bypass is only another form of competition, that private systems are most often selected in order to obtain higher service quality, and that private systems are not in widespread use for all the communications needs of customers.

The FCC's bypass study does make some attempt to quantify the potential losses due to bypass. However, the carrier sponsored bypass studies on which it relies do not cite actual losses or investment stranded because of bypass, but rather refer to a concept of "revenues at risk." Revenues at risk apparently includes all potential customer expenditures on nontelephone company communications services, rather than actual telephone company revenue decreases. For example, Pacific Bell estimated 1985 revenue losses of $115 million from service bypass and private bypass losses of only eight million dollars.[90] However, in 1985 Pacific Bell's overall revenues increased by $673 million and its net income increased by $100 million.[91] These "losses" were obviously overwhelmed by telephone company growth.

Another underlying assumption of the FCC study, and the numerous carrier sponsored bypass studies and surveys upon which it relied, is that bypass is primarily driven by price differentials. The majority of the studies submitted to the Commission assume that most bypass would be eliminated by the imposition of end user charges instead of payments effectively being made by toll services for their utilization of jointly used NTS local exchange facilities.[92] The important role of service availability and quality as a motivation for bypassing the local switched telephone network and the concomitant role of responsive telephone company service in reducing bypass are barely discussed in the FCC study and the underlying carrier submissions.

Indeed, on page 24 of its study, the FCC comments on the lack of evidence supporting the contention that bypass will be a significant problem in the near future:

> While the various studies submitted yield much evidence that bypass will be a major problem, they yield little satisfactory information on the expected timing of bypass activities. While a few respondents did try to address the timing of bypass activity, relatively little solid data was presented. Where data was submitted estimating the dates by which bypass might occur, it tended to show bypass occurring at an increasing rate.[93]

Thus, the FCC study offers no evidence of whether bypass will be a major problem for local exchange companies in the context of their continued revenue growth, what the level of such bypass might be, and when major bypass of local exchange companies will take place. The study does suggest that most of the bypass expected to occur in the near future will use telephone company private lines rather than other service vendors or private facilities--which means that such bypass revenues will stay with the local exchange company.

The second study relied on by the FCC to support its increase in the subscriber line charge is based on interviews with large volume telephone users in Colorado and Massachusetts and a review of several previous studies, including the FCC bypass study discussed above. *Telephone Communications: Bypass of the Local Telephone Companies* was published in late 1986 by the General Accounting Office in response to congressional concerns that local telephone companies could lose billions of dollars if larger customers were able to avoid using local telephone company facilities.[94] This study concluded that customers were bypassing for both price and service reasons and that up to 30 percent of large customers are already bypassing their local exchange companies to some degree. Further, it indicated that up to 53 percent of large users are considering plans to initiate or increase their bypass of local services.[95] However, even those respondents actually engaged in bypass continued to rely on their local telephone company for more than 75 percent of their telecommunications service.

The percentages of large customers engaging in some form of bypass reported in the GAO study are not inconsistent with the results of numerous other surveys. That bypass exists is clearly not at issue. Rather, the question which all bypass studies must address is whether bypass is having a deleterious effect on local telephone company revenues and earnings. With most bypassers in this study continuing to rely on the local telephone company for most of their telecommunications services, the opportunities for growth in local telephone company revenues seem bright. Indeed, no bypass study relied on by the FCC claims that the actual minutes of use of the local network for long distance access are decreasing. A regime in which both bypass and local telephone company revenues increase with the growth of demand for communications services is not inconsistent with the results of this study.

The GAO study attempts to address the potential loss of revenues to bypass by reference to two revenue loss models. A 1984 FCC model estimated four billion dollars in potential revenue losses because of bypass and a Bell Communications Research model estimated a ten billion dollar loss.[96] Both models assume "full and fair" competition in access markets, a condition which does not exist, and given the dominant market position of the local telephone operating companies, will not exist for the foreseeable future. Both these estimates provide extreme bypass estimates based on unrealistic assumptions that only price is important in the bypass decision and that local exchange telephone companies will not improve service and technology.

As in the FCC study on which the GAO study is partially based, the role of service factors in the bypass decisions of large users does not play a prominent role in the GAO study. The surveys performed by GAO did not address whether users bypass because of uneconomic pricing of switched access, or which telephone company services are bypassed. The GAO study is essentially a derivative of other studies which themselves are based on unrealistic assumptions. It offers no new insights in support of the FCC's bypass rationale for the subscriber line charge.

Another study submitted to the Subcommittee by the FCC to support its bypass rationale for subscriber line charges was conducted in 1984 by The National Regulatory Research Institute (NRRI).[97] *The Bypass Issue: An Emerging Form of Competition in the Telephone Industry* showed that both price and service are important factors in a customer's decision to bypass the local switched network. It also calls into question the implication that bypass activity necessarily reduces use of the telephone network:

> The conventional wisdom is that a company that bypasses reduces its use of all but the most basic local service. However, there is substantial question about the extent to which bypassers do, in fact, reduce their use of telephone company services.
>
> While every telephone company service has been reduced by some bypassers, in no case have all bypassers with the equivalent service capability in their bypass system reduced their use of telephone company services. This might imply that some bypass systems have been built to accommodate either growth in existing customer needs or new services needed by the customer.[98]

Other conclusions of this study also support the view that bypass is not a major threat to local telephone company revenues. For example, it recognizes that a uniform national bypass policy risks the distortion of developing competition in areas of uneven bypass potential, that a change in interstate cost allocations could reduce incentives for bypass and allow state regulatory commissions the flexibility to design locally responsive rates, and that most of the local bypass is in incremental traffic and not at the expense of current levels of local telephone system usage. NRRI posits that the market for telecommunications services will grow and that the telephone company, facing bypass of some of its local services, will be offering a different mix of services than it does today.[99]

The final major study relied on by the FCC is Peter Huber's report on competition in the telephone industry which was submitted to the Department of Justice as part of its triennial reconsideration of the restrictions placed on the Bell operating companies by the Consent Decree.[100]   Dr. Huber emphasizes the role of changing telecommunication technology in injecting competition into the provision of telephone services. In his view the restructure of the telephone industry and the migration of network intelligence away from major switching nodes and into the customers' premises equipment has caused a proliferation of possibilities, among which is bypass of the LPSN:

> The network is not yet as fully dispersed at the lower latitudes, but an equally profound restructuring is underway here too . . . The interexchange carriers . . . still receive all but a trickle of their traffic through LEC [local exchange carrier] switches, . . . interexchange carriers are methodically preparing for direct connection to end users. [101]

The Huber report relies mainly on the alleged new structure of telecommunications as a sort of "geodesic" dome in which there are many paths between switching centers as opposed to the traditional hierarchical, or "pyramidal" structure of the telephone network. This concept assumes, essentially, that the local bottlenecks presided over by local telephone companies are no longer important in providing access to originate and terminate long distance communications. Of course, this is not the situation actually facing most large telecommunications users, and clearly not the situation facing small residential and business users who have little, if any, significant bypass possibilities in the near future.

A detailed analysis of the deficiencies of the Huber report on behalf of two large user groups concludes that technical, economic, and competitive conditions in the telephone industry have not changed much since the Consent Decree was entered in 1982.[102]   The study finds that the local exchange monopoly has not been significantly eroded by technological or competitive changes.

For example, the report notes that the local access service market shares of the local operating companies range from 96 to 99 percent, and that this dominance of local services is even greater than it was at the time of the Consent Decree.[103]   The study also notes that there has been no perceptible abatement in the degree of "bottleneck control" over the local distribution in-frastructure. Also, even in states where allegedly restrictive state regulatory policies have been lifted, local access competition has not emerged to any great degree. Therefore, the Huber report is an interesting document in that its deficiencies document so effectively that bypass is not significantly more threatening to the prospects of the local exchange carriers today than it was five years ago.

B. Other Bypass Evidence

This section briefly examines some other bypass studies performed during the last few years by local exchange companies and others such as the independent analyses conducted by the Bethesda Research Institute, Ltd.[104] The extent of bypass activity and the revenues lost by the local exchange companies have been examined to varying degrees in numerous states. Bypass studies have been commissioned by telephone companies, user groups, federal and state governmental organizations, and academic institutions.   Local exchange companies have sponsored the majority of surveys of the communications requirements of large users. Of course, the Bell operating companies' (BOCs') largest customers are prime prospects for bypass because of their substantial traffic volumes and the concomitant revenues garnered by the local exchange carriers.

The bypass surveys performed to date are not standardized enough in their definitions and assumptions to allow a quantitative comparison of one area to another, or one timeframe to another. Nevertheless, attempts to measure the extent of bypass today and plans for tomorrow are essential if companies, users, and regulatory authorities are to develop strategies to deal with the opportunities and problems it may create. For example, if nonprice motivations, such as service quality, dictate a particular bypass decision, pricing changes (such as the subscriber line charge) aimed at suppressing bypass may have no effect, or could reduce user benefits by raising the cost of necessary bypass. Major changes in pricing, including the FCC's recent increase in the SLC, increases in depreciation rates, the expensing of formerly capitalized costs, and regulatory changes that allow long distance carriers to connect directly to their customers, are often justified by the alleged threat of bypass.   The failure to describe the current bypass conditions and prospects for the future could lead to ineffective or counter-productive policies.

Most of the recent studies concentrate on price related bypass motivations of large users, giving relatively less weight to nonprice factors and smaller users.   Institutional arrangements are also generally ignored, as are technological alternatives. For example, shared tenant services, joint ventures of telephone companies, and the impact of changing regulatory structures are not usually considered.

1. Local Exchange Company Studies

Bypass studies sponsored by telephone companies and industry organizations during the past four years have generally emphasized price related factors and reported a high incidence of bypass and high revenue losses. Typical of these studies are the more than 24 surveys performed by Touche Ross & Company for various local exchange companies. In a 1984 New York study[105] it offered the following main conclusions, typical of its studies in a number of states:

1. Large customers are primarily motivated to bypass by price.
2. One in three large customers of New York Telephone engage in bypass (of some form) and more than 50 percent indicate they will bypass in the future.
3. Revenue losses to bypass will increase from 47 million in 1984 to 147 million dollars by 1987, and are probably irreversible because of the capital investment in bypass systems.

However, these conclusions must be interpreted in cognizance of the perhaps unsupportable assumptions on which they are based, including an overbroad definition of bypass, the lack of a benchmark to which bypass revenue losses can be compared, and the implicit assumption that New York Telephone will not attempt to retain profitable traffic through service and price improvements.

A 1983 Peter Merrill Associates study for Chesapeake and Potomac Telephone Company of Maryland[106] concluded that 68 percent of large users would engage in bypass in the 1986 through 1988 period. Among other conclusions were the following:

1. Bypass is concentrated among large business users and can be expected to increase dramatically in the near future.
2. Cable television is likely to be a major bypass medium in the immediate future, as will cellular radio and digital termination systems.

3. LPSN rates which are not competitive will lead to uneconomic bypass.

This was one of the earliest bypass studies and its conclusions and, indeed, its basic design are quite suspect.   The study did not distinguish between the various kinds of bypass, there was no attempt to quantify revenues lost to bypass or to survey different kinds of large users.

In 1984, Bellcore (an agent of the Bell regional holding companies) studied bypass nationally with the main objective of determining the impact of end user charges on the Bell operating companies and their customers.   It assessed the vulnerability of local exchange access revenues to bypass activity.   Bellcore concluded, in part, that:

1. Without end user charges, the local exchange telephone companies could lose $10.20 per local loop line in revenues; with adoption of a $4.00 (as of June 1986 only $2.00 had been approved by the FCC) end user charge the potential revenue loss is only $4.55 per line.
2. Customers have three ways of reducing their telephone bills, all of which involve circumvention of the LPSN––the use of private lines, purchasing service from a reseller of local telephone service, and making alternative arrangements for the local access portion of a long distance call.

As discussed above, this study was one of several relied on by the General Accounting Office in its study.   It emphasized the importance of carrier bypass as a way of avoiding switched access charges, but, as do the other recent carrier sponsored studies, it ignored all causes of bypass other than price.

A 1985 study by Shooshan & Jackson, Inc., for the Bell Atlantic companies[107] suggests that current rates for large customers still provide an incentive to connect to interLATA carriers using bypass facilities or to move from the relatively expensive LPSN to private line services.   The study alleges that Bell Atlantic could lose 37 percent of switched business traffic by the end of the 1980s if switched access charges are not further reduced. According to this analysis, the subscriber line charge needs to be increased in order to discourage even greater levels of bypass activity.   It does not explain why Bell Atlantic revenues continue to increase in the face of the alleged bypass threat.   One explanation is, of course, that the occurrence of bypass is insufficient to detract much from the year to year growth of the local exchange companies.

2. Non—Exchange Company Studies

Bypass studies have also been sponsored by telecommunications user organizations, agencies of the federal government, academic institutions, various state agencies, and others.   These studies generally find that the extent of bypass is not so great as found in local telephone company sponsored studies.   One 1984 study concluded that bypass will account for only a small (5.9 percent) portion of the local loop market by 1990.[108] A user survey by the American Petroleum Institute concluded that the reasons for bypass of the public switched network were mainly related to service, nonprice factors.[109]   Still another user sponsored study noted that some services were unavailable from local telephone companies, forcing users to bypass the local network or do without needed services.[110] Table VI—A—1 lists the major reasons for bypass found in a number of studies conducted by various entities.

A 1985 report prepared for Congress's Office of Technology Assessment evaluated major bypass studies by both carriers and telecommunications users.[111]   This study concluded that levels of bypass at that time did not pose any serious threat to local telephone companies or universal service availability. A major conclusion was that bypass opportunities would increase over time, and that the most formidable entities offering bypass services were likely to be the telephone companies themselves.

MCI Telecommunications Corporation argued that bypass is neither a present nor a likely future problem.[112]   It points out that many of the local carriers and the FCC have ignored the bypass suppressing effects of the June 1, 1986 changes in WATS pricing, the reduction in carrier common line charges (CCLCs) for originating traffic, and the current subscriber line charge. MCI estimated the "crossover" point for the thirteen BOCs with the most large users, *i.e.*, the traffic level at which these companies allegedly susceptible to bypass would have at least an economic incentive to consider bypass of the LPSN. MCI found that:

> In each instance, the crossover point is more than 28,000 minutes per month per customer location. In Southwestern Bell's territory in Missouri, the crossover point exceeds 100,000 minutes per month, In other words, under this analysis, the usage levels at which a customer would find service bypass attractive after June 1, 1986 are extremely high in many regions of the country. The number of customers and minutes of use that are now vulnerable to service bypass simply is not as great as many exchange carriers claim. Moreover, much or all of whatever service bypass that does exist is likely to be economic, rather than uneconomic. In addition, many other flaws undermine the credibility of the bypass claims . . .[113]

Bypass surveys conducted by Bethesda Research Institute, Ltd., in Maryland, New York, New Jersey, and Pennsylvania have shown that quality of service factors, especially the responsiveness of the local telephone com—

Table VI–A–1

MAJOR REASONS FOR BYPASS CITED IN STUDIES

Study by:	Reason Cited:
API	Service
Assoc. of Amer. RRs	Service
Assoc. of Data Comm. Users	Service and price
Bell Atlantic	Price
The Conference Board	Service and price
ICA	Service
NRRI	Service and price
State of NJ	Service and price
NY Clearing House Assoc.	Service
Touch Ross & Co.–Telcos	Price
Util. Telecom. Council	Service
State of Wash.	Service and cost
GAO–Large Users	Service

Source: Bethesda Research Institute, Ltd. analyses.

pany to customers' needs, are most important to users in making the bypass decision. In the Maryland study, both large and small users ranked respon–siveness to customer needs as the most important factor in service selection, but ranked Chesapeake and Potomac Telephone as only "fair" to "good" in meeting these needs.[114] Note that for large users, those often said to be most likely to bypass the local exchange telephone company, price ranked sixth out of nine factors. With telephone expenditures typically a more significant proportion of their budgets, small users rated price second.

In a New York study, responsiveness to customer needs was again ranked first in importance by both large and small users, and price was ranked eighth out of eleven factors in importance to the bypass decision.[115] In a similar New Jersey study, service responsiveness was also ranked most important by large users. However, price was ranked fourth and sixth as a bypass criteria by bypassing and nonbypassing companies, respectively.[116]

Finally, a 1987 bypass study in Pennsylvania showed that the level of bypass activity was rising, but that Bell of Pennsylvania's revenues were also rising as the market for telecommunications services expands. This study showed that services, such as private lines provided by the local exchange carrier, represent the primary source of the relatively low level of bypass activity that does exist in Pennsylvania. Indeed, it showed that there is no indication that large users as a group will use local switched services less than they do today.[117]

The major Pennsylvania users surveyed in this study were asked to evaluate both the relative importance of various bypass related criteria and the performance of the local exchange telephone company based on these same criteria. Table VI–A–2 shows the importance of service related criteria in the bypass thinking of large users. Responsiveness to customer needs, technical quality of service, and maintenance performance are the top three concerns of these companies. Interestingly, Bell of Pennsylvania, which serves approximately 80 percent of Pennsylvania telephone customers, did not receive its highest ratings in the areas considered by users to be more important in the decision to bypass. Customers ranked Bell's performance in the three top criteria cited above lower than four other factors (Table VI–A–3). Price as a criterion for bypassing the local network ranked seventh in importance to large users in Pennsylvania.

Service related factors are clearly the most important in the decision of users to bypass the local telephone network. However, the Pennsylvania study also revealed the existence of an inherent and significant "price premium" advantage for Bell of Pennsylvania relative to alternative suppliers of local services. As shown on Table VI–A–4 many users will continue to use Bell local service even if charged prices are as much as 10 percent higher than the bypass option. This advantage should ameliorate the impact of bypass threats to company revenues, especially if Bell of Pennsylvania improves its service performance.

C. Monitoring Studies of RBOCs

Pursuant to the monitoring plan established by the FCC in Docket CC No. 87–339, the RBOCs filed their bypass studies at the end of April 1988.[118] The first part of the study results purported to show revenues lost to bypass and is divided into a facility bypass component and a service bypass portion. Facility bypass is defined as a connection not provided by the local exchange carrier and service bypass is the circumvention of the LPSN by use of private line services offered by the LEC. Thus, in the latter case there will be revenues gained from the provision of private line service to offset the loss of switched revenues.

Table VI–A–5 is a summary of the results of the RBOCs' submissions with respect to revenues allegedly lost to bypass. Overall, about 64 percent of the bypass revenues are associated with service while 36 percent stem from facility bypass. Among the RBOCs these percentages vary substantially as can be seen from Table VI–A–6.

The methods used by each of the RBOCs to develop the estimated revenues lost to bypass were generally comparable. For *facility bypass*, data was collected from FCC licensing information, via outside contractors or in–house personnel, that purported to represent the number of circuits available for private microwave bypass. The derived circuit capacities were then translated into bypass circuits by applying different utilization ratios along

Table VI–A–2

AVERAGE CUSTOMER RATINGS OF CRITERIA USED
IN SELECTING LOCAL COMMUNICATIONS
BRI Pennsylvania User Survey

Selection Criteria	Overall Importance Rank	Type of Organization					
		Manu- facturer	Govern- ment	Hospital	University	Bank	Total
Large start–up investment	4	9.0	9.7	7.0	9.0	9.0	8.9
Innovation performance	9	7.5	7.0	5.5	8.0	8.5	7.4
Technical quality of service	2	9.6	10.0	6.5	10.0	9.5	9.3
Reputation of the company	5	8.6	8.3	9.5	8.0	8.5	8.6
Experience of the company	6	8.4	8.3	10.0	9.0	8.5	8.6
Responsiveness to customer needs	1	9.4	10.0	9.0	10.0	8.0	9.4
Maintenance	3	9.3	10.0	9.0	10.0	9.0	9.3
Financial resources	8	7.7	9.0	6.5	7.0	8.5	8.1
Price	7	8.5	8.3	9.0	8.0	7.5	8.4
Statewide presence	11	7.2	7.0	3.5	4.0	8.5	6.7
User Control	10	6.6	8.0	6.5	6.0	8.0	6.9
Ability to share or resell communications service to others	12	4.3	5.0	5.5	7.0	5.0	4.8

Note: User ratings on a scale of one to ten, with ten being most important and one being not important at all. In turn, "overall importance" rankings are based on a composite of these ratings, such that "1" is the highest ranked and "12" is the lowest ranked.

Source: Study conducted by Bethesda Research Institute, Ltd., (c), 1988.

with other factors to further break down capacity to working lines by different types of circuits, e.g., voice/data.

The next step was to apply access rates to the pricing quantities associated with the voice and data circuits that were estimated to have been bypassed. For voice, the derived circuits were first multiplied by an assumed quantity of access minutes (MOUs) per line. Then, the MOUs were multiplied by the appropriate access rate per MOU to obtain the revenues lost. For data (private line), the number of circuits was simply multiplied by the appropriate special access rate to determine revenues lost to bypass.

Service bypass revenue losses were estimated in a more straightforward manner. The RBOCs utilized the number of voice grade private lines plus voice grade equivalencies converted from higher capacity circuits as the base

Table VI–A–3

AVERAGE USER RATINGS OF BELL OF PENNSYLVANIA
PERFORMANCE BY VARIOUS CRITERIA
BRI Pennsylvania User Survey

Selection Criteria	Overall Importance Rank	Type of Organization					
		Manufacturer	Government	Hospital	University	Bank	Total
Innovation performance	8/9	3.0	1.7	3.5	3.0	2.5	2.9
Technical quality of service	7	3.3	3.0	3.5	4.0	2.5	3.2
Reputation of the company	2/3/4	3.7	3.7	3.5	4.0	3.5	3.7
Experience of the company	2/3/4	3.7	4.0	3.5	4.0	3.5	3.7
Responsiveness to customer needs	6	3.2	3.7	3.5	3.0	3.0	3.3
Maintenance	5	3.0	3.7	3.5	4.0	2.5	3.4
Financial resources	1	3.8	4.0	4.0	4.0	3.5	3.8
Price	8/9	3.0	3.0	3.0	3.0	2.5	2.9
Statewide presence	2/3/4	3.9	4.0	4.0	3.0	3.5	3.7
All other things being equal, would users							
• Choose Bell of PA		91%	100%	100%	100%	100%	95%
• Choose alternative for their needs?		9	0	0	0	0	5

Note: User rating based on scale of excellent = 4, good = 3, fair = 2, and poor = 1.
Source: Study conducted by Bethesda Research Institute, Ltd., (c), 1988.

making the calculations. The voice grade circuits were multiplied by assumed
MOUs times the appropriate switched access rate per MOU to obtain gross
service bypass revenues lost. From these figures, special access revenues for
the lines were subtracted to obtain estimates of net revenues lost to service
bypass.

There are several problems with the methods used to derive the bypass
revenue estimates. First, there is no supporting documentation for the myriad
of utilization and other factors used to calculate the number of bypass
circuits.   For instance, Pacific Telesis used a fill factor of 80 percent[119]
whereas BellSouth used 85 percent[120] for apparently the same calculation.
There also was no justification for the MOUs utilized to develop the revenue
loss estimates. These figures vary from 5000 to 6400 MOUs per line per
month among the RBOCs. Based on a month of 22 work days of eight hours
each there are 10,560 minutes[121] available for telephone use. The 5,000 and
6,400 MOUs represent 47 percent and 61 percent of the available capacity.
The filings by the RBOCs do not demonstrate these to be reasonable figures
for each of the lines bypassing the LPSN.

The RBOCs' submitted computations distort the service bypass issue in at

Table VI–A–4

USER PERCEPTIONS OF IMPORTANCE OF PRICE VERSUS NONPRICE
FACTORS IN CARRIER SELECTION
BRI Pennsylvania User Survey

Type of Organization	Bell Percent Higher Price	Equivalent Nonprice Features	Superior Respon- siveness by Bell	Superior Technical Service by Bell	Superior Innovation Performance by Bell	Superior Financial Staying Power for Bell
Manufacturer	5	78%	100%	100%	89%	89%
	10	22	78	89	44	44
	20	0	0	22	0	0
Government	5	100	100	100	100	100
	10	0	100	100	100	50
	20	0	0	0	0	0
Hospital	5	50	50	50	50	50
	10	0	0	50	0	0
	20	0	0	0	0	0
University	5	100	100	100	100	100
	10	0	100	100	100	100
	20	0	0	0	0	0
Banks	5	100	100	100	100	
	10	100	100	100	100	
	20	0	50	50	50	
TOTAL	5	78%	94%	94%	83%	83%
	10	28	72	89	56	50%
	20	0	6	17	6	0%

Source: Study conducted by Bethesda Research Institute, Ltd., (c), 1988.

least two major ways. First, the RBOC studies assumed that all private lines represent bypass of the switched network.[122]   In fact, private line service has existed for decades and private line customers have generally been characterized as large users or those with special and unique communications requirements. These customers may represent service bypass according to the definitions established for the RBOCs' submissions, but this type of "bypass" has been going on for decades. Second, the RBOCs' contentions that price is typically the major factor in determining bypass has not been substantiated. As noted previously in this report, the price of a service is only one of many considerations that determines whether a user will bypass the LPSN, and, often, may be down the list of contributing factors. The studies do not show that price differentials caused service bypass and, thus, do not provide linkage to the higher SLCs scheduled to become effective.

Another aspect of the monitoring effort was an attempt to ascertain the reasons for bypass of the LPSN. Seven reasons were listed as possible candidates as noted in Table VI–A–7.

Table VI–A–5

RESULTS OF RBOCS' BYPASS MONITORING STUDIES
Data Submitted April 1988*
($ Million)

RBOC	Net Service Bypass	Facilities Bypass	Total Bypass
Ameritech	$ 393	$ 447	840
Bell Atlantic	511	348	859
BellSouth	273	10	283
NYNEX	330	88	418
Pacific Telesis	226	104	330
Southwestern Bell	203	240	443
U S WEST	337	37	374
	$2,273	$1,274	$3,547

* Some of the RBOCs subsequently filed revised data which are included in the table.

Table VI–A–6

BREAKDOWN OF BYPASS REVENUES

	Service	Facility
Ameritech	47%	53%
Bell Atlantic	59	41
BellSouth	96	4
NYNEX	79	21
Pacific Telesis	68	32
Southwestern Bell	46	54
U S WEST	90	10
Average	64%	36%

The submissions by the RBOCs provided results that varied considerably. For instance, Ameritech data showed the information portrayed in Table VI–A–8. Less than one–third of the customers indicated that price was a major factor, but for almost two–thirds of the users, the reason for bypass was not known.

Other RBOCs assumed that the reason for bypass was price which necessitated a coding of "1" for virtually all customers.[123]   As noted by Southwestern Bell on page 2 of its transmittal letter:

Price is necessarily a factor in each bypass example cited.
SWBT does not, however, contend that this is the only factor

Table VI–A–7

REASONS FOR BYPASS

Code	Reason
1	Economic
2	Services unavailable from LEC
3	Security
4	Control
5	Quality
6	Other
7	Unknown

Table VI–A–8

REASONS FOR BYPASS: AMERITECH

Code	Percentage
1	29.7%
2	4.4
3	0.0
4	0.2
5	0.1
6	0.2
7	65.4
	100.0%

driving bypass adoption.

Similarly, on page 6–7 of its monitoring plan submission, U S WEST states:

> 7. The reason for service bypass is assumed to be economic for this filing. However, research information developed from customer surveys indicates that price is one of several variables affecting the bypass decision–making process. Other variables which are ranked higher than price include product advantages, service advantages and network control.

These two RBOCs acknowledge that price is not always the most important factor governing bypass, even though price was listed in their monitoring reports as a factor for most customers. Without further analyses and an unbiased ranking of the "bypass reasons" it is doubtful that the results of this part of the monitoring plan have any validity.

Notes

1. That year, AT&T may have coined the word "bypass" during the FCC's investigation of charges for interstate access to local exchange facilities:

Bypass services will be attractive to large users who are in a position to take advantage of the excessive allocation of exchange access costs to interstate services.

(Comments filed August 15, 1980, n.7, in CC Docket No. 78–72, *MTS/WATS Market Structure Phase II.*)

2. The acronym "LATA" is used to denote in short form the term, "local access and transport area," a jurisdictional boundary created as part of the "Modification Final Judgement" which led to the breakup of the Bell System on January 1, 1984.

3. Supplemental Comments, p. 3, in response to the FCC's 1984 requests for data, information, studies, and comments pertaining to bypass of the public switched network.

4. Bellcore Comments, pp. 3–4; AT&T Comments, p. 4, in response to FCC requests pertaining to bypass (see n.3).

5. See FCC's Common Carrier Bureau, "Bypass of the Public Switched Network," December 19, 1984, Appendix 4, p. 4.

6. See, *e.g.,* Rural Telephone Coalition Comments in response to FCC Requests; and the Common Carrier Bureau's "First Bypass Report," Appendix F, *Third Report and Order*, CC Docket No. 78–72, Phase II, released February 28, 1983.

7. "Bypass of the Public Switched Network," p. 18. Upgrading the local network to include fiber optic and digital facilities will alter the array of such excluded services.

8. As of December 31, 1987, the BOCs accounted for 77.5 percent of all local telephone company access lines. Source: USTA "Phone Facts for the year 1987," pp. 11, 14.

9. This stipulation, of course, removes any nontelecommunications service from the ambit of "local bypass" as used in this book. Further, telecommunications services that the local exchange carrier is not equipped to provide are generally excluded. For example, where security or other reasons necessitating absolute user control are of paramount importance, the LEC may not be a viable communications source for that user. In some cases, the local carrier may not be physically able to provide a particular communications mode because of legal or other constraints (*e.g.,* cellular radio, private microwave systems) but can offer a reasonably close substitute through the local public switched network. Instances where the user chooses these modes over the LPSN would generally be regarded as bypass in our nomenclature.

The nature of the intended application of a service or system often complicates the process of defining bypass. Thus, users that employ cellular radio in lieu of the "telephones on their desks" would be engaging in bypass activity, while those subscribing to cellular instead of some other form of mobile telephony may not be viewed as circumventing the local carrier's public network. In this study, recognizing the practical difficulties of distinguishing user motivations, BRI treats cellular as a bypass technology and activity. This approach has much support from the bypass literature. See, *e.g.,* General Accounting Office, *Telephone Communications: Bypass of the Local Telephone Companies,* August 1986, esp. Appendix V. At least some telephone companies apparently concur. A study sponsored by the C&P of Maryland concluded that:

A variety of new technologies with substantial bypass potential are approaching intro-
duction into the market. One technology, cellular radio appears to have enormous potential as a full service complement to, and substitute for, the wired telephone network.

See Peter Merrill Associates, Inc., "Strategic Analysis of Local Exchange Bypass in Maryland," March 1983, p. 100. It should be noted that this treatment would tend to overstate the actual extent of bypass in a given area.

10. Although some cellular radio activity may not strictly fit this report's definition of local bypass, it is assumed herein that cellular is generally a bypass mode capable of supplanting service otherwise obtained through the LPSN. See n. 9 *supra.*

11. *Washington Post*, October 4, 1984, p. E9.

12. "University of Michigan Signs Centel for Voice Data System," *Communications Week*, September 24, 1984, p. 46.

13. "NYNEX Unit to Bypass own Telco With Fiber Networks for DEC," *Communications Week*, May 27, 1985, p. 6.

14. In 1985, the FCC's Common Carrier Bureau preempted a Texas PUC decision which restrained Atlantic Richfield Company (ARCO) from connecting its Plano, Texas building to the Dallas public switched network served by Southwestern Bell (SWB). The Bureau overturned the PUC's ruling that SWB had unlawfully provided exchange service to a customer in the franchised operating territory of General Telephone Company of the Southwest. In overriding the state commission's decision, the Bureau found that a telephone subscriber's federal right to use its terminal equipment in ways that were "privately beneficial without being publicly detrimental" had been unlawfully denied. In February 1988, the full FCC upheld the Bureau's order, asserting that the federal right to interconnection extends not only to terminal equipment but also to "communications systems provided by customers." GTE has petitioned the U.S. Court of Appeals to review the series of decisions.

15. "BellSouth and Siecor Form Fiber Optic LAN Design and Installation Firm," *Telecommunications Reports*, April 1, 1985, p. 12.

16. Ameritech 1987 *Annual Report*, p.20; *Communications Week*, January 27, 1986.

17. "Illinois Bell Bypasses Itself Using Teleport Concept," *Bellcore News*, June 6, 1984, p. 2.

18. "Regional News," *Bellcore News*, August 15, 1984, p. 3.

19. "It's Time to let America Know...We're More than Just Talk" (Bell Atlantic Advertisement, September 1988).

20. *Order*, Docket No. 11866, 27 FCC 359 (1959).

21. These may include, *inter alia*, (private) microwave, digital termination systems (DTS), cellular radio, FM subcarriers, satellites, interactive coaxial cable, fiber optics, intraoffice systems such as local or metropolitan area networks (LANs, MANs) or digital electronic switching systems, infrared light, lasers, and teleports or other "multitech" systems. Although cellular radio may have nonbypass applications, it is commonly viewed as a bypass related technology. See notes 9 and 10 *supra*. Similarly, LANs may or may not represent bypass modes, depending on the specific applications. As discussed below, private branch exchanges (PBXs) may facilitate circumvention of the LPSN, but do not pose a bypass problem in the usual sense. As discussed in the previous Chapter, many of these same technologies have been incorporated into both the long distance and local public switched networks.

22. "Surging, Price–Insensitive Demand Over Next Two Years and Strong Five–Year Picture Forecast For Cellular Industry Association, Which Sees Capacity Concerns Validated," *Telecommunications Reports*, August 15, 1988, p. 22.

23. "Results of the LAN Survey: Is There Life After Local Area Networks? (Our survey indicates that expectations for LANs far exceed benefits.)," *Communications Consultant*, August 1987, p. 52.

24. "Boston To Join Cities Sporting Teleport Facilities," *Communications Week*, October 10, 1988.

25. FCC status as of November 1, 1988.

26. *Cablevision*, March 14, 1988.

27. AT&T announced soon after divestiture that over 300 users had expressed interest in direct hook ups to the IXC's facilities. See, *e.g.*, "AT&T Seeks Tariff Change, Expected to Spur Bypass," *Communications Week*, June 18, 1984, p. 37. In September 1985, AT&T's Chairman stated that "AT&T is not trying to be an active agent of bypass but we're not going to give up business if a customer such as Merrill Lynch in New York demands that we use their own facilities" for connection to an AT&T point of presence. *Telecommunications Reports*, September 16, 1985, p. 14. Nonetheless, two years later, AT&T insists that it always includes local telco access in designing private networks for

its customers and that the company has no intention of trying to replicate local facilities.   See "What Discrepancy?" *Communications Week*, October 17, 1987, p. 8.

28. "AT&T is Tentatively Cleared to Cut Price For Major User, Hinting at Industry Shift," *Wall Street Journal*, September 9, 1988, p. 4.

29. "AT&T helps SDN user bypass BOC," *Network World*, July 6, 1987, p. 1.

30. A variation on this plan is an NTS cost "cap," whereby large users would be assessed only the specific costs caused by these customers.   Successful implementation of this method would, of course, require knowledge of the precise costs ascribable to a given user.   Moreover, strict adherence to this approach could block otherwise appropriate support of basic service rates for "needy" users.

31. See, *e.g.*, "GTE Moves Reflect New CEO's Agenda," *Communications Week*, August 8, 1988, p. 6; and "GTE selling last US Sprint price?," *Communications Week*, September 26, 1988, p. 8.

32. "Special Report; The Push For Quality," *Business Week*, June 8, 1987, p. 132.

33. "Business Week/Harris Poll: Nobody Even Comes Close to AT&T," *Business Week*, February 17, 1986, p. 90.

34. "The Quest for the Best: U.S. Firms Turn to Quality as Competitive Tool," *Washington Post*, October 2, 1988, p. H2. In the 1988 survey of 1,005 respondents, AT&T was ranked number 6 overall.

35. "Service quality–measuring the network and the customer," *Telephony*, December 9, 1985, p. 32.

36. For a listing of nearly 100 major bypass studies, see Appendix 3 to Bethesda Research Institute, Ltd., *Market and Strategic Impacts of Bypass*, Bypass Opportunities Series, Volume II (Phillips Publishing, Inc.: Potomac, Maryland, 1986).

37. BRI's experience includes surveys in several highly urbanized states and the District of Columbia, testifying before Congress and numerous state commissions, providing analyses for the Office of Technology Assessment and the General Accounting Office, and preparing nationwide assessments of the phenomenon, *e.g.*, in *Market and Strategic Impacts of Bypass*, *op. cit.*; and *Telecommunications Policy for the 1980s: The Transition to Competition* (Englewood Cliffs, New Jersey: Prentice–Hall, Inc., 1984), prepared for the Washington Program of the Annenberg Schools of Communication.

38. Slip Opinion filed July 28, 1983, *U.S. v. WECo and AT&T*, and *U.S. v. AT&T et al*, Civil Action No. 82–0192, Misc. No. 82–0025, notes 34 and 147.

39. Order, Civil Action No. 82–0192, filed September 10, 1987, pp. 34–36.

40. *Telecommunications Reports*, August 15, 1988, p. 5.

41. Address by Judge Harold H. Greene before the "Communications Week Symposium," held December 8, 1988 in Washington, D.C.; Slip Opinion filed June 13, 1989, Civil Action No. 82–0192.

42. Order, Civil Action No. 82–0–192, filed September 10, 1987, pp. 34–36.

43. See, *e.g.*, comments attributed to Senator Albert Gore (D–Tenn) in *Telecommunications Reports*, November 24, 1986, p. 12.

44. Letter from Douglas H. Ginsburg of the Department of Justice to Congressman John D. Dingell, September 1986.

45. "Bypass: FCC Chairman is not alarmed," *Communication Age*, July 1985, p. 13.

46. *Telecommunications Reports*, November 24, 1986, p. 10.

47. *Telecommunications Reports*, February 9, 1987, p. 6.

48. *Telecommunications Reports*, December 22, 1986, p. 28.

49. See, *e.g.*, "FCC Resurrects Carrier Fee For Long Distance Carriers' Originating Calls," *Communications Week*, December 19, 1988, p. 11.

50. *NTIA, Competition in the Local Exchange Telephone Service Market*, NTIA Report No. 87–210, February 1987, pp. 20–21.

51. *Id.*, pp. 21–22.

52. *Id.*, p. 22.

53. *Id.*, p. 23.

54. Some believe that growth in telephone company plant may have little relationship to bypass activity. The statistics in this regard are presented as one of several indicia whose collective trends may provide useful insights into the magnitude of bypass activity and its impact on LEC growth.

55. These estimates were reported in the RBOCs' April, 1988 monitoring reports (as amended) filed with the FCC and the Federal/State Joint Board overseeing bypass activity. As indicated in Appendix A of this report, there are concerns that the calculations may overstate the actual level of bypass.

56. "Market value" is defined as the share price on a given day in March (*i.e.*, the 21st in 1986, the 20th in 1987, and the 18th in 1988) multiplied by the latest available common shares outstanding at that time.

57. AT&T plans to make its domestic switched network 100 percent digital by the end of 1990, and major Independents such as GTE, Untied Telecom, Contel, and Centel are aiming for 95 percent digitalization by the early 1990s. Most BOCs apparently do not anticipate achieving the 95 percent level until the year 2000. See "AT&T's Third–Quarter NET Rose 17%; $5 Billion Write–Off Possible for Year," *Wall Street Journal*, October 21, 1988, p. A2; and "Independent Telcos Edge Bells in Digital Switching," *Communications Week*, September 12, 1988, p. 38.

58. "Users look to bypass nets in wake of Ill. Bell blaze," *Network World*, June 20, 1988, p. 82.

59. See, *e.g.*, "Whatever Happened to DTS?," *Data Communications*, March 1986, pp. 78–77.

60. Source: FCC's Common Carrier Bureau.

61. "AT&T, United Technologies Kill Shared–Tenant Venture," *Communications Week*, June 27, 1986, p. 1.

62. "Sale of Intelliserve signals plight of AT&T," *Network World*, January 5, 1987, p. 5.

63. NARUC *Bulletin* No. 38–1988, September 19, 1988, p. 21.

64. "WCI rumored to be quitting bypass biz," *Network World*, May 30, 1988, pp. 9–10.

65. "The Big Four Bypass Technologies," *Communications Consultant*, March 1987, p. 38.

66. "Boston to Join Cities Sporting Teleport Facilities," *Communications Week*, October 10, 1988, p. 34.

67. "Targeting bypass technologies," *Telecommunications Products & Technology*, February 1987, p. 24.

68. See, *e.g.*, "Fiber Frontier: The Local Loop," *Telephone Engineer & Management*, July 1, 1987, p. 104.

69. "Competition Squeezes Microwave Vendors," *Communications Week*, February 2, 1987, p. C1.

70. See, *e.g.*, "U.S. Companies Involved In ISDN Trials and Service Rollouts," *Communications Week*, September 19, 1988, p. C14; and "Ill. Bell To File ISDN Tariffs, McDonald's Will Start Paying," *Communications Week*, January 18, 1988, p. 1.

71. See, *e.g.*, "The Boom in Private Networks," *Teleconnect*, October 1986; and "T1 Appeal Grows As Prices Drop," *Communications Week*, September 5, 1988, p. C3.

72. NTIA, Video Program Distribution and Cable Television: Current Policy Issues and Recommendations, NTIA Report 88–233, June 1988.

73. FCC, Notice of Inquiry, CC Docket 87–266, adopted July 16, 1988.

74. See, *e.g.*, "The Rewiring of America: Scenarios for Local Loop Distribution," *Telecommunications*, January 1988, pp. 30–31, 34, 36.

75. "Another Bell Makes Non–Wireline Inroads," *Communications Week*, January 12, 1987, p. 1.

76. "Hello Anywhere," *Business Week*, September 21, 1987, p. 86.

77. "Vertical Marketing Strategy Supplants STS, at Pac Bell," *Communications Week*, April 13, 1987, p. 37.

78. *Telecommunications Reports*, September 26, 1988, p. 22; see *supra* concerning Illinois Bell and Ohio Bell.

79. "Starting from Scratch," *Communications Week*, August 8, 1988, p. 24.

80. "AT&T Offers Digital Microwave Bypass System to CPE Arms of BOCs & Other Telcos," *The Report on AT&T*, April 8, 1985, p. 6.

81. See, *e.g.*, "Independents Return to the Basics: The Telcos' Homecoming," *Communications Week*, October 10, 1988, p. 1; and "Revisiting Bell Subsidiaries: After 5 Years.   Bells Focus on Network Business," *Communications Week*, September 19, 1988, pp. 1, 46.

82. "Ill. Bell, Sprint Win Bid For $108M Illinois Network," *Communications Week*, June 13, 1988, p. 12.

83. See, *e.g.*, "N.Y. Gov't. Awards Nynex Team $108M Contract," *Communications Week*, October 17, 1988, p. 42.

84. See, *e.g.*, Market and Strategic Impacts of Bypass, *op. cit.*, especially Parts IIB(2), IIA and B. See also, *e.g.*, "Bypass Not Cost Driven," *Network World*, December 8, 1986, p. 4.   (Diebold study); "Features, Not Price, Call the Shots for Many Telephone Customers," *Communications Week*, April 4, 1988, p. 36 (McKinsey & Co. survey); and "Problems Force Users to Retrench," *Communications Week*, November 7, 1988, pp. 1, 62. It is interesting to note that Dr. Joseph Kraemer of Touche Ross, who has supervised numerous LEC sponsored user surveys which found that price was the paramount decisionmaking criterion, recently urged local exchange carriers to concentrate on marketing and customer service as market place strategies.   See "Competition in the Local Exchange: From Where to Where," presented at the April 7–8, 1988 Phillips Conference, "Local Exchange Competition," in Washington, D.C.

85. See, *e.g.*, "Users Try New Paths to Get Data to Nets," *Communications Week*, February 22, 1988, pp. 1, 62.

86. Excerpted from Bethesda Research Institute, Ltd., *Bypass and the Subscriber Line Charge*, prepared for the National Association of State Utility Consumer Advocates by Walter G. Bolter, Fred J. Kelsey and James W. McConnaughey, August 1988 (Sections IIA, B, C, and selected charts).

87. "Bypass of the Public Switched Network," Common Carrier Bureau, Federal Communications Commission, December 19, 1984.

88. *Id.*, page 14, 15.

89. *Id.*, page 15.

90. *Further Supplemental Submission of Pacific Bell*, August 30, 1984, Attachment 2, Tab 1.

91. *1985 Annual Report to Shareholders*, Pacific Telesis Group.

92. See, for example, *Supplemental Comments of Mountain States Bell, Northwestern Bell and Pacific Northwest Bell*, CC Docket 78–72, Federal Communications Commission, October 3, 1984, page 7.

93. This comment was by Pacific Bell in its *Supplemental Submission*, CC Docket 78–72, Attachment 2, Table 1, the same company cited above for its rapid growth in spite of allegedly massive losses to service bypass.

94. "Telephone Communications: Bypass of the Local Telephone Companies," GAO/RCED–86–66, United States General Accounting Office, August 1986.

95. *Id.*, page 3.

96. *Id.*, page 50.   See also, Gerald W. Brock, "Bypass of the Local Exchange: A Quantitative Assessment," OPP Working Paper No. 12, Federal Communications Commission, September 1984.

97. Racster, Wong, and Guldmann, "The Bypass Issue: An Emerging Form of Competition in the Telephone Industry,"   No. 84–17, The   National Regulatory Research Institute, Columbus, Ohio, December 1984.

98. *Id.*, page ix.

99. *Id.*, pages ix–xi.

100. Peter W. Huber, "The Geodesic Network: 1987 Report on Competition in the Telephone Industry," Prepared for the Department of Justice in accordance with the court's decision in *U.S.100. v. Western Electric Company*, 552 F. Supp. 131, 194–5 (D.D.C. 1982).

101. *Id.*, Huber report, page 1.18.

102. "Factual Predicates to the MFJ Business Restrictions: A Critical Analysis of the Huber Report," A report to the Ad Hoc Telecommunications Users Committee and the International Communications Association (ICA), Economics and Technology, Inc., March 13, 1987.

103. *Id.*, page 2.

104. See the study undertaken by the Bethesda Research Institute, Ltd. for a listing of nearly 100 major bypass studies: "Market and Strategic Impacts of Bypass," Bypass Opportunities Series, Volume II, Appendix 3, Phillips Publishing, Inc., Potomac, Maryland, 1986.

105. Testimony of Joseph S. Kraemer, Touche Ross & Co., Before the New York Public Service Commission on behalf of New York Telephone Co. (Case No. 28710), June 1984.

106. Testimony of Donald C. Hillman, Peter Merrill Associates, Before the Maryland Public Service Commission (Case No. 7450, Phase II), March 1983, and accompanying study, "Strategic Analysis of Local Exchange Bypass in Maryland," March 1983, on behalf of Chesapeake and Potomac Telephone Company of Maryland.

107. "Access Charging and Bypass Adoption," Shooshan & Jackson, Inc., a study prepared for Bell Atlantic, March 1985.

108. Perspective Telecommunications Group, "Intra–City Communications Networks," January 1983, and "Intra–City Communications Networks: II," July 1984, Paramus, New Jersey.

109. Testimony of Donald L. Walton, Central Committee on Telecommunications of the American Petroleum Institute, Before the New York Public Service Commission in Case No. 28710, May 1984.

110. Comments of the Association of Data Communications Users, filed in response to the FCC's *Request for Data, Information, and Studies Pertaining to Bypass of the Public Switched Network*, May 21, 1984.

111. Walter G. Bolter and James W. McConnaughey, "Telecommunications Bypass Policy in the United States: Description and Assessment," Bethesda Research Institute, Ltd., A report prepared for the Office of Technology Assessment, U. S. Congress, March 1985.

112. *Reply Comments of MCI Telecommunications Corporation*, CC Docket No. 78–72/80–286, Federal Communications Commission, October 9, 1986.

113. *Id., Reply Comments*, pages 5 and 6.

114. J. McConnaughey, "Summary of BRI Private Study of Local Bypass in Maryland," Bethesda Research Institute, Ltd., September 1983.

115. "Study of Local Bypass and Preliminary Customer Survey," New York State Public Service Commission, Case No. 28710, Bethesda Research Institute, Ltd., April 1984.

116. "Local Bypass in New Jersey: Survey Results and Implications," Research Studies Division, Bethesda Research Institute, Ltd., December 1984.

117. "Survey of Local Telephone Network Bypass in Pennsylvania," Research Studies Division, Bethesda Research Institute, Ltd., Rockville, Maryland, 1986.

118. Subsequent to the initial submissions, amended data was filed by some of the RBOCs.

119. "FCC Bypass Report," *Pacific Bell*, April 1988, p. 2.

120. "BellSouth Region, FCC Bypass Monitoring Report," April 29, 1988, Ex. I, Att. C, p. 1.

121. $22 \times 8 \times 60 = 10,560$.

122. PacTel mitigated the problem to some degree by only considering growth of special access circuits from 1984 rather than total circuits as was apparently done by the other RBOCs.

123. Multiple choices were allowed so that some customers could have other reasons for bypassing the LPSN in addition to price.

CHAPTER VII

GLOBAL PERSPECTIVE OF TELECOMMUNICATIONS AND SERVICES

A. Domestic Service Providers

Common carriers provide telecommunications services that are essential to all Americans. Telecommunications common carriers include telephone, tele-graph, and overseas cable companies that are required to furnish adequate service to all requesting such service, to interconnect with other carriers, and, generally to adhere to schedules of charges (rates) approved by a state regulatory commission or by the Federal Communications Commission (FCC). As the growth of computers created the need for data transmission over common carrier telephone networks originally built only for voice transmis-sion, the need for more capacity of higher quality required a reworking of the telephone networks. The relatively slow pace of the telephone common carriers in adopting computerized switching and building better transmission facilities conflicted with users' desires to connect their own equipment, especially computer terminals, to telephone company facilities. Initially banned, the FCC slowly opened telephone common carriers to both network and equipment competition, a process which continues today in the aftermath of the AT&T divestiture of its local operating companies. The basic incompatibility of computers and telecommunications systems remains both a problem from the past and a technical challenge.[1]

Universal telephone service (UTS) has been an explicit U.S. policy goal since the enactment by the U.S. Congress of Section 1, Title 1, of the 1934 Communications Act, *viz.*,

> . . . to make available, so far as possible, to all the people
> of the United States, a rapid, efficient, Nation–wide, and
> world–wide wire and radio communication service with
> adequate facilities at reasonable charges . . .

This policy evolved during a fifty year period in communications history which was characterized by broad based regulation of franchised monopolies which provided local exchange and intrastate toll services, as well as customer premises equipment (such as telephones), a single provider of inter-state long distance services, and duopolistic supply of domestic telegraphy.

Rapidly changing technology and procompetitive public policies emerged during the late 1960s and 1970s, modifying the telecommunications market structure by permitting entry of new suppliers. Deregulatory initiatives were actively implemented by the FCC beginning in the 1980s. Major areas of network technology during the era encompassed microwave, satellite and coaxial cable systems, primarily analog (voice grade) toll and local exchange circuit switching, transmission media dominated by copper wire in the local loop, and private automatic branch exchanges (PABXs), telephones, modems and other customer premises equipment (CPE) adapted to an analog public switched network.

As a result of a consent decree consummated between AT&T and the Department of Justice, the Bell System was dismantled in 1984 in the largest corporate reorganization in U.S. history. Divestiture of the 22 Bell operating companies from AT&T and their recombination into seven regional entities radically restructured the telecommunications sector, fueling the already potent forces of technological change, competitive entry, and deregulation. The new environment features multiple sources of supply for services and equipment, a brisk rate of innovation, and lower costs in many sectors.

FCC policy has emphasized unbundling subscriber rates, promoting equal access for interexchange carriers (ICs) and enhanced service providers, and embracing efficiency as the paramount agency objective.   Given the latter FCC goal, some industry observers have questioned the Commission's commitment to UTS.   Although the FCC has strongly claimed that the telephone penetration rate had, in fact, already attained record levels during the early post–divestiture years, others argued that this Census Bureau index measures possession of telephones rather than universal service.

The actual extent of bypass of the public switched network, especially at the local exchange level, also became a controversial issue during the 1980s and is discussed extensively in Chapter VI.

The new era has also witnessed technological changes which would substantially alter the nature of the telephone network.   Digital technology has begun to supplant existing analog applications in both toll and local networks, which were largely segmented by the AT&T divestiture. Digitalization has fundamentally affected switching, transmission, and terminal equipment.   The rapid movement toward digitalization and other network modernization activities has been spurred by the extremely rapid changes in integrated circuit design and the resultant major cost savings.

1.   Service Providers

During the 1970s, domestic U.S. telecommunications was dominated by the Bell System and Independent telephone companies.   Throughout that decade, the two accounted for more than 96 percent of the nation's common carrier services.   (See Table VII–1).   Total telephone industry operating revenues for 1980 were over $62 billion.

Local operating companies were franchised monopolists whose only competition was interservice (e.g., private lines vs. basic service) and private microwave systems (some 91 million circuit miles as of September 1979).[2] By 1980, local phone service revenues were $24.6 billion, and toll revenues totaled $29.0 billion.   Of these totals, Bell represented 84 percent of the local revenues and 82 percent of all toll revenues.   The Bell System also served 81 percent of U.S. telephones, yet accounted for only 38 percent of the exchanges and two percent of the existing telephone companies.[3]

Among long distance carriers, AT&T reigned supreme.   Its market share in 1980 for MTS was 88.0 percent, for WATS was 95.3 percent, and for the combined category was 89.0 percent.   The interexchange carrier also commanded 87.6 and 81.9 percent of the 1980 private line and toll services

Table VII–1

U.S. TELECOMMUNICATIONS MARKET SHARES
1972 – 1980

	Bell System and Independents	Others	Total
1972	96.7%	3.3%	100%
1973	96.8	3.2	100
1974	96.7	3.3	100
1975	96.8	3.2	100
1976	96.7	3.3	100
1977	96.6	3.4	100
1978	96.6	3.4	100
1979	96.5	3.5	100

Source: "Telecommunications in Transition: The Status of Competition in the Telecommunications Industry," a report by the majority staff of the Subcommittee on Telecommunications, Consumer protection, and Finance (Comm. Print 97–V), November 3, 1981, p. 118.

markets, respectively. In fact, the 1979 combined figure for AT&T and the Independents was 97.3 percent.[4]

The Independent companies and especially the Bell System also prevailed in the customer premises equipment market. In terms of private branch exchange (PBX) installed base, Bell captured 67 percent and the Independents 15 percent in 1978. By 1982 as competition began to make inroads, Bell's share of the market dropped to 56 percent and the independent telephone companies controlled only 13 percent of the PBX market. Between 1978 and 1982, the market share of nontelephone company suppliers, the so called "interconnect" companies had almost doubled to 31 percent. The PBX market, meanwhile, had continued its steady increase in growth, nearly eight percent in 1982.

The market share of these independent PBX system suppliers increased as a result not only of the demise of regulatory barriers to equipment market entry, but also because the interconnect companies were offering features not provided by the Bell companies. For example, companies such as Mitel, Rolm, and Northern Telecom were offering digital PBXs that were not only cheaper than Bell's models but also exceeded the performance of Bell's Centrex services at a lower price. One of these companies, Rolm, became a part of IBM's movement into communications in the early 1980s.

Behind the Bell equipment dominance prior to 1980 was Western Electric, the System's manufacturing arm. By the early 1970s, Western had secured dominant positions in the transmission equipment, central office, and CPE markets. The end of the decade showed a different picture, though, as inroads were made by competitors into CPE markets. For instance, Bell's share of the large PBX market went from 81 percent in 1973 to about 60 percent in 1980.

Since divestiture the RHCs have also been active in the CPE market. Several of the regionals have been acquiring profitable interconnect companies to bolster their own sales and corporate objectives. For instance, BellSouth has acquired NEC's leading distributor in Roanoke, Virginia and Northern telecom's direct sales operations in Atlanta. Figures VII–1 and 2 show market shares for CPE distributors at two points in time, 1987 and 1992. The data reflects the increasing role of the RHCs in this market. Aggressive acquisition strategies could expand the RHCs' market share in the late 1990s.

Figure VII–3 presents projections of market shares of distributors in the business only CPE interconnect market. The data represents three categories: the RHCs (and affiliates); independent telcos (and affiliates); and all others which includes 14 of the highest ranked remaining interconnects. The entire group is comprised of the top 25 CPE competitors with sales topping $3 billion in 1987. As the chart shows, the RHCs have the lion's share of this market which grew at double digit rates, e.g., over 20 percent annually from 1984 to 1987.

New competition in services' markets was led by MCI and Southern Pacific Communications Company (SPCC, now US Sprint) and joined by others such as ITT's U.S. Transmission Systems (USTS), the specialized common carriers (SCCs) grew using a combination of aggressive litigation and marketing. These companies started as a response to the neglect of data communications by the telephone companies, to fill customer needs in what was then a niche market. A series of favorable decisions by the courts (e.g., Execunet I and II) and the FCC (e.g., Specialized Common Carrier decision) removed formerly serious obstacles. Some firms did not survive (e.g., Datran) but the market presence of many SCCs expanded steadily during the 1970s. The SCCs laid a foundation for rapid expansion into voice communications, as well as data, in the early 1980s.

The first domestic satellite, or domsat, (Westar) was successfully launched by Western Union on April 13, 1974. Major satellite carriers in the 1970s and early 1980s were Satellite Business Systems (SBS), RCA, Western Union, AT&T, GTE, American Satellite Company (AmSat), SPCC, and USSI.

U.S. Telephone Company, Allnet, and hundreds of other companies thrived by subscribing to telephone company volume discounted services and then acting as resellers to users who would otherwise not be able to take advantage of bulk discounts.

Other telecommunications companies also began to grow. Miscellaneous common carriers (MCCs) functioned as carriers' carriers for video transmission involving broadcasting networks. Value added carriers such as Tymnet and Telenet offered specialized or enhanced services. Domestic record carriers such as Western Union transmitted data within the U.S. while international record carriers (IRCs) performed this function for those seeking international communications services.

Ownership of microwave networks by users became legal in 1959 after the FCC adopted its Above 890 decision which freed radio spectrum for such use.

Figure VII-1

DISTRIBUTORS OF NEW CPE

1987: Total Market — $8.7M

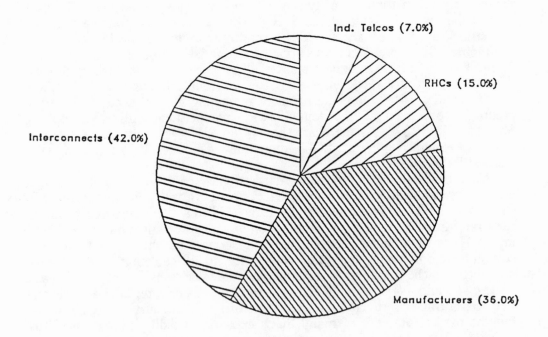

Source: <u>Communications Week</u>, April 18, 1988, p. 12.

Figure VII-2

DISTRIBUTORS OF NEW CPE

1992: Total Market — $9.8M

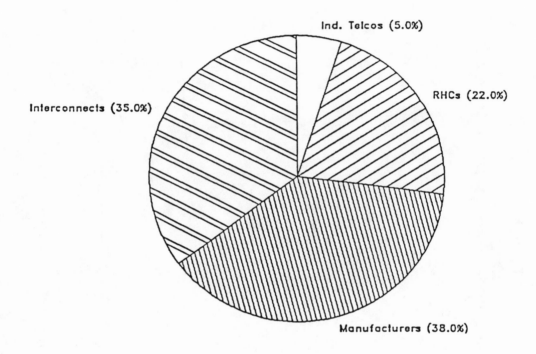

Ind. Telcos (5.0%)

RHCs (22.0%)

Interconnects (35.0%)

Manufacturers (38.0%)

Source: Communications Week, April 18, 1988, p. 12.

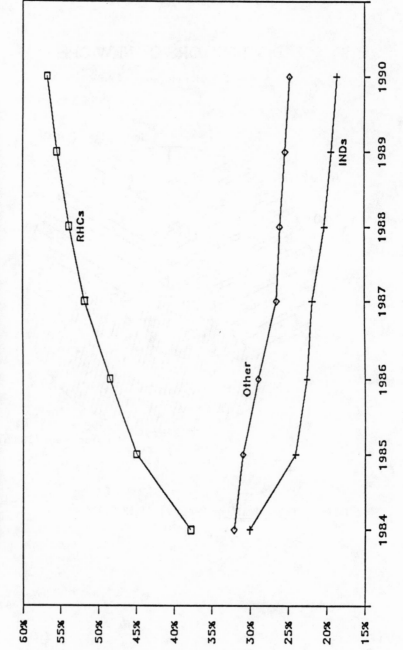

Figure VII-3

BUSINESS CPE MARKET SHARE– U.S.

Source: Telephony, May 11, 1987 and BRI estimates.

The Commission concluded that as of the late 1970s, no economic harm to the local public switched network (LPSN) had occurred.[5] From 1977 to 1982, such private microwave systems grew at an annual rate of 3.75 percent per year.[6]

By 1980, less than four percent of U.S. common carrier services were captured by an assortment of communications companies, including specialized common carriers, U.S. satellite carriers, miscellaneous common carriers, value added common carriers, domestic record carriers, and international record carriers. Specialized common carriers accounted for only one percent of the national metered toll revenues. Western Union (5.3 percent), specialized carriers (2.6 percent), domsats (4.7 percent), value added carriers (2.7 percent), and miscellaneous carriers (1.1 percent) together tallied over 16 percent of all long distance private line revenues.

During the 1970s, the various nontelephone company carriers, now known as the other common carriers (OCCs), grew at varying rates. SCCs grew most vigorously, while moderate increases were registered by satellite carriers, value added carriers, and radio common carriers (RCCs). The IRCs and MCCs did not appreciably change their relative market positions, while domestic record carriers showed a decline.

The telecommunications sector of the 1980s has, thus far, been shaped by a series of major public policy changes and continued technical progress. The Modification of Final Judgment (MFJ) disbanding the Bell System, coupled with the FCC's deregulatory initiatives established in *Computer II, Competitive Carrier, Computer VII* and other proceedings, have attempted to facilitate both competition and innovative change. According to FCC statistics, the percentage of interstate switched traffic carried by AT&T's competitors, increased from 20 percent in 1984 to about 30 percent in 1988. Technological imperatives have further promoted diversity, efficiency, and a whetting of consumer wants and needs. As a result of these forces for change, a proliferation of new services is presently being offered, representing new alternatives to existing common carrier services and products.

Interexchange usage is now growing at 13 percent annually for the industry, with OCCs exhibiting even greater growth at 33 percent. Among the companies providing interexchange services, AT&T continues to dominate interLATA communications with as much as 70 to 80 percent of the revenues. However, among larger users, AT&T's share has dropped substantially based on a late 1988 survey.[7] AT&T's percentage at these locations fell by almost 20 percent as MCI, US Sprint, Allnet, and others have gained market share. This trend could be reversed as AT&T has recently emphasized sales to large customers via creative pricing and tariff schemes.

Construction expenditures by AT&T in 1989 were expected to be $3,000 million compared to MCI's and US Sprint's expenditures of $715 million and $650 million, respectively. Although MCI's and US Sprint's construction costs are substantial and will add to present facilities, one should note that AT&T's growth is on top of an already overwhelming capacity in embedded plant facilities.

The three major players today are essentially the same as in 1981 – AT&T, MCI, and US Sprint. Allnet Communications Service, now the largest of the so–called resellers, is becoming increasingly facilities–based and, while still capturing only a small fraction of the interexchange market, is one of the top ten firms in the industry. In spite of AT&T's continued dominance, new technologies and public policy changes have supported rapid growth by AT&T's major interexchange competitors. From 1978 to the present, infant competitors such as MCI, US Sprint and Allnet have grown into companies of large absolute size in terms of revenues, assets, and customer base. Further growth may be expected to increase the market share of most of these competitors at the expense of AT&T in the postdivestiture world of equal access, but AT&T is now aggressively seeking to maintain a high market share.

Satellite carriers have grown rapidly in capacity since the first commercial communications satellite was placed in orbit in 1963. Part of this growth can be attributed to the absence of vigorous economic regulation by the FCC, but domestic satellite carriers have primarily grown because they provide base capacity that is easily adapted to almost any communications service used for long haul transmission (generally the break even distance for satellite services relative to terrestrial microwave is over 1000 miles) market. Leading satellite manufacturing firms such as Hughes and RCA have launched their own satellites. Some firms are direct competitors for consumer dollars while others sell large portions of their capacity to common carriers, private networks, DBS operators, cable television companies, broadcasting networks, and value added carriers. Increasing competition from improved terrestrial microwave systems and high capacity fiber optic communications systems, coupled with a rapid increase in the number of operational satellites and transponder capacity, has sent transponder lease rates plummeting and slowed growth.

Technical innovations in satellite communications include increasing use of higher frequencies in the Ku and Ka bands which allow the use of smaller (and cheaper) earth–based antennas, satellites with tunable antenna arrays which allow more efficient use of the available frequency spectrum, and a longer–term move toward larger and more complicated satellites which could provide true "switch–in–the sky" services. These and other improvements could reverse recent trends and hasten growth in both satellite service capacity and function.

The longstanding regulatory prohibitions against the IRCs providing domestic communications services were removed in the mid–1980s. The major IRCs have rapidly begun to integrate their international and new domestic operations, taking advantage of their existing customer base, technical exper–tise, and low costs of entry through their existing plant. Some companies have expanded domestically by merger or purchase, such as MCI's purchase of Western Union International, while others have joined with separate subsidiaries of the same parent company, such as ITT's USTS and ITT Worldcom. While the IRCs have traditionally been involved only in record communications, they are now adding voice, data, and Digital Termination Services (DTS) to both their domestic and international operations. In comparison to the major interexchange carriers, the IRCs are small, oriented toward international communications, and traditionally not as aggressive. They could, however, have a significant impact in exploiting their market niche, especially in concert with domestic companies such as MCI.

Although Judge Harold Greene of the U.S. District Court of the District of Columbia has made clear that the RHCs will not be allowed to provide interLATA, interexchange services as long as they retain local "bottleneck" monopolies, the holding companies continue to request waivers of this policy. Some observers, notably then Rep. Timothy Wirth (D.–Colorado), have suggested that the RHCs' buildup of network facilities[8] is aimed as much at positioning for entry into the interLATA market as it is at providing improved local service and local access to the current interexchange companies. Whatever their intentions *vis–à–vis* the interexchange marketplace, the RHCs in aggregate are potentially the most awesome competitors for interexchange traffic with total assets of over $160 billion, revenues of almost $75 billion, and 1988 net income of $8.8 billion. Their technical resources are also impressive, with local operating company engineering staffs backed up by technical organizations at the holding company level and by the technical and research activities of jointly owned Bellcore.

Additionally, the RHCs are already deeply involved in intraLATA toll services. Some LATAs encompass whole states (such as Maine and North Dakota), while most are extensive enough to generate toll services. For all the RHCs, 14 percent of their 1988 revenues were garnered from intraLATA toll services. Without regulatory restriction, there is little doubt that the RHCs would quickly connect their own LATAs with interexchange facilities, possibly building on their already existing internal communications facilities.

Until that time, however, the RHCs continue to expand into technologies that could at least form a part of interexchange facilities. RHC subsidiaries are extensively involved in cellular radio systems, PBX sales and service, digital termination services, fiber optics, and packet switching.

The traditional independent telephone companies are well aware of the advantages of integrating local telephone operations with long distance service. The toll revenues of these nonBell local telephone companies were $5.9 billion as early as 1980, and these independents are not restricted by the courts or the FCC from full participation in the interexchange service market as are the RHCs. The independents are aggressively moving to position themselves as integrated local/long distance providers. For instance, both GTE and United Telecom have been associated with US Sprint and Rochester Telephone established RCI.

Even Cincinnati Bell and Southern New England Telephone, formerly Bell operating companies, are beginning to assert themselves in nontraditional ways.[9] For example, Cincinnati Bell formed a subsidiary to resell AT&T long distance services, while Southern New England Telephone joined with CSX Corporation to form Lightnet, a fiber optic carrier's carrier.

The independent telephone companies are also moving into cellular radio, DTS, value–added services,[10] and the PBX markets. These markets offer tempting possibilities for integration with other local and long distance services.

By far the largest and most extensive of the interexchange carriers today is AT&T Communications, a part of AT&T set up to provide interexchange network services after the stripping of the local operating companies from the old Bell System. Variously estimated to handle from 70 to 80 percent of all intercity telecommunications, this over $50 billion (revenues) company inherited nearly all the #4 ESS digital toll switches and the entire long distance network of the Bell System. This technologically advanced network is being constantly upgraded to offer the data services demanded by large business customers. AT&T's Accunet network is the largest digital network in the world, as is the company's packet switched command and control network. AT&T is also installing fiber optic transmission facilities at a rapid pace, including new undersea cables to Hawaii and Europe. AT&T will have the technological depth and network resources to compete effectively against any other company, especially after charges for access to the local exchanges are equalized with the completion of carrier equal access to most local switches.

While virtually all interexchange and local telephone companies have adopted fiber optic transmission systems as their major transmission growth medium, carriers' carriers are concerned with wholesaling capacity to other carriers and private users rather than retailing services to end users. In the mid–1980s the top dozen companies planned to add seven billion circuit–miles, thereby increasing the capacity of the U.S. long distance network by five times. Fiber optic systems are on the cutting edge of technology, offering very high capacities at a rapidly declining cost. In this regard, some believe that satellites should be used to carry video signals and voice calls only as a backup to terrestrial facilities or on routes that carry few calls over large distances. The growing domestic fiber optic network, which does not suffer from the irritating propagation delays of satellite communications, could pose a threat to satellites as primary long distance facilities.

These carriers' carriers could themselves be in a precarious position if overcapacity develops in long distance transmission. The major interexchange carriers, AT&T, MCI, and US Sprint, and the resellers could shift traffic onto their own systems, leaving these transmission wholesalers with excess capacity. Another cloud on the horizon is that, according to a report to the FCC by the Ad Hoc Telecommunications Users Committee, AT&T itself may turn out to be the lowest–cost provider of fiber optic transmission capacity in the industry. This situation could threaten the economic viability of these wholesalers.

Nevertheless, these companies planned to spend more than $6 billion on long distance, fiber optic facilities. About a third of this amount will be spent by the industry leaders, AT&T, MCI, and US Sprint, who obviously will be providing for their own transmission needs as well as wholesaling capacity to other carriers and private networks. United Telecommunications and others also planned to build nationwide systems for wholesale at a cost of over $3 billion. Other players built regional systems, and interconnection agreements and consolidations have tied many of the regional systems into a semblance of nationwide coverage. Railroads, manufacturers, local telephone companies, financial institutions, record carriers, and the major long distance companies are all investors in the companies building these new fiber optic networks. While it seems unlikely that all these firms will survive, it is clear that fiber optics will make the largest contribution to the capacity of the interexchange network of any technology over the next decade.

VANs are carriers which combine services purchased from an interex- change carrier with some "added value" such as special protocols, features, and information content before retailing the communications circuits to customers. As a practical matter, however, VANs are becoming increasingly difficult to define, as their services are very similar to those offered by many other firms. Electronic mail, remote computing services, and many other services could well be defined as "value added." The VANs do have all the elements needed to integrate backwards into basic information transmission -- a customer base, technical expertise, and existing network facilities.

Electronic mail, computer mailbox services, and Digital Electronic Message Services (DEMS) are a relatively new category of value added services. It is a prime example of the convergence of information processing and information transmission industries. To some extent these services will continue to replace traditional telex and telegraph services long provided by Western Union and others.

A 1976 FCC decision removed virtually all legal restrictions on the resale and shared use of common carrier interstate private line services. Resale carriers were subsequently allowed to buy services from established carriers and resell them to individual users. There are hundreds of resellers operating in very different fields -- hotels reselling to their guests, colleges to their students in dormitories, long distance companies reselling to anybody, and myriads of companies reselling their excess leased communication capacity. Low entry and exit barriers, low sunk costs, and decreasing margins on resales currently prevail as interexchange common carrier pricing becomes more competitive and cost based rates make reselling an unstable marketplace function.

The larger resellers such as Allnet are increasingly acquiring actual transmission facilities and thus becoming wholesalers of capacity themselves. Interestingly, the number of smaller resellers may well increase dramatically as more and more private systems, many utilizing satellite carriers for basic interexchange communications capacity, attempt to sell their excess capacity.

The national television broadcast networks have long been large users of communications services of common carriers for the transmission of video and audio programming to their affiliated stations. Satellite program distribution is now close to universal, with most local stations having, at least, receive- only earth stations. The addition of transmission capability would create nationwide broadband networks that could provide regular communications services in addition to video programming. Services such as Starnet, using mobile antennas mounted on trucks are using satellite relay to carry live broadcasts from formerly inaccessible locations.

Broadcast and common carrier services are showing some signs of conver- gence. FCC actions have encouraged multipoint distribution services (MDS) which are beginning to attract regular telephone common carrier's interest.

While MDS has mainly been used to broadcast pay television service, two—way use of the assigned spectrum is a real possibility. Radio networks can be used to provide paging, electronic mail, and facsimile over subsidiary frequencies. Television broadcasters can offer teletext over the vertical blanking interval of this video signal and paging over this aural sideband. Full use of the broadcast spectrum, facilities, and networks could result in significant competition for common carriers in certain interexchange submarkets.

The convergence of broadcast and common carrier functions is especially sharp for direct broadcast satellites (DBS). Late at night, when not in use for direct broadcasting, the satellite transponder capacity of these systems could be used for program distribution for broadcast networks, data transmission, and other services. Essentially, DBS satellite capacity is a private network with potentially excess capacity available for wholesaling or retailing to other users. While some DBS services are now being provided, the real usefulness of DBS lies in the future as smaller earth stations make consumer reception of DBS programming increasingly economical.

Private communications networks are justified on a cost or service basis for many large organizations with large data transmission requirements. Private networks may reduce a firm's total telecommunications costs, improve the ability to budget in the face of rapid common carrier regulatory changes, and increase the ability of the firm to customize services and manage its operation. Some firms are also turning their communications system into a source of profits by reselling excess capacity or providing data services to others.

Private networks may be local, national, or even worldwide and may employ the full range of communication technologies. Today, most private networks rely on point—to—point microwave, satellites, or facilities leased from the local telephone company. It is anticipated that local area networks (LANs), designed to connect computers with high speed data links, and traditional PBXs which may be connected together by a large private telecommunications network will become more attractive economically in the future.

Financial service companies such as credit card companies, banks, brokerage firms and insurance companies generate a huge and continuous flow of data. These firms may not only have private communications networks, but also specialized networks for specific purposes. Electronic funds transfer, automated tellers, branch accounting data, stock transactions and quotes may require very reliable and extensive special communications networks. Some of these companies have expanded their networks to offer investor information, accounting software, and financial information to remote users.

Railroads and electric and gas utility companies have long utilized private microwave facilities for command and control of their network operations. Additionally, they own or control extensive rights—of—way, especially railroads whose rights—of—way connect urban centers. For these reasons, railroads have been especially active in providing rights—of—way by sale or joint venture for the construction of intercity coaxial or fiber optic transmission systems.

US Sprint, the third largest interexchange common carrier, actually developed from Southern Pacific's private microwave network. Today, the

American Association of Railroads and other trade associations advise their members on how to capitalize on their natural network structure by providing excess capacity in their private networks to resell or lease to other communications users.

Equipment manufacturers are clearly familiar with the underlying technologies. As the information processing and data transmission industries merge, integration by many manufacturers into at least some transmission markets may be seen as necessary to preserve the firm's strategic position. Thus, Mitel and American Satellite formed a joint venture, EMX Telecom, to provide end–to–end telecommunications services; and Hewlett–Packard has shown a similar interest in this area. The prime example of such integration was the IBM/SBS relationship: IBM moved to increase its management control over SBS, and SBS applied to the FCC for permission to make joint marketing presentations with IBM. Subsequently, MCI acquired control of SBS, and IBM, in turn, has made major investments in MCI.

2. Interexchange Market Structure

There are certain indications that substantial operational economies may exist in interexchange markets and that there is dominance rather than competitive market forces at work. As noted above, prior to 1984 AT&T's Bell System dominated the U.S. long distance market. With the implementation of the MFJ and the FCC's procompetition and deregulatory policies, however, has come the divestiture of Bell's local exchange operations from its interexchange (more, specifically, the interLATA) business and the inauguration of an open interconnection policy for all interexchange carriers. Despite this radical restructuring and the high expectations for the new equal access program, AT&T's long standing dominance in long distance has not thus far been overcome.

Notably, AT&T's market power has several dimensions. While market share estimates vary, AT&T's post divestiture presence has remained imposing. For example, using a toll revenue benchmark, the National Telecommunications and Information Administration (NTIA) calculated AT&T's share of the U.S. interLATA market upon divestiture, finding it to be 85 percent. Based on other estimates, intervening entry in later years has not eliminated AT&T's power. For instance, Prof. Peter Huber in his landmark study, *The Geodesic Network: 1987 Report on Competition in the Telephone Industry*, prepared at the behest of the U.S. Department of Justice, found that in 1985 AT&T possessed a commanding share of interLATA revenues (80–85 percent), business customers (88 percent), residential customers (95 percent), and toll minutes (84 percent). Presently, estimates range from 70 to 80 percent as representing AT&T's share of the market.

AT&T intends to preserve this dominance, based on remarks attributed to the Company's Chairman, who, in reporting to stockholders respecting core business such as long distance services, noted that "[w]here we are market leaders, we intend to retain and enhance our position."[11] Furthermore, "[w]here our performance has fallen short of our expectations, we intend to increase revenues by strengthening our marketing and sales efforts."[12]   This effort apparently includes individual contracts with target customers, frequently long term in nature, such as those proposed by AT&T in interstate tariff revisions for a virtual telecommunications network service (VTNS) offering for DuPont Co.[13]   Within the context of its newly devised Tariff 15 AT&T is permitted to respond to competitive bids directed at its customers on a case–by–case basis. Pricing flexibility and creativity will allow AT&T to maintain market dominance. Other similar type tariffs have been initiated by AT&T, all with the purpose of gaining or retaining large customers.

In addition, AT&T has undertaken a vigorous installation program for new technologies, including transmission and switching. For example, as of April 1987 the carrier apparently had more fiber optics in service than US Sprint (12,000 vs. 9,700 miles).   Of course, US Sprint is the third largest interexchange carrier and the best known proponent of fiber technology among long distance competitors. Also, in its 1988 third quarterly report to stockholders, AT&T's chairman, Robert E. Allen, stated that "the company is planning to accelerate its program to make the AT&T long distance network completely digital." This meant a writeoff of $6.7 billion, a sum which is staggering in terms of what its competitors could do in a similar circumstance.

Moreover, AT&T announced in 1987 that it planned to spend $6 billion during 1988 and 1989, $1 billion more than originally forecasted in January 1987, in order to expand its network. The AT&T chairman attributed this need for expansion to an increase in the number of long distance telephone calls and demand for digital business services.[14]   A company executive elaborated, observing that AT&T is experiencing annual growth in service demand of about 20 percent which represented an approximate doubling of the growth rate reported earlier.[15]   The Company intends to spend an unprecedented $15 billion on its network during the next five years, making its network 95 percent digital by 1995.[16]

Certain characteristics of the interexchange market would seem to reinforce AT&T attempts to retain control of that arena.   For example, through historical assignments by regulators, AT&T already possesses a substantial share of total microwave hops (paths) in the two primary interexchange frequency bands in the U.S., viz., 84.1 percent of 3700–4200 MHz and 31.6 percent of 5925–6425 MHz (Table VII–2).

Importantly, AT&T's major interexchange competitors have relied on others, including AT&T, for many of their facility needs. For example, in 1986 MCI spent more than a quarter billion dollars on facilities leased from AT&T and other carriers.[17]   In February 1987 US Sprint was paying AT&T directly one million dollars per day for leased lines.[18]   Although these firms have been increasingly constructing and owning their facilities, their dependence at such a late juncture belies support for the notion of a competitive industry. Indeed, the large number of competitors in the reseller segment of firms that have entered the market are by definition totally reliant on AT&T and other facilities based firms for their operating plant.

Table VII–2

DISTRIBUTION OF MICROWAVE HOPS
Primary Interexchange Frequency Bands
(January 1, 1986)

Type of Licesee	Number of Hops (Paths)		Percent of Total Hops	
	3700– 4200 MHz	5925– 6425 MHz	3700– 4200 MHz	5925– 6425 MHz
AT&T and Affiliates	12,881	11,427	84.1%	31.6%
Former BOCs	1,043	5,941	6.8	16.5
GTE Telcos	171	986	1.1	2.7
Other Telcos	175	1,893	1.1	5.2
MCI	316	5,084	2.1	14.1
GTE Sprint	8	2,041	0.1	5.6
Western Union	202	1,402	1.3	3.9
All Other	522	7,355	3.4	20.4
	15,318	36,129	100.0	100.0

Source: FCC Microwave Application System (MAPS): Path Counts Within
Frequency Bands, Jan 1, 1986.

Despite a great emphasis on price by market entrants earlier, customers
apparently still attach great importance to service quality, which is consistent
with and has been among AT&T's primary objectives. Indeed, an important
survey by the *Wall Street Journal* and NBC News revealed quality of service
to be a paramount consideration for purchasers of long distance service, and
AT&T's general perception as top rated in this area.[19]   And, a separate
survey by respected researcher Louis Harris conducted in early 1986 supported
these results.[20]

Contrary to expectations that AT&T's competitors would have proliferated
in markets not subject to dominance or operating economies, a major
shakeout has been occurring among the OCCs. For instance, MCI absorbed
number four ranked SBS in late 1985 and itself has become owned in part by
IBM. During the same period, Allnet Communications found it necessary to
combine operations with Lexitel. Other mergers were deemed essential by
major competitors, such as GTE Sprint and U.S. Telecom, which merged to
form US Sprint in mid–1986. Indeed, Fibertrak, which proposed to build a
modern fiber optics system, was forced to largely abandon its efforts in 1986
as an individual entrant. Argo Communications, a satellite based OCC targeting business customers, filed for protection under Chapter 11 of the U.S.
bankruptcy laws in early 1987 after two other regional ICs (Microtel and
Litel) cancelled their proposed merger with Argo. In 1987 the Williams
Telecommunications Group merged with LDX Net.

Industry consolidations continued in 1988. Rochester Telephone proposed to acquire ACC Corp., a company with a long distance affiliate,[21] for over $20 million. Also, SouthernNet merged with Teleconnect, Advanced Telecommunications acquired Microtel, and Lightnet extended its network by implementing traffic swapping arrangements with regional carriers rather than expanding its own network through construction.

In essence, the structure of the U.S. long distance market has been significantly shaped during the post divestiture period by the inherent advantages of incumbency perhaps as manifestations of important operating economies at the scale of activity achieved by AT&T. Apparently, ready made market dominance, an established ubiquitous network, and widespread name recognition have all redounded to AT&T's benefit during this era. And the ensuing shakeout and growing concentration within the sector seem to strongly signal market change that is concurrent if not consistent with the technological changes and economies that are being realized in transmission and switching.

Some view an oligopolistic structure to apparently be evolving in U.S. interexchange service markets. Of course, the essential feature of such an organizational form is a high degree of mutual interdependence exhibited by a relatively few number of major suppliers. But oligopoly theory suggests that prices and profits will probably be higher than those under perfect competition and monopolistic competition; yet these are lower than those which would exist under conditions of pure monopoly. Nonprice competition, *e.g.*, advertising and marketing, is the prevalent form of rivalry. Clearly, the currently rising levels of concentration in the sector and the new emphasis on service quality *vis-à-vis* price differentials are not inconsistent with the teachings of this economic theory.

The U.S. interexchange market at present appears to resemble a special type of oligopoly, *viz.*, a dominant firm price leadership structure. This form may arise in an industry where one firm possesses a substantial share of the total market, and the remaining firms are relatively small both in terms of size and market share. The dominant firm maximizes profit by equating marginal revenue to marginal cost. Smaller firms are price takers and may or may not maximize their profits, depending on the cost structure.

Notably, important conscious parallelism in pricing has been evident among the ICs. Thus, many of the rate decreases initiated by AT&T during the early 1980s were purposefully matched by OCC rate cuts. Ordered by the FCC to pass savings from lower federal access charges onto its customers, AT&T reduced its interstate long distance rates by almost 16 percent overall for the first half of 1987 and approximately 38 percent since divestiture through 1988. MCI and US Sprint have responded to these declines with multiple decreases of their own.

But, since mid 1986, the OCCs have not always attempted to match AT&T's rate reductions but, rather, to remain less expensive than AT&T. For example, MCI met AT&T's June 1, 1986 MTS rate decrease of 11.5 percent with approximately a nine percent decline for its dial–up services. Subsequent AT&T reductions of 11 percent (January 1, 1987) and five percent

(July 1, 1987) led to over 10 percent and five percent rate drops by MCI effective March 1 and August 1, 1987.

OCCs currently find themselves in a difficult position. Failure to match AT&T's price decreases may cause loss of market share. OCCs could cut costs to maintain profits, but forsaking growth could send the wrong signals to prospective customers. Thus, ICs such as MCI and US Sprint have seen their price advantage decline and, in some cases disappear.

Given the financial instability besetting OCC's in recent years and AT&T's vigorous market and service responsiveness, the sector's structure may be viewed as evolving toward an even tighter oligopoly, *e.g.*, of facilities based ICs. While numerous firms operating as resellers may exist from time to time, these entities generally represent only a small segment of the U.S. long distance market. By their very nature they are dependent on others for their facilities and, hence, can be viewed as participants of even more uncertain tenure. For instance, Allnet, the largest reseller in recent years, has recognized this tenuousness and has attempted to transfer an increasing amount of traffic to its own network leased pursuant to long term contracts.

Regardless of the final structure that eventually emerges, AT&T's grip on the U.S. long distance market may be highly sustainable. Despite considerable adverse press concerning its financial health since divestiture, AT&T has been ranked number 1 among all telecommunications firms (based on market value) by *Business Week* from 1986 to 1988 (see Chapter III). Thus, notwithstanding major public policy attempts to interject more competition into the U.S. long distance arena, AT&T's market dominance has remained largely intact. With advantages carried over from the predivestiture era helping to maintain AT&T's formidable presence and the economies of its new equipment to be felt fully in future years, AT&T's position *vis-à-vis* the OCCs should be preserved over time.

B. A Services View of Telecommunications

1. Traditional Offerings

Prior to the procompetition stance by the FCC and the 1984 Bell System divestiture, LECs provided services to customers over the local network via tariffed offerings.[22] These included, for example, services such as POTS, supplemental features, Centrex, and private line. The costs associated with the use of local facilities to originate and terminate toll calls were recovered from the long distance company offering service pursuant to the jurisdictional separations process (JSP). The JSP was implemented by maintaining agreements among the participating carriers that followed prescribed rules for making payments to the LECs for the use of local facilities.

As competition gathered momentum and competitors to AT&T's long distance services surfaced, the traditional method of reimbursing LECs was altered. Initially, both tariffs and tariffs based on negotiated agreements were delayed.[23] These tariffs did not apply to AT&T, which continued to pay for local facilities via the JSP. With the breakup of the Bell System and regulatory actions by the FCC, a system of access tariffs was instituted whereby all interstate long distance carriers, including AT&T, paid access charges to the LECs. In addition, access charges were also imposed on residential and business customers in the form of end user fees. Thus, since the inauguration of competition the composition of local market has changed from one of end users to one also including interexchange carriers.

There are two general types of carriers that provide publicly available telephone service in the United States. In the first category are the Bell and Independent local exchange companies, as well as certain miscellaneous radio and other carriers. The second group consists of interexchange carriers (ICs), such as AT&T, US Sprint, MCI, and Western Union. Several ICs offer service throughout the various states, while others are regional or serve primarily one state, such as Alascom (Alaska).

From an operating aspect, the Bell LECs are restricted to offering service within their LATAs,[24] which can include both local exchange and some toll services. ICs do not provide the broad range of traditional local exchange telephone services, but, instead, focus their attention on calls originated or terminated in a state to or from locations in other jurisdictions.

Toll carriers can be divided into two major categories. "Facilities based carriers" have their own switching and transmission facilities to provide interexchange services.[25] "Resale carriers" purchase bulk facilities from underlying carriers and resell the capacity in smaller increments to individual customers at a discount over the rates of underlying carriers.

In order for ICs to provide toll service they must obtain access to the LEC's local network since the toll carriers' facilities (owned or leased) are between their switches and do not directly connect to end users. As noted above, access to customers is obtained via tariffs filed by LECs with the appropriate regulatory agency, *e.g.*, the FCC for interstate toll.

Referring to Figure V-1, the IC portion includes toll switching (two ends) and the transmission facilities connecting the switches. The local portion includes subscriber lines (local loop), local switching, and local trunks where necessary. The connection between the local and toll facilities is included along with the local facilities in the access function provided to ICs.

Toll carriers receive two basic types of access: line side or trunk side connections. The former is designated Feature Group A (FGA) while the latter includes FGB, FGC, and FGD. Figure VII-4 depicts an illustration of FGA and Figure VII-5 shows FGB, C, and D. At the end of 1987, over 80 percent of the access lines were equipped for equal access or FGD in all of the BOCs' operating areas except NYNEX (69 percent), and in 1988 the percentages were approaching or exceeding 90 percent. See Table VII-3 for a summary of RHC equal access attainment. The apparent slower conversion of NYNEX' switches is mainly due to the relatively low number of access lines that were connected to electronic switches (47 percent) at divestiture. The company has indicated it has embarked on a $3 billion program to update its switches whereby all lines will be converted to equal access by year-end 1992.

The revenues paid by ICs and end users for access to toll services via the local network are substantial.[26] Table VII-4 establishes that the revenues

Figure VII-4

SWITCHED ACCESS WITH FEATURE GROUP A

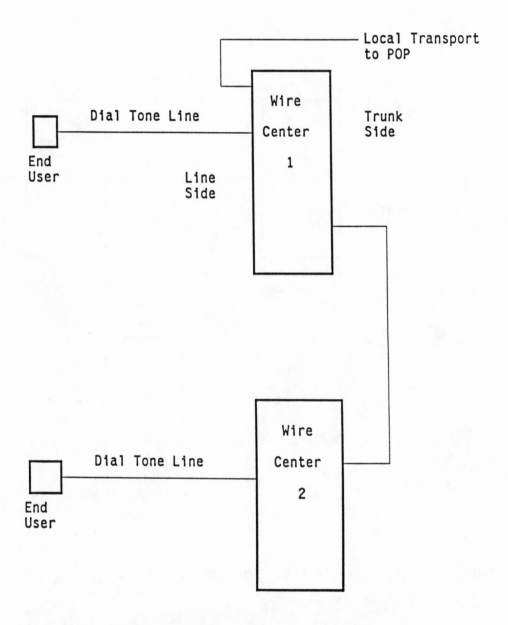

Both above end users access the OCC facilities over
a dial tone line provided out of Wire Center 1.

Figure VII-5

SWITCHED ACCESS WITH FEATURE GROUPS B, C, & D

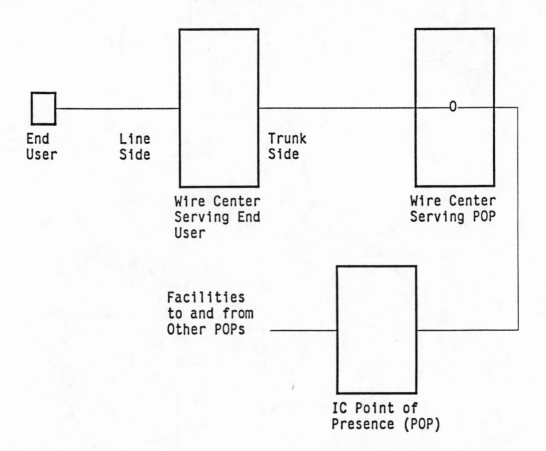

End User

Line Side

Trunk Side

Wire Center Serving End User

Wire Center Serving POP

Facilities to and from Other POPs

IC Point of Presence (POP)

Switched Access Service from End User to IC POP.

O = Hard Wired

Table VII-3

EQUAL ACCESS LINES
Regional Holding Companies

	1986	1987
Ameritech	77%	88%
Bell Atlantic	79	91
BellSouth	70	87
NYNEX	55	69
Pacific Telesis	73	93
Southwestern Bell	78	85
U S WEST	73	85
Overall	72%	85%

Source: FCC data as reported by the BOCs.

Table VII-4

PERCENTAGE OF ACCESS RELATED REVENUES

	1984	1985	1986	1987	1988
Ameritech	25.1%	26.7%	26.5%	24.8%	25.7%
Bell Atlantic	25.8	26.8	26.7	25.3	24.4
BellSouth	30.1	30.7	30.0	29.2	27.0
NYNEX	24.9	25.1	26.3	25.9	25.7
Pacific Telesis	31.9	31.9	30.0	27.7	26.6
Southwestern Bell	31.1	33.5	35.4	33.5	31.1
U S WEST	34.9	33.1	31.7	29.5	29.2
Cincinnati Bell	–	20.5	19.5	18.0	16.1
SNET	–	–	21.9	23.5	22.4
Contel	60.0	59.4	52.9	54.5	57.0
United	–	35.6	38.5	38.3	39.0

Source: Annual Reports.

received by major LECs represented a major portion of their total revenues. Table VII-5 indicates that the majority ICs paid about fifty percent of their gross revenues to LECs for access with the ratio gradually decreasing for AT&T. The monopoly position of the LECs with respect to the interconnection of ICs to the local network will result in a continuation of access fees providing a substantial source of revenues to the local companies.

This optimistic position is fortified when the growth in toll services and access lines is taken into account. For instance, ICs' revenues increased by

Table VII–5

RATIO OF ACCESS COSTS TO REVENUES

	1984	1985	1986	1987	1988
AT&T	59.1%	58.6%	53.8%	50.1%	47.5%
MCI	24.5	34.4	45.5	49.8	46.7
US Sprint	26.6	28.6	49.2	55.9	51.0

Source: Annual Reports.

Table VII–6

ACCESS LINES
(Million)

	1984	1985	1986	1987	1988
Ameritech	14.3	14.6	14.8	15.1	15.5
Bell Atlantic	14.7	15.1	15.5	16.1	16.5
BellSouth	14.0	14.5	15.0	15.7	16.4
NYNEX	13.2	13.6	14.0	14.4	14.9
Pacific Telesis	11.3	11.6	12.1	12.5	13.1
Southwestern Bell	10.7	10.9	11.1	11.1	11.3
U S WEST	10.9	11.2	11.3	11.6	11.8
GTE	12.3	12.7	13.1	13.6	14.4
Cincinnati Bell	0.7	0.7	0.7	0.7	0.8
SNET	1.6	1.7	1.7	1.8	1.8
Contel	2.2	2.2	2.3	2.4	2.5
United	3.1	3.3	3.4	3.5	3.7
Centel	1.3	1.3	1.4	1.4	1.5
Group Total	110.3	113.4	116.4	119.9	124.2

Source: Annual Reports.

about eight percent between 1986 and 1987 despite a 16 percent rate reduction by AT&T which, with its 70–80 percent market share, dominates the market. Furthermore, interstate switched access minutes continue to grow at double digit rates and AT&T predicted growth of over 11 percent for its switched services in 1988.[27] On the LECs' side of the equation, there appears to be no abatement in the historical annual growth of about three percent. Table VII–6 depicts carrier growth from 1984 to 1988 for the larger

Table VII–7

INTEREXCHANGE CARRIER CONSTRUCTION EXPENDITURES
($ Million)

	1984	1985	1986	1987	1988	1989	1990
AT&T	$1,342	$2,109	$2,557	$2,660	$3,000	$3,000	$2,900
MCI	1,157	1,000	980	1,000	750	715	650
US Sprint	1,467	1,687	1,101	996	625	650	650
NTN	5	150	550	450	100	100	200
Total	$3,971	$4,946	$5,188	$5,106	$4,475	$4,465	$4,400

Source: *Telephony*, January 18, 1988, p. 37 and January 9, 1989, p. 36.

Table VII–8

CONSTRUCTION BUDGETS OF LOCAL EXCHANGE CARRIERS
($ Million)

	1984	1985	1986	1987	1988	1989	1990
RBOCs	$13,086	$14,758	$14,376	$14,030	$13,829	$14,049	$14,304
Independ.							
Top 18	4,096	4,520	4,833	5,215	4,852	4,798	4,647
Other	723	798	725	782	728	720	697
Total	$17,905	$20,076	$19,934	$20,027	$19,409	$19,567	$19,648

Source: *Telephony*, January 18, 1988, p. 47 and January 9, 1989, p. 29.

companies which represent over 95 percent of total industry revenues.[28] This
steady growth should continue into the next century and will provide a substantial revenue base for the local telephone companies.

Further evidence of continuing growth for both ICs and LECs may be
seen by a review of their construction expenditure projections. These are
shown on Tables VII–7 (ICs) and VII–8 (LECs). For the ICs, annual
construction has remained at a fairly constant level of about $4.5–$5.0 billion.
A great deal of the more recent expenditures have been spent to develop
fiber optic based networks that now or will soon have call carrying capability
that may not be reached for many years. Thus, there will be substantial
room for growth on the IC's network which will benefit the LECs in terms of
fees collected for providing local access.

The LECs' construction expenditures are hovering in the $19–$20 billion
range and are not expected to decline in the near future. Table VII–9 shows
a general breakdown of LEC capital expenditures by major plant category for

Table VII–9

DISTRIBUTION OF 1989 CAPITAL EXPENDITURES

	RHCs	Top 18 Independents
Central Office	29%	33%
Transmission Equipment	23	14
Transmission Facilities	29	38
Land, Building, & Other Support	9	10
Other	10	5
	100%	100%

Source: *Telephony*, January 9, 1989, pp. 24 and 26.

1989. Over 80 percent of investments will be directed toward switching, transmission equipment, and transmission facilities. These costs will mainly be used to upgrade the network with digital switches, fiber optics, and electronic equipment to derive more efficient usage of facilities. The strategic deployment of these facilities reflects a response by the LECs to perceived competitive threats and anticipated growth in the local network.

The LECs' access lines and local switches are the foundation of local offerings, and provide a seemingly endless and steady stream of revenues. In addition to basic services, adjuncts and many other services are derived from the local network. The basic offerings are marketed under various names but all provide dial tone, local switching and transmission capability. Some of these traditional functions are tariffed under the following:

- Dial Tone Line
- Flat Rate – Residential/Business
- Measured Rate – Residential/Business
- Message Rate – Residential/Business
- PBX Trunk Line
- Coin Service

LECs' tariffs contain a myriad of other services held out for subscription by customers. Appendix VII–A lists many of the types of offerings that are marketed by the LECs or their parents. Some of the more significant services will be discussed in detail.

a. *Yellow Pages*

All of the RHCs and many of the independents are actively pursuing markets in this eight billion dollar industry. The incentive by the RHCs to maintain and expand their presence in this market is precipitated by outstanding growth. In 1988, growth was up 10 percent from 1987 levels, with no apparent abatement in sight. It is not only the RHCs that perceive business opportunities with financial rewards associated with Yellow Pages. There are now over 200 publishers that offer the service in one form or another. It is expected that the larger companies, such as the RHCs, will acquire and form joint ventures with many of the other firms as shakeouts take place.

The markets entered by the RHCs are not just restricted to their local operating environs. Aggressive strategies have resulted in the entrance of some of the regionals into the territories of others. Notably, Southwestern Bell invaded NYNEX territory in 1985. The incursion began with an offering aimed at senior citizens, Silver Pages, and then a second version of Yellow Pages for the area. However, this venture was not successful as Southwestern Bell announced at the end of 1988 that it was terminating its directory publishing operation in New York and two other regions. Furthermore, publication of the Silver Pages directory was discontinued nationwide in May 1988. Yet, Southwestern Bell is still involved with Yellow Pages in nationwide and oversea markets and has recently joined forces with Donnelley Directory, a major directory publisher, to enhance its position in the greater Baltimore and Washington areas.

Other strategies used to promote Yellow Pages and retain customers include the insertion of additional information within the directories such as community information and local maps. Also, many directories include coupons that provide for discounts for products sold in local business establishments.

Some of the RHCs' publishing operations are growing as a result of acquisitions. For instance, L.M. Berry & Co. was purchased by BellSouth thereby increasing the RHC's revenues to almost one billion dollars in 1986, although only 50 percent of Berry's business is associated with BellSouth's customer base. Their remaining effort relates to national and international clientele. Similarly, Southwestern Bell acquired Mast Advertising & Publishing, increasing revenues to $850 million. The LECs receive substantial revenue from Yellow Pages operations as is evident from the 1988 payments of $489 million as fees to BellSouth's two operating telephone companies for publishing rights and other services.

Foreign ventures have also been attempted by the RHCs. Southwestern Bell set up an Australian subsidiary, AD/VENT Information Services International, after receiving a five-year $1 billion contract along with another firm to sell advertising in the country. In addition, Southwestern Bell provided a directory for the Summer Olympic Games held in South Korea in September 1988. Ameritech and BellSouth have also expressed an interest in obtaining an international Yellow Pages presence.

Another important area not yet available to the RHCs is electronic publishing which is also referred to as "talking Yellow Pages." The Bell companies have been barred from the enhanced provision of Yellow Pages by the legal constraints of the MFJ. This prohibition is apparently going to be appealed as the RHCs see a potential $1 billion industry in the future. For 1988, revenues are expected to be about $83 million with growth to about one-quarter of a billion dollars in 1990. There is uncertainty with regard to when, and if, the RHCs will be allowed into this market. If they are, their vast resources and customer bases could substantially raise the anticipated total market.

Yellow Pages have become a much more competitive market in recent years. Growth in this lucrative market may slow down but as noted by Kenneth O. Johnson, president of Donnelley Directory:

> It is generally agreed that the companies that will succeed in the yellow pages competition will be those who are more aggressive, who take advantage of their competitors' shortfalls, who keep employees loyal and enthusiastic, who have a desire to win, who are equipped to change as the rules change, and who are smarter−−most definitely in a marketing sense.[29]

b.   Centrex

Centrex represents the generic name for a class of telecommunications services offered by local telephone companies. The basic service provided is usually furnished through the telephone company's central office (CO), utilizing primarily electronic switches and digital technology where available.[30] In a typical Centrex installation, each individual station line is directly connected to the CO by means of a dedicated access line local loop. This loop is identical to that employed for individual residential and business subscribers. As a core feature, Centrex provides all customer stations with direct inward and outward dialing capability, as well as calling between different intracompany stations (intercom). Increasingly, various improved CO calling features, such as call forwarding or 3−way calling, and other options are offered along with the basic service.

Private branch exchange (PBX) equipment located on a customer's premises furnishes a competitive alternative switching system to Centrex, at least for multiline customers. The location of PBX equipment permits customers to perform internal communications on their premises, as well as to access the outside world. But outside access also requires customers to obtain central office connections (PBX trunks) from the local telephone company.

Since PBX system intercom calls are internal to the customer's system, users only obtain enough telephone company trunks to satisfy their peak simultaneous external communications requirements. Thus, there is rarely, if ever, a one−to−one ratio of stations to access lines. Indeed, these ratios may be quite high, *e.g.,* from five−to−one to ten−to−one.

Centrex systems typically utilize more outside plant loops and central office capacity than a PBX system having the same number of telephone stations because of functional differences between the two offerings. Centrex services' additional facilities can be traced primarily to provision of the intercom function. In contrast, the on−premises and switching aspects of the PBX substitute for a portion of the outside plant loops and central office switching capacity which would be used by a Centrex system of comparable size.

Centrex was initially offered by the LECs in the early 1960s as an alternative to PBX vendor services. In the 1970s, PBX began its resurgence as microprocessor technology advances and the FCC's procompetitive policies gathered momentum. The FCC's decisions in the areas of equipment registration, rate unbundling, and cost based pricing fostered considerable competitive entry. As a result, by the 1980s, there was much greater emphasis on meeting customer needs and growth in the PBX sector, particularly respecting equipment offered by competitors of the Bell System.

Apparently, in an attempt to meet changed marketplace conditions and combat incursion of new competitors, the Bell System launched a marketing program in the late 1970s that has been termed the "migration strategy" (MS). Under this new strategy Centrex was deemphasized. Instead, marketing focus and development of new features was shifted to Bell's recently upgraded CPE project line (e.g., Dimension PBX). Within a few years, Centrex systems' attractive past growth and customer acceptance suffered through increasing replacement by Bell's electronic PBXs.

As evidenced in subsequent hearings by the Subcommittee on Telecommunications, Consumer Protection, and Finance (Report issued November 3, 1981), there were indications that the Bell System's strategic objectives under MS also involved the wholesale shift of customers of its installed customer premises equipment (CPE) to newer "flagship" PBX products. Adherents of this view maintained that the MS approach was consistent with preclusion of competitors' penetration of the installed CPE marketplace. That is, by inducing existing Bell CPE subscribers to enter into long term contracts, rapid erosion of Bell's traditionally dominant CPE marketplace share to competitors would be prevented. At a later point, Bell could replace its embedded equipment base with new vintages when its PBX and other CPE offerings were fully upgraded and repriced.

Allegedly, Bell's MS exploited its leading position in existing CPE marketplaces by strategically manipulating price, equipment availability, terms of offerings, treatment of returned equipment, and other marketplace variables. Of course, this strategy apparently caused great harm to Centrex in the process. Indeed, Bell System Centrex growth abated in the late 1970s and actually declined in some years.

Court approval of the proposed AT&T/Department of Justice Modification of Final Judgment in late 1982 altered these conditions and incentives dramatically. And, since that time, the BOCs have inaugurated an energetic program to remarket and upgrade their Centrex services. A moderate resurgence of Centrex in the range of 1–2 percent per year growth is expected to continue as a result of this sales push, corollary actions (e.g., a lowering of the minimum [100 line] requirement formerly imposed on Centrex users), and technological enhancements in the late 1980s. A subsequent section will describe central office LANs (CO–LANs) which take advantage of extant Centrex lines to allow the BOCs to provide an alternative offering to LANs obtained from independent suppliers. Higher growth for small business users, particularly in the 35 to 40 line range, is expected to be a primary part of the Centrex resurgence.

In this regard, the under–100 line may exhibit growth of more than 40 percent from 1986 to 1990 with the greatest growth occurring in the lower end of the range.[31]   This growth was more spectacular for Bell Atlantic, which reported that Centrex lines serving small customers increased by almost 20 percent in 1987 alone.[32]

Notably, the BOC's marketing effort may reflect both short and long terms aims, although the precise timeframe for implementation of the new push for Centrex growth may well vary among the regions. Of course, an overall constraint on BOCs' actions stems from the restricted permission granted by the Court to the regional Bell holding companies in 1984 respecting reentry of these firms into the CPE marketplace (*i.e.*, without allowing manufacturing). Some of these firms may expect continuation of the MFJ's full restrictions and thus favor a focus on Centrex over the long term over CPE options. Others may focus specifically on CPE. Yet, given the size of the holding companies, it may even be possible to advance both options. Thus, a possible Bell strategy for the foreseeable future could be to vigorously promote both Centrex and PBXs.

Of course, development of any marketing plan for Centrex could be multifaceted. For instance, one approach would be simply to reduce rates substantially. This can be accomplished by creating "rate stability" via long term contracts or by effectively eliminating, or offsetting to a large degree, the interstate subscriber line charges associated with Centrex access lines. Also, Centrex service could be repriced, such as on a customer specific or facilities basis. Another marketing approach would be to foster upgrading Centrex features, *e.g.*, by placement of newer switches and enhancing existing switches. Additionally, Centrex can be made available to customers with fewer lines (*e.g.*, less than 30 lines). Nationwide, many of these approaches have been taken. Table VII–10 provides an example of where a BOC has adjusted regular Centrex rates to meet a perceived threat of competition.

The "new look" Centrex will provide a formidable alternative to PBX due to several reasons. Technological differences between the two offerings are virtually nil due to the recent efforts of the BOCs, notably, in the area of digital COs and all of the attendant enhancements that go along with this technology.

Advantages also accrue to the BOCs on the pricing side as regulators have given the appearance of accommodating the BOCs with respect to pricing strategies. Large customers now receive preferential customer specific rate treatment, a phenomenon that is likely to filter down to medium–sized users.

The economics and risk of owning a PBX versus leasing Centrex from a BOC are other important reasons that Centrex may be a more viable option for some customers. As economic conditions have tightened, it has become more difficult to raise the substantial capital required to purchase and support PBX systems. It is simply easier to maintain and pay for a Centrex system on a month–to–month basis. In addition, and as with any state–of–the–art technology, a newly purchased PBX may become obsolete within five years whereas Centrex can be updated by the local BOC.

Lastly, the features and enhancements now associated with Centrex provide customers with substantially more hands–on control to an extent not previously available. Many basic functions such as moves, adds, changes, and

Table VII–10

ESSX–CUSTOM SERVICE
Comparison of Monthly Revenues with Centrex Service

Cust.	ESSX Custom	CTX II	Change	Change
A	$ 7,800	$ 11,100	$ (3,300)	(29.7)
B	105,500	129,200	(23,700)	(18.3)
C	76,900	130,600	(53,700)	(41.1)
D	81,900	97,100	(15,200)	(15.7)
E	113,400	129,000	(15,600)	(12.1)
F	61,400	76,000	(14,600)	(19.2)
	$446,900	$573,000	(126,100)	(22.0)

Source: BRI estimates.

station message detail recordings[33] can now be performed by users at their location. Previously, these features were not available and PBX systems had a built–in advantage over Centrex.

c. *Payphone*
Until recently, public telephone service (commonly referred to as payphones) was provided only by local telephone companies. After proceedings at the federal level, credit card public telephone service offerings by nontelephone companies were permitted by the FCC in 1981, and in 1984 customer owned coin operated telephones (COCOTs) were allowed to be connected to the public switched network. Thus, independent businesses were able to market COCOT service in competition with the entrenched carriers.

The new "smart" phones installed by COCOT providers include the intelligence to perform functions that were previously handled by manual labor. Included within the electronics of "smart" phones are the abilities to detect connect and disconnect, count coins, determine charges, provide some theft and fraud control, provide voice and/or visual instructions to customers, etc. Despite these enhanced features and the fact that privately operated coin phones are permitted in most states, COCOTS operators are having a tough time turning a profit.

One of the obvious reasons for the difficulties experienced by private payphone operators is the enormous resources of the entrenched LECs, spearheaded by the BOCs. The LECs have not let the fledgling independent payphone industry into their turf without strong opposition. They have battled vigorously in various state regulatory proceedings to maintain the dominance that has accrued over the years due to virtually no opposition. On the marketing side the BOCs have sponsored aggressive advertising campaigns and adjusted their commission payout structures to retain and attract payphone locations. In fact, it appears that the real competition is for payphone locations.   Thus, once a location is secured, the provider of payphone service has a virtual monopoly at that location.   Unless prices are controlled in some fashion, end users may not benefit from so called "competition."   Generally the rate for LEC provided local coin service is 20¢ or 25¢ which is often the ceiling established by regulators for COCOT rates.

A measure of the BOCs' success at maintaining a high market share can be seen on Table VII–11.   This exhibit indicates that even in states where there are relatively high numbers of COCOTs locations the percentage of COCOT phones is low.   For instance, in California, Illinois, and New York, COCOT telephones account for 11 percent, 15 percent, and 7 percent, respec-tively, of the total.   These ratios are most likely overstated because the telco figures generally only include the BOC in the state and not other LECs.   However, even despite the relatively low market shares of COCOT providers, some inroads have been made and further progress can be made if these independent suppliers can remain viable.

The rates and rate structures approved by state regulatory agencies vary substantially.   For instance, some states permit flat rate service while others do not.   The differences in rate levels for the dial tone element of measured rate service paid by a COCOT customer can be seen by comparing a $6 rate in one state to a $67 rate in a second state.   The usage rates also were far apart, e.g., varying from 6¢ to 25¢ for a five minute call.   Rates are often set on the basis of lost or replacement revenues to the BOCs rather than on a sound economical cost basis.

The BOCs control the bottleneck access facilities required to connect the COCOT payphone to the local network.   Thus, the BOC acts as the supplier of a crucial element in its competitors' service.   Without knowledgeable and enlightened oversight by state commissions, the anticipated battle for payphone business, with customers being the beneficiaries, could be over before it is long off the ground.   Recent decisions suggested that some state regulators have a concern about competition in the payphone industry by ruling favorably toward COCOT providers.[34]

2.   Opportunities in Emerging Markets

The breakup of the Bell system and the procompetitive stance of the telecommunications industry, both due in part to technological advances that continue unabatedly, have fostered new and emerging markets.   The services that customers are now demanding in ever increasing quantity and quality have been recognized by the BOCs and other LECs.   Several of these will be discussed at length in this section along with other emerging services.   Generally, all of these offerings are either: (1) more esoteric versions of older services that have been repackaged to meet perceived market niches; (2) services that have evolved from technological advancements; or (3) services/products that take advantage of extant in–house capabilities and expertise.

Table VII–11

COIN TELEPHONES BY STATES

State	Telco	COCOTS	State	Telco	COCOTS
AL	20,000	A	MO	33,000	60
AK	1,284	A	MT	5,095	391
AZ	20,590	603	NE	7,000	A
AR	13,000	A	NV	6,000	A
CA	157,000	20,000	NH	8,500	20
CO	23,460	558	NJ	75,000	2,000
CT	25,500	A	NM	6,953	328
DE	4,667	A	NY	170,000	13,500
DC	10,214	865	NC	20,990	652
FL	63,334	2,000	ND	4,000	A
GA	35,660	2,500	OH	73,000	2,150
HI	6,500	A	OK	22,000	A
ID	5,300	225	OR	13,000	A
IL	77,000	14,000	PA	70,000	3,500
IN	24,000	40	RI	7,000	130
IA	14,000	A	SC	16,072	346
KS	17,000	61	SD	4,500	93
KY	16,000	540	TN	28,000	1,000
LA	29,000	282	TX	124,000	4,000
ME	7,000	100	UT	8,242	103
MD	34,416	1,000	VT	3,000	A
MA	55,000	A	VA	33,434	306
MI	62,000	1,050	WA	22,000	A
MN	16,000	A	WV	8,722	0
MS	15,287	600	WI	26,000	500
			WY	4,048	A
		Total All States		1,552,768	73,503

Source: *Payphone*, "The 1988 Reference Guide," p. 42.

a. Cellular

Cellular radio is a mobile communications medium which will permit each assigned frequency channel to be used many times within a given service area through the establishment and coordination of a system of zones or "cells." As the subscriber unit (*e.g.*, a car) travels in a defined area that offers cellular service, a radio connection is handed off from cell to cell while the unit passes through the grid of cells. This maintenance of uninterrupted calling is accomplished through a central control switch called a Mobile Telecommunications Switching Office (MTSO).

A major advantage of cellular radio is that it permits more efficient use of the spectrum relative to existing mobile telephone offerings. Its availability will significantly increase service accessibility for both existing and prospective users. It can also potentially allow subscribers to make short haul toll calls at no extra charge. A shortcoming identified by many observers is that cellular technology, particularly terminal equipment, will be too expensive for all but business customers and the affluent during the next several years. Another relates to technical and cost problems encountered thus far in cellular transmission of data. From a social perspective, the unregulated provision of cellular phone service through Bell regional companies, rather than their operating telephone companies, may exacerbate deleterious effects of bypass on local revenues.

In the future, cellular radio technology may afford potential for bypass of local LEC facilities built to furnish exchange, toll, and payphone services. It will not, however, make any significant contribution to the local or interexchange movement of data. Data (medium and high–speed) and video teleconferencing traffic requires greater bandwidth than cellular systems have to offer and is generated in fixed business locations where fixed communications facilities are often readily available. Cellular radio technology promises, however, to make low–speed data and voice service available to anyone, any place by the end of this decade. Continuing price decreases have already brought the equipment costs for this service as low as $1,000, making remote and mobile service possible for many more than when comparable costs were over $3,000. Future satellite–based cellular systems providing nationwide service are also a medium–term possibility.

Limited bandwidth availability has traditionally limited the use of mobile telephones and kept their price relatively high. Although car telephones have been around since the 1940s, it was not until the early 1980s that technical developments led to the provision of new cellular technology thereby making portable telephones available for thousands of users in a given urban area. Cellular radio utilizes low power, narrow band two–way transmissions which reuse frequencies in a series of contiguous areas called cells. Each cell has its own transmit/receive antennas, and computer controls permit antenna and frequency changes as users move from cell to cell. The geographical extent of a cell could be a dozen city blocks or larger areas depending on traffic demand and technical constraints. The cellular radio system is also connected to local wirelines in order to access local telephone and long distance services.

The services provided by cellular radio companies include what one would routinely expect in an urban telephone system –– voice, low–speed data, ability to connect monitors, terminals, and small computers, and custom-calling features. While most cellular radios are now installed in vehicles, it is possible to buy units that enable the user to have telephone service anywhere –– on the construction site, in the park, or just walking down the street.

Cellular equipment costs have dropped sharply from $3,000 or more to present levels of less than $700 in some instances, and are expected to decline even further.[35] This relatively high start–up cost is believed to be the major deterrent to more widespread use of cellular. In addition, monthly costs are in the $90 to $125 range which is substantially higher than the $50 monthly price thought to be the level needed to encourage penetration of the residential market. Concurrently, the market has expanded from 88,000 subscribers in 1984 to over 2.3 million users[36] by mid–year 1989. (See Figure V–7.) Various estimates put the cellular market at over three million users by 1990 and from 11 million to over 20 million subscribers by the year 2000.[37] In the United States cellular penetration has risen to 9.4 per 1,000 people which is about twice the comparable figure in Europe. Revenues for 1988 are in the three billion dollars range and will climb commensurate with user growth.

Hundreds of manufacturers now make equipment for the new and fast–growing cellular market, while the FCC was inundated with over 5,000 applications for cellular operating licenses. Although many areas of the United States do not yet have any cellular radio service, the general plan was to initially allow service by two firms in each market, one wireline company (telephone company, RHC, etc.) and one nonwireline company. It was anticipated that the two–firm licensing in each market would create an intensely competitive environment. However, the RHCs have been buying the cellular licenses from their nonwireline rivals. As a result, the hoped for competition from nontelephone companies has not developed with the consequence that predicted declining rates may not occur in the near future, if at all. Acquisitions and consolidation is occurring at a much more rapid rate than originally expected by regulators. The end result may find the RHCs competing with each other and some very large independents. Some smaller independents may also remain to serve less dense and less lucrative markets.

To illustrate the relative strength of the RHCs, consider the top 30 cellular markets which cover almost 50 percent of the U.S. population. Between the wireline and nonwireline companies service is offered in 1,504 cells of which 57 percent are controlled directly by wireline companies. However, many of the 651 cells under the auspices of nonwireline carriers are owned by RHC subsidiaries. For instance, nonwireline companies controlled by Southwestern Bell[38] and PacTel provide service in six of the top 30 markets with a total of 164 cells, or 25 percent of the total nonwireline market. This increases the cellular market controlled by the RHCs to 68 percent.

The wireline carriers have also been able to begin service in 261 (85 percent) of the 306 markets existing at the end of 1988 whereas only 163 (53 percent) nonwireline carriers had received regulatory approval. Figures VII–6 and 7 display the "catching–up" that the nonwireline companies had to accomplish in the top 30 cellular markets. In terms of number of cells and population served the wireline carriers appear to have had a significant headstart on their competitors. The approximately two year lag might be able

Figure VII-6

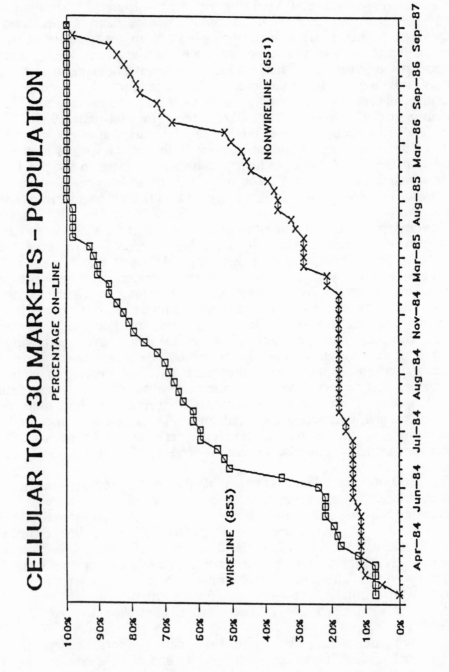

CELLULAR TOP 30 MARKETS – POPULATION

PERCENTAGE ON–LINE

NONWIRELINE (651)

WIRELINE (853)

Source: Cellular Business.

Figure VII-7

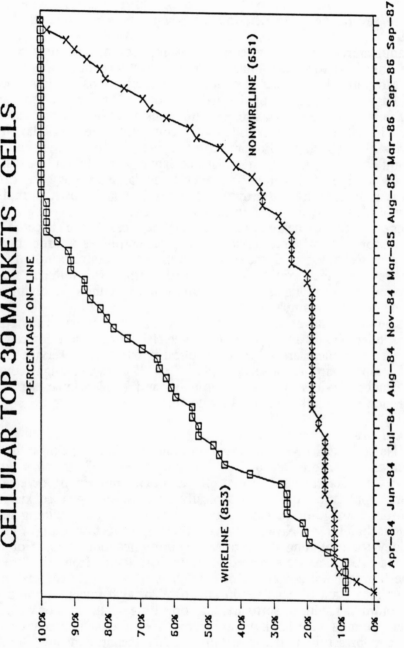

CELLULAR TOP 30 MARKETS – CELLS

PERCENTAGE ON-LINE

Source: Cellular Business.

to become overcome with superior service provided by the nonwirelines, but it will take several years to determine the winners and losers in the cellular market.

Manufacturers, telephone entities, paging companies, newspapers, and foreign firms have formed cellular companies. Many cellular applicants/operators already offer interexchange or local communications services, such as the RHCs, paging companies, and United Telecom. The foreign firms often are manufacturers of cellular equipment with substantial experience in their base markets in Japan or the Scandinavian countries where cellular service is already well established. Foreign entrants include Astroset, a joint venture of Stromberg–Carlson and Mitsubishi of Japan, and Mobira, a subsidiary of Nokia Co. of Finland. Although practical cellular technology has existed for almost two decades, its real growth may only be starting as it is implemented in the world's largest telecommunications market.

Some observers believe that cellular services could become a close substitute for local wireline service if the price continues to drop, becoming a true bypass technology. Some of the cellular operators also provide interexchange services that could be integrated with local cellular services to provide end–to–end long distance communications without involving any local telephone operating company.

Resale of cellular services is already taking place as rental car companies install cellular phones in some of their vehicles. Resale is a logical outcome of the fact that there are so many applicants for so few service franchises. Hybrid arrangements are also possible in which a reseller might contract for long distance services with one company and local cellular services from another, and then market the package to customers.

b.   Local Area Networks (LANs)

LANs are basically high speed intrafacility data pipelines that permit communication among an office's computers, as well as other intelligent devices. Use of a standard format affords interaction among diverse signals. The early application of LANs typically used twisted pair coaxial cable to provide data, image or text communications within one building or several contiguous buildings. Now, however, fiber optics is becoming a prominent technology for providing the necessary communications links. For instance, fiber optic LAN sales are expected to more than double from 1987 to 1989.

The fundamental advantage of a LAN is its ability to increase the value of the various "smart" machines in an office through integration and efficient use of common facilities, software, and operating systems. For example, this technique permits coordination and avoidance of data redundancy logjams. Deficiencies presently inherent within a LAN scenario include the fact that different types of computers currently cannot easily communicate with each other on the same local area network, the industry's unresolved quest for a standard technology, office inside wiring complexities, and the limited range of some LANs (often less than a mile.)

Several other issues dominated in 1988. The lack of an integrated, vertical LAN was an important matter in the management of LANs as managers apparently desire to move to a less diverse type of arrangement than now exists in many instances.[39] Fault tolerance is another important issue. Network failures are not tolerable in certain LAN applications and, therefore, procedures must be established to prevent their occurrence.

Security within the LAN is critical to many users. Maintaining security can be accomplished by simply using passwords or devising more sophisticated methods of keeping intruders from accessing files and data.

Gateways can provide the key to the accessing of multiple user protocols. Such a need is becoming more of a reality in a multivendor environment and as the number of LANs and the number of terminals connected within LANs continue to grow rapidly. Gateways are just now beginning to surface in the industry and will greatly aid in solving the incompatibility problems cited as a deterrent to installing LANs. Bridges are also important to users because they permit uninterrupted operation by workers as behind–the–scenes tasks take place.

Lastly, LAN users believe more and better training is necessary. A support function should be created within the particular company in order to expeditiously and economically resolve problems that arise on a day–to–day basis.

LANs also increasingly perform the local, intra–business distribution function for private or semi–private end–to–end networks. LANs may be connected to the local network or to bypass systems such as DTS and cable television. They may use rooftop antennas to directly connect to satellite interexchange carrier service nodes or satellites, or simply use the local telephone network to connect with the local nodes of AT&T, MCI, or other common carriers.

The prognosis for LANs appears good. In 1987 LAN industry sales grew to $1.5 billion, a 12–fold increase over the 1983 level of $125 million[40] and the number of LANs doubled from 1987 to 1988.[41] Phenomenal growth is expected to continue through the early 1990s as LAN shipments increase four–fold. The cost of LANs has now dropped to the point where customers are willing to take advantage of the technology which has existed for several years. Thus, lower volume applications will be viable for users where in the past the high cost to install and operate a LAN precluded most low usage customers. Table V–12 demonstrates the cost reductions of PC–compatible systems from 1985 to 1988. It is anticipated that these costs could go down even further in the future, thereby, making LANs an attractive alternative to PBXs and Centrex.

Despite these rather optimistic cost comparisons, there are "hidden" costs associated with operating a LAN which could add up to as much as $3,000 per year.[42] These costs include the network administration spent working with software updates, troubleshooting peripherals such as printers, getting soft-ware to work properly, as well as developing in–house software and applica-tions.

The number of PCs that are connected to LANs grew from 1.3 million in 1986 to 2.1 million in 1987. The number of PC LANs should continue to show

Table VII–12

COMPARISON OF LAN COSTS

Costs	1985	1986	1987	1988
PC System	$1,500	$1,200	$900	$700
LAN Board	800	600	300	100
LAN Software	2,000	2,000	600	600
Percentage of System Cost				
PC System	57%	56%	69%	78%
LAN Board	30	28	23	11
LAN Software	13	16	8	11

Source: *LAN Times*, December 1987, p. 10.

substantial growth, and whereas they constituted 39 percent of the market in 1986, by 1992 they are expected to garner a 55 percent share.[43]

The ability to economically connect PCs and synchronous terminals on a LAN is an important facet in the telecommunications plans of many firms. A late 1987 survey conducted by Datamation[44] provided enlightening information with regard to the views and experiences of about 400 computer systems managers of companies in different industries.

The general consensus (70 percent) seemed to be that although hardware and software exist to interconnect PCs and other terminals, the wherewithal is missing. The most significant problem is a common theme today throughout the industry, the lack of effective and meaningful standards. Also cited as problem areas were the user unfriendliness of current systems and the non–support from vendors in determining connectivity strategies. For instance, the study found that about one–half of the respondents inferred they received no help from vendors in this regard. Another study finding is that 37 percent of large companies reported bad experiences with alleged connectivity solutions. For all companies the figure is 16 percent.

The following shows a summary of key findings:

Full interconnection objective within company:	59% – Yes
Percentage of companies with LANs:	36%
Percentage of users on LANs in companies with LANs:	30%
Percentage of users on LANs connected to mainframe:	29%

The first item indicates that almost 60 percent of the companies have a plan for full connectivity which appears to fly in the face of reality. First, only about one–third of the firms have a LAN and of these only 30 percent are connected to the mainframe. More than 50 percent of those without LANs, *i.e.*, two–thirds of the respondents, indicated no plans to install networks

within five years. These results do not support the notion of full connectivity.

It also appears that full connectivity has not been attained even after
LANs are installed. Item three in the above table shows that only 30 percent
of computer users are connected to the network. The fourth item reflects a
relatively low 29 percent of users who are on LANs and connected to their
companies' mainframes. Again, full connectivity seems to be a nonevent at
the present time.

The Datamation survey highlights problems with the state of achieving
full connectivity as stated to be the goal of 60 percent of the companies
responding to the questionnaire. It does not appear that the objective will be
reached until barriers such as the lack of standards and vendor support are
overcome. As the installation of LANs and PCs continues to grow, these
problems should receive more attention and be resolved, thus leading to ever
greater growth.

Table VII–13 depicts market shares for the major suppliers. The market
shares on the upper portion of the exhibit must be read with a degree of
awareness. First, the data does not reflect the financial status or viability of
the vendors. For instance, some firms may not be around next year because
of the consolidation going on within the industry. And, secondly, the data
does not reflect software installation where Novell is the acknowledged
leader. This data is portrayed on the lower portion of the chart and shows
Novell has a 70 percent share of the LAN operating systems market.[45]
However, with the recent introduction of Microsoft's competitive LAN
Manager, it is anticipated that Novell's market share of operating could drop
by 15–20 percent in the early 1990s.[46]

A 1988 study conducted by The Market Information Center of 300 large
firms indicated that 41 percent have a LAN and another 29 percent expect to
acquire a LAN in the near future. The study also provided ratings of various
LANs suppliers as shown in the Table VII–14. A similar rating of the overall
performance of the vendors supplying the LANs is shown in Table VII–15.

Another recent study undertaken by Datamation, which included over
5,000 firms with small computer systems, indicated that 24 percent of the
companies had LANs and that 44 percent expected to have a LAN by the end
of 1989.[47]

c. Shared Tenant Services (STS)

Shared tenant communications and computer services, variously known as
"smart buildings" or "enhanced real estate," are joint efforts between telecommunications and information processing companies and real estate developers
to provide a broad range of communications services to tenants of office
buildings and office parks. Often, the provision of communications services
by the building, a form of shared tenant communications, can relieve
individual tenants of communications problems, provide sole source provisioning of end–to–end services, allow smaller companies access to services they
could not otherwise afford, and assure the building's owner of fully leasing
buildings.

Table VII–13

LAN MARKET SHARES

Percentage of LANs

	1988	1989
Novell	17.3%	28.0%
DEC	27.5	16.5
IBM	8.8	16.1
HP	2.5	4.6
Banyan	0.1	5.0
3 Com	5.2	4.1
Other	38.6	25.7
	100.0 %	100.0 %

Percentage of LAN Operating Systems

	1988
Novell	70%
IBM	14
Banyan	4
3 Com	6
Sun	3
Apple	1
Other	2
	100.0 %

Sources: *Datamation*, November 15, 1988, p. 21 and *Network World*, September 19, 1988, p. 19.

Participants in the new enhanced real estate market, sometimes called "smart buildings," include real estate developers, long distance resellers, and major companies. Connections with the long distance providers' node and the local telephone network by these private building systems can be provided by satellite, private leased line, or digital termination systems.

The wide acceptance and success once predicted for STS has yet to materialize. The projected $10 billion market has not even been remotely approached. The apparent failure of STS to develop as anticipated is due to several reasons, but the major causes lie with AT&T and the BOCs. Although the strategies for the two are dissimilar, the results were the same, *i.e.*, a long, if not eternal, delay in the viability of STS.

Initially, in 1984 AT&T entered into a joint venture with United Technologies Corp. to become the nation's leading provider of STS under the name

Table VII–14

RATING OF LAN PERFORMANCE BY USERS
Maximum = 100

Installation	70
Expansion	73
Response Time	70
Tech Support	65
Maintenance	63
Reliability	73
Overall Average	69

Source: *Communications News*, February 1988, p. 10.

Table VII–15

RATING OF LAN SUPPLIERS BY USERS
Maximum = 100

IBM	65
DEC	77
Novell	70
3Com	66
AT&T	71
Sytek	65
Overall Average	69

Source: *Id.*

ShareTech. In January 1986, ShareTech folded which was viewed by many as an indication that the STS market might not be profitable. Such an action by one of the industry's major players placed a damper on the notion of a viable STS marketplace. At the present time, there are only about six or seven major service providers with the largest (Realcom) having about 50 STS locations.

The BOCs, on the other hand, have aggressively fought STS, apparently believing it to be a serious threat to its local monopoly. At first, the BOCs went to their local regulators and cried "foul" by alleging that STS providers were becoming unregulated telephone companies and infringing on their franchised local exchange markets. The usual claim made by the BOCs was that local residential rates would have to be increased if developers were permitted to come in and divert revenues with no offsetting cost savings. This strategy was partially successful as STS implementation was often delayed.   Also, the rates and rate structures applicable to STS that were approved by the local public utility commissions were not always favorable to STS providers. In certain instances there appeared to be an unevenhanded-ness between the access rates for access and the BOC services.

In any event, many of the BOCs eventually resorted to a different strategy to combat STS.   They turned to creative marketing schemes that discouraged developers from purchasing PBXs to resell service for profit.   In essence, once the originally perceived evils of STS were proven to be a false alarm, the BOCs concentrated on the acumen acquired in its local markets over the year.

Generally, the BOCs have recently combatted STS by making their own Centrex offerings more attractive to real estate developers so that they will not purchase PBXs necessary to operate STS.   One such attempt is a Centrex service provided by BellSouth's subsidiary Southern Bell (SB) which is called multi–account ESSX.[48]   Essentially, this offering establishes SB as an STS provider whereby only one bill is sent to a building for all services. Individual building tenants receive price breaks because the sum of their individual bills under regular rates would be greater than their portion of the discounted bill under multi–account ESSX.[49]

Another selling point to the developer is that he does not have to be concerned about technology changes with ESSX whereas a PBX might be outdated in five years.   Also, other factors such as maintenance and the saving of building space are favorably disposed toward the developer when he purchases ESSX.

d.   Very Small Aperture Terminal (VSAT)

VSATs are small satellite earth stations with receiving dishes measuring about 1.8 meters or less in diameter. A VSAT consists of outdoor equipment, which performs radio frequency transmission functions, and indoor equipment, which performs digital baseband signal processing functions.

The substantial growth in business and personal computers and in LANs provided the impetus for VSAT networks.   This is especially the case for installation at the remote locations of companies with business operations that are geographically dispersed. VSAT networks are proving to be a convenient, cost effective means to provide data and video communications via satellite to a hub earth station at a central site within the organization. Branch offices, retail stores, and service stations are examples of remote locations that require communications capabilities to a central headquarters.

VSATs are most commonly used to collect, distribute, and manage information flow among remote locations, generally to/from a central site. Point–of–sale applications are a prime example of VSAT use. The requirement to have information readily available by managers or executives for decision making purposes is at the core of VSAT networks. Also, the rapid and timely flow of information is important to the control of companies' revenue growth and cost control.   The private VSAT networks provide other advantages to users. These include lower transmission costs, end–to–end circuit control, cost stability, improved transmission quality, system reliability, network flexibility, and the relatively short lead time needed to add reception sites to the network. Savings over terrestrial networks of up to 40 percent may be realized with VSAT networks as terrestrial private line rates have continued to escalate since the mid 1980s.

In April 1986, the FCC issued blanket licensing guidelines to govern the process of obtaining permission to operate satellites which made the implementation of VSAT systems administratively practical by removing the individual paperwork previously required for each site. Thus, it became easier for prospective private VSAT network operators to attain the necessary approval to construct their networks.

It is anticipated that the networks of VSAT will play a major role in future telecommunications strategies. The present market of 10,000 to 20,000 VSATs is expected to grow to 200,000 by 1992 according to one forecaster.[50] Earth stations located at subscribers' premises will facilitate the provision of both local network and internetwork functions in the ISDN regardless of the application. Thus, the services provided by VSAT networks could expand to include voice, conferencing, electronic mail, facsimile, data base distribution, videotex, and the like. The link of VSAT networks with ISDN is summarized in the following excerpt from a recent article describing future developments:

> The evolution of the star VSAT networks will see the integration of packet switching first and then circuit switch-ing into the VSAT hub itself. This will open the way for full mesh connectivity--anywhere to anywhere--between network users. At this point, the network will have the attributes of an ISDN network; namely, clear–channel and packet–switched bearer services. Coupled with a suitable ISDN access port interface at the VSATs, it will be able to provide end–to–end ISDN bearer services.
>
> By adding an ISDN gateway capability at the hub such a network can be interconnected to other ISDN networks. Thus, more–universal connectivity will be possible.[51]

And for further developments:

> The next stage in network evolution is likely to be an architecture whereby VSATs can be connected directly together on demand without an intermediary hub. This is likely to be possible as satellites become more powerful and the size of the RF portion of the VSAT can be reduced relative to that required to use today's satellites.
>
> Coupled with reductions in cost of the VSATs using the previously discussed technologies, the economics could make VSATs attractive for such delay–sensitive services as two–way videoconferencing and telephony, in addition to data or high–quality facsimile. Higher aggregate data rates interconnect-ing to other VSATs are likely, increasing the total traffic handling capability and expanding the high–end range of locations that can use VSATs.

The technology will be evolutionary rather than revolu- tionary, driven by user needs and expectations. Major emphasis will be on VSAT cost reduction first, then on enhanced functions and features. A key attribute for successful products will be the ability of the new versions to work in systems using older versions while offering greater capabilities or reduced costs.

e.   Software Defined Network (SDN)

The data communications needs of large users have traditionally been served by AT&T and the local telephone companies in one or more of three ways. First, the users could send data between terminals over the public switched network (PSN) at rates of up to 9.6 kilobits per second by using modems. Second, since 1974 digital data system dedicated circuits could carry data at up to 56 kilobits per second. And, third, a private line arrangement could be obtained voice or data grade service under applicable tariffs. Similarly, voice communications needs were served by the PSN under applicable MTS tariffs or under the WATS tariffs, a bulk voice offering. Historically, large networks have found private lines, both bridged or unbridged, most attractive for their dispersed and heavy traffic patterns.

During 1985 AT&T introduced a new high capacity virtual private network offering, the Software Defined Network (SDN). Unlike private lines and DDS services which use dedicated facilities, this new service uses the switched network. SDN continued the trend seen in the unswitched private line and special access tariffs toward unbundling of local access channels from the line haul function. Separate charges apply to services such as access coordination, central office connections, and nonrecurring installation and start up charges. Switched services billing differs in that it does not impose a flat monthly charge as used for private lines, but rather is billed a monthly access charge plus additional time and distance based usage charges.

The similarity of the billing system of the new service to ordinary switched telephone service is part of the competitive push toward usage based rates intended to position AT&T for increasing head-to-head competition with other interexchange companies. SDN is aimed at high volume customers, the kind of customer traditionally using private lines or WATS. SDN is also a piecepart of AT&T's evolution toward the ISDN concept which emphasizes user selection on a real time basis of only needed amounts of specific services at usage based prices. As an alternative to private line and WATS, the service allows large users to rearrange services and end points under software control for both voice and data services. SDN is at least a partial replacement for the older services, private lines, WATS, and DDS, and can be looked on as another step intended to "migrate" customers toward the ISDN, the all digital, fully switched universal network. SDN is a service that was developed for multilocation businesses, to provide for unique network design and greater customer control.

SDN, which began in late 1985, gives businesses more control over the configuration of their networks. Users can use software on their own premises to select routing patterns for their traffic which is carried over AT&T's switched network. Customers can also avail themselves of various private line features, such as speed dialing and authorization codes, on an allocated rather than dedicated basis. As presently constituted, SDN is comprised of three schedules as follows:

Schedule A: calls originated and terminated over switched access facilities

Schedule B: calls either originated over switched access and completed over special access or vice versa

Schedule C: calls originated and terminated over special access

Some adjustments have been made to the initial SDN rate structure which have seen a substantial drop in the installation charge and the establishment of a less expensive dial–up access option. These changes appear to blend in with AT&T's pricing scheme for migrating customers to virtual networks via the ISDN at any level of usage. Some of the newer SDN offerings provide a low use option for smaller customers whereby they can easily grow into less expensive services (on a unit basis) when their usage increases.

In January 1989, AT&T further revamped its SDN pricing strategy when it proposed a discount plan that will substantially reduce usage charges for large customers. The new scheme, called the Expanded Volume Plan, is intended to augment AT&T's Usage Reduction Plan, which provides for a five percent reduction on interstate and international usage charges exceeding $50,000 per month. The new plan applies to only interstate SDN services and was proposed to combat similar services offered by MCI and US Sprint. As shown in Table VII–16, the rate structure is based on usage levels and length of service. The highest discounts apply for the third and all successive years of service.

AT&T's early estimates of market acceptance of SDN fell well short of expectations. Original projections for 1986 called for revenues of $43.2 million. However, actual results were only $15.9 million or about 37 percent of the estimate. However, much of the shortfall may have been caused by a delay in the authorization of SDN rates by the FCC from April to November 1985. In 1987, the number of users increased from 28 to 70 with associated revenues greater than $50 million. Forecasts of 1988 usage were substantially above 1987 levels as indicated in Table VII–17.

3. Offerings Nascent to the Information Age

The continued growth in the information requirements of the United States and other nations' economies combined with recent advances in information storage and transmission technologies, has stimulated increased interest in deployment of high capacity communications networks. Of course, advances in computers and communications technology have already transformed the regulation and market structure of the telephone industry. Further change is likely as policymakers review court imposed line–of–business

Table VII-16

AT&T PROPOSED SDN EXPANDED VOLUME PLAN
Discounts

Above Monthly Usage Level	Years of Service		
	1	2	3
$ 50,000	10.0%	10.5%	11.0%
100,000	10.5	11.0	12.0
200,000	11.0	12.0	15.0
300,000	12.0	15.0	18.0

Table VII-17

SDN CONVERSATION MINUTES OF USE
(Millions)

Schedule	1987	1988	Percent Change
A	1.3	32.0	–
B	179.0	293.2	64%
C	106.3	477.4	349
	286.6	802.6	180%

Source: *Communications Week*, February 22, 1988, p. 48.

restrictions on the BOCs and possibly free them to compete in information services to an extent not now possible. As new services are developed based on technical advances in computers, transmission systems, network design, electronics, and optics, the need for high capacity, so-called broadband networks will increase. Fiber optic communications systems (based on light guiding fibers) are only one option for high capacity communications systems, but as the price of these systems continues to decrease their use will increase dramatically.

The trend toward all digital electronic switching is well established. Indeed, essentially all new telephone switches are digital in design both in the public switched networks of the telephone companies and in private networks. Trends in customer premises equipment are also toward all digital design. Of course, personal computers, PBXs, local area networks (LANs), metering devices, and facsimile are all becoming "digitized." These changes are being complemented by the placement of high capacity links between switching systems, including improvements in microwave radio, coaxial cable, and, most prominently, fiber optic transmission systems. These improvements are providing the telecommunications carriers and private organizations with unparalleled capacities to offer new services and to serve the growth of existing services.

Public communications systems have traditionally been divided into a switched analog voice network and one or more unswitched, overlay network(s) for private use or for higher than voice rate digital data. The development of switched broadband digital communications, as well as fiber optic and other digital transmission technologies, makes it possible to integrate voice, data, and video communications on the same network. And, the breakup of AT&T and other deregulatory actions have led to a proliferation of new companies and competitive adjustments on the part of established telecommunications firms.

Broadband networks are evolving from today's separate switched and private networks through the use of both broadband transmission technologies and new communications protocols such as packet switching. Combined networks are capable of serving the various bandwidth–hungry services which will be demanded by residential and business customers. The first steps toward this Broadband Universal Telecommunications Network (BUTN) are being taken with the installation of digital switching and high capacity transmission media such as digital microwave and fiber optics.

New business and consumer services with concomitant increased switching and transmission requirements will likely develop as computers and other digital devices are employed in more businesses and homes. Digital devices on the customer's premises generate digital information which can be communicated among devices down the hall, across town, or across the world. Although the switching systems and long distance networks of communications carriers are increasingly digital, the local plant (the loop) connecting subscribers to the switching centers is now most often voice frequency, low capacity, copper wire cable.

A step on the road to the BUTN is implementation of the Integrated Services Digital Network (ISDN) which is based on digital access lines between digital central offices and the subscribers' premises. ISDN access lines are being implemented by digitizing existing copper loops with some add–on electronics to provide two kinds of channels. The so–called "B" channels would carry up to 23 voice/data information streams. Each channel operates at 64 kilobits per second, adequate for one voice channel or the equivalent in data. A separate "D" channel would handle control information related to control and routing of information on the 23 other channels. This would replace the current system of analog tones used for signalling in conventional switched voice networks. Separate digital networks would no longer be required because a single access line would provide universal digital access by integrating several services on a single communications path.

Ultimately, ISDN services could include computer data, facsimile, videotex, electronic mail, database access, telemetry, video, and voice. Since it is essentially a digital technology, fiber optic transmission systems dovetail perfectly with the digital switching systems and digital customer premises

equipment being installed by both common carriers and users.   The benefits of the ISDN, even if implemented on upgraded copper customer loops, include:
- The ability to reallocate line capacity to serve changing communications needs.
- The ability to use existing customer lines to handle most kinds of present and future communications needs.
- Customer flexibility to expand or contract service at will.
- Improved quality for voice and data transmission.

The implementation of narrowband ISDN systems does not require fiber optic facilities unless these can be justified on economic grounds. However, as the demand for digital services increases, and the cost of fiber optic systems drops, fiber will likely be the prime transmission technology for new installations and broadband applications.

A good deal of tomorrow's service and facilities planning, and even today's markets posturing, revolves around the expected transition to the ISDN. To more fully understand ISDN's significance, this section will first provide a discussion of the concept itself, and then describe some of the services that are expected to be offered via ISDN. The services discussion will include both entirely new offerings and enhanced versions of older network products. Finally, a near term outlook for ISDN is presented in anticipation of future developments that will require policy decisions by regulators.

a. ISDN

Industry experts emphasize that ISDN is not a product or service but an engineering concept. In large measure, ISDN represents a wide scale response to what is now only a perceived need to link the diverse communications networks scattered throughout the nation and the world. But the rapidly expanding requirements for national and international communications have made many conclude that ISDN is imperative as requirements for more ubiquitous networks are established as part of a "world infrastructure." Finally, development of ISDN represents a recognition that having an integrated network could result in significant efficiencies and economies to providers and customers alike.

Detailed exploratory work regarding ISDN began in Europe and Japan in the early 1980s as a worldwide standard was sought. The United States lagged behind until 1986, and although final standards have yet to be reached, progress has been made as offerings began to appear in 1988. In Canada ISDN features are being built into telecommunications equipment and networks and Bell Canada is presently testing the feasibility of ISDN with expectations that ISDN services will be offered within two or three years. In anticipation of ISDN implementation, electronics and interface devices have been designed and built to work with the standards established to date. The most common interface to be implemented puts two "B" digitized voice (64 kbps) channels and one "D" data (16 kbps) channel on an ordinary pair of telephone wires. Figure VII-8 is a simplified diagram of ISDN.

Figure VII-8

THE INTEGRATED DIGITAL NETWORK (IDN)
ISDN Network Architecture

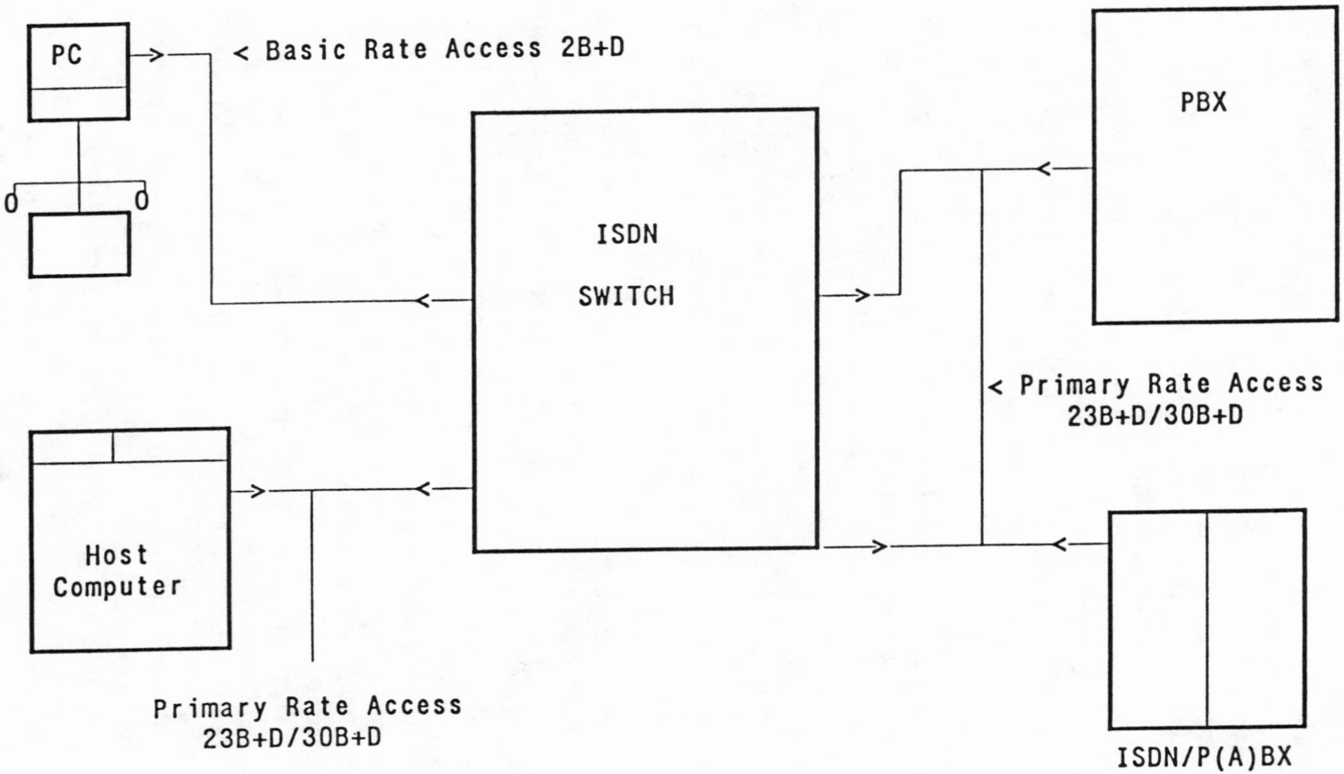

It is generally acknowledged that in the U.S. narrowband (2B+D) ISDN service, Basic Rate Interface (BRI), will be deployed first, in the 1988–1989 timeframe, with broadband (23B+D), Primary Rate Interface (PRI), following during 1990–1991. There are many advantages associated with narrowband. Some of these are as follows:

- Integration of voice, data, and video transmission over the public switched network.
- Less connect time for the transmission of data and facsimile.
- Universality with respect to all CPE.
- Greater flexibility with different terminal equipment for video, data, audio, and text applications.
- Singular interface on one transparent, open network, that is end–to–end.

Services to be provided via ISDN are numerous, and Table VII–18 provides a list of sample offerings that is not meant to be all–inclusive.

From this list it can be seen that ISDN will support existing services. It will also support newer broadband services and services yet to be developed. ISDN will most likely first be available on a case–by–case basis to large private network customers. In addition to generating greater revenues, these subscribers will be able to use their existing equipment. Smaller customers will need new equipment or other devices to utilize ISDN based services, a factor which will tend to dampen initial demand.

The strategy by the telephone companies (telcos) seems to involve initial–ly convincing large customers that ISDN is the way to go for their telecom–munications needs. This can be facilitated by conducting field experiments (ISDN trials) whereby the large customers will gain first hand experience with the "benefits" of ISDN. Next these large customers would purchase service and the telco will install the necessary equipment and facilities to the extent such plant is not in place. Then, mid–size and small business customers would be solicited based on the hope that they will ride on the coattails of the large users. Lastly, residential customers could be brought on line after the significant amounts of capital associated with ISDN have already been expended on the larger customers.

There are at least two potential stumbling blocks to this approach and any other strategy that is established to foster implementation of ISDN. These concerns are crucial in the eyes of many policy makers, as well as the ultimate users of ISDN services.

First, it is not at all clear that a significant portion of the costs to implement ISDN has not already been expended. For instance, digital switch deployment has continued at breakneck speed and by the early to mid 1990s most switched access lines will be served out of digital offices. The construction costs associated with this endeavor are now being collected from telcos' basic exchange service ratepayers. Thus, the "coattails" argument may be fallacious, at least from the cost standpoint.

Second, there is some concern that ISDN will be implemented and business customers will not support the system, thereby leaving residual revenue requirements to be recovered from residential customers. This is not

Table VII–18

SAMPLE ISDN OFFERINGS

	Narrowband	Wideband
Voice	Telephone, leased circuits, information retrieval	Music, hi–fi, stereo, radio, television–audio
Data	Packet switched, circuit switched, leased circuits, telemetry, funds transfer, information retrieval, mail box, electronic mail, alarms	High speed, computer–to–computer
Text	Telex, Teletex, leased circuits, videotex, information retrieval, mailbox, electronic mail	Teletex, electronic publishing
Video	Videotex, facsimile, information retrieval, surveillance	Teletex, video conference, videophone cable, distribution, HDTV

a spurious argument. The telcos have not been overly successful in promoting new services, especially when such services are virtually the same as present offerings. The relatively poor showing of custom calling penetration[52] is an example of telco marketing problems.

Regulators may have other reservations about ISDN as to its impact on residential service. Questions as to whether ISDN will lead to the reconfiguration of network facilities and result in stranded investment, with concomitant revenue requirements deficiencies, is an important issue. Another significant item is the question of who should pay for ISDN and how will costs be recovered if ISDN does not meet expectations. It is likely that the regulators will want to see evidence of any benefits that will accrue to residential subscribers. The issues of the impact on universal telephone service and cross subsidies are important. There will also be questions regarding the high investments of ISDN and the questionable replacement of analog electronic plant.

Results from many of the ISDN customers participating in trials in the U.S. have been portrayed as being encouraging by the industry. For example, the following advantages were noted by Southwestern Bell's customers:

1. The ability to reduce traffic sensitive expenditures. This includes the elimination of coaxial cable, pooling of modems

and access over one line to different types of data and different kinds of systems.

2. ISDN offers savings, especially in the flexibility of relocating terminals —— asynchronous and synchronous terminals can work on the same line. A PC can be moved and reconnected by making a software change. This used to cost $1,000 a move, but with ISDN, it is virtually costless.

3. ISDN gives the customer flexibility: they can have the telephone, the fax, the synchronous and asynchterminals all at one desk. ISDN is a low capital investment where users get the potential of a 64 kbps data channel, without a lot of extensive work.[53]

In Canada, a more technically complex trial began in July 1988 as Bell Canada became the first carrier in North America to provide connections between the types of ISDN services presently undergoing testing, *i.e.*, BRI and PRI. The new two year trial will allow customers participating in Bell's trial, begun in November 1987, to communicate with users at the PRI test site which encompasses selected employees at Telecom Canada's Ottawa head-quarters.

However, not all the comments have been positive. The Bundespost, the German PTT that virtually has an absolute monopoly on telecommunications in Germany identified four risk areas associated with the social aspects of ISDN:

1. The ISDN could be detrimental to the labor market, because it offers increased rationalization possibilities by reducing prices and passing on simple work processes to the customer by remote ordering.

2. The ISDN makes telehomework possible and profitable. The Germans use this word to refer to both telecommuting to the office and freelance contract labor.

   Some telehomeworkers will be self employed, and as a result, existing statutory rights regarding the protection of employ-ees, which are conditional on an employee–employer relation-ship will then only be enjoyed by a much smaller part of the labor force. Social Security will get into financial trouble owing to the declining number of contributors [and] the balance of forces between trade unions and employers will suffer because the self employed telehomeworkers could be used as strikebreakers.

3. Digital switching technology will increase the risk of communications being supervised, as this will be possible

more inconspicuously and at lower cost. If people use switched telecommunications services in more and more domains, the network provider gains knowledge, at least theoretically, about more and more facets of people's lives.

4. Technically switched communication, unlike direct person–to–person communication, emphasizes individual aspects of information and has unknown effects on human behavior. There is a risk of . . . impairing peoples' creativity and ability to communicate.[54]

b. ISDN Services

Initially, LECs will offer narrowband services via ISDN to establish a customer base and take advantage of in–place facilities. However, the extensive capacity that will exist in the public network as a result of the deployment of digital switches and fiber optic transmission has created incentives for LECs to market broadband services. These higher capacity offerings are being developed in the U.S. and European countries and some major carriers, such as AT&T, foresee all digital networks within the next several years. LECs will perceive a need to use the available capacity for strategic marketing applications in order to maintain the monopoly positions to which they have grown accustomed. The following sections show how LECs are positioning themselves, in a marketing sense, as they attempt to ease customers into the Information Age.

(1) Central Office LANs

A recent development by the Bell Regional Holding Companies (RHCs) is the central office LAN or CO–LAN offered through their telephone subsidiaries. The first one was offered by Bell Atlantic in 1985. CO–LANs utilize existing Centrex lines rather than reconfiguring facilities for a new LAN. Essentially, a CO–LAN provides the added networking benefits of a LAN with no initial investment by the customer and the BOC is responsible for installation, support, and maintenance. The system allows for the transmission of both data and voice signals, and access can be provided to internal host computers, public packet switched networks, and private networks. The functionality obtained from a CO–LAN will also provide users with an introduction to the capabilities of ISDN.

The salient features touted for CO–LANs are:
- Flexibility to add or move users.
- No long term financial or equipment commitments except for modems.
- Connection of devices and hosts without costs and problems with installation.
- Automatic technology updates by the BOC thereby removing obsolescence problems associated with CPE LANs.
- Ability of PC to PC communication.
- Space savings compared to CPE LANs.

The RHCs have jumped into the LAN marketplace by offering CO–LANs to counter CPE LAN suppliers. Bell Atlantic is the most active, having signed up more than 70 sales for its CO–LAN service, which total about 35,000 lines. The monthly cost of each port is $20, and the bulk of the lines sold were to government entities or universities.

Ameritech has two CO–LAN offerings, one for basic users and another for more sophisticated applications. This RHC conducted an on–site test for a minimal one year period to acquaint itself and customers with the service. The NYNEX companies provide CO–LAN service at rates that vary from $22 to $24 per port, and expected 10,000 ports to be in service by mid 1988. The other RHCs are at various stages of developing strategies and tariffs to meet CO–LAN demand in their regions.

(2) ISDN–Based LANs

From the user's perspective, ISDN will not provide near term benefits to large data file transfers. That is because such communications transmit in megabits per second, and the broadband interface to handle this requirement will not be available until the early 1990s. Therefore, ISDN for LAN users will initially only be beneficial for low volume transmission. Once broadband capability becomes available, the largest volume customers will be the first to take advantage of ISDN–based LANs. This is because private network controllers, i.e., the PBX, are now being installed with ISDN functionality to control voice and data services.

Suppliers of LANs also have a stake in the development of ISDN. Five of these are Apple, 3Com, DEC, Wang and IBM. Important concerns of major vendors appear to relate to a clear cut commitment by major telephone carriers plus an indication that customer demand will be forthcoming.[55] Another concern is that regulatory obstacles in a particular country could cause delays in the implementation of ISDN thereby reducing that nation's role in the Information Age.

Apple is convinced that demand exists for information service applications by small business and residential customers based on the results of the French Minitel system. They believe that the current complexities of the network which are depressing demand can be resolved by the deployment of ISDN.

3Com visualizes the bringing together of small clusters of terminals or PCs into a centralized site served by a LAN. In turn, multiple LAN connec–tivity will be enhanced by the implementation of ISDN. 3Com believes many of the technical issues are on their way to resolution, but, that the develop–ment of products and services, i.e., demand, is not readily apparent at this time.

DEC is also of the opinion that customer demand is the key element. It believes that ISDN deployment will further the installation and enhancement of wide area networks (WANs). In order to determine marketing and techni–cal data DEC has participated in ISDN trials in both the United States with the RHCs and abroad with European PTTs.

Wang's view is that ISDN will enhance but not necessarily replace existing data networks and has actively participated in field trials to help identify user applications. Wang also opines that market demand is crucial to the deployment of resources to support ISDN and the success of ISDN will hinge on its cost, ability to provide unique services and functions, nationwide availability, and a capability to solve unique telecommunications problems.

IBM has conducted extensive field trials in several European companies and in the U.S. They believe that initial demand will come from existing users to take advantage of anticipated lower rates. Once new services and applications are defined, customers will upgrade and expand their systems to take advantage of greater bandwidth, improved technical reliability, and greater flexibility. The key element to the success of ISDN will be the timing of new applications and enhanced services, according to IBM.

(3) Electronic Mail
Electronic mail (E–Mail) is expected to continue its dramatic growth as information services proliferate. For instance, the number of private E–Mail subscribers grew over 40 percent from 1986 to 1987 to a level of 5.6 million.[56] Future estimates are for 50 to 60 percent growth with revenues attaining the one billion dollar mark by the early 1990s. Growth could even be greater as the RHCs are now able to offer voice messaging services as a result of the March 1988 ruling by U.S. District Judge Harold Greene in connection with the MFJ. The advent of ISDN and the establishment of E–Mail standards so that electronic documents can easily be sent between PCs using dissimilar E–Mail services will also foster the growth of the service. The one billion dollar revenue estimate noted above does not include the sales associated with the modems, PC–based software, terminals, etc. that are required for E–Mail. These items may represent revenues of about three–billion dollars. Of course, many of these costs to customers are not incurred on a recurring basis but rather at start–up or when enhancements are required.

Over the next several years as more competitors enter the market and the industry becomes more orderly it will be faster, easier, and cheaper to transmit an electronic letter than using the postal service. Electronic document transfer of one page over a facsimile[57] or 1200 baud modem takes about 20 seconds as compared to several days associated with the mail. Of course, overnight services are available, but only at a premium cost. The transmission of an electronic document eliminates many of the bothersome steps involved with mailing a letter. For instance, envelopes need not be typed, sealed, stamped, or mailed, letters do not require folding, signature, or, in some cases, printing. On the cost side, the direct cost of the U.S. mail is 25¢ whereas by using a 2400 baud modem, six pages cost about 20¢. For slower speed modems the cost is higher, but, as noted above, rates are expected to decrease.

The recent growth of fax, which is often the type of terminal used to originate and receive electronic communications, has been significant. In the early 1980s there were only a few thousand fax machines. In 1987 the installed base had jumped to 730,000 and is expected to grow to 2.7 million by 1991. Sales in 1987 topped the 500,000 mark in the U.S. and about one million worldwide. The declining price of fax machines is a major reason for the sales explosion. Costs are now under $1,000 whereas just a few years ago it cost more than $3,000 for a fax machine.

The dissatisfaction of users with the incompatibility of the various offerings of E-Mail suppliers has hindered development and more widespread acceptance of the service. However, at the insistence of several major aerospace companies, representing a very large group of users, many E-Mail providers will conduct a trial in early 1989 so that standards can be developed to allow for manageable interconnection among the services of different suppliers. E-Mail compatibility is a key to continued growth and will facilitate the electronic exchange of information among more diverse groups of users.

(4) Packet Switching

Packet switching represents a mode of data transmission in which messages are broken into smaller increments called packets, each of which may be routed independently to the destination, and reassembled in order at the destination. The primary benefit of packet switching is its ability to permit many different types of computers to communicate thereby facilitating the exchange of information. Other advantages associated with packet switching are that it can relieve the processing load on mainframe computers and communication front-end processors, provide code and speed conversion, reduce the number of ports and lines, provide security and is universally available.

The packet switching market is expected to continue its rapid growth. The D channel of the basic 2B+D ISDN rate is a packet switching channel which suggests that packet switching will fit into the overall scheme of ISDN deployment. Of necessity, though, packet switching suppliers will have to develop ISDN related equipment interfaces.

The RHCs and Southern New England Telephone (SNET) have local packet network tariffs on file. The basic rate elements are the holding time charge for dial-in ports, a charge for traffic, protocol conversion charges, and fixed charges for the X.25 ports. The protocol conversion element is called a NURE (Network Utilization Rate Element) which was proscribed by the FCC. The rates for direct connection of X.25 ports vary among the carriers from $300 to $450 for a 9.6 kbps port and from $500 to $750 for a 56 kbps port.

(5) Other Information Services

AT&T has estimated that 85 percent of information flow on the public telephone network in the U.S. is voice originated and that by 1995, 50 million PCs will be used by the nation's work force.[58] The present use of voice communications predominates as evidence shows that firms in the RHC opera-ting areas allocate over 60 percent of their communications budgets to voice applications. The 60 percent ratio has remained relatively constant over the last several years, suggesting that there is not yet a stampede to data services.   Also, the proportion of data switched through PBXs is even lower. The figure is about 7.5 percent presently, but is expected to triple over the next two years.[59]

As requirements for information exchange increases during the next 5–10 years, the percentage of data services is expected to increase over present figures.   Under this scenario, new services will become available to meet these new requirements.   The synergistic relationship between PCs, data processing, and telecom networks will serve to enhance and enlarge network growth worldwide.   Of course, most of these applications are targeted to business customers, since the majority of residential subscribers do not own PCs or other high–tech facilities.

Many large corporations now offer nontraditional information services that often directly tie–in to their communications capabilities.   For instance, GE, Borg–Warner, and Westinghouse derive significant revenues from service based services.   This trend is not limited to the U.S. as Japanese conglomer–ates are following a similar course of action.

There are several types of new services that will be offered in the near future.   Public access to information via terminals not unlike the public telephone booth will provide a menu of various topics that are of particular interest to customers.   Included among these topics might be financial data, restaurant ratings and food specialties, sports results, etc.   Payment could be facilitated with credit cards as an added convenience to customers and as theft protection for the vendor.

Telephone companies may also become data processing resources for firms that cannot afford their own MIS (management information systems).   Their ISDN will enable connectivity among a diverse range of terminals and computers for data transfer.   The LECs can also be expected to act as the interface between information/data base providers and end users.   In other words, if a customer wishes to obtain the most recent financial data for a particular company or industry but does not know where to call, he could call his telephone company for such information and be connected almost instan–taneously.   These gateway services will aid both customers and information providers alike.

At the end of 1988 Bell Canada began to provide the gateway access to a wide range of information services from home terminals in a Montreal trial. The offerings will include home banking, home shopping, and news services. Financial institutions and local merchants will provide the actual services via the gateway and end users will access the services from terminals costing about $8 per month.   The services can also be accessed from customer owned PCs using a software package provided by Bell.   An electronic telephone directory, information, and transaction services will also be offered by Bell Canada.

In a landmark decision, U.S. District Judge Harold Greene ruled in March 1988 that the RHCs could participate in the voice messaging and electronic mail markets in a limited role.   The regionals are permitted to transmit information through a gateway system but may not generate information content nor provide electronic directory services.   All of the RHCs have jumped into the information services market with new services or with trials underway or in the planning stage. The initial offerings have generally consisted of audiotext or videotex gateway services in major markets of each RHC.

One example of the information services being offered by the RHCs can be seen from a recent proposal by the New England Telephone Company (NET) in Massachusetts. The offering, called Information Delivery Service (IDS), would permit vendors to provide information announcement services to callers who dial the announcement telephone number. End user charges were based on usage and varied from 50¢ to $1.00 per minute with maximum limits. Charges to the vendors, which represented NET's portion of total revenues collected from customers, were 10¢ for the initial minute and 6¢ for each additional minute. NET would also be reimbursed about 10¢ for performing the billing and collection functions. In order to guard against unwanted access to these services, NET proposed to implement blocking and other features.

The model for information service offerings may be the six year old Teletel videotex system established by France Telecom. The well publicized service has exhibited remarkable growth which many believe to be the result of the no-charge Minitel terminals provided to end users. At the present time there are about 3.7 million terminals, and these could grow by over 60 percent to six million by 1990. However, the no-charge aspect of the Minitels will be replaced by a small rental fee in 1989. The outcome of this strategy will provide useful insight to others who are offering information services.

It is clear, though, that the Minitel services have been successful from a sales viewpoint, although data on profitability is not readily available. At the end of 1987 Minitel penetration was about 14 percent, with a 51 percent increase in that year alone.[60] From 1985 to 1987, calls increased by almost five-fold and usage grew by about 350 percent. A breakdown of the usage by applications is shown in Table VII–19.

Of course, there is no guarantee that the 8000 information services provided on the Teletel network will take hold in the U.S. or elsewhere. Yet, the basic model may be appropriate for specific applications.

c. Near Term Outlook for ISDN

ISDN development will continue to proceed during the next several years, but much will depend on public policy guidance. Historically, industry members, especially exchange carriers in the U.S., have spearheaded technological change within the network (e.g., introduction of electronic switching), as regulators have generally accepted these programs. However, these changes could not have proceeded without formal regulatory approval.

Three basic ISDN scenarios seem plausible:

- One scenario is characterized by "market failure" whereby the lack of a quick consensus on standards would retard development of a public ISDN, resulting in disparate, incom- patible private enhanced networks.

Table VII–19

MINITEL USAGE

	Hours	Calls
Professional Applications	23%	23%
Electronic Directory	18	33
Messaging	22	8
Leisure Games	14	7
General Information	4	7
Practical Service	10	12
Banking & Finance	9	10
	100 %	100 %

Source: *Telephony,* August 8, 1988, p. 28.

- A second is the emergence of a public ISDN on a "piecemeal" basis, targeting large cities and featuring a shared facilities architecture rather than complete integration of voice, data, facsimile and other services.
- The third scenario envisions full conversion to ISDN as the technological "dream" is brought to fruition, namely, full deployment and integration based on universally accepted ISDN standards, open entry, and a myriad of wideband video and high speed data offerings, integrated packet and circuit switching, and value based (rather than cost based) pricing.

Failure to develop an appropriate public policy infrastructure for the new Information Age could result in parallel development of all three scenarios at an enormous waste of R&D funds, public monies, manufacturing resources, and public network operating systems. The possibility exists that full conversion might never be achieved without the necessary public guidance.

The demand for services provided via ISDN is a key element to the success of the concept. The cost to end users may not be the determining factor since the price of a service is not always the criterion used to select among alternative service offerings. Service quality and reliability are often more important than cost considerations. Technical criteria, such as the capability to interface different technologies and terminal types among users, are a critical factor in other situations. And, if diverse routing is required by users alternate suppliers can be used to provide such a feature.

There also appears to be a lot of uncertainty concerning the value of ISDN. Some communications managers have questioned whether ISDN will give them anything not available today. Some examples of large customers' concerns with respect to the value of ISDN can be seen from the following roundtable discussion among members of the International Communications Association (ICA):

Q. Will the ISDN evolve into a ubiquitous reality by the 1990s, as the local carriers suggest?

A. I don't think so.   I haven't heard of anything that ISDN gives me that I can't get today. I haven't figured out what we'd do with it, and as best as I can tell there is no demand for it in the company (Deere & Co.) that I work for.

A. I guess my feeling with ISDN is, why bother? There is nothing I can do with ISDN that I can't do today with something else (Bankers Trust Co.).

Q. But won't ISDN make it less expensive to do those things?

A. No. It would cost me more.[61]

Similar sentiments were set forth in a recent article appearing in *Communications Consultant*.[62] There it was noted that almost all the features provided with ISDN were included in telephone company central offices years ago and that there does not appear to be any incentive to spend more for ISDN to obtain the same features and services currently available. These concerns have led many to believe that ISDN is a solution in search of a problem. It would also appear that if the initial targets of ISDN marketing efforts, *i.e.*, large customers, are having difficulty rationalizing the use of ISDN, then there may be even less demand by residential users. Issues as to whether ISDN is cost effective or if there is even any demand for it should be resolved before large resource commitments are made. The lack of definitions and standards are leaving many potential users lukewarm at best when it comes to ISDN.

Appendix VII–A

LIST OF TARIFF SERVICES

1. Centrex Service & Service Charges
2. Channel Services and Service Charges
3. Complex Wire
4. Bellboy Service & Service Charges
5. Mobile Service & Service Charges

6. Remote Call Forward
7. Dishonored Check Charge
8. Basic Res. & Bus. Svcs w/Message Units and Service Charges
9. Public Coin Service
10. Directory Assistance

11. Touch Tone Service
12. Custom Calling Service
13. Service for Cus.–Prov. Coin & Credit Card Operated Telephones
14. Audiotex Service
15. Directory Listings

16. List Service
17. Supplemental Equipment
    a. Apartment Door Answering
    b. DID and OID
    c. PBX Night, Su. & Holidays Arrgmt
    d. Break Rotary Hunt Arrgmt
    e. Long Distance Message Res.
    f. Make Busy Arrgmts
    g. Hunting Service
    h. Data Sets
    i. Split Supervisory Drop Wire Arrgmt
    j. Special Telephone Numbers
    k. Booths
    l. Transfer Arrangements
18. Group Alerting & Dispatching Serv.
19. Intermediary Switching Arrangements
20. Preferred Telephone Numbers

21. Concentrator Identifier Equipment
22. Local Conference Service
23. Verification/Interrupt Service
24. Operator Assisted Local Calls
25. Electronic Switching System–ACD Type A

26. Protection Eq. to Power Stations
27. Concentrator & Data Access Arrangements – CPE Systems
28. Network Interface Jacks
29. Connection w/various CPE
30. Selective Class of Call Screening

31. Channels Requiring Sp. Conditioning
32. Outpulsing Facilities
33. Centrex Optional Features
34. Centrex Custom Calling Services
35. Centrex Electronic Tandem Switching Features
36. Central Office Local Area Network Service

Notes

1. K.D. Fishman, *The Computer Establishment*, McGraw Hill, 1981, pp. 294–297.

2. AT&T estimates submitted October 1984 in FCC Bypass Proceeding.

3. *Independent Phone Facts '80*, USITA, p. 11.

4. Id.

5. See "Report by the Federal Communications Commission on Domestic Telecommunications Policies," before the Chairman of the U.S. House Subcommittee on Communications, issued September 27, 1976.

6. See W. Bolter, J. Duvall, F. Kelsey, and J. McConnaughey, *Telecommunications Policy for the 1980s: The Transition to Competition*, Prentice–Hall: Englewood Cliffs, 1984, Section V, n. 126.

7. *Communications Week*, December 26, 1988, p. 20.

8. The RHCs have been building networks of wholly owned toll switching to replace intraLATA toll switching capacity they now lease on AT&T switches.

9. Cincinnati Bell and SNETCo were not subject to the AT&T consent decree because they were not wholly owned subsidiaries. AT&T, nonetheless, voluntarily "spun off" these two entities.

10. Value added services is a dated term used to describe communications services which in some way alter the information content of messages being carried. Least cost message routing and protocol conversion are sometimes considered to be value added services.

11. AT&T, *1986 Annual Report*, p. 8.

12. *Id.*

13. *Telecommunications Reports*, October 12, 1987, p. 8. AT&T also maintains similar private networks for GE and more than 300 other customers. See, *e.g.*, *New York Times*, August 28, 1987, p. D1.

14. *New York Times*, November 12, 1987, p. D5.

15. "AT&T to Accelerate Annual Investment in Digital Network to $3 Billion in 1988, 1989," *Telecommunications Reports*, November 16, 1987, p. 6.

16. *Wall Street Journal*, November 12, 1987, p. 2.

17. MCI, *Annual Report 1986*, p. 26.

18. "Sprint pays steep rent on AT&T line," *Network World*, February 16, 1987, pp. 1, 44.

19. See, *e.g.*, "Calling Long Distance: User Vote Shows Strong Support for AT&T...," *Wall Street Journal*, August 22, 1986, p. 19.

20. See, *e.g.*, "The Long–Distance Warrior," *Business Week*, February 26, 1986, p. 90.

21. ACC Corp. would be the ninth long distance affiliate acquired by Rochester Telephone.

22. There were some exceptions, such as facilities contracts with Western Union which were eventually eliminated.

23. The agreements were embodied in the Exchange Network Facilities for Interstate Access (ENFIA) tariffs filed with the FCC.

24. Local Access and Transport Areas established by the MFJ as geographical areas of operation for the BOCs.

25. In certain instances, facilities may be leased to fill out service requirements.

26. For the ICs, access revenues paid to the BOCs represent a cost of providing toll services.

27. AT&T projected growth in conversation minutes of use from 91.6 billion in 1987 to 102 billion in 1988. See *Communications Week*, February 22, 1988, p. 48.

28. From 1974 to 1983 the average annual growth rate was also about three percent.

29. "The Yellow Pages Walk into a New Marketing Age," *TE&M*, June 15, 1987, p. 113.

30. As digital technology becomes more prevalent in the local network, Centrex applications will be served to an even greater extent over such facilities to take advantage of advanced features and enhancements *vis-à-vis* analog technologies.

31. "Centrex Can Open Service Doors," *TE&M*, December 1, 1987, p. 63.

32. *Communications Week*, February 1, 1988, p. 10. Bell Atlantic attributes the substantial growth to reduced prices and feature enhancements.

33. More specifically, Centrex users can directly access a BOC's data base where lines can be added or deleted, and certain features, including the adjustment of service class, reassignment of station lines, changing of call pick up groups and speed call numbers, can be altered.

34. *Payphone*, February 1988, p. 72.

35. It is not clear whether the lower prices paid for cellular equipment are due to economies associated with lower unit production costs or subsidies designed to gain market shares.

36. The installed base has been growing by over 60,000 subscribers per month since mid–1988.

37. In this regard, Southwestern Bell's 1988 *Annual Report* (page 6) indicates that by 1994 the number of cellular customers will increase to 20 million. Similarly, NYNEX expects growth to be ten–fold by 1995 according to its *Annual Report* (page 20)

38. SWB markets its nonwireline cellular service as Cellular One which is also licensed to different companies in other markets.

39. *LAN Times*, December 1987, p. 47.

40. *Lightwave*, March 1988, p. 1.

41. *LAN Times*, December 1988, p. 5.

42. *Communications Consultant*, January, 1988, p. 48.

43. *Network World*, November 29, 1988, p. 19.

44. "The Datamation Connectivity Survey: The Haves and Have–Nots," *Datamation*, March 1, 1988, p. 70.

45. *LAN Times*, April 1988, p. 1.

46. *Network World*, November 14, 1988, p. 27.

47. *Network World*, November 15, 1988, p. 21.

48. Many of the BOCs offer enhanced and innovatively priced Centrex service under the ESSX trademark. One example is the Customer Specific Pricing (CSP) tariff of Southwestern Bell in Texas.

49. The essence of the discount relates to providing service to one large customer, say of 500 lines, versus providing service to 10 customers of 50 lines each. Under the aggregated approach all 500 lines receive the price breaks and extra features associated with large systems.

50. *TPT*, November 1988, p. 30.

51. *Communications News*, March 1988, p. 39.

52. A 1987 study found that only 29 percent of eligible customers subscribe to the LECs' custom calling features. These services have been available since the 1960s in some localities (*TE&M*, March 15, 1987, p. 80). Custom calling penetration in British Columbia Telephone Company's (Canada) operating area has fared even worse at about eight percent as noted in the CRTC's decision regarding the carrier's 1987 construction program (p. 38).

53. *CO*, January 1988, p. 32.

54. *Id.*, p. 33.

55. "The Marriage of ISDN and LANs," *Telephony*, May 9, 1988, p. 43.

56. *Network World*, November 14, 1988, p. 66.

57. Facsimile, or fax, machines are a subset of the E–Mail category of service.

58. "BOC to the Future," *CO*, December 1987, p. 33.

59. "PBX Growth Patterns Take New Directions," *TPT*, May 1988, p. 62.

60. *Telephony*, August 8, 1988, p. 25.

61. "What do Users Want?" *Telephony*, May 16, 1988, p. 37.

62. "A Telco Manager's Answer to ISDN," *Communications Consultant*, August 1988, p. 47.

CHAPTER VIII

OTHER DIMENSIONS OF INDUSTRY ANALYSIS

A. The RHCs in Foreign Markets

The seven RHCs have entered the international marketplace in hope of gaining a respectable share of what is estimated to be a $300–$400 billion market and by 1990, the market offerings could reach one trillion dollars. These companies are forming joint ventures in both Europe and Asia in addition to selling on their own behalf. Name recognition and overcoming government dominated telecommunications networks will provide challenges to the RHCs. However, the Bells have immense financial and other resources on their side to combat the negative aspects of their endeavors overseas. There is a dearth of information concerning the RHC's international operations, but PacTel appears to be the most aggressive of the regionals. The two major areas of specialization are consulting and software, which take advantage of the RHCs' in–house expertise and experience. Although the RHCs have ventured abroad, the profitability of these endeavors is not clear.

Ameritech is pursuing domestic customers who require international tele–communications capability. This company furnishes consulting services in London's mobile radio market and in Japan's paging services market. A joint relationship was established in Japan to explore technical and marketing ventures. Ameritech's publishing arm established a five year agreement to publish English–language directories in Tokyo and Osaka, beginning in 1987. Revenues for 1987 international operations, which serve customers in 40 nations, increased by 42 percent over 1986.

Bell Atlantic's international business objectives are primarily in the area of building and managing communications networks, in marketing telecom–munications service and products, and in maintaining and financing equipment. These are accomplished by providing consulting services and selling software licenses to foreign PTTs. The company views Centrex as a potential money maker and has worked with British Telecom and other PTTs to introduce the service. The Bell company has agreements with Siemens and IBM to market intelligent networks in Europe and with the Spanish Carrier, Telefonica, to provide network system support in that country.

BellSouth International's (BSI) endeavors include the signing of an 18 year agreement to provide equipment and services based on a digital PBX at Shanghai Center, the largest multi–use complex in China. The company has regional offices in Bonn, London, Metz (France), and Hong Kong and a presence in other countries such as Australia, Argentina, Guatemala, India, and China. In addition to consulting and software services, BSI is involved in mobile communications and the provision of network services.

During 1988, the firm helped form a consortium to develop and operate Argentina's first cellular communications network. The system, to become operational in 1989, is targeted at a potential market of 320,000 subscribers over a 15 year period.

BSI has recently collaborated with Digital Equipment Corporation to jointly market telecommunications systems worldwide. These systems will include emergency, directory, and toll-free service networks. BSI will also aid the Thailand government in the development of a 10 year computer application plan for use in that nation's telephone system. A presence in Australia is maintained through various subsidiaries that have a substantial share in the market for pagers with 120,000 units.

NYNEX International has one major advantage over the other RHCs' overseas operations, its U.S. operating area includes the corporate head-quarters (New York City) of a substantial number of multi-national customers. In addition, Boston and New York are two major international gateways, and both are in the NYNEX territory. The firm has offices in New York, Geneva, Hong Kong, and London and is seen as one of the more aggressive RHCs for overseas markets. Agreements were reached with telephone companies in Japan and France to develop new products and services. Similar arrangements were established in England, the Netherlands, and Taiwan. The London based BIS Group, Ltd. provides software services, information systems consulting and training, and direct marketing.

NYNEX International had a proposal for approval of its waiver request before the U.S. District Court (Judge Greene) to join with Cable & Wireless to own and operate a fiber optic link between New York and London. After a delay which resulted in the expiration of NYNEX's option to obtain the necessary licensing authority, the Department of Justice (DOJ) recommended to Judge Greene's Court that the waiver be denied. NYNEX sought to over-turn the DOJ recommendation via comments to the Court but failed. The company took a $10 million loss in early 1989 on the failed venture and it is not clear how NYNEX will pursue this lucrative market in the future.

In 1988 NYNEX obtained a contract to provide a network monitoring system for the Postal Telecommunication Administration of Shanghai. The term of the contract is 18 months during which NYNEX will provide hard-ware, software, and training for the system.

PacTel's International subsidiary, Pacific Telesis International (PTI), has focused its efforts on entering into joint ventures with other companies and administrations. It has a digital paging operation in Thailand and provides point-of-sale terminals in Korea. PTI also is working with NEC to install a cellular mobile system in Kuwait and has established a research facility in Spain in concert with Telefonica.

In November 1988, the DOJ recommended to Judge Greene's Court that PacTel be allowed to acquire a ten percent interest in a trans-Pacific cable venture via International Digital Company (IDC). This company will market international services in Japan. Apparently the difference between the above mentioned DOJ rejection of the NYNEX proposal and the acceptance of the PacTel acquisition is the size of the ownership interest and that NYNEX sought to offer international services in the U.S.

Southwestern Bell strives to enter into agreements with PTTs rather than with users. In the area of software development, the company is working with telco administrations in Germany, Norway, Sweden and the United Kingdom. The Bell firm has expanded its equipment operations to the U.K. and has publishing activity in three countries. Centrex is another area that will be pursued in Europe with the PTTs.

U S WEST is concentrating its international efforts in the marketing and sales of software, and in particular, electronic funds transfer. It has also received a contract to install point–of–sale networks in Australia New Zealand, and the U.K. The company acquired Applied Communications, Inc., a firm that develops transaction processing software for automated teller machines and point–of–sales networks. Forty percent of Applied's installed base is outside of the U.S. in 34 countries.

During 1988 U S WEST emphasized its interest in cable operations as it became part of a consortium that was awarded the cable franchise in Birmingham, England, which is touted as being the largest single cable franchise in the English–speaking world with almost a half–million households. U S WEST also acquired a ten percent interest in a growing CATV operation in France.

B. Conditions in Foreign Markets

Several of the developed nations of the world appear to be on a course of considerable liberalization of their policies concerning multiple provision of domestic telecommunications products or services. Related to these developments, worldwide growth in the use of telecommunications and, ultimately, the economic viability of a new industrial order, is the establishment of standards. In any sector, and eventually worldwide, the various countries involved must establish these parallels in interconnection and design in order to take full advantage of the technological and political breakthroughs that are occurring.

For instance, the issuance of the Green Paper on the Development of the Common Market for Telecommunications Services and Equipment by the Commission of the European Communities, the administrative arm of the 12 nation European Community (EC), has opened the door for a degree of deregulation and more liberal competitive policies in Europe. Asian nations are also moving to meet the challenges and reap the rewards of the deployment of new technologies by liberalizing regulatory policies. Japan, with Nippon Telephone and Telegraph's (NTT) $80–$120 billion fifteen year commitment to build a digital telecommunications network, is in the vanguard in the Far East. Other countries, such as Canada and Australia have also enacted more procompetitive policies.

Initially in this part of the chapter, the analysis will provide overall market and policy observations of telecommunications developments from a global perspective. Following, there is a more detailed discussion. This will center on specific issues and individual countries and the influence each exerts in the general scheme of worldwide industry change.

1. Global Perspective of Local Services
a. Technology and Services
The overall growth in worldwide access lines has been steadily increasing at an annual rate of just under five percent (See Table VIII–1). In 1987

there were slightly over 450 million access lines which are expected to grow to 520 million in 1990 and 656 million in 1995, at an average annual growth rate of about 4.7 percent.   Although percentage growth may have slowed down, the absolute additions in access lines appear to be continuing at an ever increasing pace.

For instance, from 1955 to 1982 the average annual growth world wide was 12 million lines; from 1982 to 1987 the figure was 15 million lines; and from 1987 to 1995 almost double the earlier growth at 25 million lines. This data shows that although the growth rate has abated, to some extent, and flattened out, real growth in terms of the number of access lines being added annually continues to increase substantially.   Most of the new facilities deployed to handle the growth will be comprised of digital switching and up-to-date transmission facilities.

The greatest growth in percentage terms will occur in Africa, Asia, and South America. One obvious reason for this phenomenon is that these regions are mainly populated with undeveloped nations or countries that have more recently become increasingly technologically advanced. Thus, the modernization of lifestyles and facilities, including telecommunications systems, is at an earlier stage. For example, the growth rate in Asia is just over six percent, which is one-fourth again as high as the overall world average. The largest nation in Asia in terms of access lines, is Japan, which is expected to exhibit growth of about two percent per year. However, two emerging countries from a telecommunications viewpoint, China and South Korea, exceed the Japanese growth rate by factors of four, and five, respectively. As growth in these two nations reaches maturity, it could be anticipated that growth rates will come down and flatten out.

In absolute terms, the greatest growth through 1995 will occur in Asia (75 million), Europe (67 million), and North America (37 million). The United States and the Soviet Union will lead individual countries with growth of 34 million and 25 million access lines, respectively. The USSR is starting off with a much lower base (34 million) as compared to the U.S. with its 125 million access lines, which outrank all nations and most regions.

Table VIII-2 shows that there are wide disparities in telephone penetration throughout the world as measured by main lines per 100 inhabitants. Sweden ranks highest with penetration of over 60 percent, with the U.S., Switzerland, Denmark, and Canada around 50 percent. Most countries have shown marked improvement since the mid-1970s, as reflected in the overall average which increased from 25 to 39 lines per capita from 1974 to 1985, or a 56 percent rise. Penetration in the Soviet Union in 1982 was about 10 telephones per 100 population[1] which would place it at the low end of the data in Table VIII-2.

Telephone penetration varies among countries for many reasons. Key factors are budgetary constraints, population density, economic parameters, geography, and government policy. Overall, many countries have improved the capability for new customers to be connected to their telecommunications networks. For instance, since 1974 the length of time required to add a new line decreased substantially in economically developed nations although in a

Table VIII–1

WORLDWIDE GROWTH IN NETWORK ACCESS LINES
(Million)

	1987	1990	1995
Africa	6.9	8.6	12.5
Asia	122.0	146.1	197.4
Europe	155.0	177.4	222.1
North America	138.5	151.3	175.4
Oceania	8.6	9.9	12.6
South America	22.3	26.6	35.8
Total World	453.3	519.9	655.8
U.S.	125.3	137.0	159.1
USSR	34.3	42.0	58.8
Japan	46.9	50.0	55.6
W. Germany	27.9	31.0	37.0
France	25.2	29.0	36.6
U.K.	22.9	26.0	32.2
Italy	19.2	23.0	31.1
S. Korea	8.7	12.0	20.6
Canada	12.8	14.0	16.3
Spain	10.1	12.0	16.0
China	7.1	9.0	13.5
Brazil	7.7	9.0	11.6
Australia	6.7	8.0	10.7
Netherlands	6.4	7.0	8.2
Sweden	5.4	6.0	7.2

Source: *TE&M,* January 15, 1988, p. 90, and BRI estimates.

few countries the waiting period is still relatively high. Telecommunications spending worldwide is planned to be up in 1989 to $118.0 billion from the 1988 level of $112.9 billion (see Table VIII–3). This represents a change of 4.5 percent which is a lower growth rate than experienced over recent years as can be seen from Table VIII–4.

Despite lower growth rates in 1989, the amount of expenditures continued to increase over the timeframe. North America, Europe, and the Far East will continue to be the greatest spenders, accounting for over 83 percent of total expenditures. There is a slight downward shift in the percentage of total dollars attributable to North America and the Far East which is picked up by Europe and South America. The absolute data corroborate these growth trends whereby expenditures in North America will flatten out in 1988 compared to double digit growth in the other two regions.

The largest supplier of telecommunications equipment on a global basis is

Table VIII-2

TELEPHONE MAIN LINES PER 100 INHABITANTS
Organization for Economic Cooperation and Development Countries
(Ranked on the basis of 1985 Data)

Country	1974	1980	1983	1984	1985
Sweden	49.71	58.00	60.24	61.51	62.78
United States	36.82	41.43	47.27	48.17	50.57
Switzerland	37.01	44.46	47.75	48.95	50.18
Denmark	31.71	43.43	46.98	48.24	49.74
Canada	35.27	41.44	41.90	47.03	49.18
Finland	26.45	36.40	41.62	43.08	44.68
Iceland	32.56	37.28	39.66	40.42	42.39
Luxembourg	28.49	36.26	37.98	40.16	42.08
Germany	19.61	33.35	38.34	40.22	41.94
France	11.81	29.95	38.26	40.20	41.75
Norway	21.66	28.65	36.77	39.07	41.37
Australia	24.49	32.28	37.01	38.81	40.38
Netherlands	22.62	34.57	38.02	39.12	40.20
New Zealand	31.01	35.08	37.14	37.63	39.80
Japan	26.53	33.06	35.58	36.50	37.57
United Kingdom	22.87	31.44	34.68	35.75	36.95
Austria	18.29	29.02	33.75	34.97	36.12
Belgium	18.08	25.01	28.85	29.94	31.05
Italy	16.49	23.07	27.45	28.99	30.45
Greece	17.55	23.54	27.56	29.57	30.15
Spain	12.11	19.34	22.15	23.14	24.20
Ireland	9.80	14.20	17.47	18.93	19.74
Portugal	8.00	10.07	12.42	13.08	13.75
Turkey	1.52	2.46	3.50	3.98	4.51
Average:	24.77	32.00	36.39	37.57	39.23

Source: International Telecommunications Union, *Yearbook of Common Carrier Telecommunications Statistics* (11th edition) and PTT Annual Reports.

AT&T with sales of $10 billion, $2 billion greater than its nearest competitor, Alcatel NV. Another group of six vendors is in the $3–5 billion range, while the rest are below $3 billion. However, if the virtually closed Japanese market opens up to nonJapanese firms, the competitive situation could change.

Table VIII-5 presents projections of digital facilities to be employed by various countries during 1990. The overall average for local switching of 31 percent is approximately the same as the 32 percent existing in the U.S. in 1987. The data suggests that digitalization of public networks will not be completed for many of these European countries in the near future. The worldwide problems of standardization have apparently posed a significant

Table VIII–3

TELECOMMUNICATIONS EXPENDITURES BY COUNTRY
($ Million U.S.)

Country	1987	1988	1989
Australia	$1,110	$1,903	$1,846
Austria	910	912	958
Belgium	580	572	652
Brazil	1,050	1,264	--
Canada	2,440	2,750	1,826*
France	5,710	6,220	--
India	600	610	1,805
Italy	3,870	4,331	5,762
Japan	12,180	14,408	14,400
Korea	1,530	1,837	2,148
Mexico	--	668	1,215
Netherlands	700	1,016	1,582
New Zealand	--	1,374	1,374
Norway	620	679	741
South Africa	970	776	810
Spain	2,340	3,148	--
Sweden	1,330	849	849
Switzerland	1,620	1,805	1,968
Taiwan	700	887	941
United Kingdom	3,320	4,409	4,987
United States	24,550	23,884	24,032
West Germany	8,710	9,340	9,796

* Bell Canada only.

	1988		1989	
	Amount	Ratio	Amount	Ratio
North America	$29,016	0.257	$29,105	0.247
Africa	1,905	0.017	2,042	0.017
Europe	40,778	0.361	43,972	0.373
South & Central America	3,185	0.028	4,132	0.034
USSR	7,200	0.064	7,500	0.064
Far East & Pacific	25,950	0.230	25,493	0.216
Middle East & SE Asia	4,866	0.043	5,793	0.049
Total	$112,900	1.000	$118,037	1.000

Source: *Telephony*, February 22, 1988, p. 38 and February 27, 1989, p. 21.

Table VIII–4

ANNUAL TELECOMMUNICATIONS EXPENDITURES
($ Billion)

	Amount	Change
1982	$ 68.2	NA
1983	77.8	14.1%
1984	84.3	8.4
1985	88.8	5.4
1986	94.7	6.6
1987	100.7	6.3
1988	112.9	12.1

Table VIII–5

PERCENTAGE OF DIGITAL FACILITIES IN EUROPE: 1990

Country	Transmission	Switching Local	Switching Long Distance
Belgium	50%	29%	75%
Denmark	85	23	40
France	70	70	75
W. Germany	50	10	22
Greece	15	15	25
Ireland	70	65	85
Italy	45	25	36
Luxembourg	35	8	10
Netherlands	95	35	15
Portugal	70	20	20
Spain	47	5	45
United Kingdom	100	11	11

Source: OECD planning estimates, BT and BRI estimates.

deterrent to the development and installation of a digital network in Europe which partially accounts for the less than ideal progress made to date and through 1990. Of special note are the low percentages of local switching that will have digital capability.

For the United Kingdom, the 1987 *Supplementary Report* shows electronic switching information as noted in Table VIII–6. In addition, the amount of fiber optics in the U.K. in 1987 increased over 1986 levels. In the trunk network, the future increased from 91,000 km to 140,000 km while the number

Table VIII–6

PERCENTAGE OF SWITCHING UNITS IN THE U.K.

	Total Electronic	Digital
1983	25%	0.2%
1984	29	0.8
1985	31	1.2
1986	34	3.0
1987	44	10.7

of kilometers in the junction network grew from 33,000 to 55,000. 1987 also witnessed the first deployment of fiber in the local network as 12,000 km were installed.

Operating information from the Spanish telephone company Telefonica's annual report shows limited use of fiber optic cable although the number of kilometers is growing. At the end of 1986, there were 227 km installed which is almost 2.5 times the 93 km in place at the end of 1985. Digital switches serviced only 3.3 percent of all lines in service in 1986 and five percent in 1987.   These percentages, however, are continuing to grow, up from 1.8 percent in 1985.

The advent of the information services age with its attendant and eventual deployment of ISDN has already begun in many countries. The inauguration of public text services such as videotex, facsimile, and electronic mail burst on to the scene as early as 1978. Although the technologies may have been crude by today's and tomorrow's standards, nevertheless, public access to these services became a reality, and the way was paved for technological improvements and creativity to make the offerings more closely attuned to the needs of the general public.

Tables VIII–7 and 8 show the development of public text services in selected nations.   The data indicates that some countries are significantly more advanced than others in the implementation of the services.   France with its Minitel based system far outpaces the rest of the countries with over 3.5 million users of videotex. Other nations have closely monitored the French experiment and will tailor their resources in this area of communications based on their judgment as to its success.

Facsimile terminals are expected to become more popular as ISDN is implemented and connections between unlike terminals are made easier. This is probably no more evident than in Japan where the installed base of facsimile terminals (public and private) exceeds one million. Of course, one of the reasons for this high number of facsimile terminals is the nature of the Japanese alphabet which is one more of pictures than text.

Electronic mail (E–Mail) is a recent offering in most countries. The potential growth of this service has been discussed earlier in Chapter VII, but noting the substantial number of mailboxes in Canada, which began E–mail in 1981, verifies that there appears to be a significant market for the service.

Table VIII–7

DEVELOPMENT OF PUBLIC TEXT SERVICES
Videotex and Electronic Mail
(1986 Quantities)

	Videotex		Electronic Mail	
Country	Start Date	Users	Start Date	Mailboxes
		(000)		
Austria	1981	6.2	1986	993
Belgium	1986	0.8	1987	–
Canada	1987	–	1981	75,000
Denmark	1982	1.4	1984	800
Finland	1986	3.0	1986	700
France	1982	3,000.0*	–	–
W. Germany	1983	58.0	1986	1,000
Italy	1983	6.0	1986	NA
Japan	1984	27.0	1986	2
Netherlands	1979	22.6	1986	2,300
Norway	1984	1.0	–	–
Portugal	1988	–	–	–
Spain	1984	NA	–	–
Sweden	1983	9.9	–	1,100
Switzerland	1987	4.2	–	–

* 1987.

Source: OECD data.

Value added networks (VANs) are on the rise worldwide. One estimate projects an average annual increase of 40 percent in the European market from a level of $900 million in 1986 to almost $5 billion by 1991.[2] The major users of VANs are expected to be the financial services industry. This is especially true in the U.K. where new legislation will result in additional communications requirements within the financial services industry. The U.K. and France have the largest shares of this market in Europe with 35 percent and 25 percent, respectively. VANs are also proliferating in Japan as over 400 VAN services have been introduced since 1982.

The burgeoning worldwide market of VANs has caught the attention of at least one major U.S. firm, IBM. In Europe and elsewhere, IBM strategy has been to ally itself with entities that provide both expertise and the where-withal to enter important market sectors. IBM's entrance into the VANs market fits well into the projected forthcoming opening of that market in Europe. Figure VIII–1 shows IBM's involvement in this area.

Table VIII-8

DEVELOPMENT OF PUBLIC TEXT SERVICES
Facsimile
(1986 Quantities)

Country	Start Date	Group 1-2 Terminals	Start Date	Group 3 Terminals
Austria	1979	588	1982	1,499
Belgium	1983	–	1984	2,276
Denmark	1980	10,000	1983	NA
Finland	1980	NA	1983	NA
France	1978	10,200	1981	49,800
W. Germany	1979	12,434	1982	31,365
Greece	1980	124	1982	555
Italy	1980	8,000	1983	17,000
Japan	1978	11,677*	1979	14,570*
Netherlands	1980	2,000	1982	16,000
Norway	1980	NA	1980	12,000
Spain	NA	6,080	NA	NA
Sweden	1979	1,500	1984	18,500
Switzerland	1980	658	1984	12,127

* 1985.

Source: OECD data.

Cable television (CATV) penetration in the larger European countries to date has been significantly lower than in the United States and in several smaller countries of Europe.[3] Luxembourg, Belgium, Switzerland, and the Netherlands CATV penetration was several times greater than in the larger nations such as France, West Germany, and the U.K.   In the United States cable penetration is about 50 percent which is also above that of the larger European countries.

This apparent disparity in Europe is due to geographical and political differences.   For instance, the smaller nations have readily available and inexpensive programming from neighboring countries which can blanket their entire national boundaries. In addition, the presence of multilingual audiences within small countries created instant markets for CATV as it became available. Another reason is that the high quality domestic programming existing in the larger nations was not established in the smaller countries, thereby making CATV more attractive. These factors do not exist for the most part in the larger countries, a fact which has tended to retard initial CATV growth.

The current trend of liberalization and deregulation in Europe is expected to lead to faster CATV growth in the U.K., France, and West Germany.

Figure VIII–1

IBM VAN SERVICES AND AGREEMENTS

Denmark –   Agreement with KTAS, largest of Denmark's indepen–
             dent telephone companies.

France –   Agreement with Paribas, Sema Metra, and Credit
             Agricole.

Italy –   Agreement with Fiat, agreement with STET.

Japan –   Agreement with NTT (NIC Nippon Information and
             Communication Company), agreement with Mitsubishi.

Spain –   Agreement with Telefonica and Semi Matra.

U.K. –   Agreement with British Telecom on Jove joint
             venture (prohibited by U.K. government).

Europe –   Information Network Services (INS), offering infor–
             mation exchange service for multinational SNA users
             and electronic data interexchange for trade and
             transport companies.

U.S. –   IBM Information Network established in 1984, now
             serving over 200 U.S. cities. International Market
             Net, a joint venture with Merrill Lynch proposing
             financial services based on SNA and 3270 terminals.

World Wide – Intercontinental Information Services (IIS), linking
             IBM VANs in the US, Europe and Japan.

However, penetration in these countries will probably still not reach the
levels of the smaller countries.

The penetration of cellular in the U.S. has been about twice that of the
overall European Community (see Table VIII–9). Yet, some areas of Europe
have significantly higher cellular use than their neighbors and the U.S.
Notably, penetration in the Scandinavian countries and Iceland is in the 20 to
37 per 1,000 inhabitant range whereas the overall European average is about
4.6. One reason for the difference is the geographical remoteness of areas
within these countries relative to the other European countries. Because of
this characteristic, it may be prohibitively expensive to install and maintain
normal modes of communications, thereby creating natural markets for cellular
technology in order for subscribers to receive basic telephone services.   As

Table VIII-9

CELLULAR PENETRATION IN SELECTED COUNTRIES

Country	Subscribers	Penetration per 1,000
Norway	154,410	36.76
Iceland	6,620	27.58
Sweden	249,840	29.74
Finland	108,990	22.71
Denmark	103,580	19.92
United Kingdom	527,000	9.31
Austria	38,060	5.01
Netherlands	33,050	2.28
Switzerland	33,900	5.65
Ireland	5,640	1.61
W. Germany	103,580	1.67
France	104,820	1.89
Belgium	20,260	2.05
Luxembourg	327	0.88
Italy	33,220	0.58
Spain	12,750	0.33
Total Europe	1,536,047	4.58
United States*	2,334,000	9.39

Source: *Cellular Business*, June 1989, p. 66.

competition and deregulation move forward, the prices of cellular equipment will come down to levels where potential subscribers in the other nations will see benefits to outweigh costs of owning cellular telephones for use in cars, recreation vehicles, and other transient situations. This is the scenario that has occurred in the United States.

b. Policy and Regulatory Changes
Significant changes have occurred with respect to telecommunications policy in the United States over the last several decades. More recently, these same types of changes have manifested themselves in other areas of the world, namely, Europe and the Far East. In the U.K., the former state controlled British Telecom (BT) was privatized and deregulated pursuant to the Telecommunications Acts of 1981 and 1984. At the same time, a second network carrier, Mercury,[4] was authorized to compete with BT and in the future additional firms will be allowed into the market.

The Japanese experience regarding competition (liberalism) and privatiza-tion has parallels with the policies established in both the U.K. and the U.S. In 1985 publicly run monopoly Nippon Telegraph and Telephone (NTT) was changed into Japan's largest corporation. Competitors have been permitted to compete with NTT, with two based on satellite facilities and three with terrestrial technologies setting up networks. Yet, regulatory oversight is still maintained by various government entities, some who vie for control over different parts of NTT's operations. The new policies in Japan are targeted toward making that nation the world's leader in information services.

The European community has seen initiatives taken by the European Commission (EC) in its publication of the "Green Paper" on the *Development of the Common Market for Telecommunications Services and Equipment* in June 1987. The impetus for the study was the recognition that telecommunications services are key inputs to a nation's or region's productivity and economic growth. Notably, to achieve economic growth high quality and technologically advanced services are required for the efficient transfer and dissemination of information in a society that is becoming more and more information dependent. Although there is not complete harmony with respect to the Green Paper proposals, there are a number of items that have been agreed upon:

- Separation of the regulatory and operational activities in each country.
- Liberalization of CPE and other nonvoice services.
- Acceleration of standardization agreements.
- A need for increased competition.
- Promotion of a unified broadband (ISDN) network throughout Europe.

However, there has not been accord as to which services should be open to competition. Pertinent questions such as ease of network entry by potential competitors, interconnection standards, and tariff issues are not well settled. Each of the nations of Europe has its own views on these questions and it may be some time before complete amity can be achieved.

The policy changes in Europe and Japan come after years of industry operation under regulated state owned monopolies. These entities, the Post Telephone and Telegraph administrations (PTTs) operated monopolies on telephone services and most CPE. Not only did the PTTs dictate the services offered, but they also largely determined telecommunications policy.

Under these arrangements there was little or no separation between the providers of service and their regulators. An analogy would be the situation where the predivestiture Bell System included the FCC and state regulatory agencies within its corporate structure. The PTTs also implemented government policies in other areas not related directly to telecommunications. Among these were: the redistribution of income via carefully structured tariffs; the protection of national industries by discriminating against foreign suppliers; and the support of national technological objectives by actively participating in government sponsored programs while not assisting foreign endeavors. The old regime was not unlike that extant in the U.S. before procompetition forces were exerted. Customers had virtually no choice in selecting suppliers of telecommunications services. Furthermore, private transmission facilities were forbidden and leased lines (private lines) could not be connected to public networks.

Despite the recent fervor toward liberalization there are still obstacles to overcome. As with most significant changes in policy throughout history, inertia is a key factor for the establishment and implementation of new policies. Many view the old system as workable and satisfactory, with perhaps a little tweaking here and there being necessary in order to adapt to modern technology. The new technology will tend to blur the distinctions between different types of services, *e.g.,* voice and data. The best way to realize the efficiencies and benefits of such an integrated network is through a monopoly controlled by the PTT. Another argument against liberalization is that because the size of the market in each nation is not nearly the size of the U.S. market, where competition seems to be viable, there may not be enough room for more than one supplier of telecommunications services. Of course, the PTTs believe that since they are already providing the basic service, they should also be able to provide new and additional services at lower costs than new entrants. Traditional arguments such as duplicative and wasteful use of resources have also been cited as reasons for not going forward with liberalism.

Although there has been some resistance to allowing competitors onto the turf of the PTTs, events in Japan and the U.K. suggest that the PTTs can richly share in the benefits of competition. For instance, in the U.K. the entrenched PTT, British Telecom, has reaped the rewards of opening up the enhanced services markets to all corners. This policy had spurred seven–fold growth of electronic mail boxes from about 1,000 in 1984 to 7,000 in 1986 and BT was able to develop 70 percent of this market for itself.

The experiences in the U.S., Japan, and the U.K. suggest that when competitive policies are implemented customer equipment is generally the first market where alternative vendors penetrate entrenched markets. Value added services are often the next group of services to be provided by alternative suppliers over leased facilities, followed by services offered over a mixture of leased and owned facilities, and, finally, competitors deploy their own facilities to handle most traffic. Whatever the degree of success enjoyed by new entrants in making inroads into historically controlled markets, the established carriers have striven to improve their own productivity via operating efficiencies and new up–to–date facilities. The presence of competitive offerings has also fostered innovative, creative, and enhanced service by the dominant carriers. For instance, in the U.S. AT&T has responded to competitive filings by MCI, US Sprint, etc. by offering discounted services and services based on customer specific pricing techniques.

c. *Customer Premises Equipment (CPE)*
The liberalization of CPE in Japan and the United Kingdom appears to have had a more drastic impact over a shorter timeframe than did the comparable relaxed regulation in the United States. In the U.S. it was as if inertia had to be overcome before customers would accept anything but a telephone from their local telephony company. Once the ball got rolling though, new telephones with all the "bells and whistles" have proliferated.

Perhaps the ultimate success of CPE in the U.S. provided a test case for the implementation of liberalization in other countries.

CPE liberalization in Japan began in the 1950s. At its inception in 1952 NTT was given a monopoly over the supply of telephones in Japan. In 1957 customers were permitted to provide their own extension telephones and in 1970 foreign attachments were authorized. Thus, at that time NTT retained control only over the primary instruments. With the advent of the proliferation of new telephones in the market, NTT's monopoly effectively ended and, in 1983, NTT entered the market by selling telephones on an experimental basis.

With the passage of the Telecommunications Business Law (TBL)[5] which became effective on April 1, 1985, the liberalization of CPE received a big boost. The primary instrument could then be provided by firms other than NTT for the first time. The TBL established an independent agency comprised of domestic and foreign equipment manufacturers to oversee the CPE certification process which had previously been the responsibility of NTT. The certification process for overseas imports was also streamlined in order to permit the responsiveness of foreign vendors to Japanese markets on a more timely basis.

The response by CPE suppliers and the impact on users was dramatic. Domestically, new entities were formed and production increased by almost 50 percent in 1985. Foreign manufacturers were also helped by the new policy as CPE approvals increased five–fold in 1985. Consumers benefitted as prices fell by about seven percent and the new telephones contained many optional features that had not previously been available. Similar to the American experience, public phone stores appeared thereby facilitating purchases. As an indication of the popularity and success of the new policy, telephone purchases in 1985 were 500,000 units, up 130 percent from 1984 levels. Even NTT received benefits as its residential sales increased though its overall market share fell by 23 percent.

In the U.K., British Telecom was both a manufacturer and supplier of CPE prior to liberalization in 1981 when BT's control was reduced. In addition, BT had been responsible for certifying other vendors in a competitive market place. Not surprisingly, users and vendors were not happy with the restrictive policies followed by BT in the monopolist's best interests. The Telecommunications Act established the British Approvals Board for Telecommunications (BABT) to evaluate and certify equipment, including CPE, and effectively deregulated CPE. BABT is funded by manufacturers with final approval coming from the Office of Telecommunications (OFTEL).[6]

Apparently, the transfer of the certification process from BT to BABT has not been as orderly and timely as expected. The lack of experience of the new entity has slowed down the transition much to the chagrin of equipment manufacturers. These time consuming and costly procedures have acted as barriers to the liberalism envisioned in the legislation enacted in 1981.

However, and despite these administrative problems, competition in CPE markets seems to be moving forward in the U.K. although not as fast as some would prefer. Between 1983 and 1986 telephone set prices were reduced by

30 percent while BT's sales have increased in the face of declining market shares.[7] An increase in telephone set annual growth from about two percent to seven percent was experienced from 1984 to 1986.

The number of suppliers in the complex CPE market (PBX) also changed as a result of liberalization, increasing from six in 1982 to 18 in 1986. Furthermore, prices declined during the 1984–1985 period. In the small PBX system submarket, under 100 lines, BT had been the sole provider, and it was in this area that competitors sought to enter and gain market share. The small PBX market had experienced a 70 percent turnover during the period 1981 to 1985 which would suggest unique opportunities for alternative suppliers. However, BT replaced 90 percent of the new PBXs,[8] leading to a suspicion that the administrative delays noted above had a significant impact on the ability of competitors to enter the market.

Since BT already had the lion's share of the small PBX market, it set its sights on the over 100 line submarket where previously it had no presence. Despite this apparent handicap, BT has been able to garner about 50 percent of the large PBX market in a relatively short time. BT's success is due in large part to the comprehensive and convenient maintenance service it offers to large PBX users in addition to aggressive sales strategies.

The European Commission put its 12 member nations on notice that it intends to abide by its plan to begin the liberalization of CPE on a European regional basis by mid 1988.[9] Although some members voiced concern that such a policy would benefit nonEuropean countries more than Europeans, the Commission indicated it would use regulatory remedies at its disposal if necessary. Expressing concern over the methods used by the Commission to enforce competition, the governments of France, West Germany, Belgium, and Italy have filed suits with the European Court of Justice against the Commission with regard to the CPE directive. The issue is not with CPE competition *per se* but with the tactics used by the Commission that bypassed normal channels. Initially, 11 of the 12 member nations of the EC protested the Commission's strategy as bypassing their own telecommunications ministries.

It has been estimated that liberalization would increase the $12 billion European CPE market by about seven percent annually, but as noted above, the growth, and perhaps some displacement of the current base, could go to foreign suppliers. One of the significant issues to be resolved is the policy with regard to who should provide the primary telephone instrument. Up to now the PTTs have generally had exclusive rights in this area much to the consternation of users and alternative suppliers.

d. Value Added Networks (VANs)

VANs, or enhanced services (as they are called in the U.S.) are a key feature of liberalization. In Japan, advances in technology and changes in business practices often preceded deregulatory efforts. For instance, in the early 1970s information services companies were established to take advantage of extant technology and deregulation policies whereby computers, facsimile equipment and other information related equipment could be connected to the telephone network of NTT. Strong demand for these types of data services led to the origination of VANs which were permitted by regulators for small businesses in 1982 as a temporary measure,[10] and by 1981, 4,000 privately operated VANs were in existence, often competing with NTT's services. Additional evidence of liberalization is that message exchange through CATV was allowed during the next year and the new legislation has resulted in the deployment of 400 additional LANs.

VANs, according to Japanese law, must lease switching and transmission capacity from underlying carriers. The VANs also compete with underlying carriers in addition to each other. However, many of the VANs are in niche markets such as financial services and other special interest markets, and joint ventures have been formed to provide various of the data offerings. The ongoing list of new entrants includes IBM–Mitsubishi and AT&T–Mitsui. There are also some financially sound Japanese players, Fujitsu, NEC, and Hitachi, that are offering VAN services. Growth from 1984 to 1986 saw 200 new entrants in the marketplace as various types of industries sought connections to their suppliers.

In 1981, groundwork was laid for the establishment of VANs in the U.K. And, in 1982 the task of licensing VANs was transferred from BT to the Department of Trade and Industry where fairer treatment and more expeditious processing was anticipated. The licenses were to be temporary in nature, running from 10 to 25 years, and were limited to genuine VANs, thereby eliminating resale and shared use from consideration. The removal of significant barriers to entry resulted in the initial approval of 40 VAN vendors and at the present time there are about 200.

There is a vast array of services that are offered by VAN operators in the U.K. Included are services such as: special event reservations and ticketing; customer data bases; Electronic Document Interchange (EDI); mailbox services; protocol conversion; management packages; etc. BT has reacted to VANs positively by offering its own services. For instance, before 1982 public E–Mail was virtually nonexistent. By 1986, though, BT had two–thirds of the 70,000 users in its customer base. Niche markets have developed such as the data base established and run by the British library where business has increased ten–fold since 1980.

BT also participates lucratively in joint ventures with providers of information services similar to the Dial–It services offered in the U.S.[11] BT provides the communications medium and the partner provides the voice message or other information. The profits associated with the fees collected from users of the services are split between the two entities. This service, along with all the other VAN offerings hinge upon connection to the network.

One of the objectives of the Green Paper is that supplemental, enhanced or value added services should be open to competition within the European community. At the present time, the various members appear to be in general agreement on the subject but implementation may be a different matter. Historical policies must be reviewed and analyzed before individual countries will be willing to adopt new methods of operating their telecommunications systems.

The EC decided to press the issue when on December 15, 1988 it issued a preliminary order to deregulate value added services by 1991. A final order, after consultation with all affected parties, was expected to be issued in March 1989. In this regard, several European countries have already reached accord in connection with telecommunications matters. Recently, British Telecom reached agreements with the PTTs of Spain and Italy covering value added services, network modernization, and international communications. The Spanish telephone company, Telefonica, has also obtained similar pacts with Italy and France.

2. Individual Countries

This portion of the chapter will provide information that was accumulated for different nations regarding telecommunication policy and regulatory status.

a. Australia

The domestic telecommunications monopoly, Telecom Australia, is the nation's largest employer, and a key factor in the technical and industrial development in Australia. The company is operated in an efficient manner relative to other telecom operations in other countries. For instance, Australia ranks third behind the U.S. and Canada in terms of hours required to work by the average residential customer to pay the annual costs of telephone service.

Over a recent seven year period average annual growth of seven percent for basic services has been higher than most nations. Even more spectacular was the almost 40 percent annual growth rate for data modems, indicating a trend toward information services. National videotex service has been growing and is available to serve business and farmers. Technological development is also taking place as a digital network is being installed which includes both fiber optic and microwave facilities, generally deployed on major routes. Eventually, a digital overlay over the present network is planned as the Australians prepare for a fully integrated digital network.

Australia can be characterized as a net importer of technology as its R&D is at a low level and is mainly government funded. Thus, foreign investment has played a key role in the country's economic development. Industries tend to be highly concentrated whereby protectionism is at a high level and has been sustained over a long time. All of these factors have tended to keep telecommunications competition in the background in Australia, except for CPE.

However, the advent of satellite technology in 1985 has seemingly opened the door for competition. Although Telecom owns 25 percent of the satellite system, many believe the monopolist will now take a more competitive stance. The nation is several years behind many of the other countries with respect to technological development and liberalization, but given the recent threat of an alternate mode of operation and the apparent commitment to install a digital network, competitive policies may eventually take hold in the network.

In anticipation of the liberalization of the CPE market, the two largest manufacturers in Australia (SFC and AWA) joined forces with Telecom Australia to introduce a technologically advanced standard telephone to ward off foreign entry. The government is also expected to permit competition for key telephones and small switching systems. In this regard, toward the latter part of 1988 the government established an independent regulatory group having responsibility to approve all equipment connecting to the public network and for licensing all value added services. The new entity, Austel, will begin operating in July 1989 and will take over licensing and technical regulation responsibilities from Telecom. Other of Austel's functions will be to protect Telecom's monopoly services, protect consumers from abuses by monopoly carriers, and assure service obligations are met by carriers.

b. Austria

The PTT in Austria is a legal monopoly that provides telecommunications services and has regulatory authority. Thus, it is able to control the licensing of potential competitors except for publicly switched telephone service. The policy for the approval of most CPE is considered liberal and even further relaxation will most likely occur in order to further competitive goals and improve the quality, price, and range of equipment. However, it is not evident that the Austrians believe a second common carrier is required for telephone services offered over the network. In a small country such as Austria, the theory of a natural monopoly appears to work well and may be sufficient for the well being of its citizens according to some of the nation's policymakers.

It is also recognized that new legislation may be needed to redefine the scope of the state monopoly as the country approaches and enters the Information Age. In this regard, the rush into ISDN by many other nations is not occurring in Austria. There are many unresolved issues that require answers before resources will be committed in any significant amount. Pilot projects have to be undertaken to evaluate technical and marketing concerns. Another question relates to the cost of ISDN deployment and who will be responsible for its financing. A companion issue is the relative value of ISDN to the average customer, i.e., cost–benefit analyses. At the present time, the demand required to support ISDN does not appear to exist in Austria nor is it believed that the technology is fully developed. Thus, it would seem that ISDN development will proceed cautiously. It is expected that one–sixth of the PTT's subscribers will have digital technology available by 1990 and then the pace will be escalated.

Data services are provided by the PTT with some competitive services available. In 1986 43,000 terminals were used for data applications. It is expected that many of these terminals will eventually be integrated into ISDN. As in most countries, standardization is important to attaining the potential of data communications. In this regard, Austria often depends on standards which are established abroad and imported.

Videotex is offered in Austria but has not exhibited the growth patterns that were anticipated. One reason may be the high cost of the terminal used with the service. Other reasons for the poor showing are the small number of vendors, the poor quality of information content, unduly long set–up times, and consumer fears about possible abuses of subscriber call data. The targeted household market has not developed and the major users are business establishments.

Other new services have been more successful and continue to grow. There are mobile telephone, Telefax, and cordless telephones. The cellular mobile telephone service began in 1984 and is expanding at the rate of 7,500 stations annually. This growth could have been even greater but initial demand was underestimated which led to installation backups and network bottlenecks.

Connection of Telefax terminals to the public network is relatively easy and the service is inexpensive, both of which enhance its marketability. The service has been aggressively marketed and the number of terminals was expected to increase from 3,000 to 10,000 by year end 1987.

Generally, service is good and rates are high in Austria, while telephone density might be considered on a level below average. The problem of the relatively high number of party lines is expected to diminish as the PTT's objective of eliminating them is implemented. Austria began the digitalization of its network in 1986 and by the next century the entire network will be revamped.

Many aspects of social and economic goals in Austria rely on telecom– munications policy. However, Austrians do not appear willing to leap into the Information Age without some degree of caution. It is recognized that regulatory and technological changes may have to be made, but in a gradual and methodical manner to minimize the impact on consumers. In general, Austrians believe their state run monopoly has and will continue to provide services nationwide on a profitable basis and in a satisfactory manner.

c. Belgium

The operations and regulation of the state controlled PTT (RTT) are the responsibility of the same government entity. RTT does not, however, function as a complete monopoly as regulatory relaxation has been exercised with respect to CPE since 1985. However, the primary telephone set remains under monopoly control. Extension telephones[12] as well as advanced CPE, such as multiline PBXs and fax terminals, are outside the monopoly. RTT must sanction foreign attachments to its network which gives the PTT an added degree of control over competition.

In recognition of limitations placed upon RTT by tight government control, a special commission was established to improve the PTT's ability to react expeditiously to technological developments that would benefit Belgians, not only in the area of telecommunications, but in other areas of national interest. One of the objectives was to provide RTT with more independent operating authority while retaining some control over public interest matters.

The 1986 report emanating from the Commission recommended that the basic infrastructure up to the customer's point of access should remain under monopoly control for efficient operation of the network RTT would be changed into a semigovernment body under the auspices of a ministry. Regulatory control would be administered by a separate entity which is to be responsible for public interest matters. The authorization of equipment function would be transformed from RTT to an autonomous group within the government.

With regard to CPE, the Commission proposed to liberalize all terminals located beyond the access, including the primary instrument. This process may take from three to five years to implement. RTT would be allowed to participate in the CPE market but would have to establish separations from basic services to prevent cross subsidies.

The issue of private network resale also came under scrutiny. Pure private lines dedicated to a particular subscriber would be tariffed on a flat rate basis while different treatment would apply for shared use or resale. In these instances usage based tariffs would be utilized. This strategy would authorize resale and shared use to encourage value added services while retaining revenue producing traffic on the network which could be lost under a rate structure that resells private lines under flat rates.

At the end of 1988, legislation was scheduled to be proposed that is expected to provide more autonomy for RTT and to address the deregulation of CPE and value added services. The relationships between RTT, its regulator, competitors, and consumers will change under the proposed regime. It is not clear if the policy changes will enhance Belgium's participation in the Information Age, but in their view positive steps have already been taken. Several new services have been offered over the last several years along these lines. These include a cellular system, public videotex, teletex, E–Mail, facsimile, packet switching, and videoconferencing.

d. Canada

Telecommunications policy in Canada has generally proceeded on a different track vis–à–vis developments in other nations. For example, in comparison to Europe and the U.S., Canadian policies perhaps occupy a central position between the aggressive deregulation posture of its southern neighbor and that of the Europeans, where government ownership and control has been the rule.

Within Canada, as well as throughout the rest of the world, technological changes are rapidly, taking place, fostering new services and an increasingly competitive environment. The regulation of telecommunications in Canada involves a mix of both federal and provincial jurisdictions, which is similar to the U.S. environment. Bell Canada is by far the largest telephone company. Bell services almost 60 percent of network access lines, compared to the 12 percent share held by the second largest firm, British Columbia Telephone (B.C. Tel) which is owned by GTE.

Subscribership in Canada is among the highest worldwide, with a penetration of 98.5 percent of households in 1987. Recent events have changed the telecommunications climate in Canada. These somewhat parallel actions taken in the U.S., although generally to a lesser degree and at a later date. Because of the analogies that can be drawn in telecommunications policies and development between the two countries, the U.S. experience can provide useful insight or a "laboratory environment" for choosing among alternative future Canadian policy options.

Cable television (CATV) penetration in Canada was about 78.5 percent in 1987, substantially above the comparable figure of 75 percent in 1983. During that same time frame, the number of systems increased from 520 to 812, or 56 percent. These figures are among the highest in the world and reflect the substantial emphasis on cabling and increasing the presence of cable systems throughout Canada. The major catalyst for the great number of cable subscribers is that the CATV companies were able to gain access to the outside plant facilities of telephone companies when regulatory agencies ruled against prohibitions set up by the carriers in the mid 1970s. And, given the high penetration of cable, it has been pragmatic to push forward with experiments to define the requirements of two–way interactive communications using existing cable systems.

The new technologies that have developed in the U.S. and other nations are also being deployed in Canada. Notably, there are many new and innovative services that utilize up–to–date telecommunications technologies. Some of these include the use of digital facilities, satellite mobile radio applications, fiber optic transmission, and meteor–burst technologies. The Integrated Services Digital Network (ISDN) concept has been much publicized. Indeed, Bell Canada is already conducting an ISDN field trial in the National Capital Region.

Cellular technology has been implemented under a policy similar to that in effect in the U.S. That is, two licenses were set aside for each of 23 major metropolitan areas; one for the established LEC; and the second for a company called Cantel Communications, which won the award over several other applicants in December 1983. The entrenched carrier was not permitted to get a head start over Cantel, but could begin service only after suitable interconnection arrangements were provided to Cantel. Neither entity is required to file tariffs but the telephone company must operate through a subsidiary at an arms length separation from its parent.

On the regulatory front, the Canadian Radio–television and Telecommunication Commission (CRTC) approved tariff revisions in 1987 to permit the resale and sharing provisions previously approved. The tariffs allowed for the resale and sharing of carrier services that provide local services (except public telephone service), data services, and voice services other than MTS and WATS. Also, ongoing proceedings have been in progress to develop costing information for the Commission's use in addressing regulatory issues such as cross–subsidization of competitive services by monopoly services. Partial flexible rate regulation was enacted for CNCP in 1987 as the Commission determined the firm was not a dominant carrier except for telegrams and interconnected voice services.

e. China

The development of telecommunications in China lags behind most of the industrial nations but strides are being made to modernize and improve the present system. A substantial number of cities with populations over 100,000 do not have automatic dialing and many smaller cities and villages have only one telephone. In 1984 there was less than one telephone per one hundred population in the People's Republic of China. Yet, despite these somewhat pessimistic statistics, progress is being made to bring China's telecommunications network up to current standards. The realization that a modern telephone system is essential to economic growth and the nation's well being has resulted in a determination of China's leaders to upgrade.

Starting from near ground zero, several changes are anticipated.

- A transformation of responsibility and authority within the government in telecom matters.
- The establishment of a nationwide automated information system to facilitate the goal of developing a modern telecommunications network.
- More financing will come from local jurisdictions as national funding is expected to decline in 1988.

The planned growth rate from 1986 to 1990 is 11.5 percent and includes expenditures of about $5.5 billion. The government's goal is to increase the number of telephones from 6.2 million in 1986 to 33.6 million by the year 2000 which would increase overall phone density to about three percent. In the large metropolitan areas density would increase to 25–35 percent.

Digital switches are being deployed in metropolitan areas while the rural locations will utilize second hand crossbar equipment. All of the crossbar and most of the digital switches will be imported since there is presently limited manufacturing capability in China. The overall plan is to form joint ventures until the country's needs can be met internally.

f. Denmark

The Danish domestic telecommunications network is comprised of state and regionally controlled monopolies with each company having a monopoly within its sphere of operation. Recently, organizational changes took place to improve customer service and simplify the structure of services.

Presently, the carriers have retained monopolies over the primary telephone, telex terminals, PBXs, and modems over 1200 baud. All other CPE is subject to competition although other equipment is subject to approval by another state entity tied–in with the major carrier. In response to the Green Paper, Denmark is planning to liberalize all of its terminal equipment by 1992 and in mid–1988 customers were permitted to buy, rather than lease, telephone sets. Furthermore, the certification of CPE will be conducted by a more neutral approval body.

Information services providers can use the network on a value added basis without limitation if the communication is between two parties. When a third party is involved, though, a license must be obtained by the service provider, and only if a public switched network is used can service be rendered. If the transmission is over leased circuits, third party traffic may not be transmitted unless a license containing specific stipulated terms and conditions is obtained.

Newer type services offered in Denmark include facsimile, teletex, E-Mail, packet switching, videotex, and videoconferencing, and a new high speed switched network began operation during early 1989. Initially, the network will function in areas with large concentrations of businesses.

g. France

The French PTT (DGT, renamed France Telecom) is a state controlled organization that operates both as a monopoly and under a liberal scheme respecting certain services. Telecom has a monopoly of network infrastructure and basic services with two exceptions: closed VANs and networks of public utilities. The monopoly offerings include basic telephone service, Telex, and mobile services. Neither shared use nor resale are permitted on private lines.

Competition is allowed for all CPE including the primary instrument, and Telecom competes in many markets. An independent commission within the Ministry of Post, Telecommunications, and Space is completely responsible for control over competitive services. Customers are permitted to install their own CPE, after obtaining certification from the proper authorities. Other offerings that are open to competition include mobile, paging, value added services, and certain information and transaction services such as E-Mail. Also, a second cellular supplier was expected to begin service in 1989 to provide an alternative to France Telecom's service.

The French network is heavily digitized by worldwide standards. Over 65 percent of the network, both transmission and customer-switching, is digital which has led to services and traffic volumes that do not exist in other countries. The world's largest packet switched public network, Transpac,[13] began operation in 1978 and had over 12,000 customer connections by the end of 1987. A 600 customer ISDN commercial system in Paris has been operating for over one year and nationwide expansion is planned in 1990.

France also has the largest home videotex service in the world with about four million terminals and 8,000 information services. The apparent key to the success of videotex in France is the placement of low cost Minitel terminals in homes and offices. The initial offering was promoted as an electronic telephone directory, but the facilities were subsequently used for many other information services. The general concept in France was to open the network to information providers and their computers, and collect revenues for the use of the network facilities.

The French government is trying to streamline the operations of Telecom while maintaining a competitive posture. The administration is expected to embody liberalism for value added services, local distribution of cable television which is almost nonexistent in France, public telephone booths, teleports, and mobile communications. A 1988 article[14] noted that a mistake made in the U.K. was the creation of a competitor to the established PTT, British Telecom, and this would not be done in France. However, the fate of the agenda under the former French government is uncertain under the regime put in power during 1988.

Major U.S. firms have sought corporate relationships in France to establish themselves as viable market forces. For instance, AT&T has tried to gain control of CGCT while IBM has arranged a joint venture with Sema–Metra and Paribus to supply value added services. Also, a G.E. subsidiary is seeking a partner to provide similar offerings.

h. Germany (FRG)

According to legal interpretations, telecommunications is a government responsibility in the Federal Republic of Germany. This important distinction means the government must provide for basic services. Both regulatory and operational functions are carried out by the Deutsche Bundespost (DBP) and services are provided under both monopoly and competitive conditions by the DBP.

Traditional monopolies exist in local and long distance telephone services. Also, mobile offerings are limited to provision by the DBP as is the primary telephone set. Most other CPE is either provided by the government monopo–list in competition with private vendors or the market is served only by private suppliers. Shared use and resale is permitted except that pure resale of leased lines is not allowed. Furthermore, the rates for leased line capacity used for value added services are usage sensitive to remove tariff arbitrage.

The setting of standards and the authorizations associated with CPE sold or leased by independent vendors are controlled by the DBP. The certifica–tion process tends to take a long time, thereby often placing DBP's competitors at a disadvantage. Recently there has been a relaxation of the technical approval requirements for PBXs and other new equipment which is expected to speed up the process.

In line with market changes, the German government announced in 1988, after two years of development, that it is planning legislation to liberalize and reform telecommunications policy and operations in the nation. Included is the separation of the policy and operational functions of the DBP into different entities. The complete liberalization of CPE, including the primary instrument, is part of the proposal and is expected to be implemented by July 1990. CPE certification will be further streamlined and the entire process is to be transferred to an independent office of the Bundespost.

DBP (Telekom)[15] will retain monopolies in the switched voice markets but will lower barriers to value added services by eliminating restrictions. Private suppliers will be able to offer services to third parties by leasing private lines from Telekom to connect them to their own systems for access–ing information sources and processing data. A key element of this policy change is the replacement of usage sensitive pricing for private lines with flat rates. It is also anticipated that the level of private line rates will be reduced. Another aspect of liberalism is that a second mobile phone company will be allowed to compete in the early 1990s with the present monopoly service operated by DBP. If the legislation is approved without a hitch, by

1992 competition in West Germany will exist for all CPE, business communications via satellite, mobile, and value added services.

However, the political climate appears to be such that delays in the legislative process are now anticipated. Also, the country's unions have exerted pressure to limit the amount of change to protect jobs.   Other opposition has come from individual states who want some say in telecommunications policy, especially with respect to their individual jurisdictions. Because of the apparent delay in the reform plan it is not clear whether any new legislation will be enacted.

i. Italy

Telecommunications in Italy is controlled by the government with several companies having the responsibility for operating the system. Generally, basic services are provided as monopolies, and CPE and value added services are liberalized. Although Italy aspires to participating in the information age and implementing ISDN in the future, regulatory restrictions may impede progress. For instance, neither shared use nor resale is permitted on the network. Also, links from private networks to the public network are banned as is the leasing of private line capacity to third parties. CPE in Italy is completely liberalized, and, thus, the purchase and maintenance of terminal equipment is open to competition.

Recent legislative proposals will relax some of the restrictions related to value added services. It is hoped that passage of the bill will encourage greater participation in these services by providers and, concomitantly, end users. The ultimate goal is for value added services to be offered under free competition. A 1988 law was signed that promised cost based rates and improved customer service. Although many remain skeptical, the philosophical change could be important. Another anticipated improvement would be the consolidation of the various entities that provide telecom services in Italy.

An experimental teletex service was conducted in order to gather operational and marketing information. Videotex trials have also been conducted and service was started in 1981. At the end of 1986 there were 230 information providers and 159,000 pages available to users. The PTT has initiated an ambitious modernization plan to upgrade its facilities and improve service quality. By 1992, it is anticipated that 45 percent of central office switches will be digital.

j. Japan

The Japanese major carrier, NTT, is no longer a government owned entity. The passage of the NTT Company Law in 1984 and the accompanying Telecommunications Business Law (TBL) established NTT as a semi-private corporation subject to competition from outside suppliers. The plan was to phase in up to two-thirds of public ownership of NTT. However, under privatization, NTT will still be regulated by the Ministry of Posts and Telecommunications (MPT) as it vies for business in markets such as CPE, value added services, long distance, and basic services.

The telecommunications industry in Japan consists of a network services sector and an equipment sector. The former is more closely aligned with domestic issues while the latter is export oriented. Traditionally, greater resources have been spent on the export sector thereby resulting in a somewhat inefficient domestic telephone system. Also, this dichotomy has lead to policy setting and control of NTT by two governmental bodies, MPT on the domestic side and the Ministry of International Trade and Industry (MITI) on the export side. These two forces sometimes have opposing, or at best, different, views of how NTT should be operated. Under the new regime MPT and MITI will most likely still disagree on many issues.

Under the TBL two classes of competitors were established and aptly named Class I and Class II firms.

(1) Type I Operators

These are other common carriers subject to regulation who own and operate their own transmission and switching facilities. The MPT must approve Type I operators and in carrying out this process considers financial, economic, operating, and public interest matters. NTT was established as a Type I operator under the new law, and five additional operators were authorized.

(2) Type II Operators

These operators, usually VANs, do not own underlying facilities but purchase capacity from Type I companies and are regulated to a lesser degree. Although Type II operators are not legally barred from offering voice services, there are effective restrictions limiting Type II services to data. Type II operators are further subdivided into two categories: large scale operators that have more than 5,000 lines and offer transmission speeds over 1200 bps; and smaller operators. The first category requires registration and approval by the MPT while only notification of intent to provide service is needed by the second category.

Four criteria must be satisfied by large Type II operators:

1. Universal service: all customers requesting service must be served.
2. Neither preferential treatment nor discrimination must exist between customers.
3. Tariffs must be published.
4. The service must be accessed through the public network.

The impact of the new law was not without problems and controversy. One difficulty is in maintaining clear distinctions between Type I and Type II licenses. Not surprisingly, Type I carriers, and in particular NTT the dominant carrier, wish to offer Type II services, either on a stand alone basis or via subsidiaries without the regulatory requirements of a Type I operator.

New policies and regulations would have to be established to ensure cross subsidies do not occur under such a scenario.

There are also questions about the distinction between voice and data services and whether they can be resold or not, based on restrictions in NTT's tariffs. Modern technology is starting to blur the voice/data distinction thereby leaving issues to be resolved.

NTT has begun to position itself in the new regulatory environment by establishing a number of separated subsidiaries to provide nonbasic services. Under present rules, these changes mean that NTT will have to set up an accounting and cost allocation system that allows tariffs to properly reflect underlying costs for various services. The carrier is also aggressively installing digital facilities and fiber optic technology throughout its national network, and has been offering commercial ISDN based services since 1988. NTT has initially endorsed competition in anticipation of new carriers entering the market and providing versatile and innovative services with everyone getting a piece of the larger pie. However, these expectations have yet to be attained, and actually what has occurred is that the new carriers have simply diverted business from NTT. If this scenario continues, NTT may at some future point in time change its views and policy regarding competition.

At the end of 1988, a subcommittee on administrative reform recommended increased telecommunications competition and re-evaluation of NTT's role in the industry. In light of NTT's dominant position in the domestic market, the carrier should take actions to make the market more competitive. Suggested actions were the provision of subscriber identification numbers to private common carriers, accounting changes, and the provision of more technical information.

k. Spain

The Spanish major service provider is Telefonica which is 46 percent controlled by the government and, therefore, not considered a state owned carrier. For all practical purposes, though, the government regulatory body, the DGT, exercises considerable control over telecommunications matters in Spain.

At the end of 1987 a new telecommunications law was enacted which would further liberalize some of Telefonica's offerings. Network services remained as a monopoly as did the primary telephone set. Competition is allowed for virtually all other types of CPE, including digital terminal equipment. Previously, competition for PBXs existed, but very few alternative suppliers were in the market which accounted for Telefonica's 80 percent market share. Two other factors may have contributed to the virtual monopoly position of the carrier. First, it was responsible for approving all CPE that it would compete against and, second, it is involved in equipment manufacturing through various corporate avenues. Under the new law the certification process was taken away from Telefonica and placed in an independent section of the DGT.

Value added services were opened up to competition with some restrictions and Telefonica expects to vigorously compete in these markets. The carrier now offers facsimile, teletex, packet switching, and videotex services. Previously, the resale of capacity on private lines was not allowed.

Telefonica has set out an ambitious expansion program to reach the next century as traffic is presently growing at nine percent a year. From a base of 9.8 million lines in 1986 (55 percent of households) it plans to expand to 11.5 million lines by 1990 (65 percent), and to 17 million lines by the year 2000 (90 percent). Network digitalization will also be expanded by 1990 from four percent of customer lines to 20 percent and from 13 percent to 36 percent of long distance trunks. Expenditures through 1992 are projected to be $9.5 billion. In changing from a monopoly oriented carrier to a company relying more on market factors, Telefonica will begin to offer new services such as videoconferencing, switched 64 Kbps service, information services, and new types of payphones.

l. United Kingdom

Pursuant to legislation, the former state and monopoly, British Telecom (BT), was privatized in 1984. This version of privatization was somewhat different than that which occurred in Japan. In the U.K., BT was privatized by selling 51 percent of its shares to private investors while the government retained a 49 percent ownership position. In Japan, NTT was privatized by making it into a private company that is owned by the government. Thus, BT seemingly became a carrier outside the direct control of the government. However, under the new arrangement Parliament maintained control of BT via the Office of Telecommunications (OFTEL) which was given regulatory and advisory powers over subject carriers.

Another difference in the U.K. was that a second privately owned carrier, Mercury, was also licensed as a Public Telecommunication Operator (PTO) to provide services similar to those offered by BT on a nationwide basis. Other companies were licensed to provide either particular services, *e.g.*, mobile, or services in a limited geographical area. The policy was established that no other nationwide PTOs would be allowed until 1990.

The licenses for BT and Mercury included the following important conditions.

1.   Universal service is obligatory.
2.   Tariff services for a basket of services are regulated (Retail Price Index less a productivity factor was established as an overall upper bound).[16]
3.   BT is obliged to provide interconnection for licensed systems.
4.   Undue price discrimination is prohibited.
5.   OFTEL has the power to prevent cross subsidization of equipment supply and network operations.

Significant liberalization had taken place in the U.K. since 1981 which affected virtually all services. The advent of privatization increased the degree of liberalization as BT and Mercury compete for most services. Because of its ubiquitous network, BT will most likely be the only carrier that will offer basic residential services throughout the nation. Mercury has a presence in most major business areas and in locations where it can offer service efficiently.

In order for competition to effectively work with respect to Mercury, interconnection with BT's local network was required. Arguments initially arose as to the terms and conditions of how implementation of network access would be accomplished and negotiations broke down.[17] Finally, OFTEL stepped in and decided the matter in a manner which appeared to be favorable to Mercury. The following was determined with regard to Mercury's access of BT's network:

1. Mercury could have access to any of BT's customers.
2. Customers should be able to choose which network would carry the call.
3. For access Mercury would pay the equivalent of a bulk discount on BT's costs, not tariffed rates.
4. For increased capacity, Mercury would pay 50 percent of incremental capacity costs.
5. Mercury would pay the actual cost of making connections.
6. The amount of required capacity had to be furnished by Mercury one year in advance.

BT appears to have joined the competitive fray with vigor. For instance, the carrier quickly reacted to competitive forays by Mercury into unclaimed markets by introducing premium services and reducing the waiting time for installing private lines in major business centers.

The CPE market has been completely competitive since 1984 with the exception of payphones. Approval of CPE from private vendors must be obtained from OFTEL which relies on an independent private sector entity, BABT, for evaluations.[18]

With regard to value added services, no pure resale of basic voice circuits is permitted until mid-1989. Despite this restriction, since 1981 various licenses were issued to encourage entrance into the value added market. This strategy appears to have worked since the U.K. has the largest number of value added services in Europe. The future for value added services in the U.K. is also projected to be good. In 1986 these services accounted for 3.9 percent of the total U.K. services market. The percentage is expected to increase to 7.8 percent in 1990, or double the 1986 figure.

There appears to be some question as to whether the British privatization/liberalization plan is working. A basic thesis of the plan was to encourage improved operating and economic efficiencies in the U.K.'s telecom system. By having BT operate as a normal profit seeking business it was felt that incentives were sufficient for improved operations. The RPI-3 method was supposed to provide the incentive for meeting this goal.

Table VIII-10 shows the results from 1984 to 1987 of the price changes subject to regulation.

Table VIII–10

TWELVE MONTH PERCENTAGE CHANGES AS OF NOVEMBER

	1984	1985	1986	1987
Change in RPI	5.1%	7.0%	2.5%	4.2%
RPI minus 3	2.1	4.0	(0.5)	1.2
Weighted Average Increase	2.0	3.7	(0.3)	0.0
Permitted Increase*	2.1	4.1	(0.1)	1.3

* Reflects carry–over of unused allowances from previous years.

Source: "The Regulation of British Telecom's Prices, A Consultative Document," issued by the Director   General of Telecommunications, OFTEL, January 1988, p. 5.

The overall rate increases all fell within the permitted guidelines. Therefore, the new rates did not need to be justified and no regulatory action was required.

Although the overall increase in rates shown in the above table were lower than allowed under the guidelines, price increases for basic monopoly services were substantially higher.   The rates for exchange lines have increased by over 20 percent for residential and business customers since 1984.   In addition, local calling rates for peak usage increased by 35 percent while standard rates increased by 21 percent and cheap calls increased by 10 percent.[19]

Implementation of the new regulatory regime that applies the RPI–3 formula has increased BT's profits to the point where the rate of return is over 21 percent.   The following table shows BT's rate of return on capital since 1983:[20]

1983	1984	1985	1986	1987
19.5%	17.5%	19.2%	20.2%	21.4%

There was some concern among policymakers that profits were getting excessive.

The quality of service in the U.K. has deteriorated according to various reports, and public complaints are at high levels.   A report issued by OFTEL in October 1987[21] cited numerous statistics showing that BT's service quality was declining.   Some key results of OFTEL's Quality of Service survey are shown in Table VIII–11.   The data all pointed to a worsening situation with respect to service quality.   Many believed this to be too high a price to pay for price cap regulation and privatization.

In this regard, OFTEL in mid–1988 indicated it was going to tighten its control over BT.   Service is supposed to improve and the RPI–3 formula will

Table VIII–11

SERVICE QUALITY IN THE U.K.

	March 1986	March 1987
Service Worsened	10%	23%
Service Improved	12	8

COMPLAINTS

	1985	1986	1987
Jan–Mar	2,476	3,624	4,965
Apr–Jun	2,433	4,356	4,137
Jul–Sep	2,925	4,312	9,846
Oct–Dec	2,083	3,118	4,316

change to RPI–4.5. Thus, beginning in August 1989 and extending to four years, BT's charges for the services in the price control basket are to be 4.5 percent less than the RPI. The basket of services will include current services in the basket, *e.g.*, exchange line rentals and direct dialed calls within the U.K., plus operator assisted calls and directory assistance services. The possibility also exists for establishing price caps for private line services and other services.

C. ISDN in Foreign Markets

Various countries are at different stages toward the implementation of ISDN. This section will delve more into ISDN installation from a global perspective as nations of the world position themselves for the Information Age.

A major theme weaving itself through this chapter is the liberalization, or competitive, policies being pursued by many of the PTTs throughout the world. For instance, in Europe recent developments, *e.g.*, the Green Paper, seek to unite the nations of that continent to achieve continuing economic growth. Improved and current telecommunications technologies and policies will be required to attain this goal. The overall objective is to develop a unified European market, rather than a fragmented series of interconnected individual PTTs, each with its own set of policies and operating criteria.

Although the per capita expenditures for telecommunications projects in Europe has been substantially lower than in the United States and Japan, the market of over 320 million inhabitants[22] provides a vast potential for future sales. A unified telecommunications policy might help tap this market, and

Table VIII–12

ISDN ACCESS LINES – 1993

Belgium	140,000
Denmark	125,000
France	100,000
Germany	1,250,000
Greece	170,000
Ireland	30,000
Italy	825,000
Luxembourg	7,000
Netherlands	280,000
United Kingdom	1,000,000

Source: Organization for Economic Co–operation and Develop–ment (OECD), 1988.

the implementation of ISDN could aid in the development of such an approach. Certainly as we get further into the Information Age, technological advancements will play an important role, not only in Europe, but in other nations as well.

A crucial factor to the success of ISDN on a regional or worldwide basis is the development of standards that will permit viable interconnection. Problems in this area continue to provide barriers to a unified deployment of ISDN. This can be seen from the European experience where several concerns have surfaced. For instance, the major countries, *i.e.*, France, Germany, Italy, and the U.K., are developing ISDN strategies, but technical standards are not often compatible. Also, ten Eurostandards, or NETs, have been developed to provide equipment standards throughout the continent, but approval and implementation has been slow at best. Europe is not the only area experiencing these problems as both Japan and the U.S. have yet to resolve the standards question. In any event, some progress has been made at the national level and between individual countries. Table VIII–12 illus–trates a projection of ISDN penetration by the year 1993 for several European countries.

However, there are some who do not believe ISDN will exhibit significant growth in Europe until the mid–1990s. For instance, one forecaster predicted European shipments of no more than 100,000 by 1993 with 600,000 expected by 1997.[23] The lack of standards and demand, resulting from the inability to develop cost effective applications, are expected to provide the main barriers to ISDN growth.

1. Japan

NTT, the dominant carrier in Japan, is already offering ISDN services as part of its $80–$120 billion Information Network System (INS) program which is expected to be completed by the end of the century. This immense and ambitious undertaking is part of the nation's effort to meet anticipated demand and become a leader in the provision of information services.

The overall plan bypasses a natural progression in switch technology. That is, instead of going from electromechanical central offices (crossbar) to analog electronic switches, the Japanese scheme will jump right to digital technology. The transmission part of the network is also being digitalized. Approximately one–third of long distance facilities and 15 percent of the local loop were equipped with fiber optics in early 1988.

The Japanese VAN market was expected to grow from over three and one–half billion dollars in 1985 to five and one–quarter billion dollars in 1987, or 20 percent per year. Available categories of service include: digital telephone, digital facsimile, digital videotex, data, database access, video conferencing and other video and facsimile services. Some of the individual services are shown in Figure VIII–2.

There also appears to be movement into telecommunications by Japan's power utilities. By 1987 they had over 8,000 miles of embedded fiber optics transmission facilities built along their rights–of–way. Although this capacity was initially installed for in–house capability, several of the electrics have established subsidiaries to sell regional telecommunications services as Type I carriers under the law. Offerings were originally limited to private lines for businesses, but in the future switched services may be provided. Rates for the dedicated services have generally been 15 percent to 20 percent lower than those of NTT. Ultimately, if nationwide services are to be offered, interconnection agreements with NTT and other carriers will be required. The success of such an endeavor will depend, in large part, upon the political and regulatory climate of the time.

2.   France

France is in the vanguard with respect to ISDN related services and expects to have a national network in–place by 1990 and 500,000 B–channels in service by 1995. The reason for the advanced status of France Telecom's ISDN deployment is the high state of digital technology in the country. For instance, over 65 percent of the public switching and transmission facilities are already digitized and only minor changes are required for other parts of the switching plant.

The success of videotex to date in France has brought about an aura of confidence with respect to information services' offerings in the nation. The initial strategy for developing ISDN markets is directed at business customers. The general concept is one of getting a foot–in–the–door and then selling applications to build up usage. Rates for equivalent new services are expected to be about 50 percent of current Transcom rates thereby allowing users to effectively get twice the capacity of the old service for the same price. To assist the marketing effort, France Telecom is leasing CPE that can connect to the ISDN system. Other vendors are expected to enter the market as sales grow.

Figure VIII-2

INFORMATION SERVICES: JAPAN

Home Shopping	allows users to receive information on products for sale and order goods via terminals.
Home Banking	allows users to perform banking functions and obtain pertinent financial information from the home via terminals.
Medical	allows for the transmission of diagnostic data to hospitals as well as other important information relative to particular situations, *e.g.*, accidents, emergencies, etc.
Business Handicap Security Education	allows users with specific requirements to communicate with others.
Videotex	there are various offerings which cater to different market segments. Included are: news and weather, public information, financial services, education, entertainment, business, medical, product distribution, travel, taxes and others.
Customized	two categories are provided, public and business, and are offered via 75 nationwide centers.
Facsimile	this is a large growth area, and new enhanced offerings *e.g.*, color fax, keep rolling out.
Message Services	with paging service, numbers may also be transmitted; NTT's Message Service has turned every push button telephone in Tokyo into an answering machine. Customers receive personal codes accessing NTT's central computer which may record up to 10 half-minute messages per customer at a nominal price.
Public Announcement	these are information/special message offerings geared toward specific markets such as weather, golf, skiing, etc.
Electronic Mail	this service began in early 1987 and includes a fixed monthly rate of about $21 plus charges for usage.
Computing Services	this high growth market is expected to grow from $3.7 billion in 1985 to $8.4 billion in 1991 and $12.7 billion in 1996. These services provide access to technical data and software.
Electronic Directory	allows users to obtain desired information from their terminals.

Source: BRI analysis, Phillips Publishing, and industry data.

France Telecom has already begun to offer ISDN–type services. These offerings provide data file transfers, high definition and high speed facsimile, links between computer aided design or engineering terminals and remote computers, and interconnection of LANs. Figure VIII–3 lists some of the information services available in France.

On another front, France Telecom recently joined with the DBP of West Germany in a venture to offer VAN services in Germany. This deal, which may be a precursor of additional bilateral agreements in Europe, will create new specific value added services and share in existing services. The focal point of the joint venture is to build strong foundations to nullify strong competitive incursions by the likes of IBM, GE, and others. The carrier is presently connecting ISDN services in several major cities and 150,000 customers are projected by 1992, with 500,000 by 1995. The French network is also expected to have the capability of communicating with networks in West Germany, Italy, and the U.K. in 1990 and be directly interconnected after 1992.

3. West Germany

Full digitalization of DBP's network is not expected until the year 2020 which puts it behind its neighbors. However, ISDN trials are now underway and service at selected locations is slated for early 1989. The DBP appears to recognize a need for digitizing its network as its traffic is growing at a rate whereby the current network cannot be sustained for many more years. In this regard, substantial savings in costs, space, and network capacity have been found to exist with the installation of digital equipment and facilities according to analyses undertaken by DBP[24]. Thus, the company's plans are to move ahead with digital deployment. The relatively long time horizon is due to the predominant analog technology now in use, but, DBP does intend to provide ISDN before the year 2020, though, as it will arrange facilities to connect customers to ISDN switches. The goal is that by 1993 every customer will have some access to ISDN.[25] The new services that will be offered include teletex, telefax, data, and picture transmission. Figure VIII–4 is a list of information services.

4. Canada

At the end of 1988 Bell Canada was scheduled to provide the gateway access to a wide range of information services from home terminals in Montreal. The offerings will include home banking, home shopping, and news services. Financial institutions and local merchants will provide the actual services via the gateway and end users will access the services from terminals costing about $8 per month. The services can also be accessed from customer owned PCs using a software package provided by Bell.

The technology to implement ISDN is being deployed in Bell Canada operating territory as the portion of working lines connected to digital switches increased from 24 percent in 1986 to 30 percent in 1987, a 25 per–

Figure VIII-3

INFORMATION SERVICES: FRANCE

Videotex   the number of terminals installed in homes and offices
                        are expected to increase from 2.2 million in 1986 to over
                        7.0 million in 1990. The following types of offerings are
                        available: banking, services, technological data, mailboxes,
                        consumer shopping, education, employment, recreation,
                        government services, health services, professional
                        services, real estate and social services.

Electronic   allows users to obtain desired information from their
Directory   terminals. Listings of all the nation's telephones are
                        available. First three minutes are free.

Message   allows users to send and retrieve messages from their
Services   terminals.

Facsimile   two public services are available.

Source: BRI analysis, Phillips Publishing, and industry data.

Figure VIII-4

INFORMATION SERVICES: WEST GERMANY

Videotex   over 900 different services are offered to over 1.5
                        million users. The following types of offerings are
                        available: banking services, consumer information
                        services, business oriented services, travel, leisure,
                        sports, health, and services for the handicapped.

Temex   telemetry and alarm services.

Electronic   telephone white pages and personal directories
Directory

Electronic Mail   mailbox service and access to/from telex, teletex, and
                        telefax is available. Annual subscription fee is about
                        $53.

Source: BRI analysis, Phillips Publishing, and industry data.

cent growth rate. By 1992 it is anticipated that 58 percent of lines will have
access to digital offices. Similar statistics for British Columbia Telephone
(B.C. Tel) are even more dramatic. In 1983 only about two percent of local
lines were connected to digital switches whereas in 1987 the figure had grown
to 59 percent. In 1993 about 93 percent of working lines will have digital
access.

It is clear that the major carriers in Canada are constructing and deploy-
ing digital networks. In a 1988 public hearing held in Vancouver regarding
B.C. Tel's revenue requirements, a company spokesman responded that indeed
the carrier was "in fact digitizing the network."[26] Millions of dollars have
been expended by the telcos to digitize the network, and ISDN is the focal

point of much of these costs. This is despite the fact that many important questions pertaining to the implementation of services utilizing the ISDN concept are far from resolution. As noted by B.C. Tel at the public hearing, standards for implementation of ISDN have yet to be established in Canada[27] The company witness also said that "we have yet to define any ISDN based services,"[28] thereby suggesting a certain degree of uncertainty regarding ISDN implementation.

However, as the telcos' networks become digitized, the inherent econo-mies associated with the new technologies, plus the economies of scale and scope associated with the monopoly positions of the telcos, will tend to preclude effective competition. Meanwhile, the deployment of digital technology, that has mainly been financed by monopoly ratepayers, will also create excess capacity that the telcos will try to fill up with new and attrac-tively priced services.

The Canadian carriers offer many digital, data, and enhanced services. Some of these are:

- Dataroute: a dedicated digital private line service.
- Datapac: a shared digital network service based on packet switching.
- Datalink: a pay–as–you–use shared digital service.
- Envoy 100: essentially an electronic mail service.
- iNET 2000: provides a gateway to computer oriented data bases.
- Traderoute: an electronic data exchange service.
- Exten: a voice messaging service.

Figure VIII–5 lists information services presently being provided in Canada.

5.   United Kingdom

The British Telecom version of ISDN is called IDA (Integrated Digital Access). BT has offered a single line 80 Kbps service since mid–1985. Although large customers such as IBM, DEC, and International Computers, Ltd. have subscribed to the service, projected demand has not been attained. Trials for basic ISDN type services are scheduled for 1988 after being delayed from mid–1987. One problem seen with IDA is that it is a proprietary system and may not be completely compatible with ISDN systems of other nations. Figure VIII–6 is a list of U.K. information services.

6.   Italy

The Italian network is in need of modernizing before ISDN can be implemented to any significant degree. With a telephone density of 33 percent and the percentage of digital facilities at 12 percent, Italy's PTT, STET, has plans to upgrade the network by the year 2000. Under moderniza-tion, telephone density is expected to improve to over 40 percent by 1992. ISDN tests are being conducted to ascertain if demand exists and whether ISDN services can be offered on a viable basis.

Figure VIII-5

INFORMATION SERVICES: CANADA

Videotex

various types of offerings are available. These are: information   for farmers, financial news, travel/tourism, specific weather data, education, banking, MIS, and product information.

Electronic Directory

various directories related to particular user interests can be accessed by customers free of charge.

Electronic Mail

the E-Mail market grew from $15 million in 1985 to $19 million in 1986. Mailbox services and access from fax machines are offered. User to user services are also provided.

Transactional

electronic funds transfer at point of sale is provided. Online inventory control and credit verification services are offered.

Databases

access to and retrieval from electronic databases; NET 2000 is a gateway to information services.

Private Line

customers can create and customize their own private line networks over digital facilities.

Source: BRI analysis, Phillips Publishing, and industry data.

Figure VIII-6

INFORMATION SERVICES: UNITED KINGDOM

Videotex

provides for the following types of offerings: home banking, financial, weather, education, home shopping, travel, handicapped services, legal, health, and insurance. Basic quarterly charge is about $30 for   business and $11 for residential customers.

Transactional

credit verification from retail establishments.

Computing

access to electronic databases.

Electronic Mail

Telecom Gold, BT's, E-Mail offering, is growing rapidly, 100 percent per year.

Voice Mail

voicebank was started in 1985 by BT as a computer messaging system.

Electronic Directory

various searches may be done by users free of charge.

Public Service Announcements

various PSAs and answering services are provided.

Source: BRI analysis, Phillips Publishing, and industry data.

Notes

1. *Statistical Abstract of the United States 1987,* U.S. Dept. of Commerce, 107 ed., p. 827.

2. *Communications Week,* April 11, 1988, p. 52.

3. A good deal of the information regarding Europe is developed from a paper authored by Jurgen Muller entitled "Cable Policy in Europe," *Telecommunications Policy,* September 1987, p. 259.

4. Mercury is the equivalent of MCI or US Sprint in the United States.

5. The TBL stipulated the basic principles and structure regarding telecommunications business in Japan. Notably, it abolished the domestic and international monopolies held by NTT and KDD, respectively. A second companion law, the Nippon Telegraph and Telephone Law, converted NTT to a private joint stock company.

6. Organizationally, OFTEL is the administrative arm in telecommunications matters for the Secretary of State for Industry.

7. BT still maintained a large portion of the market, though, with an 80 percent share that is expected to decline to 60 percent by 1990.

8. *Financial Times,* (London), May 17, 1985.

9. *Communications Week,* May 2, 1988, p. 6.

10. American companies such as IBM and AT&T were prime movers of VAN liberalization in Japan.

11. Under Judge Greene's pronouncement in 1988, the RHCs will have a more expanded role in the provision of information services as they will offer gateway services to information service providers.

12. Extension phones may be purchased from RTT or private vendors.

13. Transpac is a joint venture, two thirds owned by France Telecom and the remainder belongs to private investors.

14. *Communications Week,* March 28, 1988, p. 14.

15. The new name of the telecommunications entity will be Telekom.

16. This is the now famous RPI-3 formula, where three percent was chosen as the productivity factor. Debates continue as to the validity of the entire formula as well as the somewhat arbitrarily selected productivity factor. The basket of services include exchange line rentals for business and residential subscribers, as well as local and domestic trunk calls.

17. This situation was analogous to the problems between the OCCs and BOCs in the U.S. regarding access to the local network.

18. As noted earlier, BT played a major role in evaluating competitors' CPE during the initial years of the new regulatory regime.

19. *OFTEL,* p. 5.

20. *OFTEL,* p. 6.

21. "British Telecom's Quality of Service 1987," *OFTEL,* October 1987.

22. This compares to about 240 million in the U.S. and 120 million in Japan.

23. *Communications Week,* November 21, 1988, p. 28.

24. "ISDN and the telecommunications environment," reprint from the *1986 Yearbook of the Deutsche Bundespost,* p. 8.

25. *Id.*, p. 26. It would appear that remote access to ISDN switches will be provided in a number of instances.

26. Transcript of public hearing, "British Columbia Telephone Company – Revenue Requirement Proceeding for the Years 1988 and 1989," Vancouver, B.C., August 31, 1988, Vol. 7, p. 1064.

27. *Ibid.*, pp. 1067–68.

28. *Ibid.*, p. 1069.

CHAPTER IX

INDUSTRY TRENDS, POLICY ISSUES, AND FUTURE DEVELOPMENTS

A. Overview

On the eve of the 1990s, U.S. telecommunications is still seeking its new identity. Whipsawed by the technological, competitive, and policy upheaval of the 1980s, the industry is still emerging in terms of its structural orientation. The preceding eight chapters have explored in some detail the evolution of the sector through the analytical framework of industrial organization, bringing us to the present. At this juncture it seems appropriate (and perhaps brazen!) to venture a reasoned viewpoint concerning the future directions of the industry.

This prospective look is probably best attempted as it relates to the "Huberian view" of the new telecommunications industry. In *The Geodesic Network: 1987 Report on Competition in the Telephone Industry,* Peter Huber sets forth his view that the nature of the local public switched network (LPSN) is being transformed in fundamental technological ways. The exchange network historically has been pyramid like in structure such that a vertical hierarchy of switches has been developed in the basic "nodes" of the network. This form evolved because switching was much more expensive than transmission "links," and local operating companies wielded "bottleneck" control over entry to this network through the relatively few gateway switches. According to Prof. Huber, the MFJ's central premise is that local exchange service for low volume customers is a natural monopoly because of perceived steadily decreasing costs and universal access.[1]

Moreover, Huber asserts that the "horizontally stratified telecommunications marketplace" afforded by the pyramid infrastructure "will not survive."[2] Instead, the proliferation of relatively inexpensive switching compared to transmission nodes will lead to a profusion of nodes and links called a "geodesic network." The product of significant technological changes, the latter construct causes processing and control functions to be decentralized. The resulting dispersion of electronic intelligence is perceived to be irreversible, and the geodesic network would be "managed by a small number of giant, vertically integrated firms, AT&T among them."[3] Thus, the "central paradox of the information age" in Huber's view is that the "dispersion of consumption is matched by consolidation of production."[4] Bottleneck control would be eroded through the emergence of a geodesic network which could support multiple interconnected, vertically integrated suppliers.

Concerning specifically the local exchange, the Huber report observes that its:

> . . . assessment of entry–level network nodes, switching capacities, and economic and regulatory indicators all support the same conclusion. Competition in local switching services has begun to take root, but remains patchy . . . serious competition to serve smaller users has not arrived [but] [l]arge users may draw on a much more significant range of available switching options . . . . large users now use as much private [*i.e.,* PBX] as public switching capacity.[5]

The analysis emphasizes that the "building blocks" for competition in the local exchange are "falling into place."[6]   With loyalties having ostensibly "faded quickly," the former Bell System companies are portrayed as engaging in extraregional "head–to–head" competition in such areas as shared tenant services (STS), yellow pages, pay phones, and PBXs v. Centrex (see Figure IX–1).[7] Huber emphasizes that local competition will likely develop at a rapid pace during the next few years.   Networking is seen as "highly contagious": as the number of new nodes increases, the interconnection possibilities grow geometrically.[8]   The report stresses that state regulations that hinder the emergence of new nodes are "still regrettably common," and that in combination with the MFJ's line of business restrictions, will impliedly prevent the vigors of competition to fully take hold.[9]

Some claim that this theory is basically flawed. For example, AT&T asserts that the geodesic model is fundamentally at odds with the principles of engineering and network design which were stipulated to by the parties to *United States* v. *Am. Tel. & Tel. Co.*[10]   Others, *e.g.*, Economics and Technology, Inc., aver that switching costs are declining *more slowly* than transmission costs and that there is no evidence supporting the Huber contention that business dial tones are "more likely" to be generated by PBXs than by central office switches.[11]

It would certainly appear that even if the Huber model is an accurate predictor of future occurrences, the theory's premise of a substantial erosion of the BOCs' bottleneck control over their respective local exchanges has thus far not been achieved. Numerous studies of the incidence of bypass have been undertaken which have shown that existing levels do not represent significant incursions into local operating companies' (especially BOC) exchange markets.[12] In many cases, revenue growth by local companies has at least partially offset or even exceeded in magnitude the losses attributable to bypass. As discussed in Chapter VI, a number of public policy makers apparently do not believe that the current level of use of nonLEC services represents a threat to either universal telephone service or the financial viability of the local companies.

For example, Judge Greene of the MFJ court continues to believe that it would be premature to remove existing line of business restrictions because there is "overwhelming evidence" that the local exchange monopoly has not sufficiently eroded.[13] Earlier, in specific response to the Huber report, he pointed to the

> . . . complete lack of merit of arguments that economic,
> technological, or legal changes have substantially eroded or
> impaired the Regional Company bottleneck monopoly power
> . . . It is clear, therefore that no substantial competition
> exists at the present time in the local exchange service.[14]

Other government decision makers tend to agree about retention of local bottleneck control by the BOCs. Since divestiture, the House Small Business Committee (1984), NTIA (1987), and even the FCC (1985–1988) and the Justice Department (1986) have concluded that local bypass activity has not been significant.[15]

Figure IX-1

COMPETITION AMONG FORMER BELL SYSTEM ENTITIES

AMERITECH (AM)

SWB	Yellow Pages
AT&T	Pay Phones
AT&T	PBX vs. CTX
BS	STS
USW	Yellow Pages
BS	Yellow Pages

BELL ATLANTIC (BA)

SWB	Yellow Pages
AT&T	PBX vs. CTX
AT&T	Pay Phones
NY	Yellow Pages
BS	Yellow Pages
BS	STS
AM	STS
USW	Yellow Pages

BELLSOUTH (BS)

SWB	Yellow Pages
AM	Yellow Pages
AT&T	Pay Phones
AT&T	PBX vs. CTX
USW	Yellow Pages
AM	STS

PACIFIC TELESIS (PT)

SWB	Yellow Pages
AT&T	Pay Phones
AT&T	PBX vs. CTX
BS	STS
AM	STS
USW	Yellow Pages
BS	Yellow Pages
NY	Yellow Pages

SOUTHWESTERN BELL (SWB)

AT&T	Pay Phones
AT&T	SH Bypass
AT&T	PBX vs. CTX
AM	Yellow Pages
BS	STS
AM	STS
USW	Yellow Pages
BS	Yellow Pages

U S WEST (USW)

SWB	Yellow Pages
AM	Yellow Pages
AT&T	Pay Phones
AT&T	PBX vs. CTX
BS	STS
AM	STS
BS	Yellow Pages
NY	Yellow Pages

NYNEX (NY)

SWB	Yellow Pages
AT&T	Pay Phones
AT&T	SH Bypass
AT&T	PBX vs. CTX
BS	STS
AM	STS
USW	Yellow Pages
BS	Yellow Pages

Source: Annual Reports and P. Huber, The Geodesic Network: 1987 Report on Competition in the Telephone Industry, Fig. L. 11.

Moreover, in a March 1987 report critiquing the Huber analysis, the Ad Hoc Telecommunications Users Committee and the International Communications Association cite data from *The Geodesic Network* which demonstrates the dominance retained by the BOCs.[16] More particularly, the two large user organizations identify a 96 to 99 percent market share range for the Bell entities with respect to access services, and greater than 99 percent for local exchange services.[17]

Thus, the direct customer–to–customer connectivity predicted by Prof. Huber has apparently not materialized thus far as local exchange facilities remain an integral part of an overwhelming majority of communications traffic in this country.   In short, the so-called "dispersion of consumption" has not developed to a substantial degree.

In addition, the evidence appears to lend only limited support to Huber's "consolidation of production" hypothesis. As documented in Chapters VI and VII, industry concentration in the local exchange and interexchange service markets remains high during the post divestiture era. In the former case, the individual franchised local carriers have demonstrated varying degrees of vertical integration. The BOCs and their affiliates, of course, are barred from engaging in long distance services and manufacturing, as well as information content. The RBOCs have recently been permitted by the MFJ court to provide information "gateways" and other low level transport, and these entities have subsequently introduced a number of such services. With respect to interexchange and manufacturing, one can only speculate as to RBOC activity in these areas if they were permitted unfettered entry; for at least certain of the companies (*e.g.*, Pacific Telesis), the interest in such integration appears to be less than for information services.[18]

For other, less constrained local operating companies, the attitude toward vertical integration is mixed. GTE, for one, is retreating from its traditional interexchange service and manufacturing businesses. By agreement, GTE will relinquish all ownership interest in US Sprint to United Telecom by 1990 and its portion of the joint venture with AT&T to develop and manufacture central office switching systems by the year 2004.[19] At the same time, GTE continues to pursue the information services market. On the other hand, United is obviously strengthening its commitment to interexchange provisioning, and such companies as Cincinnati Bell and Southern New England Telephone Company, the former Bell System entities, continue to participate in the market.

On balance, the available evidence would not appear to validate the geodesic network thesis in the current environment. Significant erosion of the local exchange bottleneck has not yet occurred, as acknowledged by both Prof. Huber and the Justice Department.[20] Although Huber's anticipated "small number of giant, vertically integrated firms" may well emerge, especially if the RBOCs' line of business constraints are removed, this predicted structural form does not currently exist. Instead, dominant firms prevail in their respective local exchanges. Further, no substantial correlation between state recision of entry barriers and the emergence of effective competition in the local exchange has apparently been established.

There is also no *de facto* consensus at present that "switching is cheap" and "transmission is expensive," which is an essential element of any developing geodesic network.[21]   Thus far, the vision of "multilateral connectivity" directly between end users has not been realized as LECs aggressively protect their markets with new central office based offerings that afford customers the network control they seek.

The past may not be prologue, of course, but certain signs suggest that the geodesic world of dissipated market power may not actually develop, at least in the short term. Substantial advantages of incumbency may represent significant impediments to effective competition in a dominant firm setting, at least in the short run. For example, one such advantage revealed during Bethesda Research Institute, Ltd.'s surveys of users in Maryland, New York, New Jersey, Pennsylvania, and the District of Columbia (see above) centers on the notion of "ceteris paribus." Specifically, participants were asked, "other things being equal, would you choose the local telephone company or a bypass provider as the supplier of your local communications needs?" In all five surveys, an overwhelming majority of respondents chose the local exchange carrier.

Considerable evidence exists that *nonprice* factors are typically more important than price in user decisions about choice of local service providers, and this finding in tandem with "brand loyalty" manifestations may tend to preserve an incumbent firm's market dominance.[22] In BRI's surveys of users in the four states, "responsiveness to customer needs" was ranked first, on average, in each of these states. In the District of Columbia, "technical quality of service" was accorded number one priority.[23] In Maryland, large users also rated technical service quality, financial resources of supplier, experience of supplier, and the provider's reputation ahead of price, which was ranked second by small users (see Table IX–1). In New York, for the large users polled, price followed such nonprice factors as responsiveness to needs, maintenance, technical quality of service, experience, reputation, user control, and financial resources (Table IX–2).

BRI's New Jersey study disaggregated respondents by "bypassers" and "nonbypassers." The former group placed price behind responsiveness, technical service quality, and reputation, while nonbypassers deemed responsiveness, maintenance, experience, reputation, and technical service quality to be more important than price (Table IX–3). In Pennsylvania, the responsiveness factor also earned first place, but this criterion and five others (technical quality of service, maintenance, large startup investment, reputation, and experience) ranked higher than price (see Table IX–4). In the District of Columbia, customer responsiveness ranked first for nonbypassers who also rated price number seven. For bypassers, however, technical service quality, maintenance, and responsiveness were the top three criteria, while price finished eleventh out of twelve (Table IX–5).

The greater weighting assigned to *nonprice* factors by users is critical to local operating companies' ability to successfully meet the bypass challenge: service quality and other related factors by nature are subject to the control of the companies themselves. Unlike price, which must typically be approved

Table IX–1

BYPASS DECISION MAKING CRITERIA
AVERAGE RANKINGS
BRI Maryland User Survey

	Ranking	
Criterion	Large Users	Small Users
Responsiveness to Customer Needs	1	1
Technical Quality of Service	2	5
Financial Resources of Supplier	3	4
Experience of Supplier	4	8
Reputation of Supplier	5	7
Price	6 (tie)	2
Statewide Presence	6 (tie)	6
Large Start–Up Cost	8	3
Innovation Performance	9	9

Table IX–2

BYPASS DECISION MAKING CRITERIA
AVERAGE RANKINGS
BRI New York User Survey

Criterion	Ranking
Responsiveness to Customer Needs	1
Maintenance	2
Technical Quality of Service	3 (tie)
Experience of Supplier	3 (tie)
Reputation of Supplier	5
User Control	6 (tie)
Financial Resources of Supplier	6 (tie)
Price	8
Large Start–Up Costs	9
Statewide Presence	10
Innovation Performance	11

by the relevant regulatory commission, these other criteria allow the BOCs and Independent telephone companies to have much more autonomy in determining their market place destinies.

Even for those customers who consider price to be a major criterion in choosing their local service provider, the local exchange carriers apparently enjoy a "premium price" advantage. For example, in both Pennsylvania and the District of Columbia numerous users indicated that they would continue to

Table IX–3

BYPASS DECISION MAKING CRITERIA
AVERAGE RANKINGS
BRI New Jersey User Survey

	Ranking	
Criterion	Bypassers	NonBypassers
Responsiveness to Customer Needs	1	1
Technical Quality of Service	2	5
Reputation of Supplier	3	4
Price	4	6
Maintenance	5	2
Financial Resources of Supplier	6	7
Experience of Supplier	7	3
Statewide Presence	8	11
User Control	9	10
Large Start–Up Cost	10	8
Innovation Performance	11	9

Table IX–4

BYPASS DECISION MAKING CRITERIA
AVERAGE RANKINGS
BRI Pennsylvania User Survey

Criterion	Ranking
Responsiveness to Customer Needs	1
Technical Quality of Service	2
Maintenance	3
Large Start–Up Cost	4
Reputation of the Company	5
Experience of the Company	6
Price	7
Financial Resources	8
Innovation Performance	9
User Control	10
Statewide Presence	11
Ability to Share or Resell to Others	12

subscribe to the local Bell company if that entity had prices as much as 10 percent higher than the prospective bypass provider (Tables IX–6 and IX–7). In New York and New Jersey a similar price advantage was found (Maryland respondents were not asked this line of questioning).

Table IX–5

BYPASS DECISION MAKING CRITERIA
AVERAGE RANKINGS
BRI District of Columbia User Survey

	Ranking	
Criterion	Bypassers	NonBypassers
Technical Quality of Service	1	3
Maintenance	2	2
Responsive to Customer Needs	3	1
Financial Resources	4	4 (tie)
Reputation of the Company	6 (tie)	4 (tie)
Geographic Coverage	6 (tie)	10
Large Start–Up Cost	8	8
User Control	9 (tie)	9
Innovation Performance	9 (tie)	11
Price	11	7
Ability to Share or Resell to Others	12	12

Thus, Huber's prophecy that traditional loyalties have faded quickly is inaccurate. These findings regarding incumbency would seem to suggest that the market dominance currently enjoyed by local exchange carriers, particularly the Bell entities, can be largely preserved through carrier attentiveness to the service and feature needs of their customers. Indeed, current BOC and GTE programs to accelerate the introduction of fiber optics into the local loop and the deployment of ISDN capabilities appear to be just as a potent market strategy. Successful implementation of this approach would solidly position these incumbents for participation in the nascent Information Age.

Such advantages of incumbency coupled with the *Geodesic Network's* prediction of a "few gigantic firms" do not seem to sustain Huber's claim that "the geodesic network will support both integration and competition."[24] While some notion of competition is possible in a tight oligopoly, economic theory would suggest that mutual interdependence and conscious parallelism would be the result. Nonprice rivalry and "me too" pricing would likely be the hallmarks of such an arrangement as interdependence supplants "full" competition.

Real world examples of such mutual interdependence may include the interexchange service industry and the vaunted IBM–AT&T rivalry. As discussed earlier, the IX market appears to fit the dominant firm price leadership model, with AT&T's price changes generally eliciting parallel "me too" responses from MCI and US Sprint.[25] Despite the hoopla surrounding the anticipated showdown between AT&T and IBM,[26] confrontation seems to have given way to coexistence. The battle for each other's turf has been anything but spectacular. Since divestiture, AT&T has formally attempted

Table IX-6

USER PERCEPTIONS OF IMPORTANCE OF PRICE VERSUS NONPRICE
FACTORS IN LOCAL CARRIER SELECTION
Bell of Pennsylvania

Percent of Users Staying with Bell Services

Type of Organization	Bell Percent Higher Price	Equivalent Nonprice Features	Superior Responsiveness by Bell	Superior Technical Service by Bell	Superior Innovation Performance by Bell	Superior Financial Staying Power for Bell
Government	5	100%	100%	100%	100%	100%
	10	0	100	100	100	50
	20	0	0	0	0	0
Hospital	5	50	50	50	50	50
	10	0	0	50	0	0
	20	0	0	0	0	0
Manufacturing	5	78	100	100	89	89
	10	22	78	89	44	44
	20	0	0	22	0	0
University	5	100	100	100	100	100
	10	0	100	100	100	100
	20	0	50	0	0	0
Banks	5	100	100	100	100	-
	10	100	100	100	100	-
	20	0	50	50	50	-
TOTAL	5	78%	94%	94%	83%	83%
	10	28%	72%	89%	56%	50%
	20	0%	6%	17%	6%	0%

Table IX-7

USER PERCEPTIONS OF IMPORTANCE OF PRICE VERSUS NONPRICE
FACTORS IN LOCAL CARRIER SELECTION
C&P Telephone Company

Percent of Users Staying with C&P Services

Type of Organization	C&P Percent Higher Price	Equivalent Nonprice Features	Superior Responsiveness by C&P	Superior Technical Service by C&P	Superior Innovation Performance by C&P	Superior Financial Staying Power for C&P
Government	5	50%	100%	100%	100%	100%
	10	0	33	0	0	0
	20	0	0	0	0	0
Services	5	68	100	95	79	89
	10	42	79	84	42	67
	20	5	38	37	16	17
Manufacturing	5	50	100	100	75	100
	10	0	33	75	0	50
	20	0	0	0	0	0
Regulated Entities	5	50	100	100	100	75
	10	0	67	75	0	25
	20	0	33	0	0	0
Financial Organizations	5	75	75	75	75	75
	10	25	75	75	25	50
	20	0	25	0	0	0
Retail	5	100	100	100	100	100
	10	0	67	50	0	50
	20	0	0	0	0	50
Construction	5	100	100	100	100	100
	10/20	0	0	0	0	0
TOTAL	5	67%	98%	94%	83%	88%
	10	25%	67%	77%	26%	53%
	20	0%	27%	20%	9%	12%

entry into the computer equipment business, losing one billion dollars before taxes in 1986 and $300 million in 1987. IBM has essentially withdrawn from the long distance business that it once sought to participate in extensively through ownership interests in first, Satellite Business Systems (SBS), and subsequently MCI. Notwithstanding these cross market forays, AT&T remains primarily a service company, deriving some 80 percent of its net income from long distance offerings.   In turn, IBM's major arena is still computer equipment, deriving 60 percent of its operating profits from mainframe computers alone.[27]

Interestingly, the two giant firms shed contrasting light on the validity of Prof. Huber's hypotheses. For example, he predicts that during the evolution to the geodesic network, the

> . . . major market survivors will not look like MCI . . . They will look like MCI–Rolm–IBM. Or, for that matter, like the AT&T that was still is, and will be even more so in the future -- a vertically integrated provider of end–to–end connections.[28]

In fact, this nexus has been largely severed as MCI has repurchased IBM's common stock holdings in the long distance company, and IBM has sold the bulk of its Rolm division's PBX assets which had been acquired in 1985 to Siemens AG.[29] However, the latter and IBM have agreed to form a joint PBX sales unit.

AT&T continues its quest for integration of communications capability. For example, as asserted in a recent advertisement:

> In 1908, AT&T announced its vision of the future: universal service . . . "a phone in every home."

> On February 12, 1985 at a major telecommunications conference, AT&T Network Systems announced a revolution- ary new vision of the future for the telecommunications industry: universal information services . . . So that network providers everywhere can give any customer any kind of voice, data or image service in any place, at any time, in any combination, with maximum convenience and economy.

This "vision" is apparently being implemented through internal diversification and acquisition, but also through numerous domestic and international joint ventures (see *supra*).

Thus, certain current trends may be perceived as lending support to the Huber model, at least on the supply side. As discussed above, large busi- nesses and residences are very much attracted to the concept of "one stop shopping," *i.e.*, reliance on a single source, for their telecommunications needs. The RBOCs, AT&T, and many Independents have indicated their belief in this corporate objective.[30] For example, under *Computer III,* BellSouth and Ameritech telephone companies have been able to combine their service and

CPE operations.[31]   Similarly, AT&T and such Independents as Rochester Telephone Company have sought one stop capability.[32] Some companies have teamed together to win lucrative contracts, *e.g.,* the $108 million award to Illinois Bell/US Sprint to build a new "backbone" voice, data and video network.[33]

Vertical integration would be one means of accomplishing this. Moreover, the Independent telephone industry may be on the verge of another consolidation movement reminiscent of the mid–to–late 1960s. Pressures for such an acquisition movement would include, *inter alia,* the Independents' desire for growth in a mature business and the ability to boost stock prices through restructuring.[34]   Consolidation of the local telephone company industry, too, would be consistent with the notion of "a small number of giant firms," whether achieved through the pursuit of growth, diversification, or scale economies.

Thus, a plausible telecommunications market structure for the remainder of the century might be a hierarchy of firms offering a variety of information services and associated premises equipment. The larger "core" entities would attempt to offer a panoply of services through a broadband fiber–based ISDN network, while much smaller firms would seek "niches" in which to market their specialized wares.

Unlike in the Huber model, however, considerable market power would likely persist. This would obtain especially for "core" telephone companies such as the RBOCs, Independents, and AT&T, whose resources, technical "know–how," aggressiveness, and advantages of incumbency (*e.g.,* "familiarity" to the public as "the telephone company") would attract overwhelmed small users and many large ones as well. These customers would essentially be seeking "safe harbor" and noncomplex yet "full service" sources of supply. Customer premises equipment would abound in the form of personal and larger computers, often in a LAN setting, and "fax" machines in the typical business environment and in many homes.

For reasons of security, specialized needs or cost,[35] some large users would develop their own private networks, utilizing electronic digital switching, T–1 systems and broad fiber. However, all would continue to subscribe to the modern public switched network, which would meet their growing needs for data as well as voice services. The network would also afford a high level of user control without the network management headaches of a private system. Hence, the geodesic network premise of a dispersed demand would be realized only in part as customers across the user spectrum continue to rely heavily on a sophisticated public switched network for local and long distance needs. A pullback by some major users, *e.g.,* Merrill Lynch, Texas Air Corp., from reliance on private networks in favor of alternative (carrier) solutions has already begun.[36] Reasons for the change apparently center on cost and the difficulty of hiring the necessary skilled staffs to operate and maintain in–house networks.[37]

Given this broad brush forecast of industrial organization and demand characteristics, the following will discuss the anticipated role of regulation and antitrust enforcement.

B. New System of Access Charges, ONA, Collocation

As described in earlier chapters, U.S. telecommunications policy during the post divestiture era has undergone a number of fundamental changes. With the onset of interexchange competition and the breakup of AT&T's Bell System, a new system of local carrier recovery of exchange access costs was developed as a replacement for the "division of revenues" (DRs) type of reimbursement. Implemented initially in 1984, access charges were to be paid by both interexchange carriers ("carrier common line charges," or CCLC) and by end users ("customer access line charges," or CALC).

The FCC has established four basic goals for its access charge program: (1) preservation of universal service; (2) elimination of discrimination; (3) removal of incentives for exchange bypass; and (4) encouragement of network efficiency. Embracing this credo, the Commission's long term objective is to decrease carrier charges (especially for switched services) and to boost end user prices (now called the subscriber line charge, or SLC). Ultimately it is intended that CCLC would be reduced to zero while residences and small businesses, and possibly large users, would be charged rising end user rates. The SLC will increase to as much as $3.50 per month per line by April 1, 1989.

Coupled with a fully implemented "equal access" program for IXCs, the access charge system employed by the FCC and certain states should tend to deter large, price–conscious users from abandoning the LPSN and to bolster IXC competition. These actions should help to preserve universal service, ameliorate some amount of the low–level bypass that currently exists, and keep users on the public network during the transition to the "network of the future" (*viz.,* broadband ISDN).

Open network architecture (ONA) is a form of equal access for enhanced service providers. On February 1, 1988 the Regional Companies and AT&T filed their ONA plans as directed by the FCC. As shown in Appendix IX–A, the Bell Companies submitted a variety of "basic service elements" (BSEs) as required by the Commission, as well as the less unbundled "basic serving arrangements" (BSAs).[38] The BSEs, which the FCC requires that the Regionals make available to customers within one year of regulatory approval of their plans, are grouped under BSAs with complementary network services (CNSs) and ancillary services.

In the RBOCs' submissions, there are five typical BSAs, *viz.,* three types of circuit switched access, packet switched access, and dedicated private line access. The actual numbers in the February 1 plans range from four (Ameritech) to 14 (NYNEX) for those who developed basic serving arrangements; one Regional (U S WEST), however, did not propose any new or separate BSAs. In turn, basic service elements, which may be available under more than one BSA, apparently range as high as 91, including both existing (75) and new (16) BSEs (NYNEX).

Users, enhanced service providers, and manufacturers who filed comments, however, generally urged the FCC to reject or at least collect more information concerning the Regional Companies' plans. For example, International

Communications Association (ICA) criticized the FCC for a "lack of leader-ship" and the BOCs for insufficient unbundling of basic service elements, a general absence of cost based pricing, and limited geographic availability.[39] The Association of Data Processing Service Organizations (ADAPSO), a union of enhanced service providers, asserted that:

> . . . rather than being a regulatory safeguard, ONA has been transformed into a vehicle for anticompetitive mischief.[40]

In turn, the Independent Data Communications Manufacturers Association (IDCMA) deemed the plans to be "fundamentally flawed" "because the level of unbundling is inadequate and because enhanced service providers are generally barred from collocating their equipment in the BOC's central offices.[41] Moreover, the National Telecommunications and Information Administration (NTIA) has dismissed the Bell plans as "unnecessarily confusing and complex" and urged the formation of an inter-industry committee to ensure the long term success of ONA.[42] Further comments or remarks by members of state commissions indicated their displeasure with both the BOC plans and the FCC over the most appropriate way to enforce ONA.[43]

In reply, the Bell companies argued that their plans fully comply with the FCC's requirements.   In fact, they stated that critics of the submissions attempt to move the companies beyond these requirements, which is neither warranted nor supported. Complaints about inadequate unbundling of network service elements are regarded as invalid, and it was pointed out that excessive unbundling could lead to an extreme lack of uniformity in the seven Bell regions. The companies seemed to agree with the U S WEST assessment that ONA "is an evolutionary process that cannot be achieved immediately."

In November 1988, the Commission approved the basic Bell ONA models but directed the RBOCs to submit key revisions by May 1989. In the decision released December 22, 1988 in "Phase I" of Docket 88-2, the agency approved the RBOCs' common ONA model." Under the model, an enhanced service provider must first subscribe to an access connection (BSA) before it could order unbundled network functionalities (BSEs). The Commission also called for full federal tariffing of interstate BSEs and state tariffing of intrastate ONA services. Further, existing state tariffed access arrangements would not be preempted by the FCC, and enhanced service providers would continue to be granted exemption from federal access charges. Jurisdictional issues would be addressed by federal-state Joint Board under Section 410(b) of the Communications Act.

In a companion order, the Commission approved AT&T's proposal to offer noncollocated enhanced services without filing service specific "comparably efficient interconnection" (CEI). The one exception was for "REDI-ACCESS" a co-marketed enhanced service featuring protocol conversion, for which CEI requirements must be met. Where AT&T seeks to collocate an enhanced service which it offers, compliance with CEI conditions would also be required.

Highly acclaimed as a concept, ONA as developed by the FCC has been criticized for its lack of specificity and for its slow development.

The pivotal importance of ONA is widely recognized by the telecommunications industry. The Regional Companies see a significant market opportunity in successful implementation of the process. For example, an executive at Southwestern Bell recently observed:

> Increasing the use of the network--even by just 1 percent--promises far more revenue potential than anything we could gain by providing enhanced services ourselves . . . ONA can aid economic development by creating a telecommunications market rich in Information Age services. New businesses or existing businesses considering relocation will look at whether an area offers a progressive environment that promotes the advantages of the Information Age.[44]

Enhanced service providers are also cognizant of this potentially lucrative market. Potential users regard the process as a means to have their information service needs better met. Public policy makers at the FCC envision ONA as an "equal access" approach to promoting competition and assuring a more rapid and efficient delivery of Information Age services to the public.

The concept is a key element in the FCC's *Computer III* program of relaxed regulation; without its successful implementation, separate subsidiary requirements will be retained for enhanced service provision by Bell companies. This network architecture and its interim counterpart, comparably efficient interconnection (CEI), represent essential elements of the much touted broadband ISDN network of the 1990s and beyond.

Collocation, *i.e.*, the physical location of enhanced service providers' equipment at a local telephone company's central office, is viewed by some as a crucial component of the ONA program. Although most of the RBOCs have seemed to balk at offering such an option, U S WEST has asserted that it endorses the concept. In May 1988, the company and Telenet announced their intent to initiate collocation at a Mountain Bell central office in Phoenix, Arizona; one month later, the physical connection was completed. Ultimately, such collocation may become more widespread as the cost of expensive interconnection between the local telephone company and the value added carrier is lowered, circuit quality is improved, and the lucrative nature of the arrangement becomes evident. In the FCC's December 22, 1988 ONA order, the agency refused to institute mandatory collocation.

C. Deregulation of All But Basic Services in the States

As discussed at some length in Chapter IV, many of the states have embraced regulatory reforms with respect to telecommunications services offered in their respective jurisdictions. One state, Nebraska, has virtually deregulated all telephone services, including basic local exchange except for a five year limit on the size of local rate increases. An alternative adopted in Vermont is a "social contract" whereby New England Telephone Company has agreed to stabilize its basic telephone rates, limit increases for certain telephone services, maintain high service quality, and modernize the network statewide. Deregulatory policies for toll and other services have been tied to competitive classifications in Illinois and a number of U S WEST territories (*e.g.,* Washington).   Virtually all states have undergone or are currently undergoing re–examination of traditional methods of regulation, particularly since the AT&T divestiture of 1984.

No consensus about a single "correct" type of regulatory program will likely be forthcoming among the 50 states and the District of Columbia because of different needs, philosophies, and statutes. However, the press of technology and, in some instances, federal preemption by the FCC or the courts, will likely lead many of the jurisdictions to seek to remove public policy obstacles to introduction of information services to the states' users. Varying degrees of regulatory oversight will continue to occur as states seek to balance universal service concerns with other objectives tailored to their specific needs.

Nationally, public policy makers differ on the perspicacity of continued state regulation. The FCC under Mark Fowler (1981–87) urged the adoption of virtually total deregulation by state jurisdictions on a three year trial basis.[45]   The Department of Justice's consultant, Peter Huber, laments the "still regrettably common" impedance of new network nodes by state regulatory policies.[46]   On the other hand, he observes that "the RBOCs, like the many other phone companies already involved in information services, surely could work some anticompetitive mischief at the edges of the market," and "close, continuing regulatory vigilance is therefore in order."[47]

Judge Greene's views in this area are unequivocal. On February 21, 1988, he told the Communications Committee of the National Governors' Association that:

> One question we might wish to consider is what the states
> and local policy makers and regulators can do in the
> telecommunications environment so greatly changed by the
> AT&T divestiture. One subject stands out above all: the
> need for vigilance to make certain that local ratepayers are
> not overcharged to subsidize the many outside ventures that
> the Bell companies are increasingly entering.[48]

Speculation in such matters would apparently be ill–advised in view of the many relevant variables. However, given the universal service mandate of Section 1 of the 1934 Communications Act, as amended, and the seriousness with which states view this responsibility[49] it would seem most unlikely that *complete* deregulation of all U.S. telecommunications will ever be achieved on a large scale. Prospects for regulatory oversight limited to provision of basic exchange services, however, seem good, and carrier planning on this basis would apparently not be imprudent. A promising means of effectively limiting regulation to basic services is discussed below.

D. Stand Alone Costing

A major issue in many states that will be important as market forces and regulatory flexibility become more prevalent is how to assign costs to major service categories for purposes of establishing dichotomies such as regulated/

unregulated and competitive/monopoly. Once services have been categorized as to their status relative to these demarcations, associated costs must be apportioned properly. Stand alone cost analyses can provide a reasonable and economically valid method of accomplishing the task. The stand alone costing method has, in fact, a long history of application in regulatory economics, dating at least from the regulation of federal water control projects in the 1930s. It is regarded by economists as a fair and economically efficient means of recovering costs.

The stand alone cost of a service represents what it would cost to provide that service alone, independent of the provision of any other service. The same concept, of course, applies to groups of services, such that the stand alone cost for a group is the cost of providing only that group of services, independent of all others. Given complete market freedom, no consumer or group of consumers would reasonably agree to pay more for a service or group of services than it would cost them to provide those services themselves, independently of the network. Thus, stand alone costs serve as a surrogate for competitive market forces, by forcing a competitive standard on service prices even in the absence of real competition.

The notion of stand alone costs has been used before as a tool for setting rates in regulated industries. Their practical application dates at least from the 1930s, when they were used in setting rates for the public use of federal water control projects. They have also been used extensively in the transportation industry.

As an example of the use of stand alone costs, it may help to illustrate the use of the procedure by referring to the original allocation of joint costs for the Tennessee Valley Authority (TVA). This series of federally funded dams on the Tennessee River provided three vital services – navigation, flood control and power generation. Table IX–8 shows the stand alone costs for these services. The cost of building dams to meet only navigational requirements was known to be approximately $160 million, while flood control projects built in isolation would have cost $140 million and power projects would have cost $250 million. If the system had been built to meet the requirements of both navigation and flood control, while excluding only power generation, some scale economies would have been realized and it would have cost $200 million, considerably less than the total of the separate stand alone costs for navigation and flood control. This, then, was the stand alone cost for a two–service system, and similar calculations were made for other combinations. The cost of the total system, serving all three needs, was $400 million, and this was the amount that was distributed using the stand alone costs.

Since the stand alone cost for a combined flood control and power system was $310 million, no more than that amount could be assigned to those services, in total. To satisfy this constraint, no less than $90 million ($400 million – $310 million) had to be assigned to the other service, navigation. Similarly, the minimum assignment to flood control was $75 million, because the maximum that could be assigned to navigation and power was $325 million. For power, the minimum was $200 million ($400 million – $200 million). The

Table IX–8

STAND ALONE COSTS FOR
THE TENNESSEE VALLEY AUTHORITY
($ Million)

	Stand Alone Costs	
Navigation	160	
Flood Control	140	
Power	250	
Navigation & Flood Control		200
Flood Control & Power		310
Power & Navigation		325
Navigation, Flood Control, & Power			400

Extreme Solutions:

Navigation	Flood Control	Power	Total
90	75	235	400
90	110	200	400
125	75	200	400

Source: P. Fanara, Jr. and C. M. Grimm, "Stand–Alone Cost: Use and Abuse in Determining Maximum U.S. Railroad Rates," *Transportation Research*, vol. 19A, No. 4, pp. 297–303, 1985, based on data from the Engineering Report of the Joint Committee Investigating the Tennessee Valley Authority (76th Congress, 1st session, doc. 56, 1939), pp. 10–12, 42–51.

same kind of procedure was used to determine the upper limit on the cost assignment for each service.

The procedure resulted in a range of acceptable cost distributions, with each service receiving no less than its minimum and no more than its maximum and the total adding to $400 million. Each solution would be economically efficient and subsidy free, so the TVA was free to choose among them on the basis of other criteria, such as equity.

The primary advantage of using stand alone costs for setting rates is that they are economically efficient, as well as fair. As explained above, using stand alone costs insures that services will be priced at levels below the cost of independent supply. Since the cost of independent supply represents the cost that a competitor would face if one appeared to provide a service, stand alone costs constrain prices to competitive levels even for those services where no competition actually exists. Stand alone costs also provide regulators with a reliable means of identifying any possible cross subsidies, thus eliminating a very important source of possible inefficiency.

Stand alone costs can contribute to the identification of cross subsidies. Prices are always subsidy–free if no group of customers pays more than its stand alone costs. If a group pays more than what it would cost to provide the same service in isolation, they must, by definition, be subsidizing another service, which would then be paying less than its incremental costs. This was illustrated with the example of TVA cost assignments provided above.

With regard to telephony, it has often been claimed that basic local exchange service has been and continues to be subsidized by toll services. However, a more realistic view of the nature of toll services' use of exchange plant and facilities suggests that such is not the case.

The illusion of a toll subsidy is due entirely to the method used to make the jurisdictional assignment of nontraffic sensitive (NTS) costs. Under separations procedures, the costs of nontraffic sensitive plant are assigned to the interstate jurisdiction at a rate that is greater than the amount that would be assigned under a directly proportional allocation scheme.[50] For this reason proponents of the toll subsidy theory claim that exchange services receive unwarranted subsidies.

The notion of various services "contributing to the support of basic services" has also been reinforced by the embedded costing methods employed by the LECs. The results of these studies typically show that exchange services have a poor revenue to cost ratio, thereby suggesting that the customers of other service(s) are paying more than their fair share of company incurred costs.

The embedded cost results are less than accurate for several reasons, but most importantly, because of the fact that most NTS costs are assigned to local exchange services despite the fact that both interstate and state toll services are provided over local NTS facilities. As a practical matter, without local exchange facilities there would be no viable means of connecting interexchange services to the majority of customers' premises.

To see why this is true, consider that interexchange carriers would have to build local facilities in order to serve customers unable to provide interconnection via their own means, and each and every entity that sought to offer interexchange services, whether intrastate or interstate, would require separate facilities. It appears obvious that the availability of the local network for toll use is a benefit to interexchange carriers and all toll customers. The sole assignment of NTS costs to local services would seem to be unreasonable and unfair under these circumstances. Yet the telephone industry, led by the LECs, has steadfastly attempted to eliminate the "toll subsidy" and reduce the claimed burden on competitive services.

Stand alone studies in telephony recognize the inherent benefits of plant used jointly by customers of various telephone services. Intuitively, it seems logical that the multiservices sharing of common facilities should reduce overall costs of operating each service as compared to the case where each service is provided over its own unique facilities. Thus, for example, the joint use of local loop plant by local and toll services has a beneficial impact on each service individually. Clearly, it is less costly to purchase and maintain one "set" of loop plant rather than two or three.

A stand alone study analyzes, to the extent possible, the costs of the local exchange plant used by services provided over that plant. The purpose of the study is to reflect the benefits accruing to each service from the joint use of common plant and fairly distribute these benefits among the services. One way of viewing the beneficial nature of joint use plant is to estimate and compare the difference in the costs of providing each service on a stand alone basis with the costs allocated to these services under traditional methods.

The results of stand alone studies often show that the relationship between exchange and toll services, based on the stand alone analysis, is far from that portrayed by the industry. For instance, see Table IX–9 which presents the results of a stand alone study for a hypothetical LEC. This data reflects the allocation of revenues, expenses, and rate base on the basis of stand alone methods. If one were to view exchange, interstate toll, and state toll as three distinct offerings, the costs of each system required to provide service would not be as dissimilar as suggested by previous embedded cost studies.

It is important to recognize that stand alone cost studies are not merely a means of distributing NTS costs. They are complete systems for calculating service costs. In fact, while the impact of stand alone studies is most dramatic in the assignment of NTS costs, they may also have a significant effect on the assignment of traffic sensitive (TS) costs. An example of the stand alone approach as it applies to traffic sensitive costs will help to illustrate the general method.

For instance, a marker is a switching control unit, with an average installed cost of about $10,000 to $12,000, that locates the calling line and marks a path through the switch to the called line. The more calls there are passing through the switch, the greater the number of markers needed, so it is classified as a traffic sensitive piece of equipment. The standard practice in engineering a switch is to select the number of markers based on the amount of traffic, expressed in marker holding time, using a formula such as that described by the figures in Table IX–10.

The marker holding time that each type of call demands is known (.55 seconds for a basic local call and .36 seconds for a toll call[51]). If the number of calls that each service generates during the ten busiest days in a given office is also known (data collected routinely by most local telephone companies), a determination of what each service would have to invest in markers if it were standing alone can be made. For example, in an office with 13,000 local calls (71.5 CCS[52] of marker holding time), 1,500 state toll calls (5.4 CCS) and 1,250 interstate toll calls (4.5 CCS), the marker investment for stand alone system would look like the figures shown in Table IX–11.

Thus, the independent operation of these services would require a total of eight markers, at a cost of $88,000. However, if the three services were using a single switch, the total volume of 15,750 calls (81.4 CCS of marker holding time) would only require five markers at a cost of $55,000. Clearly, the savings from sharing a single switch are substantial in this case. The benefits from the shared use of common facilities would be $33,000.

Table IX–9

STAND ALONE RESULTS
DISAGGREGATED STAND ALONE COSTING APPROACH
($ Million)

| | | MESSAGE | | | PRIVATE LINE | | |
| | | Toll | | | Toll | | |
	Total	IS	ST	Exch	IS	ST	Exch
Revenues	$ 501	$ 155	$ 126	$ 191	$ 18	$ 6	$ 5
Expenses	330	105	93	113	9	8	2
Taxes	79	23	18	33	4	0	1
Earnings	92	27	15	45	5	(2)	2
Rate Base	835	257	269	251	26	27	5
Earnings Ratio	11.0%	10.5%	5.6%	17.9%	19.2%	(7.4)%	40.0%

Combined Total Toll	8.0%	5.7%

Source: BRI analysis.

Table IX–10

DETERMINATION OF THE NUMBER OF MARKERS

Average CCS During The Ten Busiest Days	Markers Required
0–20	2
21–47	3
48–76	4
77–108	5
etc.	etc.

The objective of the stand alone costing method is to distribute these benefits in an equitable manner by assigning them to each service in direct proportion to the costs the services would incur operating independently. Thus, in this example, the cost of the shared markers would be distributed as shown in Table IX–12.

This contrasts with other costing approaches, which distribute traffic sensitive costs entirely on the basis of some usage measurement such as relative conversation minutes, regardless of whether the equipment in question is actually engineered on that basis. In this case, given the average duration of calls is 3.7 minutes for local, 10.4 minutes for state toll and 17.0 minutes for interstate toll, the conversation minutes would be 48,100 for local service,

Table IX–11

STAND ALONE MARKER INVESTMENT

	Unit Cost	Markers Required	Required Investment
Exchange	$11,000	4	$44,000
State Toll	11,000	2	22,000
Interstate Toll	11,000	2	22,000
Totals		8	$88,000

Table IX–12

DISTRIBUTION OF COMMON SUPPLY SAVINGS
BY STAND ALONE COST ALLOCATION

	Stand Alone Investment	Allocation	Savings	
Exchange	$44,000	$27,500	$16,500	37.5%
State Toll	22,000	13,750	8,250	37.5
Interstate Toll	22,000	13,750	8,250	37.5
Totals	$88,000	$55,000	$33,000	37.5%

15,600 for state toll and 21,250 for interstate toll. An allocation based on these minutes would result in a very different distribution of the common supply savings as shown in Table IX–13.

The contrast between stand alone cost calculations and results obtained from other methods, such as those often used by LECs, is even more dramatic when the analysis turns to NTS costs. If services were operating over physically separate systems and companies providing the services wanted to reach every customer they can reach today through the existing common facilities, most of the NTS facilities would have to be replicated entirely.

It is clear that each of the three service categories noted above relies on the use of the common equipment and facilities, and could not be provided without them. Taking access lines as an example, if any of these three services were deprived of the existing access lines, service could be continued only if a replacement system of access lines were installed for the exclusive use of that service. Since this would be much costlier than operating all services over a single set of access lines, each service benefits from the joint use arrangement.

The treatment of access lines in cost allocation studies is a good example of the application of the stand alone method. Access lines should be treated as precisely what they are, an essential part of any telecommunications service. Until recently, most carriers had always recognized this relationship

Table IX–13

DISTRIBUTION OF COMMON SUPPLY SAVINGS
BY RELATIVE USAGE COST ALLOCATION

	Stand Alone Investment	Usage Allocation	Savings	
Exchange	$44,000	$31,142	$12,858	29.2%
State Toll	22,000	10,100	11,900	54.1
Interstate Toll	22,000	13,758	8,242	37.5
Totals	$88,000	$55,000	$33,000	37.5%

between usage and lines. The old Bell System, for example, included among its "Fundamental Characteristics Affecting Telephone Rates," published in 1947, the precept that "a telephone has little or no value except as it is used to make and receive calls." It is simply impossible for a consumer to receive other telephone services without having some means of access, and there is a reason for that: access is an integral part of each telephone service.

Perhaps the best evidence that access does not warrant separate classification as a service is the fact that it is also virtually impossible to define the incremental cost of anything called "access service". The cost of an access line or a group of access lines can be calculated, and included in the costs assigned to other services, but developing an incremental cost for access service would require that other services exist in the absence of access. An acceptable definition of incremental costs makes this quite clear. Thus, the incremental costs of an existing service are the costs that would be saved in the long run if the service were discontinued but demand for other services remained the same. Incremental costs for a potential new service are the amount that the company's costs must increase to provide that service. It is difficult to imagine how access could be discontinued while "demand for other services remained the same." It is equally impossible to define a stand alone cost for other services existing in the absence of access. And, of course, the idea of access existing in the absence of other services is completely meaningless.

E. Phase–Out of MFJ Restrictions

A complete removal of existing line of business restrictions on the Regional Bell Companies may occur in the "long run," but the near term likelihood seems relatively low. Throughout the MFJ implementation process, Judge Greene has repeatedly stressed that the BOCs' bottleneck monopoly has remained largely intact, affording these entities substantial market power. This power, it is feared, may be potentially leveraged to cross subsidize Bell ventures in various competitive markets.

Certain areas, such as interexchange services or manufacturing, have been considered verboten by the Court with respect to the RBOCs because these endeavors would re–establish incentives for abuse that were documented regarding the old Bell System.   Until the September 10, 1987 and March 7, 1988 orders, information services were similarly off limits for the Bell entities.   Those decisions partially relaxed this prohibition, permitting provision of such voice storage and retrieval (VSR) services as electronic and voice mail, and voice messaging; in short, transmission of information services would be allowed, but manipulation of content would not.   This modification was justified on the basis that transmission of information services –– unlike the supply of information content, telecommunications manufacturing, and the long distance market –– requires RBOC participation to help assure their commercial viability.   However, recent requests by three Bell entities to provide information content services such as electronic publishing and electronic directories were denied by the MFJ court on June 13, 1989.[53]

No appreciable erosion of Regional Company market power relating to the local exchange network has apparently occurred. Besides the support for this assessment embodied in numerous bypass studies (see above), other evidence of present and expected dominance exists. For example, an analyst at Salomon Brothers, Inc., recently declared that the "local exchange business may be one of the most recession – resistant businesses that you'll find in America."[54] In turn, the Chairman of one RBOC (BellSouth) labeled its local operating telephone companies (Southern Bell, South Central Bell) as "two powerhouses" and a "firm foundation for the future."[55] Perhaps commenting on the future as well as the present, Judge Greene has averred that:

> Local telephone service is a natural monopoly because it is
> not possible, for reasons of technology and economic reality,
> to run more than one set of wires to every home, office, or
> factory in a city or town.[56]

Apparently at least one of three avenues for change must be successfully negotiated before the MFJ restrictions will be rescinded. First, the prohibitions could be removed legislatively, as has been attempted in the Dole, Wyden, and Swift–Tauke Congressional bills. Such efforts have not resulted in the enactment of any "corrective" laws, to date. Secondly, a public policy override could occur through an appellate court action overturning Judge Greene's rulings concerning such proscribed activities as manufacturing or provision of interexchange or certain information services.[57] Thus far, only the MFJ Court's decision relating to BOC involvement in extra regional exchange services has been negated by a higher court.

Thirdly, the MFJ Court itself could modify or eliminate the existing line of business bans. This would be done "upon a showing by the petitioning BOC that there is no substantial possibility that it could use its monopoly power to impede competition in the market it seeks to enter" (Section VIII(C) of the MFJ decree). In Judge Greene's Court, this would presumably require a demonstration that the BOCs' bottleneck control has sufficiently declined (through, e.g., technological advances or changed user requirements) or that regulatory monitoring would bridle the potential for anticompetitive conduct by the local exchange carriers. As discussed earlier, the Court has not yet perceived a significant erosion of exchange based market power.

The Judge has also plainly stated his lack of faith in the ability of the FCC to effectively regulate the Bell Companies. In its recommendations to drop the market restrictions, the Justice Department has relied heavily on such Commission policies as its *Joint Cost* methodologies for separating costs for regulated and unregulated Bell operations, and the interconnection requirements of ONA and CEI. The Court unequivocally rejected this reliance as misplaced. Judge Greene asserted that:

> . . . for a number of years the FCC was unable to prevent or to remedy major anticompetitive abuses by the Bell System achieved through the activities of its local affiliates.
>
> . . .
>
> To the extent that there has been any recent change in the regulatory picture itself, it has been to weaken the regulations governing telecommunications carriers, not to strengthen them.[58]

Furthermore, the Court pointed to the "fewer resources" possessed by the current FCC relative to earlier regimes, and the present emphasis on deregulatory programs.[59]   Overall, existing regulations are "entirely inadequate" because they either have already been revealed at the *AT&T* case hearing to be "ineffective"; are "not sufficiently comprehensive"; exhibit "large loopholes"; or are not even implemented.[60]

In sum, for the reasons just discussed, the probability of Congress, a higher court, or Judge Greene seeking to eliminate the extant line of business safeguards seems remote for the near term. Any conscious phase−out of these restrictions by public policy makers, then, must await significantly changed circumstances.

F. Divestiture of the RBOC Local Exchange "Pipes"

One possible scenario for the future which is less well known than the previous four areas of public policy already discussed would be a redefinition of the natural monopoly elements of the local public switched network. This might be accomplished through a reassessment of the concept in terms of (1) services; (2) network facilities; or (3) a combination of the two.

In the post divestiture world of telecommunications, it is likely that not all local exchange services will remain monopolistic in nature. Examples of this may be specialized data transmission services or broadband teleconferencing. A case can be made that voice grade switched local exchange services will be the sole offering in the long run that will remain noncompetitive, and accordingly should be separately addressed by public policy makers. Some states, such as Idaho, have already mandated that segments of voice grade services be split off from other offerings.

More specifically, these basic voice grade services (VGS) could be isolated for regulatory purposes, and "stand alone" costs could be determined as benchmarks for ratemaking.[61] Subsequently, only those costs incurred specifically to benefit voice grade services would be assigned to this category. To prevent possible circumvention of this regulatory segregation, funds provided through VGS revenue requirements should be tied to that operation. For example, depreciation funds could be targeted to provide only new facilities intended to furnish basic voice offerings. All costs unrelated to VGS supply would be allocated to other service categories.

A second approach would identify the facilities of a local exchange carrier that *currently* exhibit "natural monopoly" cost characteristics.[62] In modern U.S. telecommunications, local loop facilities seem to possess these characteristics, especially given the scale economies that apparently obtain with the increasing use of fiber optics in the loop.[63] In contrast, local switching and ancillary central office equipment seemingly do not feature such cost traits. Separate access companies could be created to handle the loop portion of the network.

Under this scenario, regulation would be confined to the distribution, transport and access interface services provided by these access entities. Providers of other services interconnecting with the loop would be totally deregulated since they lack control of bottleneck facilities and, hence, wield little market power. Interservice cross subsidization, which is the bane of current regulators, would cease to be a problem.

A hybrid of the above two conceptualizations might also merit consideration as a means to restructure the industry and tailor public policy to the new market organization. For example, the national objective of maintaining universal telephone service with respect to VGS offerings could be tied to the operation of the aforementioned access companies. The latter would be required to provide access *and* basic VGS services pursuant to regulation.

Given the multiservice nature of modern telecommunications networks, it would be virtually impossible short of certification rules or affidavits to prevent other suppliers from offering local voice grade services. However, the regulated VGS offerings would exist as benchmarks for any competitive services and presumably because of scale or scope economies, could be priced on a cost basis below the rates charged by others. The access companies would function as a public utility and be required to serve as a carrier of last resort in assuring the continuing achievement of universal telephone service.

These approaches and other variants would feature equal access, regula-tion of monopoly elements, and maintenance of universal service. If implemented, such a setting would potentially have salient effects on ratepayers, established service providers, and new entrants.

These VGS and access companies would, of course, be subject to some form of regulation. Besides a costing basis such as a stand alone methodology (see above), a system of flexible price based regulation may well be implemented. This approach is the subject of the next section.

G. Price Based Regulation of Dominant Carriers

The Federal Communications Commission under Chairmen Mark S. Fowler (May 1981– April 1987) and Dennis R. Patrick (April 1987–Present) has embarked on a number of deregulatory initiatives. For example, in October 1983, the FCC inaugurated an inquiry into the long term regulation of AT&T's interstate services and rates (Docket 83–1147). In December 1986 a new, broader proceeding (Docket 86–421) was begun which attempts to extend the agency's *Competitive Carrier* rulings and supersedes Docket 83–1147. In its *Notice of Proposed Rulemaking,* the Commission indicated that it would seek to deregulate certain basic services provided by dominant carriers such as the Bell companies or AT&T. The FCC perceives that two such services are already ripe for streamlined tariff regulation: data transmission services utilizing packet switching networks, and services provided under contract pursuant to competitive bids. "Border patrol" regulation is envisioned whereby a dominant carrier is fully regulated in some service areas, but subject to streamlined regulation in others.

Besides presiding over the initiation of these proceedings and the phasing out of *Computer II* in favor of *Computer III* and nonstructural safeguards, Chairman Fowler advocated a three–year experimental suspension of regulation of all telecommunications goods and services in participating states. Dubbed "Back to the Future," the proposed total deregulation trial was expected to simultaneously accelerate the transition to a competitive telecommunications market place and avoid the costs of a gradualist approach to deregulation.[64]

Fowler's successor, Chairman Patrick, has actively sought alternatives to traditional rate of return/rate base regulation for dominant carriers. Figure IX–2 sets forth his overall credo that "deregulation is not an end in itself" and six broad objectives he has established for his stint as Chairman. One of the major tasks for the FCC under his regime is the successful implementation of Open Network Architecture and other *Computer III* platforms. The capstone of his tenure at the Commission, if endorsed by both his agency *and* Congress, would be the "price cap" system of regulation.

In August 1986, largely at his urging, the Commission initiated a Notice of Proposed Rulemaking concerning a proposed price cap ratemaking system. More specifically, the FCC recommended replacing rate of return regulation for dominant carriers other than Comsat with ceilings on prices charged for use of interstate services. The agency tentatively concluded that this new regulatory approach would apply initially to AT&T and later to the interstate and foreign basic services of local exchange carriers and Alascom, Inc.

The Commission believes that the price cap model is a superior form of regulation relative to the traditional reliance on rate base–rate of return–cost of service oversight. Legally, the FCC asserts that it is under no compulsion to continue using such a regulatory scheme for dominant carriers if a more effective or comparably effective, but less costly, alternative exists; it is believed that the "model offering the greatest promise is one under which ceilings would be imposed on a carrier's service rates."[65] Arguing that rate of return regulation establishes "powerful incentives for carriers to behave inefficiently," the Commission states that price cap regulation would overcome the incentive of subject carriers to "pad" their rate bases (*i.e.,* overinvest as per the Averch–Johnson effect) or generate operating expenses at nonoptimal levels.[66] Ideally, the price cap method of rates would assure

Figure IX-2

OBJECTIVES OF FCC CHAIRMAN DENNIS PATRICK

OVERALL

"While I firmly believe the public has benefitted from the deregulatory path
the Commission has pursued we should never confuse the end with the means.
Deregulation is not an end in itself, but has validity only insofar as it
services the public interest."

SIX BROAD OBJECTIVES

(1) Promote, Whenever Possible, A Competitive Marketplace For The
    Development And Use of Communications Facilities And Services
(2) Provide A Regulatory Framework Which Permits Markets For Communica-
    tions Services To Function Effectively, While Eliminating Regulations
    Which Are Unnecessary Or Inimical To The Public Interest
(3) Promote Efficiency In The Allocation, Licensing And Use Of The
    Electromagnetic Spectrum
(4) Protect And Promote The Interests Of The American Public In
    International Communications
(5) Provide Service To The Public In The Most Efficient, Expeditious Manner
    Possible
(6) Eliminate Government Action Which Infringes Upon Freedom Of Speech
    And The Press

protection of the ratepayer, promote service efficiency and technological
innovation, reduce if not eliminate incentives to cross subsidize, and afford
simple administration by the regulatory commission. Under the plan, initial
ceilings would be set on prices for all existing services, and periodic adjustments in the caps based on various factors, such as productivity changes or
inflation.

Despite support from NTIA, AT&T, the Bell Companies, and most other
telephone companies, the FCC proposal encountered a firestorm of protest
from competitors, users, and particularly members of Congress. Criticisms
centered on the concern that AT&T and the Regional Bell Companies would be
able to boost profits at the expense of others, and that the Commission's
August 1987 proposal lacked essential details. Other perceived problems
related, inter alia, to maintenance of service quality, the lack of safeguards
against dominant carrier abuses, the inappropriateness of using existing
inefficient rates as the initial capped prices, the proper level of service
aggregation, treatment of new services, the likelihood of higher-not lower-
prices under the plan, and the nature of the proper adjustment mechanism.

Responding to these concerns, Chairman Patrick announced in February
1988 that the FCC would issue a new, more detailed price cap plan and solicit
more public comment. On May 12, 1988 the Commission did adopt a
considerably more elaborate proposal through a Further Notice of Proposed
Rulemaking in CC Docket 87-313. Under the new plan, price caps would
apply to all existing federally tariffed AT&T services and local exchange
carriers' interstate access services but not individualized offerings, e.g.,
AT&T's custom designed network services. Carrier earnings for the latter
type of service would be held separate for purposes of reviewing carriers'
performances. New services would not be included under the price cap plan

for up to one annual tariff filing cycle, and the FCC would apply a "net revenue test" to evaluate such services.

Moreover, services would be grouped into "baskets," each subject to a price cap. The local exchange carriers' baskets would be special access and switched access, while AT&T's categories would be private line and switched services. Rates would be decreased annually to reflect a calculated 3 percent productivity factor. This percentage is derived from a projected 2.5 percent productivity gain for telecommunications relative to the overall economy, plus a 0.5 percent "consumer productivity dividend" (CPD) which would redound to the benefit of users.

Under the plan, each rate element of a service would be subject to bands which would limit annual changes to 5 percent. Failure to remain within this zone would prevent carriers from receiving only a streamlined tariff review by the FCC. If any capped rate is found by the Commission to be unlawful, then refunds may be ordered and the cap may be adjusted.

The May 1988 FCC proposal envisioned an April 1, 1989 initiation date for the plan, using existing rates as a starting point. The system would apply to AT&T and subject local exchange carriers but not to Alascom and Comsat. Participation would be voluntary and the plan would be employed on a trial basis for four years, saving customers an estimated $1.6 billion during that period.

In response to the Further Notice, parties to the Docket 87–313 proceeding submitted more than 5,000 pages of comments to the FCC. Opposition to the plan remained strong, particularly from Congressional members and users. For example, the Democratic staff of the House telecommunications subcommittee issued a highly critical report in November 1988. Among other things, the report concluded that the "price–cap proposal represents a radical and unjustified departure" from traditional methods of federal regulation and that the "adoption of such a regulatory scheme is beyond the commission's authority."[67] Criticism from opponents continued to focus on a productivity factor believed to be too low, the unjustified use of existing prices as the plan's starting point, the perceived opportunities for price discrimination, and concerns about deteriorating service quality under the plan.

Consequently, the agency deferred action on the proposal, first until early December 1988, then January 1989, and finally until mid March 1989. FCC Chairman Patrick testified before Senate and House subcommittees in February and March 1989, and intense negotiations occurred between the Commission and Congress. Telephone companies continued to vigorously support the concept of price caps, and the Rand Corporation released a favorable study on the subject.[68]

On March 16, 1989 the FCC adopted a revised price cap plan for AT&T.[69] As before, the price cap formula would include, *inter alia*, a three percent annual decrease for rates in each basket. The three percent would be based on a 2.5 percent historical productivity rate and a 0.5 percent consumer productivity dividend.

Largely as a result of Congressional pressure, several major changes were incorporated into the May 1988 proposal. First, the agency increased the number of service "baskets" from two to three. One of the baskets includes six separate categories of residential and small business services: daytime Message Telecommunications Services (MTS); evening MTS; night/weekend MTS; international; "Reach Out America" calling plans; and miscellaneous services (e.g., operator assistance and credit card calling). A second basket is for "800" (formerly Inward WATS) services, where AT&T was found to retain substantial market power. The final basket consists of all other AT&T services, i.e., the ones perceived to be most competitive. Services in each of the baskets are generally limited to a five percent increase or decrease relative to the change in the price cap index, either as a maximum (e.g., residential services) or as a trigger for closer FCC scrutiny ("800" and other-services baskets). The price floor component of the limit was implemented in response to demands from Congress.

Several safeguards specifically targeting consumers were adopted. For example, AT&T can only raise evening and night/weekend MTS rates by four percent per year above the change in the price cap index. Moreover, an average residential rate for all AT&T services in the residential basket must be calculated, and this rate shall not increase by more than one percent per year. And generally, local exchange carrier (LEC) access charge reductions will be flowed through to customers in proportion to their usage.

Projected by the Commission to save consumers some $700 million and businesses approximately $200 million during the four-year trial period start-ing July 1, 1989 the new plan does not apply to AT&T's customized tariffs or other "one-of-a-kind" services such as special construction. Price changes within the set limits for applicable services may be instituted under a stream-lined tariff process essentially requiring a simple 14-day notice. Proposed changes outside the prescribed limits would necessitate a regular tariff review by the FCC. AT&T filed its new tariffs on May 17, 1989, pursuant to the price cap order.

The agency reiterated its commitment to geographic rate averaging as a general principle, but would study de-averaging on a tariff-by-tariff basis. In addition, the price cap plan would complement but not replace existing Commission policies such as open network architecture, Uniform System of Accounts, and jurisdictional separations. Further, the FCC's ongoing program intended to preserve universal telephone service and to support high-cost telephone companies would be continued.

On June 30, 1989, the FCC affirmed the basic framework of the March 1989 price cap plan on reconsideration.

Concurrent with the adoption of the AT&T price cap regime, the FCC inaugurated another Notice of Proposed Rulemaking relating to a suggested approach for local exchange carriers.[70] The delay was established in order for the Commission to further study the productivity experiences of the various local companies. For participating LECs, the price cap plan would begin one year after the start of the AT&T regulatory scheme, viz., July 1, 1990. The plan would be mandatory for the largest carriers, i.e., the "tier 1" companies such as the RBOCs and GTE companies with annual revenues in excess of $100 million. For other LECs, the use of price caps would be elective; those choosing not to be regulated under such a system would continue with a rate of return framework.

Similar to AT&T, three baskets would be used for LEC interstate services. One proposed basket would consist of carrier common line (CCL) offerings, which are the nontraffic sensitive (NTS) access services obtained by interexchange carriers from local companies. A second grouping would be the traffic sensitive (TS) basket, while the third would pertain to all other LEC services such as special (private line) access and "corridor" offerings. Tentatively excluded from price caps under the proposal are special construction and individual–case–basis services, which would be subject to traditional tariff review procedures. Otherwise, LECs would be subject to the same tariff requirements as AT&T, except that their annual filing would be made on 90 rather than 60 days' notice. The five percent cap would apparently apply to services in each of the three baskets.

A new price cap feature developed particularly for possible applicability to LECs is an "automatic stabilizer." This mechanism would adjust price cap levels downward if a carrier's earnings exceeded the current authorized rate of return by more than two percent and upward with a two percent shortfall. As an alternative that might be less intrusive to the inherent price cap system of incentives, more frequent FCC reviews of LEC caps may be undertaken. Somewhat ironically, given the increasing deregulatory trend at the federal level in recent years, the Commission proposed to expand its current service monitoring efforts from the BOCs to all LECs participating in a price cap regime. Initial comments by large users, state commissions, IXCs and some LECs indicated strong opposition to at least certain parts of this initial FCC proposal.

Notwithstanding the modifications to its original price cap plan, however, the FCC's new system represents the most fundamental regulatory change at the federal level since cost–of–service/rate of return regulation was instituted in the early 1960s. For large local exchange carriers such as the Bell Companies, GTE Corporation's operating carriers, and United Telecommunications' telephone companies, a basically new set of incentives would be established, creating new opportunities and risks. Coupled with other modified "ground rules," such as the myriad changes occurring among the states in their public policy approaches and the ramifications of the recent FCC ruling in the *ARCO* case permitting customers to interconnect their private systems to the local exchange of their choice,[71] the telecommunications environment for local carriers and their competitors promises new horizons and substantial uncertainty.

Appendix IX–A.1

PROPOSED BELL COMPANY
OPEN NETWORK ARCHITECTURE (ONA) PLANS
Ameritech

A. **Proposed BSAs***
    Voice Grade–Line–Circuit Switched
    Voice Grade–Trunk–Circuit Switched
    Packet Switched
    Dedicated–Network Access Link

B. **Proposed BSEs****
    Calling Billing Number Delivery (ANI)
    Called Directory Number Delivery
    Customer Facilities Usage Information
    Central Office Announcements
    Make Busy Arrangements
    Uniform Call Distribution
    Queuing
    Regular Multi–Line Hunt Group
    Circular Multi–Line Hunt Group
    Multi–Line Hunt Group Overflow
    Individual Access to Each Port in a Hunt Group
    Remote Activation of Message Waiting
    Three Way Call Transfer
    Call History Package Delivery (SMDI)
    Call Detail Recording
    Reverse Billing
    Notification of Subscriber Line Breaks (Alarm)
    Packet–Fast Select Acceptance
    Packet–Closed User Groups
    Packet–Data Hunt Groups
    Packet–Call Redirection

* BSAs, or "Basic Serving Arrangements," are network access arrangements for enhanced service provision that are offered pursuant to existing tariffs.
** BSEs, or "Basic Service Elements," are FCC–mandated tariffed offerings which must be provided to enhanced service providers on a separate and unbundled basis.

Appendix IX–A.2

PROPOSED BELL COMPANY
OPEN NETWORK ARCHITECTURE (ONA) PLANS
Bell Atlantic Corp.

A. **Proposed BSAs***
    Voice Grade–Line–Circuit Switched
    Voice Grade–Trunk–Circuit Switched
    Digital Grade–Circuit Switched
    Packet Switched
    Dedicated–Private Line

B. **Proposed BSEs****
    Calling Number Identification (CNI)
    Call Block
    Automatic Recall
    Automatic Call Back
    Central Office Trace
    Selective Call Forwarding
    Distinctive Ringing
    Call Forwarding on Busy Line
    Call Forwarding on Don't Answer
    Call Forwarding–Variable Ring Count
    Remote Control–Call Forwarding
    Cancel Call Waiting
    One Number Service
    Message Desk
    Multiline Hunting
    Automatic Call Distribution
    Line (Loop) Supervision Service
    Direct Inward Dialing
    Group Make Busy/Transfer
    Dynamic Routing
    Secondary Channel
    Route Diversity
    Automatic Protection Switching
    Private Line Conditioning
    Bridging
    Closed User Groups
    Hunt Groups

* BSAs, or "Basic Serving Arrangements," are network access
arrangements for enhanced service provision that are offered pursuant
to existing tariffs.
** BSEs, or "Basic Service Elements," are FCC–mandated tariffed offerings which must be provided to enhanced service providers on a
separate and unbundled basis.

Appendix IX–A.3

PROPOSED BELL COMPANY
OPEN NETWORK ARCHITECTURE (ONA) PLANS
BellSouth Corp.

A. **Proposed BSAs***
Voice Grade–Line–Circuit Switched
Voice Grade–Trunk–Circuit Switched
Digital–Line–Circuit Switched
Packet Switching
Dedicated–Private Line

B. **Proposed BSEs****
Automatic Protection Switching
Route Diversity
DS1/Analog or DSO Multiplexer
DS3/DS1 Multiplexer
Derived Channel Multiplexer
Access to Data Service
Activation of Call Forwarding Without Call Completion
Call Distribution Functions Including Queue
Call Forward–Busy Line–Intraoffice
Call Forward–Busy Line–Interoffice
Call Forward Don't Answer–Intraoffice
Call Forward Don't Answer–Interoffice
Call Forward–Variable
Call Forward Don't Answer with Variable Ring Counts
Call Forward–Multiple Simultaneous Calls
Call Forward–Variable–Selected Numbers
Called/Calling Number Information–Automatic Number Identification
Called/Calling Number Information–Bulk Calling Line Identification
Called/Calling Number Information–Message Desk Service
Called/Calling Number Information–Simplified Message Desk Interface
Call Waiting
Carrier Selection on Reverse Charging
Customer Control of Call Forward–Busy Line Don't Answer
Custom Service Areas
Direct Inward Dialing
Distinctive Ringing
Multi–Frequency Signaling on DID
Make Busy/Night Transfer

Appendix IX–A.3(cont.)

PROPOSED BELL COMPANY
OPEN NETWORK ARCHITECTURE (ONA) PLANS
BellSouth Corp.

B.   **Proposed BSEs****
Multiline Hunt Groups
Network Reconfiguration
Packet Switch Options–Call Redirection
Packet Switch Options–Closed User Group
Packet Switch Options–Direct Call
Packet Switch Options–Fast Select
Packet Switch Options–Hunt Group
Remote Activation of Call Forwarding
Screening
Speed Calling
User Transfer
Uniform Access Numbers for Business Lines
Warm Line
800 Service to DID Lines

* BSAs, or "Basic Serving Arrangements," are network access arrangements for enhanced service provision that are offered pursuant to existing tariffs.
** BSEs, or "Basic Service Elements," are FCC–mandated tariffed offerings which must be provided to enhanced service providers on a separate and unbundled basis.

Appendix IX–A.4

PROPOSED BELL COMPANY
OPEN NETWORK ARCHITECTURE (ONA) PLANS
NYNEX

A. **Proposed BSAs***
Circuit Switched–Line Side
Circuit Switched–Trunk Side
Packet Switched–Line Side
Packet Switched–Trunk Side
Dedicated–Metallic
Dedicated–Telegraph Grade
Dedicated–Voice Grade
Dedicated–Program Audio
Dedicated–Video
Dedicated–Digital Data
Dedicated–High Capacity
Dedicated–Superpath Optical
Dedicated–DOV Access
Dedicated–Alarm Services Transport

B. **Proposed BSEs****
Call Forward Busy/Don't Answer
Call Forward Don't Answer with Variable Ring Count
Customer Control of Call Forward Busy Line/Don't Answer
Simplified Message Desk Interface
Information Delivery Services
Line Circuit Switched with T1 Transport
Tandem Routing
Automatic Number Identification
Trunk Circuit Switched with T1 Transport
Trunk Group Make Busy
Alternate Routing
Diagnostic Channel on DSO Lines
Reconfigurable Private Network Service
Call Redirection
Gateway Services
Exchange Carrier Billing for ESPs

* BSAs, or "Basic Serving Arrangements," are network access arrangements for enhanced service provision that are offered pursuant to existing tariffs.
** BSEs, or "Basic Service Elements," are FCC–mandated tariffed offerings which must be provided to enhanced service providers on a separate and unbundled basis.

Appendix IX-A.5

PROPOSED BELL COMPANY
OPEN NETWORK ARCHITECTURE (ONA) PLANS
Pacific Telesis Group

A. **Proposed BSAs***
Voice Grade-Line-Circuit Switched
Voice Grade-Trunk-Circuit Switched
Digital Grade-Line-Circuit Switched
Dedicated-Private Line
Packet Switched

B. **Proposed BSEs****
Ability to Reconfigure Private Non Switched Networks
Answer Supervision
Billing Number Delivery
Bridging
Call Distribution Functions (Without Queue)
Call Distribution Functions Including Queue
Call Forwarding Busy Line/Don't Answer – Third Party Ordering/Billing
Call Forwarding Busy Line – Third Party Ordering/Billing
Call Forwarding Don't Answer – Third Party Ordering/Billing
Call Redirection (Packet)
Calling Directory Number Delivery
Closed User Group (Packet)
Diagnostic Channel on DSO and Subrate Lines –
Direct Call (Packet)-Third Party Ordering/Billing
Direct Connection-Third Party Ordering/Billing
Distinctive Ringing-Third Party Ordering/Billing
Fast Select (Packet)
Forward Call Information (FCI), or
     Simplified Message Desk Interface (SMDI)
Forward Call Information-Multiple Users
Hunt Group (Packet)
Message Waiting Indication-Activation
Message Waiting Indication-Third Party Ordering/Billing
Multiline Hunt Groups
Private Line Conditioning
Remote Speed Call Menu Access Translator (Packet
Restriction of Outgoing Calls (Packet)
Selected Call Forward-Third Party Ordering/Billing
Selected Call Rejection-Third Party Ordering/Billing
Three Way Call Transfer
Trunk Group Make Busy
Warm Line-Third Party Ordering/Billing

* BSAs, or "Basic Serving Arrangements," are network access
arrangements for enhanced service provision that are offered pursuant
to existing tariffs.
** BSEs, or "Basic Service Elements," are FCC-mandated tariffed offerings which must be provided to enhanced service providers on a
separate and unbundled basis.

Appendix IX–A.6

PROPOSED BELL COMPANY
OPEN NETWORK ARCHITECTURE (ONA) PLANS
Southwestern Bell Corp.

A. **Proposed BSAs***
Voice Grade–Circuit Switched I
Voice Grade–Circuit Switched–Digital Multiplexed I
Packet Access
Dedicated–Low Speed
Dedicated–Voice Grade
Dedicated–Audio Program Channel
Digital Data Service
Dedicated–Digital 1.544 Mbps
Dedicated–Digital Above 1.544 Mbps
Voice Grade–Circuit Switched II
Voice Grade–Circuit Switched–Digital Multiplexed II

B. **Proposed BSEs****
Call Distribution With Queuing
Calling Number Identification
Called Number Identification
Multiline Hunt Group
Multiline Hunt Group–Very Large Size
Trunk Side Access with Remote Make Busy
Customer Alerting
Remote Make Busy/Night Transfer
Three Way Calling with Ability to Add a Help Line
Routing–Dynamic Control of Exchange Networks by ESP
DDS–Access to Secondary Channel
Network Reconfiguration Under ESP Control
Route Diversity
Automatic Protection Switching
Conditioning on Private Lines
Bridging
Multiplexing
Packet Closed User Group
Conditioning on Switched Lines
Expedited Testing
Recorded Announcements

* BSAs, or "Basic Serving Arrangements," are network access arrangements for enhanced service provision that are offered pursuant to existing tariffs.
** BSEs, or "Basic Service Elements," are FCC–mandated tariffed offerings which must be provided to enhanced service providers on a separate and unbundled basis.

Appendix IX–A.7

PROPOSED BELL COMPANY
OPEN NETWORK ARCHITECTURE (ONA) PLANS
U S WEST, Inc.

A. **Proposed BSAs***
    –– No New tariffs proffered

B. **Proposed BSEs****
    Call Forwarding Variable
    Call Forwarding Don't Answer
    Call Forwarding Busy Line
    Call Forwarding Busy Line Don't Answer
    Expanded Call Forwarding Don't Answer
    Expanded Call Forwarding Busy Line
    Expanded Call Forwarding Busy Line Don't Answer
    Abbreviated Activation of Call Forwarding
    Remote Call Forwarding
    Speed Calling (8 numbers)
    Speed Calling (30 numbers)
    Abbreviated Access (1 Digit)
    Abbreviated Access (2 Digit)
    Three Way Call Transfer
    Call Waiting
    Message Waiting Indication
    Hunting
    Make Busy
    Automatic Call Distribution
    DID Trunk Queuing
    Call Number Information Service (CNIS)
    Message Delivery Service
    Facility Monitoring
    Command A Link – Network Reconfiguration
    Automatic Loop Transfer
    Hot Line
    Warm Line
    Packet Switching–Closed User Group
    Packet Switching–Fast Select Acceptance
    Packet Switching–Multi Point Hunt Group
    Packet Switching–Call Backup/Redirection
    Packet Switching–Auto Call

* BSAs, or "Basic Serving Arrangements," are network access
arrangements for enhanced service provision that are offered pursuant
to existing tariffs.
** BSEs, or "Basic Service Elements," are FCC–mandated tariffed offer-
ings which must be provided to enhanced service providers on a
separate and unbundled basis.

Notes

1. *The Geodesic Network: 1987 Report on Competition in the Telephone Industry, op. cit.,* p. 21.

2. *Id.,* p. 1.2

3. *Id.,* p. 1.6.

4. *Id.,* p. 2.12.

5. *Id.,* p. 2.12.

6. *Id.,* p. 2.25.

7. *Id.,* p. 2.12.

8. *Id.,* pp. 2.25, 2.26.

9. *Id.*

10. See September 10, 1987 Opinion in *U.S.A. v. Western Electric Company, Inc. et al., op. cit.,* n. 60.

11. See Economics & Technology, Inc., *Factual Predicates to the MFJ Business Restrictions: A Critical Analysis of the Huber Report;* A Report to the Ad Hoc Telecommunications Users Committee and the International Communications Association, March 13, 1987, pp. 16–18, 35–36.

12. See Appendix A to Chapter VI.

13. December 8, 1988, Address, "Communications Week Symposium," *op. cit.,* pp. 14, 15.

14. Order, Civil Action No. 82–0192, filed September 10, 1987, pp. 34–36.

15. See "Bypass Evidence and Prospects: An Overview" in Chapter VI.

16. "Factual Predicates to the MFJ Business Restrictions: A Critical Analysis of the Huber Report," *op. cit.*

17. *Id.,* pp. 25, 60.

18. See, *e.g.,* A.M. Rutkowski, "The Geodesic Network," *Telecommunications,* April 1987, p. 46 (interview with PacTel Vice Chairman Sam Ginn).

19. See, *e.g.,* "Reaction mixed to announcement that United Telecom will buy majority interest in US Sprint joint venture," *Telecommunications Reports,* July 25, 1988, pp. 4–6; and "AT&T and GTE Launched Joint Venture," *Communications Week,* January, 9, 1989, p. 4.

20. "Report of the United States Concerning the Line of Business Restrictions Imposed on the Bell Operating Companies by the Modification of Final Judgment" January 30, 1987, p. 42.

21. Certain factors tend to militate against generalizations about such relative costs. For example, scale economics may vary widely depending on the demand in a given market.

22. See, *e.g.,* Market and Strategic Impacts of Bypass, op. cit., especially Parts IIB(2), IIA and B. See also, *e.g.,* "Bypass Not Cost Driven," *Network World,* December 8, 1986, p. 4. (Diebold study) and "Features, Not Price, Call the Shots for Many Telephone Customers," *Communications Week,* April 4, 1988, p. 36 (McKinsey & Co. survey). It is interesting to note that Dr. Joseph Kraemer of Touche Ross, who has supervised numerous user surveys which found that price was the paramount decision-making criterion, recently urged local exchange carriers to concentrate on marketing and customer service as market place strategies. See "Competition in the Local Exchange: From Where to Where," presented at the April 7–8, 1988 Phillips Conference, "Local Exchange Competition," in Washington, D.C.

23. See Appendix.

24. *Id.*, p. 1.9.

25. See Chapters II and VII, and Charts VII–6, VII–7.

26. See, *e.g.*, "Ma Bell vs. IBM? Squaring Off at Each Other in Data Communications," *Barrons*, February 9, 1976, pp. 3, 14, 16, 17, 22; "The odds in a Bell–IBM bout," *Business Week*, January 25, 1982, pp. 22–23; "Ma Blue: IBM's Move Into Communications," *Fortune*, October 15, 1984, pp. 52–54, 58, 62, "The Big Face–Off: AT&T versus IBM," December 1985, pp. 64, 75, 77, 78.

27. 1987 data.

28. *The Geodesic Network*, *op. cit.*, pp. 1.20, 1.21.

29. See, *e.g.*, "MCI Will Buy IBM's 16% Stake for $677 million," *Wall Street Journal*, July 15, 1988, p. 3; and, "Siemens, IBM join forces to tackle tough PBX problems," *Telephony*, December 19, 1988, p. 10.

30. See, *e.g.*, "The CPE Marketplace Is a Dog–Eat–Dog World," *Telephony*, May 11, 1987, pp. 30–54.

31. See, *e.g.*, "Ameritech announces consolidation of Ameritech Communications, Telco sales subsidiaries," *Telecommunications Reports*, December 19, 1988, p. 15; and "With structural separation rules lifted, BellSouth Telcos reintegrate services, CPE," *Telecommunications Reports*, January 23, 1989, p. 39.

32. See, *e.g.*, "Rivals fear AT&T's return to full strength," *The Arizona Republic*, October 13, 1985; and "One–Stop Shopping Keeps Customers Satisfied" *Telephony*, September 28, 1987, pp. 160–161.

33. "Ill. Bell, Sprint Win Bid for $108 M Illinois Network," *Communications Week*, June 13, 1988, p. 12.

34. For a good discussion of the likelihood of this merger spree, see "The Coming Consolidation of the Independent Telephone Industry," *Telecommunications*, April 1988, pp. 48, 51, 54, 55, and 63.

35. Another reason might be the need for backup communications. The recent fire in an Illinois Bell central office in a Chicago suburb interrupted service to some 35,000 customers and their callers for more than a week.

36. See, *e.g.*, "Problems Force Users to Retrench," *Communications Week*, November 7, 1988, pp. 1, 62; and "Red Ink Downs Net," *Communications Week*, November 21, 1988, p. 1, 43.

37. See, *e.g.*, "Reconsidering Private Nets," *Communications Week*, November 21, 1988, p. 13.

38. BSAs are network access arrangements for enhanced service provision that are usually offered pursuant to existing tariffs; they define the central office switch connection and generally include connections for voice grade line, circuit–switched line, voice grade trunk and circuit–switched, packet switched and dedicated network access link. In turn, BSEs are FCC–mandated tariffed offerings which must be provided to enhanced service providers on a separate and unbundled basis; these may include such components as uniform call distribution, call detail recording, reverse billing, and call history package delivery.

39. "Bell's ONA Proposals Deemed Unacceptable As ICA Calls For Increased FCC Leadership," *Communications Week*, May 23, 1988, pp. 42, 43.

40. "Bells' ONA Proposals Garner Thumbs–Down Reviews," *Communications Week*, April 25, 1988, pp. 31, 32.

41. *Id.*, p. 33.

42. "NTIA: BOC ONA Model Is Needlessly Confusing," *Communications Week*, May 30, 1988, p. 8.

43. See, *e.g.*, "D.C. Commissioner Berates FCC As State–Federal Differences Over ONA Hit New High," *Communications Week*, April 4, 1988, pp. 10, 11; and "States, Feds in New Battle," *Communications Week*, May 2, 1988, p. 12.

44. Remarks given by Richard J. Vehige, Southwestern Bell Assistant Vice President, before the Columbia University Telecommunications and Information Seminar, June 29, 1987, p. 2.

45. "'Back to the Future': A Model for Telecommunications," *op. cit.*

46. *The Geodesic Network, op. cit.*, p. 2.25.

47. *Id.*, p.

48. H. Greene, paper presented before the National Governors' Association, February 21, 1988, p. 10.

49. For example, a California PUC administrative law judge opined in 1984 that: "In the stormy turbulent circumstances of divestiture, there is one beacon that guides us – universal service." *Proposed Decision 83–06–91*, p. 190.

50. Under revised separations procedures the interstate NTS allocator will be set at 25 percent in all states. An eight year phase–in period has been established, beginning in 1986, to lessen and spread out the impact on ratepayers in states with relatively high allocation factors at the present time.

51. Bell System Practice 218–060–200, p. 18.

52. The term CCS represents one hundred call seconds. Thus, if each local call occupies a marker for .55 second and there are 13,000 local calls, there would be a total of 7,150 seconds of marker use, or 71.5 hundred call seconds.

53. See March 7, 1988, *Slip Opinion, op. cit.*, pp. 13–14, n.15, and June 13, 1989 *Slip Opinion, op. cit.*

54. "Four insiders analyze the telecommunications industry," *Telephony*, January 4, 1988, p. 30.

55. "Clendenin Tells Financial Analysts Telcos Represent Firm Foundation for the Future," *Tele-communications Reports*, June 1, 1987, p. 15.

56. H. Greene, "Keynote Address to Legal Symposium," Forum 87, Fifth Quadrennial World telecommunication Forum, October 21, 1987, p. 8.

57. Also at risk in this context could be the furnishing of shared tenant services (STS) or "least cost routing" by BOCs. The latter would involve selection of one or more interexchange carriers among a "menu" of IXCs in order to complete a given call in the most economic manner available.

58. *Slip Opinion*, issued September 10, 1987, *op. cit.*, pp. 116, 121

59. *Id.*, pp. 123–125.

60. *Id.*, p. 150.

61. See Walter G. Bolter, "Restructuring in Telecommunications and Regulatory Adjustment," *Public Utilities Fortnightly*, July 5, 1984, pp. 21–22, and discussion *supra*.

62. See Jerry B. Duvall, "The Evolution of Competition in the Market for Local Telecommunica-tions Services: A Proposal for Industry Organization in the 21st Century," presented before U.S. Telephone Association Conference, *Survival Strategies for the Future: Planning for Change and Consolidation*, Arlington, Virginia, June 29, 1987.

63. In view of the wideband, digital transmission capability of fiber optics, it is not improbable that a single loop facility to each business or residence could be used to provide a continuum of voice, data, or video services. Duvall, *op. cit.*, p. 13.

64. Mark S. Fowler, Albert Halprin, and James D. Schlicting, "Back to the Future: A Model for Telecommunications," *Federal Communications Law Journal*, Vol. 38, No. 2, August 1986.

65. *Policy and Rules Concerning Rates for Dominant Carriers, NPRM,* 2 FCC Rcd. 5212 (1987).

66. See "Response to Questions by Chairmen Dingell and Markey for the Record of the November 1987 Hearing of the Subcommittee on Telecommunications and Finance on the FCC's Price Cap Proceeding, CC Docket No. 87–313," dated April 15, 1988, Enclosure p. 1.

67. "FCC may slow price–cap action as new challenges are mounted," *Telephony*, December 5, 1988, p.10.

68. Rand Corporation, "Price Caps in Telecommunications Regulatory Reform," February 1989.

69. Report and Order and Second Further Notice of Proposed Rulemaking, adopted March 16, 1989, CC Docket No. 87–313.

70. *Id*.

71. In 1985, the FCC's Common Carrier Bureau preempted a Texas PUC decision which restrained Atlantic Richfield Company (ARCO) from connecting its Plano, Texas, building to the Dallas public switched network served by Southwestern Bell (SWB). The Bureau overturned the PUC's ruling that SWB had unlawfully provided exchange service to a customer in the franchised operating territory of General Telephone Company of the Southwest. In overriding the state commission's decision, the Bureau found that a telephone subscriber's federal right to use its terminal equipment in ways that were "privately beneficial without being publicly detrimental" had been unlawfully denied. In February 1988 the full FCC upheld the Bureau's order, asserting that the federal right to interconnection extends not only to terminal equipment but also to "communications systems provided by customers." GTE has petitioned the U.S. Court of Appeals to review the series of decisions.

CHAPTER X

LOCAL EXCHANGE CARRIER TRENDS: FINANCIAL

The future financial performance for the major firms providing local telephone services looks promising. Under all but the most dire scenarios, the local exchange market would apparently continue to be profitable and least subject to loss of their control. Indeed, it appears unlikely that competition will fully develop in this market for a long time, if ever. Notably, if the RHCs or largest independents sold all their unregulated enterprises, their core businesses would perform better than many other companies in the U.S.

The combination of regulated and unregulated businesses should enable the major telephone companies to sustain their strong financial performance over the long term. Evidence indicates that the telecommunications industry has been well managed relative to other utility sectors. For example, the difficulties of the electric industry, in which imprudent nuclear power management appears to have led to billions of dollars in losses due to abandonment, are largely absent in the telecommunications industry. Compared with other industrial and service industries, telecommunications fares very well in the context of growth and opportunities.

The sustainability of the RHCs and other major LECs is evident from a review of key financial information. Table X–1 shows assets of these firms from 1984 to 1988 and indicates steady but unspectacular growth patterns. These firms had assets of over $200 billion by year–end 1988 with overall growth of 4.9 percent from 1984. On the other hand, Table X–2 shows that revenues over the same period have generally grown faster at a 6.3 percent rate. With the exception of U S WEST, the ratio of assets to revenues has declined since divestiture for all of the RHCs, indicating that these LECs are making more efficient use of their plant. In 1988, SWB improved its ratio substantially and appears to have turned its operation around. On the other hand, the independents as a group do not show the improved efficiencies exhibited by the RHCs. This may indicate that the independents have not moved as swiftly in a competitive mode.

Efficiency and productivity measures were also noted in Chapter V (see Tables V–4 and 5). These charts show that lines per telephone company employee and revenues per employee have increased steadily since 1984.

Chapter VII noted the vast amounts of capital being employed by the LECs to implement their construction plans, about $20 billion annually. These enormous requirements can be financed entirely from internal means for virtually all of the LECs listed on Table X–3. This ability to internally generate construction funds provides significant flexibility and market power to the LECs in their quest to maintain dominant positions in the telecommunications marketplace.

Tables X–4 and 5 show how dividends (DPS) and earnings (EPS) have grown for the LECs since 1984. These indicators all suggest that these local

Table X–1

ASSETS
Local Exchange Companies

($ Billion)

	1984	1985	1986	1987	1988
Ameritech	$ 17.6	$ 18.1	$ 18.7	$ 18.8	$ 19.2
Bell Atlantic	18.8	20.0	22.2	23.6	24.7
BellSouth	23.7	25.0	26.2	27.4	28.5
NYNEX	19.9	20.7	22.0	23.0	25.4
Pacific Telesis	18.4	19.6	20.5	21.4	21.2
Southwestern Bell	18.0	19.3	20.3	21.5	21.0
U S WEST	17.1	18.4	20.0	21.0	22.4
GTE	20.0	20.9	22.0	22.9	24.3
Cincinnati Bell	0.9	0.9	1.0	1.1	1.3
SNET	2.3	2.5	2.6	2.8	3.1
Contel	3.8	3.9	4.1	4.2	4.5
United	4.7	4.7	4.7	4.7	4.9
Centel	1.7	1.7	1.7	1.8	1.8
	$166.9	$175.7	$186.0	$194.2	$202.3

Growth

Annual		5.3%	5.9%	4.4%	4.2%
1984–1988					4.9%

Table X–2

REVENUE GROWTH
Local Exchange Companies

($ Billion)

	1984	1985	1986	1987	1988
Ameritech	$ 8.4	$ 9.1	$ 9.4	$ 9.5	$ 9.9
Bell Atlantic	8.1	9.1	10.1	10.7	10.9
BellSouth	9.7	10.7	11.5	12.3	13.7
NYNEX	9.6	10.3	11.3	12.1	12.7
Pacific Telesis	7.8	8.5	9.0	9.2	9.5
Southwestern Bell	7.2	7.9	7.9	8.0	8.5
U S WEST	7.3	7.8	8.4	8.7	9.2
GTE	9.2	10.1	10.8	11.2	11.7
Cincinnati Bell	0.4	0.5	0.5	0.6	0.7
SNET	1.3	1.4	1.4	1.5	1.6
Contel	1.6	1.7	1.9	2.0	2.1
United	2.2	2.3	2.3	2.4	2.5
Centel	0.8	0.8	0.8	0.8	0.9
	$73.6	$80.2	$85.3	$89.0	$93.9

Growth

Annual		9.0%	6.4%	4.3%	5.5%
1984–1988					6.3%

Source: Annual Reports.

Table X–3

INTERNAL FUNDING OF CONSTRUCTION
Local Exchange Companies

	1984	1985	1986	1987	1988
Ameritech	150%	145%	143%	148%	155%
Bell Atlantic	133	135	135	137	137
BellSouth	140	138	138	137	139
NYNEX	137	136	135	123	120
Pacific Telesis	116	117	137	127	182
Southwestern Bell	131	130	136	180	220
U S WEST	132	121	111	139	137
GTE	103	111	138	134	126
Cincinnati Bell	212	155	168	164	197
SNET	151	144	122	91	122
Contel	118	120	134	112	95
United	115	81	102	151	106
Centel	———	131	169	127	119

Table X–4

DIVIDENDS PER SHARE
Local Exchange Companies

	1984	1985	1986	1987	1988
Ameritech	$2.00	$2.20	$2.40	$2.55	$2.76
Bell Atlantic	3.20	3.40	3.60	3.84	4.08
BellSouth	1.72	1.88	2.04	2.20	2.36
NYNEX	3.00	3.20	3.48	3.80	4.04
Pacific Telesis	1.35	1.43	1.52	1.64	1.76
Southwestern Bell	1.87	2.00	2.13	2.32	2.48
U S WEST	2.70	2.86	3.04	3.28	3.52
GTE	2.03	2.08	2.20	2.48	2.60
Cincinnati Bell	0.75	0.78	0.88	0.96	1.12
SNET	2.66	2.74	2.82	2.91	3.03
Contel	1.70	1.78	1.86	1.97	2.06
United	1.88	1.92	1.92	1.92	1.92
Centel	1.04	1.06	1.09	1.13	1.17

Source: Annual Reports.

Table X–5

EARNINGS PER SHARE
Local Exchange Companies

	1984	1985	1986	1987	1988
Ameritech	$3.39	$3.67	$3.94	$4.24	$4.55
Bell Atlantic	4.97	5.47	5.85	6.24	6.83
BellSouth	2.85	3.13	3.38	3.46	3.51
NYNEX	5.05	5.42	6.01	6.26	6.63
Pacific Telesis	2.12	2.27	2.51	2.21	2.81
Southwestern Bell	3.01	3.33	3.42	3.48	3.53
U S WEST	4.62	4.84	4.86	5.31	6.24
GTE	3.55	(.63)	3.53	3.29	3.58
Cincinnati Bell	1.44	1.55	1.77	2.01	2.63
SNET	4.03	3.81	4.46	4.54	4.99
Contel	2.51	2.94	3.02	0.55	3.50
United	2.42	0.24	1.88	(.55)	4.95
Centel	1.93	2.05	1.73	2.40	2.13

Source: Annual Reports.

companies will continue to do well financially and shareholders will reap the benefits of profitable operations as earnings mount.

That the RHCs are financially successful can also be seen by a comparison of their profits to those of a broader group of large U.S. firms. Since divestiture, the RHCs as a group have outperformed the *Business Week* top 1,000 corporations as measured by the ratio of net income to assets. This is shown in Table X–6.

The RHCs' long term financial standing will be affected in part by their ability to provide information services. It is expected that these constraints will eventually be removed.[1] This could be as early as 1990, when the Department of Justice makes its second triennial review of the MFJ, and contingent upon the implementation of open network architecture and other safeguards.

Once the Regional companies are given more freedom from existing constraints, the information services market will likely enhance long term profitability. It is generally believed that earnings would be robust because the infrastructure is already in place to provide such services. This market is at the embryonic stage of development, with pent–up demand that is expected to manifest itself as regulation is relaxed and the carriers actively pursue market share. Pinpointing the amount of revenues that could come from information services, however, is difficult because this sector is not clearly defined.

Table X–6

Comparisons of Net Income to Assets

	RHC Average	B.W. Top 1000	RHC Exceeds Top 1000
1984	5.1%	3.2%	1.9%
1985	5.3	2.6	2.7
1986	5.4	2.4	3.0
1987	5.3	2.5	2.8
1988	5.5	3.0	2.5

The RHCs' future opportunities would be affected by removal of the manufacturing restraint, but it would influence profitability indirectly. Providing proprietary technology to the RHCs individually is the role that manufacturers will likely play. The Regional companies will seek network capabilities that differentiate themselves from each other since they are interested in the benefits of technology, not in creating it.

Bellcore's R&D efforts may gradually decrease as the RHCs seek to fund projects that are designed to meet their own particular needs. Bellcore is currently set up to provide technical expertise to the RHCs as a group, although the entity has recently made moves to tailor some of its projects more closely to specific member requirements. It is not clear that this organization will be able to perform research and development for the individual companies without a conflict of interest.

Several of the RHCs have established R&D facilities to address their own perceived needs. For instance, NYNEX opened its Science and Technology Center in White Plains, N.Y. with more than 200 scientists and researchers. At the center various projects are being studied such as speech recognition, machine vision, cellular network monitoring, and wireless LANs. U S WEST has also made a major commitment to R&D as it broke ground on a $45 million facility in Colorado during 1988.

The cellular communications business has an excellent chance of being a long term profitable service for the RHCs and independents. Within the last year or two, the companies have avoided building cellular communications systems. Instead they have purchased properties or entered into joint ventures in the U.S. and abroad that are either operational or near completion. Eventually, the acquisition trend may result in all of the nonwireline franchises in the major markets being owned either by an RHC or other large telephone carriers. Once the initial investment has been made and the system is running, future demand is expected to render these operations very profitable. A major reason for anticipated profitability is that the wireline franchise will likely have the edge because of such factors as ratepayer familiarity and loyalty.

The yellow pages directory and publishing businesses will sustain their historical profits for the Bell companies for the most part. There are two significant trends, however, that will affect the future. The first is the increasing competition that is taking place as discussed in detail in Chapter VII. Some of the RHCs have fortified their directory publishing subsidiaries to compete in territories outside of their own regions and even outside of the U.S. and others have ceased publication of unprofitable directories, *i.e.,* Southwestern Bell's Silver Pages. But, competition is likely to continue to occur only in large metropolitan cities. And, thus far, competition has apparently stimulated additional demand instead of displacing profits. Over time, growth will peak and the ensuing battle will turn into some price competition and lower profit margins, but these may still total higher returns for all of the Bell players than before these markets opened.

Importantly, the white and yellow pages directories within the next few years may be offered electronically by the RHCs, *i.e.,* if MFJ shackles can be removed. Of course, the independents have no such constraints and some already offer "talking" Yellow Pages. Although there presumably will always be a need to have a printed directory, it is not clear how advertising revenues will be affected by electronic capability. It is inevitable that the RHCs will face competitors that offer similar electronic directories.[2] But, they will also compete for lucrative business formerly left to newspaper and local leaflet advertisements, with the likely result that the overall directory business will be profitable.

The equipment subsidiaries will continue to be a low margin business. In 1987 the Bell companies realized total sales in the CPE distribution market of $650 million with a ten percent market share. It is very unlikely that the RHCs that have not attempted a separate nationwide equipment sales effort thus far will do so in the future. Instead, the companies will concentrate on selling equipment as part of a larger effort to sell integrated systems and as part of information service offerings, *e.g.,* teletex and videotex terminals. To develop their system's expertise, the RHCs and independents will continue to search for software companies with an expertise in end user interfaces, IBM's SNA (system network architecture) and system integration.

The international arena is another area where the RHCs and independents have begun to focus as noted in Chapter VIII. The telephone companies' biggest asset will probably be their technical ability to design and construct networks. Funds that are becoming increasingly available from the World Bank to developing countries will create consulting opportunities. As information services become more prevalent, the companies may attempt to sell their expertise in this area to some of the developing nations. It will not be surprising if within the next ten years, one or more of the RHCs will be an international carrier.

From a future perspective, each of the individual companies hopes to transform itself from a "public utility" into a diversified corporation. Their current strategic design will push them in a number of directions that will fashion characteristics that are distinguishing. Yet, the primary thrust of their business will remain local exchange service. The companies basically recognize this fact and, indeed, claim that diversification is simply a method to augment the exchange business and increase shareholder earnings. The vital part played by LECs' traditional services in generating revenues can be seen on Table X–7. The data shows continued growth in nontelecom revenues from 1984 to 1988, but for most of the companies the portion of these revenues is less than or around the 20 percent level. Thus, 80 percent of revenues still are derived from basic communications services. The success of new services and regulatory policies will be the major factors that determine the growth of nontelecom offerings.

Although nontelecom revenue growth for the RHCs has slowed from the apparent initial frenzy of diversification that occurred after divestiture, this growth remains greater than that for traditional telephone services. To illustrate, consider that from 1984 to 1988 telephone revenues increased by about four percent per year whereas nontelecom revenues grew 18.4 percent annually. It is instructive to project RHC revenues utilizing these growth rates to emphasize the importance of traditional telephone service revenues and dispel notions that basic services will not play a key role in the RHCs' strategic planning.[3]

Table X–8 depicts the breakdown of total revenues of the RHCs between traditional and other services through the year 2000. The growth of traditional services was kept constant at the overall level since 1984, i.e., four percent while nontelecom growth was estimated at two different levels. Eighteen percent was used as being representative of the upper limit of growth since divestiture and ten percent was utilized to reflect a waning growth rate. In both instances traditional telephone services maintain a substantial share of total revenues.

It is useful to qualitatively review how the RHCs' and independents' present diversification endeavors will impact the future. Based on current strategies, the long term outlook for the RHCs and several independents is explored as these companies appear to have refocused their efforts toward their core businesses.

A. Ameritech

Ameritech now has a strategy of developing its core business and taking advantage of its strong Midwest presence. The company initially acquired ADR (Applied Data Research) in 1985 to fill a perceived void that continues to affect some of the other RHCs. It was believed that the acquisition would be instrumental in helping Ameritech develop its systems integration business. ADR's expertise in IBM computers and presence in some of America's largest companies were expected to open the door for Ameritech to provide a host of other consulting services.

However, anticipated synergies between ADR and the RHC did not take place and ADR was sold in October 1988 to Computer Associates International, Inc. for $170 million. The selling price was about $45 million less than what

Table X–7

PERCENTAGE NONTELECOM REVENUES
Local Exchange Companies

	1984	1985	1986	1987	1988
Ameritech	12.5%	13.4%	14.0%	16.1%	16.2%
Bell Atlantic	12.7	15.6	17.7	21.7	22.6
BellSouth	12.7	14.5	15.4	17.7	23.1
NYNEX	11.0	11.7	13.3	16.6	18.4
Pacific Telesis	12.9	14.4	14.8	15.4	17.3
Southwestern Bell	16.7	16.9	13.5	13.8	17.9
U S WEST	11.5	14.8	18.3	19.5	19.7
GTE	15.6	18.0	18.8	19.1	20.0
Cincinnati Bell	7.6	15.0	19.3	27.4	34.9
SNET	13.8	18.3	20.8	20.1	26.6
Contel	8.4	9.7	23.3	22.2	20.6
United	6.4	16.6	13.7	13.2	11.6
Centel	13.2	14.2	14.5	16.6	18.9

Table X–8

PROJECTION OF RHC REVENUE DISTRIBUTION
($ Billions)

Year	10% Growth of Other		18% Growth of Other	
	Traditional Telephone	Other	Traditional Telephone	Other
1984	87.2%	12.8%	87.2%	12.8%
1985	85.6	14.4	85.6	14.4
1986	84.7	15.3	84.7	15.3
1987	82.6	17.4	82.6	17.4
1988	80.5	19.5	80.5	19.5
1989	79.6	20.4	80.0	20.0
1990	78.6	21.4	77.9	22.1
1992	76.7	23.3	73.3	26.7
1995	73.5	26.5	65.2	34.8
2000	67.7	32.3	49.9	50.1

Assumptions: four percent annual growth for traditional revenues and as
noted for other revenues.

Source: Annual Reports.

was paid for the Princeton, New Jersey firm in 1985. This action by Ameritech serves to represent its belief that communications services in its region are its strength and the company's major profit makers.

Ameritech has focused on the service industries in the Great Lakes region, but has not ignored other areas. The company has not made any dramatic diversification moves, and it is not expected that it will do so as flair does not appear to be its management's style. Rather, the holding company seems content to move cautiously in developing its unregulated businesses, ensuring that new ventures fit well with core services.

Ameritech's regulated business will grow modestly from an increased demand for telecommunications services as opposed to population growth which will tend to be stagnant. Ameritech's network services will benefit immensely from the fast growing industry segments of banking finance, health care and transportation, and to a lesser degree, auto manufacturing. The positive regulatory climate will accrue to the company's long term benefit.

It is expected that Ameritech's equipment business will not enjoy extraordinary success, but it has and should continue to fare well in a very competitive marketplace. The equipment subsidiary now has a liaison organization that was set up to deal with independent consultants, which will encourage third parties to recommend Ameritech's equipment systems.

The company's cellular business will mature well because of the number of large cities in its region and in 1988 it served 15 markets and 130,000 customers in the Midwest. The Chicago market is profitable and will likely be a strong money maker due to its size and makeup. The company currently does not have any cellular properties outside of its territory,[4] apparently choosing to confine itself to its own geographic region.

The publishing subsidiary has strong ties to industry giant R.H. Donnelley, which may stave off competitors from other regions. Ameritech's strategy in the publishing business appears to be oriented toward the secondary markets. It now owns Old Heritage, a small directory publishing firm that is concentrated in small cities outside of the region. If Ameritech moves further into the small city market, it will be largely noncompetitive and potentially profitable. This would appear to be a smarter strategy than to compete head on with other RHCs outside of Ameritech's region.

Internationally, the company obtained permission from Judge Greene to engage in manufacturing abroad. Although it has stated it had no immediate plans to manufacture, Ameritech will have the flexibility to enter into arrangements with foreign firms without waiting for the MFJ restrictions to be lifted. These efforts will be aimed at developing specific applications. Additionally, this kind of activity will give Ameritech an entree to the international market which will payoff in the long run.

From 1984 to 1988 the company's earnings increased by 5.7 percent per year but only a 4.1 percent increase was experienced in 1988 as shown on Table X–9. During the next five years, it is believed that Ameritech's net income will rise moderately in the 5–6 percent range. Compared to the other RHCs, Ameritech is one of the more stable companies in terms of growth.

Table X-9

CASH FLOW ANALYSIS
Ameritech
($ Million)

	1984	1985	1986	1987	1988
Net Income	$ 991	$1,078	$1,138	$1,188	$1,237
Depreciation	1,347	1,603	1,665	1,793	1,757
Other	275	204	158	(93)	(65)
TOTAL OPERATING FUNDS	2,613	2,885	2,961	2,888	2,929
Dividends	586	645	691	712	737
Capital Exp.	1,747	1,991	2,076	1,956	1,895
CASH FLOW	280	249	194	220	297
ADJUSTED CASH FLOW+					
Net Cash from Operations*	NA	NA	3,264	2,802	2,920
CASH FLOW	NA	NA	497	134	288

+ 1986 and 1987 adjusted to reflect new accounting practices.
* Includes cash and cash equivalents.

Source: Annual Reports.

The company's cash flow will rise steadily over the next four years, but may dip slightly because of capital expenditures required to implement digital technologies. Furthermore, it is likely that additional acquisitions will be made which would tend to lower cash flow.

Ameritech can be expected to forge ahead of the other RHCs in the systems and equipment business, and it would not be surprising to see the company purchase another software firm despite its experience with ADR. Ameritech is apparently committed to substantial research and development in communications software and will continue to pursue this avenue if it can match-up with a suitable partner. The emphasis on systems and software will posture Ameritech as a provider of data and information services, and its emphasis on new technology will probably continue.

B. Bell Atlantic

Many telecommunications industry observers believe that Bell Atlantic clearly has one of the best planned strategies of the seven RHCs. Bell Atlantic's upper management has a vision of where it wants to take the company in the long run. Bell Atlantic has also identified business ventures that do not fit into their long term strategies, *e.g.*, CompuShop (computer distributor) and A Beeper (paging), and has sought to sell them. Recognition of alternative and more profitable uses of the company's resources and the ability to act decisively will be an asset to the RHC over the long haul.

In connection with this underlying diversification strategy, Bell Atlantic heavily stresses its network services such as Centrex, and other advanced capabilities. Like Ameritech, Bell Atlantic has formed a group to interface with independent consultants to promote the company's products and services. The region's economic growth and strong service sector will keep demand for telecommunications services high. In short, Bell Atlantic is building its strength on its biggest asset, namely the network, which will position the company well for the provision of information services.

Bell Atlantic is geographically well suited to profitably enter the long distance market in its region. Traffic among Pittsburgh, Philadelphia, Baltimore and Washington, D.C., is heavy. Additionally, since its service territory includes New Jersey, Bell Atlantic could capture the traffic between these four cities and New York.

But Bell Atlantic is not sitting tight waiting for MFJ relief. The company already has agreements to link its operating companies' networks with the facilities of several interexchange carriers to offer its public data network (packet switched) service. This service is presently available in many of the company's 19 LATAs. The RHC is also in the vanguard with its participation in information services offerings.

The other unregulated subsidiaries have performed respectably. Bell Atlantic may expand its cellular communications company beyond its region, but will have few choices because of the consolidation that has already taken place. At the same time, the company's cellular division will probably compete more aggressively in its present markets and revenues increased by 48 percent in 1988. It also has been more aggressive in the paging business by expanding its operating area. In addition, the RBOC has been successful leasing and managing real estate. The company apparently will continue to run the directory businesses through the operating companies. Computer maintenance, both at home and abroad, is an area pursued by the RHC, and its 1988 purchase of the Bell Canada Enterprise companies positions Bell Atlantic in the international market.

Bell Atlantic's activities in the international market have generally been kept under wraps, presumably for strategic reasons. The company is providing consulting advice in the UK regarding Centrex service to London's financial community, and in 1988 won a contract to install a network management system in Spain. Bell Atlantic's geographic locations render it an ideal candidate to become a multinational telecommunications carrier by purchasing one of the international record companies. Bell Atlantic serves the nation's capital, which originates and terminates a tremendous amount of international traffic, and its service territory is adjacent to the international gateway of New York City.

Table X–10

CASH FLOW ANALYSIS
Bell Atlantic
($ Million)

	1984	1985	1986	1987	1988
Net Income	$ 973	$1,093	$1,167	$1,240	$1,317
Depreciation	1,194	1,484	1,927	2,117	2,354
Other	370	347	2	(117)	(70)
TOTAL OPERATING					
FUNDS	2,537	2,924	3,096	3,240	3,601
Dividends	629	679	717	762	796
Capital Exp.	1,913	2,163	2,291	2,364	2,620
CASH FLOW	(5)	82	88	114	185
ADJUSTED CASH FLOW+					
Net Cash from					
Operations*	NA	NA	3,424	3,592	3,481
CASH FLOW	NA	NA	416	466	230

+ 1986 and 1987 adjusted to reflect new accounting practices.
* Includes cash and cash equivalents.

Source: Annual Reports.

Bell Atlantic's earnings outlook appears to be positive (see Table X–10). Net income growth averaged almost eight percent since divestiture and could even go higher through 1992. After 1992, earnings may level off to the seven to eight percent range.

Depreciation can also be expected to rise continuously. Cash flow will also rise steadily unless there are additional acquisitions. The company has given strong indications that more purchases are on the way, thereby reducing cash flow. Also tending to lower Bell Atlantic's cash flow will be the company's increasing construction expenditures. Bell Atlantic will likely maintain its commitment to network modernization, which will probably pay off handsomely in the long run.

Bell Atlantic appears poised to be a very formidable force in the telecommunications industry in years to come. Over the next five years, it can be expected that this company will be one of the top performers among the Regional companies.

C. BellSouth

BellSouth could do well over the next few years regardless of managerial ability because of the economic climate in its territory. The growth in access

Table X–11

CASH FLOW ANALYSIS
BellSouth
($ Million)

	1984	1985	1986	1987	1988
Net Income	$1,257	$1,418	$1,589	$1,665	$1,666
Depreciation	1,536	1,802	1,936	2,498	2,682
Other	400	398	378	(54)	(114)
TOTAL OPERATING					
FUNDS	3,193	3,618	3,903	4,109	4,234
Dividends	766	847	955	1,059	1,104
Capital Exp.	2,274	2,624	2,835	3,008	3,207
CASH FLOW	153	147	113	42	(77)
ADJUSTED CASH FLOW+					
Net Cash from					
Operations*	NA	NA	4,172	3,998	4,240
CASH FLOW	NA	NA	382	(69)	(71)

+ 1986 and 1987 adjusted to reflect new accounting practices.
* Includes cash and cash equivalents.

Source: Annual Reports.

lines alone over the next five years should sustain the company's strong results. But since the company appears to be well managed, some securities analysts and telecommunications industry observers expect that BellSouth will be a top performer in basic regulated services over the next five years. The company is also one of the leaders in information service offerings and other new technology services. In order to optimize business opportunities, BellSouth has revamped its marketing program. The new structure will enable the company to market both telephone equipment and network services through a single organization thereby establishing one–stop shopping for customers. Strategic alliances continue to be formed that should ultimately enhance BellSouth's profitability.

BellSouth's net income will continue to be among the highest, although flat for 1988, and its cash flow will remain strong despite large capital expenditures (see Table X–11). Depreciation expense growth may be lower after 1988, but will still contribute to the large amount of available cash.

BellSouth's strongest unregulated subsidiary is its publishing division, BellSouth Advertising and Publishing Co. (BAPCO). The vertically integrated nature of the operation, in which every aspect of the business except distribution is performed, along with its acquisition of L.M. Berry, will position BAPCO strategically as a national force. Over the next five years, the publishing division will probably become more aggressive outside of the BellSouth region.

Although BAPCO does not have the national presence that Southwestern Bell has, some anticipate that the publishing company will have more success in its own region than Southwestern Bell will experience in its five states. The lurking hazard that BellSouth's publishing arm potentially faces in the future is competition from other RHCs in major markets. This scenario would probably result eventually in price competition once growth demand is satisfied. BAPCO could hedge its position by fully developing its secondary markets.

The other nonregulated area in which BellSouth has expended considerable effort is in cellular communications where it serves 35 major metropolitan areas and has established a presence in foreign markets. BellSouth has acquired a number of nonwireline franchises outside of its territory including a substantial ownership share in the lucrative Los Angeles market. Although confronted by some competition, the company's cellular business is expected to continue to grow as equipment costs decline, and the service becomes affordable to new customers.

BellSouth may be one of the more aggressive RHCs in the international market, especially mobile communications. The company seems to have established a niche in the Pacific Basin and will probably continue to expand its presence in this and other areas.

D. NYNEX

NYNEX has taken a comprehensive approach to serving its large business community, which should prove to be beneficial for the company in the long run. NYNEX has acquired several software companies, including one that is oriented toward integrated systems. Complementing the software companies is its chain of stores acquired from IBM and Datago that sell computers, CPE and other business products. NYNEX has become more aggressive in enhancing its network and transmission facilities because of the burgeoning competition in the area of intelligent services and integrated systems. For instance, from 1984 to 1988, the company increased its digitally served customers tenfold, increased fiber miles by a factor of six, and over the past five years NYNEX invested more than $11 billion to upgrade facilities.

The long term outlook for sustaining the computer stores outside of New York and New England, however, is questionable. NYNEX has undertaken substantial risk by attempting to use the stores as a base to sell business products and to establish a nationwide marketing force without network support. The company's efforts could be more efficiently expended by targeting its resources toward its own territory. NYNEX may decide to sell some of the stores within several years if the computer equipment market remains intensively competitive.

NYNEX's failed attempt at a joint venture in a transAtlantic optical fiber cable undertaking was initially lauded as a worthy enterprise with tremendous

Table X–12

CASH FLOW ANALYSIS
NYNEX
($ Million)

	1984	1985	1986	1987	1988
Net Income	$ 986	$1,095	$1,215	$1,277	$1,315
Depreciation	1,202	1,433	1,655	2,031	2,154
Other	402	304	365	(83)	(120)
TOTAL OPERATING FUNDS	2,590	2,832	3,235	3,225	3,349
Dividends	593	647	705	774	791
Capital Exp.	1,854	2,115	2,402	2,551	2,784
CASH FLOW	153	70	128	(100)	(226)
ADJUSTED CASH FLOW+					
Net Cash from Operations*	NA	NA	3,178	3,134	3,147
CASH FLOW	NA	NA	71	(191)	(428)

+ 1986 and 1987 adjusted to reflect new accounting practices.
* Includes cash and cash equivalents.

Source: Annual Reports.

potential profitability. Over 60 percent of the U.S. European traffic origin–ates and terminates in New York, and Boston is another large international gateway and NYNEX's participation in the venture was expected to aid the firm's bottom line. In early 1989 NYNEX took a $10 million loss on its thwarted bid to acquire 50 percent of the cable and it is not clear how NYNEX will pursue this lucrative market in the future.

NYNEX's leverage in the international market could be considerably increased if it were to acquire one of the international record carriers. This would gain NYNEX operating agreements with foreign carriers and it would capture some of the public switched traffic as well as revenues from the private undersea fiber optic cable. Additionally, the working relationships that would be built with foreign carriers could lead to other business in which NYNEX has demonstrated expertise. The international market is an area that apparently holds considerable promise for the company.

NYNEX has a profitable cellular system in New York City, but the others will likely remain unprofitable for the next couple of years. Its directory publishing subsidiary has one company that operates on the west coast, but NYNEX is not likely to be a major player in this business. In fact, NYNEX will seemingly have its hands full competing in its own territory with Southwestern Bell.

NYNEX's earnings will probably be strong over the next five years and then gradually level off. The company's net income could be one of the highest among the RHCs (see Table X–12) as it grew at an average rate of about 7.5 percent per year since 1984. NYNEX's cash flow will also improve when construction growth stabilizes and as income continues to grow. Available cash could be lower if NYNEX continues to buy into joint ventures and make the large acquisitions that it has in the past.

What could also negatively affect cash flow would be a reversal in the trend of generous depreciation expenses by the regulatory commissions in the jurisdictions NYNEX serves. Conversely, given the social contract in Vermont, incentive regulation in New York, and possible changes in Massachusetts, regulatory treatment will probably be favorable. Therefore, NYNEX can be expected to fare well financially over the next five years.

E. Pacific Telesis Group

Pacific Telesis is centered in a market where growth and prosperity will enhance the company's long term future. Unlike most of the other regions, basic exchange service for both the business and residential sectors in California will continue to grow. In 1988, access line growth was about four percent, which compares favorably with the industry average of three percent. Given the state of the economy and the high personal income, information services will have a strong demand once they become available.

Consequently, Pacific Telesis' earnings have grown about 9.4 percent annually since 1984 (see Table X–13). Pacific Telesis' cash flow will probably rise because of the anticipated rise in net income over the next five years. Due to anticipated population growth in California, however, it is possible that construction expenditures will experience a growth increase after 1989 which will tend to retard cash flow. Another factor that could negatively affect cash flow would be a decrease in depreciation expense growth. Given the unpredictable nature of the regulatory climate in California, this is entirely possible. On the other hand, the California Commission recently provided PacBell with pricing flexibility for certain competitive services. This action should aid the company's bottom line.

Pacific Telesis has developed a strong cellular business with 262,000 customers. The Los Angeles market is flourishing and with the other California sites there are one–quarter million subscribers which should add to profitability. The company has purchased nonwireline cellular franchises in major cities outside of California and Nevada and operates in five of the top ten U.S. markets. As a group, the long term profitability outlook for the cellular properties is very good. Pacific Telesis may emerge as the nation's leader in cellular communications.

The company's third strength is its international business. Thus far, Pacific Telesis has used its west coast presence effectively. It already has established excellent working relationships in the Far East countries of China,

Table X–13

CASH FLOW ANALYSIS
Pacific Telesis
($ Million)

	1984	1985	1986	1987	1988
Net Income	$ 829	$ 929	$1,079	$ 950	$1,188
Depreciation	1,084	1,238	1,511	1,707	1,845
Other	430	466	283	(86)	(144)
TOTAL OPERATING FUNDS	2,343	2,633	2,873	2,571	2,889
Dividends	531	594	654	705	673
Capital Exp.	2,082	2,257	2,103	2,028	1,500
CASH FLOW	(270)	(218)	116	(162)	776
ADJUSTED CASH FLOW+					
Net Cash from Operations*	NA	NA	3,185	2,846	2,929
CASH FLOW	NA	NA	428	113	756

+ 1986 and 1987 adjusted to reflect new accounting practices.
* Includes cash and cash equivalents.

Source: Annual Reports.

Japan, Korea, and Thailand, and has concentrated on providing services there which the company is currently prohibited from selling domestically.   The company's participation in the transPacific fiber optic cable venture will give the company increased visibility in the Far East.   Because the Pacific Basin is not as developed as the European markets, the potential for growth is enormous.   Therefore, this area represents the largest opportunity for Pacific Telesis in the long run.

Pacific Telesis' weak area has been the systems integration business. The company introduced Pactel Spectrum Services, a division that was to offer network management services, but subsequently sold it to IBM in 1988.   It also formed a joint venture with Northern Telecom to provide for integrated office systems sales and service. The company also sought to merge with ABI American Businessphones, Inc., a firm that sells and services small PBXs and key systems.   Considerable resources still have to be directed toward this business.

F. Southwestern Bell

Even though signs of improvement are now evident, the residual effects of the economic problems of the Southwest will continue to depress the financial performance of Southwestern Bell.   The company's earnings will continue to be sluggish over the next year or two (see Table X-14).   Thereafter, net income should grow at a higher pace and then level off as the region's economy continues to rebound.   At the same time, the company's depreciation expense will rise steadily.

Despite the languishing economy in its service territory, Southwestern Bell has continued to invest heavily in plant modernization and must continue to do so since it had the lowest proportion of digital lines and switches of the BOCs in mid-1988, 18 percent and 20 percent, respectively.   At some point, the oil and agriculture industries will recover and many of the region's new businesses will have matured.   When this happens, markets will develop and the company will be capable of offering new and innovative services.

Southwestern Bell has been one of the leaders in providing ISDN technology to large business customers.   The company has also announced trials for mass market and data gateways as SWB gears up for its participation in the information services market.   The company hopes to gain a significant share of the projected $250 million voice messaging market in its operating territory.

Another company strategy that should pay off in the long run is its persistent telecommunications equipment and systems subsidiary.   In 1987 its Freedom Phone line increased sales by 130 percent and shipped its one millionth unit and in 1988 it shipped its two millionth product.   During 1988 a Freedom Phone outlet was opened in the UK.   This division operates in highly competitive markets and its long term profitability potential is questionable.   But the company has stuck with it as part of its overall objective to maintain control of its accounts.

Southwestern Bell's unregulated bailiwick will continue to be its directory publishing business.   The company seems wise to have expanded its directory operations beyond its five state territory because of the region's economic state, and a growing problem of uncollectible directory revenues due to failing businesses.

1987 was the first year for production of Southwestern Bell's competitive, extraterritorial directories.   The verdict on whether there is a market for two yellow pages directories in large cities has yet to come as advertisers evaluate the effectiveness of the initial year's operation.   In 1988, the company withdrew its nationwide senior citizens directory and also left three of the five competitive markets outside its five-state area.   Even if the outside directory business is successful, the traditional high margins are going to disappear in competitive markets, which gives the business an element of uncertainty in the long run.   To remain profitable, Southwestern Bell may have to avoid engaging in price wars and pick markets in which cost is a secondary concern to advertisers.

The publishing division has also expanded its operations internationally.   It is now doing business in Australia and Israel.   Additionally, this subsidiary has discussions ongoing with other countries and can be expected to make further inroads into other foreign markets during the next several years.   The

Table X–14

CASH FLOW ANALYSIS
Southwestern Bell
($ Million)

	1984	1985	1986	1987	1988
Net Income	$ 883	$ 996	$1,023	$1,047	$1,060
Depreciation	1,141	1,302	1,387	1,650	1,845
Other	416	422	221	(21)	(217)
TOTAL OPERATING					
FUNDS	2,440	2,720	2,631	2,676	2,688
Dividends	549	598	638	698	644
Capital Exp.	1,804	2,090	1,970	1,484	1,222
CASH FLOW	87	33	23	494	822
ADJUSTED CASH FLOW+					
Net Cash from					
Operations*	NA	NA	2,571	2,478	2,530
CASH FLOW	NA	NA	(37)	296	664

+ 1986 and 1987 adjusted to reflect new accounting practices.
* Includes cash and cash equivalents.

Source: Annual Reports.

international marketplace is an area where Southwestern Bell has a unique opportunity to develop its directory business.

The acquisition of the Metromedia cellular properties gave Southwestern Bell national prominence in the mobile communications business, and perhaps provided the struggling cellular industry with a much needed boost in valuation. Over the long term, the purchase should become a profitable venture for the company. Due to the extravagant price, however, the payback period will be increased beyond the normal cycle.

G. U S WEST

In the long run, the competitive fervor that pervades U S WEST will probably make this company successful. In the short run, the company will have to develop a coordinated strategy. U S WEST has learned the hard way that diversification endeavors too decentralized or too far away from the home base can be disastrous.

Fortunately, the company has recognized its own lack of direction and appears to be a little more focused. The company recently formed a strategic marketing group to consolidate the organization's planning functions. It also

Table X-15

CASH FLOW ANALYSIS
U S WEST
($ Million)

	1984	1985	1986	1987	1988
Net Income	$ 887	$ 926	$ 924	$1,006	$1,132
Depreciation	1,106	1,276	1,400	1,641	1,760
Other	345	332	208	6	259
TOTAL OPERATING FUNDS	2,338	2,534	2,532	2,653	3,151
Dividends	518	546	578	612	636
Capital Exp.	1,774	2,089	2,282	1,908	2,294
CASH FLOW	46	(101)	(328)	133	221
ADJUSTED CASH FLOW+					
Net Cash from Operations*	NA	NA	2,868	2,907	2,990
CASH FLOW	NA	NA	8	387	60

+ 1986 and 1987 adjusted to reflect new accounting practices.
* Includes cash and cash equivalents.

Source: Annual Reports.

formed a technologies group to organize activities directed at developing proprietary research opportunities.

Like most of the RHCs, U S WEST is not particularly strong in systems integration. To address this weakness, the company acquired a software firm to strengthen U S WEST's systems integration capabilities. U S WEST also acquired a financial services operation during 1988 that was ranked as the 58th largest in the nation. This addition to the Financial Services division is expected to bolster profits, but such an outcome is not clear at this point.

After cutting back its nationwide CPE business, U S WEST has directed its diversification efforts toward directory publishing. The company has purchased a string of publishing concerns that compete in the smaller markets. This area looks promising in the long run, but falls short of the lofty expectations projected by the management.

Since 1984 saw net income increased by 4.1 percent annually,[5] and, whether this level can be sustained or not, U S WEST has most likely seen the worst of its financial performances. It can be expected that the company's net income will grow in the four to six percent range over the next five years, and then stabilize at about 6.5 percent in subsequent years.

But U S WEST will probably trail most of the other RHCs in profits and overall performance (see Table X–15).

The cash flow, however, will continue to rise because of increasing depreciation expenses and very limited growth in construction expenditures. The 14 state region will not experience much growth in population, and the territory's economic climate will not lend itself to stimulation of additional demand.

H. GTE

GTE's depressed earnings over recent years have in large part been due to losses sustained by US Sprint and its predecessors. From 1984 to 1988 net income has only increased by about 1.6 percent per year and earnings per share (EPS) showed no growth. In 1988, GTE sought to alleviate this problem by selling a substantial portion of its 50 percent share in US Sprint to the other co–owner, United Telecommunications, thereby leaving GTE with a 19.9 percent share in US Sprint. Also, the company has begun a reorganization to combine operating companies into four operating areas to take advantage of economies of operation. GTE is also planning massive force reductions to effectuate greater operating efficiencies. The company recently announced the planned sale of its Consumer Communications Products division (CPE, answering devises) to concentrate on service offerings.

The independent recently formed GTE Information Services which has acquired businesses in the health care, education, and retail sector. The company also is in the cellular business and at the end of 1987 ranked fourth among the nation's 44 cellular companies in the size of potential customers. GTE Directories is in the publications business and recently entered into an agreement with Bell Atlantic to sell Yellow Pages advertising. GTE also provides communications management services and satellite services. GTE's largest operation is its telephone companies with about 14 million access lines in 31 states, Canada, and the Dominican Republic. The largest LEC is located in California where an expanding economy and relaxed regulation should help to improve profits. Productivity continues to improve, thereby strengthening the bottom line.

In a somewhat unique endeavor, GTE and AT&T agreed in 1988 to a joint venture to facilitate ISDN introduction to GTE's digital switching systems. The proposal, which must be approved by the U.S. government, establishes a new company that would include the network switching business of GTE and various AT&T 5ESS digital switch and other technology licenses. The entity would develop enhanced features and capabilities for GTE's popular digital switches.

The strategies currently being implemented by GTE should turn the company's profit growth around. The firm is apparently attacking its recent sluggish growth from both the demand and cost sides of the problem. If its efforts are successful, growth should pick up.

I. Southern New England Telecommunications

Since 1984 SNET's net income has improved at an average annual rate of 5.5 percent. However, 1988 growth has been about ten percent as the company's subsidiaries are now turning a profit. One of SNET's disadvantages from a growth viewpoint is the limited franchise area for its basic telephone business, *i.e.*, the state of Connecticut.

SNET Cellular appears to be the most lucrative nonregulated subsidiary with positive income first being realized in 1987. This operation conducts its business within the state of Connecticut and derives substantial revenues from users traveling the busy New York to Boston corridor.

SNET's joint venture with CSX to form the LIGHTNET fiber optic communications network was barely profitable. In early 1989, SNET announced it was planning to sell its share of LIGHTNET to the Williams Telecommunications Group, Inc. by April 1989. The company indicated that LIGHTNET was too much of a drain on overall profits and that it would begin to focus its resources on the telecommunications business in Connecticut. This is another instance of a telephone company "conglomerate" returning to its basic mission, *i.e.*, the provision of local telephone service.

The company's equipment subsidiary has not been nearly as successful as anticipated. Its losses have decreased each year but it is not clear whether this subsidiary will be a major contributor to SNET profits. SNET's major nontelecom revenue source is its directory publication operation which continues to do well. Directory revenues increased by over 16 percent in 1987.

The former Bell company derives most of its revenues and net income from its telephone operations. Connecticut's economy continues to expand and its proximity to New York City and Boston bode well for continued growth. However, SNET's limited operating area will tend to keep growth constant, within its historical ranges. Also, some recent funding for capital projects came from external sources suggesting that SNET may not be in as favorable a position as other telephone companies to actively pursue an acquisition strategy.

J. Cincinnati Bell

Cincinnati Bell (CBI) is the other former Bell company not affected by divestiture to the same degree as the seven RHCs. This firm has exhibited extraordinary growth as it has expanded into information services outside its small operating area, both nationally and worldwide. This strategy is in stark contrast to the approach taken by SNET.

From 1984 to 1988 CBI's net income has soared by 85 percent or 17 percent per year. In 1988 alone, profits were up 39 percent. This has occurred despite the rather mediocre annual increase in access lines of about two percent. The growth has come from unregulated ventures, particularly

Cincinnati Bell Information Systems (CBIS). To reach this position, CBI has aggressively pursued nontraditional telephone business and been successful.

CBIS provides information services in the U.S. and foreign countries whereby it designs, markets, and manages information systems for clients. The company has acquired firms to augment its expertise in the information services market.   During 1988, CBIS was awarded a contract with Japan's major domestic telephone company, NTT, to help manage its telephone operations.   CBIS also provides billing systems and customer account management for the mobile telephone business and claims a 70 percent market share of North American systems.

CBI appears to be on the right track as the nation enters the Information Age. Its growth in earnings should continue at high levels as its unregulated businesses prosper. This company has aggressively pursued what it perceives to be the "wave of the future" with rewarding results. CBI also generates substantial funding from internal operations from which it can completely finance its construction projects. Excess funds could be used for further acquisitions.

K. Contel

Contel is a company that appears to be struggling with its nonregulated operations. The firm became involved in many ventures and has finally realized that its telephone business is where its focus should lie. In recent years net income has been sluggish and in 1987 there was a substantial drop as management sought to eliminate unprofitable operations. The actions taken have resulted in improved financial results in 1988.

The company's telephone operations continue steady growth both from a revenue and income viewpoint. Contel Cellular is one of the few cellular companies that are profitable and its growth continues unabated.

The other sectors of Contel have not fared well. The Federal Systems sector lost money in 1987 and has barely been profitable in 1988. Expectations are that this business will pick up but in this competitive field such hopes are not easily attained.

Contel's Information Systems sector has sustained losses in most years and continues to do so. The company has recognized the problems with this business and decided to dispose of the Business Systems subsidiary which sells computer based information systems. Cost reductions and management changes were made within the sector to improve profits.

Contel's telephone operations also include a tenant services division which acquired Realcom, the former IBM affiliate. A new entity was formed, Contel Office Communications, which provides service to over 900 businesses. As noted in an earlier chapter, shared tenant services (STS) have not exploded onto the scene as many predicted. However, Contel now has the bulk of the business and is in a good position if the market expands.

Contel's telephone business appears to be ready for the Information Age with 79 percent digital lines and 54,000 miles of fiber optics. The company is winding down its major construction program and may be able to use resources to better develop its overall strategies. The company's cash flow status deteriorated somewhat in 1988 but with the paring of some unprofitable subsidiaries improvements can be expected. It may take a few years for Contel to recoup its losses but the company's new strategy should help turn the profit picture around.

L. United Telecom

United's net profits have been growing at a five percent rate since 1984, and in 1987 and 1988 this rate has been exceeded. As noted above, United now has an 80 percent share of US Sprint. Although this long distance carrier has historically been a drain on earnings, recent results have shown improvements. Also, the awarding of a substantial portion of a multi-year contract by the federal government will enhance US Sprint's and United's earnings.

Telenet, the packet switching subsidiary of US Sprint, is the largest of its kind in the world and introduced an Integrated Digital Network (IDN) in 1987. Telenet provides products and services in the U.S. and internationally, and holds almost 50 percent of the estimated $400 million U.S. public packet switched network market.

United's telephone operations have maintained excellent growth rates and access lines are presently expanding well above the industry average. The company appears to be well positioned, in a technological sense, with over 70 percent digital access lines and an increasing number of fiber miles. The company also offers long distance service through its reseller that operates in several states. In 1988, United sold its cellular and paging operations to Centel, and the funds from the sale were used to purchase the additional 30 percent share of US Sprint from GTE.

United's complementary businesses were profitable in 1987, up 43 percent from 1986 figures. This company has seemingly chosen a good mix of offerings as compared to many of the other telephone companies providing nonregulated services. United's directory publications operation has been expanded outside of the company's basic operating territories, resulting in an increase of revenues of 61 percent in 1987. North Supply Company, United's telecommunications distribution subsidiary, has continued to add to corporate profits at an ever increasing rate.

United's growth should continue, perhaps at an increased pace, as US Sprint begins to realize its potential and core businesses maintain current trends. With a good deal of the company's modernization in place, funds may be available for further strategic acquisitions.

Notes

1. In March 1988 Judge Greene's Court provided some relaxation of the prohibition of the RHCs' participation in the information services market.

2. Under open network architecture, the Bell operating companies will have to offer the same information to outside firms that the carriers offer to a holding company's directory subsidiary.

3. Of course some might argue that the RHCs will utilize the substantial revenue streams from basic services to develop and support nontelecom services. In any event, revenues from traditional telephone services will dominate well into the future.

4. During the first quarter of 1988 Ameritech sold its interest in Cantel, a leading cellular company in Canada.

5. Excluding a one time gain from the sale of NewVector common stock in 1988.

INDEX

ABOUT THE AUTHORS

WALTER G. BOLTER teaches in the Department of Business Administration and Economics at Flagler College in St. Augustine, Florida, and is a director of the Bethesda Research Institute, a firm specializing in market research, regulatory, and public policy issues. Dr. Bolter was formerly Chief Economist for the House of Representatives' Subcommittee on Telecommunications and has also served as Chief of the Economics Division of the Federal Communications Commission and Senior Economist of the Office of Telecommunications in the U.S. Department of Commerce.

He earned M.A. and Ph.D. degrees in Economics from the University of Maryland, and degrees of Master of Science in Industrial Management and Bachelor of Mechanical Engineering from the Georgia Institute of Technology.

FRED J. KELSEY is a special consultant to the Bethesda Research Institute. He has also worked in supervisory and industry research positions for the Common Carrier Bureau of the Federal Communications Commission, the Western Union Telegraph Company, and the Long Island Lighting Company.

Kelsey holds degrees in engineering from C.W. Post College and in applied science from Adelphi University, and an M.B.A. from Loyola College.

JAMES W. MCCONNAUGHEY completed work on this book while serving as Research Studies Manager with the Bethesda Research Institute. He previously worked with the Federal Communications Commission.

He has degrees from the University of Maryland and The George Washington University.

Kelsey, McConnaughey, and Bolter coauthored *Setting Telecommunications Policy for the 1980s: The Transition to Competition.*

DATE DUE

~~AUG 0 8 2002~~		~~MAY 1 5 2004~~	
		~~OCT 2 3 2006~~	
~~DEC 0 2 2002~~			
		~~JUN 1 8 2007~~	
~~MAY 0 2 2003~~			
~~SEP 1 2 2004~~			
~~JAN 0 4 2005~~			
~~AUG 3 0 2005~~			
~~FEB 1 8 2007~~			
~~SEP 0 0 2~~			
			Printed in USA

HIGHSMITH #45230

95

TELE ⬤ COMMUNI-CATIONS POLICY for the 1990s and beyond